Fodor's 7th Edition

Virginia and Maryland

The Guide for All Budgets

Completely Updated

Where to Stay, Eat, and Explore

On and Off the Beaten Path

When to Go, What to Pack

Maps, Travel Tips, and Web Sites

Fodor's Travel Publications • New York, Toronto, London, Sydney, Auckland
www.fodors.com

Fodor's Virginia and Maryland

Editor: John D. Rambow

Editorial Contributors: Gail Doyle, Michelle Gienow, Kathryn McKay, Kevin Myatt, Pete Nelson, Greg Tasker, CiCi Williamson
Editorial Production: Kristin Milavec
Maps: David Lindroth, Inc.; Mapping Specialists, *cartographers;* Rebecca Baer and Bob Blake, *map editors*
Design: Fabrizio La Rocca, *creative director;* Guido Caroti, *art director;* Jolie Novak, *senior picture editor;* Melanie Marin, *photo editor*
Cover Design: Pentagram
Production/Manufacturing: Angela L. McLean
Cover Photo (Autumn at Sharp Top Peak): David Muench/Corbis

Copyright

Seventh Edition

ISBN 1-4000-1132-9

ISSN 1075-0711

Important Tip

Although all prices, opening times, and other details in this book are based on information supplied to us at press time, changes occur all the time in the travel world, and Fodor's cannot accept responsibility for facts that become outdated or for inadvertent errors or omissions. So **always confirm information when it matters,** especially if you're making a detour to visit a specific place.

Special Sales

Fodor's Travel Publications are available at special discounts for bulk purchases for sales promotions or premiums. Special editions, including personalized covers, excerpts of existing guides, and corporate imprints, can be created in large quantities for special needs. For more information, contact your local bookseller or write to Special Markets, Fodor's Travel Publications, 1745 Broadway, New York, New York 10019. Inquiries from Canada should be directed to your local Canadian bookseller or sent to Random House of Canada, Ltd., Marketing Department, 2775 Matheson Boulevard East, Mississauga, Ontario L4W 4P7. Inquiries from the United Kingdom should be sent to Fodor's Travel Publications, 20 Vauxhall Bridge Road, London SW1V 2SA, England.

PRINTED IN THE UNITED STATES OF AMERICA

10 9 8 7 6 5 4 3 2 1

CONTENTS

Maps

ON THE ROAD WITH FODOR'S

A trip takes you out of yourself. Concerns of life at home completely disappear, driven away by more immediate thoughts—about, say, what marvels will beguile the next day, or where you'll have dinner. That's where Fodor's comes in. We make sure that you know all your options, so that you don't miss something that's around the next bend just because you didn't know it was there. Mindful that the best memories of your trip might have nothing to do with what you came to Virginia or Maryland to see, we guide you to sights large and small all over the region. You might set out to be enveloped by Colonial Williamsburg, but back at home you find yourself unable to forget racing up Skyline Drive at dawn or chowing down on some Southern Maryland crab cakes. With Fodor's at your side, serendipitous discoveries are never far away.

About Our Writers

Our success in showing you every corner of Virginia and Maryland is a credit to our extraordinary writers. Although there's no substitute for travel advice from a good friend who knows your style, our contributors are the next best thing—the kind of people you would poll for travel advice if you knew them.

Greg Tasker, who updated the Smart Travel Tips and Frederick and Western Maryland chapters, is a frequent contributor to the *Baltimore Sun*'s travel section and other regional magazines and newspapers. He is the former Western Maryland correspondent for the *Baltimore Sun.*

CiCi Williamson has been a food and travel writer and syndicated newspaper columnist for more than two decades. The author of six books, she updated our chapters on Northern Virginia and the Richmond and Northern Neck area. A resident of McLean, Virginia, in suburban Washington, D.C., and the daughter of a U.S. Naval officer, her inherited wanderlust has enticed her to visit every U.S. state and more than 80 countries on 6 continents.

Kathryn McKay updated our chapter on D.C.'s Maryland suburbs. A resident of Montgomery County, her ancestors settled in Prince George's County 300 years ago, and she's had family in Maryland ever since. Kathryn wrote Fodor's *Around Washington, D.C. with Kids* and also contributes to local newspapers.

Kevin Myatt, who lives in Roanoke, Virginia, updated the chapter on Charlottesville, the Shenandoah Valley, the Blue Ridge, and Southwest Virginia. As hiking columnist for www.roanoke.com, he has gained an intimate knowledge of western Virginia's many hills and hollers and the communities they contain. A newspaper writer and editor for 14 years, Kevin is advertising operations manager for the *Roanoke Times.*

Our updater for the Williamsburg and Hampton Roads area, Virginia-native **Gail Doyle,** has worked in the local travel industry for more than 20 years. The former public relations director for the Richmond Convention and Visitors Bureau has authored two books about the state and has updated chapters in *Fodor's Healthy Escapes.*

Photographer and writer **Michelle Gienow** travels the globe for her work but always returns happily to her native Baltimore. When not painting her window screens or rooting for the Orioles, she freelances for the *New York Times, Washington Post,* Discovery Channel, and many other national media clients.

Pete Nelson, a resident of the northern Chesapeake Bay area since the early 1980s, covered Maryland's and Virginia's Eastern Shore for this edition. After more than 20 years in hospitality marketing in the Washington, D.C., area as well as outside the United States, he now writes regularly for local and regional lifestyle magazines. In 2001, he updated the southernmost region of Chile and most of Venezuela for Fodor's.

You can rest assured that you're in good hands—and that no property mentioned in the book has paid to be included. Each has been selected strictly on its merits, as the best of its type in its price range.

How to Use This Book

Up front is **Smart Travel Tips A to Z,** arranged alphabetically by topic and loaded with tips, Web sites, and contact infor-

Virginia and Maryland

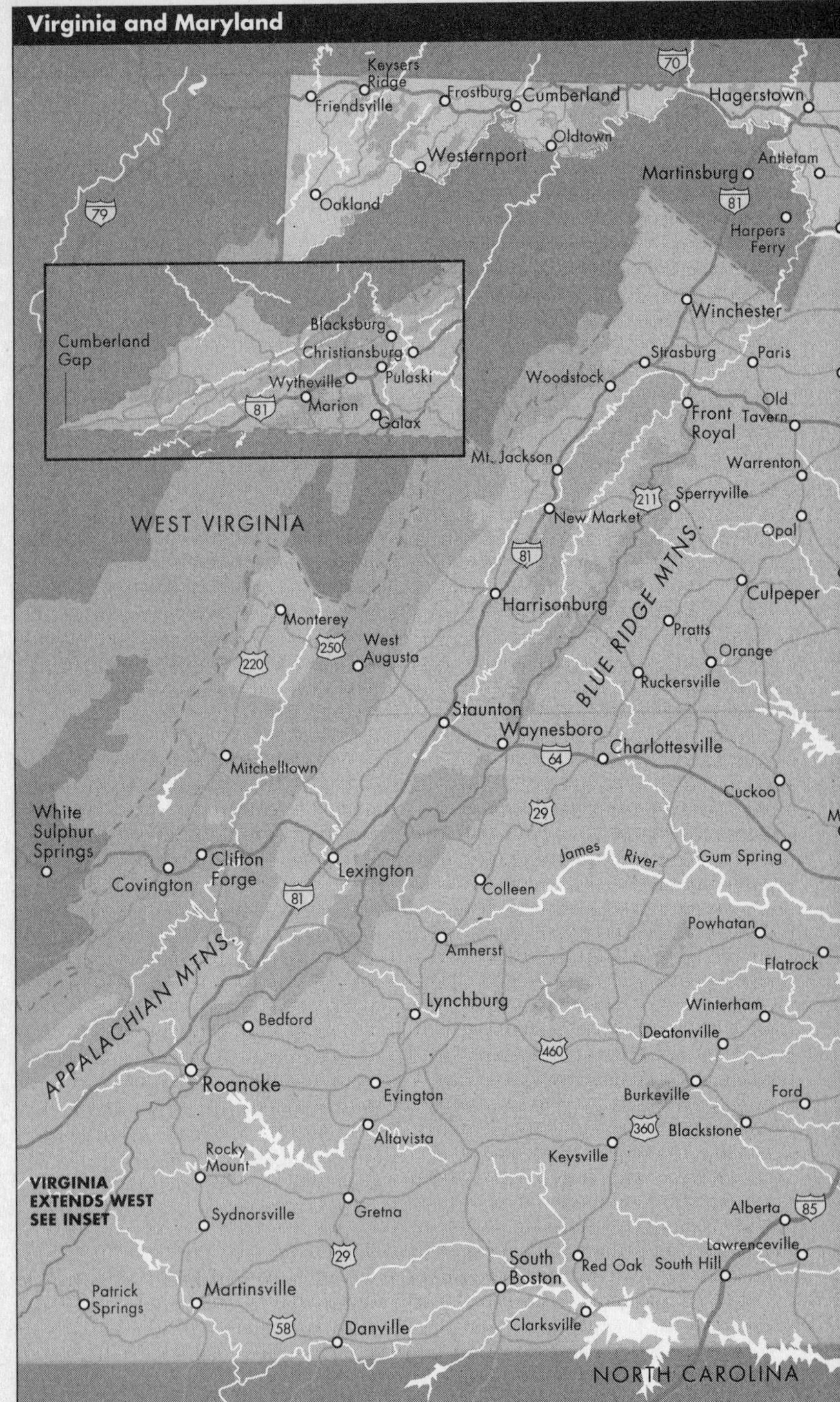

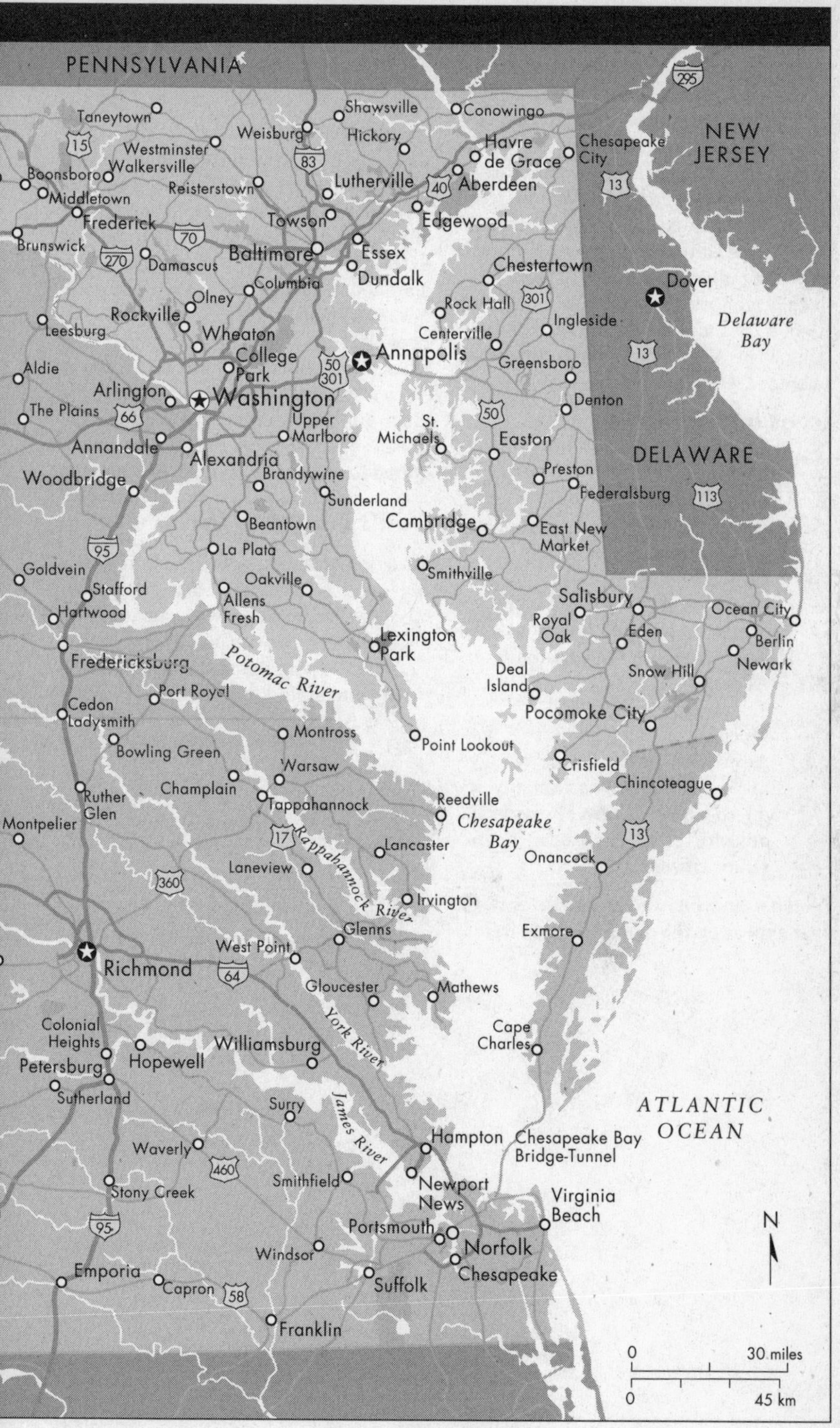
PENNSYLVANIA
NEW JERSEY
DELAWARE
Delaware Bay
Chesapeake Bay
ATLANTIC OCEAN
Potomac River
Rappahannock River
York River
James River
Taneytown
Westminster
Walkersville
Boonsboro
Middletown
Frederick
Brunswick
Damascus
Weisburg
Shawsville
Hickory
Conowingo
Havre de Grace
Chesapeake City
Reisterstown
Lutherville
Aberdeen
Towson
Edgewood
Baltimore
Essex
Dundalk
Chestertown
Columbia
Olney
Rockville
Leesburg
Wheaton
College Park
Annapolis
Rock Hall
Ingleside
Centerville
Greensboro
Dover
Aldie
Arlington
Washington
The Plains
Upper Marlboro
St. Michaels
Easton
Denton
Annandale
Alexandria
Woodbridge
Brandywine
Sunderland
Preston
Federalsburg
Beantown
Cambridge
East New Market
La Plata
Goldvein
Stafford
Hartwood
Oakville
Allens Fresh
Smithville
Salisbury
Royal Oak
Ocean City
Eden
Berlin
Newark
Lexington Park
Fredericksburg
Deal Island
Snow Hill
Port Royal
Pocomoke City
Cedon
Ladysmith
Montross
Point Lookout
Bowling Green
Warsaw
Crisfield
Chincoteague
Ruther Glen
Champlain
Tappahannock
Reedville
Montpelier
Lancaster
Onancock
Laneview
Irvington
Glenns
Exmore
West Point
Richmond
Gloucester
Mathews
Colonial Heights
Cape Charles
Williamsburg
Hopewell
Petersburg
Sutherland
Surry
Hampton
Chesapeake Bay Bridge-Tunnel
Waverly
Smithfield
Newport News
Virginia Beach
Stony Creek
Portsmouth
Norfolk
Windsor
Chesapeake
Emporia
Capron
Suffolk
Franklin
15
83
40
13
295
70
270
301
50
66
113
95
17
360
64
460
58
N
0
30 miles
0
45 km

mation. "Destination: Virginia and Maryland" helps get you in the mood for your trip. Subsequent chapters in *Fodor's Virginia and Maryland* are arranged regionally. All regional chapters are divided geographically; within each area, towns are covered in logical geographical order, and attractive stretches of road between them are indicated by the designation En Route. The Baltimore chapter begins with exploring information, with a section for each neighborhood (each recommending a good tour and listing sights alphabetically). The A to Z section that ends every chapter lists additional resources.

Icons and Symbols

- ★ Our special recommendations
- ✕ Restaurant
- 🏨 Lodging establishment
- ✕🏨 Lodging establishment whose restaurant warrants a special trip
- ⛺ Campgrounds
- 🦆 Good for kids (rubber duckie)
- ☞ Sends you to another section of the guide for more information
- ✉ Address
- ☎ Telephone number
- ⏲ Opening and closing times
- 🎟 Admission prices (those we give apply to adults; substantially reduced fees are almost always available for children, students, and senior citizens)

Numbers in white and black circles ③ ❸ that appear on the maps, in the margins, and within the tours correspond to one another.

For hotels, you can assume that all rooms have private baths, phones, TVs, and air-conditioning unless otherwise noted and that all hotels operate on the European Plan (with no meals) if we don't specify another meal plan. We always list a property's facilities but not whether you'll be charged extra to use them, so when pricing accommodations, do ask what's included. For restaurants, it's always a good idea to book ahead; we mention reservations only when they're essential or are not accepted. All restaurants we list are open daily for lunch and dinner unless stated otherwise; dress is mentioned only when men are required to wear a jacket or a jacket and tie.

Don't Forget to Write

Your experiences—positive and negative—matter to us. If we have missed or misstated something, we want to hear about it. We follow up on all suggestions. Contact the Virginia and Maryland editor at editors@fodors.com or c/o Fodor's at 1745 Broadway, New York, New York 10019. And have a fabulous trip!

Karen Cure
Editorial Director

ESSENTIAL INFORMATION

AIR TRAVEL

US Airways links the major airports in the region. Commuter flights shuttle between the Eastern Shore and Baltimore-Washington International Airport.

CHECK-IN AND BOARDING

Always **ask your carrier about its check-in policy.** Plan to arrive at the airport about two hours before your scheduled departure time for domestic flights and 2½ to 3 hours before international flights. Assuming that not everyone with a ticket will show up, airlines routinely overbook planes. When everyone does, airlines ask for volunteers to give up their seats. In return, these volunteers usually get a certificate for a free flight and are rebooked on the next flight out. If there are not enough volunteers, the airline must choose who will be denied boarding. The first to get bumped are passengers who checked in late and those flying on discounted tickets, so **get to the gate and check in as early as possible,** especially during peak periods.

Always **bring a government-issued photo I.D. to the airport;** even when it's not required, a passport is best.

ENJOYING THE FLIGHT

For better service, **fly smaller or regional carriers,** which often have higher passenger-satisfaction ratings. Sometimes you'll find leather seats, more legroom, and better food.

State your seat preference when purchasing your ticket, and then repeat it when you confirm and when you check in. For more legroom, you can request one of the few emergency-aisle seats at check-in, if you are capable of lifting at least 50 pounds—a Federal Aviation Administration requirement of passengers in these seats. Seats behind a bulkhead also offer more legroom, but they don't have under-seat storage. Don't sit in the row in front of the emergency aisle or in front of a bulkhead, where seats may not recline.

Ask the airline whether a snack or meal is served on the flight. If you have dietary concerns, **request special meals when booking.** These can be vegetarian, low-cholesterol, or kosher, for example. It's a good idea to pack some healthful snacks and a small (plastic) bottle of water in your carry-on bag. On long flights, try to maintain a normal routine, to help fight jet lag. At night, **get some sleep.** By day, **eat light meals, drink water** (not alcohol), and **move around the cabin** to stretch your legs. For additional jet-lag tips consult *Fodor's FYI: Travel Fit & Healthy* (available at bookstores everywhere).

Smoking policies vary from carrier to carrier. Many airlines prohibit smoking on all of their international flights; others allow smoking only on certain routes or certain departures. Ask your carrier about its policy.

FLYING TIMES

Flying time to Baltimore-Washington International Airport is nearly one hour from New York; approximately two hours from Chicago; and five hours, 40 minutes from Los Angeles. Flying time to Richmond International Airport is approximately 1½ hours from New York, two hours from Chicago, and 6½ hours from Los Angeles. A flight to D.C. is a little less than an hour from New York, about 1½ hours from Chicago, three hours from Denver and Dallas, and five hours from San Francisco. Those flying from London can expect a trip of about six hours. A trip from Sydney takes about 20 hours.

HOW TO COMPLAIN

If your baggage goes astray or your flight goes awry, complain right away.

Most carriers require that you **file a claim immediately.** The Aviation Consumer Protection Division of the Department of Transportation publishes *Fly-Rights,* which discusses airlines and consumer issues and is available on-line. At PassengerRights.com, a Web site, you can compose a letter of complaint and distribute it electronically.

➤ AIRLINE COMPLAINTS: **Aviation Consumer Protection Division** (✉ U.S. Department of Transportation, Room 4107, C-75, Washington, DC 20590, ☎ 202/366–2220, WEB www.dot.gov/airconsumer). **Federal Aviation Administration Consumer Hotline** (☎ 800/322–7873).

RECONFIRMING

Check the status of your flight before you leave for the airport. You can do this on your carrier's Web site, by linking to a flight-status checker (many Web booking services offer these), or by calling your carrier or travel agent.

AIRPORTS

There are several major airports to choose from. Virginia has Richmond International Airport, 10 mi east of Richmond; the busy Ronald Reagan Washington National Airport, 3 mi south of downtown Washington; and Washington Dulles International Airport, 26 mi northwest of Washington. Maryland's Baltimore-Washington International (BWI) Airport is about 25 mi northeast of Washington and 10 mi south of Baltimore. Amtrak and commuter trains stop at BWI's station. Fares into Richmond are often more expensive than those into D.C. or BWI.

Greater Cumberland Regional Airport serves western Maryland; Easton Airport, with Maryland Airlines, services Maryland's middle Eastern Shore. Ocean City Municipal Airport offers private facilities close to Maryland's Atlantic seashore; Salisbury-Ocean City-Wicomico Regional Airport provides service to Maryland's lower Eastern Shore, and Washington County Regional (Hagerstown) Airport has flights that go to Pittsburgh and throughout Maryland.

➤ AIRPORT INFORMATION: **Baltimore-Washington International Airport** (BWI; Exit 2 off Baltimore-Washington Pkwy., ☎ 410/859–7100, WEB www.bwiairport.com). **Richmond International Airport** (RIC; ✉ Exit 197 off I–64, ☎ 804/226–3000). **Ronald Reagan Washington National Airport** (DCA; ✉ Airport exit off Rte. 1, ☎ 703/417–8000, WEB www.metwashairports.com/tableof.htm). **Washington Dulles International Airport** (IAD; ✉ Dulles Access Rd. off I–66, ☎ 703/572–2700, WEB www.metwashairports.com/tableof.htm).

➤ COMMUTER AIRPORTS: **Easton Airport** (ESN; ✉ 29137 Newnam Rd. Unit 1, Easton, MD, ☎ 410/770–8055). **Greater Cumberland Regional Airport** (✉ CBE; Rte. 1, Wiley Ford, WV, ☎ 304/738–0002). **Ocean City Municipal Airport** (OXB; ✉ 12724 Airport Rd., Berlin, MD, ☎ 410/213–2471). **Salisbury-Ocean City-Wicomico Regional Airport** (SBY; ✉ 5485 Airport Terminal Rd. Unit A, Salisbury, MD, ☎ 410/548–4827). **Washington County Regional (Hagerstown) Airport** (HGR; ✉ 18434 Showalter Rd.,.Hagerstown, MD, ☎ 240/313–2777).

TRANSFERS BY BUS

Reagan National, Dulles, and BWI airports are served by SuperShuttle, which will take you to a specific hotel or residence. Make reservations at the ground transportation desk. Fares vary depending on the destination. Drivers accept major credit cards in addition to cash.

➤ BUS INFORMATION: **SuperShuttle** (☎ 800/258–3826).

BIKE TRAVEL

Getting around major cities and suburbs is tricky—roads are congested and, for the most part, there are no bicycle lanes. Outside the urban areas, you'll find terrain more suited for bicycling, including flat coastal plains, gentle hills, and mountains. Popular bicycling trails include the Baltimore and Annapolis Trail Park and the towpath of the C&O Canal, which runs parallel to the Potomac River on the Maryland shore, from Georgetown in Washington, D.C., to Cumberland in western

Maryland. Touring bikes are available in resort towns along the Maryland and Virginia shorelines; mountain bikes are offered at ski resorts and in the mountains.

The Maryland State Highway Administration can provide details concerning statewide bike routes. In Virginia, contact the State Bicycle Coordinator.

➤ INFORMATION: The **Maryland State Highway Administration** (✉ Bicycle and Pedestrian Coordinator, Mailstop C-502, State Highway Administration, 707 N. Calvert St., Baltimore, MD 21203, ☎ 410/545–5656, WEB www.sha.state.md.us). In Virginia, contact the **State Bicycle Coordinator** (✉ Virginia Department of Transportation, 1221 E. Broad St., Richmond, VA 23219, ☎ 804/786–2801, WEB virginiadot.org).

BIKES IN FLIGHT

Most airlines accommodate bikes as luggage, provided they are dismantled and boxed; check with individual airlines about packing requirements. Airlines sell bike boxes, which are often free at bike shops, for about $15 (bike bags start at $100). International travelers often can substitute a bike for a piece of checked luggage at no charge; otherwise, the cost is about $100. Domestic and Canadian airlines charge $40–$80 each way.

BOAT AND FERRY TRAVEL

Water sports and activities are popular recreational pursuits in Virginia and Maryland, which share the expansive Chesapeake Bay and the Potomac River. Harbor and river cruises are offered in Baltimore, St. Michaels, Annapolis, Washington, D.C. (along the Potomac), Hampton, and Norfolk, to name a few starting points. Sailboats and other pleasure craft can be chartered for trips on the Chesapeake Bay or inland rivers. Popular ports include Rock Hall, Havre de Grace, and Solomons in Maryland, and Newport News and Chincoteague in Virginia.

In Baltimore, one of the best ways to get to the neighborhoods and sights that border the harbor is by water taxi. After paying a $5 fee, you can use one of several private water taxis all day.

BUS TRAVEL

A bus is a fairly practical way to get to a one-stop resort destination such as Ocean City or Virginia Beach, but many of Maryland's and Virginia's attractions lie outside the cities served by bus routes. Municipal buses do provide point-to-point transportation in Baltimore and Richmond.

Greyhound Lines serves the following locations (among others) in Maryland: Baltimore, Cambridge, Cumberland, Easton, Frederick, Hagerstown, Salisbury, Silver Spring, and Ocean City. In Virginia it serves Abingdon, Arlington, Charlottesville, Fairfax, Fredericksburg, Hampton, Lexington, Norfolk, Richmond, Roanoke, Springfield, Staunton, Virginia Beach, and Williamsburg, as well as other towns.

➤ BUS INFORMATION: **Greyhound Lines** (☎ 800/231–2222, WEB www.greyhound.com).

BUSINESS HOURS

The business week runs from 9 to 5 weekdays, and in some instances, on Saturday in the metropolitan regions of Virginia and Maryland. Stores, restaurants, and other services maintain longer hours. Hours vary in small towns and resort areas, especially those dependent on seasonal visitors. In rural areas, many retail establishments close on Sundays.

Most businesses in the area close for many religious holidays and all holidays that are celebrated on a Monday. However, shopping malls and plazas, as well as restaurants, remain open.

MUSEUMS AND SIGHTS

The major art and historical museums in the region are open from 10 or 11 to 5 or 6, Monday through Saturday, and noon to 5 on Sunday. Some museums are closed on Monday and/or Tuesday. Many parks and historical homes tend to have varied hours according to the season, with later closing hours in the summer. Some close during the winter months. In this book's sight reviews, open hours are denoted by a clock icon.

PHARMACIES

Major chain pharmacies have longer hours than independent pharmacies in suburban and rural communities. Some chain stores offer 24-hour and drive-through service daily in the more populated regions. Most independent pharmacies are closed on Sunday.

SHOPS

In the metropolitan areas, retail stores and shopping malls are open 10–9, Monday through Saturday, and 11–6 on Sunday. Outlet shopping centers maintain the same hours. In suburban Baltimore, Washington, and Richmond, grocery stores and superstores often are open 24 hours. Retailers in small towns and in the downtown office districts close earlier and are often not open on Sunday.

CAMERAS AND PHOTOGRAPHY

The *Kodak Guide to Shooting Great Travel Pictures* (available at bookstores everywhere) is loaded with tips.

➤ PHOTO HELP: **Kodak Information Center** (☎ 800/242–2424, WEB www.kodak.com).

CAR RENTAL

Rates in Virginia and Maryland begin at $30–$40 a day and $105 a week for an economy car with unlimited mileage. This does not include tax on car rentals, which is 8% in Virginia and 11½% in Maryland.

INSURANCE

When driving a rented car you are generally responsible for any damage to or loss of the vehicle. You may also be liable for any property damage or personal injury that you may cause while driving. Before you rent, see what coverage you already have under the terms of your personal auto-insurance policy and credit cards.

For about $15 to $20 a day, rental companies sell protection, known as a collision- or loss-damage waiver (CDW or LDW), that eliminates your liability for damage to the car; it's always optional and should never be automatically added to your bill. In Maryland the car-rental agency's insurance is primary; therefore, the company must pay for damage to third parties up to a preset legal limit, beyond which your own liability insurance kicks in. However, **make sure you have enough coverage to pay for the car.** If you do not have auto insurance or an umbrella policy that covers damage to third parties, purchasing liability insurance and a CDW or LDW is highly recommended.

REQUIREMENTS AND RESTRICTIONS

In Virginia and Maryland you must be 21 to rent a car.

CAR TRAVEL

Unless you are visiting central Baltimore or Ocean City, a car is by far the most convenient means of travel throughout Maryland and Virginia, and in many areas it is the only practical way to get around. (Where it exists, public transportation is clean and comfortable, but too often it bypasses or falls short of travel high points.)

HIGHWAYS

Interstate 95 runs north–south through Maryland and Virginia, carrying traffic to and from New England and Florida and intermediate points. U.S. 50 links I–95 with Annapolis and Maryland's Eastern Shore. U.S. 97 links Baltimore with Annapolis. I–64 intersects I–95 at Richmond and runs east–west, headed east toward Williamsburg, Hampton Roads, and the bridge-tunnel to Virginia's Eastern Shore, and west toward Charlottesville and the Shenandoah Valley. At Staunton, I–64 intersects I–81, which runs north–south. Interstate 70 runs west from Baltimore's Beltway, I–695, to Hancock in western Maryland. I–68 connects Hancock to Cumberland and Garrett County. Also, U.S. 40—the National Pike—travels east and west, the entire length of Maryland. Interstate 83 journeys south from Pennsylvania to the top of I–695, the Baltimore Beltway.

ROAD MAPS

The state tourist offices of Maryland and Virginia (☞ Visitor Information) publish official state road maps, free for the asking, that contain directories and other useful information. For the excellent, free *Maryland Scenic Byways* guide, call 877/632–9929 or look for one at a state welcome center.

RULES OF THE ROAD

The maximum speed limit is 65 mph on stretches of major highways in both states. Radar detectors are legal in Maryland, but are not permitted in Virginia, so don't forget to put it away once you cross into Virginia. Front-seat passengers in both states must wear seat belts.

In Virginia and Maryland, you may turn right at a red light after stopping if there is no oncoming traffic. When in doubt, wait for the green. Be alert for one-way streets, "no left turn" intersections, and blocks closed to car traffic.

CHILDREN IN VIRGINIA AND MARYLAND

Be sure to plan ahead and **involve your youngsters** as you outline your trip. When packing, include things to keep them busy en route. On sightseeing days try to schedule activities of special interest to your children. Maryland publishes *The Official Chesapeake Bay Activity Book–Fun From the Bridge to the Beach* free upon request at the Bay Bridge toll booths.

If you are renting a car, don't forget to **arrange for a car seat** when you reserve. For general advice about traveling with children, consult *Fodor's FYI: Travel with Your Baby* (available in bookstores everywhere).

➤ AGENCIES: **Tidewater Babysitters** (✉ Norfolk, VA, ☎ 757/489–1622). **Homecare Connection** (✉ Richmond, VA, ☎ 804/379–9314).

FLYING

If your children are two or older, **ask about children's airfares.** As a general rule, infants under two not occupying a seat fly at greatly reduced fares or even for free.

Experts agree that it's a good idea to use safety seats aloft for children weighing less than 40 pounds. Airlines set their own policies: U.S. carriers usually require that the child be ticketed, even if he or she is young enough to ride free, since the seats must be strapped into regular seats. Do **check your airline's policy about using safety seats during takeoff and landing.** Safety seats are not allowed everywhere in the plane, so get your seat assignments as early as possible.

When reserving, **request children's meals or a freestanding bassinet** (not available at all airlines) if you need them. But note that bulkhead seats, where you must sit to use the bassinet, may lack an overhead bin or storage space on the floor.

LODGING

Most hotels in Virginia and Maryland allow children under a certain age to stay in their parents' room at no extra charge, but others charge for them as extra adults; be sure to **find out the cutoff age for children's discounts.**

SIGHTS AND ATTRACTIONS

Places that are especially appealing to children are indicated by a rubber-duckie icon (🐤) in the margin. Many historic attractions make every effort to engage children with hands-on activities and entertaining costumed reenactors. At Williamsburg you can even rent period costumes for children, so that they can get into the spirit.

TRANSPORTATION

If you are renting a car, don't forget to **arrange for a car seat** when you reserve. Always **strap children under age 6 or under 40 lbs. into approved child-safety seats.** This is the law in Virginia; in Maryland the maximum age for a child-safety seat is 4. In both states, children under 15 must wear seat belts regardless of where they're seated.

CONSUMER PROTECTION

Whether you're shopping for gifts or purchasing travel services, **pay with a major credit card** whenever possible, so you can cancel payment or get reimbursed if there's a problem (and you can provide documentation). If you're doing business with a particular company for the first time, **contact your local Better Business Bureau and the attorney general's offices** in your state and (for U.S. businesses) the company's home state as well. Have any complaints been filed? Finally, if you're buying a package or tour, always **consider travel insurance** that includes default coverage (☞ Insurance).

➤ BBBs: **Council of Better Business Bureaus** (✉ 4200 Wilson Blvd., Suite 800, Arlington, VA 22203, ☎ 703/276–0100, FAX 703/525–8277, WEB www.bbb.org).

DINING

The restaurants we list are the cream of the crop in each price category. Properties indicated by an ✕🏨 are lodging establishments whose restaurant warrants a special trip. Seafood, from blue crabs to oysters to rockfish, is a staple in the coastal towns of Maryland and Virginia. Inland waterways, too, provide meals for the table: duck, goose, shellfish, and terrapin (turtle). The best ethnic restaurants are in Baltimore, suburban Washington, D.C., and Richmond. Pennsylvania Dutch influences can be found on the menus of restaurants in parts of northern Maryland, and traditional Southern fare is common in Virginia beyond the Washington suburbs.

In general, when you order a regular coffee, you get coffee with milk and sugar.

CATEGORY	COST*
$$$$	over $32
$$$	$22–$32
$$	$12–$22
$	under $12

**per person for a main course at dinner*

RESERVATIONS AND DRESS

Reservations are always a good idea; we mention them only when they're essential or not accepted. Book as far ahead as you can, and reconfirm as soon as you arrive. (Large parties should always call ahead to check the reservations policy.) We mention dress only when men are required to wear a jacket or a jacket and tie.

SPECIALTIES

The treasure of the Chesapeake Bay is the blue crab. In Maryland and Virginia, the locals like crabs steamed in the shells, seasoned by the bushel, and dumped on brown-paper-covered tables in spartan crab houses. They use wooden mallets to crack the shells, and nimble fingers to reach the meat. Crab cakes, crab imperial (enriched crabmeat stuffed back into shells), crab soup, and a host of other such dishes can be found throughout the region. Rockfish (striped bass) is another seafood delicacy, harvested in summer and fall.

In Virginia, country ham, biscuits, collard greens, and fried chicken—Southern staples—are popular Sunday meals. Grits (often served for breakfast) and pecan and sweet potato pies are other popular Southern foods.

WINE, BEER, AND SPIRITS

Though Maryland and Virginia vineyards have been producing it for hundreds of years, most of the region's wines remain obscure. Wineries in both states, though, routinely win national awards. Most of Maryland's dozen or so wineries are in the central part of the state, where the spring and fall are more temperate. You can visit most of them on weekend tours. The state's wine industry is touted every fall at the Maryland Wine Festival in Westminster. The state also has more than 20 brew pubs.

Wineries are spread throughout Virginia's varied terrain, from the coastal plains to the Blue Ridge Mountains. Two notable wineries are Jefferson Vineyards near Charlottesville, the site of Thomas Jefferson's first plantings of European vinifera vines; and Williamsburg Winery, popular with those visiting Colonial Williamsburg. The Dominion State also has about a dozen brew pubs. One of the most successful is the Capital City Brewing Co., which sells handcrafted beers in D.C., suburban Virginia, and Baltimore.

DISABILITIES AND ACCESSIBILITY

Destination Maryland, a guidebook published by the Maryland Office of Tourism, labels individual historic sites, attractions, hotels, and restaurants that are accessible to the disabled. The Virginia Tourism Corporation publishes the free *Virginia Travel Guide for Persons with*

Disabilities, which provides information on parking, accessibility, and other needs of disabled travelers at attractions, parks, lodgings, campgrounds, and outdoor recreation and shopping centers.

➤ LOCAL RESOURCES: **Maryland Office of Tourism** (☎ 800/634–7386, WEB www.mdisfun.org). **The Virginia Tourism Corporation** (☎ 804/371–0327 or 800/742–3935, WEB www.virginia.org).

LODGING

Despite the Americans with Disabilities Act, the definition of accessibility seems to differ from hotel to hotel. Some properties may be accessible by ADA standards for people with mobility problems but not for people with hearing or vision impairments, for example.

If you have mobility problems, ask for the lowest floor on which accessible services are offered. If you have a hearing impairment, check whether the hotel has devices to alert you visually to the ring of the telephone, a knock at the door, and a fire/emergency alarm. Some hotels provide these devices without charge. Discuss your needs with hotel personnel if this equipment isn't available, so that a staff member can personally alert you in the event of an emergency.

If you're bringing a guide dog, get authorization ahead of time and write down the name of the person you spoke with.

RESERVATIONS

When discussing accessibility with an operator or reservations agent, **ask hard questions.** Are there any stairs, inside *or* out? Are there grab bars next to the toilet *and* in the shower/tub? How wide is the doorway to the room? To the bathroom? For the most extensive facilities meeting the latest legal specifications, **opt for newer accommodations.** If you reserve through a toll-free number, consider also calling the hotel's local number to confirm the information from the central reservations office. Get confirmation in writing when you can.

➤ COMPLAINTS: **Aviation Consumer Protection Division** (☞ Air Travel) for airline-related problems. **Departmental Office of Civil Rights** (for general inquiries, ✉ U.S. Department of Transportation, S-30, 400 7th St. SW, Room 10215, Washington, DC 20590, ☎ 202/366–4648, FAX 202/366–3571, WEB www.dot.gov/ost/docr). **Disability Rights Section** (✉ NYAV, U.S. Department of Justice, Civil Rights Division, 950 Pennsylvania Ave. NW, Washington, DC 20530; ☎ ADA information line 202/514–0301 or 800/514–0301; 202/514–0383 TTY or 800/514–0383 TTY, WEB www.usdoj.gov/crt/ada/adahom1.htm).

TRAVEL AGENCIES

In the United States, the Americans with Disabilities Act requires that travel firms serve the needs of all travelers. Some agencies specialize in working with people with disabilities.

➤ TRAVELERS WITH MOBILITY PROBLEMS: **Access Adventures** (✉ 206 Chestnut Ridge Rd., Scottsville, NY 14624, ☎ 716/889–9096, dltravel@prodigy.net), run by a former physical-rehabilitation counselor. **Accessible Vans of America** (✉ 9 Spielman Rd., Fairfield, NJ 07004, ☎ 877/282–8267; 888/282–8267 reservations, FAX 973/808–9713, WEB www.accessiblevans.com). **Flying Wheels Travel** (✉ 143 W. Bridge St., Box 382, Owatonna, MN 55060, ☎ 507/451–5005, FAX 507/451–1685, WEB www.flyingwheelstravel.com).

DISCOUNTS AND DEALS

Be a smart shopper and **compare all your options** before making decisions. A plane ticket bought with a promotional coupon from travel clubs, coupon books, and direct-mail offers or purchased on the Internet may not be cheaper than the least expensive fare from a discount ticket agency. And always keep in mind that what you get is just as important as what you save.

CREDIT-CARD BENEFITS

When you use your credit card to make travel purchases you may get free travel-accident insurance, collision-damage insurance, and medical or legal assistance, depending on the card and the bank that issued it. American Express, MasterCard, and

Visa cards often provide one or more of these services, so **get a copy of your credit card's travel-benefits policy.** If you are a member of an auto club, always **ask hotel and car-rental reservations agents about auto-club discounts.** Some clubs offer additional discounts on tours, cruises, and admission to attractions.

DISCOUNT RESERVATIONS

To save money, **look into discount reservations services** with Web sites and toll-free numbers, which use their buying power to get a better price on hotels, airline tickets, even car rentals. When booking a room, always **call the hotel's local toll-free number** (if one is available) rather than the central reservations number—you'll often get a better price. Always ask about special packages or corporate rates.

➤ AIRLINE TICKETS: ☎ **800/AIR-4LESS.**

➤ HOTEL ROOMS: **RMC Travel** (☎ 800/245–5738, WEB www.rmcwebtravel.com). **Turbotrip.com** (☎ 800/473–7829, WEB www.turbotrip.com).

PACKAGE DEALS

Don't confuse packages and guided tours. When you buy a package, you travel on your own, just as though you had planned the trip yourself. Fly/drive packages, which combine airfare and car rental, are often a good deal.

GAY AND LESBIAN TRAVEL

For details about the gay and lesbian scene, consult *Fodor's Gay Guide to the USA* (available in bookstores everywhere).

In Maryland, Baltimore's Mount Vernon, north of the Inner Harbor, has several gay and lesbian nightclubs and bars, as well as Lambda Rising, a gay and lesbian bookstore.

Gays and lesbians are generally accepted in Virginia and Maryland's larger cities and in the suburbs of D.C. Caution should be exercised in some of the more rural and mountainous regions of both states, however, which may be less accepting.

➤ GAY- AND LESBIAN-FRIENDLY TRAVEL AGENCIES: **Different Roads Travel** (✉ 8383 Wilshire Blvd., Suite 902, Beverly Hills, CA 90211, ☎ 323/651–5557 or 800/429–8747, FAX 323/651–3678, lgernert@tzell.com). **Kennedy Travel** (✉ 314 Jericho Turnpike, Floral Park, NY 11001, ☎ 516/352–4888 or 800/237–7433, FAX 516/354–8849, WEB www.kennedytravel.com). **Now, Voyager** (✉ 4406 18th St., San Francisco, CA 94114, ☎ 415/626–1169 or 800/255–6951, FAX 415/626–8626, WEB www.nowvoyager.com). **Skylink Travel and Tour** (✉ 1006 Mendocino Ave., Santa Rosa, CA 95401, ☎ 707/546–9888 or 800/225–5759, FAX 707/546–9891, WEB www.skylinktravel.com), serving lesbian travelers.

GUIDEBOOKS

Plan well and you won't be sorry. Guidebooks are excellent tools—and you can take them with you. You may want to check out *Fodor's Road Guide USA: Delaware, District of Columbia, Maryland, Pennsylvania, Virginia,* with comprehensive restaurant, hotel, and attractions listings for driving vacations.

HOLIDAYS

Independence Day is naturally a big affair in Maryland and Virginia, both among the original 13 Colonies and also crossroads of the Civil War. Patriotic music, along with fireworks and cannon volleys, celebrate independence at the annual Maryland Symphony Orchestra performance at Antietam National Battlefield, the site of a decisive Civil War battle. Colonial Williamsburg honors the occasion with a reading of the Declaration of Independence, along with a military salute to the 13 Colonies.

Major national holidays include New Year's Day (Jan. 1); Martin Luther King Jr. Day (3rd Mon. in Jan.); Presidents' Day (3rd Mon. in Feb.); Memorial Day (last Mon. in May); Independence Day (July 4); Labor Day (1st Mon. in Sept.); Thanksgiving Day (4th Thurs. in Nov.); Christmas Eve and Christmas Day (Dec. 24 and 25); and New Year's Eve (Dec. 31).

INSURANCE

The most useful travel-insurance plan is a comprehensive policy that includes coverage for trip cancellation and interruption, default, trip delay, and medical expenses (with a waiver for preexisting conditions).

Without insurance you will lose all or most of your money if you cancel your trip, regardless of the reason. Default insurance covers you if your tour operator, airline, or cruise line goes out of business. Trip-delay covers expenses that arise because of bad weather or mechanical delays. Study the fine print when comparing policies.

U.K. residents can buy a travel-insurance policy valid for most vacations taken during the year in which it's purchased (but check preexisting-condition coverage).

Always **buy travel policies directly from the insurance company**; if you buy them from a cruise line, airline, or tour operator that goes out of business you probably will not be covered for the agency or operator's default, a major risk. Before making any purchase, **review your existing health and home-owner's policies** to find what they cover away from home.

➤ TRAVEL INSURERS: In the U.S.: **Access America** (✉ 6600 W. Broad St., Richmond, VA 23230, ☎ 800/284–8300, FAX 804/673–1491 or 800/346–9265, WEB www.accessamerica.com). **Travel Guard International** (✉ 1145 Clark St., Stevens Point, WI 54481, ☎ 715/345–0505 or 800/826–1300, FAX 800/955–8785, WEB www.travelguard.com).

LODGING

The lodgings we list are the cream of the crop in each price category. We always list the facilities that are available, but we don't specify whether they cost extra; when pricing accommodations, always ask what's included and what costs extra.

CATEGORY	COST*
$$$$	over $225
$$$	$150–$225
$$	$100–$150
$	under $100

**All prices are for a standard double room, excluding state tax.*

Properties are assigned price categories based on the range from their least-expensive standard double room at high season (excluding holidays) to the most expensive.

Assume that hotels operate on the **European Plan** (EP, with no meals) unless we specify that they use the **Continental Plan** (CP, with a Continental breakfast), **Breakfast Plan** (BP, with a full breakfast), **Modified American Plan** (MAP, with breakfast and dinner), or the **Full American Plan** (FAP, with all meals).

Properties marked ✕🏨 are lodging establishments whose restaurants warrant a special trip.

APARTMENT AND HOUSE RENTALS

If you want a home base that's roomy enough for a family and comes with cooking facilities, **consider a furnished rental.** These can save you money, especially if you're traveling with a large group. Home-exchange directories list rentals (often second homes owned by prospective house swappers), and some services search for a house or apartment for you and handle the paperwork. Some send an illustrated catalog; others send photographs only of specific properties, sometimes at a charge. Up-front registration fees may apply.

At shoreline resorts, as well as Deep Creek Lake in western Maryland, real estate agents generally handle apartment, condo, and town house rentals. Developers and individual owners make arrangements in the mountain resorts of Virginia.

➤ LOCAL AGENTS: **Bed & Breakfast Accommodations Ltd.** (☎ 413/583–9998 or 800/899–7533) has Virginia and Maryland listings. **Atkinson Realty** (☎ 757/428–4441) arranges rentals in Virginia Beach. **Bud Church Coldwell Banker** (☎ 800/851–7326) for Ocean City. **Moore Warfield & Glick** (☎ 800/289–2821) for Ocean City. **Coldwell Banker** (☎ 301/387–6187) or **Railey Mountain Lake Vacations** (☎ 800/846–7368) for Deep Creek Lake in Maryland.

➤ RENTAL AGENTS: **Property Rentals International** (✉ 1008 Mansfield Crossing Rd., Richmond, VA 23236, ☎ 804/378–6054, FAX 804/379–2073). **Hideaways International**

(✉ 767 Islington St., Portsmouth, NH 03801, ☎ 603/430–4433 or 800/843–4433, FAX 603/430–4444; membership $99) is a club for travelers who arrange rentals among themselves.

BED-AND-BREAKFASTS

Houses in this region make it a natural area for bed-and-breakfast accommodations. The majority of B&Bs in Virginia and Maryland are Victorian structures with fewer than 10 rental units; a full or a Continental breakfast is typically included in the lodging rate, and rooms rarely have their own TV. Most rooms, however, have private bathrooms.

➤ RESERVATION SERVICES: **Bed & Breakfast Accommodations Ltd. of Washington, DC** (✉ Box 12011, Washington, DC 20005, ☎ 202/328–3510, FAX 431/582–9669) has lodgings in Washington, Virginia, and Maryland. **Virginia Division of Tourism Reservation Service** (☎ 800/934–9184).

CAMPING

Camping is popular in the Shenandoah and Blue Ridge mountains in Virginia, and at state forests and parks in western Maryland. Be aware that black bears abound in these regions. State-maintained sites include primitive and full-service sites (with showers, bathrooms, and hook-ups). Private campgrounds offer more amenities.

Assateague Island State Park in Maryland and the Assateague Island National Seashore (in Maryland and Virginia) are both popular campgrounds, largely because of the pristine beaches and ocean swimming, and the opportunity to camp near wild ponies. Mosquitoes are nuisances throughout the summer months.

HOME EXCHANGES

If you would like to exchange your home for someone else's, **join a home-exchange organization,** which will send you its updated listings of available exchanges for a year and will include your own listing in at least one of them. It's up to you to make specific arrangements.

➤ EXCHANGE CLUBS: **HomeLink International** (✉ Box 47747, Tampa, FL 33647, ☎ 813/975–9825 or 800/638–3841, FAX 813/910–8144, WEB www.homelink.org; $106 per year).**Intervac U.S.** (✉ Box 590504, San Francisco, CA 94159, ☎ 800/756–4663, FAX 415/435–7440, WEB www.intervacus.com; $93 yearly fee includes one catalog and on-line access).

HOSTELS

No matter what your age, you can **save on lodging costs by staying at hostels.** In some 4,500 locations in more than 70 countries around the world, Hostelling International (HI), the umbrella group for a number of national youth-hostel associations, offers single-sex, dorm-style beds and, at many hostels, rooms for couples and family accommodations. Membership in any HI national hostel association, open to travelers of all ages, allows you to stay in HI-affiliated hostels at member rates; one-year membership is about $25 for adults (C$35 for a two-year minimum membership in Canada, £13 in the U.K., A$52 in Australia, and NZ$40 in New Zealand); hostels run about $10–$30 per night. Members have priority if the hostel is full; they're also eligible for discounts around the world, even on rail and bus travel in some countries.

With few exceptions, hostels in Virginia and Maryland are near popular outdoor spots or resort communities. In Maryland, the Harpers Ferry Lodge is near the Appalachian Trail in Knoxville, across the Potomac River from Harpers Ferry. Virginia's Bears Den Lodge is near the Appalachian Trail in Bluemont, the Blue Ridge Mountains is near the Blue Ridge Parkway in Galax, and Angie's Guest Cottage Hostel is in Virginia Beach.

➤ HOSTELS: **HI-Angie's Guest Cottage Hostel** (✉ 302 24th St., Virginia Beach, VA 23451, ☎ 757/428–4690, WEB www.angiescottage.com). **HI-Bears Den Lodge** (✉ Virginia Hwy. 601, 18393 Blueridge Mountain Rd., Bluemont, VA 20135, ☎ 540/554–8708, FAX 540/554–8708). **HI-Blue Ridge Mountains** (✉ Blue Ridge

Parkway at milepost 214½, east side, Galax, VA 24333, ☎ 276/236–4962). **HI-Harpers Ferry Lodge** (✉ 19123 Sandy Hook Rd., Knoxville, MD 21758, ☎ 310/834–7652, FAX 301/834–7652, WEB www.harpersferryhostel.org).

➤ ORGANIZATIONS: **Hostelling International—American Youth Hostels** (✉ 733 15th St. NW, Suite 840, Washington, DC 20005, ☎ 202/783–6161, FAX 202/783–6171, WEB www.hiayh.org). **Hostelling International—Canada** (✉ 400–205 Catherine St., Ottawa, Ontario K2P 1C3, ☎ 613/237–7884 or 800/663–5777, FAX 613/237–7868, WEB www.hihostels.ca). **Youth Hostel Association of England and Wales** (✉ Trevelyan House, Dimple Rd., Matlock, Derbyshire DE4 3YH, U.K., ☎ 0870/870–8808, FAX 0169/592–702, WEB www.yha.org.uk). **Youth Hostel Association Australia** (✉ 10 Mallett St., Camperdown, NSW 2050, ☎ 02/9565–1699, FAX 02/9565–1325, WEB www.yha.com.au). **Youth Hostels Association of New Zealand** (✉ Level 3, 193 Cashel St., Box 436, Christchurch, ☎ 03/379–9970, FAX 03/365–4476, WEB www.yha.org.nz).

HOTELS

The large hotels of Baltimore, Richmond, Norfolk, and the Virginia suburbs of Washington, D.C., are in competitive markets: standards (and prices) remain high. The beach and mountain resorts in the region are among the oldest, largest, and most expensive in the country. Accommodations at beach resorts in Maryland and Virginia can be difficult to find during summer holiday weekends—be sure to make reservations.

All hotels listed have a private bath unless otherwise noted.

MEDIA

NEWSPAPERS AND MAGAZINES

Chesapeake Bay and *Chesapeake Life* are monthly magazines with features about natural and human history and boating. The publication is available on newsstands in Maryland, Virginia, Pennsylvania, and Washington, D.C.

Maryland's largest newspaper, the *Baltimore Sun,* covers predominately metropolitan Baltimore and the Eastern Shore, and lists arts and entertainment events in its *Live* section on Thursday. Maryland and Virginia's Washington suburbs look to the *Washington Post* for international and national news. The *Post* packages weekend events and entertainment in its Friday *Weekend* insert.

MONEY MATTERS

Generally, lodging, restaurants, and attractions are most expensive in Baltimore, Richmond, and the metropolitan regions and resort areas, especially Ocean City and Virginia Beach. Gas prices tend to be higher in the rural and mountainous regions. Lodging and restaurants costs are considerably less expensive in the western Maryland mountains and rural Virginia.

Coupons for hotel discounts and services in Virginia can be printed at www.travelcoupons.com. Select the area you'll be visiting.

Prices throughout this guide are given for adults. Substantially reduced fees are almost always available for children, students, and senior citizens. For information on taxes, *see* Taxes.

ATMS

ATMs are very common throughout metropolitan Baltimore, Washington, Richmond and their suburbs. Although ATMs are not as prevalent in western Maryland and rural Virginia, travelers should have no trouble finding them at banks and grocery stores. Banks generally have 24-hour machines.

➤ ATM LOCATIONS: **Cirrus** (☎ 800/424–7787). **Plus** (☎ 800/843–7587).

CREDIT CARDS

Should you use a credit card or a debit card when traveling? Both have benefits. A credit card allows you to delay payment and gives you certain rights as a consumer (☞ Consumer Protection). A debit card, also known as a check card, deducts funds directly from your checking account and helps you stay within your budget. When you want to rent a car, though, you may still need an old-fashioned credit card. Although you can always *pay* for your car with a debit card, some agencies will not allow you to *reserve* a car with a debit card.

Otherwise, the two types of plastic are virtually the same. Both will get you cash advances at ATMs worldwide if your card is properly programmed with your personal identification number (PIN).

Throughout this guide, the following abbreviations are used: **AE,** American Express; **D,** Discover; **DC,** Diners Club; **MC,** MasterCard; and **V,** Visa.

➤ REPORTING LOST CARDS: **American Express** (☎ 800/441–0519). **Discover** (☎ 800/347–2683). **Diners Club** (☎ 800/234–6377). **MasterCard** (☎ 800/622–7747). **Visa** (☎ 800/847–2911).

NATIONAL AND STATE PARKS

Look into discount passes to save money on park entrance fees. For $50, the National Parks Pass admits you (and any passengers in your private vehicle) to all national parks, monuments, and recreation areas, as well as other sites run by the National Park Service, for a year. (In parks that charge per person, the pass admits you, your spouse and children, and your parents, when you arrive together.) Camping and parking are extra. The $15 Golden Eagle Pass, a hologram you affix to your National Parks Pass, functions as an upgrade, granting entry to all sites run by the NPS, the U.S. Fish and Wildlife Service, the U.S. Forest Service, and the Bureau of Land Management (BLM). The upgrade, which expires with the parks pass, is sold by most national-park, Fish-and-Wildlife, and BLM fee stations. A percentage of the proceeds from pass sales funds National Parks projects.

Both the Golden Age Passport ($10), for U.S. citizens or permanent residents who are 62 and older, and the Golden Access Passport (free), for those with disabilities, entitle holders (and any passengers in their private vehicles) to lifetime free entry to all national parks, plus 50% off fees for the use of many park facilities and services. (The discount doesn't always apply to companions.) To obtain them, you must show proof of age and of U.S. citizenship or permanent residency—such as a U.S. passport, driver's license, or birth certificate—and, if requesting Golden Access, proof of disability. The Golden Age and Golden Access passes, as well as the National Parks Pass, are available at any NPS-run site that charges an entrance fee. The National Parks Pass is also available by mail and via the Internet.

➤ PASSES BY MAIL: **National Park Service** (✉ National Park Service/Department of Interior, 1849 C St. NW, Washington, DC 20240, ☎ 202/208–4747, WEB www.nps.gov). **National Parks Pass** (✉ 27540 Ave. Mentry, Valencia, CA 91355, ☎ 888/GO–PARKS or 888/467–2757, WEB www.nationalparks.org).

➤ STATE PARK INFORMATION: In Maryland: **Office of Tourism Development** (✉ 217 E. Redwood St., 9th floor, Baltimore 21202, ☎ 410/767–3400 or 800/634–7386). **State Forest and Park Service** (✉ Maryland Department of Natural Resources, Tawes State Office Bldg., 580 Taylor Ave., Annapolis 21401, ☎ 410/260–8367). In Virginia, the Division of State Parks, **Department of Conservation and Recreation** (✉ 203 Governor St., Suite 213, Richmond 23219, ☎ 804/786–1712).

OUTDOORS AND SPORTS

CANOEING AND KAYAKING

Canoeing and kayaking are popular paddle sports in Maryland and Virginia. Many outfitters offer kayaking excursions on the Chesapeake Bay and its tributaries, including the Rappahannock and James rivers in Virginia, and the Patapsco and St. Mary's rivers in Maryland. The water is equally placid on Maryland's Eastern Shore and stretches of the Potomac River. White-water enthusiasts will find challenge along the Shenandoah River in Virginia and the Youghiogheny and Savage rivers in western Maryland. A rugged stretch of the Potomac River near Washington, D.C., offers some of the best white-water kayaking in the region.

➤ INFORMATION: **Virginia Tourism Corporation** (✉ 901 E. Byrd St., Richmond, VA 23219, ☎ 804/786–2051). Maryland's **Office of Tourism Development** (✉ 217 E. Redwood

St., Baltimore, MD 21202, ☎ 800/543–1036).

FISHING

Virginia does not require a license for saltwater fishing in the ocean, in the bay, or in rivers up to the freshwater line. A license is required for freshwater fishing in rivers, lakes, and impoundments; a license valid for one year costs $30.50 for nonresidents, $12.50 for residents.

Maryland fishing licenses valid for one year are $9 from the Department of Natural Resources. You can download a license form off its Web site. Fishing licenses can also be obtained at many sporting-goods stores; these licenses, valid for five days, cost $6 or more.

➤ INFORMATION: **Virginia Department of Game and Inland Fisheries** (✉ Box 1104, Richmond 23230, ☎ 804/367–1000). **Maryland Department of Natural Resources** (✉ 580 Taylor Ave., Box 1869, Annapolis 21401, ☎ 410/260–8100, WEB www.dnr.state.md.us).

SAILING

Finding places to sail is as easy as looking at a map of the states and finding big coastal cities—Baltimore, Annapolis, Newport News, and Hampton. Charter companies abound in the coastal communities, including Solomons, St. Michaels, and Ocean City in Maryland, and Virginia's Norfolk and Virginia Beach. Sailing regattas can be seen on the Chesapeake Bay throughout the summer. Because demand is heavy from mid-May through October, it's a good idea to reserve boats as soon as you know your plans.

➤ INFORMATION: **Annapolis Sailing School** (✉ 601 6th St., Box 3334, Annapolis, MD 21403, ☎ 800/638–9192). **Guide to Cruising Chesapeake Bay** ($29.95 plus $3 postage) is published by *Chesapeake Bay Magazine* (✉ 1819 Bay Ridge Ave., Suite 200, Annapolis, MD 21403, ☎ 410/263–2662).

SKIING

In the Shenandoah Valley, the Homestead Resort in Hot Springs started the southern ski industry in the 1950s and has since been joined by Wintergreen near Waynesboro, Massanutten near Harrisonburg, and other Virginia resorts. The Department of Conservation and Recreation provides further information on skiing facilities and seasons.

Wisp Ski Area, in far western Maryland, rises nearly 3,100 ft above sea level and overlooks Deep Creek Lake. It has 23 slopes and 14 mi of trails, from novice to expert. It is easily accessible for weekenders from Baltimore and Washington. There are additional cross-country ski trails in the region.

➤ INFORMATION: In Virginia, the **Department of Conservation and Recreation** (✉ 203 Governor St., Suite 213, Richmond, VA 23219, ☎ 804/786–1712, WEB ww.dcr.state.va.us).

➤ SKI AREA: **Wisp Ski & Golf Resort** (✉ 290 Marsh Hill Rd., McHenry, MD 21541, ☎ 301/387–4911, WEB www.skiwisp.com).

PACKING

If you're visiting the mountains and the caverns of Virginia, prepare for colder-than-average temperatures. Hiking along the Appalachian Trail, even during spring and fall, frequently requires a coat. A sweater is in order for a visit to Luray Caverns or Shenandoah Caverns in all seasons of the year.

Where dress is concerned, Baltimore and Richmond are relatively conservative. In the more expensive restaurants, men are expected to wear jacket and tie; in such public areas as art museums and theaters, patrons who are not neatly dressed and groomed are liable to feel conspicuous.

At the bay and ocean resorts, "formal" means long trousers and a collared shirt for men, and shoes for everybody. A tie might never get tied during a stay in these areas.

In your carry-on luggage, **pack an extra pair of eyeglasses or contact lenses and enough of any medication** you take to last a few days longer than the entire trip. You may also ask your doctor to write a spare prescription using the drug's generic name, since brand names may vary from country to country. In luggage to be checked, **never pack prescription drugs or valuables.** And don't forget to carry with you the addresses of offices that handle refunds of lost traveler's checks. Check *Fodor's How to Pack* (available in bookstores everywhere) for more tips.

To avoid customs and security delays, carry medications in their original packaging. Don't pack any sharp objects in your carry-on luggage, including knives of any size or material, scissors, manicure tools, and corkscrews, or anything else that might arouse suspicion.

SENIOR-CITIZEN TRAVEL

To qualify for age-related discounts, **mention your senior-citizen status up front** when booking hotel reservations (not when checking out) and before you're seated in restaurants (not when paying the bill). Be sure to have identification on hand. When renting a car, ask about promotional car-rental discounts, which can be cheaper than senior-citizen rates.

➤ EDUCATIONAL PROGRAMS: **Elderhostel** (✉ 11 Ave. de Lafayette, Boston, MA 02111-1746, ☎ 877/426–8056, FAX 877/426–2166, WEB www.elderhostel.org).

SHOPPING

KEY DESTINATIONS

Shoppers looking for discount clothes in Maryland and Virginia should head to the outlets. Potomac Mills Value Outlet Mall in Woodbridge, Virginia, is a destination for many, with more than 200 well-known manufacturers' stores. In Maryland, Prime Outlets near Hagerstown attracts hordes of shoppers. Another Prime Outlets branch is off I–95 in suburban Baltimore.

SMART SOUVENIRS

Handmade pottery, wood items, and jewelry can be found at the Allegheny Highlands Arts & Crafts Center in the Appalachian Mountains near Clifton Forge, Virginia. In western Maryland, the Spruce Forest Artisan Village showcases the work of local potters, weavers, stained-glass artists, and wood-carvers.

STUDENTS IN VIRGINIA AND MARYLAND

Student discounts are prevalent at attractions, on sightseeing excursions, and at state and national parks in Maryland and Virginia. Student identification is usually required.

➤ I.D.S AND SERVICES: **STA Travel** (☎ 212/627–3111 or 800/781–4040, FAX 212/627–3387, WEB www.sta.com). **Travel Cuts** (✉ 187 College St., Toronto, Ontario M5T 1P7, Canada, ☎ 416/979–2406 or 888/838–2887, FAX 416/979–8167, WEB www.travelcuts.com).

TIME

Maryland and Virginia are in the eastern time zone. Daylight saving time is in effect from early April through late October; eastern standard time, the rest of the year. Clocks are set ahead one hour when daylight saving time begins, and back one hour when it ends. The area is three hours ahead of Los Angeles, one hour ahead of Chicago, five hours behind London, and 14 hours behind Sydney.

TOURS AND PACKAGES

Because everything is prearranged on a prepackaged tour or independent vacation, you spend less time planning—and often get it all at a good price.

BOOKING WITH AN AGENT

Travel agents are excellent resources. But it's a good idea to collect brochures from several agencies, as some agents' suggestions may be influenced by relationships with tour and package firms that reward them for volume sales. If you have a special interest, **find an agent with expertise in that area**; the American Society of Travel Agents (ASTA; ☞ Travel Agencies) has a database of specialists worldwide.

Make sure your travel agent knows the accommodations and other services of the place being recommended. Ask about the hotel's location, room size, beds, and whether it has a pool, room service, or programs for children, if you care about these. Has your agent been there in person or sent others whom you can contact?

Do some homework on your own, too: local tourism boards can provide information about lesser-known and small-niche operators, some of which may sell only direct.

BUYER BEWARE

Each year consumers are stranded or lose their money when tour operators—even large ones with excellent reputations—go out of business. So **check out the operator.** Ask several travel agents about its reputation, and try to **book with a company that has a consumer-protection program.** (Look for information in the company's brochure.) In the United States, members of the National Tour Association and the United States Tour Operators Association are required to set aside funds to cover your payments and travel arrangements in the event that the company defaults. It's also a good idea to choose a company that participates in the American Society of Travel Agents' Tour Operator Program (TOP); ASTA will act as mediator in any disputes between you and your tour operator.

Remember that the more your package or tour includes, the better you can predict the ultimate cost of your vacation. Make sure you know exactly what is covered, and **beware of hidden costs.** Are taxes, tips, and transfers included? Entertainment and excursions? These can add up.

➤ TOUR-OPERATOR RECOMMENDATIONS: **American Society of Travel Agents** (☞ Travel Agencies). **National Tour Association** (NTA; ✉ 546 E. Main St., Lexington, KY 40508, ☎ 859/226–4444 or 800/682–8886, WEB www.ntaonline.com). **United States Tour Operators Association** (USTOA; ✉ 275 Madison Ave., Suite 2014, New York, NY 10016, ☎ 212/599–6599 or 800/468–7862, FAX 212/599–6744, WEB www.ustoa.com).

TRAIN TRAVEL

Amtrak trains run out of Baltimore, Maryland, north toward Boston and south toward Washington, D.C., along the busy "northeast corridor." A rail station at Baltimore-Washington International Airport serves both Baltimore (about 15 mi to the north) and Washington, D.C. (about 30 mi to the south). Some trains running between New York and Chicago stop at Charlottesville, Virginia, and at two locations in western Virginia. Trains run between Newport News, Virginia, and New York City, stopping in northern Virginia, Richmond, and Williamsburg in between. Stops in Richmond and northern Virginia are also made on runs between New York City and Florida.

The Maryland State Railroad Administration, or MARC, operates daily commuter trains between Baltimore's Penn Station and D.C.'s Union Station. It also operates trains from Baltimore's downtown Camden Station and from Union Station in Washington, D.C. There is free bus transportation between the Baltimore-Washington International Airport Rail Station and the airport passenger terminal.

Virginia Railway Express, or VRE, provides workday commuter service between Union Station in Washington and Fredericksburg and Manassas, with additional stops near hotels in Crystal City, Alexandria, and elsewhere.

➤ TRAINS: **Amtrak** (☎ 800/872–7245, WEB www.northeast.amtrak.com). **Maryland State Railroad Administration** (MARC; ☎ 800/325–7245). **Virginia Railway Express** (VRE; ☎ 800/743–3873, WEB www.vre.org).

TRANSPORTATION AROUND MARYLAND AND VIRGINIA

The best way to see these two states is by car. Interstates traverse the region, allowing easy access to the mountains and beaches. The metropolitan regions should be avoided during morning and afternoon rush hours.

The major attractions in Baltimore, which hug the Inner Harbor, are easily navigable by foot or water taxi. Neighborhoods and suburbs are accessible by reliable bus and light-rail.

Attractions in Annapolis and Frederick in Maryland and Charlottesville and Fredericksburg in Virginia are accessible by foot.

TRAVEL AGENCIES

A good travel agent puts your needs first. Look for an agency that has been in business at least five years, emphasizes customer service, and has someone on staff who specializes in your destination. In addition, **make sure the agency belongs to a professional trade organization.** The American Society of Travel Agents (ASTA)—the largest and most influential in the field with more than 24,000 members in some 140 countries—maintains and enforces a strict code of ethics and will step in to help mediate any agent-client disputes involving ASTA members if necessary. ASTA (whose motto is "Without a travel agent, you're on your own") also maintains a Web site that includes a directory of agents. (If a travel agency is also acting as your tour operator, *see* Buyer Beware *in* Tours and Packages.)

➤ LOCAL AGENT REFERRALS: **American Society of Travel Agents** (ASTA; ✉ 1101 King St., Suite 200, Alexandria, VA 22314, ☎ 800/965–2782 24-hr hot line, FAX 703/739–3268, WEB www.astanet.com). **Association of British Travel Agents** (✉ 68–71 Newman St., London W1T 3AH, ☎ 020/7637–2444, FAX 020/7637–0713, WEB www.abtanet.com). **Association of Canadian Travel Agents** (✉ 130 Albert St., Suite 1705, Ottawa, Ontario K1P 5G4, ☎ 613/237–3657, FAX 613/237–7052, WEB www.acta.ca). **Australian Federation of Travel Agents** (✉ Level 3, 309 Pitt St., Sydney, NSW 2000, ☎ 02/9264–3299, FAX 02/9264–1085, WEB www.afta.com.au). **Travel Agents' Association of New Zealand** (✉ Level 5, Tourism and Travel House, 79 Boulcott St., Box 1888, Wellington 6001, ☎ 04/499–0104, FAX 04/499–0827, WEB www.taanz.org.nz).

VISITOR INFORMATION

For city and local tourism offices, *see* Visitor Information *in* the A to Z sections at the end of each chapter.

➤ STATE TOURISM OFFICES: **Baltimore Area Convention & Visitors Association** (✉ 100 Light St., Baltimore, MD 21202, ☎ 410/659–7300, WEB www.bacva.org). **Maryland Office of Tourism Development** (✉ 217 E. Redwood St., 9th floor, Baltimore, MD 21202, ☎ 410/767–3400 or 800/634–7386, FAX 410/333–6643, WEB www.mdisfun.org). **Ocean City Convention & Visitors Bureau** (✉ 4001 Coastal Hwy., Ocean City, MD 21842, ☎ 410/289–8181 or 800/626–2326). **Virginia Tourism Corporation** (✉ 901 E. Byrd St., Richmond, VA 23219, ☎ 804/786–2051 or 800/847–4882; 800/935–9184 for B&B information, FAX 804/786–1919, WEB www.vatc.org).

➤ NATIONAL PARK SERVICE: The **National Park Service** (✉ National Capital Region, 1100 Ohio Dr. SW, Washington, DC 20242, ☎ 202/619–7222, FAX 202/619–7062, WEB www.nps.gov/parks.html).

➤ IN THE U.K.: **Maryland Office of Tourism** (✉ Spittal Barn, Main St., Great Burton, Oxon PX171QL, ☎ 0129/575–0789). **Virginia Corporation** (✉ 182–184 Addington Rd., 1st floor, Selsdon, South Croydon, Surrey CR28LB, ☎ 0181/651–4743, FAX 0181/651–5702).

WEB SITES

Do check out the World Wide Web when planning your trip. You'll find everything from weather forecasts to virtual tours of famous cities. Be sure to **visit Fodors.com** (www.fodors.com), a complete travel-planning site. You can research prices and book plane tickets, hotel rooms, rental cars, vacation packages, and more. In addition, you can post your pressing questions in the Travel Talk section. Other planning tools include a currency converter and weather reports, and there are loads of links to travel resources.

Civil War buffs should check out www.civilwartraveler.com for information on battlefields and war-related sites and events. Wine enthusiasts can learn the basics of Virginia wines (including winery locations) at www.virginiawinecountry.com. For Maryland wines, www.marylandwine.com offers a comprehensive list of state-produced wines and wineries.

WHEN TO GO

Spring brings horse racing to Baltimore, northern Virginia, and the Virginia Piedmont; the Preakness Stakes in Baltimore is a highly festive occasion, but many point-to-points and steeplechases are more interesting to watch and visit. Public gardens are in full bloom and offer free visitations; garden clubs conduct tours of private properties throughout both states. In Shenandoah National Park, Skyline Drive overlooks a blooming panorama that is as stirring as the autumn colors. If you happen to travel to Baltimore in early May, don't miss Sherwood Gardens, well known for hundreds of thousands of tulips (planted freshly each year), azaleas, pansies, and blossoming trees.

Summer draws the largest numbers of visitors, particularly at Virginia Beach, Ocean City, and other resorts on the bay and the ocean. Historical buildings and museums in both states tend to schedule longer opening hours to serve the crowds. Baltimore's Inner Harbor can be thronged with tourists and yachtsmen. On warm days, the promenade is filled with visitors from around the world.

Autumn brings spectacular colors in the foliage of the rolling Piedmont region of Virginia and the Catoctin Mountains west of Baltimore; the temperatures become more comfortable for hiking and biking. Equestrian events resume, and in Maryland the sailboat and powerboat shows in Annapolis and the Waterfowl Festival in Easton attract thousands of people in October and November.

Winter temperatures may make it too cold to swim, yet the major resorts continue to draw vacationers with seasonal peace and quiet at much lower off-season rates. Other travelers come for romantic seclusion at a B&B in a little town. Virginia was the first Southern state to develop skiing commercially, and now both downhill and cross-country skiing are popular activities at resorts in the Shenandoah Valley and western Maryland. Elsewhere in the region heavy snow is rarely seen, and because local residents are unaccustomed to driving under such conditions, a snowfall is a serious traffic hazard in this area.

CLIMATE

The best time to visit is in the spring and fall, when the temperatures are cooler. The summers in both states are hot and humid, making sightseeing very unpleasant, though the mountainous regions tend to be 10 to 15 degrees cooler. Resorts and lodging in the higher elevations usually don't have air-conditioning. Winters are rainy and damp, and winter sports are often an iffy proposition.

BALTIMORE, MARYLAND

Jan.	43F	6C	May	74F	23C	Sept.	79F	26C
	29	–2		56	13		61	16
Feb.	43F	6C	June	83F	28C	Oct.	67F	19C
	29	–2		65	18		50	10
Mar.	52F	11C	July	86F	30C	Nov.	54F	12C
	36	2		70	21		40	4
Apr.	63F	17C	Aug.	85F	29C	Dec.	45F	7C
	45	7		67	19		31	–1

NORFOLK, VIRGINIA

Jan.	49F	9C	May	76F	24C	Sept.	81F	27C
	34	1		58	14		65	18
Feb.	50F	10C	June	83F	28C	Oct.	70F	21C
	34	1		67	19		56	13
Mar.	58F	14C	July	88F	31C	Nov.	61F	16C
	40	4		72	22		45	7
Apr.	67F	19C	Aug.	85F	29C	Dec.	52F	11C
	49	9		70	21		36	2

➤ FORECASTS: **Weather Channel Connection** (☎ 900/932–8437), 95¢ per minute from a Touch-Tone phone.

FESTIVALS AND SEASONAL EVENTS

➤ EARLY DEC.: During **Illuminations,** (☎ 800/447–8679, WEB www.history.org) in Williamsburg, Virginia, 18th-century entertainment is performed on four outdoor stages. A military tattoo signals the lighting of candles in windows of the Colonial city's historic buildings.

➤ LATE DEC.: The **Candlelight Tour of Historic Houses of Worship** (☎ 301/663–8687, WEB www.visitfrederick.org), in downtown Frederick, is a self-guided tour of historic churches and a synagogue, most of them within walking distance of one another. The churches are decorated for the holidays, and Christmas music and refreshments add to the festivities.

➤ DEC. 31: **New Year's Eve** (☎ 410/752–8632, WEB www.bop.org) festivities in Baltimore include a concert at the Harborplace amphitheater and a midnight fireworks display over Inner Harbor. **First Night Annapolis** (☎ 410/268–8553, WEB www.firstnightannapolis.org) is a family-oriented, alcohol-free, and affordable celebration of the lively arts. The state capital is transformed into a stage with about 300 performances in historic homes and public buildings.

➤ LATE JAN.: **Lee-Jackson-King Day,** the third Monday of the month, commemorates the birthdays of the Confederate generals Robert E. Lee (Jan. 19) and Stonewall Jackson (Jan. 21) and civil rights leader Martin Luther King Jr. with celebrations all over Virginia. Maryland's **Annapolis Heritage Antiques Show** (☎ 410/222–1919 or 410/961–5121, WEB www.armacostantiquesshows.com) is one of the major mid-Atlantic events of its kind and lasts three days.

➤ LATE FEB.: **George Washington's Birthday** (☎ 703/549–7662, WEB www.washingtonbirthday.net) is celebrated in Alexandria, Virginia, with a parade—175 floats and marching units—and a reenactment of a Revolutionary War skirmish at Fort Ward nearby.

➤ MAR.: **Military Through the Ages** (☎ 757/253–4838, WEB www.historyisfun.org), in Jamestown, Virginia, uses authentic weapons in a series of reenactments of battles from the Middle Ages to the 20th century.

➤ MID-APR.: Norfolk's **Azalea Festival** (☎ 757/282–2801, WEB www.azaleafestival.org) salutes NATO through battleship tours, a parade, an air show, outdoor concerts, a ball, and the crowning of a queen from the year's honored NATO member nation.

➤ MID–LATE APR.: **Historic Garden Week** (☎ 804/644–7776, WEB www.vagardenweek.org) throughout Virginia is a time when several hundred grand private homes, otherwise closed to the public, open their doors and grounds to visitors. The **Celtic Festival and Highland Gathering of Southern Maryland** (☎ 443/404–7319, WEB www.cssm.org), which takes place south of Annapolis in St. Leonard, includes piping and fiddling competitions, dancing, games, and the foods and crafts of the United Kingdom, Ireland, and Brittany.

➤ LATE APR.–EARLY MAY: **Virginia Waterfront International Arts Festival** (☎ 757/282–2822, WEB www.vaintlartsfest.com) showcases performances by the Virginia Symphony, Virginia Opera, and out-of-state orchestras and artists.

➤ EARLY MAY: **Virginia Gold Cup** (☎ 540/347–2612 Ext. 12, WEB www.vagoldcup.com) steeplechase horse races, held near Middleburg in Northern Virginia, have been among the most prominent social and sporting events of the state since the 1920s.

➤ MID-MAY: Baltimore's **Maryland Preakness Celebration** (☎ 410/542–9400, WEB www.preakness.com) is a weeklong festival including, among the more than 100 events, parades, street parties, fund-raisers, and hot-air-balloon races. The celebration culminates in the annual running of the Preakness Stakes at Pimlico Racetrack, on the third Saturday in May.

➤ MID–LATE MAY: The **Chestertown Tea Party** (☎ 410/778–0416, WEB www.chestertownteaparty.com) on Maryland's Eastern Shore commemorates patriots' 1774 act of hurling

British tea into the Chester River. **Commissioning Week** (☎ 410/293–2292, WEB www.usna.edu/Schedules/commweek.html) at the United States Naval Academy in Annapolis, Maryland, is a time of dress parades, traditional stunts such as the Herndon Monument Climb, and a spectacular aerobatics demonstration by the navy's famous Blue Angels precision flying team.

➤ MID-JUNE: The **Fiddlers' Convention at the Carroll County Farm Museum** (☎ 410/876–2667), an annual gathering in Westminster, Maryland, attracts some of the nation's finest bluegrass entertainers and fiddlers.

➤ LATE JUNE: The **Hampton Jazz Festival** (☎ 757/838–4203, WEB www.hamptoncoliseum.org) in Hampton, Virginia, brings together top performers in the various styles of jazz.

➤ LATE JULY: The **Pony Swim and Auction** (☎ 757/336–6161, WEB www.chincoteaguechamber.com) in Chincoteague, Virginia, is the annual roundup of wild ponies from Assateague Island; the foals are auctioned off to support the volunteer fire department.

➤ LATE JULY–EARLY AUG.: The two-week-long **Virginia Highlands Festival** (☎ 800/435–3440 or 276/676–2282, WEB www.vahighlandsfestival.org) in Abingdon celebrates Appalachia with juried displays and demonstrations of arts and crafts, exhibitions of animals, sales of antiques, and performances of country music. The **Dorchester Chamber Seafood Feast-i-val** (☎ 410/228–1211, WEB www.tourdorchester.org) in Cambridge, Maryland, is an all-you-can-eat extravaganza on the shore of the Choptank River. During the first three weekends of August, "Shakespeare at the Ruins" at **Barboursville Vineyards** (☎ 540/832–3824, WEB www.barboursvillewine.com) brings outdoor performances of the Bard's classics to these beautiful vineyards, between Charlottesville and Orange in Virginia.

➤ LATE AUG.: During the **Virginia Wine Festival** (☎ 410/267–6711, WEB showsinc.com/vawf) in the Plains you can taste vintages from roughly 50 wineries. There's also grape stomping and musical entertainment. The **Maryland State Fair** (☎ 410/252–0200, WEB www.marylandstatefair.com), in Timonium, is 10 days of horse racing, livestock judging, live entertainment, agricultural displays, farm implements, and plenty of food. The **Maryland Renaissance Festival** (☎ 410/266–7304 or 800/296–7304, WEB www.rennfest.com/mrf) celebrates 16th-century England with entertainment, food, and craft shops. The grounds near Annapolis include a 5,000-seat jousting area and 10 stages. The event continues through late October.

➤ EARLY SEPT.: **Defenders' Day** (☎ 410/962–4290, WEB www.nps.gov/fomc) celebrations at Fort McHenry in Baltimore commemorate—with music, drilling, mock bombardment, and fireworks—the battle that led to the writing of the national anthem. Crisfield, Maryland's **National Hard Crab Derby** (☎ 410/968–2500, WEB www.crisfield.org) celebrates—what else?—the Eastern Shore's crabs with a crab race, steamed crabs, and the crowning of Miss Crustacean.

➤ MID-SEPT.: The **Apple Harvest Festival** (☎ 540/662–3996) in Winchester, Virginia, is a weekend of arts and crafts that celebrates an important regional crop.

➤ LATE SEPT.: The **Virginia State Fair** (☎ 804/228–3200, WEB www.statefair.com), in Richmond, is a classic conglomeration of carnival rides, livestock shows, displays of farm equipment, and lots of food for sale. Ocean City, Maryland, celebrates the quest for endless summer with **Sunfest Kite Festival** (☎ 410/289–7855, WEB www.kiteloft.com/sunfest.asp), a four-day blowout with all sorts of entertainment, kite contests, and a crafts show. The **Maryland Wine Festival** (☎ 410/876–2667, WEB ccgov.carr.org/farm-mus), at the Carroll County Farm Museum, Westminster, brings representatives from Maryland's wineries to display their products, offer tastings, and give seminars on wine making. The **Baltimore Book Festival** (☎ 410/837–4636 or 800/282–6632, WEB www.bop.org), held in the historic Mount Vernon neighborhood, celebrates books and Baltimore's literary past.

➤ EARLY–MID-OCT.: The **Autumn Glory Festival** (☎ 301/387–4386), held in Oakland in Maryland's westernmost county, is a celebration of the peak fall foliage and includes state banjo and fiddle championships, Oktoberfest festivities, arts, crafts, and antiques. The **October Homes Tour and Crafts Exhibit** (☎ 540/882–3018, WEB www.waterfordva.org) in Waterford, Virginia, draws tens of thousands to this historic community. The first Saturday of October, Bethesda restaurants sell samples of their fare at the food festival, **Taste of Bethesda** (☎ 301/215–6660, WEB www.bethesda.org). The **United States Sailboat and Powerboat Shows** (☎ 410/268–8828, WEB usboat.com), the world's largest events of their kind, take place in Annapolis, Maryland. The **Chincoteague Oyster Festival** (☎ 757/336–6161, WEB www.chincoteaguechamber.com), on Virginia's Eastern Shore, typically sells out months in advance.

➤ LATE OCT.: **Yorktown Day** (☎ 757/898–2410, WEB www.nps.gov/colo) observances in Yorktown, Virginia, celebrate the Colonial victory in the American War of Independence (October 19, 1781) with 18th-century tactical demonstrations, patriotic exercises, and a wreath-laying ceremony. The **Virginia Film Festival** (☎ 800/882–3378, WEB www.vafilm.com), in Charlottesville, Virginia, is becoming a major event in the motion picture industry, with screenings of important new movies and appearances by their stars.

➤ EARLY NOV.: The **Waterfowl Festival** (☎ 410/822–4567, WEB www.waterfowlfestival.org) in Easton, Maryland, involves decoy exhibitions, carving demonstrations, duck-calling contests, and retriever exercises during a three-day weekend.

➤ LATE NOV.: **Waterfowl Week** (☎ 757/336–6122, WEB www.chincoteaguechamber.com) in Chincoteague, Virginia, is when the National Wildlife Refuge opens nature trails to motor vehicles, allowing drivers to watch the Canada and snow geese on their southward migration.

➤ DEC.: Alexandria's **Scottish Christmas Walk** (☎ 703/549–0111, WEB www.campagnacenter.org) is a parade with marchers from more than 100 clans. Musical performances and the selling of wreathes and other greens also take place during the event. The **Historic Alexandria Candlelight Tour** (☎ 703/838–4242, WEB www.funside.com) is a visit to historic houses for light refreshment and performances of period music of the season.

1 DESTINATION: VIRGINIA AND MARYLAND

The Planter and the Waterman

What's Where

Pleasures and Pastimes

Fodor's Choice

Great Itineraries

THE PLANTER AND THE WATERMAN

THE PLANTER AND THE WATERMAN—two curious types, one long extinct, the other now endangered. Standing side by side, they evoke the histories and express the personalities of Virginia and Maryland.

The Virginia planter was very much connected to the land, at least to his own plantation. Many plantations in various stages of restoration, some of them still going concerns, can be toured today throughout the northern, eastern, and central parts of the state—Washington's august Mount Vernon, Jefferson's ingenious Monticello, and others less well known but also memorable. The heirloom silver in their grand dining rooms (and the dirt floors of their slave quarters) are eloquent evocations of antebellum Virginia.

Two centuries of life on the plantation go far to explain the curious combination of hauteur and hospitality that marks the Virginian personality to this day. Eighteenth-century aristocrats such as William Byrd of Westover and his friends the Carters (whose descendants still live at the nearby Shirley plantation) used to show off their wealth by throwing lavish parties and taking solicitous interest in the affairs of their dependents and other inferiors. The condescension of one class and the deference of another melded into a common courtesy that persists in the reserve and the gracious speech of museum docents and waitresses alike.

Of all the crops raised on Virginia plantations, the most abundant was tobacco. But so was liberty. This paternalistic, slave-holding system cultivated the interests and ideas that brought the American Revolution. The rising landed gentry of Virginia composed the House of Burgesses (its chamber is now on view inside the reconstructed capitol in Williamsburg), which gave the Colonists a long preparatory exercise in self-government. Though ultimately the Revolution meant far more than the self-interest of a certain class, it was crucial that plantation owners, alienated from a Crown that coveted their landed wealth, formed the preeminent Virginia contingent of revolutionaries.

The hard-won liberty was inequitably distributed, of course. The "peculiar institution" of slavery was perhaps more entrenched in Deep South states such as South Carolina and Georgia—after all, James Madison and George Mason, both Virginians, had included abolition in an early draft of the Constitution. But when rancor over the issue erupted into the Civil War, the Old Dominion took the lead in the rebellion.

The capital of the Confederacy was in Richmond; the top commander of its army was the Virginian Robert E. Lee; and two-thirds of Civil War battles were fought here. Petersburg and Richmond were especially ravaged, but few places lay untouched. Today every town has at least one amateur historian who can point out the scenes of skirmishes or tell which buildings survived and which burned down.

But though they revere the past, Virginians nevertheless prefer building to brooding. Jamestown's Captain John Smith told the very first generation of Virginia gentlemen, "Who does not work does not eat," and in a gentler tone the defeated but resilient Lee, after Appomattox, wrote to his relations at Shirley, "There is nothing left for us but work." Such industry has brought about change, often of a nature that would have startled Lee.

The landscape has been markedly altered, in many respects shamefully. On the rolling plains in Albemarle and Orange counties ("Mr. Jefferson's Country") and in the still-remote southwestern highlands (a region through which the Wilderness Road once coursed), the roadsides pass by a profusion of fast-food outlets and discount malls. Yet many Virginians regard the landscape itself as their preeminent luxury, and violations of it offend their sense of place. Manassas, where nearly 29,000 men died in two Civil War battles, recently avoided becoming a development full of luxury homes—although some homes will be built, a large section of the battlefield will be preserved forever. Other large tracts of Virginia are legally protected from disfigurement: more than a million acres are dedicated to national and state parks, a designation that includes mountains, marshes, forests, and seashore.

In the beginning, all of America was Virginia—even Plymouth Rock, where the Pilgrims landed in 1620, was officially in northern Virginia. All of English North America had been named in honor of Elizabeth I, the Virgin Queen. Maryland, which was subtracted from Virginia and set up as its own Colony in the 18th century, was named not for a reigning monarch but for his consort, Charles I's wife (and daughter of Henry IV), Queen Henrietta Maria. In the 3½ centuries since, it has lost border disputes with all its neighbors—Pennsylvania, West Virginia, and Virginia—to end up in its ungainly current shape, a quarter of the size of Virginia.

But maps tell only one side of history. Maryland's largest city, Baltimore, has roughly twice as many people as Virginia Beach, the Old Dominion's largest city, and Maryland has three-quarters the inhabitants of its grand southern neighbor. Though there is much less of it, Maryland has a terrain just as varied as Virginia's, from the mountains in the west through the central plateau to the jagged coast around the Chesapeake Bay.

Although the Chesapeake also makes boundaries for Virginia, the Chesapeake is far more important in determining Maryland's geography, separating its Eastern from its Western shores. Divided by water, the inhabitants of the two shores have preserved quite different accents and customs. On the Western Shore itself, the Patuxent River separates Calvert and St. Mary's counties, which maintain subtly distinct identities and manners. On the Eastern Shore, the winding shoreline prolongs distance; in many cases it takes several times as long to drive to the next town as to sail to it across an inlet.

Most Marylanders lead terrestrial lives, but in spirit they are a waterborne people bearing the legacy of a prominent maritime past. "Virginia is for lovers" was a hit promotional slogan in the 1970s; a Maryland T-shirt manufacturer matched it with, "Maryland is for crabs." The second motto has the advantage, besides being a mildly witty double entendre, of concrete truth: crabs, along with oysters and other seafood from the Chesapeake Bay, remain a major Maryland industry (the catch, however, is constantly dwindling).

Baltimore, on the Patapsco River, was an 18th- and 19th-century shipbuilding center, famous for the speedy Clippers employed in privateering, drawing particular ire from the British in the early 1800s. When, in the War of 1812, British ships bombarded Fort McHenry in the harbor, Baltimoreans stood firm, and their flag-waving defiance inspired "The Star-Spangled Banner." Now Baltimore is one of the busiest ports on the East Coast (its rival is Norfolk), and since renovations and enhancements in the late '70s and early '80s, its Inner Harbor has been an attractive waterside recreation area, with shops, restaurants, museums, and an exemplary aquarium that draw millions of locals and out-of-towners alike each year.

Annapolis, on the banks of the Severn River, is one of the most important sailing cities in the world and home of the U.S. Naval Academy. All along both shores of the bay, towns such as St. Michaels, Tilghman's Island, and Solomons thrive on the weekend pleasures of yachters.

Maryland's mythic hero—its cowboy, if you will—is the waterman, who prowls the Chesapeake in his skipjack, dredging oysters from the decks of America's last fleet of working sailboats. In the 1880s there were more than 1,500 of these native flat-bottom sloops. Today, fewer than three dozen still ply the Chesapeake waters, and the oyster harvest is a fraction of its former self because of MSX disease, which in the 1950s caused a widespread oyster kill-off. (The protozoa that causes the disease arrived in the bilgewater of a foreign merchant ship.)

On one hand, a waterman's life—spending days and nights on the water with colleagues and returning home to an isolated bay-side or island village—is an anomaly in a state where half the population is concentrated in the Baltimore metropolitan area. But the waterman is a rich symbol of contemporary Maryland society: not in the manner in which he sets off to work but in the variety of the catch he hauls back to the dock. Maryland has always been a land of diversity.

It is said that Maryland was founded as a Catholic Colony. Cecil Calvert, the second Lord Baltimore, who organized the first expedition of Colonists in 1633, was Roman Catholic; half the members of that expedition were as well. But Puritans and Anglicans were made welcome, too, a courtesy not reciprocated in most of the other English Colonies. In fact, through its Toleration Act (1649), Maryland was the first Colony to guarantee freedom of religion, at least for Christians.

Diversity has been cause for turmoil. During the Civil War the state was dangerously ambivalent. Sitting below the Mason-Dixon Line, with an economy based equally on agriculture and industry, Maryland found its popular sentiment divided between the South and the North. The consensus was, in the tradition of tolerance, for compromise: to somehow preserve the Union without coercing the South. There was rioting (and the first bloodshed of that war) when Union troops appeared in Baltimore, and President Lincoln saw fit to incarcerate some city officials. The state faced itself on the field of battle when the First Maryland Regiment of the Union army fought the First Maryland Regiment of the Confederate army at Front Royal, Virginia.

Between Virginia and Maryland, nature carved out the Chesapeake Bay, and politics carved out the District of Columbia. Maryland teeters between the cultures of North and South; it has been called the northernmost Southern state and the southernmost Northern state. But Virginia is quintessentially Southern. It is tempting to draw further distinctions: Virginians are gracious, Marylanders fractious; Virginians are tragic, Marylanders sassy; Virginians are stalwart, Marylanders mercurial. There is plenty of evidence to disprove all such generalizations. Nevertheless, such comparisons help us to understand both states. Virginia and Maryland are best visited in tandem.

The planter and the waterman: one is patrician, landed, and gregarious; the other plebeian, afloat, and solitary. Both are enterprising and jealous of their independence, but they have proved to be good neighbors as well as spirited rivals.

WHAT'S WHERE

Northern Virginia

Much more than a satellite of the nation's capital, northern Virginia is a repository of Colonial and Civil War history. Alexandria's Old Town holds a substantial number of historic buildings, churches, and museums; and Arlington, Fairfax, and Loudoun counties are sprinkled with historic sites and monuments such as Mount Vernon, Arlington Cemetery, and the Manassas battlefield (also known as Bull Run). Loudoun County is also Virginia's horse country, with handsome towns that include Middleburg and Leesburg. And from Great Falls Park you can view the splendid waterfalls of the Potomac.

D.C.'s Maryland Suburbs

Part of suburbia's sprawl, Montgomery and Prince George's counties are where you'll find the Washington Redskins, Six Flags America, the College Park Aviation Museum, and Strathmore Hall Arts Center. Naturalists appreciate the area's great green spaces, including the C&O Canal National Historical Park and Piscataway Park. Diners from Washington, D.C., and both sides of the Potomac River head to Bethesda and Silver Spring to sample cuisine from all over the world, especially Thailand and elsewhere in Asia.

Charlottesville, the Blue Ridge, the Shenandoah Valley, and Southwest Virginia

Mountains rule the horizons here. The evening sun sets over the Blue Ridge for those in the cultural center of Charlottesville; nearby is Thomas Jefferson's "little mountain," Monticello. Skyline Drive and the Blue Ridge Parkway trace the spine of the Blue Ridge, creating many vistas within Shenandoah National Park and the George Washington National Forest. The Shenandoah Valley, once the home of early European settlers and later a Civil War thoroughfare, rests between the Blue Ridge and the Allegheny mountains. Farther south, inside a bowl-shaped depression encircled by bluish ridgelines, is bustling Roanoke. To the west and south of that bustling city are the New River Valley and the gorge-incised Appalachian Plateau, from whose hollows old-time mountain music still echoes.

Richmond, Fredericksburg, and the Northern Neck

Richmond, capital of the commonwealth and former capital of the Confederacy, is not only full of historic sites but also one of the South's preeminent art cities and a major industrial center. Among its appealing restored neighborhoods is the turn-of-the-20th-century Fan District. At Petersburg, south of Richmond, the Confederacy made its last stand. In Fredericksburg, midway between Richmond and Washington, D.C., are historic 18th- and 19th-century homes, antiques shops, and Civil War battlefields. The rural peninsula of the Northern Neck extends east from Fredericksburg to the Chesapeake.

Williamsburg and Hampton Roads

Colonial Williamsburg, a re-created 18th-century American city complete with historic buildings, working shops, and costumed interpreters, is Virginia's most-visited attraction. Nearby are three other historical treasures: Historic Jamestowne, where the first permanent English settlers made their home; Jamestown Settlement, a re-creation of the original ships and fort; and Yorktown, site of the final major battle in the American War of Independence. Even for those with extremely limited time to spend in Virginia, these ought to be visited. Hampton Roads—the channel where the James, Elizabeth, and Nansemond rivers meet—is surrounded by small towns that include the historic settlements of Hampton and Portsmouth; Newport News, builder of the navy's biggest nuclear ships; the port town of Norfolk; and the busy resort town of Virginia Beach, the state's largest city.

Baltimore

Known as the jewel of the Patapsco River, Baltimore is a busy port city with newly revitalized appeal. Lively Inner Harbor, with its constellation of attractions such as the National Aquarium and the American Visionary Art Museum, is in many ways the city's heart, though Charles Street is the more established part of town. Fells Point, the center of shipbuilding in the 18th and 19th centuries, and Federal Hill are among the cobblestone neighborhoods worth exploring.

Frederick and Western Maryland

Rugged, scenic mountains dominate the landscape of western Maryland. They frame cities such as Frederick and Cumberland; they wall in pastoral valleys, state forests, and parks; they even set the stage for a popular train excursion, the Western Maryland Scenic Railroad. Once crossed by the nation's first pioneers on their westward journey, these mountains are rich with remnants of an earlier time; today you can still hike along what was once the towpath for the Chesapeake and Ohio (C&O) Canal—the region's main trade route in the mid-19th century.

Annapolis and Southern Maryland

Maryland traces its origins to the Chesapeake Bay's Western Shore, where English Colonists arrived in the 1600s. Today, Annapolis, the state capital, is rich with Colonial architecture and history. Tobacco fields, once the livelihood of early Colonists, still blanket the gentle landscape of the southern part of the state, although more sparsely than before.

The Eastern Shore

Separated from mainland Maryland by the Chesapeake Bay and bounded on the east by the Atlantic Ocean, this peninsula is a land apart. Marshy wildlife refuges, isolated islands, and rivers traversed by fishermen and sailors set the stage for a quieter way of life. (However, you'll have to share the Atlantic with quite a crowd at the thriving resort town of Ocean City.) Virginia's Eastern Shore, which extends south from Maryland and is also accessible from Virginia Beach via the Chesapeake Bay Bridge-Tunnel, is a largely undisturbed area of tiny towns and abundant wildlife, including the wild "ponies" on Assateague Island.

PLEASURES AND PASTIMES

American History

These two original Colonies are full of historical attractions, from entire re-created Colonial towns to Civil War battlefields to remnants of the routes that pioneers followed on their westward treks. You can explore Colonial beginnings in Virginia's Williamsburg or Maryland's Historic St. Mary's City; amble through Richmond, Fredericksburg, Baltimore, and Frederick, where some neighborhoods appear virtually unchanged from the 18th and 19th centuries; stroll tiny Eastern Shore harbors where the waterman's way of life is now supplemented by pleasure tours on old fishing boats; or stand on the battlefields of Yorktown, Antietam, or Manassas. At Mount Vernon and Monticello you can step into the homes—and perhaps even the minds—of two of the country's most important former presidents; in Maryland, you can follow the region's former trade route by walking a portion of the historic C&O Canal, now a national park.

Biking and Hiking

The three regions of Maryland and Virginia—coastal plain (or Tidewater), Piedmont, and mountains—are great for cyclists and hikers seeking an abundance of choices. National and regional trails such as the famed Appalachian Trail cross both states. In Virginia, the 500-mi section of the Trans-America Bicycle Trail extends from Breaks Interstate Park at the western fringe of the state to Yorktown on the coast; in addition, a 280-mi segment of the Maine-Richmond and Richmond-Florida coastal tracks crosses the state. In Maryland, trails, canal towpaths, and even old railroad routes are popular biking and hiking routes.

National Parks and Forests

From the mountains to the seashore, many scenic and historical national parks lie within these states. In Virginia's Shenandoah Mountains lies the lovely Skyline Drive, a popular 105-mi route through Shenandoah National Park. In Maryland's smaller Catoctin Mountains sits Catoctin Mountain Park. The place is good enough for the president—Camp David, the presidential retreat, is somewhere within. Blackwater National Wildlife Refuge, southeast of Annapolis, is one of the East Coast's premier spots for viewing migratory waterfowl, bald eagles, and ospreys. The Potomac River, the waterway that divides Maryland and Virginia, is the route of the 185-mi linear park, the C&O Canal National Historical Park. It's a favorite with hikers and bicyclists.

Seafood

The Chesapeake Bay, the estuary that separates mainland Maryland and Virginia from their respective Eastern Shores, provides a cornucopia of seafood. Steamed hard-shell crabs cracked with a mallet on paper-covered tables, to the accompaniment of plenty of beer, are as traditional as crab cakes seasoned with Old Bay seasoning or garlic. Cream-of-crab soup, Maryland crab soup, crab balls, crab dip, and crab imperial are just a few of the other odes to this creature. Also on the menu, in season, are bluefish, rockfish, oysters, and mussels.

Wineries

Since the 1980s, Virginia has come from way behind to its spot as fifth in the nation for grape production. The state's 75 wineries, most in picturesque and historic buildings, are distributed throughout the state. Both states have wine festivals, most of which occur in the fall. Virginia alone has more than 400 annual festivals and wine-related events.

FODOR'S CHOICE

Even with so many special places in Virginia and Maryland, Fodor's writers and editors have their favorites. Here are a few that stand out.

Historic Buildings and Restorations

Appomattox Court House, Virginia. In this village, now restored to its 1865 appearance, General Robert E. Lee surrendered his Confederate troops to General Ulysses S. Grant.

Colonial Williamsburg, Virginia. Once the state's capital, this restored 18th-century city is full of skilled craftspeople, orators, and actors who bring history to life (and encourage you to join in).

Hammond-Harwood House, Annapolis, Maryland. Nearly all of this pre-Revolutionary mansion is original. It's one of the finest examples of the Colonial architecture of its time.

Monticello, Virginia. Thomas Jefferson's unique home, outside of Charlottesville, reflects the intense and multifaceted mind of this president and statesman.

Mount Vernon, Virginia. Overlooking the Potomac River, George Washington's house and farm is the most visited—and one of the most important—museums of its kind in the United States.

Battlefields and Monuments

Antietam National Battlefield, Sharpsburg, Maryland. The bloodiest fight of the Civil War took place here in 1862. When it was over, more than 23,000 soldiers had either died or been wounded.

Ft. McHenry, Baltimore, Maryland. This fort made of brick and earth saw battle during the War of 1812; its bombardment inspired "The Star-Spangled Banner."

Manassas National Battlefield Park, Virginia. Also known as Bull Run, this battlefield was the site of two of the most important victories for the Confederates.

Arlington National Cemetery, Virginia. The burial site of John F. Kennedy and a quarter of a million people who have served during wartime, Arlington National is a solemn site for contemplating a nation's sorrows and determination.

Hotels

Harbor Court Hotel, Baltimore, Maryland. Next to the Inner Harbor, this eight-story, redbrick hotel is known for its English country-house interiors and fine service. *$$$$*

The Homestead, Hot Springs, Virginia. Eight presidents have stayed in this luxurious hotel set among the Appalachians—you can, too. *$$$–$$$$*

Kent Manor Inn, Stevensville, Maryland. What was once a manor house and then a Victorian summer hotel is on 226 acres of farmland and near a creek. *$$–$$$$*

Colonial Houses, Williamsburg, Virginia. You can step back in time (and still retain modern amenities) at these charming lodgings within Colonial Williamsburg. *$$–$$$*

Linden Row Inn, Richmond, Virginia. A row of 1840s Greek revival town houses filled with antiques and reproductions makes up this charming inn. *$–$$$*

Museums

American Visionary Art Museum, Baltimore, Maryland. The passionate creations of unconventional artists are displayed in seven galleries inside a former warehouse.

Calvert Marine Museum, Solomons, Maryland. The history of the Chesapeake Bay and the fishing, boat construction, and other industries that rely on it are explored at this southern Maryland museum.

Virginia Air and Space Center, Hampton, Virginia. Inside a nine-story waterfront building are an *Apollo 12* command capsule, a lunar lander, a dozen aircraft, and an IMAX theater. Also within is the Hampton Roads History Center.

Yorktown Victory Center, Yorktown, Virginia. This museum, next to the battlefield on which the Revolutionary War ended, helps capture what the moment meant for contemporaries.

Natural Sights

Assateague Island National Seashore. This 37-mi-long barrier island on the border of Virginia and Maryland is a good place to find pristine beaches, wild ponies, deer, and 300 species of birds.

Natural Bridge of Virginia. Twenty miles south of Lexington, Virginia, is what Native Americans called the "Bridge of God": it's a graceful, 21-story limestone arch that now supports part of a highway.

Skyline Drive, Virginia. For more than 100 mi this highway winds up the Blue Ridge in Shenandoah National Park. It's got multiple vantage points for spectacular scenery, especially in the fall.

Sunsets at Ocean City, Maryland. Savor them outside or take a seat at any number of bay-side bars and restaurants—they're unforgettable.

Restaurants

Hamptons, Baltimore, Maryland. A view of Baltimore's Inner Harbor, elegant furnishings, and an innovative menu have earned this restaurant widespread acclaim. *$$$$*

Inn at Little Washington, Washington, Virginia. Since 1978 chef Patrick O'Connell and his partner have been turning out New American food that wins raves from all over. *$$$$*

L'Auberge Provencale, White Post, Virginia. Nationally known for its French cuisine, the bed-and-breakfast is well worth a stop for its prix-fixe dinners. *$$$$*

Métropolitain, Charlottesville, Virginia. With owners from West Virginia and Burgundy, France, the Métropolitain brings to the table an intriguing fusion of New American and French cuisine. *$$–$$$*

The Homeplace, Catawba, Virginia. In a mountain hamlet near Roanoke, the old-time country home serves mounds of fried chicken, potatoes and gravy, biscuits, and other Southern specialties. The lemonade is unlimited—and delicious. $

GREAT ITINERARIES

If you don't have time for an extended itinerary, consider the Eastern Shore or the Shenandoah Valley. They're both great choices for long weekends spent outdoors, with stops for galleries and antiques shops.

Maryland

3 Days

Baltimore, the geographical and cultural center of Maryland, is a must-see for first-time visitors. Take in some of the major sights that are clustered around the colorful Inner Harbor. On Day 2, revisit Maryland's Colonial past in Annapolis, the state capital. On the third day, head farther south to view the ongoing archaeological and reconstruction work at St. Mary's City. You can overnight in Solomons, a longtime getaway for those who love boating and the Chesapeake Bay. If you want to learn more about how the bodies of water affect those who live around here, cross the expansive Chesapeake to the Eastern Shore, stopping in such small towns as Easton and St. Michaels.

5 Days

Spend your first couple of days in Baltimore before heading south to Annapolis. Historic St. Mary's City, Solomons, and other towns in St. Mary's and Calvert counties will take care of Day 4. On your last day, either cross the Chesapeake Bay to visit the Eastern Shore or head west to Frederick, a vibrant city in the foothills of the Catoctin Mountains.

Virginia

3 Days

Start in the northern part of the state. Spend a day exploring the sights of Alexandria and Mount Vernon, George Washington's home; then take a nighttime drive across the river for a glimpse of the illuminated monuments of Washington, D.C. On the second day visit Manassas National Battlefield Park before heading west to the Shenandoah Valley for a spectacular drive south along Skyline Drive. Stay overnight in or outside Charlottesville, and allow at least three hours for Thomas Jefferson's plantation home, Monticello, the next morning.

5 Days

Follow the three-day tour above and then proceed to Virginia's capital, Richmond, for another full day. From Richmond, it's a short jaunt south to Petersburg and Pamplin Historical Park, where General Lee's defenses were routed. The impressive museum there holds many Civil War artifacts. If you prefer, you could instead spend the fifth day in Fredericksburg's historic center.

Five days is also a fair amount of time to do justice to the historic sights surrounding Williamsburg without limiting yourself to them. Squeeze the early English settlements of Jamestown and Yorktown attractions into one full day. Allow the next two days for the museums and living history of Colonial Williamsburg. On Day 4 examine the important maritime history of the area at the Mariner's Museum in Newport News before heading across Hampton Roads to the impressive collection of the Chrysler Museum of Art in Norfolk. After these two museums, find a beach to relax at—either in Cape Charles at the tip of the Eastern Shore, or in the busy resort town of Virginia Beach.

7 Days

Start your trip in Richmond and spend the day visiting its many museums and Civil War sites. On the second day, head west on I–64 to Charlottesville, where you can survey the lush, rolling countryside from Thomas Jefferson's mountaintop home, Monticello. On Day 3, take a side trip northeast up Route 20 to Orange to see Montpelier, the home of James Madison, and to tour the area's wineries. On Day 4, head west again on I–64 toward the Blue Ridge Mountains and visit Staunton; the Museum of American Frontier Culture re-creates the beginnings of agrarian life in the Shenandoah Valley. On your fifth day, take the Blue Ridge Parkway south to Lexington, home to Washington and Lee University and the Virginia Military Institute. On Day 6, stop in Roanoke for a dose of culture or head to Jefferson National Forest to commune with nature. On your final day, continue south on the scenic Blue Ridge Parkway to Abingdon for a taste of the rugged Highlands.

Virginia and Maryland

10 Days

Ten days is enough time to explore the Colonial and maritime pasts of Virginia and Maryland and to visit two major cities, Baltimore and Richmond. In a concentrated area such as the triangle of Jamestown, Williamsburg, and Yorktown, five days are the minimum to see the sights and have time to unwind.

Spend your first two days exploring Baltimore's Inner Harbor sights, art museums, and historic neighborhoods. On Day 3 visit Maryland's state capital, Annapolis, and perhaps the U.S. Naval Academy there before crossing the Chesapeake to the laidback pace of the Eastern Shore. Spend the third night in Easton and wake up well after the area's fishermen have set off. Take a day to meander through harbor towns and wildlife areas before watching the sunset from Chincoteague Island. The fifth day make your way down and off the Eastern Shore to overnight in the Hampton Roads area. Spend the next three days experiencing Virginia's Colonial past in Williamsburg, Jamestown, and Yorktown. After a day on the rides of Busch Gardens, buckle down with some history again in Richmond, Virginia's capital and the capital of the Confederacy.

A Civil War Tour

11 days

Civil War sites are among the most compelling reasons to visit Virginia and Maryland, and the Civil War itinerary below covers the standout attractions. When Virginia seceded from the Union in 1861, it doomed itself to become a major battleground. Thus, much of this tour is in Virginia, with a brief foray across the Mason-Dixon Line into Maryland. Richmond is the tour's hub.

Day One: Start at Hampton, on the Virginia Peninsula, where the Union general George McClellan launched his drive toward Richmond. Across the channel is Fort Monroe—the Union stronghold in which the president of the Confederacy, Jefferson Davis, was imprisoned.

Day Two: Drive northwest on I–64 up the peninsula to Richmond's Museum and White House of the Confederacy and the Richmond National Battlefield Park Visitor Center. Proceed 20 mi south on I–95 to Petersburg, the city that was under an extended siege by Grant's army. Visit Petersburg National Battlefield, the Siege Museum, and Pamplin Historical Park.

Days Three to Five: From Richmond proceed north on I–95 to Fredericksburg, which has blocks of historic Civil War–era homes. Detour to see four battlefields at Fredericksburg/Spotsylvania National Military Park. Detour an hour outside of town to see Stratfold Hall plantation, where Robert E. Lee was born. Then return to I–95 and drive northwest to Manassas National Battlefield Park, site of two important Confederate victories.

Days Six and Seven: Continue on I–95 north into Arlington and see Arlington National Cemetery and Arlington House (Lee's home for 30 years, before the Union army confiscated it and turned the grounds into the cemetery). Then head north on I–270 into Maryland. North of Frederick catch Route 34 out of Boonsboro and follow it to the Antietam National Battlefield. Return to Frederick. If you have time, visit the National Museum of Civil War Medicine, then drive southeast to Monocacy National Battlefield.

Days Eight to Eleven: Drive back to Richmond and then southwest from the city on U.S. 360 to U.S. 460. Proceed west into Appomattox Court House, where Lee surrendered to Grant. From Appomattox you can continue west on U.S. 460 to Lynchburg's Monument Terrace, a Civil War memorial. Then take U.S. 29 north to U.S. 60 northwest into Lexington, where you can visit the Lee Chapel and Museum, where Lee is buried, and the Virginia Military Institute Museum, which has displays on Stonewall Jackson.

2 NORTHERN VIRGINIA

Historic treasures abound between the District of Columbia and the Blue Ridge Mountains: Mount Vernon, Arlington National Cemetery, Manassas National Battlefield, and the Chesapeake and Ohio Canal National Historical Park. Old Town Alexandria alone has more than 2,000 18th- and 19th-century buildings. To the west, Loudoun County is the state's horse country, with handsome towns and a number of vineyards.

Updated by CiCi Williamson

CLOSE TO D.C. IN MORE WAYS THAN ONE, this unique region extends westward from the capital to the Blue Ridge Mountains. With much of Northern Virginia's business and residential life taking its cue from Washington, the area has prospered. Alexandria and Arlington counties were Virginia's contribution to the District of Columbia when it was created, and their history together is complicated and tightly bound. The areas were in Fairfax County before the District was formed. After many years without any federal construction, the Virginia portion of the District was returned to the state and became Alexandria County rather than reverting to Fairfax County. Alexandria City separated from the county in 1869, and in 1920 the confusion between the county and city names was resolved when the county renamed itself Arlington.

Cosmopolitan Northern Virginia sometimes feels more affinity for Washington than for Richmond. But its residents still take pride in being Virginians, and in protecting the historic treasures they hold in trust for the rest of the nation.

Buildings in the Old Town portion of Alexandria are reminiscent of the Federal period (1790–1820); its more than 2,000 18th- and 19th-century buildings are listed collectively on the National Register of Historic Places. Nearby areas have grown significantly and have modern housing, government, and office buildings. Tysons Corner in Fairfax County serves more than 400 corporations employing 70,000 people. Northern Virginia contains some of America's most precious acreage, including Mount Vernon and Arlington National Cemetery. Manassas (Bull Run), 26 mi from Washington, was the site of two of the most significant battles of the Civil War. In Loudoun County the gracious lifestyle of the rural Old South survives, and elite diversions still include fox hunting and steeplechasing.

Exploring Northern Virginia

Northern Virginia is generally defined as the area close to and south and west of the Potomac River, including Arlington and Alexandria, Fairfax County, Loudoun County, and Prince William County, to the south.

Pleasures and Pastimes

Dining and Lodging

DINING

CATEGORY	COST*
$$$$	over $32
$$$	$22–$32
$$	$12–$22
$	under $12

**per person for a main course at dinner*

LODGING

CATEGORY	COST*
$$$$	over $225
$$$	$150–$225
$$	$100–$150
$	under $100

**All prices are for a standard double room, excluding state tax.*

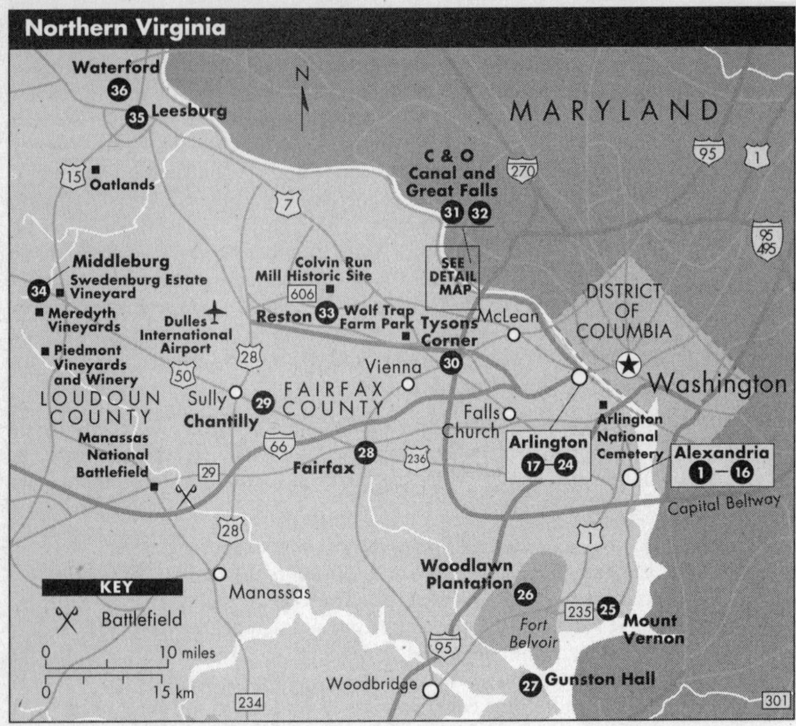

ALEXANDRIA

The city of Alexandria remains distinct from the younger Washington, D.C., across the Potomac. Founded in 1749 by Scottish merchants eager to capitalize on the booming tobacco trade, Alexandria emerged as one of the most important ports in Colonial America. (The city dwarfed Georgetown—Washington's oldest neighborhood—in the days before the Revolution.) The city's history is linked to the most significant events and personages of the Colonial, Revolutionary, and Civil War periods. Members of the Lee family of Revolutionary and Civil War fame lived here, and George Washington had a town house and attended church in Alexandria, though he lived a few miles south in Mount Vernon.

This vibrant past is still alive in the historic district of Old Town Alexandria—an area of cobbled streets, restored 18th- and 19th-century homes, churches, and taverns. The main arteries of this district are Washington Street (the GW Parkway as it passes through town) and King Street. Most points of interest are on the east (Potomac) side of Washington Street. Visit them on foot if you are prepared to walk for 20 blocks or so; parking is usually scarce, especially close to the river, and the parking police seem to catch every violation, but parking garages within walking distance of Ramsay House provide some relief. On Saturday, parking costs $2 all day; it's $3 after 6 PM.

Numbers in the text correspond to numbers in the margin and on the Old Town Alexandria map.

A Good Walk

Start your walk through Old Town at the Alexandria Convention & Visitors Association, in **Ramsay House** ①, the oldest house in Alexandria. Across the street, near the corner of Fairfax and King streets, is the **Stabler-Leadbeater Apothecary** ②, the country's second-oldest apothecary. It was the equivalent of a corner drugstore to Alexandrians, including George Washington and the Lee family. Two blocks south on Fairfax Street, just beyond Duke Street, stands the **Old Presbyterian Meetinghouse** ③, where Scottish patriots met during the Revolutionary War. Walk back up Fairfax Street one block and turn right on Prince Street to Gentry Row, the block between Fairfax and Lee streets. The striking edifice at the corner of Prince and Lee streets is the **Athenaeum** ④. Many of the city's sea captains built their homes on the block of Prince Street between Lee and Union, which became known as **Captain's Row** ⑤. Walk a block north on Union to King Street, where there are many shops and restaurants. One of Alexandria's most popular attractions is the **Torpedo Factory Arts Center** ⑥, a collection of art studios and galleries in a former munitions plant (on Union at the foot of King Street). Also here is the Alexandria Archaeology Museum, with exhibits of artifacts found during excavations in Alexandria. Take Cameron Street away from the river. **Carlyle House** ⑦, built in 1753, is at the corner of Cameron and North Fairfax streets.

One block west along Cameron, at Royal Street, is **Gadsby's Tavern Museum** ⑧, where Washington attended parties. Continue west on Cameron Street for two blocks, turn right on St. Asaph Street, and walk up to Oronoco Street. Two historic Lee homes are on the short stretch of Oronoco between North Washington and St. Asaph streets. On the near side of Oronoco is the **Lee-Fendall House Museum** ⑨; the **boyhood home of Robert E. Lee** ⑩ is across Oronoco on the St. Asaph Street corner.

Although they were a tiny minority, there were in fact 52 free blacks living in Alexandria in 1790. This population grew to become a significant factor in Alexandria's successful development. The **Alexandria Black History Resource Center** ⑪, two blocks north and two blocks west of Lee's boyhood home, tells the history of African-Americans in Alexandria and Virginia. Head back to North Washington Street and go south to the corner of Queen Street. The **Lloyd House** ⑫, a fine example of Georgian architecture, is owned by the city of Alexandria. At the corner of Cameron and North Washington streets, one block south, stands the Georgian country-style **Christ Church** ⑬. Walk south two blocks to the **Lyceum** ⑭ at the corner of South Washington and Prince streets; it now houses two art galleries and a museum focusing on local history. The Confederate Statue is in the middle of South Washington and Prince streets, and two blocks to the west on South Alfred Street is the **Friendship Fire House** ⑮, restored and outfitted like a typical 19th-century firehouse. It's a long walk (or a quick ride on Bus 2 or 5 west on King Street) but worth the trouble to visit the **George Washington Masonic National Memorial** ⑯ on Callahan Drive at the King Street Metro station 1 mi west of the center of the city. In good weather, the open ninth-floor observation deck allows for good views.

TIMING

The Alexandria tour should take about four hours, not counting a trip to the George Washington Masonic National Memorial. Add another hour for a round-trip visit to the memorial (or add just a half hour if you don't plan to return to Old Town but wish to leave the area on the King Street Metro, across the street from the memorial); budget yet another hour to take the tour.

Sights to See

⓫ **Alexandria Black History Resource Center.** The history of African-Americans in Alexandria and Virginia from 1749 to the present is recounted here with photographs, drawings, and written accounts. The federal census of 1790 recorded 52 free blacks living in the city, and

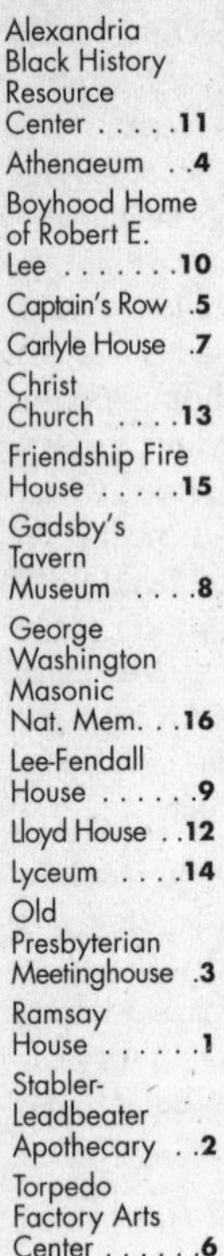

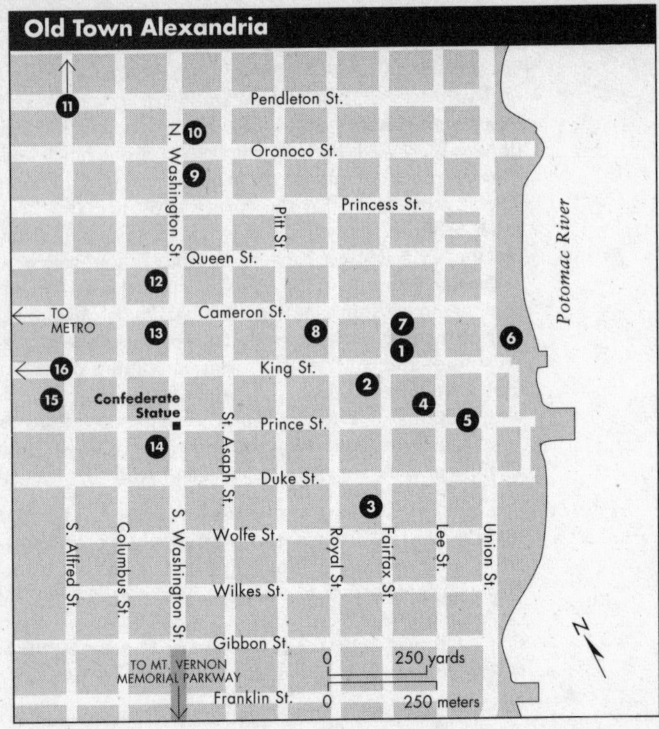

the port town was one of the largest slave exportation points in the South, with at least two bustling slave markets. Panels with photographs, drawings, and writing recount the black history of Alexandria. ✉ *638 N. Alfred St., Old Town,* ☎ *703/838–4356.* 🎫 *Free.* 🕒 *Tues.–Sat. 10–4, Sun. 1–5.*

4 **Athenaeum.** One of the most noteworthy structures in Alexandria, the Athenaeum is a striking, reddish-brown Greek revival edifice at the corner of Prince and Lee streets contrasts with its many redbrick Federal neighbors. Built in 1851 as a bank, it now houses the gallery of the Northern Virginia Fine Arts Association. This block of Prince Street between Fairfax and Lee streets is known as **Gentry Row,** after the 18th- and 19th-century inhabitants of its imposing three-story houses. ✉ *201 Prince St., Old Town,* ☎ *703/548–0035.* 🎫 *Free.* 🕒 *Wed.–Fri. 11–4, Sat. 11–1, Sun. 1–4.*

10 **Boyhood home of Robert E. Lee.** The childhood home in Alexandria of the commander in chief of the Confederate forces, Robert E. Lee, is a fine example of a 19th-century town house with Federal architecture. The home was sold in 2000 to private owners who have made it their home, over the objections of many Virginians, including the governor. Although it's not possible to tour the house, some of the home's furnishings are now displayed at the Lyceum. ✉ *607 Oronoco St., Old Town.*

5 **Captain's Row.** Many of Alexandria's sea captains once lived on this block. The cobblestones in the street were allegedly laid by Hessian mercenaries who had fought for the British during the Revolution and were held in Alexandria as prisoners of war. ✉ *Prince St. between Lee and Union Sts., Old Town.*

7 **Carlyle House.** The grandest of Alexandria's older homes, the Georgian-style Carlyle House was modeled after a Scottish country manor

house. The structure was completed in 1753 by Scottish merchant John Carlyle. General Edward Braddock met here with five royal governors in 1755 to plan the strategy and funding of the early campaigns in the French and Indian War. The interior remains 18th century, with the original woodwork and Chippendale furniture throughout, and decorative items that include Chinese export porcelain. An architectural exhibit on the second floor explains how the house was built. ⊠ *121 N. Fairfax St., Old Town,* ☎ *703/549–2997,* WEB *www.carlylehouse.org.* 🎫 *$4.* ⊙ *Tues.–Sat. 10–4:30, Sun. noon–4:30; tour every ½ hr.*

★ 13 **Christ Church.** Both Washington and Robert E. Lee were pewholders in this Episcopal church, which remains in nearly original condition. (Washington paid £36 and 10 shillings—a lot of money in those days—for Pew 60.) Built in 1773, Christ Church is a fine example of an English Georgian country-style church. It has a fine Palladian window, an interior balcony, and an English wrought-brass-and-crystal chandelier. Docents give tours during visiting hours. ⊠ *118 N. Washington St., Old Town,* ☎ *703/549–1450,* WEB *www.historicchristchurch.org.* 🎫 *Free.* ⊙ *Mon.–Sat. 9–4, Sun. 2:00–4; services Sun. at 8, 9, 11:15, and 5. Occasionally closed weekends for private events.*

Confederate Statue. In 1861, when Alexandria was occupied by Union forces, the 800 soldiers of the city's garrison marched out of town to join the Confederate Army. This memorial marks the place where the soldiers assembled. Based on John A. Elder's painting *Appomattox,* the statue is of a lone soldier glumly surveying the battlefields after General Robert E. Lee's surrender. The names of 100 Alexandria Confederate dead are carved on the base. ⊠ *Middle of Washington and Prince Sts., Old Town.*

15 **Friendship Fire House.** Alexandria's showcase firehouse dates from 1855 and has the appearance and implements of a typical 19th-century firehouse. According to local lore, George Washington helped found the volunteer fire company in 1774. Among early fire engines on display are a hand pumper built in Baltimore in 1851, and an Amoskeag steam pumper built in Manchester, NH, in 1860. ⊠ *107 S. Alfred St., Old Town,* ☎ *703/838–3891,* WEB *oha.ci.alexandria.va.us.* 🎫 *Free.* ⊙ *Fri.–Sat. 10–4, Sun. 1–4.*

8 **Gadsby's Tavern Museum.** This museum is housed in the old City Tavern and Hotel, which was a center of political and social life in the late 18th century. George Washington went to birthday celebrations in the ballroom here. Other noted patrons included Thomas Jefferson, John Adams, and the Marquis de Lafayette. The taproom, dining room, assembly room, ballroom, and communal bedrooms have been convincingly restored to how they probably appeared in the 1780s. The tours on Friday evenings are led by a costumed guide using a lantern. ⊠ *134 N. Royal St., Old Town,* ☎ *703/838–4242,* WEB *www.gadsbys.com.* 🎫 *$4, lantern tour $5.* ⊙ *Oct.–Mar., Tues.–Sat. 11–4, Sun. 1–4 (last tour 3:15); Apr.–Sept., Tues.–Sat. 10–5, Sun. 1–5 (last tour 4:15); tours 15 min before and 15 min after the hr. Lantern tour Mar.–Nov., Fri. 7–9:30.*

★ 16 **George Washington Masonic National Memorial.** Because Alexandria, like Washington, D.C., has no really tall buildings, the spire of this memorial dominates the surroundings and is visible for miles. The building fronts King Street, one of Alexandria's major east–west arteries; from the ninth-floor observation deck (reached by elevator) you get a spectacular view of Alexandria, with Washington D.C., in the distance. The building contains furnishings from the first Masonic lodge in Alexandria. George Washington became a member of it in 1752 and held the high rank of Worshipful Master at the same time he served as president. If you don't wish to walk, the site can also be reached by DASH bus west on King Street. ✉ *101 Callahan Dr., Old Town,* ☎ *703/683–2007,* WEB *www.gwmemorial.org.* 🎫 *Free.* ⏲ *Daily 9–5; 50-min guided tour of building and observation deck daily at 9:30, 10:30, 11:30, 1, 2, 3, and 4.*

9 **Lee-Fendall House.** The short block of Alexandria's Oronoco Street between Washington and St. Asaph streets is the site of two Lee-owned houses. One is this house from 1785, the home of several illustrious members of the Lee family, and the other is the boyhood home of Robert E. Lee. The Lee-Fendall House's interior, done in several different styles, contains some family furniture. The labor leader John L. Lewis lived here from 1937 to 1969. ✉ *614 Oronoco St., Old Town,* ☎ *703/548–1789,* WEB *www.leefendallhouse.org.* 🎫 *$4.* ⏲ *Tues.–Sat. 10–4, Sun. 1–4; last tour 3. Sometimes closed weekends.*

12 **Lloyd House.** A fine example of Georgian architecture, Lloyd House was built in 1797. It can only be admired from the outside. ✉ *220 N. Washington St., Old Town.* 🎫 *Free.*

14 **Lyceum.** Built in 1839, the Lyceum is one of Alexandria's best examples of Greek revival design. It has served as the Alexandria Library, a Civil War hospital, a residence, and an office building. Restored in the 1970s, it now houses a museum devoted to the area's history. Some travel information for other parts of the state is also available here. ✉ *201 S. Washington St., Old Town,* ☎ *703/838–4994,* WEB *www.alexandriahistory.org.* 🎫 *Free.* ⏲ *Mon.–Sat. 10–5, Sun. 1–5.*

3 **Old Presbyterian Meetinghouse.** Except for a six-decade hiatus, the red-brick Old Presbyterian Meetinghouse has been an active house of worship since 1774, when Scottish pioneers established the church; a Presbyterian congregation still meets at 8:30 and 11 on Sunday morning. As its name suggests, however, the building has been more than a church. It was a gathering place in Alexandria vital to Scottish patriots during the Revolution. Eulogies for George Washington were delivered here on December 29, 1799. The Tomb of the Unknown Soldier of the American Revolution lies in a corner of the churchyard, where many prominent Alexandrians—including Dr. James Craik, physician to Washington, Lafayette, and John Carlyle—are interred. Still a very active congregation, the Presbyterian Meetinghouse is the site of sacred and secular "Concerts with a Cause" every month or so. ✉ *321 S. Fairfax St., Old Town,* ☎ *703/549–6670,* WEB *www.opmh.org/history.htm.* 🎫 *Free.* ⏲ *Sanctuary weekdays 9–3 (key available at church office, 316 S. Royal St.).*

1 **Ramsay House.** The best place to start a tour of Alexandria's Old Town is at the **Alexandria Convention and Visitors Association,** inside the home of the town's first postmaster and lord mayor, William Ramsay. The yellow clapboard structure was built in 1724 in Dumfries (about 25 mi south along the Potomac, and once an important port until its harbor silted up in the 1880s) and moved here in 1749; it is believed to be the oldest house in Alexandria. Travel counselors provide information, brochures, and maps for self-guided walking tours. You can also obtain a free 24-hour parking permit for the two-hour metered zones (you must furnish your license plate number). ✉ *221 King St., Old Town,* ☎ *703/838–4200 or 800/388–9119,* WEB *www.funside.org.* 🎫 *Free.* ⏲ *Daily 9–5.*

2 **Stabler-Leadbeater Apothecary.** Once patronized by George Washington and the Lee family, Alexandria's Stabler-Leadbeater Apothecary is the second-oldest pharmacy in the country (the oldest is reputedly

in Bethlehem, Pennsylvania). It was here, on October 17, 1859, that Lieutenant Colonel Robert E. Lee received orders to take command of some marines from the Washington barracks and move to Harpers Ferry to suppress John Brown's insurrection. The shop now houses a small museum of 18th- and 19th-century apothecary memorabilia, including one of the finest collections of apothecary bottles in the country (some 800 bottles in all). ✉ *105–107 S. Fairfax St., Old Town,* ☎ *703/836–3713,* WEB *www.apothecary.org.* 🎫 *$2.50.* ⏲ *Mon.–Sat. 10–4, Sun. 1–5.*

★ ❻ **Torpedo Factory Arts Center.** Torpedoes were manufactured here by the U.S. Navy during both world wars. Now the building houses the studios and workshops of about 160 artists and artisans and has become one of Alexandria's most popular attractions. You can view the workshops of printmakers, jewelry makers, sculptors, painters, and potters, and most of the art and crafts are for sale for reasonable prices. The Torpedo Factory complex also houses the Alexandria Archaeology Program, which displays such artifacts as plates, cups, pipes, and coins from an early tavern, and Civil War soldiers' equipment. ✉ *105 N. Union St., Old Town,* ☎ *703/838–4565,* WEB *www.torpedofactory.org.* 🎫 *Free.* ⏲ *Daily 10–5.*

Dining

$$$$ ✕ **Elysium.** There's no sign on the street, but the dining room of the elegant Morrison House hotel in Old Town Alexandria is worth seeking out. If you choose the restaurant's "A Chef of Your Own" prix-fixe meal ($67), a chef will work with you to design a meal of your choice from the fresh ingredients of the day. Menu items can also be ordered à la carte. The menus mix down-home American, traditional French, and Southwestern influences, combining first-rate ingredients with culinary imagination. ✉ *116 S. Alfred St., Old Town,* ☎ *703/838–8000. AE, DC, MC, V. No dinner Sun.–Mon.*

$$–$$$ ✕ **Gadsby's Tavern.** In the heart of the historic district, this circa 1792 tavern provides a taste of the interior decoration, cuisine, and entertainment of Colonial days. There's a strolling balladeer making the rounds on Tuesday and Wednesday nights, for instance. The tavern was a favorite of George Washington, who is commemorated on the menu ("George Washington's Favorite Duck" is half a duck roasted with peach apricot dressing and served with Madeira sauce). Other period offerings are Gentlemen's Pye (made with veal), Sally Lunn bread, and a rich English trifle. ✉ *138 N. Royal St., Old Town,* ☎ *703/548–1288,* WEB *www.gadsbys.com. D, DC, MC, V.*

$$–$$$ ★ ✕ **La Bergerie.** Opened in 1974 by two brothers from the Basque region of southwest France, this white-tablecloth restaurant has long been famous for its French cuisine and regional Basque specialties. (A *bergerie* is a sheltered area where a shepherd keeps his sheep during a storm.) Inside a historic brick warehouse, the main dining room has crystal chandeliers, leather banquettes, and large-leafed potted plants around wooden columns. Offerings include duck confit and a dish of assorted seafood in a light garlic tomato sauce, *Galette Basque* (almond tart with Sabayon sauce), and raspberry soufflé. ✉ *218 Lee St., Old Town,* ☎ *703/683–1007. AE, DC, MC, V. Closed Sun.*

$$–$$$ ✕ **Las Tapas.** A big, bright authentic Spanish restaurant, Las Tapas specializes in, what else? Tapas! There are 74 of these appetizers on the menu, besides substantial entrées, including three kinds of paella. Come on Tuesday or Thursday night for flamenco ($5 cover). ✉ *710 King St., Old Town,* ☎ *703/836–4000. AE, D, DC, MC, V.*

$$–$$$ ✕ **Le Refuge.** At this small restaurant, popular selections include trout, bouillabaisse, frogs' legs, and beef Wellington. The prix-fixe lunch ($12.95) is available daily; the prix-fixe dinner ($18.95) is served until 7 Tuesday–Thursday and anytime Monday. ✉ *127 N. Washington St., Old Town,* ☎ *703/548–4661. AE, DC, MC, V. Closed Sun.*

$$–$$$ ★ ✕ **Majestic Cafe.** Opened in 1932, the original Majestic Cafe stayed open 24 hours during World War II to serve the workers at the nearby Torpedo Factory—now an art center. The restaurant closed in 1978, but in 2001 was renovated down to its mostly original terrazzo floor, art deco facade, and original neon sign in the front window. Specialties include halibut, soft-shell crabs, and cracker-crusted pork chops as well as excellent vegetable dishes and luscious desserts. ✉ *911 King St., Old Town,* ☎ *703/837–9117,* WEB *www.majesticcafe.com. AE, D, DC, MC, V.*

$$–$$$ ★ ✕ **Stella's.** Across Diagonal Road from the King Street Metro station, Stella's is set back in a pleasant courtyard. The old-fashioned wide bar with several domestic and European beers on tap is just the place to relax and wait for the end of rush hour. The "New Virginia" cuisine served here takes fresh Virginia produce, meats, and seafood and uses them in nonlocal dishes, such as paella. ✉ *1725 Duke St., Old Town,* ☎ *703/519–1946. AE, D, DC, MC, V.*

$–$$ ✕ **Hard Times Café.** Piped-in country-and-western music and framed photographs of Depression-era Oklahoma set the tone at this casual, crowded hangout. Three kinds of chili—Texas (spicy), Cincinnati (sweeter), and vegetarian—are offered. Texas chili is typically served over spaghetti—a "chili-mac"; Cincinnati comes with cheese, onions, beans, or all three. A tuna sandwich, chicken salad, and chicken wings are alternatives to the more combustive cuisine. About 30 domestic and Mexican beers are available. ✉ *1404 King St., Old Town,* ☎ *703/683–5340. Reservations not accepted. AE, MC, V. No lunch Sun.*

$–$$ ✕ **Il Porto.** Inside an old building two blocks from the Potomac, Il Porto's mostly wood interior is reminiscent of an 18th-century ship. There are many Italian entrées to choose from, including veal, seafood, pasta, and chicken. ✉ *121 King St., Old Town,* ☎ *703/836–8833,* WEB *www.ilporto.com. AE, D, DC, MC, V.*

$–$$ ✕ **King Street Blues.** Not the place for power-lunching, this informal, relaxed café just off King Street is popular for its hearty, quirky Southern menu. The whimsical neon and papier-mâché constructions are a good foil for the waiters hustling around in T-shirts and shorts. Diners come for the baked pecan-crusted catfish, Thai chicken and noodle salad, glazed pork chops, and the daily "blue plate" and fish specials; wash your choice down with the excellent house beer. ✉ *112 N. St. Asaph St., Old Town,* ☎ *703/836–8800. AE, D, DC, MC, V.*

$–$$ ★ ✕ **Taverna Cretekou.** Whitewashed stucco walls and colorful macramé tapestries bring a bit of the Mediterranean to the center of Old Town. On the menu are lamb baked in a pastry shell and swordfish kabob. All the wines served are Greek, and in the warm months you can dine in the canopied garden. A buffet brunch is served on Sunday. ✉ *818 King St., Old Town,* ☎ *703/548–8688. AE, MC, V. Closed Mon.*

Lodging

$$$ ★ **Morrison House.** The architecture, parquet floors, crystal chandeliers, sconces, and furnishings of the stunning Morrison House, built in 1985, are so faithful to the Federal period (1790–1820) that it's often mistaken for a renovation of an old building. Guest rooms blend the Early American charm of four-poster beds and armoires with modern conveniences. A piano player tinkles the ivories in the Grill piano bar, Thursday–Saturday nights. The King Street Metro is seven blocks away. ✉ *116 S. Alfred St., Old Town, 22314,* ☎ *703/838–8000 or 800/367–0800,* FAX *703/684–6283,* WEB *www.morrisonhouse.com. 42 rooms, 3 suites. 2 restaurants, room service, piano bar, parking (fee). AE, DC, MC, V.*

$$–$$$ **Embassy Suites Olde Town Alexandria.** Across from the George Washington Masonic Temple is this modern all-suite hotel, where the light-filled atrium lobby has hanging foliage, waterfalls, and a gazebo. Suites are decorated in green and rose with mahogany furniture. Train buffs should request a suite overlooking the historic Alexandria train station, where Amtrak and freight trains pass. A free shuttle takes you to Old Town or elsewhere within 2 mi. There's a free cocktail reception every evening. ✉ *1900 Diagonal Rd., Old Town, 22314,* ☎ *703/684–5900 or 800/362–2779,* FAX *703/684–1403,* WEB *www.embassy-suites.com. 268 suites. Restaurant, kitchenettes, indoor pool, hot tub, 2 gyms, sauna, recreation room, laundry facilities, laundry service, business services, meeting rooms; no-smoking rooms. AE, D, DC, MC, V. BP.*

$$–$$$ ★ **Holiday Inn Select Old Town.** The distinctive mahogany-paneled lobby of this chain hotel suggests a club room, and the guest rooms follow this motif, with hunting-and-horse prints on the walls. Service is extraordinary here: staff will bring exercise bicycles to rooms on request and provide touring bicycles for use in the area without charge. Some rooms on the fifth and sixth floors have views of the roofs of 18th- and 19th-century buildings and the river beyond—but only after the trees have shed their leaves. ✉ *480 King St., Old Town, 22314,* ☎ *703/549–6080 or 800/368–5047,* FAX *703/684–6508,* WEB *www.oldtownhis.com. 227 rooms. Restaurant, in-room data ports, indoor pool, hair salon, sauna, bicycles, lobby lounge. AE, D, DC, MC, V.*

$ ★ **Travelers Motel.** Built in 1954, the Travelers Motel is not a glossy chain motel but rather a friendly, reasonable place run by the original manager. It's at a very convenient location near the Wilson Bridge and Capital Beltway (I–495/I–95), and shuttle service is provided to the Huntington Metro station during the day. ✉ *5916 Richmond Hwy. (Beltway exit 1A), Alexandria South, 22303,* ☎ *703/329–1310 or 800/368–7378,* FAX *703/960–9211. 29 rooms, 1 suite. Pool, free parking. AE, DC, MC, V.*

Nightlife and the Arts

Bars and Pubs

The **Fishmarket** (✉ 105 King St., Old Town, ☎ 703/836–5676, WEB www.fishmarketoldtown.com) is a rambling, two-story collection of dining rooms and bars in a historic warehouse at the river end of King Street. There is a piano bar ($3 cover charge) Thursday–Saturday nights.

Murphy's Irish Pub (✉ 713 King St., Old Town, ☎ 703/548–1717) has authentic Irish entertainment most nights, two groups on weekends (one downstairs, one upstairs), and a blazing fire when winter comes.

Jazz

At **219 Basin Street Lounge** (✉ 219 King St., Old Town, ☎ 703/549–1141), jazz combos perform Tuesday through Saturday in an attractive Victorian-style bar. Musicians from local bands often stop by to sit in. The cover charge is $5 on Friday and Saturday.

The **Birchmere** (✉ 3701 Mt. Vernon Ave., Arlandria, ☎ 703/549–7500) is one of the leading folk clubs in the country. Bluegrass, country, and jazz-fusion bands also play.

Outdoor Activities and Sports

Huntley Meadows, a 1,460-acre refuge ½ mi off U.S. 1 south of the Beltway, is a birder's delight. More than 200 species of birds—from ospreys to owls, egrets to ibis—can be spotted here (much of the park is wetlands). A boardwalk circles through a marsh, putting you in sight of beaver lodges, and almost 4 mi of trails wend through the park, making it possible to spot deer, muskrats, and, sometimes even river otters. ✉ *3701 Lockheed Blvd., Alexandria South,* ☎ *703/768–2525.* *Free.* *Park daily dawn–dark; visitor center closed Tues. (call for hrs other days).*

The **Mount Vernon Trail** is a favorite with Washington runners and bikers. The northern section begins near the pedestrian causeway leading to Theodore Roosevelt Island (directly across the river from the Kennedy Center) and goes past Ronald Reagan Washington National Airport and on to the Alexandria waterfront. This stretch is approximately 9½ mi one way. South of National Airport, the trail runs down to the Washington Sailing Marina. The southern section of the trail (approximately 9 mi) takes you along the banks of the Potomac from Alexandria all the way to George Washington's home, Mount Vernon. It passes Jones Point (under the Wilson Bridge), the southern apex of the original District of Columbia, just before entering protected wetlands for about 2 mi beginning at Hunting Creek.

Shopping

Old Town Alexandria is dense with antiques shops—many of them quite expensive—that are particularly strong in the Federal and Victorian periods. The Alexandria Convention and Visitors Association has maps and lists of the dozens of stores.

The **Saturday Morning Market at Market Square** (City Hall) is the country's oldest operating farmers' market. Vendors sell baked goods, fresh produce, plants, flowers, and high-quality crafts. Come early; the market opens at 5 AM, and by 9:30 AM everything has been packed up.

ARLINGTON

The Virginia suburb of Arlington County was once part of the District of Columbia. Now connected to Washington by four bridges, Arlington remains a virtual part of the capital.

Carved out of the Old Dominion when Washington was created, Arlington was returned to Virginia along with the rest of the land west of the Potomac in 1845 and until 1920 was the county of Alexandria. In the 18th century members of the Custis family, including Martha Washington's first husband, had extensive land holdings in the area. Arlington was also the home of Robert E. Lee. Since the end of World War I, the county has evolved from a farming community to an urban conglomeration of large corporations, Defense Department buildings, and large-scale retailing.

Numbers in the text correspond to numbers in the margin and on the Arlington map.

A Good Walk

Begin at the visitor center of **Arlington National Cemetery** ⑰. Detailed maps of the cemetery and directions to specific graves are available here. Walk out the main door to Memorial Avenue and turn left. Immediately ahead, at the end of Memorial Avenue, is the Women in Military Service for America memorial. Leaving the memorial, turn left and proceed through the gate along Schley Drive and keep walking to the crosswalk. Turn left up Custis Walk to the first cross street. A left turn here (Sheridan Drive) takes you to the **Kennedy graves** ⑱, where President John Kennedy, two of his children, and his wife Jacqueline Bouvier Kennedy Onassis, are buried. To one side is the grave of President Kennedy's brother Robert Kennedy.

From the Kennedy graves, return to Custis Walk and continue uphill to the top of the walk to **Arlington House** ⑲. Long before it was a cemetery, this land was part of the 1,100-acre estate of George Washington Parke Custis, whose daughter married Robert E. Lee. The couple lived in this fine Greek revival house. Leaving the house, continue along the path in front of the house, around the south flower garden to Crook Walk; turn left and continue past row upon row of simple white headstones, following the signs to the **Tomb of the Unknowns** ⑳. Here the remains of unknown servicemen from Korea, Vietnam, and both world wars are buried. The changing of the honor guard occurs night and day, though more frequently during daylight. Below the Tomb of the Unknowns is **Section 7A** ㉑, where many distinguished veterans are buried. To reach the main gate or grave sites at the northern end of the cemetery, or to make your way into the Rosslyn section of Arlington, walk downhill on Roosevelt Drive to Eisenhower Drive, and turn left past the Women's Memorial and the Memorial Gate to Custis Walk. Turn right on Custis Walk to a pedestrian gate. On your way you'll pass **Section 27** ㉒. About 1,500 United States Colored Troops of the Civil War are buried here, as are 3,800 former slaves who lived in Freedmen's Village during and shortly after the Civil War.

Leaving the cemetery through the pedestrian gate, cross Marshall Drive carefully and walk to the 49-bell **Netherlands Carillon** ㉓, where, even if your visit doesn't coincide with a performance, you can enjoy a good vista of Washington. To the north is the **United States Marine Corps War Memorial** ㉔, better known as the Iwo Jima Memorial, which honors all U.S. Marines who lost their lives while serving their country.

TIMING

Visiting the sites at Arlington National Cemetery could take a half day or longer, depending on your stamina and interest.

Sights to See

19 **Arlington House.** It was in Arlington that the two most famous names in Virginia history—Washington and Lee—became intertwined. George Washington Parke Custis—raised by Martha and George Washington, his grandmother and step-grandfather—built Arlington House (also known as the Custis-Lee Mansion) between 1802 and 1817 on his 1,100-acre estate overlooking the Potomac. After his death, the property went to his daughter, Mary Anna Randolph Custis. In 1831, Mary married Robert E. Lee, a graduate of West Point. For the next 30 years the Custis-Lee family lived at Arlington House.

In 1861, Lee was offered command of the Union forces. He declined, insisting that he could never take up arms against his native Virginia. The Lees left Arlington House that spring, never to return. Federal troops crossed the Potomac not long after that, fortified the estate's ridges, and turned the home into the Army of the Potomac's headquarters. Arlington House and the estate were confiscated in May 1864 and sold to the federal government when the Lees failed to pay $92.07 in property taxes in person. (Eventually, Lee's heir Custis Lee sued the government for ownership, and after the Supreme Court ruled in his favor he was paid $150,000 for the land.) Union forces built three fortifications on the

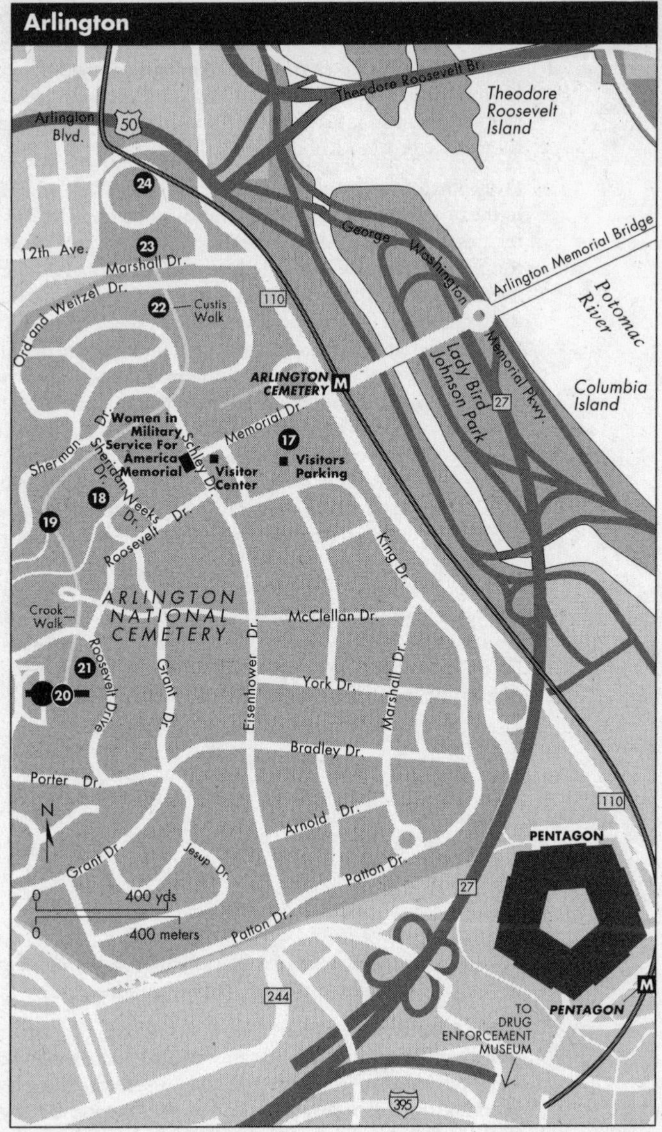

land, and 200 nearby acres were set aside as a national cemetery. Sixty-five soldiers were buried there on June 15, 1864, and by the end of the Civil War more than 16,000 headstones dotted Arlington plantation's hills. Soldiers from the Revolutionary War and the War of 1812 were reinterred at Arlington after their bodies were discovered in other resting places.

Arlington House's heavy Doric columns and severe pediment make it one of the area's best examples of Greek revival architecture. The plantation home was designed by George Hadfield, a young English architect who, for a while, supervised construction of the Capitol. The view of Washington from the front of the house is superb. It looks much as it did in the 19th century, and a quick tour takes you past objects once owned by the Custises and the Lees.

In front of Arlington House, next to a flag that flies at half staff whenever there is a funeral in the cemetery, is the flat-top **grave of Pierre**

L'Enfant, designer of the Federal City. L'Enfant died in 1825, a penniless, bitter man who felt he hadn't been recognized for his planning genius. He was originally buried in Maryland, but his body was moved here with much ceremony in 1909. ✉ *Between Lee and Sherman Drs.,* ☎ *703/557–0613.* 🎟 *Free.* 🕓 *Daily 9:30–4:30.*

★ 17 **Arlington National Cemetery.** More than 250,000 American war dead, as well as many notable Americans (among them presidents William Howard Taft and John F. Kennedy, General John Pershing, and Admiral Robert E. Peary), are interred in these 612 acres across the Potomac from Washington, established as the nation's cemetery in 1864. While you're at Arlington there's a good chance you might hear the clear, doleful sound of a trumpet playing taps or the sharp reports of a gun salute. Approximately 20 funerals are held daily (it's projected that the cemetery will be filled in 2020). Although not the largest cemetery in the country, Arlington is certainly the best known, a place where you can trace America's history through the aftermath of its battles.

To get here, you can take the Metro, travel on a Tourmobile bus, or walk across Arlington Memorial Bridge (southwest of the Lincoln Memorial in D.C.). If you're driving, there's a large paid parking lot at the skylighted **visitor center** on Memorial Drive. Stop at the center for a free brochure with a detailed map of the cemetery. If you're looking for a specific grave, the staff can consult microfilm records and give you directions to it. You should know the full name of the deceased and, if possible, his or her branch of service and year of death.

Tourmobile tour buses leave from just outside the visitor center April through September, daily 8:30–6:30, and October through March, daily 8:30–4:30. You can buy tickets here for the 40-minute tour of the cemetery, which includes stops at the Kennedy grave sites, the Tomb of the Unknowns, and Arlington House. Touring the cemetery on foot means a fair bit of hiking, but it can give you a closer look at some of the thousands of graves spread over these rolling Virginia hills. If you decide to walk, head west from the visitor center on Roosevelt Drive and then turn right on Weeks Drive. ✉ *West end of Memorial Bridge,* ☎ *703/607–8052,* WEB *www.arlingtoncemetery.org.* 🎟 *Cemetery free; parking $1.50 for the first three hours. Tourmobile tour $4.75.* 🕓 *Apr.–Sept., daily 8–7; Oct.–Mar., daily 8–5.*

★ 18 **Kennedy graves.** An important part of any visit to Arlington National Cemetery is a visit to the graves of John F. Kennedy and other members of his family. JFK is buried under an eternal flame near two of his children who died in infancy and his wife, Jacqueline Bouvier Kennedy Onassis. The graves are a short walk west of the visitor center. Across from them is a low wall engraved with quotations from Kennedy's inaugural address. The public has been able to visit JFK's grave since 1967; it's now the most-visited grave site in the country. Nearby, marked by a simple white cross, is the grave of his brother Robert Kennedy. ✉ *Sheridan and Weeks Drs.*

23 **Netherlands Carillon.** A visit to Arlington National Cemetery affords the opportunity for a lovely and unusual musical experience, thanks to a 49-bell carillon presented to the United States by the Dutch people in 1960 in gratitude for aid received during World War II. Guest carillon players perform on Saturday afternoon May through September and on July 4. Times vary; call for details. For one of the most inclusive views of Washington, look to the east across the Potomac. From this vantage point, the Lincoln Memorial, the Washington Monument, and the Capitol appear in a side-by-side formation. ✉ *Meade and Marshall Drs.*

Pentagon. This office building, the headquarters of the United States Department of Defense, is the largest in the world. It has three times the floor space of the 102-floor Empire State Building in New York, and the national Capitol could fit into any one of its five wedge-shape sections. Approximately 23,000 military and civilian workers arrive daily. Astonishingly, this mammoth office building was completed in 1943 after less than two years' worth of construction.

Through determination and concerted effort, contractors rebuilt the section damaged after the September 2001 crash of hijacked American Airlines Flight 77 into the northwest side of the building. On the first anniversary of the terrorist attacks, it was formally dedicated to those who lost their lives. Tours of the building are given on a very limited basis to educational groups by advance reservation; tours for the general public have been suspended indefinitely. ✉ *I–395 at Columbia Pike and Rte. 27,* ☎ *703/695–1776,* WEB *www.defenselink.mil/pubs/pentagon.*

21 **Section 7A.** Many distinguished veterans are buried in this area of Arlington National Cemetery near the Tomb of the Unknowns, including boxing champ Joe Louis, ABC newsman Frank Reynolds, actor Lee Marvin, and World War II fighter pilot Colonel "Pappy" Boyington. ✉ *Crook Walk near Roosevelt Dr.*

22 **Section 27.** More than 3,800 former slaves are buried in this part of Arlington National Cemetery. They're all former residents of Freedman's Village, which operated at the Custis-Lee estate for more than 30 years beginning in 1863 to provide housing, education, and employment training for ex-slaves who had traveled to the capital. In the cemetery, the headstones are marked with their names and the word "Civilian" or "Citizen." Buried at grave 19 in the first row of section 27 is William Christman, a Union private who died of peritonitis in Washington on May 13, 1864. He was the first soldier interred at Arlington National Cemetery during the Civil War. ✉ *Ord and Weitzel Dr., near Custis Walk.*

★ 20 **Tomb of the Unknowns.** Many countries established a memorial to their war dead after World War I. In the United States, the first burial at the Tomb of the Unknowns took place at Arlington National Cemetery on November 11, 1921, when the Unknown Soldier from the "Great War" was interred under the large white-marble sarcophagus. Unknown servicemen killed in World War II and Korea were buried in 1958. The unknown serviceman killed in Vietnam was laid to rest on the plaza on Memorial Day 1984 but was disinterred and identified in 1998. It was then decided to leave the Vietnam War unknown crypt vacant. Soldiers from the Army's U.S. 3rd Infantry ("The Old Guard") keep watch over the tomb 24 hours a day, regardless of weather conditions. Each sentinel marches exactly 21 steps, then faces the tomb for 21 seconds, symbolizing the 21-gun salute, America's highest military honor. The guard is changed with a precise ceremony during the day—every half hour from April through September and every hour the rest of the year. At night the guard is changed every two hours.

The Memorial Amphitheater west of the tomb is the scene of special ceremonies on Veterans Day, Memorial Day, and Easter. Decorations awarded to the unknowns by foreign governments and U.S. and foreign organizations are displayed in an indoor trophy room. Across from the amphitheater are memorials to the astronauts killed in the *Challenger* shuttle explosion and to the servicemen killed in 1980 while trying to rescue American hostages in Iran. Rising beyond that is the mainmast of the USS *Maine,* the American ship that was sunk in Havana Harbor in 1898, killing 299 men and sparking the Spanish-American War. (The foremast is on the grounds of the U.S. Naval Academy in Annapolis.) ✉ *End of Crook Walk.*

24 **United States Marine Corps War Memorial.** Better known simply as "the Iwo Jima," this memorial, despite its familiarity, has lost none of its power to stir the emotions. Honoring marines who have given their lives since the Corps was formed in 1775, the statue, sculpted by Felix W. de Weldon, is based on Joe Rosenthal's Pulitzer Prize–winning photograph of five Marines and a Navy corpsman raising a flag atop Mt. Suribachi on the Japanese island of Iwo Jima on February 19, 1945. By executive order, a real flag flies 24 hours a day from the 78-ft-high memorial. On Tuesday evening at 7 from late May to late August there's a Marine Corps sunset parade on the grounds of the memorial. On parade nights a free shuttle bus runs from the Arlington Cemetery visitors' parking lot. Note that it is not safe to visit the memorial after dark.

Women in Military Service for America Memorial. What is now this memorial next to the visitor center was once the Hemicycle, a huge carved retaining wall faced with granite at the entrance to Arlington National Cemetery. Built in 1932, the wall was restored, with stairways added leading to a rooftop terrace. Inside are 16 exhibit alcoves showing the contributions that women have made to the military—from the Revolutionary War to the present—as well as the history of the memorial itself. A 196-seat theater shows films and is used for lectures and conferences. A computer database has pictures, military histories, and stories of thousands of women veterans. A fountain and reflecting pool front the classical-style Hemicycle and entry gates.

Dining and Lodging

Bragging rights to some of the D.C. area's best Asian restaurants go to Arlington, where Wilson Boulevard is lined with popular Vietnamese establishments and branches of D.C. restaurants. The Clarendon Metro station makes these Asian restaurants readily accessible; the King Street Metro station is a 15-minute walk from most Old Town Alexandria eateries.

$$–$$$ ✕ **Carlyle Grand Cafe.** This restaurant and bar stand out from among the several in the little Shirlington area of Arlington. The bustling downstairs bar and the sleek art deco dining room upstairs serve almost the same menu but feel like two different restaurants. Both serve an imaginative, generous interpretation of contemporary American cooking. You might start with lobster pot stickers (dumplings that have been browned and then cooked in broth) and then progress to entrées such as sea bass with shiitake mushroom crust or sea scallops with potato hash. The chocolate waffle is the most popular dessert. If you like the bread, you can buy more at the restaurant's bakery, the Best Buns Bread Company, next door. Free, off-street parking is plentiful. ✉ *4000 S. 28th St.,* ☎ *703/931–0777. AE, MC, V.*

$–$$$ ★ ✕ **Aegean Taverna.** The Aegean Taverna serves authentic Greek food indoors and outside in good weather. Good menu choices are *pastitsio* (baked ziti pasta with ground beef and cheese topped with béchamel sauce), moussaka, and spanakopita. Greek musicians perform Friday and Saturday nights from 7:30 to 11:30. Parking is free and easy in a large adjoining lot. ✉ *2950 Clarendon Blvd.,* ☎ *703/841–9494. AE, D, DC, MC, V.*

$ ✕ **Pho 75.** The soup of the same name is the only dish at Pho 75, a cafeteria-style eatery in the Rosslyn section of Wilson Boulevard. To refer to pho (pronounced *fuh*) as mere soup would be a disservice to the delightful procession of flavors that come with every mouthful—but that is essentially what pho is: a Hanoi-style beef soup packed with noodles and thin slices of meat that are cooked in seconds by the steaming broth. A plate of fresh bean sprouts, mint leaves, lemon, and green chiles comes with every order so that you may spice your feast-in-a-bowl as you wish. ✉ *1721 Wilson Blvd.,* ☎ *703/525–7355. No credit cards.*

$ ★ ✕ **Queen Bee.** Arlington's Little Saigon area has several Vietnamese restaurants, and this unassuming spot is one of the best. The service is cordial, and the food is always excellent. The *cha gio* (spring rolls) are wonderful. The green-papaya salad (with squid or beef jerky) and the Saigon pancake—accented with a mix of crab, pork, and shrimp—are two other reasons that diners often wait for a table. ✉ *3181 Wilson Blvd.,* ☎ *703/527–3444. AE, MC, V.*

$ ✕ **Red Hot & Blue.** Photos of famous customers, including several blues singers, adorn the walls of this barbecue restaurant, where patrons order pork ribs and shoulders prepared Memphis style—smoked, then spiced or sauced—or pulled-pork sandwiches. Beans, coleslaw, potato salad, and french fries make up the side choices. ✉ *1600 Wilson Blvd.,* ☎ *703/276–7427. AE, MC, V.*

$$$–$$$$ ★ **Ritz-Carlton, Pentagon City.** This 18-story Ritz-Carlton at the Pentagon City Metro stop is more convenient to downtown Washington than many D.C. hotels. Inside, the hotel looks to Virginia horse country for its inspiration, and public spaces are full of art and antiques, mostly from the 18th and 19th centuries. The lobby lounge offers an afternoon tea of extensive variety, and serves cocktails and light fare. Guest rooms have mahogany furnishings, and the upper rooms have views of the monuments across the river. The hotel connects to the upscale Fashion Centre at Pentagon City. ✉ *1250 S. Hayes St., 22202,* ☎ *703/415–5000 or 800/241–3333,* FAX *703/415–5061,* WEB *www.ritzcarlton.com. 345 rooms, 21 suites. Restaurant, room service, in-room data ports, in-room fax, in-room safes, minibars, indoor pool, health club, bar, lobby lounge, business services, meeting rooms, parking (fee). AE, DC, MC, V.*

$$–$$$ **Residence Inn Pentagon City.** This all-suite high-rise has a magnificent view across the Potomac of the D.C. skyline and the monuments. Adjacent to the Pentagon, it's one block from a Metro stop and the Fashion Centre at Pentagon City. The teal-and-burgundy suites have fully equipped kitchens. Complimentary are grocery shopping service, daily newspaper, an extensive Continental breakfast, and transportation to Ronald Reagan Washington National Airport. ✉ *550 Army-Navy Dr., 22202,* ☎ *703/413–6630 or 800/331–3131,* FAX *703/418–1751,* WEB *www.residenceinn.com. 299 suites. In-room data ports, kitchenettes, indoor pool, gym, hot tub, dry cleaning, laundry facilities, laundry service, meeting rooms, airport shuttle, parking (fee); no-smoking rooms. AE, D, DC, MC, V. CP.*

$–$$$ **Quality Inn Iwo Jima.** Within walking distance of the Marine Corps memorial and the Rosslyn Metro, the Quality Inn Iwo Jima is a consistently well-regarded budget hotel with easy access to Georgetown, the Pentagon, and Ronald Reagan Washington National Airport. The older original section has outside entrances and larger rooms with double-sink bathrooms. The high-rise rooms are business-class and include a work table, data ports, and a 25-inch television set. Local calls, coffee, and a morning copy of *The Washington Post* are free. ✉ *1501 Arlington Blvd. (Rte. 50), 22209,* ☎ *703/524–5000 or 800/221–2222,* WEB *www.qualityinniwojima.com,* FAX *703/522–5484. 141 rooms. Restaurant, room service, indoor pool, gym, bar, laundry service, free parking. AE, D, DC, MC, V.*

$$ **Holiday Inn Rosslyn Westpark.** A comfortable, economical hotel, the Westpark is two blocks from the Rosslyn Metro and a leisurely stroll across Key Bridge to Georgetown's restaurants and nightclubs. But the

best thing about this hotel may be the view of Washington's monuments from the Vantage Point restaurant's panoramic windows. The hotel is also near Fort Myer, the Marine Corps memorial, and Arlington National Cemetery. ✉ *1900 N. Fort Myer Dr., 22209,* ☎ *703/807–2000 or 800/368–3408,* FAX *703/522–8864,* WEB *www.basshotels.com/holiday-inn. 306 rooms. Restaurant, café, in-room data ports, in-room safes, indoor pool, health club, laundry facilities, laundry service, meeting rooms, free parking. AE, D, DC, MC, V.*

$ **Travelodge Cherry Blossom.** This economical, three-story lodging is less than 2 mi from the Pentagon, Fashion Centre at Pentagon City, and two Metro stations (a city bus stops in front). Wallpapered rooms are done in navy and wine fabrics and have the usual motel furniture, coffeemakers, and hair dryers. Local calls, complimentary coffee, HBO, a microwave oven on request, and Continental breakfast are included. The Rincome, a Thai restaurant, is on the premises, and more than 50 other restaurants are within walking distance. ✉ *3030 Columbia Pike, 22204,* ☎ *703/521–5570 or 800/578–7878,* FAX *703/271–0081,* WEB *www.travelodge.com. 76 rooms. Restaurant, some kitchenettes, cable TV, gym, laundry facilities, meeting rooms, free parking; no-smoking rooms. AE, D, DC, MC, V. CP.*

Nightlife and the Arts

MUSIC

Iota (✉ 2832 Wilson Blvd., ☎ 703/522–8340) presents many different kinds of live music nightly. You'll hear everything from alternative rock to folk. Cover charges start at $5, and there are no advance ticket sales.

Outdoor Activities and Sports

Arlington's 36 mi of multiuse trails and 50 mi of connecting bicycle lanes and routes take you along the Virginia side of the Potomac from Key Bridge to Mount Vernon. Contact the **Arlington Department of Parks, Recreation and Community Resources** (☎ 703/228–4747, WEB www.co.arlington.va.us) for a map of the Arlington County Bikeway System.

Shopping

The **Fashion Centre at Pentagon City** (✉ 1100 S. Hayes St., ☎ 703/415–2400, WEB www.fashioncentrepentagon.com) has more than 170 stores on three shopping levels, a food court, and six cinemas. Anchors include Macy's and Nordstrom; other large stores include Abercrombie & Fitch, Ann Taylor, Banana Republic, Crate & Barrel, and Williams-Sonoma. In the skylit Food Court are international specialties both familiar and exotic. Seven full-service restaurants provide an additional selection of good food.

MOUNT VERNON, WOODLAWN, AND GUNSTON HALL

Long before Washington was planned, the shores of the Potomac had been divided into plantations by wealthy traders and gentleman farmers. Most traces of the Colonial era were obliterated as the capital grew in the 19th century, but several splendid examples of plantation architecture remain on the Virginia side of the Potomac, just 15 mi or so south of D.C. In just one day you can easily visit three such mansions: Mount Vernon, the home of George Washington and one of the most popular sites in the area; Woodlawn, the estate of Washington's step-granddaughter; and Gunston Hall, the home of George Mason, author of the document on which the Bill of Rights was based. On hillsides overlooking the river, these estates offer magnificent vistas and

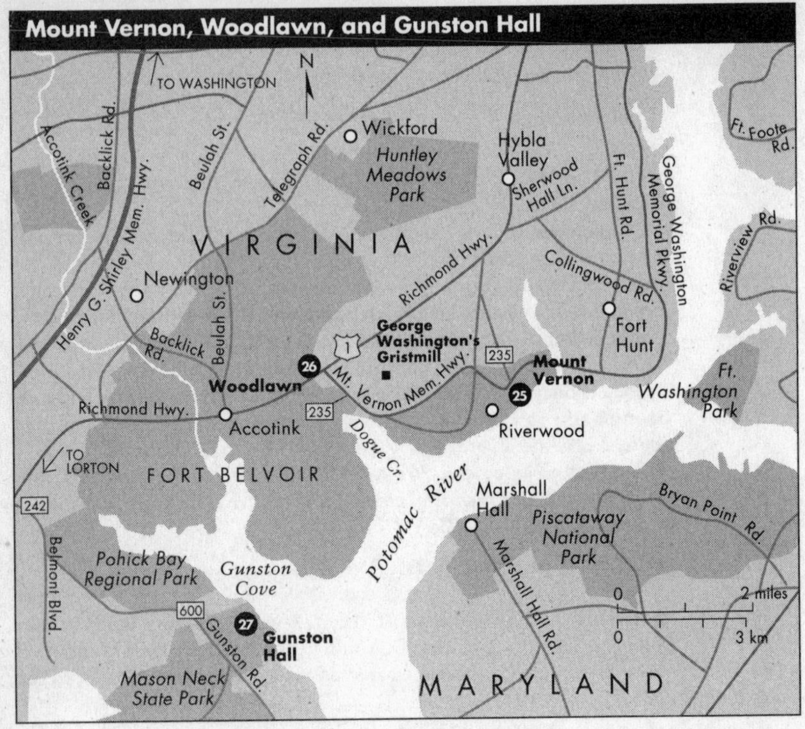

bring a bygone era to vivid life. A bit farther south is Woodbridge, which has a more modern attraction: the Potomac Mills outlet mall.

Numbers in the margin correspond to points of interest on the Mount Vernon, Woodlawn, and Gunston Hall map.

Mount Vernon

★ 25 *16 mi southeast of Washington, D.C., 8 mi south of Alexandria, VA.*

Mount Vernon and the surrounding lands had been in the Washington family for nearly 90 years by the time George inherited it all in 1761. Before taking over command of the Continental Army, Washington was a yeoman farmer managing the 8,000-acre plantation, of which more than 3,000 acres were under cultivation. He also oversaw the transformation of the main house from an ordinary farm dwelling into what was, for the time, a grand mansion. The inheritance of his widowed bride, Martha, is largely what made that transformation possible.

The red-roofed main house is elegant though understated, with a yellow pine exterior that's been painted and coated with layers of sand to resemble white-stone blocks. The first-floor rooms are quite ornate, especially the formal large dining room, with a molded ceiling decorated with agricultural motifs. The bright colors of the walls, which match the original paint, may surprise those who associate the period with pastels. Throughout the house are smaller symbols of the owner's eminence, such as a key to the main portal of the Bastille—presented to Washington by the Marquis de Lafayette—and Washington's presidential chair. As you tour the mansion, guides are stationed throughout the house to describe the furnishings and answer questions.

The real treasure of Mount Vernon is the view from around back: beneath a 90-ft portico, the home's dramatic riverside porch overlooks an expanse of lawn that slopes down to the Potomac. In springtime the view of the river (a mile wide where it passes the plantation) is framed by dogwood blossoms. Protocol requires United States Navy and Coast Guard ships to salute when passing the house during daylight hours. Although not required, foreign naval vessels often salute, too.

You can stroll around the estate's 500 acres and three gardens, visiting the workshops, the kitchen, the carriage house, the greenhouse, the slave quarters, and—down the hill toward the boat landing—the tomb of George and Martha Washington. There's also a pioneer farmer site: a 4-acre hands-on exhibit with a reconstruction of George Washington's 16-sided treading barn as its centerpiece. Among the souvenirs sold at the plantation are stripling boxwoods that began life as clippings from bushes planted in 1798, the year before Washington died. A tour of house and grounds takes about two hours. A limited number of wheelchairs is available at the main gate. Private, evening candlelight tours of the mansion with staff dressed in 18th-century costumes can be arranged.

After many years of research, George Washington's Gristmill opened in 2002 on the site of his original mill and distillery. During the guided tours, led by historic interpreters, you'll meet an 18th-century miller and watch the water-powered wheel grind grain into flour just as it did 200 years ago. The mill is 3 mi from Mount Vernon on Route 235 between Mount Vernon and U.S. Rte. 1. Tickets can be purchased either at the gristmill itself or at Mount Vernon's Main Gate. ✉ *Southern end of George Washington Pkwy., Mount Vernon, VA,* ☎ *703/780–2000; 703/799–8606 evening tours,* FAX *703/799–8609,* WEB *www.mountvernon.org.* 🎟 *$11; $4 gristmill; $13 combination ticket.* ⏲ *Mar. and Sept.–Oct., daily 9–5; Apr.–Aug., daily 8–5; Nov.–Feb., daily 9–4.*

Woodlawn

㉖ *3 mi west of Mount Vernon, 15 mi south of Washington, D.C.*

Woodlawn was once part of the Mount Vernon estate. From here you can still see traces of the bowling green that fronted Washington's home. The house was built for Washington's step-granddaughter, Nelly Custis, who married his favorite nephew, Lawrence Lewis. (Lewis had come to Mount Vernon from Fredericksburg to help Uncle George manage his five farms.)

The Lewises' home, completed in 1805, was designed by William Thornton, a physician and amateur architect from the West Indies who drew up the original plans for the U.S. Capitol. Like Mount Vernon, the Woodlawn house is constructed wholly of native materials, including the clay for its bricks and the yellow pine used throughout its interior. In the tradition of Southern riverfront mansions, Woodlawn has a central hallway that provides a cool refuge in summer. At one corner of the passage is a bust of George Washington set on a pedestal so the crown of the head is at 6 ft, 2 inches—Washington's actual height. The music room has a ceiling that's approximately 2 ft higher than any other in the house, built that way to improve the acoustics for the harp and harpsichord recitals that the Lewises and their children enjoyed.

After Woodlawn passed out of the Lewis family's hands it was owned by a Quaker community, which established a meetinghouse and the first integrated school in Virginia here. The property was acquired by the National Trust for Historic Preservation in 1957, which had been operating it as a museum since 1951. Every March, Woodlawn hosts an annual needlework exhibit with more than 700 items on display.

Also on the grounds of Woodlawn is the **Pope-Leighey House.** One of Frank Lloyd Wright's "Usonian" homes, it was designed in part as a showcase of affordable housing for people of modest means. The house was built in 1940 and moved here from Falls Church, Virginia, in 1964. ✉ *9000 Richmond Hwy., Mt. Vernon,* ☎ *703/780–4000,* WEB *www.nthp.org/main/sites/leighey.htm.* *$7.50 for either Woodlawn or Pope-Leighey House; $13 combination ticket.* *Apr.–Dec., daily 10–5; tour every ½ hr (last tour at 4:30); Mar., daily 10–5; lunch served daily 11:30–2:30 Mar. only (no tours owing to the annual needlework show).*

Gunston Hall

27 *12 mi south of Woodlawn, 25 mi south of Washington, D.C.*

Gunston Hall Plantation, down the Potomac from Mount Vernon, was the home of another important George. Gentleman farmer George Mason was a colonel of the Fairfax militia and author of the Virginia Declaration of Rights, the model for the U.S. Bill of Rights, which called for freedom of the press, tolerance of religion, and other fundamental democratic principles. Mason was a framer of the Constitution but refused to sign the final document because it didn't stop the importation of slaves, adequately restrain the powers of the federal government, or include a bill of rights. Mason's objections spurred the movement for the inclusion of the Bill of Rights into the Constitution.

Mason's home was built circa 1755. The Georgian-style mansion has some of the finest hand-carved ornamented interiors in the country. It's the handiwork of the 18th century's foremost architect, William Buckland, who also designed the Hammond-Harwood and Chase-Lloyd houses in Annapolis. Gunston Hall is built of native brick, black walnut, and yellow pine. The style of the time demanded absolute symmetry in all structures, which explains the false door set into one side of the center hallway and the "robber" window on a second-floor storage room. The house's interior, with carved woodwork in styles from Chinese to Gothic, has been meticulously restored, with paints made from the original formulas and carefully carved replacements for the intricate mahogany medallions in the moldings. Restored outbuildings include a kitchen, dairy, laundry, and smokehouse, and a schoolhouse has also been reconstructed.

The formal gardens, under excavation by a team of archaeologists, are famous for their boxwoods—some, now 12 ft high, are thought to have been planted during George Mason's time, making them among the oldest in the country. The Potomac is visible past the expansive deer park. Also on the grounds is an active farmyard with livestock and crop varieties that resemble those of Mason's time. Special programs—such as history lectures and hearth cooking demonstrations—are offered throughout the year. A tour of Gunston Hall takes at least 45 minutes; tours begin at the visitor center, which includes a museum and gift shop. ✉ *10709 Gunston Rd., Mason Neck,* ☎ *703/550–9220 or 800/811–6966,* WEB *www.gunstonhall.org.* *$7.* *Daily 9:30–5; tours every 30 min, beginning at 10 AM, last tour at 4:30.*

Shopping

Nine miles from Gunston Hall, **Potomac Mills** (✉ 2700 Potomac Mills Circle, Woodbridge, ☎ 703/490–5948) is a mile-long mall off I–95. It bills itself as Virginia's leading tourist attraction. There are 220 outlet stores here, including Nordstrom Rack, T. J. Maxx, and Burlington Coat Factory. Anchoring the mall is Swedish furniture giant IKEA.

FAIRFAX COUNTY

In 1694 King Charles II of England gave the land that would become Fairfax County to seven English noblemen. It became a county in 1741 and was named after Thomas, sixth Lord of Fairfax. Widespread tobacco farming, the dominant industry in the 18th century, eventually depleted the land and helped steer the county toward a more industrial base. Today Fairfax County has one of the highest per capita incomes in the country. The only national park dedicated to the performing arts is here, and throughout the year it draws concertgoers from miles around.

Fairfax

28 *10 mi west of Arlington.*

Fairfax is completely independent of the county of the same name that surrounds it. It's a convenient place to stay while visiting the county's sights, as well as the rest of northern Virginia.

The National Rifle Association's **National Firearms Museum** has exhibits on the role guns have played in the history of America. The permanent collection includes muzzle-loading flintlocks used in the Revolutionary War, high-tech pistols used by Olympic shooting teams, and weapons that once belonged to American presidents, including Teddy Roosevelt's .32-caliber Browning pistol and a Winchester rifle used by Dwight Eisenhower. ✉ *National Rifle Association, 11250 Waples Mill Rd.,* ☎ *703/267–1600,* WEB *www.nrahq.org/museum.* 🎫 *Free.* ⏲ *Daily 10–4.*

Lodging

$$$ **The Bailiwick Inn.** Red brick and green shutters distinguish this small luxury hotel in an 1812 building opposite the historic Fairfax County Courthouse. Expect to be pampered: there are nearly twice as many staff members as rooms. Named for prominent Virginians, guest rooms have antique and reproduction furniture, period detail, and luxurious, modern bathrooms. Four rooms have fireplaces; two have whirlpool baths. The restaurant is open Wednesday through Sunday for dinner, and lunch is served Friday. Room rates include a very fine breakfast and afternoon tea daily. Tea is open to the public on Thursday and Sunday. ✉ *4023 Chain Bridge Rd., 22030,* ☎ *703/691–2266 or 800/366–7666,* FAX *703/934–2112,* WEB *www.bailiwickinn.com. 13 rooms, 1 suite. Restaurant, minibars, bar; no kids. AE, MC, V. BP.*

Chantilly

29 *8 mi northwest of Fairfax.*

The main attraction for those who come to Chantilly is a Federal-period home called **Sully.** The house has changed hands many times since it was built in 1794 by Richard Bland Lee, Northern Virginia's first representative to Congress. Citizen action in the 20th century saved it from destruction during construction of nearby Dulles Airport. In the 1970s the house and its outbuilding were restored to their original appearance, with a representative kitchen and flower gardens. A 45-minute tour is offered every hour on the hour. Educational programs, craft demonstrations, and living history events are on offer throughout the year. ✉ *Rte. 28 (3601 Sully Rd.),* ☎ *703/437–1794,* WEB *www.co.fairfax.va.us/parks/sully.* 🎫 *$5.* ⏲ *Mar.–Dec., Wed.–Mon. 11–4; Jan.–Feb., Wed.–Mon. 11–3.*

OFF THE BEATEN PATH

MANASSAS NATIONAL BATTLEFIELD PARK – The Confederacy won two important victories—in July 1861 and August 1862—at Manassas National Battlefield Park, or Bull Run. General Thomas Jonathan Jackson earned his nickname Stonewall here, when he and his brigade "stood like a stone wall." When the second battle ended, the Confederacy was at the zenith of its power. President Taft led a peaceful reunion of thousands of veterans here in 1911—50 years after the first battle. The "Peace Jubilee" continues to be celebrated in Manassas every summer. A self-guided tour of the park begins at the visitor center, whose exhibits and audiovisual presentations greatly enhance a visit. Bull Run is a 26-mi drive from Washington; from Arlington and Fairfax take I–66 west (use I–495 to get to I–66 from Alexandria) to Route 234 North (don't be fooled by the earlier Manassas exit for Route 28). The visitor center is ½ mi north on the right. ✉ *12521 Lee Hwy., north of I–66 Exit 47,* ☎ *703/361–1339,* WEB *www.nps.gov/mana.* 🎫 *$2.* ⏲ *Park daily dawn–dusk; visitor center daily 8:30–5.*

McLean

15 mi northeast of Fairfax, 12 mi northwest of Alexandria.

The home of ambassadors, members of Congress, business magnates, and the CIA, McLean is the wealthiest suburb in Virginia. There's not much of a town—just some banks, upscale groceries, and other stores near the intersection of Chain Bridge Road and Old Dominion Drive. But at about a 20-minute drive from the Capitol, McLean has the benefits of proximity to the District and the feel of country living with its rolling land and winding roads.

The only privately operated national park in the country, the **Claude Moore Colonial Farm** portrays family life on a small farm in 1771. A walk around the farm—in the tall woods across the street from the high security fences of the CIA—is just under ¾ of a mile and passes the barn and tobacco field, the livestock, and the family's home, a one-room log building tucked between the apple orchard and the kitchen garden. On the third full weekends of May, July, and October, thousands of people join the costumed farm family and period craftsmen, entertainers and merchants in an 18th-century Market Fair. ✉ *6310 Georgetown Pike,* ☎ *703/442–7557,* WEB *www.1771.org.* 🎫 *$2 (slightly higher for special events).* ⏲ *Apr.–mid-Dec., Wed.–Sun. 10–4:30.*

Tysons Corner

30 *11 mi northwest of Alexandria.*

A highly developed commercial area of office buildings, hotels, restaurants, and two major shopping centers, Tysons Corner is a fashionable address in the Washington, D.C., area. Beware of the grating traffic jam hitting every road, side street, and parking lot at rush hour. Routes 123 and 7, Gallows Road, and International Drive, are the worst; I–495, the Beltway, is less affected.

Dining and Lodging

$–$$$ ✕ **Clyde's of Tysons Corner.** A branch of a popular Georgetown pub, Clyde's has four art deco dining rooms. The Palm Terrace has high ceilings and lots of greenery; another room is a formal dining room. The lengthy, eclectic menu always includes fresh fish dishes, such as trout Parmesan. The wine list is equally long. Quality is high, and service attentive. ✉ *8332 Leesburg Pike,* ☎ *703/734–1900. AE, D, DC, MC, V.*

$$$ 🏨 **Ritz-Carlton, Tysons Corner.** Rooms here are large, with antique furniture, 19th-century lithographs, and trademark elegance. Booking a room in the concierge level gives you access to an exclusive club with sweeping views of the Virginia countryside. On the third floor, the Eden Spa has everything from a juice bar to a pool with lap lanes. The lobby lounge's dark paneled walls and safari animal bronzes make it feel like a club room. The bar's innovative menu includes pizzettes with goat cheese and smoked duck. The restaurant, at the foot of a grand double staircase, serves contemporary American cuisine. ✉ *1700 Tysons Blvd., McLean 22102,* ☎ *703/506–4300,* FAX *703/506–4305,* WEB *www.ritzcarlton.com. 366 rooms, 33 suites. Restaurant, minibars, indoor pool, health club, spa, bar, business services, meeting rooms. AE, D, MC, V.*

Shopping

Tysons Corner Center (✉ 1961 Chain Bridge Rd., ☎ 703/893–9400 or 888/289–7667, WEB www.shoptysons.com), at the junction of Routes 7 and 123, contains 240 retailers, including Bloomingdale's, Nordstrom, and Hecht's department stores. Children make a trip to the **Disney Store** (☎ 703/448–8314) a sightseeing adventure.

The **Galleria at Tysons II** (✉ 1714 International Dr., ☎ 703/827–7730, WEB www.tysons2.com/galleria.html), across Route 123 from the Tysons Corner Center, has 125 stores, including Saks Fifth Avenue, Neiman Marcus, and F. A. O. Schwarz.

Wolf Trap Farm Park for the Performing Arts

13 mi west of Alexandria.

A major venue in the greater D.C. area, **Wolf Trap Farm Park for the Performing Arts** is the only national park devoted to the performing arts. In warmer months drama, dance, and music performances are given in a partially covered pavilion, the Filene Center, and in the Barns of Wolf Trap—two 18th-century barns transported from upstate New York—the rest of the year. Many food concessions are available; picnicking is permitted on the lawn, but not in the fixed seating under the pavilion.

Children's programs are emphasized at the outdoor Theater in the Woods, including mime, puppetry, animal shows, music, drama, and storytelling. (Be aware that no food or drink other than water is allowed in the theater.) A major event in September is the International Children's Festival. At any event, allow extra time for parking, and expect a traffic jam after the performance. The 100-odd acres of hills, meadows, and forests here are closed to general use from two hours before to one hour after performances. ✉ *1551 Trap Rd., off Rte. 7,* ☎ *703/255–1860 or 703/255–1900; 703/255–1827 Theatre in the Woods; 703/938–2404 Barns of Wolf Trap,* WEB *www.nps.gov/wotr.* 🎫 *Varies with event.* ⏲ *Daily 7 AM–dusk.*

C&O Canal National Historic Park and Great Falls Park

20 mi northwest of Alexandria.

The Potomac River was and still is a highway for transporting goods. In the 18th and early 19th centuries, it was the main transport route between vital Maryland ports and the seaports of the Chesapeake Bay. Though it served as an important link with the country's western territories, the Potomac had a major drawback for a commercial waterway: rapids and waterfalls along its 190 mi made navigation of the entire distance by boat impossible.

To make the flow of goods from east to west more efficient, engineers proposed that a canal with elevator locks be built parallel to the river. George Washington founded a company to build the canal, and in 1802 (after his death) the firm opened the Patowmack Canal on the Virginia side of the river.

In 1828 Washington's canal was replaced by the Chesapeake and Ohio Canal, known as the C&O. Stretching from downtown Washington to Cumberland, Maryland, barges moved through 75 locks of the canal, and by the mid-19th century it carried a million tons of goods a year. But by the time it had opened, newer technology was starting to make canals obsolete. The Baltimore and Ohio Railroad—which had opened the same day as the C&O—finally put the canal out of business in 1924. After Palisades residents defeated a 1950s proposal to build a highway over it, the canal was reborn as the lovely Chesapeake & Ohio Canal National Historical Park in 1971.

Numbers in the margin correspond to points of interest on the C&O Canal and Great Falls Park map.

Fletcher's Boat House, on the D.C. side of the Potomac, rents rowboats, canoes, and bicycles and sells tackle, snack foods, and D.C. fishing licenses. Here you can catch shad, perch, catfish, striped bass, and other freshwater species. Canoeing is allowed in the canal and, weather permitting, in the Potomac. There's a large picnic area along the riverbank. ✉ *4940 Canal Rd., at Reservoir Rd., Georgetown,* ☎ *202/244–0461.* ⏲ *Late Mar.–May, daily 7:30–7; June–Aug., daily 9–7; Sept.–Nov., daily 9–6. Closed Dec.–early Mar. and during severe weather.*

31 The **Chain Bridge** links the District of Columbia with Virginia. Named for the chains that held up the original structure, the bridge was built to enable cattlemen to bring Virginia herds to the slaughterhouses on the Maryland side of the Potomac. The Virginia side of the river in the area around Chain Bridge is known for its good fishing and narrow, treacherous channel.

Upriver about 8 mi from the Chain Bridge, the C&O Canal National Historic Park—on the Washington, D.C., and Maryland side of the Po-
32 tomac River—faces its sister national park **Great Falls Park**—on the Virginia side. Here the steep, jagged falls of the Potomac roar into the narrow Mather Gorge, the rocky narrows that make the Potomac churn.

The 800-acre park is a favorite for outings; here you can follow trails past the old Patowmack Canal and among the boulders and forests lining the edge of the falls. Horseback riding is permitted—maps are available at the visitor center—but you can't rent horses in the park. Swimming, wading, overnight camping, and alcoholic beverages are not allowed, but you can fish (a Virginia, Maryland, or D.C. license is required for anglers 16 and older), climb rocks (climbers must register at the visitor center beforehand), or—if you're an experienced boater with your own equipment—go white-water kayaking (*below* the falls only). As is true all along this stretch of the river, the currents are deadly. Despite frequent signs and warnings, there are those who occasionally dare the water and drown.

A tour of the visitor center and museum takes 30 minutes. Staff members conduct special tours and walks year-round. Maryland's Great Falls Tavern, discussed in Chapter 3, serves as a museum and has displays of canal history and a platform from which to view the falls. You can get to C&O Canal National Historical Park from Alexandria or Arlington by taking Chain Bridge to MacArthur Boulevard, then driving northwest, or by taking Exit 41 off the Beltway and following the signs to Carderock. ✉ *Rte. 193 (Exit 13 off Rte. 495, the Capitol Beltway) to Rte. 738, and follow the signs,* ☎ *703/285–2966,* WEB *www.nps.*

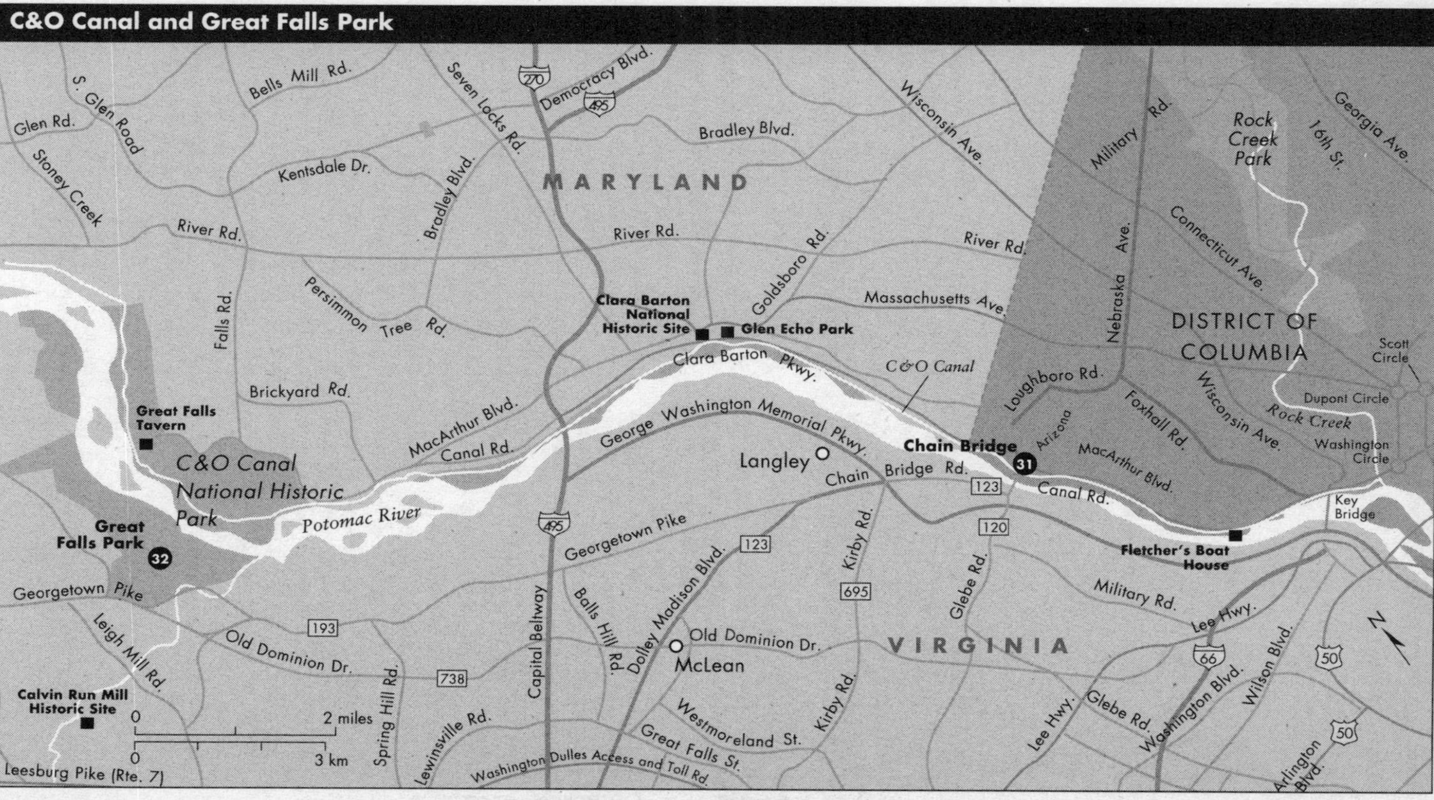
C&O Canal and Great Falls Park
Bells Mill Rd.
S. Glen Road
Glen Rd.
Stoney Creek
Kentsdale Dr.
Seven Locks Rd.
270
Democracy Blvd.
495
Bradley Blvd.
Bradley Blvd.
MARYLAND
Wisconsin Ave.
Military Rd.
Rock Creek Park
16th St.
Georgia Ave.
River Rd.
River Rd.
River Rd.
Connecticut Ave.
Nebraska Ave.
Persimmon Tree Rd.
Falls Rd.
Goldsboro Rd.
Massachusetts Ave.
Clara Barton National Historic Site
Glen Echo Park
DISTRICT OF COLUMBIA
Scott Circle
Clara Barton Pkwy.
C&O Canal
Loughboro Rd.
Dupont Circle
Brickyard Rd.
Rock Creek
Great Falls Tavern
MacArthur Blvd.
Canal Rd.
George Washington Memorial Pkwy.
Foxhall Rd.
Wisconsin Ave.
Washington Circle
Arizona
Chain Bridge
31
MacArthur Blvd.
C&O Canal National Historic Park
Langley
Chain Bridge Rd.
123
Canal Rd.
Key Bridge
Potomac River
495
Georgetown Pike
120
Great Falls Park
32
123
Kirby Rd.
Fletcher's Boat House
Dolley Madison Blvd.
Glebe Rd.
695
Military Rd.
Georgetown Pike
Balls Hill Rd.
Lee Hwy.
193
Capital Beltway
Old Dominion Dr.
VIRGINIA
Leigh Mill Rd.
Old Dominion Dr.
McLean
66
50
738
Wilson Blvd.
Calvin Run Mill Historic Site
Spring Hill Rd.
Kirby Rd.
Washington Blvd.
0
2 miles
Lewinsville Rd.
Westmoreland St.
Lee Hwy.
Glebe Rd.
50
0
3 km
Great Falls St.
Leesburg Pike (Rte. 7)
Washington Dulles Access and Toll Rd.
Arlington Blvd.

Close-Up

WINE MAKING IN VIRGINIA

IN 1609, ENGLISH SETTLERS in Jamestown, Virginia, produced the first wine—however humble—in America. In the centuries that have followed, it has been either sink or swim for the state's wine industry—mostly sink. But after numerous tries, Virginia can proudly claim some 70-odd wineries.

In 1611 the Virginia Company, which was eager to establish wine making in the Colonies, sent over French winegrowers along with slips and seeds of European vine stocks. For the next two centuries, French viticulturists attempted but failed to transplant European rootstock to the New World. In 1769, the Virginia Assembly appointed the Frenchman Andrew Estave as wine maker and viticulturist. Although he couldn't get the European stock to take either, he did realize that the problem lay with Virginia's harsher climate of cold winters and hot, humid summers. Estave believed that growers should therefore use native American grapes, which were more likely to flourish.

Thomas Jefferson was anxious to promote grape growing, both to encourage wine drinking for itself and to create a cash-crop alternative to tobacco. Although he appreciated European wines, Jefferson believed that successful wine making in America would depend on native varietals. By 1800, he and other Virginians had begun developing hybrids of American and European varieties, resulting in grapes that combined American hardiness with European finesse and complexity. The most popular are still grown today.

A strong wine-making industry developed in Virginia between 1800 and the Civil War. Unfortunately, the war's fierce battles destroyed many vineyards. As recently as 1950, only 15 acres of grapes were being grown. In the 1960s, the Virginia grape industry began a revival that has made it the sixth-largest wine-producing state. Although the revival began with American hybrids, it has shifted to French hybrids, with the cultivation of vinifera varietals appealing to more sophisticated palates.

Today Virginia's wines are winning national and international acclaim. The state produces more than 300,000 cases of wine yearly from 2,100 acres of wine grapes. The most popular variety grown, Chardonnay, comes as a medium- to full-bodied dry white wine. It may be fruity, with a hint of apples or citrus. Other whites include Riesling, Gewürztraminer, Sauvignon Blanc, Seyval Blanc, and Vidal Blanc. Virginia's reds include Cabernet Sauvignon, Merlot, Pinot Noir, and Chambourcin. Virginia's wineries are spread around the state in six viticultural areas. The wine industry begun by Jefferson is in the Monticello region in central Virginia. Other areas are the Shenandoah, Northern Neck George Washington Birthplace, North Fork of Roanoke, Rocky Knob, and Virginia's Eastern Shore. Each area has been designated for its unique wine-growing conditions.

The 400 wine festivals and events that take place each year attract half a million visitors. A 16-page booklet, "Virginia Wineries Festival & Tour Guide," is available free at visitor information centers in the state. The guide also lists each of the state's wineries; many offer tours and tastings. You can request a copy by contacting the **Virginia Wine Marketing Program** (✉ Virginia Department of Agriculture and Consumer Services, Division of Marketing, Box 1163, Richmond 23218, ☎ 800/828–4637, WEB www.virginiawines.org).

— CiCi Williamson

gov/gwmp/grfa. 🎫 *$4 per vehicle, good for 7 days.* ⏲ *Year-round, daily 7–dusk. Visitor center Apr.–Oct., daily 10–6; Nov.–Mar., daily 10–4.*

Colvin Run Mill Historic Site dates from the first decade of the 19th century, although the country store was added in the early 20th. In addition to the restored mill, there's a small museum inside the miller's home. It offers hourly tours, educational programs, special events, and outdoor concerts. You can picnic on the grounds, feed the ducks, and learn about America's technological roots. The Colvin Run Mill General Store originally served the local community and today offers penny candy, freshly ground cornmeal and wheat flour, popcorn, and various old-fashioned goods. The mill itself usually operates the first and third Sunday afternoons from March to November. ✉ *Rte. 7 and 10017 Colvin Run Rd., Great Falls,* ☎ *703/759–2771,* WEB *www.co.fairfax.va.us/parks/crm.* 🎫 *$4.* ⏲ *Mar.–Dec., Wed.–Mon. 11–5.*

Dining

$$$$ ★ ✕ **L'Auberge Chez François.** The building, made of white stucco and dark exposed beams, does resemble a French *auberge* (country inn). It's set on 6 acres, and a garden can be seen from the dining room. Three fireplaces, flowered tablecloths, and stained glass set the mood for such Alsatian specialties as salmon soufflé—a fillet of salmon topped with a mousse of scallops and salmon and a white-wine or lobster sauce. If you want to eat here near a holiday or other busy time, make reservations four weeks in advance. ✉ *332 Springvale Rd. (Rte. 674), Great Falls,* ☎ *703/759–3800,* WEB *www.laubergechezfrancois.com. Reservations essential. Jacket required. AE, D, DC, MC, V. Closed Mon. No lunch.*

Reston

33 *20 mi northwest of Alexandria.*

This planned community was the brainchild of Robert E. Simon Jr. (his initials form the first syllable of the town's name). Reston's Town Center has become a gathering place for the area, and the outdoor pavilion here hosts music shows, a farm dinner in late July, and an Oktoberfest in late September.

Dining

$–$$$ ✕ **Clyde's of Reston.** From spring to fall, farmers in Virginia, Maryland, and Pennsylvania grow fresh produce for the various outposts of Clyde's (there's another in Tysons Corner, for instance). The interior evokes a turn-of-the-20th-century saloon through silver gas sconces, handblown glass shades, and leather-upholstered mahogany furniture. One dining room has model airplanes from the '20s and '30s suspended from the ceiling. The menu changes daily but a few repeating specialties are Shenandoah Valley trout, Bay rockfish, and buffalo from the Valley's Georgetown Farm. ✉ *11905 Market St.,* ☎ *703/787–6601,* WEB *www.clydes.com. AE, D, DC, MC, V.*

Outdoor Activities and Sports

Reston National Golf Course (✉ 11875 Sunrise Valley Dr., ☎ 703/620–9333), a 6,480-yard, par-71 course widely considered the best public course in the metropolitan area, is about a half-hour drive from downtown Washington. Well maintained, it is heavily wooded but not too difficult for the average player. Greens fees, which include a cart, are $35–$70 weekdays and $40–$80 on weekends, depending on your start time and whether you're playing the full course or 9 holes.

LOUDOUN COUNTY

Loudoun County, capital of Virginia's horse country and just a half hour away from D.C., abounds with historic villages and towns, shops, wineries, farms, and heritage sites. The Potomac River borders the county on the north. The countryside is littered with stables, barns, and stacked-stone fences. In the major towns in Loudoun, such as Leesburg, Middleburg, and Waterford, old Virginia carries on with gracious living, fox hunts, and steeplechases.

Numbers in the margin correspond to points of interest on the Northern Virginia map.

Middleburg

34 *40 mi west of Alexandria.*

The area that is now Middleburg was surveyed by George Washington in 1763, when it was known as Chinn's Crossroads. It was considered strategic because of its location midway on the Winchester–Alexandria route (roughly what is now U.S. 50). Many of Middleburg's homes include horse farms, and the town is known for its steeplechases and fox hunts in spring and fall. Attractive boutiques and stores line U.S. 50, the main street, and polo matches are played on Sundays June through Labor Day.

The vineyards in this area often have tastings and tours. Three mi south of Middleburg, **Piedmont Vineyards and Winery** has 25 acres of vines. Construction on the manor house here began around 1740. Piedmont specializes in Chardonnay, and Semillon, both whites, but also makes some red wine. ✉ *Rte. 626,* ☎ *540/687–5528,* WEB *www.piedmontwines.com.* ⏲ *Tours Apr.–Dec., daily 11–5; Jan.–Mar., Wed.–Sun. 11–5; tasting room Mon.–Sat. 10–5; Sun. 11–5.*

Just 1 mi east of Middleburg is the **Swedenburg Estate Vineyard.** The winery's modern building sits on the working Valley View Farm, which raises Angus beef cattle and grows crops. The Bull Run mountains form a backdrop for the vineyards. Swedenburg vineyard grows Chardonnay, Cabernet Sauvignon, Pinot Noir, and Reisling. ✉ *Rte. 50,* ☎ *540/687–5219,* WEB *www.swedenburgwines.com.* ⏲ *Daily 10–4.*

Lodging

$$$ **Middleburg Country Inn.** This three-story structure, built in 1820 and enlarged in 1858, was the rectory of St. John's Parish Episcopal Church until 1907. Its medium-size rooms are furnished with antiques and period reproductions and have working fireplaces. A full country breakfast is served, and, when weather permits, you can eat your meal alfresco. ✉ *209 E. Washington St., Box 2065, 22117,* ☎ *540/687–6082 or 800/262–6082,* FAX *540/687–5603,* WEB *www.midcountryinn.com. 5 rooms, 3 suites. Hot tub. AE, D, MC, V. BP.*

$$–$$$ **Middleburg Inn and Guest Suites.** Though not in a historic building, the Middleburg Inn still carries with it a whiff of 18th-century-style living. Suites (named for famous race horses locally owned and bred) have living rooms and kitchens, and many amenities. Furnishings include canopied beds, antiques, and period reproductions. ✉ *105 W. Washington St., 22117,* ☎ *540/687–3115 or 800/432–6125,* WEB *www.middleburgonline.com/mgs. 4 suites, 1 cottage. MC, V.*

En Route Five miles south of Leesburg on Route 15, **Oatlands** is a former 5,000-acre plantation built by a great-grandson of Robert "King" Carter, one of the wealthiest pre-Revolution planters in Virginia. The Greek revival manor house was built in 1803; a stately portico and half-octagonal stair wings were added in 1827. The house, a National Trust Historic Site, has been meticulously restored, and the manicured fields that remain host public and private equestrian events from spring to fall. Among these is the Loudoun Hunt Point-to-Point in April, a race that brings out the entire community for tailgates and picnics on blankets. The terraced walls here border a restored English garden of 4½ acres. ✉ *20850 Oatlands Plantation La., (Rte. 15),* ☎ *703/777–3174,* WEB *www.oatlands.org.* 🎫 *$8 (additional fee for special events).* ⏲ *Apr.–Dec., Mon.–Sat. 10–5, Sun. 1–5.*

Leesburg

35 *36 mi northwest of Alexandria.*

A staging area during George Washington's push to the Ohio Valley during the French and Indian War (1754–60), Leesburg is one of the oldest towns in northern Virginia. Its numerous fine Georgian and Federal buildings now house offices, shops, restaurants, and homes. In an early sign of changing allegiances, "George Town" changed its name to Leesburg in 1758 to honor Virginia's illustrious Lee family. When the British burned Washington during the War of 1812, James and Dolley Madison fled to Leesburg with many government records, including official copies of the Declaration of Independence and the U.S. Constitution.

The history of the Loudoun County area is detailed in the **Loudoun Museum and Gift Shop,** which displays art and artifacts of daily life from the time preceding the town's existence on through the present. ✉ *16 W. Loudoun St. SW,* ☎ *703/777–7427,* WEB *www.visitloudoun.com.* 🎫 *$3.* ⏲ *Mon.–Sat. 10–5, Sun. 1–5.*

Within the 1,200 acres that make up **Morven Park** is the Westmoreland Davis Equestrian Institute (a private riding school) and two museums: Morven Park Carriage Museum and the Museum of Hounds and Hunting. The mansion, the work of three architects in 1781, is a Greek revival building that bears a striking resemblance to the White House (completed in 1800), so much so that it's been used as a stand-in for it in films. Two governors have lived here. The price of admission includes entrance to the two museums and to 16 rooms in the Morven Park mansion. ✉ *Rte. 7, 1 mi north of Leesburg,* ☎ *703/777–2414,* WEB *www.morvenpark.org.* 🎫 *$6.* ⏲ *Apr.–Oct., Tues.–Fri. noon–5, Sat. 10–5, Sun. 1–5; Nov., weekends noon–5; Christmas tours during the 1st 3 wks of Dec., Tues.–Sun. noon–5.*

Dining and Lodging

$$–$$$$ ✕ **Lightfoot Restaurant.** Housed in a Romanesque-revival building (1888), this restaurant was the Peoples National Bank for more than half a century. Restored to its original grandeur, the restaurant was named in honor of Francis Lightfoot Lee, a signer of the Declaration of Independence. The wine "cellar" is actually the bank's vault. The seasonal American cuisine, based on local ingredients, includes Blue Ridge spinach salad, a variation on oysters Rockefeller, lamb T-bones marinated in garlic, and many kinds of seafood. ✉ *11 N. King St.,* ☎ *703/771–2233,* WEB *www.lightfootrestaurant.com. AE, D, DC, MC, V.*

$$$$ ★ ✕🏨 **Lansdowne Conference Resort.** This modern resort sits on 205 acres of hills and tall trees bordered by the Potomac River. Lansdowne specializes in outdoor activities and has miles of hiking and jogging trails. Polished wood furniture, carpets, handsome wall decorations, and marble-accented bathrooms help make the property elegant. Tall windows in the Lansdowne Grille ($$$–$$$$) look out on Sugarloaf Mountain. The many menu items include surf and turf (Maine lobster tail with a filet mignon), seafood, and steaks and chops with seasonal side dishes. The Riverside Hearth, a café overlooking a Robert Trent Jones Jr. 18-hole golf course, serves American cuisine breakfast through dinner. Its Sunday brunch buffet is renowned. A third eatery, at the course's midpoint, specializes in sandwiches and deli items. ✉ *44050 Woodridge Pkwy., off Rte. 7, 22075,* ☎ *703/729–8400 or 800/541–4801,* FAX *703/729–4096,* WEB *www.landsdowneresort.com. 291 rooms; 14 suites. Restaurant, 2 cafés, 18-hole golf course, tennis court, pool, indoor pool, gym, billiards, racquetball, volleyball, bar. AE, D, DC, MC, V.*

Waterford

36 *5 mi northwest of Leesburg, 45 mi northwest of Alexandria.*

The historic community of Waterford was founded by a Quaker miller and for many decades has been synonymous with fine crafts; its annual Homes Tour and Crafts Exhibit, held the first weekend of October, includes visits to 18th-century buildings. Waterford and more than 1,400 acres around it were declared a National Historic Landmark in 1970 in recognition of its authenticity as an almost original, ordinary 18th- century village.

NORTHERN VIRGINIA A TO Z

To research prices, get advice from other travelers, and book travel arrangements, visit www.fodors.com.

ADDRESSES

Founded as a colonial port city, Alexandria was first settled along the Potomac River. It is this oldest area that's now called Old Town. Although the city sprawls west across I–395, this area mostly contains modern homes and shopping areas, so it's not host to any sites listed in this chapter. Although the city limits end at the I–495 "Beltway" many of the housing developments south of the Beltway still have an Alexandria postal address. If you take the G. W. Parkway toward Mount Vernon, you'll traverse this area called Alexandria South.

AIRPORT

Three major airports serve northern Virginia and Washington, D.C. The busy and often crowded Ronald Reagan Washington National Airport, 10 mi south of downtown Washington in Virginia, has scheduled daily flights by all major U.S. carriers. Washington Dulles International Airport, 26 mi northwest of Washington, is a modern facility served by the major U.S. airlines and many international carriers. Baltimore-Washington International Airport is 26 mi northeast of the capital.

➤ AIRPORT INFORMATION: **Ronald Reagan Washington National Airport** (DCA; ☎ 703/417–8000, WEB www.metwashairports.com/National). **Washington Dulles International Airport** (IAD; ☎ 703/572–2700, WEB www.metwashairports.com/Dulles). **Baltimore-Washington International Airport** (BWI; ☎ 410/859–7100, WEB www.bwiairport.com).

TRANSFERS

Alexandria is only a few miles from Ronald Reagan Washington National Airport. It's possible to transfer there via Metro, taxi, or public buses. Taking a taxi to Washington Dulles ($55) or Baltimore ($90) airports is extremely expensive. Baltimore is more than an hour away, but from Union Station in Washington, D.C., MARC commuter trains and many Amtrak trains stop near the airport, where a free shuttle bus transfers you to the terminal. The cheapest way to reach Washington Dulles airport is via a shuttle bus—either from Alexandria or from the Vienna Metro stop.

➤ CONTACTS: **SuperShuttle** (☎ 800/258–3826, WEB www.supershuttle.com). **United Airport Transportation Service** (☎ 703/801–4884). **Washington Flyer** (☎ 703/685–1400, WEB www.washfly.com).

BIKE TRAVEL

A great place to rent a bike is at the idyllic Washington Sailing Marina, which is right on the Mount Vernon Bike Trail. A 12-mi ride south will take you right up to the front doors of Mount Vernon, and a 6-mi ride north across the Memorial Bridge will put you at the foot of the Washington Monument. All-terrain bikes rent for $6 per hour or $22 per day; cruisers cost $4 per hour or $16.50 per day. The marina is open 9–5 daily.

Fletcher's Boat House rents bicycles on the D.C. side of the Potomac. The C&O Canal paths connect to the Virginia bike paths. The boat house is open late March–May, daily 7:30–7; June–August, daily 9–7; September–November, daily 9–6. It's closed December–early March and during severe weather.

➤ BIKE RENTALS: **Fletcher's Boat House** (✉ 4740 Canal Rd. at Reservoir Rd., Washington, D.C., ☎ 202/244–0461). **Washington Sailing Marina** (✉ 1 Marina Dr., George Washington Memorial Pkwy., Alexandria, ☎ 703/548–9027, WEB www.guestservices.com/wsm).

BUS TRAVEL

From Fredericksburg, Richmond, Norfolk, and other major Virginia cities as well as from many other point, Greyhound Lines provides scheduled service to Fairfax, Arlington, and Springfield, 8 mi west of Alexandria. Station hours are limited to daytime. There are several buses daily. Within Northern Virginia, local buses and the Metro are the best, cheapest, most frequent service, running several times an hour for all routes. For some areas, such as Leesburg and Middleburg, there is no bus service at all. A car is the only way to get to these pastoral areas.

Metrobus connects passengers throughout Arlington, Alexandria, and Fairfax County to Washington, D.C., and Maryland, either via transfers or Metrorail. Cue, the City of Fairfax bus, connects passengers between the Vienna Metro station and Fairfax City, George Mason University, and Fair City Mall. Fairfax Connector is Fairfax County's bus system with more than 50 routes all over the county, including Mount Vernon. Buses and the Metro leave every few minutes.

➤ BUS DEPOTS: **Arlington** (✉ Pentagon). **Fairfax** (✉ Fairfax Vienna Metrorail station, I–66 and Nutley St.). **Springfield** (✉ Metro, ☎ 703/971–7598).

➤ BUS LINES: **Cue** (☎ 703/385–7859, WEB www.ci.fairfax.va.us). **Fairfax Connector** (☎ 703/339–7200, WEB www.fairfaxconnector.com). **Metrobus** (☎ 202/637–7000, WEB www.wmata.com).

BUS TRAVEL WITHIN ALEXANDRIA

DASH is the Alexandria Transit Company's local bus service. Various routes connect Old Town Alexandria; the Eisenhower and Van Dorn Metro stations; Landmark Shopping Mall; and major streets in the city.

FARES AND SCHEDULES

DASH's base fare is $1. Transfers are free, but there's a 25¢ surcharge to get to the Pentagon. Among the several passes and tickets honored by DASH are the Regional One Day Bus Pass and the Metrorail-to-bus transfer (along with an additional 25¢).

➤ INFORMATION: **DASH** (☎ 703/370–3274). **Fairfax** (✉ Fairfax Vienna Metrorail station, I–66 and Nutley St.). **Greyhound Lines** (☎ 800/231–2222).

CAR TRAVEL

I–95 runs north–south along the eastern side of the region. I–395 begins in D.C. and joins I–95 as it crosses I–495, the Capital Beltway, which circles the District of Columbia through Virginia and Maryland, providing a circular—albeit very clogged—bypass around Washington for north- or southbound drivers. Avoid it during morning and evening rush hours. The main interchange where I–395, I–95, and I–495 converge is undergoing a major alteration, and although traffic is not being detoured, the volume of vehicles traveling through this area can cause backups, especially during rush hour.

I–66 runs east–west between Washington, D.C., and I–81 near Front Royal, which takes you south through the Shenandoah or north to West Virginia. Note that HOV restrictions prohibit single–person vehicles on I–66 inside the Beltway eastbound during morning rush hour and westbound during evening rush hour.

Once you have reached Northern Virginia, it's convenient to use the area's excellent, clean, and safe Washington Metropolitan Area Transit Authority (WMATA) system (buses and subway) or local jurisdictions' bus systems, or travel by biking or walking. In the farther-out suburbs, a car is necessary.

PARKING

At the Alexandria Convention and Visitors Association, you can obtain a free 24-hour parking permit for the two-hour metered zones (you must furnish your license plate number). Giving parking tickets is one of the things Capital-area police forces do best, so if you park at meters throughout Northern Virginia and D.C., watch the time religiously and keep the meter fed lest you acquire an expensive bill stuck under your wiper blade. Also read parking signs carefully. There are many variations, and they are often quite confusing. Parking in the curb lane on major arteries during rush hour may result in your car being towed.

TRAFFIC

Visitors and residents alike can be baffled by the Capital Area's tangle of highway interchanges, the sometimes confusing signage, the ongoing road repairs/improvements, and some of the nation's worst traffic. Morning and evening rush hours (6:30–9:30 and 4–7) exacerbate the situation, so avoid driving toward downtown Washington or Tysons Corner at these times. It would be prudent to select lodging north of the I–95/I–495 interchange if you plan to spend most of your time in downtown Washington or within the Beltway. The roads around Tysons Corner move very slowly during rush hours, particularly at quitting time.

DISABILITIES AND ACCESSIBILITY

With the eyes of the federal government watching from across the Potomac, you can expect Northern Virginia to be almost 100% accessible, the exception being the second or third floors of historic buildings. All streets have curb cuts and many public buildings have ramps.

DISCOUNTS AND DEALS

Alexandria's Key Pass provides for 15% off regular ticket prices to the historic estates of Virginia. The pass, valid April–December, includes admission to Mount Vernon, Gunston Hall, and Woodlawn plantations. It costs $20 for adults, $11 for children 6–17, and is free for children under 5. The passes can be purchased from the Alexandria Convention and Visitors Association either in person or over the phone.

The Alexandria Very Important Patriot (VIP) Pass saves 20% on admission to a guided walking tour of Old Town, a boat cruise on the Potomac, and four of Old Town Alexandria's most popular attractions. The attractions are Gadsby's Tavern Museum, Carlyle House, Lee-Fendall House Museum and Garden, and the Stabler-Leadbeater Apothecary Museum. The passes, valid May–September, cost $26 for adults and $14 for children 11–17. These passes are also available from the Alexandria Convention and Visitors Association.

➤ CONTACT: **Alexandria Convention and Visitors Association** (✉ Ramsay House, 221 King St., Alexandria 22314, ☎ 703/838–5005 or toll free 866/300–6044, WEB www.funside.com).

EMERGENCIES

Formerly named Arlington Hospital, Virginia Hospital Center—Arlington is a teaching hospital long associated with Georgetown University's School of Medicine. It has a medical staff of more than 700 physicians.

➤ CONTACTS: **Emergency** (☎ 911). **Fire** (☎ 703/838–4660). **Police** (☎ 703/838–4444).

➤ HOSPITALS: **Alexandria Hospital** (✉ 4320 Seminary Rd., Alexandria, ☎ 703/504–3000, WEB www.inova.com). **Inova Fair Oaks Hospital** (✉ 3600 Joseph Siewick Dr., Fairfax, ☎ 703/391–3600, WEB www.inova.com). **Inova Fairfax Hospital and Inova Fairfax Hospital for Children** (✉ 3300 Gallows Rd., Falls Church, ☎ 703/698–1110 and 703/204–6777, WEB www.inova.com). **Inova Mount Vernon Hospital** (✉ 2501 Parker's La., Alexandria, ☎ 703/664–7000, WEB www.inova.com). **Virginia Hospital Center—Arlington** (✉ 1701 N. George Mason Dr., Arlington, ☎ 703/558–5000, WEB www.virginiahospitalcenter.com).

➤ 24-HOUR PHARMACIES: **CVS** (✉ 5101 Duke St., Alexandria, ☎ 703/823–7411, pharmacy 703/823–7430, WEB www.cvs.com). **Rite Aid** (✉ 6711 Richmond Hwy., Alexandria, ☎ 703/768–7233, WEB www.riteaid.com).

LODGING

BED-AND-BREAKFASTS

Princely Bed & Breakfast Ltd. will arrange accommodations in historic homes in Alexandria.

➤ RESERVATIONS SERVICES: **Princely Bed & Breakfast Ltd.** (✉ 2822 Avenham Ave., Roanoke 24014, ☎ 540/343–0100 or 800/470–5588, FAX 540/343–6250, WEB www.princelybandb.com).

MAIL AND SHIPPING

Alexandria's main post office is open weekdays 8–6:30 and Saturday 9–4.

At Atomic Grounds Coffeehouse & Cyberlounge, Internet access costs $7 an hour. If you head to the Mouse Trap Internet Cafe, free coffee comes with the use of the computers ($9 an hour). It's open 10–10 Monday–Thursday, 10–11 Friday–Saturday, and noon–8 on Sunday.

➤ POST OFFICE: **Alexandria Main Post Office** (✉ 1100 Wythe St., ☎ 703/684–7168, WEB www.usps.gov).

➤ INTERNET CAFÉS: **Atomic Grounds Coffeehouse & Cyberlounge** (✉ 1555 Wilson Blvd., Arlington, ☎ 703/524–2157, WEB www.atomic-grounds.com). **Mouse Trap Internet Cafe** (✉ 2336 Wilson Blvd., Arlington, ☎ 703/294–4008, WEB www.mousetrapdc.com).

TAXIS

➤ TAXI COMPANIES: **Alexandria Diamond Cab** (☎ 703/549–6200). **Alexandria White Top Cab** (☎ 703/683–0594). **Alexandria Yellow Cab** (☎ 703/549–2500).

TOURS

The Alexandria Convention and Visitors Association runs walking tours that leave from its office 10:30 AM Monday through Saturday and 2 PM Sunday; tickets are $10. Doorways to Old Virginia leads guided walking tours of historic Alexandria by reservation. Ghost-and-graveyard tours (reservations not required) are conducted Friday, Saturday, and Sunday nights.

➤ WALKING TOURS: **Doorways to Old Virginia** (☎ 703/548–0100).

TRAIN TRAVEL

Amtrak has scheduled stops in Alexandria. Virginia Rail Express provides workday commuter service between Union Station in Washington and Fredericksburg and Manassas, with additional stops near hotels in Crystal City, Alexandria, and elsewhere.

➤ TRAIN STATIONS: **Alexandria** (✉ 110 Callahan Dr.).

➤ TRAIN LINES: **Amtrak** (☎ 800/872–7245; Metroliner Service, 800/523–8720; Union Station, 202/484–7540, WEB www.amtrak.com). **Virginia Rail Express** (VRE; ☎ 800/743–3873 or 703/497–7777, WEB www.vre.com).

VISITOR INFORMATION

Most visitor centers are open 9–5 daily.

➤ TOURIST INFORMATION: **Alexandria Convention and Visitors Association** (✉ Ramsay House, 221 King St., Alexandria 22314, ☎ 703/838–4200 or 800/388–9119, WEB www.funside.com). **Arlington County Visitor Center** (✉ 735 S. 18th St., Arlington 22202, ☎ 703/228–5720 or 800/677–6267, WEB www.stayarlington.com). **Fairfax County Convention and Visitors Bureau** (✉ 8300 Boone Blvd., Suite 450, Vienna 22182, ☎ 703/790–3329, WEB www.visitfairfax.org). **Fairfax County Visitors Center** (✉ 8180A Silverbrook Rd., Lorton 22182, ☎ 800/732–4732, WEB www.visitfairfax.org). **Loudoun Tourism Council** (✉ 108D South St. SE, Leesburg 22075, ☎ 703/771–2617 or 800/752–6118, WEB www.visitloudon.org). **Manassas Visitor Center** (✉ 9431 West St., Manassas, ☎ 703/361–6599, WEB www.visitpwc.com). **Prince William Visitor Center** (✉ 200 Mill St., Occoqua, ☎ 703/491–4045, WEB www.visitpwc.com). **Waterford Foundation** (✉ Main and 2nd Sts., ☎ 540/882–3018, WEB www.waterfordva.org).

3 D.C.'S MARYLAND SUBURBS

In between and beyond Washington's sprawling suburban housing developments lies parkland; a nature preserve; a major amusement park; and historic homes, two named after women—one known as an "angel"; the other hanged by the federal government.

By Kathryn McKay

SUBURBAN MARYLAND IS D.C.'S BACKYARD. In 1791, Montgomery and Prince George's counties ceded 90 square mi to the new United States government to create the nation's capital, then called simply Washington. Montgomery County is to the west and north of the capital's sharply drawn boundaries, and Prince George's County is to the east. Because of their proximity to D.C., the counties are the most densely populated in Maryland, and many residents consider themselves Washingtonians. After all, what happens on Capitol Hill often has an immediate effect on residents: many people work for the federal government or are politically active.

Aside from locals commuting daily to the capital, Washington also comes to the suburbs themselves. Federal agencies that maintain offices in the area include the National Institutes of Health, the Internal Revenue Service, and the National Aeronautic Space Administration. Even the Washington Redskins play in Prince George's County.

One of the most affluent counties in the country, Montgomery County is known for Bethesda's bounty of restaurants and a breathtaking view of the powerful Potomac River and Great Falls. Prince George's County, which many African-American professionals call home, also holds the University of Maryland's College Park campus; historic houses, such as the Surratt House Museum; and great green spaces that include Fort Washington Park, the Colonial Farm, and the Merkle Wildlife Sanctuary.

Pleasures and Pastimes

Dining

CATEGORY	COST*
$$$$	over $32
$$$	$22–$32
$$	$12–$22
$	under $12

**per person for a main course at dinner*

Lodging

CATEGORY	COST*
$$$$	over $225
$$$	$150–$225
$$	$100–$150
$	under $100

**All prices are for a standard double room, excluding state tax.*

Exploring Suburban Maryland

An automobile is a must to travel throughout the counties, but avoid the Capital Beltway (Interstate 495) during morning and afternoon rush hours. At those times the congestion is second only to Los Angeles. Most attractions, restaurants, and shops in Montgomery County are clustered "down-county" in areas closest to D.C. In Prince George's County, places to explore are sprinkled throughout the area.

MONTGOMERY COUNTY

Numbers in the margin correspond to points of interest on the Montgomery County map.

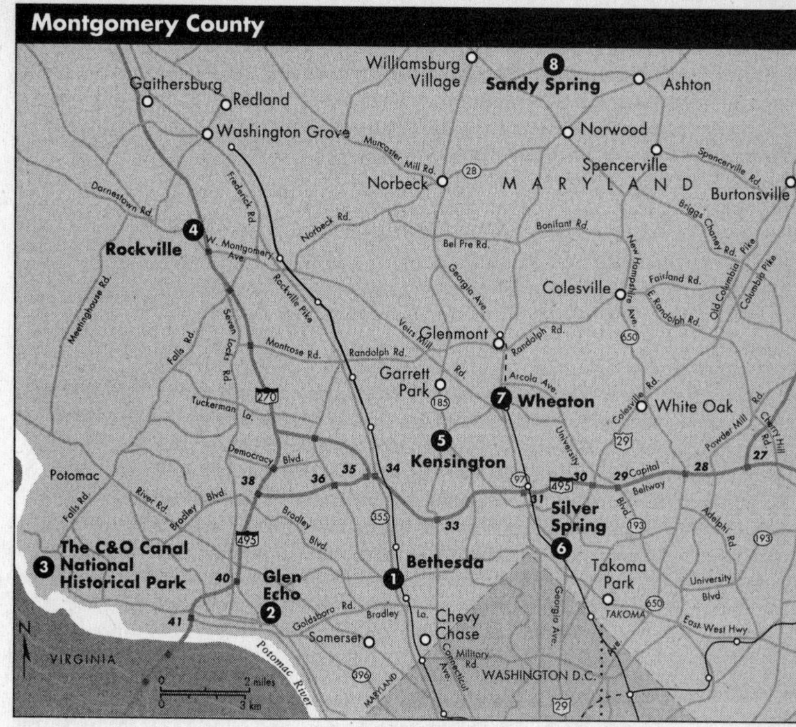

Montgomery County, named after Revolutionary War hero General Richard Montgomery, became (in 1776) the first Maryland county to drop the custom of naming jurisdictions after royalty. In between housing developments, strip malls, and office parks, the northern portion of the county retains traces of the area's agrarian beginnings.

Bethesda

❶ *2 mi north of Washington, D.C.*

Bethesda was named in 1871 after the Bethesda Meeting House, which was built by the Presbyterians. The name alludes to a biblical pool that had great healing power. Today, people seek healing in Bethesda at the National Institutes of Health and meet here to enjoy the burgeoning restaurant scene. Bethesda has changed from a small community into an urban destination, but in certain ways time has stood still east of Bethesda in Chevy Chase, a tony town of exclusive country clubs, stately homes, and huge trees.

One of the world's foremost biomedical research centers, the **National Institutes of Health (NIH)** opens its doors to the curious during one-hour tours of the National Library of Medicine. Although best known for its books and journals—there are more than 6 million—the library also houses historical medical references dating back to the 11th century. The tour includes a video presentation, lecture, and question and answer session. You can also view historical documents; the library's databases; and their "visible human," which provides a view of everything from how the kneecap works to how physicians use surgical simulators. But what most people find most helpful are the tips the guides give on how to start medical searches. To conduct library research, arrive at least 1½ hours before closing time. ✉ *Visitor Information Center, 9000 Rockville Pike, Bldg. 10,* ☎ *301/496–1776 visitor information;*

301/496–6308 library; ✉ *National Library of Medicine, 8600 Rockville Pike, Bldg. 38A,* ☎ *301/496–6308,* WEB *www.nlm.nih.gov.* 🎫 *Free.* ⏲ *Library tours weekdays 1:30. Library weekdays 8:30–5, Sat. 8:30–12:30. Memorial Day–Labor Day library is open until 9* PM *on Thurs. Metro: Medical Center.*

More than 750 varieties of azaleas bloom at **McCrillis Gardens and Gallery** from late March through July, and usually peak around May 1. This premier shade garden also has choice ornamental trees and shrubs. Bulbs, ground cover, and shade-loving perennials add ongoing color and texture. A small art gallery hosts monthly exhibitions by local artists. ✉ *6910 Greentree Rd.,* ☎ *301/365–1657,* WEB *www.mc-mncppc.org/parks/brookside/mccrilli.shtm.* 🎫 *Free.* ⏲ *Gardens daily 10–sunset; gallery Feb.–Nov., Tues.–Sun. noon–4.*

In a low, white building in the midst of high-rise office buildings, **Montgomery Farm Women's Cooperative Market** is a vestige of Montgomery County's agricultural community. During the Great Depression, women gathered goods from their gardens to sell to residents of D.C. and its growing suburbs. Today the tradition of farm women continues as farmers bring in baked goods, fresh fruits, and vegetables. Crafts and flea market goods are sold on Sunday. A view of the market in the 1930s is depicted in a mural on the wall of the Bethesda Post Office at 7400 Wisconsin Avenue. ✉ *7155 Wisconsin Ave.,* ☎ *301/652–2291,* WEB *montgomerycountymd.com/events/montgomery_market.htm.* ⏲ *Wed. and Sat. 7–3, flea market weekends 8–5.*

A self-guided nature trail winds through a verdant 40-acre estate and around the **Audubon Naturalist Society.** You're never far from the trill of birdsong here, as the society has turned the grounds into something of a nature preserve, forbidding the use of pesticides and leaving some areas in a natural state. The estate is known as Woodend, as is the mansion, which was designed in the 1920s by Jefferson Memorial architect John Russell Pope. The society leads wildlife identification walks, environmental education programs, and—September through June—a weekly Saturday "bird walk" at its headquarters. Birders interested in new local avian sightings may want to call for the Audubon Society's Voice of the Naturalist tape recording. The bookstore stocks titles on conservation, ecology, and birding, as well as bird feeders, birdhouses, and nature-related gifts such as jewelry and toys. ✉ *8940 Jones Mill Rd., Chevy Chase,* ☎ *301/652–9188; 301/652–1088 for naturalist tape,* WEB *www.audubonnaturalist.org.* 🎫 *Free.* ⏲ *Grounds daily sunrise–sunset, bookstore weekdays 10–5, Sat. 9–5, Sun. noon–5.*

Dining

You can nibble your way around the world in Bethesda. The largest concentration of restaurants (about 75) are within the Woodmont Triangle, whose boundaries are formed by Old Georgetown Road, Woodmont Avenue, and Rugby Road. Bright blue signs identify parking; on weekends you can park for free in public garages.

For information about a Bethesda dining guide, Taste of Bethesda, and other special events, contact the **Bethesda Urban Partnership** (☎ 301/215–6660, WEB www.bethesda.org).

$$–$$$ ★ ✕ **Cafe Bethesda.** The modern American cuisine is conservative yet creative, and the service is attentive at this intimate restaurant. Most tables are next to flower-laden window boxes. Specialties include a fresh rack of lamb crusted in basil and served with ratatouille and the sautéed Atlantic salmon with caramelized shallots and spinach strudel. Make reservations for Friday and Saturday nights. ✉ *5027 Wilson La.,* ☎ *301/657–3383. AE, D, MC, V.* ⏲ *Closed on Mon. No lunch weekends.*

$$–$$$ ★ ✕ **Thyme Square.** The predominantly vegetarian menu at this hip and healthful joint is even paired with an organic wine list. Although the menu changes seasonally, Brazilian shellfish stew—shrimp, mussels, and fish in a spicy tomato and coconut broth—remains a constant favorite. There's always a chicken option, too. ✉ *4735 Bethesda Ave.,* ☎ *301/657–9077. AE, D, MC, V.*

$$–$$$ ✕ **Andalucia.** *Zarzuela*, a seafood stew, is one of Andalucia's traditional Spanish specialties. The spartan Rockville location (hidden in an office-and-shopping strip) was popular enough to spawn the more formal Bethesda branch, which has a tapas bar and a tempting dessert cart. Although the restaurants are run separately, their menus are similar. Free parking is available behind the Bethesda restaurant. Flamenco dancers entertain on Thursday night in Rockville. ✉ *4931 Elm St., Bethesda,* ☎ *301/907–0052; 12300 Wilkins Ave., Rockville,* ☎ *301/770–1880. AE, D, DC, MC, V. No lunch weekends; Rockville location closed Mon.*

$$ ✕ **Bacchus.** The lamb dishes and appetizers are excellent at this Lebanese restaurant, which is much bigger—and some say better—than its location in Washington, D.C. Outdoor seating is available. ✉ *7945 Norfolk Ave.,* ☎ *301/657–1722. AE, D, MC, V.*

$–$$ ★ ✕ **Cottonwood Café.** As at its Boston counterpart, the stylish Cottonwood Café cooks up an innovative blend of Santa Fe, Texas, and New American dishes. The blue-cornmeal calamari appetizer is a must. Entrées are generous: try "fire and spice" linguine with andouille sausage and shrimp, the grilled chicken and shrimp marinated in barbecue sauce with a baked banana, or the classic grilled fajitas. ✉ *4844 Cordell Ave.,* ☎ *301/656–4844. AE, MC, V. No lunch Sun.*

$–$$ ✕ **Tara Thai.** Blue walls and paintings of sea life reflect the owner's childhood home in Huahin, Thailand: so does the extensive menu, whose many seafood dishes include fresh flounder and rockfish. Pictures of chili peppers on the menu mark the spiciness of each entrée. Favorites include the mild and traditional pad thai, and the spicy Goong Phuket, grilled black tiger shrimp topped with crabmeat and chicken sauce. ✉ *4828 Bethesda Ave., Bethesda,* ☎ *301/657–0488;* ✉ *12071 Rockville Pike, Rockville,* ☎ *301/231–9899. AE, D, DC, MC, V.*

$ ✕ **California Tortilla.** Friendly, quick service and red chili-pepper lights hanging from the ceiling make this counter-service restaurant a local favorite. The blackened chicken Caesar burrito outsells other items three to one. Add spice to your meal with a dash or two from 75 hot sauces lined up on the wall, and grab a seat inside or out. On Monday nights, spin the Burrito Wheel for discounts and freebies. The Bethesda branch gave birth to locations in Rockville and Potomac. ✉ *4862 Cordell Ave., Bethesda,* ☎ *301/654–8226;* ✉ *199 E. Montgomery Ave., Rockville,* ☎ *301/610–6500;* ✉ *7727 Tuckerman La., Potomac,* ☎ *301/765–3600. MC, V.*

$ ✕ **Tastee Diner.** The Tastees are part of a dying breed in the Washington area. As 24-hour diners go, they are sentimental favorites among many area residents. Patronage has less to do with the food than with the sense of old-fashioned community each place evokes. Students and others on low budgets (or little sleep) ignore the dust and relish the coffee, which flows endlessly. ✉ *7731 Woodmont Ave.,* ☎ *301/652–3970. Reservations not accepted. MC, V.*

Lodging

Even with six hotels within a mile of downtown Bethesda, it's best to book your room in advance. Occupancy rates are high, and you'll pay only a little less than you would in Washington. Tourists coming to see Washington's cherry blossoms make spring the busiest season. December and January tend to be the slowest and least expensive months, except around a presidential inauguration.

$$$$ **Embassy Suites.** Shopping and sightseeing couldn't be more convenient at this all-suite hotel, which is adjacent to the upscale Chevy Chase Pavilion and an elevator ride up from the Friendship Heights Metro Station. Each suite includes a bedroom and separate living room with a sleep sofa, kitchen space with microwave, and a table suitable for dining and working. The fitness center has more than 20 exercise stations and a personal trainer available at no charge. Complimentary breakfast and evening cocktails are offered daily in the sun-filled atrium. A dozen restaurants are within walking distance. ✉ *4300 Military Rd., Washington, D.C. 20015,* ☎ *202/362–9300 or 800/362–2779,* FAX *202/686–3405,* WEB *www.embassysuites.com. 198 suites. Room service, indoor pool, health club, laundry service, parking (fee); no-smoking rooms. AE, D, DC, MC, V. BP.*

$$$$ **Hyatt Regency Bethesda.** The atrium lobby, with glass elevators and ferns, contrasts with the masculinity of the rooms, which are decorated in burgundy and gold with black-and-white photographs of Washington, D.C., on the walls. The real-life sights of downtown D.C. are about 15 minutes away by Metro; the Bethesda Metro stop adjoins the hotel. An adjacent plaza has a small ice rink, open in winter. The room rates drop considerably on the weekend. Many restaurants and shops are within walking distance. For an extra $20, the staff will equip your room with a fax machine and offer you free access to printers and unlimited copies from their business center. ✉ *1 Bethesda Metro Center (on the 7400 block of Wisconsin Ave.), 20814,* ☎ *301/657–1234 or 800/233–1234,* FAX *301/657–6453,* WEB *www.hyatt.com. 390 rooms, 5 suites. Restaurant, café, room service, in-room data ports, cable TV, indoor pool, gym, health club, bar, lobby lounge, laundry service, business services, convention center, meeting rooms, parking (fee). AE, D, DC, MC, V.*

$$–$$$$ **Residence Inn by Marriott.** In the heart of downtown Bethesda, this all-suite hotel is designed for extended stays. Each room has a living room and fully equipped kitchen, complete with standard-size refrigerator and dishwasher, plates, and utensils—and comfortable furnishings in the one- and two-bedroom suites, which the staff will stock with groceries. The many complimentary services also include a breakfast buffet and evening social hours Monday through Thursday. The longer you stay, the more your rates go down. ✉ *7335 Wisconsin Ave., 20814,* ☎ *301/718–0200 or 800/331–3131,* FAX *301/718–0679,* WEB *www.residenceinn.com. 187 suites. In-room data ports, kitchens, cable TV, pool, gym, sauna, laundry facilities, business services, airport shuttle, parking (free), some pets allowed (fee). AE, D, DC, MC, V. CP.*

$$–$$$ **Holiday Inn Chevy Chase.** A short walk from the Friendship Heights Metro on the D.C. border, this comfortable hotel is in the heart of one of the area's most upscale shopping districts. The Avenue Deli and Julian's restaurant are in the hotel, the nearby Chevy Chase Pavilion and Mazza Gallerie malls have expanded family dining options, and you'll find a wealth of good dining choices one Metro stop away in Bethesda or a 10-minute drive down Wisconsin Avenue into Georgetown. A large outdoor swimming pool is set near the hotel's beautiful rose garden terrace, a popular spot for weddings. Booking in advance can bring the rates down, and children under 18 stay free. Use of the laundry facilities in the hotel is free of charge. Rates may dip to as low as $100 during December. ✉ *5520 Wisconsin Ave., Chevy Chase 20815,* ☎ *301/656–1500 or 800/465–4329,* FAX *301/656–5045,* WEB *www.sixcontinentshotels.com. 204 rooms, 12 suites. Restaurant, deli, room service, in-room data ports, cable TV, pool, gym, hair salon, bar, laun-*

dry facilities, business services, meeting rooms, parking (fee), some pets allowed. AE, D, DC, MC, V. CP.

$-$$ **American Inn of Bethesda.** At the north end of downtown Bethesda, the American Inn sets no new fashion for motel decor, but the rooms are clean, generally bright, and affordable. The hotel houses Guapo's restaurant, serving moderately priced Tex-Mex fare. Many other restaurants and nightclubs are within walking distance; the Bethesda Metro is a 10-minute walk away. Use of the business center—including access to the Internet and e-mail service—is free. The hotel also provides a free shuttle to the National Institutes of Health and the Naval Hospital. ✉ *8130 Wisconsin Ave., 20814,* ☎ *301/656–9300 or 800/323–7081,* FAX *301/656–2907,* WEB *www.american-inn.com. 75 rooms, 1 suite. Restaurant, breakfast room, refrigerators, cable TV, pool, bar, laundry facilities, laundry service, free parking; no-smoking floors. AE, D, DC, MC, V. CP.*

Nightlife and the Arts

On weekends from Memorial Day through Labor Day, you can dance to the beat of live bands at free concerts held at the intersection of Wisconsin Avenue, Old Georgetown Road, and East West Highway.

NIGHTLIFE

Arcade games provide the most action at **Dave & Buster's** (✉ White Flint Mall, 11301 Rockville Pike, ☎ 301/230–5151), but this 60,000-square-ft entertainment complex also includes billiard tables, shuffleboards, interactive video games and simulators, a casual restaurant, and two bars. Every other Saturday at 8 PM, a murder mystery dinner adds to the usual amusement choices. Patrons under 21 must leave by 10 PM.

DJs at the **Shark Club** (✉ 4915 St. Elmo Ave., ☎ 301/718–4030) draw a diverse crowd with tunes designed to get people moving: Top 40, Latin, disco, and high-energy dance music. Tune in to the tango on Sunday nights. After the salsa lessons on Tuesday, there's a Latin dance party.

Enormously popular with well-dressed singles over 30, the **Yacht Club** (✉ 8111 Woodmont Ave., ☎ 301/654–2396) is the brainchild of irrepressible entrepreneur and matchmaker Tommy Curtis, who measures his success by the number of engagements and marriages spawned here (at last count it was 128). Jacket and tie or turtleneck required except on Wednesday and summer evenings, when the attire is casual. The club is closed Sunday–Tuesday.

THE ARTS

Opened in 2002, the 347-seat **Round House Theatre** (✉ 7501 Wisconsin Ave., ☎ 240/644–1100, WEB www.round-house.org) primarily showcases quirky, contemporary, off-Broadway plays. At least one classic play is done a year, and every December brings a musical.

Local and national artists exhibit in the galleries, and musicians perform year-round at **Strathmore Hall Arts Center** (✉ 10701 Rockville Pike, North Bethesda, ☎ 301/530–0540), a mansion built at the turn of the 20th century. On Tuesday and Thursday evenings during the summer, concertgoers spread out on the expansive lawn to listen to free music—everything from classical to Cajun and world beat. Make reservations for Strathmore's Tea ($18), served in a well-lit wood-paneled salon, Tuesday and Wednesday at 1, every month but August. During July and August, "Backyard" theater performers entertain children. Construction of a 2,000-seat concert hall is expected to be complete by 2005. The metro stop is Grovesnor/Strathmore.

Outdoor Activities and Sports

The paved **Capital Crescent Trail** runs along the old Georgetown Branch, a B&O Railroad line completed in 1910 that saw its last train in 1985. Bicyclists, walkers, rollerbladers, and strollers take the 7½-mi route from near Key Bridge in Washington's Georgetown to Bethesda and Woodmont avenues in central Bethesda. The trail picks up again at a well-lit tunnel near the Thyme Square Restaurant (✉ 4735 Bethesda Ave.) and continues into Silver Spring. From Bethesda to the outskirts of Silver Spring, the 3½-mi trail is gravel. The Georgetown Branch Trail, as this section is officially named, connects with the Rock Creek Trail, which goes to Rockville in the north and Memorial Bridge past the Washington Monument in the south. On beautiful weekends, all sections of the trails tend to be crowded. For more information, contact the Coalition for the Capital Crescent Trail (☎ 202/234–4874, WEB www.cctrail.org).

One of the best playgrounds in the Washington area, **Cabin John Regional Park** (✉ 7400 Tuckerman La., ☎ 301/299–0024) has plastic slides, bouncing wooden bridges, swings, and mazes to delight both toddlers and preteens. On the park grounds, there's also an ice rink, indoor and outdoor tennis courts, a nature center, hiking trails, trains that operate seasonally, and a 700-seat Shirley Povich Baseball Field. Free military concerts join the chorus of cicadas every summer.

Shopping

Bethesda isn't known for bargains; shoppers who love discounts should head north on Wisconsin Avenue to Rockville Pike (Route 355). Four of the area's seven regional malls are in Bethesda and the Chevy Chase section of Washington, D.C. Bookworms appreciate downtown Bethesda's 13 bookstores, including a huge Barnes & Noble.

CLOTHING

Lemon Twist. You'll find classic women's wear and children's clothes, gifts, and more from designers such as Lilly, C. J. Lang, Susan Bristal, and CanvasBack. But most of all this boutique has been known for its customer service since 1977. ✉ *8534 Connecticut Ave., Chevy Chase,* ☎ *301/986–0271.*

Wear It Well. From funky jackets and slacks to tailored business suits, this local shop specializes in items that wear well and travel well. ✉ *4816 Bethesda Ave., Bethesda,* ☎ *301/652–3713.*

DEPARTMENT STORES

Most national department stores can be found at shopping malls throughout the county.

Filene's Basement. The Boston-based upscale fashion discounter attracts bargain hunters looking for steep discounts on Calvin Klein, Hugo Boss, and other designer men's and women's labels. Off-price shoes, perfume, and accessories are sold as well. ✉ *5300 Wisconsin Ave. NW, Washington, D.C.,* ☎ *202/966–0208. Metro: Friendship Heights.*

Saks Fifth Avenue. Despite its New York origin and name, Saks is a Washington institution. It has a wide selection of European and American couture clothes; other attractions are the shoe, jewelry, fur, and lingerie departments. ✉ *5555 Wisconsin Ave., Chevy Chase,* ☎ *301/657–9000. Metro: Friendship Heights.*

MALLS

Chevy Chase Pavilion. Across from Mazza Gallerie is the newer, similarly upmarket Chevy Chase Pavilion. Its exclusive women's clothing stores include Koffi Agosu and the Steilmann European Selection (which carries KS separates). Other retail shops of note here are Pottery Barn and Country Road Australia. ✉ *5335 Wisconsin Ave. NW, Washington, D.C.,* ☎ *202/686–5335. Metro: Friendship Heights.*

Mazza Gallerie. This four-level mall is anchored by the ritzy Neiman Marcus department store and the discounter Filene's Basement. Other draws include Williams-Sonoma's kitchenware and a seven-screen movie theater. ✉ *5300 Wisconsin Ave. NW, Washington, D.C.,* ☎ *202/966–6114. Metro: Friendship Heights.*

Montgomery Mall. Stores in the county's largest mall include Crate & Barrel, Sears, Hecht's, and Nordstrom. It is not convenient to a metro stop, but is just off I–270 and I–495. ✉ *7101 Democracy Blvd.,* ☎ *301/469–6000.*

White Flint Mall. Bloomingdale's, Lord & Taylor, and Borders Books & Music pull in the serious shoppers. The other 125 stores and amenities include Coach Store, Sharper Image, Eddie Bauer, a movie theater, and Dave & Buster's. Children enjoy the Kids Zone. ✉ *11301 Rockville Pike, North Bethesda,* ☎ *301/231–7467. Metro: White Flint.*

Glen Echo

❷ *4 mi west of downtown Bethesda, 2½ mi from the Capital Beltway.*

Glen Echo, now a charming village of Victorian houses, was founded in 1891 by Edwin and Edward Baltzley, inventors of the eggbeater. The brothers fell under the spell of the Chautauqua movement, an organization that promoted liberal and practical education. To further their dream, the brothers sold land and houses, but the Glen Echo Chautauqua lasted only one season.

The Baltzley brothers' compound, **Glen Echo Park,** was once noted for its whimsical architecture, including a stone tower, from the Chautauqua period. The area was later the site of an amusement park, and you can still see the skeletons of the once thriving rides. Only the splendid 1921 Dentzel **carousel** still runs (May–September, Wednesday and Thursday 10–2, weekends noon–6), and the musical accompaniment is from a rare Wurlitzer military band organ. The National Park Service administers the 10-acre property, which is the site of folk festivals as well as a puppet company and a children's theater that operate year-round. Discovery Creek children's museum plans nature activities every weekend. Dances are held Friday–Sunday nights and Sunday afternoons. In summer 2003, the dances will move back to the Spanish Ballroom, renovated to its original ornate glory of 1933. For scheduling information, check the Weekend section in Friday's *Washington Post.* ✉ *7300 MacArthur Blvd.,* ☎ *301/492–6229; 301/492–6282 events hot line.* *Carousel rides 50¢, puppet shows $5, plays $6, cost of dances vary.* *Daily.*

The **Clara Barton National Historic Site** is a monument to the founder of the American Red Cross. Known as the "angel of the battlefield" for nursing wounded soldiers during the Civil War, Barton used the striking Victorian structure at first to store Red Cross supplies (it was built for her by the Glen Echo founders, and later became both her home and the organization's headquarters). Today the building is furnished with many of her possessions and period artifacts. Access is by guided tours, which last approximately 35 minutes. ✉ *5801 Oxford Rd., next to Glen Echo Park parking lot, Glen Echo,* ☎ *301/492–6245.* *Free.* *Daily 10–4:30; tours on the hr 10–4.*

Dining

$$–$$$ ★ ✕ **Inn at Glen Echo.** This turn-of-the-century inn has played various roles in its time. In the 1960s it was a biker bar. In the '80s the inn be-

came an intimate place to enjoy fine American cuisine. It's still cozy, with eight dining rooms; each has between one and six tables. ✉ *6119 Tulane Ave.,* ☎ *301/229–2280. AE, D, DC, MC, V.*

Potomac

8 mi north of Glen Echo, 7 mi northwest of Bethesda.

The popular translation of the Native American name "Patawomeck" is "they are coming by water." One of the best places to view the mighty Potomac River is by hiking along the towpath of the C&O canal and climbing the rocks at Great Falls, which Maryland and Virginia share a view of on opposite banks. Potomac is also known for its elegant country estates and homes.

3 **The C&O Canal National Historical Park** extends along the Potomac River 184.5 mi from Washington, D.C., to Cumberland, Maryland. Three miles south of the town of Potomac, the **Great Falls Tavern,** a museum and visitor center, serves as the park's local anchor. Barge trips and a vista on the powerful Great Falls are the draws here. A ½-mi, wheelchair-accessible walkway to the platform on Olmsted Island provides a spectacular view of the churning waters. During mule-drawn canal boat rides ($8), costumed guides can teach you a thing or two about life along the canal in the 1800s. On the canal lock walls are grooves worn by decades of friction from boat towlines. Swimming and wading are prohibited, but you can fish (a Maryland license is required for anglers 16 and older), climb rocks, or go white-water kayaking below the falls (experienced boaters only). All along this stretch of the river, the currents are deadly. Despite frequent signs and warnings, people occasionally dare the water and drown. Bring your own picnic if you plan to lunch here, or head for the snack bar (open March–November) a few paces north of the tavern. ✉ *11710 MacArthur Blvd.,* ☎ *301/299–3613.* *$5 per vehicle, $3 per person without vehicle (good for 3 days on MD and VA sides of the park).* ⏲ *Park, daily sunrise–sunset; tavern and museum, daily 9–4:45; barge trips Apr.–Oct., call for hrs.*

Dining and Lodging

$$$–$$$$ ★ ✕ **Old Angler's Inn.** The inn, where Civil War soldiers from the North and South found respite and Teddy Roosevelt stopped after hunting and fishing, was restored in 1957 as a fine restaurant. The menu changes daily, but you'll have a dozen entrées and 100 wines to choose from. ✉ *10801 MacArthur Blvd.,* ☎ *301/299–9097,* WEB *www.oldanglersinn.com. AE, D, MC, V. Closed Mon.*

$$–$$$ ★ ✕ **Normandie Farm.** The French provincial cuisine here is served in romantic, rustic surroundings reminiscent of a country French farm. Many locals head to Normandie Farm to celebrate special occasions. On a menu that has remained constant for many years, the most popular dishes are beef Wellington, poached salmon, and lamb chops accompanied by fabulous popovers. Daily specials may include a grilled veal rib chop, broiled twin lobster tails, or soft-shell crabs. ✉ *10710 Falls Rd.,* ☎ *301/983–8838. AE, DC, MC, V. Closed Mon.*

Rockville

4 *5 mi northeast of Potomac, 8 mi north of Bethesda.*

Montgomery County's seat is the second-largest city in Maryland. At the historic Beall-Dawson home, docents tell about life before shopping centers took over the town. Locals say if you can't find what you're looking for on the Rockville Pike, it probably doesn't exist. Literature lovers may be interested to know that the graves of F. Scott and Zelda

Fitzgerald are in an enclosed area near the front of the chapel at **St. Mary's Cemetery** (✉ 520 Viers Mill Rd.).

The **Beall-Dawson House and Stonestreet Medical Museum** is where a prominent Rockville family and its slaves lived during the early 1800s. A few paces away from the Federal-style town house is the one-room medical office of Dr. Stonestreet, who practiced medicine from 1852 to 1903. The office is set up to resemble a 19th-century exam room with displays of medical equipment, including an amputation kit. ✉ *103 W. Montgomery Ave.,* ☎ *301/762–1492,* WEB *www.montgomeryhistory.org.* *$3.* ⏲ *Tues.–Sun. noon–4.*

Dining and Lodging

$$–$$$ ★ ✕ **Addies.** Come here for an alfresco meal, taken under the shade of an umbrella. Inside, there's room for 40 to dine in three rooms of this 1930s house. Hardwood floors, fresh flowers at every table, and bright-color walls with dozens of clocks add to the whimsy. But food is taken seriously here: 70% of the produce comes from local farmers, all desserts are baked in-house, grilling takes place over a hardwood grill, and the menu changes seasonally. Besides salmon fillets, crab cakes, and Angus steak, the menu sometimes includes grilled ostrich. ✉ *11120 Rockville Pike,* ☎ *301/881–0081. AE, D, DC, MC, V. No lunch Sun.*

$$–$$$$ **DoubleTree Hotel and Executive Meeting Center.** The soothing sounds of the one-story waterfall in the soaring atrium can be heard throughout the corridors. The atrium also includes a 200-seat dining room and a gazebo with a bar and large-screen television. In the rooms, a floral spread covers the bed and floral prints adorn the walls. More than a dozen restaurants are within walking distance of the hotel. The conference center's 13 rooms are equipped with computers, copiers, and Internet access, and are staffed. Across the street in the back of hotel is the Twinbrook Metro station. Rates drop considerably on weekends. ✉ *1750 Rockville Pike, 20852,* ☎ *301/468–1100 or 800/222–8733,* FAX *301/468–0308. 315 rooms, 17 suites. Restaurant, indoor-outdoor pool, gym, laundry service; no-smoking rooms. AE, D, DC, MC, V.*

Kensington

❺ *7 mi southeast of Rockville, 4 mi northeast of Bethesda.*

Established in 1890, Kensington is one of Montgomery County's earliest villages. Many elaborate Victorian houses are in both Kensington and its neighbor Garrett Park, which even has a few "Chevy houses": built in 1930, they came with a Chevrolet in the driveway.

The **Temple of the Church of Jesus Christ of Latter-day Saints** is impossible to miss from the Beltway near Silver Spring. One of its white towers is topped with a golden statue of the Mormon angel Moroni. It's closed to non-Mormons, but a visitor center provides a lovely view of the mammoth white-marble temple and runs a film about the temple and what takes place inside. Tulips, dogwoods, and azaleas bloom in the 57-acre grounds each spring. In December locals of all faiths enjoy the Festival of Lights—400,000 of them—and a live Nativity scene. ✉ *9900 Stoneybrook Dr.,* ☎ *301/587–0144.* ⏲ *Grounds and visitor center daily 10–9.*

Dining

$ ✕ **Café Monet.** Yellow walls and impressionist paintings lend charm to this little counter-service restaurant, a favorite of local ladies of all ages who linger over espresso, scones, and muffins. Homemade Turkish spinach *borek* (filled puff pastry) and guacamole tortillas add to the appeal. Outdoor seating is available. ✉ *10417 Armory Ave.,* ☎ *301/946–9404. AE, D, MC, V. No dinner.*

Shopping

At Kensington's **Antique Row** (✉ Howard Ave., ☎ 301/949–5333), east of bustling Connecticut Avenue, more than 75 antiques dealers in 42 shops sell jewelry, china, silver, and furniture in buildings as old as some of the items. On the west side of Connecticut Avenue, Howard Avenue alternates auto body repair shops with 100,000 square ft of antiques warehouses that specialize in furniture from Belgium, England, Italy, France, and the United States. For a listing of the **Antique Dealers of West Howard Avenue,** visit www.westhowardantiques.com.

Silver Spring

❻ *5 mi southeast of Kensington via Rte. 97.*

With a population of some 220,000, the greater Silver Spring area is one of the Washington area's largest suburbs. Silver Spring was named when Francis Preston Blair, editor of the *Washington Globe* and a friend of President Andrew Jackson, was riding his horse through the countryside, looking for a pastoral retreat from Washington. His horse threw him, and as he looked for his mount, he noticed a spring in which sand and mica shone like silver. In 1842, he built a second home in "Silver Spring." (Blair House, his Washington home across from the White House, is the nation's official guest quarters.)

Permanent and changing exhibits at the **George Meany Memorial Archives** document work life and United States labor history. The archives preserve the historical record of the American Federation of Labor and Congress of Industrial Organizations (AFL-CIO); Meany was their first president. ✉ *10000 New Hampshire Ave.,* ☎ *301/431–5451,* WEB *www.georgemeany.org/archives.* *Free.* ⏲ *Weekdays 9–4:30.*

Dining and Lodging

$$$–$$$$ ✕ **Mrs. K's Toll House.** In one of the last tollhouses in Montgomery County, Mrs. K's has welcomed diners since 1930 and continues to be a favorite of senior citizens. Antique furniture, "Historic Old Blue" Staffordshire plates, and Nicholas Lutz glass are on display in the original tollhouse location. Complete American fare lunches and dinners are served here—nothing is à la carte. Both the menu and the decorations change seasonally. Smoking is not permitted. ✉ *9201 Colesville Rd.,* ☎ *301/589–3500. AE, D, DC, MC, V.*

$–$$$$ ✕ **The Original Crisfield Seafood Restaurant.** With not much more elegance than a neighborhood barbershop, the prices here might seem absurd. Yet you get your money's worth: no-nonsense seafood and an eyeful of Old Maryland arrested in time. Crab cakes don't get any more authentic than these, presented with just enough structural imperfection to guarantee they're made by hand; the clam chowder—creamy, chunky, and served with a bottomless bowl of oyster crackers—is rendered with similar, down-home care. The fancier (and pricier) location in Lee Plaza has an art deco style and also serves chicken and steak. It's under separate management. ✉ *8012 Georgia Ave.,* ☎ *301/589–1306;* ✉ *Lee Plaza, 8606 Colesville Rd.,* ☎ *301/588–1572. AE, MC, V. Original closed Mon. No lunch weekends at Lee Plaza.*

$$–$$$ 🏨 **Holiday Inn.** Four blocks from the Silver Spring Metro, this chain hotel uses the same neutral palette in each of its guest rooms. Some have refrigerators, double sinks, couches, or recliners. A shuttle bus runs within a 4-mi radius on weekdays. ✉ *8777 Georgia Ave., 20910,* ☎ *301/589–0800,* FAX *301/587–4791. 221 rooms, 10 suites. Restaurant, room service, outdoor pool, gym, bar, free parking. AE, D, DC, MC, V.*

Wheaton

❼ *4 mi north of Silver Spring.*

Although the main distinction between Wheaton and Silver Spring is largely a line on a map, there are also more Wheaton sights.

A selection of the capital's historic trolleys have been rescued and restored at the **National Capital Trolley Museum,** along with streetcars from Europe, Canada, and elsewhere in America. The museum is run by volunteers whose childhood fascination with trains never left them at the station. For a nominal fare you can go on a 2-mi ride through the countryside. ✉ *Bonifant Rd. between Layhill Rd. and New Hampshire Ave.,* ☎ *301/384–6088.* *Museum free; trolley ride $2.50.* ⏲ *Jan.–mid-Mar. and mid-May–Nov., weekends and Memorial Day, July 4, and Labor Day noon–5; mid-Mar.–mid-May, Thurs. and Fri. 10–2, weekends noon–5. Last train leaves the station ½ hour before closing time.*

At rolling 50-acre **Brookside Gardens,** formal seasonal displays of bulbs, annuals, perennials, and a sprawling azalea garden flourish. Inside, the blossoming continues in two conservatories housing seasonal displays and exotic tropicals throughout the year. The visitor center has an auditorium, classrooms for adults and children, a 3,000-volume horticulture library, a gift shop, and an information booth. ✉ *1800 Glenallan Ave.,* ☎ *301/949–8230,* WEB *www.brooksidegardens.org.* *Free, class fees $7–$35.* ⏲ *Daily; conservatories 10–5, visitor center 9–5, gift shop 10–4, horticulture library 10–3.*

Sandy Spring

❽ *10 mi northwest of Rockville, 10 mi north of Wheaton.*

Best known for the refuge that the Society of Friends gave slaves here as part of the Underground Railroad, Sandy Spring is still the home of an active Quaker community. To design your own tour of this town purchase a map at Sandy Spring Museum. Of the town's dozens of buildings, five homes were associated with the Underground Railroad. Unfortunately only one of the homes, Woodlawn (16501 Norwood Rd.), is open for visitors and it's only to see the grounds.

Sandy Spring Museum houses a hodgepodge of items that includes Native American arrowheads and such early 20th-century memorabilia as a buggy and town-store items. A carriage museum and blacksmith shop opened on the grounds in 2002. ✉ *17901 Bentley Rd.,* ☎ *301/774–0022,* WEB *www.sandyspringmuseum.org.* *$3.* ⏲ *Mon., Wed., and Thurs. 9–4, weekends noon–4.*

PRINCE GEORGE'S COUNTY

Named in 1695 for Denmark and Norway's prince (the husband of the heir to the throne of England, Princess Anne), the county was once famous for its tobacco auctions, which are still held in its southern end. Tobacco created a wealthy leisure class who enjoyed cricket; fox hunting; and horse racing, a sport still popular in the area. The county today, where nearly 60% of the population is African-American, remains affluent.

Nature lovers will enjoy the National Wildlife Visitor Center and the Merkle Wildlife Sanctuary. Flight fans can check out the world's oldest airport in College Park. For those who prefer 60-second thrills, Six Flags is full of roller coasters, water slides, and kiddie rides. Sports fans may not be able to see the Redskins, but they can get a fix at a Maryland Terrapins game, or at a Bowie Baysox minor-league baseball

Prince George's County

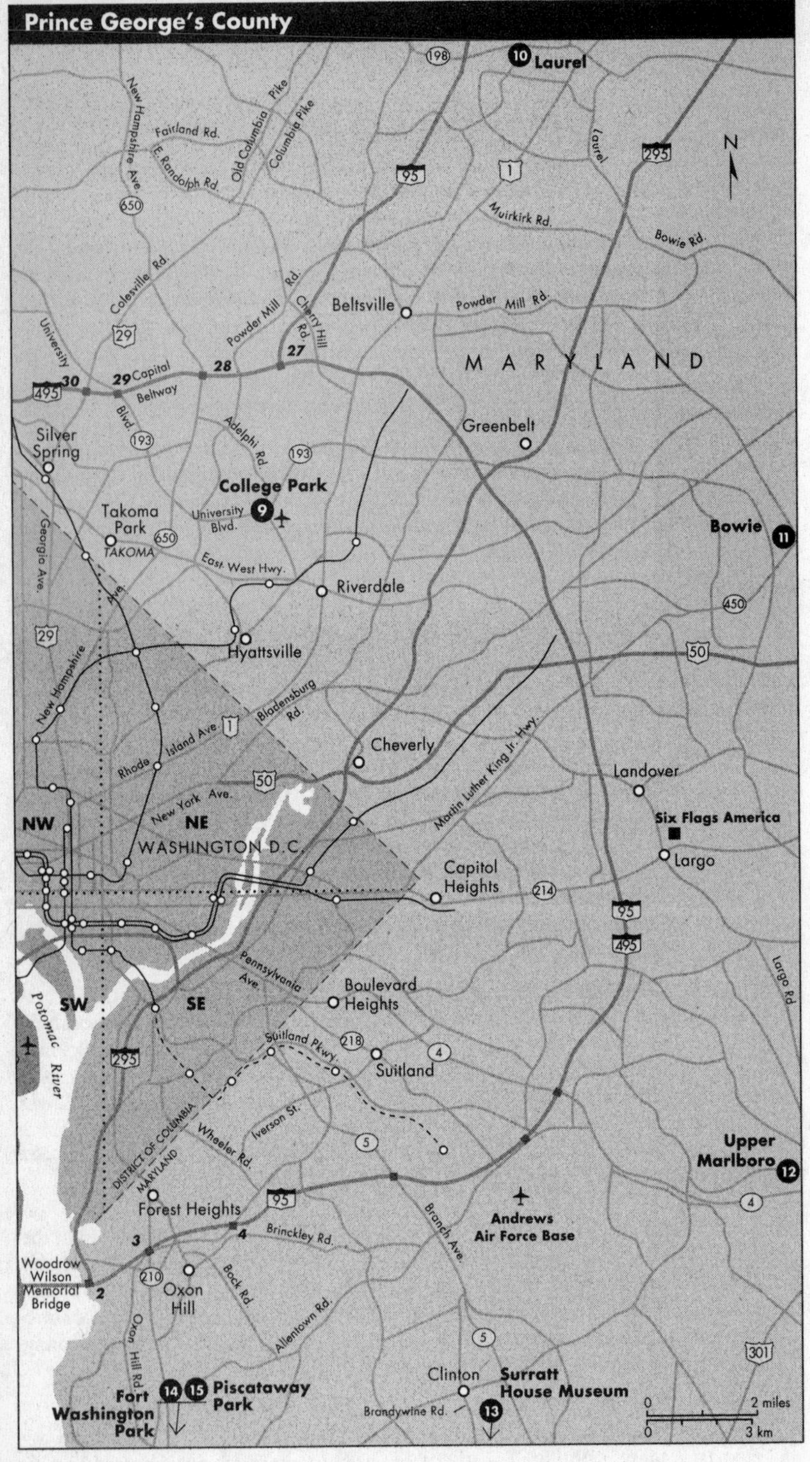

game. Historic sites, including the Surratt House Museum, are peppered throughout the county.

To tour the county, start in College Park and work your way up to Laurel. Then head south to the heart of the county before visiting sites along the Patuxent and Potomac rivers.

College Park

❾ *6 mi east of Silver Spring via I–495, 9 mi north Washington, D.C.*

As its name implies, College Park is primarily a university town on gently rolling terrain. One of the largest campuses in the country, **University of Maryland at College Park** has an enrollment of 34,000. The College Park campus began as an agricultural college in 1856, and became part of the University of Maryland in 1920. The university's athletic teams participate in the highly competitive Atlantic Coast Conference and draw large crowds to Byrd Stadium and the 17,100-seat Comcast Center. Graduates and Marylanders from all over the state cheer on the Maryland Terrapins. The men's basketball team is almost always in contention for national championships. In Turner Hall, visitor center staff provide information about the university and maps for getting around the sprawling campus of 1,580 acres and 270 buildings. At the dairy, ice cream made from campus cows' milk is available by the cone or carton. ✉ *Turner Hall, U.S. Rte. 1 and Rossborough La.,* ☎ *301/314–7777,* WEB *www.umd.edu.* ⏲ *Turner Hall weekdays 8–5, Sat. 9–3. Dairy Oct.–Apr., weekdays 8–5; May–Sept., weekdays 8–5, Sat. noon–3.*

The Wright Brothers once trained military officers to fly at College Park Airport, the world's oldest continuously operating airport. The **College Park Aviation Museum** is a tribute to the Wright Brothers and early aviation memorabilia. Children can spin propellers and dress up like aviators. A "Speaking of Flight" lecture series is held in the spring and fall. At the Peter Pan program, preschoolers make airplanes and hear stories on the second and fourth Thursdays from 10:30 to noon. ✉ *College Park Airport, 1985 Corporal Frank Scott Dr.,* ☎ *301/864–6029; 301/861–4765 TDD.* 🎫 *$4.* ⏲ *Daily 10–5.*

Dining and Lodging

$–$$ ✕ **Ledo's.** Students, alumni, and locals have made Ledo's pizza popular throughout the state. There are dozens of Ledo's franchises in Maryland, but many insist that the best pizza—with smoked provolone so gooey you need a knife and fork—comes from the original restaurant, which opened in 1955 and is still family run. Adelphi is just outside of College Park city limits. ✉ *2420 University Blvd., Adelphi,* ☎ *301/422–8622. MC, V.*

$–$$ ✕ **R. J. Bentley's.** Most walls are covered with license plates and gas pump memorabilia, and jerseys from the university's past star athletes hang on the "wall of fame." Students and alumni head to this hangout for beer, chili, wings, and sandwiches; the bar packs in fans after home games. ✉ *7323 Baltimore Ave.,* ☎ *301/277–8898. AE, MC, V.*

$$ 🏨 **The Inn and Conference Center/ University of Maryland and University College.** In a redbrick, Georgian building topped by a cupola, the inn easily blends in with the rest of the campus. Run by Marriott, the hotel is in the old Adult Education Center. Those staying here receive free use of the campus recreation center and indoor pool. Predictably, parents start booking rooms months before graduation ceremonies are held in late May or early June. The hotel is less than 10 minutes from both the College Park and Prince George's Plaza Metro stops. ✉ *3501 University Blvd. E, at Adelphi Rd., 20783,* ☎ *301/985–*

7300 or 800/727–8622, FAX *301/985–7850,* WEB *www.umuc.edu/icc. 111 rooms. 2 restaurants, gym, bar, business services, parking (fee). AE, D, MC, V.*

Greenbelt

4 mi northeast of College Park.

Planned as part of a New Deal program during the Great Depression, Greenbelt was one of three communities built for low- and middle-income families (the others are outside of Milwaukee and in Ohio). These "greenbelt" communities, constructed and planned by the U.S. Department of Agriculture, were also meant to serve as models of good suburban development.

One of the world's largest and most diversified farms in the world, the Agricultural Research Service's (ARS) **Beltsville Agricultural Research Center** has yielded many improvements in foods that Americans take for granted, such as disease-resistant potatoes, meatier turkeys, and leaner pork. Some of the biggest and newest environment chambers installed here are for the study of environmental stress, such as the depletion of the ozone. After a brief orientation at the visitor center, inside a log lodge built in 1937 by the Civilian Conservation Corps, you tour the farm by van or bus. Tours, which can be tailored to interests such as nutrition and genetic engineering, take at least two hours. Because of their length and technical nature, tours are not recommended for children below middle-school age (Field Day, held the first Saturday of June, includes hay rides, farm equipment, and lab displays and is good for all ages). Although the researchers work to develop heartier, safer, and sometimes tastier foods, there are no free samples and no cafeterias on site. ✉ *10300 Baltimore Ave., Bldg. 302, Beltsville, 3 mi northeast of Greenbelt,* ☎ *301/504–9403.* 🎫 *Free.* ⏲ *Weekdays 8:30–4. Reservations essential. Call two weeks in advance.*

Laurel

10 *7 mi north of Greenbelt.*

Four Maryland counties claim a section of this town: Anne Arundel, Howard, Montgomery, and Prince George's, but most of the suburb resides in Prince George's County.

Set on 75 acres of rolling parkland, **Montpelier Mansion** is a masterpiece of Georgian architecture. The mansion was built and owned by the Snowdens, who earned their wealth through tobacco and an iron foundry. George Washington and Abigail Adams were among the mansion's early visitors. Interesting features include a 35- by 16-ft reproduction of a hand-painted floor cloth and an offset central hall staircase. Also on the property is a summerhouse where ladies took their tea, boxwood gardens, an herb and flower garden with plants grown in the 1800s, and a cultural arts center with three galleries and artists' studios. After the one-hour tour you can stroll the property's primarily gravel paths and visit the Little Teapot gift shop, which sells loose tea and imported packaged foods. A full English tea is served at the mansion about once a month: call the Little Teapot for details. ✉ *Rte. 197 and Muirkirk Rd.,* ☎ *301/953–1376; 301/953–1993 arts center; 301/498–8486 Little Teapot.* 🎫 *$3.* ⏲ *Dec.–Feb., Sun. tours at 1 and 2; Mar.–Nov., Sun.–Thurs. noon–3, tours on the hr. Art center daily 10–5.*

One of the Department of the Interior's largest science and environmental education centers, the **Patuxent National Wildlife Visitor Center** showcases interactive exhibits on global environmental issues, migratory bird routes, wildlife habitats, and endangered species. A viewing station overlooks a lake area that beavers, bald eagles, and Canada geese use as a habitat. Weather permitting, you can take a 30-minute tram tour through meadows, forests, and wetlands and take your own tour on the trails. The paved Loop Trail runs ⅓ mi; another 4 mi of trails, covered with wood chips and other natural materials, crisscrosses the property. The center lies between Laurel and Bowie. *10901 Scarlet Tanager Loop, off Powder Mill Rd., ☎ 301/497–5760. Free; tram ride $3. Daily 10–5:30; tram mid-Mar.–late June and early Sept.–mid-Nov., weekends 11:30–3:30; late June–late Aug., daily 11:30, 12:30, 1:30, and 2:30.*

Bowie

11 *13 mi southeast of Laurel, 15 mi east of College Park.*

It grew up around a railroad junction in 1870, but today Bowie has more than 53,000 residents and is the home of Bowie State University, a historically black college within the University of Maryland system.

Built in the mid-1700s as a country retreat for Maryland governor Samuel Ogle, the Georgian-style **Belair Mansion** was owned in the early 1900s by William Woodward, one of the first people to bring thoroughbred horses to the United States from England. In 1914, Woodward added on to the home and built **Belair Stable,** which is also open to the public. One-hour tours of the mansion and stable emphasize the contributions of the families and their horses to racing history. ✉ *12207 Tulip Grove Dr., ☎ 301/809–3088. Free. Wed.–Sun. noon–4.*

Outdoor Activities and Sports

FedEx Stadium (✉ 1600 FedEx Way, Landover, ☎ 301/276–6000, WEB www.redskins.com) is where the Washington Redskins play, but all the tickets are owned by season pass holders. Football fans who don't have megabucks to buy a ticket (they're often sold through the classifieds or through on-line auction sites) may be able to get tickets for other events. The Rolling Stones, George Strait, and other superstars have all performed at this 86,000-seat stadium.

Bowie Baysox (✉ 4101 N.E. Crain Hwy., ☎ 301/805–6000), the AA affiliate of the Baltimore Orioles, plays at the 10,500-seat Prince George's Stadium. Children have major-league fun off the field at a carousel, child-oriented concession stands, and a playground. Fireworks light up the sky at every home game held on Saturday evening between April and Labor Day, as well as those on Thursday night in July and August. Tickets cost $8.

Upper Marlboro

12 *14 mi south of Bowie, 11 mi east of Suitland.*

The county seat of Prince George's County was once famous for its tobacco auctions. Although tobacco is still bought and sold here, business today mostly revolves around the local government.

Merkle Wildlife Sanctuary is named after the conservationist Edgar A. Merkle, who began a breeding program and habitat improvement program to bring Canada geese to Maryland's Patuxent River. Thousands of geese return here each September and remain through late February or early March; another 80–100 stay year-round. You can check out the geese and other fauna by hiking the nature trails or from observation decks at the visitor center, which has a discovery room where children can make crafts and observe turtles and snakes. On Sunday, from 10 to 3, the sanctuary sponsors a driving tour of the marshlands, woodlands, farm ponds, and creeks. To reach the sanctuary take Route 301 south to Route 382 and turn left on St. Thomas Church Road. ✉ *11704 Fenno Rd.,* ☎ *301/888–1377.* *$2 per vehicle.* ⊙ *Daily dawn–dusk; visitor center Mon. and Fri. 10–4; weekends 10–5 (hrs subject to change).*

Clinton

10 mi southwest of Upper Marlboro.

The origin of the name Clinton is unclear—the town used to be called Surrattsville for Mary Surratt's husband, the postmaster John Surratt.

13 The **Surratt House Museum,** once a house and tavern, is where John Wilkes Booth sought refuge after assassinating President Abraham Lincoln. For her role in the conspiracy, Mary Surratt became the first woman to be executed by the federal government. She was said to have told one of her tenants to get the "shooting irons ready" for Booth after he shot Lincoln at Ford's Theater in Washington, D.C. You can trace Booth's escape route on an electronic map at the visitor center. Costumed docents give tours of the house, talk about 19th-century life in Prince George's County, and discuss the Civil War, but they won't get into debates about Surratt's innocence or guilt. The Surratt Society, reachable through the museum, sponsors a 12-hour John Wilkes Booth escape route tour in April and September that covers the 12 days Booth spent on the run in Maryland, Virginia, and Washington, D.C. ✉ *9118 Brandywine Rd.,* ☎ *301/868–1121,* WEB *www.surratt.org.* *$3.* ⊙ *Thurs.–Fri. 11–3, weekends noon–4; tours every ½ hr.*

Oxon Cove Park preserves 19th-century farm life on a site where the Piscataway Native Americans once lived. Children can feed chickens, milk cows, and take a hayride. There's also a fine view of Washington over the Potomac River. Throughout the year, the National Park Service offers programs such as sheep shearing in May, cider making in September, and "Talking Turkey"—when kids can learn about domestic and wild turkeys and get to feed them—in November. ✉ *6411 Oxon Hill Rd., 5 mi northwest of Clinton,* ☎ *301/839–1176,* WEB *www.nps.gov/nace/oxhi.* *Free.* ⊙ *Daily 8–4:30.*

Fort Washington Park

14 *5 mi southwest of Clinton, 7 mi south of Oxon Hill.*

George Washington chose this site on a narrow portion of the Potomac River for the first fort to protect the nation's capital. It was destroyed during the War of 1812, only five years after its completion; the current fort was completed in 1824. Half-hour tours of the fort are given on weekend afternoons and upon request on weekdays. One Sunday per month, costumed volunteers re-create military life in the mid-1800s by firing the cannons. If you cross the drawbridge over the moat, you'll see the 7-ft-thick stone and masonry walls, gun positions, and other defenses. Although the fort is impressive, most people visit the park for no other reason than to picnic along the river. ✉ *13551 Fort Washington Rd.,* ☎ *301/763–4600.* *$5 per vehicle, early Apr.–late Sept.; free weekdays early Oct.–early Apr., $5 on weekends.* ⊙ *Early Apr.–late Sept., daily 9–5; early Oct.–early Apr., daily 9–4:30.*

Accokeek

10 mi south of Fort Washington.

By fighting off developers in the 1950s, the Accokeek Foundation helped keep the view from Mount Vernon as George Washington would have seen. Today, the once-rural area is being developed into a suburban community. Locals call Piscataway Park, tucked away at the end of the road by the river, a hidden treasure.

On 4,000 acres of land bought to protect the view from Mount Ver-
15 non, **Piscataway Park** attracts history buffs, horticulturists, naturalists, hikers, and families. At **National Colonial Farm,** you can walk through an 18th-century farm dwelling and tobacco barn, and reproductions of a smokehouse and out-kitchen. Guides point out the farmhouse's most valuable materials: the glass in the windows and its nails. Whenever a house burned down in the 18th century, the owners would rummage through the remains for the nails. Old-time animal breeds and heirloom crop varieties are both raised here. Also on hand is an herb garden as well as bluebirds, great blue herons, and bald eagles. If you want to compare and contrast National Colonial Farm with Mount Vernon, board the *Potomac,* a dory boat that runs every weekend between mid-June and mid-September. ✉ *3400 Bryan Point Rd. (5 mi south of Fort Washington Park),* ☎ *301/283–2113 Accokeek Foundation; 301/283–0112 National Park Service.* *$2; $7 ferry rides; $16 ferry ride includes admission to Mount Vernon.* *Park daily, dawn–dusk; National Colonial Farm mid-Mar.–mid-Dec., Tues.–Sun. 10–4, tours weekends at 11, 1, and 3; ferry rides mid-June–mid-Sept., weekends at 10, noon, 2, and 4; ferry tickets must be picked up 15 min before boarding. Reservations recommended.*

SUBURBAN MARYLAND A TO Z

To research prices, get advice from other travelers, and book travel arrangements, visit www.fodors.com.

AIRPORTS

Three major airports serve both suburban Maryland and the Washington, D.C., area. Baltimore-Washington International (BWI) Airport, 10 mi south of Baltimore off I–95 and Route 295, is closer to Montgomery and Prince George's counties than Ronald Reagan National Airport or Washington Dulles International Airport.

➤ AIRPORT INFORMATION: **Baltimore-Washington International (BWI) Airport** (☎ 410/859–7111).

BIKE TRAVEL

The Capital Crescent Trail and the canal towpath are both very popular for biking excursions. You can rent bikes at Big Wheel Bikes. Ten miles away along the towpath and 5 mi away via Falls and River roads from the Great Falls Tavern is Swain's Lock, another rental option.

➤ BIKE RENTALS: **Big Wheel Bikes** (✉ 6917 Arlington Rd., Bethesda, ☎ 301/652–0192). **Swain's Lock** (✉ 10700 Swain's Lock Rd., Potomac, ☎ 301/299–9006).

BUS TRAVEL

Greyhound Lines provides scheduled service to Silver Spring Station only. Metrobus makes local stops in both counties and in Washington, D.C. Ride-On, Montgomery County's own bus service, has service on more than 70 roads. Look for the blue-and-white bus stop signs throughout the county.

➤ BUS DEPOTS: **Silver Spring Station** (✉ 8100 Fenton St., ☎ 301/585–8700).

➤ BUS LINES: **Greyhound Lines** (☎ 800/231–2222). **Metrobus** (☎ 202/637–7000). **Ride-On** (☎ 240/777–7433).

CAR TRAVEL

The primary transportation link throughout suburban Maryland is the Capital Beltway (I–495), which runs east–west. Interstate 95 runs north–south. Interstate 270, which intersects with I–495 in Montgomery County, reaches destinations north of Rockville in Montgomery County. Roads that run through the region and into downtown Washington include Wisconsin, Connecticut, Georgia, New Hampshire, and Pennsylvania avenues; Routes 1 and 50 (the latter turns into New York Avenue upon entering the District); Baltimore Washington Parkway; and I–295.

DISABILITIES AND ACCESSIBILITY

The Metro rail system is generally accessible, but stations have only one elevator each.

➤ INFORMATION: **Washington Metropolitan Area Transit Authority** (☎ 202/962–1212 elevator information).

EMERGENCIES

Suburban Hospital is the designated trauma center for Montgomery County.

CVS's hot line can tell you which of its 24-hour pharmacies are near you.

➤ CONTACT: **Police, Fire, Ambulance** (☎ 911).

➤ HOSPITALS: **Holy Cross Hospital** (✉ 1500 Forest Glen Rd., Silver Spring, ☎ 301/754–7000). **Suburban Hospital** (✉ 8600 Old Georgetown Rd., Bethesda, ☎ 301/896–3100). **Washington Adventist Hospital** (✉ 7600 Carroll Ave., Takoma Park, ☎ 301/891–7600).

➤ 24-HOUR PHARMACIES: **CVS Pharmacy** (☎ 800/746–7287).

SUBWAY TRAVEL

Montgomery County is served by Metro subway system's Red Line, the system's busiest. Prince George's County is served by the Blue, Orange, and Green lines. Traveling from one country on the subway involves going through downtown Washington and transferring trains.

➤ INFORMATION: **Metrorail** (☎ 202/637–7000, WEB www.wmata.com).

TRAIN TRAVEL

Amtrak has scheduled stops in New Carrollton and at BWI Airport as part of its East Coast service. The MARC commuter train has two lines that go through Montgomery and Prince George's counties.

➤ TRAIN STATIONS: **New Carrollton** (✉ 4300 Garden City Dr., ☎ 202/906–3764).

➤ TRAIN LINES: **Amtrak** (☎ 800/872–7245, WEB www.amtrak.com). **MARC** (☎ 800/325–7245, WEB www.mtamaryland.com).

VISITOR INFORMATION

➤ TOURIST INFORMATION: **Bethesda Urban Partnership** (✉ 7906 Woodmont Ave., Bethesda 20814, ☎ 301/215–6660, FAX 301/215–6664, WEB www.bethesda.org). **Montgomery County Conference & Visitors Bureau** (✉ 11820 Parklawn Dr., Suite 380, Rockville 20852, ☎ 301/428–9702 or 800/925–0880, FAX 301/428–9705, WEB www.cvbmontco.com). **Prince George's County Conference & Visitors Bureau** (✉ 9200 Basil Ct., Suite 101, Largo 20774, ☎ 301/925–8300 or 888/925–8300, FAX 301/925–2053, WEB www.visitprincegeorges.com).

4 CHARLOTTESVILLE, THE BLUE RIDGE, THE SHENANDOAH VALLEY, AND SOUTHWEST VIRGINIA

In Virginia's western half, presidents' homes and Civil War battlefields compete for attention with trails and roads that roll over one magnificent Appalachian mountaintop after another. The Blue Ridge forms the region's spine, giving travelers a bird's-eye view over the Shenandoah Valley and the Piedmont area. World-class music and theater are found in cities such as Charlottesville (home of Monticello) and Roanoke, but also in smaller towns such as Abingdon and Staunton.

Revised by Kevin Myatt

THE NATURAL BEAUTY OF THE SHENANDOAH VALLEY is well known—so much so that the region's towns and cities, rich pockets of history and culture, are all too often bypassed by travelers skimming along Skyline Drive and Blue Ridge Parkway. About 150 mi long, the Shenandoah Valley lies between two ranges of the Appalachians—the Alleghenies to the west and the Blue Ridge to the east—in northwestern Virginia, parallel to the western edge of the state and extending to Harpers Ferry in West Virginia. In the heights east of the valley, Shenandoah National Park's nearly 200,000 acres stretch more than 80 mi along the Blue Ridge, providing stunning vistas, more than 500 mi of hiking trails (including a section of the Appalachian Trail), and trout fishing in rushing streams. From the roads and trails, you might see wild turkeys, white-tailed deer, and sometimes even a black bear.

Charlottesville, 71 mi northwest of Richmond, is the core of what Virginians call Mr. Jefferson's country. Although the influence of the third president of the United States is inescapable throughout the commonwealth (and far beyond its borders), Jefferson's legacy is especially strong in Albemarle and Orange counties. Here are buildings and sites associated with him and the giants among his contemporaries.

Since 1819, when Jefferson founded the University of Virginia in Charlottesville, the area has been a center of culture. In recent years the countryside has been discovered by celebrities, including the actress Sissy Spacek and best-selling author John Grisham, and a growing community of writers, artists, and musicians. They and others were drawn by the history as well as the peaceful backdrop of the Blue Ridge Mountains.

The Shenandoah Valley and the Blue Ridge meet Southwest Virginia at Roanoke, a bustling city that owes its existence to the railroads. Today, it's a commercial and medical center for the area and within easy reach of natural attractions. To the west of Roanoke is the New River Valley (named, ironically, for one of the world's oldest rivers) a region that takes pride in its inhabitants' vigorous outdoor lifestyle, its rapid growth, and Virginia Tech, the state's largest university. The Blue Ridge continues south from Roanoke to Mt. Rogers, Virginia's highest peak at 5,729 ft, then on into North Carolina. Abingdon, the oldest town west of the Blue Ridge, offers well-preserved 18th- and 19th-century buildings, two major regional festivals, and the state theater of Virginia, the Barter Theatre. Covering Virginia's southwestern tip, the Appalachian Plateau is heavily wooded and incised with gorges. One of them is the legendary Cumberland Gap, which leads into Kentucky and Tennessee.

Pleasures and Pastimes

Dining

CATEGORY	COST*
$$$$	over $32
$$$	$22–$32
$$	$12–$22
$	under $12

**per person for a main course at dinner*

Lodging

CATEGORY	COST*
$$$$	over $225
$$$	$150–$225
$$	$100–$150
$	under $100

**All prices are for a standard double room, excluding state tax.*

Exploring Charlottesville, the Blue Ridge, the Shenandoah Valley, and Southwest Virginia

At the foot of the Blue Ridge in the small, thriving city of Charlottesville, witness Thomas Jefferson's architectural genius—Monticello and the University of Virginia. To the south, the restored Civil War–era village of Appomattox Court House is a peek back in time. Along the western rim of Virginia in the Shenandoah Valley is Winchester, which changed hands no fewer than 72 times during the Civil War. Farther south is Lexington, known for its ties to Confederate generals Robert E. Lee and Stonewall Jackson. In Roanoke, Virginia's largest city west of Richmond, Market Square provides a rich cultural anchor for Southwest Virginia. In this area you can hike and camp in the George Washington and Jefferson national forests, float the New River, and photograph wild ponies near the state's highest mountain. Newbern and Tazewell offer remnants of life in the pioneer days, and Abingdon draws crowds to the Barter Theatre and the annual Virginia Highlands Festival.

CHARLOTTESVILLE AND THE FOOT OF THE BLUE RIDGE

Surrounded by a lush countryside of hills and valleys, Charlottesville is the most prominent city in the foothills of the Blue Ridge Mountains. Thomas Jefferson's mountaintop home and the enterprise of his last years, the University of Virginia, are draws for appreciators of architecture. Twenty-five miles northeast, Orange County is where you'll find the estate of Jefferson's friend and compatriot James Madison. The tiny town of Washington, 30 mi beyond Orange, bears the stamp of another president: George Washington surveyed and plotted out this slice of wilderness in 1749. Lynchburg, Charlottesville's neighbor to the south, is the site of Jefferson's retreat home, the octagonal Poplar Forest. Within the Blue Ridge itself is popular Shenandoah National Park, the park's spectacular but often-crowded Skyline Drive, and Wintergreen Resort, a haven for outdoor sports.

Numbers in the margin correspond to points of interest on the Charlottesville, the Blue Ridge, the Shenandoah Valley, and the Southwest Virginia map.

Charlottesville

1 *71 mi northwest of Richmond (via I–64).*

Charlottesville, in the heart of verdant wine country, is the epitome of Virginia's hilly Piedmont—the large, gently hilly countryside in the center of the state. The city's downtown pedestrian mall, a brick-paved street of restored buildings that stretches along six blocks of Main Street, is its legal and financial hub as well as a big draw for residents and visitors alike. Outdoor restaurants and cafés, concerts, and impromptu theatrical events keep things lively. Just 2 mi southeast of Charlottesville

Charlottesville, the Blue Ridge, the Shenandoah Valley, and Southwest Virginia

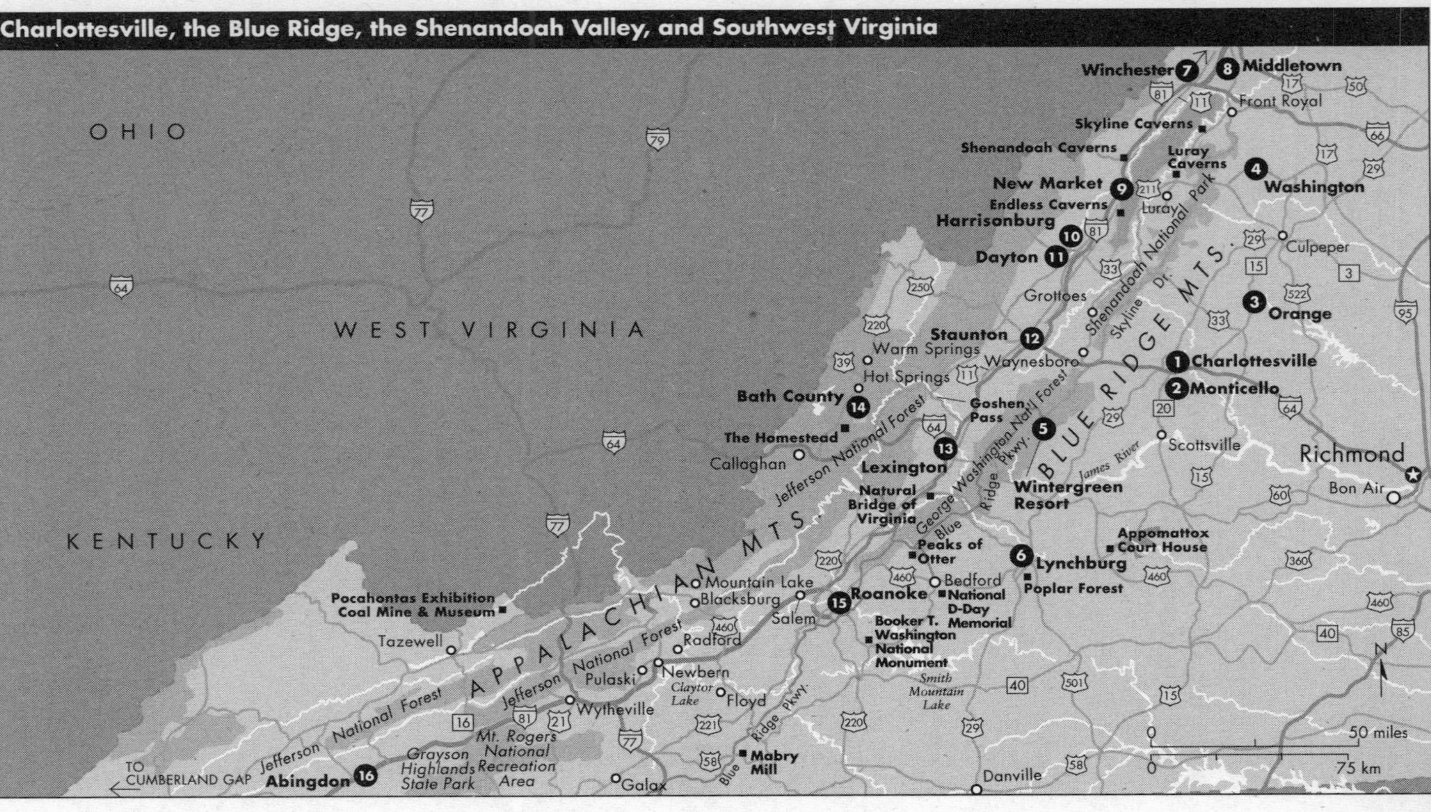

is Monticello, the distinguished home that Thomas Jefferson designed and built for himself.

A stop at the **Monticello Visitors Center** is a must, either before or after visiting the estate, since much of the history of Jefferson's home is not explained on the house tour. A wide assortment of personal memorabilia and artifacts recovered during recent archaeological excavations at Monticello is on display. The free, 35-minute film delves into Jefferson's political career. ✉ *Rte. 20 S from Charlottesville (I–64 Monticello, Exit 121),* ☎ *434/977–1783.* ⏲ *Mar.–Oct., daily 9–5:30; Nov.–Feb., daily 9–5.*

★ ❷ **Monticello,** the most famous of Jefferson's homes and a sort of monument to himself, was constructed from 1769 to 1809. Typical of no single architectural style, Monticello is primarily a neoclassical repudiation of the prevalent English Georgian style and the Colonial mentality behind it. As you might expect of Jefferson, every detail in the house makes a statement. The staircases are narrow and hidden because he considered them unsightly and a waste of space, and contrary to plantation tradition, his outbuildings are in the back and not on the east side (the direction from which his guests would arrive). Throughout the house are Jefferson's inventions, including a seven-day clock and a two-pen contraption that allowed him to make a copy of his correspondence as he wrote it—without having to show it to a copyist. On site are re-created gardens, the plantation street where his slaves lived, and a gift shop. Arrive early to avoid a long wait for a tour of the house, and don't plan on seeing everything in one visit. ✉ *Rte. 53,* ☎ *434/984–9800,* WEB *www.monticello.org.* 🎫 *$11.* ⏲ *Mar.–Oct., daily 8–5; Nov.–Feb., daily 9–4:30.*

Two miles from Monticello, the modest **Ash Lawn–Highland** is—like its grand neighbor—marked by the personality of the president who lived in it. But the building is no longer the simple farmhouse built in 1799 for James Monroe, who lived in the L-shape single story at the rear: a later owner added on a more prominent two-story section. (The furniture, however, is mostly original.) The small rooms inside are crowded with gifts from notable people and with souvenirs from Monroe's time as envoy to France. Such coziness befits the fifth U.S. president, the first to come from the middle class. Ash Lawn–Highland today is a 535-acre farm where peacocks and sheep roam. The outdoor Ash Lawn–Highland Summer Festival, at which one of the country's top-ranked summer opera companies performs, draws music aficionados June through August. ✉ *1000 James Monroe Pkwy. (Rte. 795 southwest of Monticello),* ☎ *434/293–9539,* WEB *monticello.avenue.org/ashlawn.* 🎫 *$8.* ⏲ *Apr.–Oct., daily 9–6; Nov.–Mar., daily 10–5.*

★ At the west end of Charlottesville, the **University of Virginia,** one of the nation's most notable public universities, was founded and designed by a 76-year-old Thomas Jefferson, who called himself its "father" in his own epitaph. A poll of experts at the time of the U.S. bicentennial designated this complex "the proudest achievement of American architecture in the past 200 years." Only the most outstanding students qualify for the coveted rooms that flank the Lawn, a green, terraced expanse that flows down from the Rotunda, a half-scale replica of the Pantheon in Rome. Behind the Pavilions, where senior faculty live, serpentine walls surround small, flowering gardens. Edgar Allan Poe's room—where he spent one year as a student until debts forced him to leave—is preserved on the West Range at No. 13. Tours begin indoors in the Rotunda, whose entrance is on the Lawn side, lower level. The **Bayly Art Museum** (✉ 155 Rugby Rd., ☎ 434/924–3592; 🎫 free; ⏲ Tues.–Sun. 1–5), one block north of the Rotunda, exhibits art from

Close-Up

THOMAS JEFFERSON

ONE OF THE NATION'S foremost statesmen, Jefferson is best known for his first contribution to the country: drafting the Declaration of Independence in 1776. The sum of the 33-year political career that followed is better remembered than its milestones, which do bear repeating. His first office of weight was that of governor of his beloved Virginia, beginning in 1779. In 1790 he served as secretary of state under his friend George Washington (and resigned in 1793). A Republican presidential candidate in 1796, he lost by just three electoral votes to Federalist John Adams, and as rules then dictated, Jefferson became vice president. By the 1800 race, tensions between the Federalist and Republican parties were high and debilitating to a nation still finding its way. Jefferson won the nation's third presidency at this critical juncture and served two terms, after which he retired for good to Monticello.

The breadth of Jefferson's skills is bewildering to our highly specialized age. This Enlightenment man had many talents: statesman, farmer and zealous gardener, writer, scientist, musician, and philosopher. One admiring contemporary described Jefferson as a man who could "calculate an eclipse, survey an estate, tie an artery, plan an edifice, try a cause, break a horse, dance a minuet, and play a violin." As a lover of great wine, Jefferson introduced European vinifera grapes to Virginia but failed as a vintner. Today his native state's wineries are helping fulfill his vision. He has even been hailed as the father of the American gastronomic revolution, importing from France olive oil, Parmesan cheese, raisins, and pistachios. The *Garden Book,* which he kept for upward of half a century, contains a wealth of minutiae, from planting times to the preferred method of grafting peach trees. He kept a separate accounting book that recorded every item of cash expenditure.

It is often noted that this architect of democracy was also a slave owner (he owned about 200 slaves at any given time, and freed only seven after his death). One of the most enduring mysteries surrounding Jefferson has been whether he had a liaison with Sally Hemings, one of his slaves. DNA tests from 1998 showed that a member of the Jefferson family—many believe Thomas Jefferson himself—fathered her youngest son, Eston. Jefferson went through an inquiry into his conduct during his last year as governor of Virginia, and once he was president, Federalists accused him of improper relations with a white woman and also with Hemings. A Richmond journalist was the first to publicly allege the relationship in 1802. In 1816 Jefferson confided in a letter, "As to Federal slanders, I never wished them to be answered, but [by] the tenor of my life, half a century of which has been on a theater at which the public have been spectators and the competent judges of its merit."

Virginians love Jefferson because he loved Virginia. Monticello, hiexperiment in architecture that had him making changes until the day before he died, attracts 500,000 people every year. The University of Virginia, which Jefferson called "the hobby of my old age," is now one of the nation's elite public universities. Charlottesville honors its most famous resident in a number of ways. On April 13—Jefferson's birthday—the Thomas Jefferson Center for the Protection of Free Expression presents the Muzzle Award to those guilty of trying to quash free speech. On the anniversary of his death, Independence Day, Monticello is the site of a naturalization ceremony for new Americans.

around the world from ancient times to the present day. ✉ *University of Virginia,* ☎ *434/924–3239,* WEB *www.virginia.edu.* 🎫 *Free; 30-min to 1-hr historic tours daily at 10, 11, 2, 3, and 4.* ⏲ *Rotunda open daily 9–4:45. University closed during winter break Dec.–Jan. and during spring exams the first three weeks of May.*

Housed in a converted 1916 school building, **McGuffey Art Center** contains the Second Street Gallery and the studios of painters, printmakers, metalworkers, and sculptors, all of which are open to the public. Dance performances are occasionally put on here. ✉ *201 2nd St. NW, Downtown,* ☎ *434/295–7973,* WEB *monticello.avenue.org/Arts/McGuffey.* 🎫 *Free.* ⏲ *Tues.–Sat. 10–5, Sun. noon–5.*

At the **Virginia Discovery Museum** children can step inside a giant kaleidoscope or watch bees in action in a real hive. The hands-on exhibits are meant to interest children in science, the arts, history, and the humanities. The computer lab and "make-it-and-take-it" art studio (for ages 2–10) are big attractions. ✉ *524 E. Main St., Downtown,* ☎ *434/977–1025,* WEB *www.vadm.org.* 🎫 *$4.* ⏲ *Tues.–Sat. 10–5, Sun. 1–5.*

In 1773 Thomas Jefferson gave the land that became the **Jefferson Vineyards** to Italian wine maker Filippo Mazzei. Jefferson wanted him to establish a European-style vineyard; Mazzei is said to have found the soil and climate of Virginia better than Italy's. The modern-day operation has consistently produced widely appreciated wines. The winery is open daily for tastings and for free tours, conducted on the hour. ✉ *1353 Thomas Jefferson Pkwy.,* ☎ *434/977–3042 or 800/272–3042,* WEB *www.jeffersonvineyards.com.* 🎫 *Free.* ⏲ *Daily 11–5.*

Oakencroft Vineyard & Winery, with the Blue Ridge Mountains and a lake with geese and other waterfowl as a backdrop, has produced chardonnays, cabernet sauvignons, and clarets. Free tours are offered during open hours. Tastings are $1. ✉ *1486 Oakencroft La.,* ☎ *434/296–4188,* WEB *www.oakencroft.com.* 🎫 *Free.* ⏲ *Apr.–Dec., daily 11–4:30; Mar., weekends 11–4:30.*

Dining and Lodging

$$$–$$$$ ✕ **OXO.** Just off the Downtown Mall, this chic restaurant has created a gastronomic fervor among Charlottesvillians since it opened in 1999. Chef-owner John Haywood puts a modern twist on classic French cuisine and changes the menu every few weeks. Notable entrées include oven-roasted beef tenderloin with truffles, mashed potatoes, and sautéed spinach, and pan-seared snapper wrapped in potato crêpes. The extensive wine list is mostly Californian. ✉ *215 W. Water St., Downtown,* ☎ *434/977–8111. AE, D, MC, V. No lunch.*

$$–$$$ ★ ✕ **C&O Restaurant.** A boarded-up storefront hung with an illuminated Pepsi sign conceals one of the best restaurants in town. The formal dining room upstairs (seatings begin at 6:30), the lively bistro downstairs, and the cozy mezzanine in between share a French-influenced menu that has Pacific Rim and American Southwest touches. For a starter try the veal sweetbreads simmered in cream; the entrées include steak *chinois* (flank steak panfried with soy sauce and fresh ginger cream). The wine list is 300 strong. ✉ *515 E. Water St., Downtown,* ☎ *434/971–7044,* WEB *www.candorestaurant.com. AE, MC, V.*

$$–$$$ ✕ **Duner's.** This former motel diner 5 mi west of Charlottesville fills up early. The fanciful menu, which changes daily, emphasizes fresh, seasonal fare in its seafood and pasta dishes. Appetizers may include lamb and green peppercorn pâté with grilled bread. For an entrée, try morel-mushroom risotto cakes or shrimp in lemongrass and coconut milk over linguine. The red-tile floor and decorative copper pots on the walls keep things bright and warm. The Sunday brunch is an

equally big draw. ✉ *Rte. 250 W, Ivy,* ☎ *434/293–8352. Reservations not accepted. MC, V. No lunch.*

$$–$$$ ★ ✕ **Eastern Standard.** Chef Janet Jospe's fusion cuisine incorporates the cooking of many cultures, especially Asia and the Pacific Rim. Specialties in the formal dining room upstairs include pan-seared duck breast in a barbecue glaze and loin of lamb with mint pesto. Curries and stir-fry Asian dishes are also available. Escafé, a popular bistro downstairs with a big bar and hip furnishings, serves pastas and light fare. ✉ *Downtown Mall, 102 Old Preston Ave., Downtown,* ☎ *434/295–8668,* WEB *www.easternstandard.com. AE, D, DC, MC, V. No lunch. Closed Sun.–Tues.*

$$–$$$ ★ ✕ **Métropolitain.** The kitchen is right in the middle of this airy restaurant, where diners can watch their meal take shape from a relaxed distance. The cuisine is eclectic French-American and reflects the diverse tastes of the restaurant's two owners—one hails from the mountains of West Virginia, the other from Burgundy, France. Especially popular dishes include shrimp cakes with Thai sauce and salmon "filet mignon" with horseradish crust, potato risotto, spinach, and cabernet glaze. Fried grits are also on the menu. ✉ *214 W. Water St., Downtown,* ☎ *434/977–1043. AE, D, MC, V. No lunch.*

$–$$ ★ ✕ **Crozet Pizza.** With up to 35 toppings to choose from, including seasonal items such as snow peas and asparagus spears, this out-of-the-way parlor 12 mi west of Charlottesville is renowned for having some of Virginia's best pizza. On the weekend, takeout must be ordered hours in advance. Diners in the red clapboard restaurant find things rustic, with portraits of the owners' forebears and one wall covered with business cards from around the world. ✉ *Rte. 240, Crozet,* ☎ *434/823–2132. No credit cards. Closed Sun.–Mon.*

$–$$ ✕ **Hamilton's at First and Main.** A local favorite, this Downtown Mall eatery has a warm terra-cotta interior and an eclectic cuisine. Try the pan-roasted halibut on Cuban black bean cake with a citrus salsa, or, if you're a pasta lover, the farfalle tossed with shrimp, country ham, sweet peppers, shiitake, and asparagus. In warmer weather, the outdoor patio doubles as a great perch to people-watch. ✉ *101 W. Main St., Downtown,* ☎ *434/295–6649. MC, V. Closed Sun.*

$ ✕ **Continental Divide.** A neon sign in the window of this locals' favorite says "Get in here"—you might miss the small storefront restaurant otherwise. The food is Southwestern cuisine, with quesadillas, burritos, spicy pork tacos, and enchiladas. The margaritas are potent. Cactus plants decorate the front window, and the booths have funky lights. It can get crowded and convivial, but customers like it that way. ✉ *811 W. Main St., Downtown,* ☎ *434/984–0143. Reservations not accepted. MC, V. No lunch.*

$$$–$$$$ ✕🏨 **Boar's Head Inn.** Set on 55 acres in west Charlottesville, this local landmark resembles an English country inn, with flower gardens, ponds, and a gristmill from 1834. The rooms have king-size four-poster beds and Italian Anichini linens; many have balconies. Some suites have fireplaces. In addition to many other activities, even hot-air ballooning is available, through a nearby outfitter. The Old Mill Room restaurant ($$$$) serves new American cuisine ranging from venison to seafood; the grilled filet mignon is a savory favorite. ✉ *U.S. 250W, Box 5307, 22905, Ednam Forest,* ☎ *434/296–2181 or 800/476–1988,* FAX *434/972–6019,* WEB *www.boarsheadinn.com. 171 rooms, 11 suites. 3 restaurants, cable TV with movies and video games, 18-hole golf course, 20 tennis courts, 4 pools, health club, spa, fishing, racquetball, squash, shop, Internet, meeting rooms. AE, D, DC, MC, V.*

$$–$$$ ★ ✕🏨 **Silver Thatch Inn.** Four-poster beds and period antiques are just part of what give charm to this 1780 white-clapboard Colonial farmhouse, 8 mi north of town. The friendly hosts help their guests arrange

outdoor activities at nearby locations. The popular restaurant ($$$–$$$$) serves contemporary cuisine and has a very fine wine cellar; reservations are required. The chef's grilled beef tenderloin is renowned. ✉ *3001 Hollymead Dr., 22911,* ☎ *434/978–4686 or 800/261–0720,* FAX *434/973–6156,* WEB *www.silverthatch.com. 7 rooms. Restaurant, pool; no room phones, no room TVs, no kids under 14, no smoking. AE, DC, MC, V. BP.*

$$$$ ★ **Keswick Hall at Monticello.** This 1912 Tuscan villa on 600 lush acres 5 mi east of Charlottesville is a luxurious, cosmopolitan retreat. Guest rooms and common areas are decorated in Laura Ashley fabrics and wallpapers, and each room is furnished with English and American antiques. Some have whirlpool baths and balconies. The 18-hole golf course, designed by Arnold Palmer, spreads across the rear of the estate. There is no check-in desk here; you are welcomed inside as if you are entering someone's home. The facilities of the private Keswick Club are open to those staying overnight. ✉ *701 Club Dr., Keswick 22947,* ☎ *434/979–3440 or 800/274–5391,* FAX *434/977–4171,* WEB *www.keswick.com. 44 rooms, 4 suites. 2 restaurants, dining room, cable TV with movies, 18-hole golf course, 5 tennis courts, 2 pools (1 indoor), health club, spa, fishing, bicycles, croquet, meeting rooms, some pets allowed (fee). AE, DC, MC, V.*

$$$–$$$$ ★ **Clifton, the Country Inn.** In this circa 1800 manor house lived Thomas Mann Randolph, a son-in-law of Thomas Jefferson who served as governor of Virginia and as a member of the U.S. Congress. Each guest room retains its original fireplace (plentifully stocked with firewood), and down comforters cover the antique beds, making the quarters cozy. The former livery and carriage houses have been converted into rustic hideaways, as has Randolph's law office overlooking the Rivanna River, which is now the honeymoon cottage. The dining room's menu changes nightly. A five- or six-course prix-fixe meal costs $55 on weekdays and $65 on Friday and Saturday. ✉ *1296 Clifton Inn Dr., 7 mi east of Charlottesville on U.S. 250, 22911,* ☎ *434/971–1800 or 888/971–1800,* FAX *434/971–7098,* WEB *www.timeandplacehomes.com/properties/charlottesville/cliftoninn. 7 rooms, 7 suites. Restaurant, tennis court, pool, lake, hot tub, fishing, croquet, hiking, volleyball; no room TVs, no smoking. MC, V. BP.*

$$–$$$ **Omni Charlottesville.** This attractive member of the luxury chain looms over one end of the Downtown Mall. The triangular rooms at the point of the wedge-shape building get light from two sides. Blond wood and maroon fabrics, in a mixture of modern and Colonial styles, decorate the guest quarters, and potted plants soften the look of the bright seven-story atrium lobby. ✉ *235 W. Main St., Downtown, 22902,* ☎ *434/971–5500 or 800/843–6664,* FAX *434/979–4456,* WEB *www.omnihotels.com. 204 rooms, 7 suites. Restaurant, cable TV with movies and video games, 2 pools (1 indoor), gym, hot tub, sauna, bar, Internet. AE, DC, MC, V.*

$$–$$$ **200 South Street Inn.** Two houses, one of them a former brothel, have been combined and restored to create this old-fashioned inn in the historic district, one block from the Downtown Mall. Furnishings throughout are English and Belgian antiques. Several rooms come with a canopy bed, sitting room, fireplace, and whirlpool. ✉ *200 South St., Downtown, 22901,* ☎ *434/979–0200 or 800/964–7008,* FAX *434/979–4403,* WEB *www.southstreetinn.com. 17 rooms, 3 suites. Cable TV, Internet; no smoking. AE, MC, V. BP.*

$–$$$ **High Meadows Vineyard Inn.** Two styles of architecture are joined by a hall in this bed-and-breakfast (and working vineyard). Listed on the National Register of Historic Places, the inn is 15 mi south of Monticello. Five rooms in the Victorian section, three rooms in the Federal section, and four rooms in the Queen Anne section have curtains and bed hangings with a handcrafted look. The kitchen will prepare hot take-out meals with dishes such as crêpes and quiche Monday through Wednesday. Dinner is served in the dining room by reservation Thursday through Sunday. Hors d'oeuvres and samples of Virginia wines are available on the weekend. ✉ *55 High Meadows La., Scottsville 24590,* ☎ *434/286–2218 or 800/232–1832,* FAX *434/286–2124,* WEB *www.highmeadows.com. 9 rooms, 2 suites, 3 cottages. Dining room, some pets allowed. AE, D, MC, V. BP.*

$ **Best Western Cavalier Inn.** This facility's best feature is its location, directly across the street from the grounds of the University of Virginia and one block from the sports arena. Rates include a deluxe Continental breakfast. ✉ *105 Emmet St., University, 22905,* ☎ *434/296–8111,* FAX *434/290–3523,* WEB *www.bestwestern.com. 118 rooms. Restaurant, cable TV, pool, lounge, Internet, meeting rooms, airport shuttle, some pets allowed. AE, D, DC, MC, V. CP.*

$ **English Inn.** A model treatment of the B&B theme on a large but comfortable scale, the English Inn has a three-story atrium lobby with cascading plants. The suites have a sitting room, wet bar, king-size bed, and reproduction antiques; other rooms have modern furnishings. ✉ *2000 Morton Dr., 22901,* ☎ *434/971–9900 or 800/786–5400,* FAX *434/977–8008,* WEB *www.wytestone.com. 67 rooms, 21 suites. Cable TV, indoor pool, gym, sauna. AE, DC, MC, V. BP.*

Nightlife and the Arts

For listings of cultural events, music, and movies, and a guide to restaurants, pick up a free copy of the *C-Ville Weekly* (WEB www.c-ville.com) an arts and entertainment newspaper available in restaurants and hotels throughout the city. If you are near the University of Virginia campus, grab a free copy of the student newspaper the *Cavalier Daily* (WEB www.cavalierdaily.com) for the latest on college sports and events.

BARS AND CLUBS

Miller's (✉ 109 W. Main St., Downtown Mall, Downtown, ☎ 434/971–8511), a large and comfortable bar, hosts blues, folk, and jazz musicians. Rock musician Dave Matthews used to tend bar here. **Tokyo Rose** (✉ 2171 Ivy Rd., University, ☎ 434/295–7673) is a sushi bar that doubles as a performance space for up-and-coming independent rock bands.

COFFEEHOUSES

Prism Coffeehouse (✉ 214 Rugby Rd., University, ☎ 434/977–7476, WEB www.theprism.org) has been a venue for folk music since a group of university students opened it in 1966. National acoustic acts range from Appalachian string band to bluegrass to Irish music. No smoking or alcohol is allowed. It's closed July–August.

MUSIC AND THEATER

Every autumn, Charlottesville hosts the **Virginia Film Festival** (☎ 800/882–3378, WEB www.vafilm.com), with screenings of important new movies, panel discussions, and appearances by stars of the cinema. The movies are shown at four sites around the university and downtown.

Outdoor Activities and Sports

CANOEING AND KAYAKING

James River Runners Inc. (✉ 10082 Hatton Ferry Rd., Scottsville, ☎ 434/286–2338), about 35 minutes south of Charlottesville, offers canoe, kayak, tubing, and rafting trips down the James.

Shopping

Charlottesville ranks as one of the top 10 book markets nationally (and claims the top spot for the most avid-reading households). The city's independent bookstores, especially those that specialize in used and antiquarian books, are great for a visit. Whether it's a rare first edition you are seeking or just some unique bargains, try **Blue Whale Books** (✉ 115 W. Main St., Downtown, ☎ 434/296–4646). Run by an antiquarian book dealer, the shop has thousands of books in all categories and price ranges, from one dollar to several hundred. **Daedalus Bookshop** (✉ 123 4th St. NE, Downtown, ☎ 434/293–7595) has three floors of books crammed into every nook and cranny.

The **Downtown Mall** (✉ Main St., Downtown) is a six-block brick pedestrian mall with specialty stores, cinemas, art galleries, restaurants, and coffeehouses in restored 19th- and early 20th-century buildings.

En Route Between Charlottesville and Orange, **Barboursville Vineyards** was the first vineyard in the state to grow only vinifera grapes (vinifera are of European origin; other vineyards were using American hybrids at the time) and one of its top award winners. The grapes were planted in 1976 by the sixth generation of an Italian viticulturalist dynasty on the former plantation of James Barbour, governor of the commonwealth from 1812 to 1814. His house, designed by Jefferson to resemble Monticello, was gutted by fire in 1884; the ruins remain. During the first three weekends of August, "Shakespeare at the Ruins" presents outdoor performances of the Bard's classics in this impressive setting. *✉ 17655 Winery Rd. (near intersection of Rtes. 20 and 23), Barboursville, ☎ 540/832–3824, WEB www.barboursvillewine.com. 🎫 Tours free, tastings $3. Theater performances $14. ⏲ Tastings Mon.–Sat. 10–5, Sun. 11–5. Tours weekends 10–4.*

Orange

❸ *25 mi northeast of Charlottesville (via Rte. 20), 60 mi northwest of Richmond.*

Orange is a fertile agricultural area bearing reminders of the Civil War. Among the many estates dotting the countryside is the home of our nation's fourth president.

The **James Madison Museum** presents a comprehensive exhibition on the Founding Father most responsible for the Constitution (Madison became president in 1809). The collection includes some of the china and glassware recovered from the White House before the British torched it during the War of 1812. The fourth president's tiny Campeachy chair, an 18th-century piece made for him by his friend Thomas Jefferson, reveals his small stature. *✉ 129 Caroline St., ☎ 540/672–1776. 🎫 $4. ⏲ Mar.–Nov., weekdays 9–4, Sat. 9–1, Sun. 1–4; Dec.–Feb., weekdays 9–4.*

St. Thomas's Episcopal Church (1833), the one surviving example of Jeffersonian church architecture, is a replica of Charlottesville's demolished Christ Church, which Jefferson designed. It is here that Robert E. Lee worshiped during the winter of 1863–64. The church's biggest decorative asset is its Tiffany window. *✉ 119 Caroline St., ☎ 540/672–3761. 🎫 Donation. ⏲ Tours by appointment.*

During the Civil War, a handsome Greek revival hotel, now the **Exchange Hotel Civil War Museum,** was transformed into a Confederate receiving hospital for wounded and dying soldiers. They were brought by the trainload from nearby battlefields to the railroad platform in front of the hotel. In addition to numerous weapons, uniforms, and personal effects of both Union and Confederate soldiers, the museum displays the often crude medical equipment used for amputations, tooth extractions, and bloodletting. One room re-creates a military surgery room, complete with a straw-covered floor to soak up blood.

Another re-creates a hospital ward; an estimated 70,000 soldiers were treated here between 1862 and 1865. ✉ *400 S. Main St., Gordonsville,* ☎ *540/832–2944.* 🎫 *$4.* ⏲ *Mar.–May and Sept.–Dec., Tues.–Sat. 10–4; June–Aug., Tues.–Sat. 10–4, Sun. 1–4.*

Just outside of Orange is **Montpelier,** the former residence of James Madison (1751–1836), the fourth president of the United States. Yet Montpelier in its current state has more to do with its 20th-century owners, the Du Pont family, who enlarged and redecorated it. This dual legacy poses a dilemma in the restoration; today, the house only vaguely resembles the way it was in Madison's time. Markings on walls, floors, and ceilings, which show the locations of underlying door and window frames and other features, are part of the slow and diligent restoration in progress by the National Trust. A tour begins at the visitor center with a short film about the house and Madison's legacy. As you walk around the mostly empty rooms, you can hear about various aspects of the property through headphones. The landscape walking tour includes a stop at the cemetery where James and his wife, Dolley, are buried. The annual Montpelier Hunt Races, which are a steeplechase, have been held since 1934. When they run, on the first Saturday in November, the house tour is canceled. Admission to the races is $15. ✉ *Rte. 20, 4 mi southwest of Orange,* ☎ *540/672–2728,* WEB *www.montpelier.org.* 🎫 *$9.* ⏲ *Apr.–Nov., daily 9:30–5; Dec.–Mar., daily 9:30–4:30.*

Dining and Lodging

$$$$ ★ ✕🏨 **Willow Grove Inn.** This carefully preserved 1778 Virginia plantation house, an example of Jeffersonian classical revival architecture, served as an encampment during the Revolutionary War and lay under siege during the Civil War. On 37 acres 1 mi north of Orange, the inn has antique four-poster beds and heirloom furnishings from the 18th and 19th centuries. Rooms in the weaver's cottage and two-room schoolhouse have fireplaces and private verandas. A baby grand piano accompanies the candelight dining in the formal dining room ($$$$), where prix-fixe dinners are served. The frequently changing menu's regional Southern dishes may include smoked Rappahannock trout cakes, toasted peanut- and pecan-crusted rack of lamb, or grilled quail with corn pudding, maple-grilled breast of duck, pan-seared salmon with country ham, and Carolina shrimp creole. Clark's Tavern ($) is more casual, with items such as panfried catfish and crayfish étouffée. ✉ *14079 Plantation Way, 22960,* ☎ *540/672–5982 or 800/949–1778,* FAX *540/672–3674,* WEB *www.willowgroveinn.com. 5 rooms, 5 suites. Restaurant, bar, pub, Internet, some pets allowed. AE, D, DC, MC, V. MAP.*

$$–$$$$ 🏨 **Mayhurst Inn.** An architectural rarity in the South, this Italianate Victorian mansion was built in 1859 by a grandnephew of James Madison, and generals Stonewall Jackson and Robert E. Lee were early guests. Now Mayhurst is a cozy and comfortable B&B surrounded by 37 acres of woods with hiking trails. Its rooms have floor-to-ceiling windows, marble fireplaces, and antique furnishings. Some have whirlpool baths. The inn is on U.S. 15 in Orange. ✉ *12460 Mayhurst La., 22960,* ☎ *540/672–5597 or 888/672–5597,* FAX *540/672–7447,* WEB *www.mayhurstinn.com. 5 rooms, 2 suites. Fishing, hiking; no TV in some rooms, no smoking. AE, MC, V. BP.*

Washington

❹ *63 mi north of Charlottesville.*

Known as Little Washington to differentiate it from its big sister, this tiny town packs in antiques shops, galleries, custom jewelry shops, and two theaters in roughly five blocks—perfect for an afternoon stroll.

Dining and Lodging

$$$$ ★ ✕🏨 **The Inn at Little Washington.** What began as a small-town eatery in 1978 has grown into a legend. The rich interior of the three-story white-frame inn is the work of Joyce Conway-Evans, who has designed theatrical sets and rooms in English royal houses. Plush canopy beds, marble bathrooms, and fresh flowers make the rooms sumptuous. Chef Patrick O'Connell's much-loved New American food is served in a slate-floor dining room with William Morris wallpaper. The seven-course dinner costs $128 per person on Saturday, $108 on Friday and Sunday, and $98 on weekdays, not including wine and drinks. ✉ *Middle and Main Sts., 22747,* ☎ *540/675–3800,* FAX *540/675–3100. 11 rooms, 3 suites. Restaurant, in-room safes, bicycles. MC, V. Hotel and restaurant closed Tues. except in May and Oct. CP.*

$$–$$$ ✕🏨 **Bleu Rock Inn.** This renovated farmhouse is set on 80 bucolic acres against a backdrop of the Blue Ridge Mountains, with a fishing pond, rolling pastures, and 7½ acres of vineyards spread across the foreground. An equestrian center on site boards horses (you may bring your own) and trains them for riders; there's also a polo ring and steeplechase course. The guest rooms, simply furnished with light woods and lace curtains, are pleasing; the four upstairs have private balconies. Reservations are taken no later than three months in advance for the hotel, but the French country-style food ($$–$$$) is the real star here. The dishes include roasted salmon with a tapenade crust and niçoise polenta with a red wine sauce. Delicious seasonal desserts include, in the summer, key lime cake with fresh strawberry sauce. The restaurant is closed Monday and Tuesday. ✉ *12567 Lee Hwy., 22747,* ☎ *540/987–3190,* FAX *540/987–3193,* WEB *www.bleurockinn.com. 5 rooms. Restaurant, fishing, hiking, horseback riding, pub, some pets allowed; no room phones, no room TVs. AE, D, DC, MC, V. BP.*

Wintergreen Resort

❺ *25 mi southwest of Charlottesville, via I–64 and Rte. 151 (Exit 114), 13 mi south of southern entrance of Shenandoah National Park, via Blue Ridge Pkwy.*

With 6,700 acres of forest, six restaurants, and three golf courses, Wintergreen is more like a community in itself than just a resort. Skiing and snowboarding are the central attractions, with 20 downhill slopes and five chairlifts. Wintergreen's snowmaking crew has been featured on The Weather Channel for its ability to keep the slopes white even when Old Man Winter isn't cooperative. On milder winter weekends you can even ski and golf on the same day for the price of a lift ticket. In summer, the stunning Blue Ridge location means that hiking, mountain biking, horseback riding, golf, tennis, and swimming can all be done in the cool that comes with a high elevation. One of the golf courses, at nearly 4,000 ft, is the highest in Virginia.

OFF THE BEATEN PATH

CRABTREE FALLS – A series of cascades falls a distance of 1,200 ft. Taken together, Virginia claims these cascades as the highest waterfall east of the Rockies, though no single waterfall within the series would qualify as such. Whatever the superlatives or qualifications, the falls are a wondrous sight. A trail winds up a steep mountainside all the way to the top, but the first overlook is an easy stroll just 700 ft from the lower parking lot. The best time to see the waterfalls is winter through spring, when the water is high. ✉ *Rte. 56, 6 mi east of Blue Ridge Pkwy., or 19 mi from Wintergreen by following Rte. 151 south and then Rte. 56 west at Roseland.*

Dining and Lodging

$$–$$$$ **Wintergreen Resort.** Accommodations at the resort include everything from studio apartments to seven-bedroom houses. Most rooms have fireplaces and full kitchens; the housing units' wood exteriors blend into the surrounding forest. ✉ *Rte. 664, Wintergreen 22958,* ☎ *434/325–2200 or 800/266–2444,* FAX *434/325–8003,* WEB *www.wintergreenresort.com. 305 units. 6 restaurants, 2 18-hole golf courses, 9-hole golf course, 24 tennis courts, 2 pools (1 indoor), lake, gym, spa, boating, bicycles, hiking, horseback riding, downhill skiing, bar, convention center. AE, MC, V.*

Lynchburg

❻ *66 mi southeast of Charlottesville (via Rte. 29), 110 mi west of Richmond.*

Although the city's founder, John Lynch, was a Quaker pacifist, its most prominent landmark is Monument Terrace, a war memorial: at the foot and head of the 139 limestone and granite steps that ascend to the Old City Courthouse are statues honoring a World War I doughboy and a Confederate soldier. If you're hesitant to make the climb, at least catch the dramatic view from the bottom of Court House Hill, at Main and 9th streets. Self-guided walking tours designed by the Lynchburg Visitors Information Center cover the historic Riverfront and Diamond Hill sections.

At the **Anne Spencer House** you can step into "Edankraal," the studio of this late poet of the Harlem Renaissance. Hers is the only work of a Virginian to appear in the *Norton Anthology of Modern American and English Poetry.* A librarian at one of Lynchburg's segregated black schools, Spencer (1882–1975) penned most of her work in this backgarden sanctuary, which has been left completely intact with her writing desk, bookcases, mementos, and walls tacked with photos and news clippings. ✉ *1313 Pierce St.,* ☎ *434/847–1459.* *$5.* *Tours by appointment.*

At the **Legacy Museum of African-American History,** the rotating exhibits focus on such themes as health and medicine, education, business, the civil rights struggle, and the contributions African-Americans have made to society, the arts, and politics. ✉ *403 Monroe St.,* ☎ *434/845–3455.* *$2.* *Thurs.–Sat. noon–4, Sun. 2–4.*

The **Pest House Medical Museum** is on the grounds of the **Confederate Cemetery,** where a garden of 60 rosebushes has varieties dating from 1565 to 1900. The museum provides a brief but informative look into medical practices and instruments at the time of the Civil War and later. The 1840s frame building was the office of Dr. John Jay Terrell. ✉ *4th and Taylor Sts.,* ☎ *434/847–1465.* *Free.* *Daily dawn–dusk.*

The mansion on Daniel's Hill, **Point of Honor,** was built in 1815 on the site of a duel. Once part of a 900-acre estate, this redbrick house surrounded by lawns retains a commanding view of the James River. The facade is elegantly symmetrical, with two octagonal bays joined by a balustrade on each of the building's two stories. The interiors have been restored and furnished with pieces authentic to the early 19th-century Federal period, including wallpaper whose pattern is in the permanent collection of New York's Metropolitan Museum of Art. ✉ *112 Cabell St.,* ☎ *434/847–1459,* WEB *www.pointofhonor.org.* *$5.* *Daily 10–4.*

★ Less than 5 mi southwest of Lynchburg, **Thomas Jefferson's Poplar Forest** is an impressive piece of octagonal architecture, now surrounded by only a few remaining poplars. Conceived and built by Jefferson as his "occasional retreat" (he sometimes stayed here between 1806 and 1813), this Palladian hermitage exemplifies the architect's sublime sense of order that is so evident at Monticello. Erected on a slope, the house has a front that's one story high, with a two-story rear elevation. The octagon's center is a square, skylit dining room flanked by two smaller octagons. As the ongoing restoration continues, additions made by later owners of the estate are being undone and the property is gradually being returned to Jefferson's original design. Every July 4, there's a free celebration that includes a reading of the Declaration of Independence and living-history exhibits. ✉ *Rte. 661, Forest,* ☎ *434/525–1806,* WEB *www.poplarforest.org.* 🎫 *$7.* ⏲ *Apr.–Nov., daily 10–4.*

OFF THE BEATEN PATH

APPOMATTOX COURT HOUSE – Twenty-five miles east of Lynchburg, the village of Appomattox Court House has been restored to its appearance of April 9, 1865. It was on that day that the Confederate General Lee surrendered the Army of Northern Virginia to General Grant. There are 27 structures in the national historical park; most can be entered. A highlight is the reconstructed McLean House, in whose parlor the articles of surrender were signed. The self-guided tour is well planned and introduced by exhibits and slide shows in the reconstructed courthouse. Interpreters cast as soldiers and villagers answer questions in the summer. ✉ *3 mi north of Appomattox, on State Rte. 24,* ☎ *434/352–8987.* 🎫 *$4.* ⏲ *June–Aug., daily 9–5:30; Sept.–May, daily 8:30–5.*

RED HILL–PATRICK HENRY NATIONAL MEMORIAL – In the town of Brookneal is the final home of Revolutionary War patriot Patrick Henry, whose "Give me liberty or give me death" speech inspired a generation. The 1770s house has been reconstructed on its original site and contains numerous furnishings owned by the Henry family. Other buildings, including a coachman's cabin and stable, stand near a formal boxwood garden. Henry's grave is on the property. ✉ *35 mi southeast of Lynchburg, off Rte. 619, Brookneal,* ☎ *434/376–2044.* 🎫 *$6.* ⏲ *Apr.–Oct., daily 9–5; Nov.–Mar., daily 9–4.*

Dining

$–$$ ✕ **Meriwether's Market Restaurant.** Here you'll find American dishes generally made with local and regional ingredients, from game to seafood. For an entrée, try the spicy shrimp and grits, or a specialty pizza. A lighter "intermezzo" menu is available to carry you through the lull between lunch and dinner (2:30–5:30). ✉ *4925 Boonsboro Rd.,* ☎ *434/384–3311,* WEB *www.meriwethers.com. AE, D, MC, V. Closed Sun.*

Outdoor Activities and Sports

BIKING

Lynchburg's fine municipal "greenway" system of trails is open to both bicyclists and hikers. The **Blackwater Creek Natural Area** has more than 12 mi of trails, most of them level and asphalt, that wind through a pleasant tree-shaded natural area within the city limits. One trail goes through a 500-ft tunnel. The **Percival's Island Trail,** only three blocks from one edge of the natural area and in the shadow of the downtown skyline, extends for more than a mile along a narrow strip of land in the middle of the James River. To rent a bike or get more information on greenways, contact **Blackwater Creek Bike Rental** (✉ 1611 Concord Turnpike, ☎ 434/845–4030, ⏲ weekdays 1–6, weekends 9–sunset).

Shenandoah National Park

Southern entrance 18 mi west of Charlottesville (via I–81); northern entrance at Front Royal.

This "Daughter of the Stars," which is the translation for the Native American word *Shenandoah,* extends more than 80 mi south along the Blue Ridge Mountains, with several gaps in the range forming passes between the Shenandoah Valley on the west and the Piedmont on the east. Within the park's boundaries are some 60 peaks.

Hardwood and pine forests cover the slopes, where mountain meadows full of wildflowers open up to gorgeous panoramas that can be viewed from numerous turnoffs. Hikers and campers find beautiful terrain just yards from the highway, trout fishers may wade into more than 25 streams in seven counties, and riders can rent horses for wilderness trail rides. Those who want to know more about the area's flora and fauna may want to take a guided hike, which naturalists lead daily throughout the summer. The seasonal activities of the park are outlined in the *Shenandoah Overlook,* a free newspaper you can pick up on entering the park. The park parallels I–81; the northern limit at Front Royal is close to I–66, and the southern end at Waynesboro is close to I–64. ✉ *Park Superintendent, Box 348, Rte. 4, Luray 22835,* ☎ *540/999–3500,* WEB *www.nps.gov/shen or www.visitshenandoah.com.* 🎟 *Park (and Skyline Dr.) $10 car; $5 motorcycle, bicycle, or pedestrian; tickets are valid for 7 days.*

Most people see Shenandoah National Park from **Skyline Drive,** a spectacular route that winds 105 mi south from Front Royal to Waynesboro over the mountains of the park. Beauty has its price: holiday and weekend crowds in spring through fall can slow traffic to much less than the 35 mph speed limit. Winter brings many closed facilities and occasionally ice and snow that can close parts of the drive. Nevertheless, for easily accessible wilderness and exciting views, few routes can compete with this one. Just come during the fine weather—and bring a sweater, because temperatures can be brisk.

Outdoor Activities and Sports

CANOEING

Front Royal Canoe (✉ U.S. 340, near Front Royal, ☎ 540/635–5440 or 800/270–8808, WEB www.frontroyalcanoe.com) offers a $14 tube trip as well as canoe, kayak, and raft trips of one hour up to three days for $30–$116. The company also rents boats and sells fishing accessories. At **Downriver Canoe** (✉ Rte. 613, near Front Royal, ☎ 540/635–5526, WEB www.downriver.com), day and overnight trips start at $29 per canoe (or $32 per kayak, $14 per tube, and $59 per raft). **Shenandoah River Outfitters** (✉ Rte. 684, 6502 S. Page Valley Rd., Luray 22835, ☎ 540/743–4159, WEB www.shenandoahriver.com) rents canoes and kayaks starting at $20.

FISHING

To take advantage of the trout that abound in the 50 streams of Shenandoah National Park, you will need a Virginia fishing license; a five-day license costs $5 ($12 for a year) and it's available in season (early April to mid-October) at concession stands along Skyline Drive.

HIKING

The **Appalachian Trail** zigzags back and forth across Skyline Drive through the park, offering easy access by car, variable hike lengths from a few feet to many miles, and connections with the more than 500 mi of the park's own trail network. Volunteers assist the National Park Service in upkeep of the AT, which generally has a smooth surface and gentle grade through the park. Three-sided shelters provide places for long-distance hikers to sleep overnight—or for day hikers to dodge a rain shower. If you're here in May or June, expect to see "thru-hikers" with heavy backpacks trudging on their 2,000-mile journey from

Georgia to Maine. But you don't have to hike 2,000 mi, or even 2,000 ft, to experience the joyous sights of the wilderness—glorious foliage, rock formations, vistas, and perhaps a deer or even a bear.

Lodging

$$–$$$ **Jordan Hollow Farm.** The oldest of the four buildings here is a 1790 farmhouse, now a restaurant serving American regional cuisine. The youngest structure, built of hand-hewn logs almost 200 years later, contains four of the inn's most luxurious rooms, which include a fireplace, whirlpool, and TV. The 150-acre horse farm is near the tiny town of Stanley, 6 mi from Luray and 15 mi from Shenandoah National Park. From here you can gaze out over pastures full of horses and playful llamas toward a backdrop of the Blue Ridge Mountains. The only "pets" allowed are horses: the farm has stables where they may be boarded. Nearby trails are good for both hiking and mountain biking. ✉ *326 Hawksbill Park Rd., Stanley 22851,* ☎ *540/778–2285 or 888/418–7000,* FAX *540/778–1759,* WEB *www.jordanhollow.com. 8 rooms, 7 suites. Restaurant, cable TV, bicycles, hiking, bar, meeting rooms; no smoking. D, DC, MC, V. BP.*

$–$$ **Skyland Lodge.** At the highest point on Skyline Drive (3,680 ft), with views across the Shenandoah Valley, this facility has lodging that ranges from rustic cabins and motel-style rooms to suites. There's no air-conditioning, but days above 80 degrees are rare at these heights. ✉ *Milepost 41.7 on Skyline Dr., 22835,* ☎ *540/999–2211 or 800/999–4714,* FAX *540/999–2231. 177 rooms. Restaurant, bar, Internet, meeting rooms; no a/c, no room phones, no TV in some rooms. AE, D, DC, MC, V. Closed Dec.–mid-Mar.*

$ **The Mimslyn.** Nicknamed "The Grand Old Inn of Virginia," this magnificent antebellumlike hotel just 9 mi west of the park is the place for those who wish to mix their wilderness fun with elegant lodging and dining, at relatively inexpensive rates. Soak in the Blue Ridge scenery while sitting on the column-graced veranda, which has its own bar. Or keep an eye on the gardens from inside the solarium. All rooms are furnished in a traditional manner and have plush beds. The restaurant ($–$$) serves classical American cuisine with a Virginia flair, such as venison, seared quail, and smoked apple pheasant sausage served on steamed red cabbage. ✉ *401 W. Main St., Luray 22835,* ☎ *540/743–5105 or 800/296–5105,* FAX *540/743–2632,* WEB *www.svta.org/mimslyn. 40 rooms, 9 suites. Restaurant, cable TV, lounge, shop, meeting rooms, some pets allowed (fee). AE, D, DC, V, MC.*

Shenandoah National Park. Shenandoah has more than 600 campsites in four campgrounds, plus a fifth primitive campground (Dundo) for large educational groups. The Big Meadows Campground, at the approximate midpoint of the park, accepts reservations; other campsites are available on a first-come, first-served basis. ✉ *Shenandoah National Park, Box 727, Luray 22835,* ☎ *540/999–3231; 800/365–2267 for Big Meadows reservations,* FAX *540/999–3601,* WEB *www.nps.gov/shen. 53 tent-only sites; 164 RV or tent sites, 7 sites for educational groups. Flush toilets, dump station, drinking water, laundry facilities, showers.* *Tent or RV sites $14–$17 per night, group sites $30. AE, D, MC, V.* ⏲ *Spring through Nov.*

En Route Two miles west of the northern entrance to Skyline Drive, **Skyline Caverns** is known for the anthodites, or spiked nodes, growing from its ceilings at an estimated rate of 1 inch every 7,000 years, and for its chambers, which have descriptive names such as the Capital Dome, Rainbow Trail, Fairytale Lake, and Cathedral Hall. ✉ *U.S. 340 S, Front Royal,* ☎ *540/635–4545 or 800/296–4545,* WEB *www.skylinecaverns.com.* *$12.* ⏲ *Mid-Mar.–mid-June, weekdays 9–5, weekends 9–6;*

mid-June–Labor Day, daily 9–6:30; Labor Day–mid-Nov., weekdays 9–5, weekends 9–6; mid-Nov.–mid-Mar., daily 9–4.

Luray Caverns, 9 mi west of Skyline Drive on U.S. 211, are the largest caverns in the state. For millions of years water has seeped through the limestone and clay to create rock and mineral formations. The world's only "stalacpipe organ" is composed of stalactites (calcite formations hanging from the ceilings of the caverns) that have been tuned to concert pitch and are tapped by rubber-tip plungers. The organ is played electronically for every tour and may be played manually on special occasions. A one-hour tour begins every 20 minutes. ✉ *U.S. 211, Luray,* ☎ *540/743–6551,* WEB *www.luraycaverns.com.* 🎫 *$16.* ⏲ *Mid-Mar.–Mid-June, daily 9–6; Mid-June–Labor Day, daily 9-7; Labor Day–Nov., daily 9–6, Nov.–Mid-Mar.*

SHENANDOAH VALLEY

The fertile hills of the Shenandoah Valley reminded Colonial settlers from Germany, Ireland, and Britain of the homelands they left behind. They brought an agrarian lifestyle and Protestant beliefs that eventually spread across much of the Midwest. Today, the valley is full of historic, cultural, and geological places of interest, including Civil War sites; Woodrow Wilson's birthplace, and a reproduction of Shakespeare's Globe Theatre, both at Staunton; many beautifully adorned caverns; and the famous hot mineral springs in the aptly named Bath County.

Winchester

❼ *129 mi north of Charlottesville, 136 mi northwest of Richmond.*

Winchester's small size belies its historical importance. Established in 1752, it served as a headquarters for Col. George Washington during the French and Indian War when it began two years later. During the Civil War, it was an important crossroads near the front line. It changed hands 72 times during the war, and was Gen. Stonewall Jackson's headquarters for nearly two years.

Things are more peaceful today; the biggest attraction is the Shenandoah Apple Blossom Festival in May. Specialty boutiques, regional art galleries, and antiques stores are located throughout the town's 45-block historic district, especially on the six-block pedestrian mall. Winchester's biggest claim to 20th-century fame is as the birthplace of country music legend Patsy Cline; thousands visit her gravesite each year at the Shenandoah Memorial Park cemetery, where a bell tower memorializes her.

Home of Winchester's founder, Colonel James Wood, who called it his "glen of streams," **Glen Burnie Manor House and Gardens** is a 1736 Georgian country estate surrounded by 25 acres of formal gardens. A self-guided tour lets you meander through the beautifully designed rose, pattern, and perennial gardens; a Chinese garden stocked with koi; and even a water garden trickling with waterfalls over mossy rocks. Inside the house are fine antiques, paintings, and decorative objects collected by the last family member to live here, Julian Wood Glass Jr., who died in 1992. ✉ *100 W. Piccadilly St.,* ☎ *540/662–1473.* 🎫 *$8.* ⏲ *Apr.–Oct., Tues.–Sat. 10–4, Sun. noon–4.*

Stonewall Jackson's Headquarters Museum is a restored 1854 home. Jackson used this as his base of operations during the Valley Campaign in 1861–1862. Among the artifacts on display are his prayer book and camp table. The reproduction wallpaper was a gift from the actress Mary Tyler Moore; it was her great-grandfather Lt. Col. Lewis T.

Moore who lent Jackson the use of the house. A $7.50 block ticket purchased at the museum also includes entry to two nearby historical attractions: **George Washington's Office Museum,** a preserved log cabin where Washington briefly lived during the French and Indian War, and **Abram's Delight Museum,** the oldest residence in Winchester. The stone house was owned by Isaac Hollingsworth, a prominent Quaker. ✉ *415 N. Braddock St.,* ☎ *540/667–3242,* WEB *www.winchesterhistory.org.* *$3.50.* ⏲ *Apr.–Oct., Mon.–Sat. 10–4; Sun. noon–4; Nov.–Mar., Fri–Sat. 10–4, Sun. noon–4.*

Dining and Lodging

$$–$$$ ✕ **Violino Ristorante Italiano.** Homemade pasta—about 20 different kinds—fills the menu in this cheery, yellow-stucco restaurant in the city's Old Town. Owners Franco and Marcella Stocco and their son Riccardo (the men are chefs; Marcella manages the dining room) serve up their native northern Italian cuisine, including lobster *pansotti* (lobster-filled ravioli in a sauce of white wine and lemon sauce). A strolling violinist entertains diners on the weekends. The outdoor patio, enclosed by potted plants, is a quiet spot in the midst of street bustle. ✉ *181 N. Loudoun St.,* ☎ *540/667–8006,* WEB *www.nvim.com/violino. AE, D, DC, MC, V. Closed Sun.*

$$–$$$$ ★ ✕ **L'Auberge Provencale.** Chef-owner Alain Borel and his wife, Celeste, of Avignon, France, bring the warm elegance of the south of France to this 1750s country inn, originally a sheep farm owned by Lord Fairfax. Rooms are eclectically decorated with French art and fabrics, and Victorian wicker and antiques; some have fireplaces. Breakfast includes fresh homemade croissants and apple crêpes with maple syrup. The acclaimed prix-fixe restaurant serves authentic Provençale cuisine ($70 per person; reservations essential on weekends). Memorable entrées include fois gras with mango and ginger, and lobster in a vanilla butter sauce. The restaurant serves dinner only and is closed Monday and Tuesday. ✉ *Rte. 340, White Post 22663,* ☎ *540/837–1375 or 800/638–1702,* FAX *540/837–2004,* WEB *www.laubergeprovencale.com. 10 rooms, 4 suites. Restaurant, pool; no room phones, no room TVs, no kids under 10, no smoking. AE, D, MC, V. Closed Jan. BP.*

Middletown

❽ *6 mi south of Winchester.*

Middletown has one of the area's loveliest historic homes. **Belle Grove,** an elegant farmhouse and 100-acre working farm, is a monument to the rural and the refined, two qualities that exist in harmony in the architecture here and throughout the region. Constructed in 1797 out of limestone quarried on the property, the building reflects the influence of Thomas Jefferson, said to have been a consultant. Originally built for Maj. Isaac Hite and his wife, Nelly (President James Madison's sister), this was the headquarters of the Union general Philip Sheridan during the Battle of Cedar Creek (1864), a crucial defeat for the Confederacy. Part of the battle was fought on the farm, and an annual reenactment is held in October with as many as 2,000 participants. Call for the Christmas candlelight tour schedule. ✉ *Rte. 11,* ☎ *540/869–2028,* WEB *www.bellegrove.org.* *$7.* ⏲ *Apr.–Oct., Mon.–Sat. 10–3:15, Sun. 1–4:15.*

Lodging

$$–$$$ **Wayside Inn.** This inn has been welcoming travelers since 1797, when it was a popular stagecoach stop. The 18th century is preserved through the extensive collection of antiques and fine art, which serve to make each room distinct. Some rooms have small bathrooms and lack a view, but all are pleasingly decorated. The dining room offers regional cuisine, such as spoon bread, peanut soup, and country ham. ✉ *7783 Main*

St., 22645, ☎ 540/869–1797, FAX 540/869–6038, WEB www.waysideofva.com. 20 rooms, 2 suites. Restaurant, cable TV, bar, Internet, meeting rooms; no smoking. AE, D, DC, MC, V.

En Route The **Strasburg Antique Emporium** (✉ 150 N. Massanutten St., Strasburg, ☎ 540/465–3711; ⏲ Fri.–Sat. 10–7, Sun.–Thurs. 10–5), 5 mi south of Middletown, covers 1.4 acres. It's in the quirky and historic downtown of Strasburg, which was settled by Germans. Inside the emporium, more than 100 dealers and artisans sell everything from furniture to jewelry to vintage clothing.

Adjacent to the Strasburg Antique Emporium, the **Museum of American Presidents** (✉ 130 N. Massanutten St., Strasburg, ☎ 540/465–8175; 🎟 $3 for president's museum; $8 for both museums; ⏲ Mon.–Sat. 10–5, Sun. 1–5) displays memorabilia of each American president from George Washington to George W. Bush. The prized possession is a desk where James Madison wrote some of his most important papers. Upstairs, the **Jeane Dixon Museum** includes the possessions, furnishings, books, and papers from the last apartment of the famous psychic.

New Market

❾ *35 mi southwest of Middletown (via I–81).*

At New Market the Confederates had a victory at the late date of 1864. Inside the Hall of Valor, in the 260-acre **New Market Battlefield Historical Park,** a stained-glass window mosaic commemorates the battle, in which 257 Virginia Military Institute cadets, some as young as 15, were mobilized to improve the odds against superior Union numbers; 10 were killed. This circular building contains a chronology of the war, and a short film deals with Stonewall Jackson's legendary campaign in the Shenandoah Valley. A farmhouse that figured in the fighting still stands on the premises. The battle is reenacted at the park each May. ✉ *I–81 (Exit 264),* ☎ *540/740–3101.* 🎟 *$8.* ⏲ *Daily 9–5.*

The **New Market Battlefield Military Museum** stands in the area where the New Market battle began in May 1864. The front of the building is a reproduction of Arlington, Robert E. Lee's house outside of Washington, D.C. The museum has more than 3,000 artifacts from American wars, from the Revolution through modern conflicts. Two-thirds deal with the Civil War, but the museum's most curious possession may be the camouflage fatigues worn by Panamanian dictator Manuel Noriega. A 35-minute movie on the Civil War is shown. ✉ *9500 Collins Dr., off U.S. 211,* ☎ *540/740–8065.* 🎟 *$7.* ⏲ *Mid-Mar.–Dec., daily 9–5.*

OFF THE BEATEN PATH

SHENANDOAH CAVERNS – The spectacular calcite formations found here, including a series resembling strips of bacon, were formed by water dripping through long, narrow cracks in the limestone. The colored lighting effects help differentiate the sparkling calcite crystals. The caverns are accessible to those in wheelchairs. Also on the grounds is **American Celebration on Parade,** an exhibit of floats from parades across America throughout the last 50 years. ✉ *261 Caverns Rd. (I–81, Exit 269),* ☎ *540/477–3115,* WEB *www.shenandoahcaverns.com.* 🎟 *$13 for caverns only; $8 for float exhibit only; $17.50 for both.* ⏲ *Mid-June–Labor Day, daily 9–6:15; Labor Day–Oct., 9–5:15; Nov.–mid-Apr., 9–4:15; mid-Apr.–mid-June, 9–5:15.*

ENDLESS CAVERNS – These caverns were discovered in 1879 by two boys and a dog chasing a rabbit. Opened to the public in 1920, the seemingly endless configurations of the caverns have baffled numerous explorers. The tour is enhanced by lighting effects, especially at "Snow

Drift," where a sudden illumination emphasizes the white powdery appearance of the "drift" in a room tinted brown and yellow. ✉ *3 mi south of New Market on Rte. 11 (Exit 264 or 257 off I–81),* ☎ *540/896–2283,* WEB *home1.gte.net/endless.* 💳 *$12.* ⏲ *Mid-Mar.–mid-June and Labor Day–early Nov., daily 9–5; mid-June–Labor Day, daily 9–7; mid-Nov.–mid-Mar., daily 9–4.*

Dining

$$ ✕ **Parkhurst Restaurant.** The main dining room's white walls are decorated with baskets and mirrors, and in the glass-enclosed porch, meals are served within sight of greenery all year long. The menu, international in character, may include grilled quail; curried chicken accompanied by fresh-fruit condiments; or veal Oscar (with Alaskan king crab, asparagus, and béarnaise). Local vintages are available by the glass, and many microbrews are also on hand. ✉ *U.S. 211 W,* ☎ *540/743–6009. AE, DC, MC, V.*

Outdoor Activities and Sports

FISHING

Murray's Fly Shop (✉ 121 Main St., Edinburg, ☎ 540/984–4212), 15 mi north of New Market, is the place for advice on fishing the Shenandoah River or local trout streams. The store sells more than 30,000 flies and has hundreds of rods and reels to choose from.

Harrisonburg

⑩ *18 mi southwest of New Market (via Exit 251 from I–81).*

Though the workaday market town is often bypassed for the rich farmlands that surround it, Harrisonburg is worth a visit. Settled in 1739, it's a stronghold of Mennonites, who wear plain clothes and drive horse-drawn buggies. The city is also a center of higher education, with James Madison University and Eastern Mennonite College in town and Bridgewater College nearby.

At the **Virginia Quilt Museum,** you can see examples of quilts made throughout the mid-Atlantic region and learn about the international heritage of quilting. ✉ *301 S. Main St., Harrisonburg,* ☎ *540/433–3818.* 💳 *$4.* ⏲ *Mon. and Thurs.–Sat. 10–4, Sun. 1–4.*

Dining and Lodging

$$ ★ ✕🏨 **Joshua Wilton House.** A row of trees guards the privacy of this circa 1888 B&B, decorated in the Victorian style and set on a large yard at the edge of the "Old Town" district. The sunroom and back patio are built for relaxation. Ask for Room 4; it has a lace-draped canopy bed and a turret sitting area with a view of the Blue Ridge Mountains looming over Main Street. Room 2 has a fireplace. The restaurant's menu changes daily, its components supplied by many small, local organic farmers. As an appetizer, try the smoked salmon on apple potato cake with dill crème fraîche; for a main dish, try the grilled stuffed pork tenderloin. More casual dining is offered in the café. ✉ *412 S. Main St., 22801,* ☎ *540/434–4464,* FAX *540/432–9525. 5 rooms. Restaurant, café, some in-room data ports; no room TVs, no kids under 8, no smoking. AE, DC, MC, V. BP.*

Shopping

The dozens of **antiques shops** in the Harrisonburg area are generally on or near Route 11. Contact the Harrisonburg-Rockingham Convention and Visitors Bureau for a list, or just keep an eye open while driving through communities such as Bridgewater, Dayton, Elkton, Mount Crawford, Mount Sydney, Verona, and Weyer's Cave.

OFF THE BEATEN PATH

NATURAL CHIMNEYS REGIONAL PARK – In Mount Solon, 23 mi south of Harrisonburg, these seven freestanding limestone pylons stand from 65 to 120 ft tall and are slender like the pillars of an Egyptian temple ruin. The 500-million-year-old formations were created by some form of natural action, though their exact origins are unknown. Facilities include connecting nature trails and a swimming pool. Every June and August a jousting tournament is held at the site. ✉ *I–81 (Exit 240 W), Mount Solon 22843,* ☎ *540/350–2510.* *$3 per person; $6 maximum fee per car.* ⏲ *Daily 9–dusk.*

Dayton

⓫ *2 mi west of Harrisonburg (via Rte. 33 off I–81).*

Dayton is best known for its large Mennonite population, whose black horse-drawn buggies share the road with latter-day SUVs. At the **Shenandoah Valley Folk Art & Heritage Center,** multimedia folk art reflects the largely German and Scotch-Irish culture of the valley. Among the various displays is a Civil War exhibit with an electric map that traces Stonewall Jackson's famous 1862 Valley Campaign. ✉ *382 High St.,* ☎ *540/879–2616 or 540/879–2681,* WEB *www.heritagecenter.com.* *$5.* ⏲ *Mon.–Sat. 10–4.*

Also known as the Daniel Harrison House, **Fort Harrison** (from circa 1749) is of fortified stone and decorated in prosperous frontier style. Costumed interpreters discuss how the furnishings—beds with ropes as slats and hand-quilted comforters—were made. Artifacts on display come from recent excavations undertaken adjacent to the house. ✉ *Rte. 42,* ☎ *540/879–2280.* *Free; donation encouraged.* ⏲ *Mid-May–Oct., weekends 1–5.*

Shopping

The **Dayton Farmers Market** (✉ Rte. 42, south of Dayton, ☎ 540/879–9885), an 18,000-square-ft area, has homemade baked goods and fresh fruits and vegetables as well as butter churns and ceramic speckleware, made by the Mennonites who live in the area. It's one place to mingle with the craftspeople, as well as with students from James Madison University in nearby Harrisonburg. It's open Thursday–Sunday.

Staunton

⓬ *27 mi south of Dayton (via I–81), 11 mi west of southern end of Skyline Dr. at Waynesboro (off I–64).*

Staunton (pronounced *stan*-ton) is a town with a distinguished past. This was once the seat of government of the vast Augusta County, which formed in 1738 and encompassed present-day West Virginia, Kentucky, Ohio, Illinois, Indiana, and the Pittsburgh area. After the state's General Assembly fled here from the British in 1781, Staunton was briefly the state's capital. Woodrow Wilson (1856–1924), the nation's 27th president and the eighth president from Virginia, is a native son.

The **Woodrow Wilson Birthplace and Museum** has period antiques, items from Wilson's political career, and some original pieces from when this museum was the residence of Wilson's father, a Presbyterian minister. Wilson's presidential limousine, a 1919 Pierce-Arrow sedan, is on display in the garage. ✉ *24 N. Coalter St.,* ☎ *540/885–0897 or 888/496–6376.* *$7.* ⏲ *Mon.–Sat. 10–5, Sun. noon–5.*

★ The **Frontier Culture Museum,** an outdoor living museum, re-creates agrarian life in America. The four illustrative farmsteads, American, Scotch-Irish, German, and English, were painstakingly moved from their original site and reassembled on the museum grounds. The livestock and plants here resemble the historic breeds and varieties as closely as possible. Special programs and activities, held throughout the year, include soap and broom making, cornhusking bees, and supper and barn dances. ✉ *1250 Richmond Rd. (off I–81, Exit 222 to Rte. 250 W),* ☎ *540/332–7850,* WEB *www.frontiermuseum.org.* *$8.* ⏲ *Dec.–mid-Mar., daily 10–4; mid-Mar.–Nov., daily 9–5.*

OFF THE BEATEN PATH

GRAND CAVERNS – Discovered in 1804 and opened to the public just two years later, Augusta County's Grand Caverns, 23 mi from Staunton, is America's oldest show cave. Thomas Jefferson paid an early visit, and Civil War troops from both sides were among those who descended into the subterranean wonderland. One highlight: an underground room that's one of the largest of its kind in the East. ✉ *I–81 (Exit 235),* ☎ *540/249–5705.* *$13.50.* ⏲ *Apr.–Oct., daily 9–5; Mar., weekends 9–5.*

Dining and Lodging

$–$$ ★ ✕ **Mrs. Rowe's Restaurant.** A homey restaurant with plenty of booths, Rowe's has been operated by the same family since 1947 and enjoys a rock-solid reputation for inexpensive and delicious Southern meals. The fried chicken—skillet-cooked to order—is a standout. A local breakfast favorite is oven-hot biscuits topped with gravy (your choice of sausage, tenderloin, or creamy chipped beef). For dessert, try the mince pie in the fall or the rhubarb cobbler in summer. ✉ *I–81 (Exit 222),* ☎ *540/886–1833,* WEB *www.mrsrowes.com. D, MC, V.*

$$–$$$$ ✕ **Belle Grae Inn.** The sitting room and music room of this restored 1870 Victorian house have been converted into formal dining rooms, with brass wall sconces, Oriental rugs, and candles at the tables. The menu ($$$$), which changes weekly, has Continental cuisine with a regional flair. Accommodations are furnished with antique rocking chairs and canopied or brass beds; a complimentary snifter of brandy awaits in each one. ✉ *515 W. Frederick St., 24401,* ☎ *540/886–5151 or 888/541–5151,* FAX *540/886–6641,* WEB *www.bellegrae.com. 8 rooms, 7 suites, 2 cottages. Restaurant, some microwaves, Internet; no smoking. AE, MC, V. MAP.*

$–$$$ **Frederick House.** Six restored town houses dating from 1810 make up this inn in the center of the historic district. All rooms are decorated with antiques, and some have fireplaces and private decks. A pub and a restaurant are adjacent. ✉ *28 N. New St., 24401,* ☎ *540/885–4220 or 800/334–5575,* FAX *540/885–5180,* WEB *www.frederickhouse.com. 9 rooms, 11 suites, 1 cottage. Cable TV, meeting rooms; no smoking. AE, D, DC, MC, V. BP.*

$$ **Sampson Eagon Inn.** Across the street from Woodrow Wilson's birthplace in the Gospel Hill section of town, this restored Greek revival (circa 1840) has a lot of period charm. In the spacious guest rooms are antique canopy beds, cozy sitting areas, and modern amenities. Don't miss the Kahlúa Belgian waffles for breakfast. ✉ *238 E. Beverley St., 24401,* ☎ *540/886–8200 or 800/597–9722,* WEB *www.eagoninn.com. 5 rooms (one with shower only). Cable TV with movies; no kids under 12, no smoking. AE, MC, V. BP.*

Nightlife and the Arts

THEATER

Experience Shakespeare's plays the way the Elizabethans did at **Blackfriars Playhouse** (✉ 10 S. Market St., ☎ 540/885–5588, WEB www.shenandoahshakespeare.com), a near-duplicate of the Globe Theatre that has rapidly gained worldwide acclaim for its attention to detail. Like those in 17th-century London, most seating consists of benches (modern seat backs and cushions are available), and some stools are right on stage.

Shopping

Virginia Made Shop (✉ I–81, Exit 222, ☎ 540/886–7180) specializes in Virginia-made products, from pottery and wind chimes to peanuts and wine. At **Virginia Metalcrafters** (✉ 1010 E. Main St., I–64 Exit 94, Waynesboro, ☎ 540/949–9400 or 800/368–1002) you can find a broad line of gifts and decorative accessories that are hand-cast in brass, iron, bronze, and pewter. All are made using the same techniques employed since the company was founded in 1890.

Lexington

13 *30 mi south of Staunton (via I–81).*

Two deeply traditional Virginia colleges sit side by side in this town, each with a memorial to a soldier who was also a man of peace.

Washington and Lee University, the ninth-oldest college in the United States, was founded in 1749 as Augusta Academy and later renamed Washington College in gratitude for a donation from George Washington. After Robert E. Lee's term as its president (1865–70), it received its current name. Today, with 2,000 students, the university occupies a campus of white-column, redbrick buildings around a central colonnade. The campus's **Lee Chapel and Museum** contains many relics of the Lee family. Edward Valentine's statue of the recumbent general, behind the altar, is especially moving: the pose is natural and the expression gentle, a striking contrast to most other monumental art. Here one can sense the affection and reverence that Lee inspired. ✉ *Jefferson St. (Rte. 11),* ☎ *540/463–8768,* WEB *www2.wlu.edu.* *Free.* *Chapel open Apr.–Oct., Mon.–Sat. 9–5, Sun. 1–5; Nov.–Mar., Mon.–Sat. 9–4, Sun. 1–4; campus tours Apr.–Oct., weekdays 10–4, Sat. 9:45–noon; Jan.–Mar., weekdays 10 and noon, Sat. 11.*

Adjacent to Washington and Lee University are the imposing Gothic buildings of the **Virginia Military Institute** (VMI), founded in 1839 and the nation's oldest state-supported military college. With an enrollment of about 1,300 cadets, the institute has admitted women since 1997. The **Virginia Military Institute Museum** in the lower level of Jackson Memorial Hall displays 15,000 artifacts, including Stonewall Jackson's stuffed and mounted horse, Little Sorrel, and the general's coat, pierced by the bullet that killed him at Chancellorsville. ✉ *Letcher Ave.,* ☎ *540/464–7232,* WEB *www.vmi.edu.* *Free.* *Daily 9–5.*

The **George C. Marshall Museum** preserves the memory of the World War II army chief of staff. Exhibits trace his brilliant career, which began when he was aide-de-camp to John "Black Jack" Pershing in World War I and culminated when, as secretary of state, he devised the Marshall Plan, a strategy for reviving postwar Western Europe. Marshall's Nobel Peace Prize is on display; so is the Oscar won by his aide Frank McCarthy, who produced the Academy Award–winning Best Picture of 1970, *Patton.* An electronically narrated map tells the story of World War II. ✉ *VMI campus, Letcher Ave.,* ☎ *540/463–7103.* *$3.* *Daily 9–5.*

Confederate general Jackson's private life is on display at the **Stonewall Jackson House,** where he is revealed as a dedicated Presbyterian who was devoted to physical fitness, careful with money, musically inclined, and fond of gardening. The general lived here only two years, while teaching physics and military tactics to the cadets, before leaving for his command in the Civil War. This is the only house he ever owned; it is furnished now with period pieces and some of his belongings. ✉ *8 E. Washington St.,* ☎ *540/463–2552,* WEB *www.stonewalljackson.*

org. 🎫 *$5.* ⏲ *Sept.–May, Mon.–Sat. 9–5, Sun. 1–5; June–Aug., Mon.–Sat. 9–6, Sun. 1–6.*

The inventor of the first mechanical wheat reaper is honored at the **Cyrus McCormick Museum,** which sits about a mile off I–81. Follow the signs to Walnut Grove farm; now a livestock research center, this mill farmstead is where McCormick did his work. In addition to the museum and family home, you can tour a blacksmith shop and gristmill. All are registered as national historic landmarks. ✉ *State Rte. 606, 5 mi north of Lexington,* ☎ *540/377–2255.* 🎫 *Free.* ⏲ *Daily 8:30–5.*

OFF THE BEATEN PATH

NATURAL BRIDGE OF VIRGINIA – About 20 mi south of Lexington, this impressive limestone arch (which supports Route 11) has been gradually carved out by Cedar Creek, which rushes through 215 ft below. The Monacan Native American tribe called it the Bridge of God. Surveying the structure for Lord Halifax, George Washington carved his own initials in the stone; Thomas Jefferson bought it (and more than 150 surrounding acres) from George III. The after-dark sound-and-light show may be overkill, but viewing and walking under the bridge itself and along the wooded pathway beyond are worth the price of admission. On the property are dizzying caverns that descend 34 stories, a wax museum, and an 18th-century village constructed by the Monacan Indian Nation. ✉ *I–81 S (Exit 180), I–81 N (Exit 175),* ☎ *540/291–2121 or 800/533–1410,* WEB *www.naturalbridgeva.com.* 🎫 *Bridge $10; all attractions $17.* ⏲ *Mar.–Nov., daily 8 AM–dark.*

Dining and Lodging

$$–$$$ ✕ **Wilson-Walker House.** This stately 1820 Greek revival house is ideal for eating elegant regional cuisine. Seafood dishes are a specialty—try the pan-seared, potato-encrusted trout. The restaurant is not as expensive as one might expect, and is particularly affordable during the $5 chef's-special luncheon. ✉ *30 N. Main St.,* ☎ *540/463–3020. Reservations essential. AE, MC, V. Closed Sun.–Mon.*

$ ✕ **The Palms.** Once a Victorian ice cream parlor, this full-service restaurant in an 1890 building has indoor and outdoor dining. Wood booths line the walls of the plant-filled room: the pressed-metal ceiling is original. Specialties on the American menu include broccoli-cheese soup, charbroiled meats, and teriyaki chicken. ✉ *101 W. Nelson St.,* ☎ *540/463–7911. Reservations not accepted. D, MC, V.*

$$–$$$ ✕🏨 **Maple Hall.** For a taste of Southern history, spend a night at this country inn of 1850. Once a plantation house, it's set on 56 acres 6 mi north of Lexington. All rooms have period antiques and modern amenities; most have gas log fireplaces as well. Dinner is served in three ground-floor rooms and on a glassed-in patio; the main dining room ($$–$$$) has a large decorative fireplace. Among notable entrées on the seasonal menu are beef fillet with green peppercorn sauce; veal sautéed with mushrooms in hollandaise sauce; and chicken Chesapeake, a chicken breast stuffed with spinach and crabmeat. ✉ *Rte. 11, 24450,* ☎ *540/463–6693 or 877/463–2044,* FAX *540/463–7262,* WEB *www.lexingtonhistoricinns.com/maplehall.htm. 17 rooms, 4 suites. Restaurant, tennis court, pool, fishing, hiking, meeting rooms. D, MC, V. BP.*

$–$$ 🏨 **Natural Bridge Hotel.** Within walking distance of the spectacular rock arch of the same name (there's also a shuttle bus), the Colonial-style brick hotel has a beautiful location as well as numerous recreational facilities. Long porches with rocking chairs allow leisurely appreciation of the Blue Ridge Mountains. Rooms are done in a Colonial Virginia style. ✉ *Rte. 11, Box 57, Natural Bridge 24578,* ☎ *540/291–2121 or 800/533–1410,* FAX *540/291–1896,* WEB *www.naturalbridgeva.com. 180 rooms. Restaurant, snack bar, some microwaves, cable TV with movies* *and video games, miniature golf, 2 tennis courts, pool, hiking, bar, meeting rooms. AE, D, DC, MC, V.*

Nightlife and the Arts

The **Theater at Lime Kiln** (✉ Lime Kiln Rd., ☎ 540/463–7088) stages musicals, concerts, and performances as varied as Russian clowns and Vietnamese puppeteers. The Kiln's solid rock walls create a dramatic backdrop. Original musicals are staged Tuesday through Saturday, and contemporary music concerts are given on Sunday throughout the summer. To get here from I–81, follow U.S. 60 west 0.4 mi past the Washington and Lee University pedestrian bridge, turn left on Borden Road, and follow it 0.2 mi.

En Route The drive to Bath County on the 35-mi stretch of Route 39 north and west from Lexington provides a scenic trip through 3-mi **Goshen Pass,** a dramatic gorge that follows the boulder-strewn Maury River through the Allegheny Mountains. Before the coming of railroads, it was the principal stagecoach route into Lexington. In May, the scene becomes lush with rhododendrons and other flowering plants; in October, the colors of the rainbow paint the maples and oaks that fill the gorge. A day-use park enables picnickers to bask in this forest preserve, where the river allows for fishing, swimming, and tubing.

Bath County

⓮ *20 mi northwest of Lexington (via Rte. 39).*

As residents are proud to point out, there are no traffic lights in all of Bath County and only 10 year-round inhabitants per square mile. In fact, there often seem to be almost as many visitors as inhabitants here, particularly around the historic Homestead resort in Hot Springs. The healing thermal springs were what originally brought visitors to town in the 1700s. Although they're less fashionable today, the sulfurous waters still flow at Warm Springs, Hot Springs, and Bolar Springs, their temperatures ranging from 77°F to 104°F. Try "taking the cure" at the Jefferson Pools in Warm Springs, where the rustic men's and ladies' bathhouses (built in 1761 and 1836, respectively) are largely unchanged.

Dining and Lodging

$$–$$$ ★ ✕ **Waterwheel Restaurant.** Part of a complex of five historic buildings, this restaurant is in a gristmill that dates from 1700. A walk-in wine cellar, set among the gears of the original waterwheel, has 100 wine selections; diners may step in and choose for themselves. The dining area is decorated with Currier & Ives and Audubon prints. Some menu favorites are fresh smoked trout and chicken Fantasio (breast of chicken stuffed with wild rice, sausage, apple, and pecans). Desserts include such Old Virginny recipes as a deep-dish apple pie baked with bourbon. On Sunday, look for the hearty but affordable brunch. ✉ *Grist Mill Sq., Warm Springs,* ☎ *540/839–2231. D, MC, V. Closed Tues. Nov.–May.*

$$$–$$$$ ★ 🏨 **Homestead.** Host to a prestigious clientele since 1766, the Homestead has evolved from a country spa to a 15,000-acre resort and conference facility. From the glorious columns of the entry hall to the stunning views of the Appalachian Mountains, magnificence surrounds those here from the first moment to the last. Rooms in the sprawling redbrick building, built in 1891, have Georgian-style furnishings; some have fireplaces. As for what to do, there's 4 mi of streams stocked with rainbow trout, 100 mi of riding trails, skeet and trap shooting, and nine ski slopes (snowboarding allowed). The Homestead was the site of the South's first downhill skiing in 1959, and one of the golf courses, laid out in 1892, includes the oldest tee in continuous use in the United

States. An orchestra plays nightly in the formal dining room (dinner is included in the room rate), where Continental cuisine and regional specialties take their place in its six-course extravaganzas. ✉ *Rte. 220, Hot Springs 24445,* ☎ *540/839–1766 or 800/838–1766,* FAX *540/839–7670,* WEB *www.thehomestead.com. 429 rooms, 77 suites. 6 restaurants, cable TV with movies and video games, 3 18-hole golf courses, 8 tennis courts, 2 pools (1 indoor), spa, bicycles, bowling, horseback riding, downhill skiing, ice-skating, cinema, video game room, Internet, meeting rooms, airport shuttle. AE, D, DC, MC, V. MAP.*

$–$$ ★ **Inn at Gristmill Square.** Occupying five restored buildings at the same site as the Waterwheel Restaurant, the rooms of this state historical landmark inn are in a Colonial Virginia style. Four units are in the original miller's house; others occupy the former blacksmith's shop, hardware store, gristmill, and cottage. Some of the rooms have fireplaces and patios. ✉ *Rte. 645, Box 359, Warm Springs 24484,* ☎ *540/839–2231,* FAX *540/839–5770,* WEB *www.gristmillsquare.com. 12 rooms, 5 suites, 1 apartment. Restaurant, cable TV, 3 tennis courts, pool, sauna, bar, meeting rooms. D, MC, V. BP.*

$$–$$$ **Milton Hall.** This 1874 Gothic brick house, built as an elegant country retreat by English nobility, is on 44 acres. It's close to the George Washington National Forest and its abundant outdoor activities. The spacious rooms have Victorian furnishings and large beds. Box lunches can be ordered in advance. ✉ *207 Thorny La., Covington 24426, (I–64 [Exit 10] at Callaghan),* ☎ *540/965–0196 or 877/764 –5866,* WEB *www.milton-hall.com. 6 rooms, 1 suite. Cable TV with movies, hiking; no smoking. D, MC, V. BP.*

$ **Roseloe Motel.** The modest and clean lodgings in this motel from the '50s are all homey and conventionally decorated. The Roseloe is halfway between Warm Springs and Hot Springs, where the fresh mountain air is bracing. ✉ *Rte. 1 (Box 590), Hot Springs 24445,* ☎ *540/839–5373. 14 rooms. Some kitchenettes, refrigerators, cable TV. AE, D, MC, V.*

Nightlife and the Arts

Garth Newel Music Center (✉ Rte. 220, Warm Springs, ☎ 540/839–5018, WEB www.garthnewel.org) has weekend chamber-music performances in summer; you can make reservations and plan to picnic on the grounds.

Outdoor Activities and Sports

HIKING AND MOUNTAIN BIKING

The Warm Springs Ranger District of the **George Washington and Jefferson National Forests** (☎ 540/839–2521) has information on hundreds of miles of local trails. At **Douthat State Park** (Exit 27, 7 mi north of I–64 near Clifton Forge, ☎ 540/862–8100), there are more than 40 mi of well-signed, smoothly groomed, and sometimes steep trails for hiking and biking. The trails pass by waterfalls and majestic overlooks.

SOUTHWEST VIRGINIA

Southwest Virginia is a rugged region of alternating mountain ridges and deep valleys. Modern urban life is juxtaposed with spectacular scenery in the Roanoke and New River valleys. Other areas retain the quiet charm of yesteryear: they have many pleasant meadows, old country churches, and towns with just one stop sign. The gorge-incised Appalachian Plateau in far southwest Virginia is abundant in coal. Interstate 81 and Interstate 77 form a kind of "X" across the region, and the Blue Ridge Parkway roughly defines Southwest Virginia's eastern edge.

Roanoke

15 *49 mi south of Lexington (via I–81).*

The bowl-shape Roanoke Valley, although considered the geological southern end of the Shenandoah Valley, has historic and cultural ties that link it more closely to rugged Southwest Virginia than to the genteel Shenandoah. Roanoke, population 95,000, is Virginia's largest city west of Richmond and in many ways the area's capital. The metropolitan area of 230,000 has enough city flavor to provide a degree of culture and elegance, but its location between the Blue Ridge Parkway and Appalachian Trail means that the wilds aren't too far away either; mountains dominate its horizons in all directions. Salem, next door to Roanoke, is its smaller and older neighbor in the valley. Fiercely independent, Salemites hate to have their town called a suburb.

Even in daylight, the Roanoke skyline is dominated by a star. The 100-ft-tall **Mill Mountain Star,** which was the world's largest man-made star when constructed in 1949, stands in a city park 1,000 ft above the Roanoke Valley. From either of the park's two overlooks, Roanoke, the "Star City of the South," looks like a scale model of a city. From the overlooks you can also see wave after wave of Appalachian ridgelines. *Mill Mountain Park, follow Walnut St. south 2 mi from downtown Roanoke; or take Parkway Spur Rd. 3 mi north from Blue Ridge Pkwy. at milepost 120.3.*

Sharing the mountaintop with the star is the **Mill Mountain Zoo,** one of only two nationally accredited zoos in Virginia. Asian animals are center stage here, including a rare Siberian tiger, snow leopards, and red pandas. ✉ *Mill Mountain Park, follow Walnut St. south 2 mi from downtown Roanoke; or take Parkway Spur Rd. 3 mi north from Blue Ridge Pkwy. at milepost 120.3,* ☎ *540/343–3241,* WEB *www.mmzoo.org.* *$6.* *Daily 10–5 (gate closes at 4:30).*

Market Square is the heart of Roanoke, with Virginia's oldest continuous farmer's market, a multiethnic food court inside the restored City Market Building, and several restaurants, shops, and bars. A restored warehouse called Center in the Square (✉ One Market Sq. SE, ☎ 540/342–5700, WEB www.centerinthesquare.org) contains the Mill Mountain Theatre and three museums.

The **Science Museum of Western Virginia and Hopkins Planetarium** has displays on Virginia's natural history plus interactive exhibits on science and new technology that are especially appealing to youngsters. Shows are given in the planetarium, and a MegaDome theater screens large-format 70mm films. ✉ *Center in the Square, One Market Sq. SE,* ☎ *540/342–5710,* WEB *www.smwv.org.* *Museum $6; with planetarium $8; with MegaDome $9.* *Tues.–Sat. 10–5.*

The **History Museum of Western Virginia** displays regional artifacts, including relics of the local Native Americans, whose word for "shell wampum" forms the root of "Roanoke." The permanent exhibit examines the heritage of Southwest Virginia from prehistoric times to the present. Rotating exhibits focus on the people and events that have shaped the area's development. ✉ *Center in the Square, One Market Sq. SE,* ☎ *540/342–5770.* *$2.* *Tues.–Fri. 10–4, Sat. 10–5, Sun. 1–5.*

The **Art Museum of Western Virginia** has holdings that are strongest in regional works, including Appalachian folk art and modern photography. In the second-floor gallery, rotating shows of traditional and contemporary art are mounted. ✉ *Center in the Square, One Market Sq. SE,* ☎ *540/342–5760,* WEB *www.artmuseumroanoke.org.* *Free.* *Tues.–Sat. 10–5.*

Near Market Square, the **Virginia Museum of Transportation** has the largest collection of diesel and steam locomotives in the country—not surprising, considering Roanoke got its start as a railroad town and was once the headquarters of the Norfolk & Western railroad. The dozens of original train cars and engines, many built here in town, include a massive Nickel Plate locomotive—just one of the many holdings that constitute an unabashed display of civic pride. ✉ *303 Norfolk Ave.,* ☎ *540/342–5670,* WEB *www.vmt.org.* 🎫 *$6.30.* ⏲ *Wed.–Sat. 10–5; Sun. noon–5.*

The **To The Rescue Museum** is the national emergency medical services/rescue museum, celebrating Roanoke's claim as the birthplace of the modern EMS system. Julian Stanley Wise founded a volunteer rescue unit in Roanoke in 1928; within years the concept spread across the nation and around the world. EMS workers who died on duty, including the 10 who died in the September 11, 2001, terrorist attack on New York City, are memorialized with gold leaves on the museum's "Tree of Life." Interactive exhibits give a realistic sense of rescue work, including what it's like to dispatch rescuers on actual 911 calls. ✉ *Tanglewood Mall, 4428 Electric Rd.,* ☎ *540/776–0364,* WEB *www.naemt.org/ttrescue.* 🎫 *$2.* ⏲ *Tues.–Sat. noon–9, Sun. 1–6.*

Dixie Caverns is unusual in that, rather than descending into the cave, you first must walk upstairs into the heart of a mountain. The spacious Cathedral Room, formations dubbed Turkey Wing and Wedding Bell, and an earthquake fault line are among the sights. There's also a mineral and fossil shop attached to the caverns. ✉ *5753 W. Main St. (take I–81 to Exit 132, which links up with Rte. 11/460), Salem,* ☎ *540/380–2085.* 🎫 *$7.50.* ⏲ *May–Sept. daily 9:30–6; Oct.–Apr. daily 9:30–5.*

OFF THE BEATEN PATH

NATIONAL D-DAY MEMORIAL – When Allied forces landed at Normandy on June 6, 1944, in what would be the decisive military move of World War II, the small town of Bedford lost nearly an entire generation of its young men. The town of 3,200 lost 19 on D-Day, and four more in days to come. Because its losses on D-Day were proportionally heavier than any other U.S. community, Bedford was chosen as the site of this memorial. Its focal point is a huge granite arch and flag plaza on a hill overlooking the town. There are also granite statues of soliders in combat and a reflecting pool that periodically shoots up spurts of water, as if struck by bullets. ✉ *U.S. 460, Bedford (27 mi east of Roanoke),* ☎ *800/351–3329,* WEB *www.dday.org.* 🎫 *$10.* ⏲ *Daily 10–5.*

BOOKER T. WASHINGTON NATIONAL MONUMENT – This restored tobacco farm 25 mi southeast of Roanoke and 21 mi south of Bedford is a National Monument. Washington (1856–1915), born into slavery on this farm, was a remarkable educator and author who went on to advise Presidents McKinley, Roosevelt, and Taft and to take tea with Queen Victoria. More important, he started Tuskegee Institute in Alabama and inspired generations of African Americans. Covering 224 acres, the farm's restored buildings; tools; crops; animals; and, in summer, interpreters in period costume all help show what life during slavery was like. ✉ *Rte. 122 (21 mi south of Bedford),* ☎ *540/721–2094,* WEB *www.nps.gov/bowa.* 🎫 *Free.* ⏲ *Daily 9–5.*

Dining and Lodging

$$–$$$ ★ ✕ **Carlos Brazilian International Cuisine.** High on a hill with a spectacular view, this lively restaurant has French, Italian, Spanish, and Brazilian dishes. Try the *porco reacheado* (pork tenderloin stuffed with spinach and feta cheese) or the *moqueca mineira* (shrimp, clams, and

whitefish in a Brazilian sauce). Brazilian radio often accompanies the meal. ✉ *4167 Electric Rd.,* ☎ *540/345–7661. AE, MC, V. Closed Sun.*

$$–$$$ ✕ **The Library.** This quiet, elegant restaurant in the Piccadilly Square shopping center is decorated with shelves of books. Its frequently changing menu specializes in seafood dishes. Expect dishes such as sautéed Dover sole with almonds, fillet of beef with béarnaise sauce, and lobster tail. ✉ *3117 Franklin Rd. SW,* ☎ *540/985–0811. Reservations essential. AE, DC, MC, V. Closed Sun.–Mon. No lunch.*

$–$$ ✕ **Mac 'N' Bob's.** The enormous growth in seating since 1980, from 10 to 250, testifies to the popularity of this establishment in downtown Salem. Sports memorabilia lines the walls of the attractive red-brick building near Roanoke College, and sporting events are likely to be on the TVs near the bar. The menu runs from hamburgers to steak to seafood to pizza. If you have a big appetite, try a fully loaded calzone. For an unusual zing on your taste buds, order the sweet and spicy Montreal salsa chicken. ✉ *316 E. Main St., Salem,* ☎ *540/389–5999. AE, D, MC, V.* ⏲ *No dinner Mon.–Sat.*

$ ★ ✕ **The Homeplace.** Bring a big appetite with you on the drive up and over Catawba Mountain to get to the Homeplace. Famished Appalachian Trail hikers in grimy shorts and suave diners in their Sunday best eat side by side in this farm home in a tiny country hamlet—come as you are. Old-fashioned cooking is dished up grandma style, with all you-can-eat fried chicken, mashed potatoes and gravy, green beans, pinto beans, baked apples, hot biscuits, and an extra meat selection of your choice is served to each table for $11 a person (throw in another dollar for yet another meat selection). No alcohol is served, but the lemonade is delicious. Though you will wait to be seated most days, you can spend the time admiring mountain scenery from a front-porch swing or in a pagoda under towering shade trees. ✉ *7 mi west of Salem on Rte. 311 N (Exit 141 off I–81), Catawba,* ☎ *540/384–7252. Reservations not accepted. MC, V.* ⏲ *No lunch Thurs.–Sat., no dinner Sun.*

$$$ ✕🏨 **Hotel Roanoke and Conference Center.** This elegant Tudor revival building, listed on the National Register of Historic Places, was built in 1882 by the Norfolk & Western Railroad. The richly paneled lobby has Florentine marble floors and ceiling frescos. The formal restaurant serves regional Southern cuisine ($$–$$$); perennial favorites include peanut soup and steak Diane, prepared table-side. The Market Square Bridge, a glassed-in walkway, goes from the hotel to downtown attractions. ✉ *110 Shenandoah Ave., 24016,* ☎ *540/985–5900,* FAX *540/345–2890,* WEB *www.hotelroanoke.com. 313 rooms, 19 suites. 2 restaurants, cable TV with movies and video games, pool, gym, bar, Internet, convention center, meeting rooms, airport shuttle. AE, D, DC, MC, V.*

$$–$$$ 🏨 **Bernard's Landing.** A resort set on Smith Mountain Lake 45 minutes southeast of Roanoke, Bernard's rents one- to three-bedroom condominiums with water views and two- to five-bedroom town houses (all waterfront) for periods of up to two weeks. Because the units are separately owned, the way they are furnished varies widely, but all units have full kitchen facilities and private decks. Conferences are scheduled here year-round, and summer vacationers come for the various sports available. ✉ *775 Ashmeade Rd., Moneta 24121,* ☎ *540/721–8870 or 800/572–2048,* FAX *540/721–8383,* WEB *www.bernardslanding.com. 60 units. Restaurant, kitchens, microwaves, cable TV, 6 tennis courts, 2 pools, gym, sauna, boating, fishing, racquetball, playground, Internet, meeting rooms. AE, D, MC, V.*

Nightlife and the Arts

BARS AND CLUBS

Roanoke's nightlife centers on the Market Square area of downtown, which is often bustling and lively on weekend nights. Near the Square,

Corned Beef and Co. (✉ 107 Jefferson St., ☎ 540/342–3354) has live jazz and funk music on Friday and Saturday nights. For something a bit out of the ordinary, try **Kara O'Caen's Irish Pub** (✉ 303 S. Jefferson St., ☎ 540/344–5509), where live Irish folk music plays many nights.

MUSIC

The **Roanoke Symphony** (☎ 540/343–9127, WEB www.rso.com) presents classical, chamber orchestra, pops, and educational concerts throughout the year at two locations in Roanoke.

Outdoor Activities and Sports

HIKING

The **Appalachian Trail** is north and west of Roanoke, crossing the valley at Troutville, 5 mi to the north. Two of the most photographed formations on the entire 2,000-mi route from Georgia to Maine, McAfee Knob and Dragon's Tooth, are accessible from trailheads on the Virginia 311 highway, west of the valley. The **Star Trail** (trailhead on Riverland Road, 2 mi southeast of downtown Roanoke) winds through a forest oasis amid the metropolitan area as it works its way up 1½ mi to the Mill Mountain Star. Other trails can be found along the Blue Ridge Parkway to the east and south and in the George Washington and Jefferson national forests to the north and west. For more information contact the national forests' **Supervisor's Office** (✉ 5162 Valleypointe Pkwy., Roanoke, ☎ 540/265–5100 or 888/265–0019).

SPECTATOR SPORTS

Each April and October, **Martinsville Speedway** (✉ U.S. 220, Ridgeway, ☎ 276/638–7332 or 276/627–1900, WEB www.martinsvillespeedway.com) fills its 86,000 seats with those who want to see NASCAR's top drivers in the Winston Cup series races held here, 50 mi south of Roanoke.

Shopping

Head to Market Square for offbeat stores, including **The Binaba Shop** (✉ 120 Campbell Ave. SE, ☎ 540/376–7064), which sells African artifacts, clothing, and jewelry. **Wertz's Country Store** (✉ 215 Market St. SE, ☎ 540/342–5133), beside the downtown farmer's market, sells country hams, homemade jams and jellies, sorghum molasses, and many sorts of nuts. For a furry companion that nevertheless doesn't bite or growl, visit **Blue Ridge Bears & Gifts** (✉ 3109 Brambleton Ave. SW, ☎ 540/989–4995, WEB www.nvo.com/blueridgebears), where the bears range in size from an inch to 3 ft tall.

Blue Ridge Parkway

5 mi east of Roanoke.

The Blue Ridge Parkway takes up where Skyline Drive leaves off at Waynesboro, weaving south for 471 mi to Great Smoky Mountains National Park in North Carolina. The parkway goes up to higher elevations than the drive, up to 4,200 ft at Apple Orchard Mountain, and even higher in North Carolina. Roanoke is the largest city along its entire route; with the exception of Asheville, N.C., the rest of the parkway bypasses populated areas, as was the intention of its New Deal–era designers. In Virginia, the parkway is especially scenic between Waynesboro and Roanoke, winding through the George Washington National Forest, visiting numerous ridge-top overlooks that provide views of crumpled-looking mountains and patchwork valleys. South of Roanoke, the route becomes more gently rolling as the Blue Ridge becomes more like a plateau on its way to North Carolina. (Call the National Park Service's office in Vinton [☎ 540/857–2490] for information on Virginia's section of the Blue Ridge Parkway.)

Peaks of Otter Recreation Area, 25 mi northeast of Roanoke, offers a close-up view of cone-shape Sharp Top Mountain, which no less an authority than Thomas Jefferson once called America's tallest peak. At 3,875 ft it's not even the tallest in the park—nearby Flat Top is 4,004 ft. You can hike to both peaks (the Sharp Top trail is often crowded on weekends) and to little brother Harkening Hill, as well as to Fallingwater Cascades, a thrilling multitier waterfall. For those not up to the climb, a bus heads most of the way up Sharp Top hourly throughout the day. The peaks rise about the shores of Abbott Lake, a bucolic picnic spot. A pleasant lakeside lodge and campground along the placid lake below are an ideal base for local trekking. ✉ *Blue Ridge Pkwy., mile marker 86,* ☎ *540/586–4357,* WEB *www.peaksofotter.com.* 🎫 *Free.*

Explore Park, a 1,100-acre recreational park near Roanoke, depicts life in Virginia from three distinct periods between 1671 and 1850. Costumed interpreters represent early Native American life, the Colonial frontier experience, and the life of a 19th-century settlement, with schoolhouse and blacksmith's shop. The park has 6 mi of hiking trails along the Roanoke River gorge as well as good opportunities for mountain biking, fishing, canoeing, and kayaking. Inside the park is the **Blue Ridge Parkway Visitors Center,** open 9–5 daily year-round. ✉ *1½ mi north of milepost 115 on the Blue Ridge Pkwy.,* ☎ *540/427–1800 or 800/842–9163,* WEB *www.explorepark.org.* 🎫 *$8.* ⏲ *May–Oct., Wed.–Sat. 10–5, Sun. noon–5.*

Mabry Mill, north of Meadows of Dan and the Blue Ridge Parkway's junction with U.S. 58 at milepost 176, 55 mi south of Roanoke, is one of the parkway's most popular stops for photographers. The restored water-powered, weather-worn gristmill grinds cornmeal and buckwheat flour, which are for sale. There are regular demonstrations of blacksmithing and other trades. A short hiking trail rings the property. ✉ *Blue Ridge Pkwy., milepost 176,* ☎ *276/952–2947.* 🎫 *Free.* ⏲ *May–Oct., daily 8–6.*

OFF THE BEATEN PATH

CHÂTEAU MORRISETTE WINERY INC. – With the Rock Castle Gorge nearby, this winery has spectacular surroundings. Tours of the facilities are given, and the tastings allow you to sample the dozen different wines produced here. A natural amphitheater on the property is the site of the annual Black Dog Jazz Festival. ✉ *Winery Rd., off Rte. 726, west of Blue Ridge Pkwy. at milepost 171.5, Meadows of Dan,* ☎ *540/593–2865,* WEB *www.chateaumorrisette.com.* 🎫 *$2 for tour and tasting.* ⏲ *Mon.–Thurs. 10–5, Fri.–Sat. 10–8, Sun. 11–5.*

Lodging

$$–$$$$ **Doe Run Lodge.** This resort at Groundhog Mountain, a rustic lodge on the crest of the Blue Ridge, has grand views of the Piedmont. Golfing, skiing, and hunting are all nearby. Each unit has a fireplace and kitchen, and floor-to-ceiling windows allow for full appreciation of the view. ✉ *Milepost 189, Box 280, Fancy Gap 24328,* ☎ *276/398–2212 or 800/325–6189,* FAX *276/398–2833,* WEB *www.doerunlodge.com. 39 chalets, 3 villas, 2 cabins. Restaurant, some microwaves, 3 tennis courts, pool, sauna, fishing, basketball, hiking, volleyball, meeting rooms, some pets allowed (fee); no a/c in some rooms. AE, MC, V.*

$ **Peaks of Otter Lodge.** This unpretentious, peaceful lodge is so popular that reservations are accepted beginning October 1 for the following year. Every room looks out on Abbott Lake from a private terrace or balcony, and their interiors have a folksy quality. The restaurant's big draw is the Friday night seafood buffet for $21.95. ✉ *Milepost 86, Rte. 664, Box 489, Bedford 24523,* ☎ *540/586–1081 or 800/542–5927,* FAX *540/586–4420,* WEB *www.peaksofotter.com. 63 rooms. Restaurant,* *fishing, hiking, bar, pub, meeting rooms; no room phones, no room TVs. MC, V.*

New River Valley

41 mi southwest of Roanoke (via I–81).

Despite its name, derived from being "new" to explorers when it was first discovered, the New River is actually one of the oldest rivers in the world: legend says only the Nile is older. The only river that flows from south to north completely through the Appalachian Mountains, it may have been there before the mountains came, some 300 million years ago. In Virginia, the New River cuts a bluff-graced valley for 60 mi from Galax near the North Carolina line to Pearisburg, just over the West Virginia line. With an economy centered on research at Virginia Tech and manufacturing, the once-small towns of Blacksburg, Christiansburg, Radford, and Pulaski at the heart of the valley now sprawl together until it's hard to tell where one ends and the other begins. Visitors will find cozy downtown areas in each and many opportunities for outdoor recreation just outside the towns' limits.

With 26,000 students, **Virginia Tech** is Virginia's largest university. A small college just a few decades ago, Tech is now known for top-notch research programs and its Hokies football team, regularly ranked in the top 10. The focal point of the sprawling campus is the Drillfield, a vast green space surrounded by hefty neo-Gothic buildings built of what is known locally as "Hokie Stone" masonry. The **Virginia Museum of Natural History** (✉ 428 N. Main St., ☎ 540/231–3001) presents rotating exhibits on local and national wildlife; a separate geology museum in Deering Hall displays gems and minerals. ✉ *Blacksburg,* ☎ *540/231–6000,* WEB *www.vt.edu.*

Almost a century before Virginia Tech's founding in 1872, the **Historic Smithfield** plantation was built on what was then the frontier wilds. Aristocratic colonist and Revolutionary War patriot William Preston moved his family to the estate in 1774, a year before the war began. Among his descendants were three Virginia governors and four U.S. senators. Today, costumed interpreters, authentic period furniture, and Native American artifacts reveal how different life in the New River Valley was more than two centuries ago. (✉ *100 Smithfield Plantation Rd., Blacksburg,* ☎ *540/231–3947,* WEB *www.civic.bev.net/smithfield.* 🎫 *$5.* ⏲ *Apr.–Dec., Thurs.–Sun. 1–5.*

What is now the **Wilderness Road Regional Museum** was once lodgings for settlers making their way west on a Native American route that went from Pennsylvania through the Cumberland Gap. The man who founded the town of Newbern built this house in the same year, and the structure has since served as a private home, a tavern, a post office, and a store. Today the house contains antique dolls, swords and rifles, an old loom, and other artifacts of everyday life. A self-tour map of Newbern, the only Virginia town entirely within a National Register of Historic Places district, is available at the museum. ✉ *I–81 (Exit 98), Newbern,* ☎ *540/674–4835,* WEB *www.rootsweb.com/~Evanrhs/wrrm.* 🎫 *$2.* ⏲ *Mon.–Sat. 10:30–4:30, Sun. 1:30–4:30.*

Each October, the **Radford Highlanders Festival** brings Scotland to the New River Valley through bagpipes, games, parades, dancing, crafts, and sheep dog demonstrations. Men in traditional kilts challenge each other's machismo in the caber toss and hammer throw. Clan gatherings and genealogists on site help visitors trace their Scottish roots. ✉ *Radford (I–81, Exit 109),* ☎ *540/831–5021 or 540/831–5324,* WEB *www.radford.edu/festival.* 🎫 *Free.*

OFF THE BEATEN PATH

AUDIE MURPHY MONUMENT – On May 28, 1971, America's most decorated World War II veteran, who later became an actor, died when his plane struck Brush Mountain amid thick fog. A peaceful half-mile ridgetop walk leads to a simple monument, built by the Christiansburg Veterans of Foreign Wars, that marks the site of the crash and summarizes Audie Murphy's life. An overlook below the monument has a fine view of the Craig Creek Valley. Although the path to the monument is relatively smooth, the road to the top of Brush Mountain is winding, steep, and rocky; the monument is also accessible via a steep 4-mi Applachian Trail climb. ✉ *Forest Service Rd. 188.1. From Blacksburg, follow Mount Tabor Rd. [Rte. 624] 12 mi east, turn left onto Rte. 650 at the sign, follow it 5 mi as it becomes a forest service road to the dead end on top of Brush Mountain.*

Dining and Lodging

$ ✕ **Boudreaux's Restaurant.** What started as a project in business marketing for a pair of Virginia Tech students is now an established part of Blacksburg's downtown. The canopied rooftop is a particularly relaxing area to enjoy jambalaya or Cajun catfish, all the while watching playful sparrows pick up the crumbs. Live bands often perform in the evenings. ✉ *205 N. Main St., Blacksburg,* ☎ *540/961–2330,* WEB *www.boudreauxs.com. AE, D, MC, V.*

$ ✕ **The Cellar.** A gathering place and watering hole near the Virginia Tech campus, this storefront restaurant serves eclectic, inexpensive dishes. Try the Greek spaghetti with sautéed feta, garlic, and olives, or the "Mac Daddy": a single large meatball in marinara sauce and Parmesan. In the basement tavern you can choose from a particularly large list of beers; local bands often play there into the wee hours. ✉ *302 N. Main St., Blacksburg,* ☎ *540/953–0651,* WEB *www.the-cellar.com. MC, V.*

$$$–$$$$ **Mountain Lake.** Centered around the highest natural lake east of the Mississippi, this resort has more than 20 different types of accommodations, including spartan cottages and plush suites in a majestic sandstone hotel from 1930 (the resort itself predates the Civil War). Atop 4,000-ft Salt Pond Mountain, Mountain Lake resort has an overwhelming number of outdoor activities available: you can hike, mountain bike, ride horses, swim, and boat within the 2,500-acre Mountain Lake Wilderness, which surrounds the hotel and is operated by a nonprofit organization. The adjacent Jefferson National Forest offers even more recreation, including a segment of the Appalachian Trail. Resort guests can jump in the back of truck for a hayride at no charge, or get pulled along in a horse-drawn carriage for a fee. ✉ *115 Hotel Circle, 7 mi north of U.S. 460 on Rte. 700, Pembroke, 24136,* ☎ *540/626–7121,* WEB *www.mountainlakehotel.com. 28 cottages, 16 lodge rooms, 43 hotel rooms. Dining room, some microwaves, some refrigerators, pool, hot tub, bicycles, archery, hiking, video game room, shop, meeting rooms, Internet; no a/c, no room TVs. AE, D, MC, V. MAP. Closed Dec.-Apr.*

$–$$$ **Four Points by Sheraton.** This hotel is particularly distinguished for its location, across the street from Virginia Tech, with a golf course, movie theater, numerous restaurants and shopping areas, and even a beach volleyball court nearby. The rooms are modern and comfortable, with two phone lines in each one. ✉ *900 Prices Fork Rd., Blacksburg 24060,* ☎ *540/552–7001,* FAX *540/552–0827,* WEB *www.bnt.com/4Points. 147 rooms, 1 suite. Restaurant, dining room, cable TV with movies and video games, tennis court, 2 pools (1 indoor), lounge, recreation room, Internet, meeting rooms, airport shuttle. AE, D, DC, MC, V.*

$ **Best Western Radford Inn.** Service and amenities (such as a bathroom phone) distinguish this facility from the other highway motels it resembles in the same area. The Colonial-decorated rooms have views of the Blue Ridge Mountains that are not utterly spoiled by the surrounding parking lot. ✉ *1501 Tyler Ave. (Rte. 177), Radford 24141,* ☎ FAX *540/639–3000,* WEB *www.bestwestern.com. 104 rooms. Restaurant, microwaves, cable TV, indoor pool, gym, sauna, bar, Internet, meeting rooms, some pets allowed. AE, D, DC, MC, V.*

Outdoor Activities and Sports

BIKING

The 52-mi **New River Trail,** Virginia's narrowest state park, runs from Pulaski to Galax following what was once a railroad bed. It parallels the river for 39 of those miles, passing through two tunnels. The trail is also open to hikers and horseback riders. **Mountain Lake** resort (✉ 115 Hotel Circle, 7 mi north of U.S. 460 on Rte. 700, Pembroke, ☎ 540/626–7121, WEB www.mountainlakehotel.com) has more than 20 mi of mountain bike trails, with bicycles available at the hotel. The Jefferson National Forest's **Pandapas Pond Recreation Area,** on the edge of Blacksburg, is a popular place for mountain biking.

CANOEING, KAYAKING, AND FISHING

The **New River** is open to canoeing, kayaking, and fishing. For more information, or to rent or buy boats or fishing gear, contact any of the following local outfitters: **Back Country Ski & Sport,** (✉ 3710 S. Main St., Blacksburg, ☎ 540/552–6400, www.bcski.com); **New River Adventures,** (✉ 1007 N. 4th St., Wytheville, ☎ 276/228–8311 or 276/699–1034, www.newriveradventures.com); **Tangent Outfitters,** (☎ 540/731–5202, WEB www.newrivertrail.com).

HIKING

The 4-mi loop at **Cascades Recreation Area** (✉ Jefferson National Forest, off U.S. 460, 4 mi north of Pembroke on Rte. 623) passes a rushing stream and a 60-ft waterfall. This hike is popular locally and becomes crowded on weekends when the weather's good. The **Appalachian Trail** crosses the New River Valley, visiting overlook sites such as Angel's Rest and Wind Rock. For more information on area hikes in the Jefferson National Forest, contact the **Blacksburg Ranger Station** (✉ 110 Southpark Dr., Blacksburg, ☎ 540/552–4641).

SPECTATOR SPORTS

Virginia Tech competes in the Big East conference in several varsity NCAA Division I sports, including football, baseball, and basketball. Its football team, commonly ranked in the top 10, plays in 65,000-seat **Lane Stadium** (☎ 540/231–6731 tickets).

Abingdon

16 *135 mi southwest of Roanoke (via I–81).*

Abingdon, near the Tennessee border, is a cultural crossroads in the wilderness: the town of nearly 7,000 draws tens of thousands of people each year because of a fine theater company and exuberant local celebrations. By far the most popular event here is the **Virginia Highlands Festival** during the first two weeks of August: 200,000 people come to hear live music performances ranging from bluegrass to opera, to visit the exhibitions of mountain crafts, and to browse among the wares of more than 100 antiques dealers. This is followed by the **Burley Tobacco Festival,** held in September, during which country-music stars perform and prize farm animals are proudly displayed.

Regional artists exhibit their folk art and crafts at the **William King Regional Arts Center,** which also has an outdoor sculpture garden. ✉ *415 Academy Dr.,* ☎ *276/628–5005.* 🎫 *Free.* 🕐 *Tues. 10–9, Wed.–Fri. 10–5, weekends 1–5.*

Close-Up

MOUNTAIN MUSIC

SOUTHWEST VIRGINIA'S HILLS and valleys have long reverberated with the sounds of fiddles, banjoes, mandolins, and acoustic guitars. Scotch-Irish settlers brought these sounds with them, and for the generations before radio and television, front-porch gatherings and community dances entertained local families isolated, geographically and culturally, from the rest of civilization.

Whether called bluegrass, roots, or old-time country, the notes first plucked in the rugged hollers of Appalachia now echo much farther. This straightforward music scored global success when the sound track to the movie *O Brother, Where Art Thou?* first went quadruple-platinum in sales, then won best album at the 2002 Grammys. Produced by T Bone Burnett, this collection of old-time country and gospel songs mixed with a touch of blues had little in the way of airplay. For Southwest Virginia, it was a case of local boys conquering the world. The lead singer of the album's hit single, "Man of Constant Sorrows," Dan Tyminski, resides in Ferrum, 25 mi south of Roanoke; another singer on the album, bluegrass legend Ralph Stanley, lives in Coeburn, about 40 mi northwest of Abingdon.

It's in the Virginia-Tennessee border town of Bristol that some people mark the start of the commercial country-music industry. In 1927, a makeshift recording studio was set up downtown by the talent scout Ralph Peer. Peer advertised for musicians to play and have their songs recorded. From these sessions came such seminal acts as the Carter Family and Jimmie Rodgers. "Hillbilly music" had come out of the hollers, eventually sparking a multibillion-dollar industry.

Today, whether in regular performances, informal gatherings, Sunday morning worship services in country churches, or festivals that attract thousands, the rich sounds cultivated by generations are still played. Two centers are Galax and Floyd, though many other towns, large and small, have festivals or events. Here are a few other local places for the finest in old-time country and bluegrass music:

Carter Fold (✉ Hiltons, U.S. 58/421, 19 mi west of Bristol, ☎ 276/386–6054, WEB www.fmp.com/orthey/carter.html; 🎟 $4 for shows, $18 for festival): At this 1,000-seat auditorium, live music is performed on Saturday night; a two-day festival is held each August. A museum in an adjacent old store building nearby displays memorabilia from the Carter family; descendants often perform in the shows.

Old Fiddlers Convention (✉ Galax, ☎ 276/236–2184, WEB www.oldfiddlersconvention.com; 🎟 $5 Mon.–Thurs., $8 Fri., $10 Sat. or $30 for the week): Hundreds of musicians and thousands of fans gather the second week of August for performances, contests, camaraderie, and informal jam sessions that last until early morning.

Rex Theatre (✉ 113 E. Grayson St., Galax, ☎ 276/238–8130 or 276/236–0668; 🎟 free): Bluegrass, country, and gospel music is broadcast from here each Friday night on WBRF, FM-98.1.

Blue Ridge Music Center, (✉ Blue Ridge Pkwy. milepost 213, near N.C. line, WEB www.nps.gov/blri/BRMC.htm). This center launched an ambitious concert series at its outdoor amphitheater in summer 2002 that included the likes of Ricky Skaggs and Doc Watson.

Floyd Country Store (✉ Floyd, ☎ 540/745–4563, WEB www.floydcountrystore.com; 🎟 $3). What were once just sessions have evolved into a Friday Night Jamboree attended by local folks and visitors from far off. In summer, music often breaks out all around the store as well. "Granny Rules" are in effect—"no smokin', no cussin', and no drinkin'." But clogging on the dance floor is fine.

Dining and Lodging

$$–$$$ ✕ **The Starving Artist Cafe.** This eatery, which doubles as an art gallery, has many seafood and pasta dishes. The Friday and Saturday menu includes Cajun-style prime rib. ✉ *134 Wall St. NW,* ☎ *276/628–8445. AE, MC, V. Closed Sun. No dinner on Mon.*

$$–$$$ ✕ **The Tavern.** Inside a building from 1779 you'll find this cozy restaurant. The three dining rooms and cocktail lounge all have fireplaces, stone walls, and brick floors. In warm weather you can dine outdoors on a balcony overlooking historic Court House Hill or on a brick patio surrounded by trees and flowers. The menu includes rack of lamb and fresh seasonal seafood such as stuffed trout. ✉ *222 E. Main St.,* ☎ *276/628–1118. AE, D, MC, V.*

$$$–$$$$ ★ ✕🏨 **Camberley's Martha Washington Inn.** Constructed as a private house in 1832, turned into a college dormitory in 1860, and then used as a field hospital during the Civil War, the Martha Washington finally became an inn in 1935. Across from the Barter Theater, the inn has rooms furnished with Victorian antiques; some have fireplaces. The restaurant's contemporary American cuisine ($$$) includes roasted rainbow trout with crayfish, loin of lamb with hominy cheese grits, and—for dessert—Martha's marbled strawberry shortcake. There is complimentary afternoon tea on Friday and Saturday on the porch of the inn. ✉ *150 W. Main St., 24210,* ☎ *276/628–3161 or 800/555–8000,* FAX *276/628–8885,* WEB *www.marthawashingtoninn.com. 50 rooms, 11 suites. Restaurant, meeting rooms, bar. AE, D, DC, MC, V.*

$ 🏨 **Alpine Motel.** The spacious, modern rooms of this clean motel have striking views of Virginia's highest mountain peaks: Mt. Rogers and Whitetop. The motel is set far back from the road and is therefore popular with families, as well as traveling salespeople. The Barter Theatre is nearby. ✉ *882 E. Main St., 24210,* ☎ *276/628–3178,* FAX *276/628–3179. 19 rooms. Cable TV, Internet. AE, D, MC, V.*

Nightlife and the Arts

From April through the Christmas season, audiences flock to the prestigious **Barter Theatre** (✉ 133 W. Main St., ☎ 276/628–3991, WEB www.bartertheatre.com), America's longest-running professional repertory theater. Founded during the Depression by local actor Robert Porterfield, the theater got its name in the obvious way: early patrons who could not afford the 40¢ tickets could pay in produce. Kevin Spacey, Ned Beatty, and Gregory Peck are among the many stars who began their careers at the Barter, which today presents the classics of Shakespeare as well as works by contemporary playwrights such as David Mamet. Although times have changed since Noël Coward was given a Virginia ham for his contributions, the official policy still permits you to barter for your seat. But don't just show up at the box office with a bag of arugula—all trades must be approved by advance notice. Plays change every four weeks.

Outdoor Activities

HIKING

At the end of Abingdon's Main Street is the beginning of the 34-mi **Virginia Creeper Trail,** a former railbed of the Virginia-Carolina Railroad. You can hike it, bike it, or take to it on horseback. The trail has sharp curves, steep grades, and 100 trestles and bridges. It joins the Appalachian Trail at Damascus, a town known for its friendly attitude and the many businesses targeted toward hikers and cyclists. In May the town celebrates Trail Days, a festival celebrating hikers. ✉ *Trailhead at end of Main St.,* ☎ *540/676–2282 or 800/435–3440.*

Wild ponies on open grasslands studded with rocky knobs give the area around **Mt. Rogers** an appearance distinct from any other in Virginia.

At 5,729 ft, Mt. Rogers is Virginia's highest point, but you don't need to hike all the way to its summit to experience the grandeur of Western-like terrain—a short walk of about a mile from **Grayson Highlands State Park** (✉ U.S. 58, 20 mi east of Damascus, ☎ 276/579–7092, 🎫 $2) into the adjacent **Mount Rogers Recreation Area** is all that's required. Through the 5,000-acre state park and 120,000-acre recreation area run an extensive network of riding and hiking trails; the Appalachian Trail passes through on its way to North Carolina and Tennessee, just south. Hunting and fishing are permitted in season; permits are available in most sporting goods stores. ✉ *Mount Rogers National Recreation Area, 3714 Hwy. 16, Marion 24354,* ☎ *276/783–5196.* 🎫 *Free.*

Appalachian Plateau

About 60 mi west of Abingdon (via Alternate U.S. Rte. 58).

Gorges and "hollers" cut deeply into this elevated land in the far southwestern tip of Virginia. **Cumberland Gap National Historic Park** and **Breaks Interstate Park,** both on the Virginia-Kentucky line, preserve two of the better known of these valleys. Like neighboring Kentucky and West Virginia, coal has long been the driving force here; the area has suffered as coal mining jobs have dwindled amid mechanization and environmental concerns. Nevertheless, the plateau is inviting and inspiring country, evoking some sense of how Virginia was in the time of the pioneers. George Washington Vanderbilt loved mountain-encircled Burke's Garden near Tazewell so much that he wanted to build a huge country mansion there; he was rebuffed by suspicious locals and instead chose Asheville, N.C., for Biltmore, his estate. And the mountains around the town of Big Stone Gap inspired the 1908 novel and later movie *The Trail of the Lonesome Pine,* by John Fox Jr.

Next to the Lonesome Pine theater is the 1880s **June Tolliver House.** Rooms are furnished from the period, and local arts and crafts, including coal carvings and quilts, are for sale. ✉ *Climpon Ave., Big Stone Gap,* ☎ *276/523–4707.* 🎫 *Free.* ⏲ *Mid-May–mid-Dec., Tues.–Sat. 10–5, Sun. 2–6.*

In a Victorian mansion built during the coal boom of 1888–93, the **Southwest Virginia Historical Museum** holds a mine-manager's home furnishings and other exhibits. ✉ *10 W. First St. [Rte. 58 Alternate],* ☎ *276/523–1322,* 🎫 *$3.* ⏲ *Memorial Day–Labor Day, Mon.–Thurs. 10–4, Fri. 9–4, Sat. 10–5, Sun. 1–5; Labor Day–Dec. and Mar.–Memorial Day, Tues.–Thurs. 10–4, Fri. 9–4, Sat. 10–5, Sun. 1–5.*

On 110 acres that were once part of a hunting ground for the Shawnee and Cherokee nations, **Crab Orchard Museum and Pioneer Park** presents visitors with relics of many different historical periods. An archaeological dig at the site yielded many Native American tools and pieces of furniture. The history that followed the arrival of the Europeans is also illustrated through artifacts, as are the social changes caused by farming and regional mining. Among the diverse exhibits are an early European map showing the Pacific Ocean in West Virginia, the remains of a woolly mammoth, and an instrument used to bleed patients. Farm buildings and crafts shops nearby are fully accessible to people with disabilities. To get to Tazewell, take Exit 45 of I–81 at Marion, then go north 30 mi on Route 16. ✉ *Rtes. 19/460, Tazewell,* ☎ *276/988–6755,* WEB *histcrab.netscope.net.* 🎫 *$7.* ⏲ *Tues.–Sun. 1–5.*

Visitors can get their best glimpse of the coal mining life at **Pocahontas Exhibition Coal Mine and Museum.** Inside this former mine is a 13-ft-tall coal seam that helps you understand how mammoth an operation it once was. Opened in 1882, the mine produced more than 44 million tons of coal during its 73-year existence; its famous "Pocahontas No. 3" coal was the fuel of choice for the U.S. Navy. Guides explain the story of mining and how hand-loading succumbed to mechanization. The town of Pocahontas, once with a population of 5,000 as it bustled with coal miners who came from Hungary, Wales, Russia, Poland, and Italy, now has a population of fewer than 500. From Tazewell, take U.S. 460 northeast to Rte. 102. ✉ *Rte. 644, off Rte. 102, Pocahontas,* ☎ *276/945–2134.* 🎫 *$6.* ⏲ *Apr.–Oct., Mon.–Sat. 10–5, Sun. noon–6.*

CHARLOTTESVILLE, THE BLUE RIDGE, THE SHENANDOAH VALLEY, AND SOUTHWEST VIRGINIA A TO Z

To research prices, get advice from other travelers, and book travel arrangements, visit www.fodors.com.

AIRPORTS

The region's three largest airports are small and relatively hassle-free, so, except during peak holiday periods, travelers need allow no more time than for the typical security clearances. Regional carriers using small jets and turboprops are the norm, though larger jets sometimes serve Roanoke. The regional carriers primarily offer access to Washington, Charlotte, and Atlanta, but flights to and from Chicago, Pittsburgh, Cincinnati, New York, and Detroit are also available. Many travelers to western Virginia prefer to fly into international airports in Washington, Richmond, and Greensboro, N.C., then commute by rental car; all three major city airports are within two hours' drive of western Virginia destinations. Tri-City Regional Airport is just across the state line in Blountville, Tenn., for easy access to the Abingdon area.

➤ AIRPORT INFORMATION: **Charlottesville-Albemarle Airport** (✉ 8 mi north of Charlottesville at the intersection of Rtes. 606/649 off Rte. 29, ☎ 434/973–8342, WEB www.gocho.com). **Lynchburg Regional Airport** (✉ Rte. 29 S., ☎ 434/582–1150, WEB www.ci.lynchburg.va.us/airport). **Roanoke Regional Airport** (✉ off I–581, ☎ 540/362–1999, WEB www.roanokeairport.com). **Tri-City Regional Airport** (✉ Blountville, TN, ☎ 423/325–6000, WEB www.triflight.com).

TRANSFERS

Van on the Go shuttles guests from the Charlottesville airport to hotels, downtown, and area tourist attractions. Reservations are required. Several taxi services also serve the airport (*see* Taxis).

➤ CONTACT: **Van on the Go** (✉ Charlottesville-Albermarle Airport, ☎ 434/975–8267 or 877/973–7667).

BIKE TRAVEL

Though biking is an increasingly popular activity in this beautiful region, bicycles as a means of travel have yet to catch on widely in Virginia. Virginians by and large are gracious to cyclists, but there are still many local residents who adamantly believe that bikes have no place on roads. Visitors, however, will find the many winding two-lane roads of the region pleasant for bike touring.

With several bike lanes in existence and more in development, plus a steady college population and a pedestrian-oriented downtown, Charlottesville is relatively bike-friendly. The city even offers free bikes for use by the community: for more information, contact the Charlottesville Area Biking Alliance.

Despite its size and proximity to outdoor recreation, including abundant mountain biking and road cycling in surrounding areas, bike travel is not convenient within Roanoke. Bike lanes are nearly nonexistent, and the city's greenway system, although ambitious, is still in its infancy. Lynchburg offers the area's premier city greenway system, with more than 14 mi of tree-shrouded trails convenient to, but hidden from, the urban core, accommodating both travel and recreation.
➤ CONTACTS: **Charlottesville Area Biking Alliance** (WEB chaba.homestead.com).

BUS TRAVEL

Greyhound Lines serves Charlottesville. It also schedules several trips daily to and from Abingdon and Roanoke on its transcontinental routes between major U.S. cities. Buena Vista, just east of Lexington, and Staunton have daily service to and from New York City and points south.
➤ BUS LINES: **Greyhound Lines** (☎ 800/231–2222, WEB www.greyhound.com).

BUS TRAVEL WITHIN CHARLOTTESVILLE

The city of Charlottesville and the University of Virginia are served by separate transit systems. The Charlottesville Transit Service runs 10 routes during the day, covering much of the city and into parts of surrounding Albemarle County, and six at night. Buses run hourly; fare is 75¢. CTS also offers a free trolley service daily between downtown and the university. The University Transit Service at the University of Virginia has service to and from university buildings and parking lots, the hospital, on- and off-campus student housing, and the Barracks Road shopping center.
➤ INFORMATION: **Charlottesville Transit Service** (✉ 315 4th St. NW, ☎ 434/296–7433). **University Transit Service at the University of Virginia** (✉ 1101 Millmont St., ☎ 434/924–7231).

CAR RENTALS

Airports in Charlottesville, Roanoke, and Lynchburg are served by national car rental firms. Travelers in Charlottesville might want to consider Autorent, a smaller company that serves several central and eastern Virginia cities. The company meets passengers at the airport, bus station, and train station, and has four-wheel-drive vehicles, convertibles, and a 15-seat activity bus among its fleet of rentals.
➤ LOCAL AGENCIES: **Autorent** (✉ 1744 Rio Hill Shopping Center [Rte. 29 N], ☎ 434/973–1144 or 877/467–3681, WEB www.gorent.com).

CAR TRAVEL

The many pleasant highways and routes that snake through western Virginia's rolling countryside make driving a particularly good way to travel. The region's interstates (I–64, I–81, and I–77) are remarkably scenic, but the same mountainous terrain that contributes to their beauty can also make them treacherous. Dense valley fog banks, mountain-shrouding clouds, and gusty ridge-top winds are concerns at any time of the year, and winter brings ice and snow conditions that can change dramatically in a few miles when the elevation changes.

Charlottesville is where U.S. 29 (north–south) meets I–64. Lynchburg is the meeting point of U.S. 460 between Richmond and Roanoke and Route 29 south from Charlottesville. U.S. 460 meets I–81 at Roanoke.

Interstate 81 and Route 11 run north–south the length of the Shenandoah Valley and continue south into Tennessee. Interstate 66 west from Washington, D.C., which is 90 mi to the east, passes through Front

Royal to meet I–81 and Route 11 at the northern end of the valley. Interstate 64 connects the same highways with Charlottesville, 30 mi to the east. Route 39 into Bath County connects with I–81 just north of Lexington. Interstate 77 cuts off the southwest tip of the state, running north–south and crossing I–81 at Wytheville. Interstate 77 crosses two major ridges and passes through two mountain tunnels in Virginia.

PARKING

On-street parking in Charlottesville is tight and often hard to come by in downtown and near the University of Virginia. There are several pay parking lots and parking garages on Water Street and on the corner of Market Street and 5th Street NE.

➤ CONTACTS: **Charlottesville Parking Center** (☎ 434/977–1812).

TRAFFIC

Travelers will rarely find bumper-to-bumper traffic jams in Charlottesville or any other city in the region. The major exception: autumn Saturdays when the University of Virginia has a home football game. Virginia Tech games can similarly snarl traffic in the Roanoke–New River Valley area, including on I–81.

EMERGENCIES

Charlottesville is served by six locations of CVS. Pharmacies inside Kroger and Wal-Mart are also open 24 hours a day.

➤ DOCTORS AND DENTISTS: **Martha Jefferson Hospital, Physician Referral Services** (☎ 434/982–8450).

➤ EMERGENCY SERVICES: **Albemarle County Office of Emergency Services** (☎ 434/971–1263). **Ambulance, Fire, Police** (☎ 911).

LODGING

Both locally owned and major chain motels and hotels are plentiful along the interstate highways (I–81, I–64, I–77, I–66), with a particularly heavy concentration in the Charlottesville and Roanoke areas.

BED-AND-BREAKFASTS

Guesthouses can arrange accommodations for you. For $1 you can get a brochure about local B&Bs.

Accommodations in private homes and converted inns are available through Blue Ridge Bed & Breakfast Reservation Service.

➤ RESERVATION SERVICES: **Blue Ridge Bed & Breakfast Reservation Service** (✉ 2458 Castleman Rd., Berryville 22611, ☎ 540/955–1246 or 800/296–1246, FAX 540/955–4240). **Guesthouses** (✉ Box 5737, Charlottesville 22905, ☎ 434/979–7264, WEB www.va-guesthouses.com).

MAIL AND SHIPPING

Charlottesville's main post office is on U.S. 29, north of downtown. The Jefferson-Madison Regional Library has computers with Internet access. The central branch is downtown.

➤ POST OFFICE: **U.S. Post Office, Charlottesville** (✉ 1155 Seminole Trail, ☎ 434/978–7610).

➤ INTERNET ACCESS: **Jefferson-Madison Regional Library** (✉ 201 E. Market St., ☎ 434/979–7151).

OUTDOORS AND SPORTS

There are plentiful golf courses in the hills that dominate the region. Downhill skiing is available, typically from December to March, with start and end dates highly dependent on the whims of a variable climate, at four locations: Wintergreen, Bryce, Massanutten, and Homestead resorts.

With two sprawling national forests and a number of streams and rivers flowing out of the mountains, hunting and fishing are among the most popular outdoor sports in western Virginia.

➤ GOLF: **Virginia State Golf Association** (✉ 600 Founders Bridge Blvd., Midlothian 23113, ☎ 804/378–2300, WEB www.vsga.org).

➤ HUNTING AND FISHING: **Virginia Department of Game and Inland Fisheries** (✉ 4010 W. Broad St., Richmond 23230, ☎ 804/367–1000, WEB dgif.state.va.us).

TOURS

For $16, the Lexington Carriage Company will take visitors around town in a horse-drawn carriage for 45–50 minutes, from April through October. Tours begin and end at the Lexington Visitor Center. A self-guided walking-tour brochure of town is available from the Lexington Visitor Center. The Historic Staunton Foundation offers free one-hour walking tours Saturday morning at 10, Memorial Day through October, departing from the Woodrow Wilson Birthplace at 24 North Coalter Street. A brochure for a self-guided tour is available from the Staunton/Augusta Travel Information Center.

Contact the Jeffersonian Wine Grape Growers Society for brochures about vineyards in the foothills around Charlottesville. The Virginia Department of Agriculture has a statewide guide to wineries and festivals.

➤ HORSE-DRAWN TOURS: **Lexington Carriage Company** (☎ 540/463–5647).

➤ WALKING TOURS: **Historic Staunton Foundation** (☎ 540/885–7676). **Lexington Visitor Center** (✉ 102 E. Washington St., ☎ 540/463–3777).

➤ WINERY TOURS: **Jeffersonian Wine Grape Growers Society** (✉ 1455 Oakencroft Circle, Charlottesville 22901, ☎ 434/296–4188). **Virginia Department of Agriculture** (☎ 800/828–4637).

TRAIN TRAVEL

Amtrak has service three days a week to Charlottesville and Staunton, en route from New York and Chicago. The same train stops at Clifton Forge for the Homestead resort in Bath County. A complimentary shuttle bus on Sunday, Wednesday, and Friday connects Roanoke (Campbell Court and Roanoke Airport Sheraton) and Clifton Forge Rail Station. Amtrak's *Crescent* runs between New York City and New Orleans and stops daily in Lynchburg and Charlottesville.

➤ TRAIN STATIONS: **Clifton Forge** (✉ 400 Ridgeway St.). **Kemper Street Station** (✉ 825 Kemper St. , Lynchburg, ☎ 434/847–8247). **Staunton** (✉ 1 Middlebrook Ave.). **Union Station** (✉ 810 W. Main St., Charlottesville, ☎ 434/296–4559).

➤ TRAIN LINES: **Amtrak** (☎ 800/872–7245, WEB www.amtrak.com).

VISITOR INFORMATION

➤ TOURIST INFORMATION: **Abingdon Convention & Visitors Bureau** (✉ 335 Cummings St., Abingdon 24210, ☎ 276/676–2282, WEB www.abingdon.com/tourism). **Bath County Chamber of Commerce** (✉ Rte. 220, Box 718, Hot Springs 24445, ☎ 540/839–5409 or 800/628–8092, WEB www.bathcountyva.org). **Charlottesville/Albemarle Convention and Visitors Bureau** (✉ Rte. 20 S, Box 178, Charlottesville 22902, ☎ 434/977–1783 or 877/386–1102, WEB www.charlottesvilletourism.org). **Front Royal/Warren County Chamber of Commerce and Visitors Center** (✉ 414 E. Main St., Front Royal 22630, ☎ 540/635–3185, WEB www.frontroyalchamber.com). **Harrisonburg-Rockingham Convention and Visitors Bureau** (✉ 800 Country Club Rd., Harrisonburg 22801, ☎ 540/434–3862, WEB www.hrchamber.org). **Lexington Visitor Center**

(✉ 106 E. Washington St., Lexington 24450, ☎ 540/463–3777 or 877/453–9822, WEB www.lexingtonvirginia.com). **Lynchburg Regional Convention and Visitors Bureau** (✉ 216 12th St., Lynchburg 24504, ☎ 434/847–1811 or 800/732–5821). **New River Valley Visitors Alliance** (✉ 7502 Lee Hwy., Radford 24141, ☎ 540/633–6788 or 888/398–8988). **Roanoke Valley Convention and Visitors Bureau** (✉ 114 Market St., Roanoke 24011, ☎ 540/342–6025 or 800/635–5535, WEB www.visitroanokeva.com). **Shenandoah Valley Travel Association** (✉ Box 1040, New Market 22844, ☎ 540/740–3132 or 877/847–4878, WEB www.shenandoah.org). **Staunton/Augusta Travel Information Center** (✉ Box 810, Staunton 24401, ☎ 540/332–3972 or 800/342–7982, WEB www.stauntonva.org). **Winchester–Frederick County Chamber of Commerce/Convention and Visitors Bureau** (✉ 1360 S. Pleasant Valley Rd., Winchester 22601, ☎ 540/662–4135 or 800/662–1360, WEB www.winchesterva.org).

5 RICHMOND, FREDERICKSBURG, AND THE NORTHERN NECK

Virginia's capital is rich with remnants of the past, but its appealing restored neighborhoods and lively arts scene show how Richmond also embraces the present. At Petersburg, to the south, the Confederacy made its last stand. In Fredericksburg you'll find lovely 18th- and 19th-century homes, antiques shops, and Civil War battlefields. The Northern Neck peninsula gave birth to three presidents and the Confederates' commander in chief, and also nurtured their love of state and country.

Updated by CiCi Williamson

A **HOST OF PATRIOTS AND PRESIDENTS** have lived and worked in the heart of the Old Dominion, an area that takes in Richmond, Fredericksburg, Petersburg, and the Northern Neck. The birthplaces, boyhood homes, or burial places of notable figures such as George Washington, James Monroe, John Tyler, and Robert E. Lee can be found here, and the area has many associations with other leaders, including Patrick Henry and Thomas Jefferson. Serving as Virginia's capital since 1779, Richmond is also the former capital of the Confederacy. Besides numerous Revolutionary War and Civil War sites, the city proudly claims a gaslight district full of 19th-century homes and the Thomas Jefferson–designed Virginia state capitol.

Half an hour south of Richmond, Petersburg is a delightful antebellum city with many historic attractions. Besieged by the Union Army in 1864, the townspeople bravely did their best to protect the Confederacy. Less than an hour north of Richmond sits the appealing city of Fredericksburg, a history buff's dream, containing hundreds of impressive 18th- and 19th-century homes. The nearby Fredericksburg/Spotsylvania National Military Park presents the story of the area's role in the Civil War.

East of Fredericksburg, away from the blood-soaked and fought-over grounds, peace and quiet reign in a 90-mi-long, million-acre peninsula Virginians call "The Northern Neck." This outdoorsman's escape was the birthplace of three presidents, including the Father of Our Country. Here, wide rivers and the briny Chesapeake Bay entice water lovers and sports anglers. Gazing across the peaceful property where Washington was born, it's easy to see why he longed to choose a life at Mount Vernon instead of serving two terms as our first president.

Exploring Richmond, Fredericksburg, and the Northern Neck

Richmond, 100 mi south of Washington, D.C., on the James River, is the state's historic capital. It's easy to get here on I–95. Petersburg, with its Civil War history, is a mere half hour south of Richmond. Midway between Washington and Richmond (50 mi from each) on I–95, Fredericksburg is a lovely place to relax and retrace 18th- and 19th-century history in homes and museums and on nearby battlefields. About 20 mi east of Fredericksburg, the Northern Neck begins. There is no public transportation to this rural area, but a car affords the freedom to wander at will to its many historic sites and water views.

Pleasures and Pastimes

Dining

CATEGORY	COST*
$$$$	over $32
$$$	$22–$32
$$	$12–$22
$	under $12

**per person for a main course at dinner*

Lodging

CATEGORY	COST*
$$$$	over $225
$$$	$150–$225
$$	$100–$150
$	under $100

**All prices are for a standard double room, excluding state tax.*

RICHMOND

Centered on the fall line of the James River, about 75 mi upriver from the Chesapeake Bay, Richmond completes the transition from Tidewater Virginia into the Piedmont, the central section of rolling plains that reaches toward the mountain barrier in the west. Not only is Richmond the capital of the Commonwealth, but it was also the capital of the Confederacy. As a result, the city is studded with historic sites.

At the start of the Civil War, Richmond was the most industrialized city in the South, and it remains an important city for national industries. After years of urban decay, Richmond transformed itself into a lively and sophisticated modern town, adding high technology to traditional economic bases that include shipping and banking. It's one of the South's preeminent art cities, flourishing with avant-garde painting and sculpture in addition to artifacts and magnificent traditional works, such as the Fabergé eggs in the Virginia Museum of Fine Arts.

Richmond is also a gold mine for genealogy and history researchers. The following libraries or archives are interesting stops for the casual browser as well as for those in search of ancestors: the Library of Virginia, Virginia Historical Society Museum of Virginia History, Beth Ahabah Museum and Archives, American Historical Foundation Museum, and Black History Museum & Cultural Center of Virginia.

Downtown

Richmond's historic attractions lie north of the James River, which bisects the city with a sweeping curve. The heart of old Richmond is the Court End district downtown. This area, close to the capitol, contains seven National Historic Landmarks, three museums, and 11 additional buildings on the National Register of Historic Places—all within eight blocks.

Running west from the Court End district is Main Street, lined with banks; stores are concentrated along Grace Street, to the north. Cary Street, an east–west thoroughfare, becomes, between 12th and 15th streets, the cobblestone center of Shockoe Slip. This area (once the city's largest commercial trading district) and Shockoe Bottom (on land formerly a Native American trading post) are unique restored areas filled with trendy shops, restaurants, and nightlife. Shockoe Bottom landmarks include the 17th Street Farmers' Market, operating since 1775, and Main Street Station, an elaborate Victorian structure capped by red tiles that was Richmond's first train station. To the east above the James River is Church Hill, a fashionable neighborhood of restored 18th- and 19th-century homes and churches.

Drive west beyond the historic downtown and you'll find a fascinating group of close-in, charming, and distinctive neighborhoods. Not far from the capitol is Jackson Ward, called the "Home of Black Capitalism," a cultural and entrepreneurial center after the Civil War.

Numbers in the text correspond to numbers in the margin and on the Richmond map.

A Good Tour

Because the historic sites in Richmond are fairly spread out, it's best to do a series of walks, either driving or taking public transportation between groups of attractions. On weekends from May through November, you can take the Museum Connector ($1), which shuttles between museums and attractions. It's also worth noting that the city's many one-way streets may make for a circuitous route to some sights.

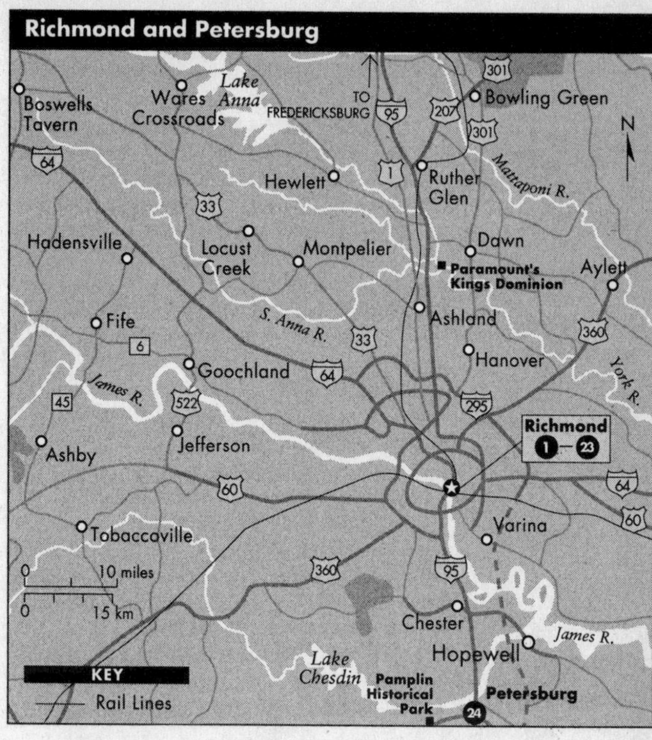

A good place to start is at the east side of downtown on Church Hill. At the **Chimborazo Medical Museum** ①, one of the National Park Service's five Richmond-area visitor centers, you can pick up information about Richmond and the Civil War battlefields nearby.

Drive nine blocks west on Broad Street and visit **St. John's Episcopal Church** ②. If you're comfortable walking uphill, walk south three blocks to Main Street, turn right, and walk five blocks downhill to the **Edgar Allan Poe Museum** ③. Walk back up to your car and head west to downtown. Parking downtown can be difficult, but you can park free near the **Museum and White House of the Confederacy** ④. To get here drive west on Broad Street and turn right on 11th Street, then right on Clay Street. Parking is free in the adjacent hospital parking garage with ticket validation at this museum or at the nearby **Valentine Museum** ⑤, which deals with city history. From here you can walk south on 10th Street and then right on Marshall to reach the **John Marshall House** ⑥. Across the street is the **Library of Virginia** ⑦, which has free underground parking.

A short walk down 9th Street will bring you to the **Virginia State Capitol** ⑧. If you want to take in a view rather than moving on to another museum, stroll **Canal Walk** ⑨, beginning south of the capitol at 12th and Main streets and following the locks on the James River. The Shockoe Slip area of upscale shops starts at Cary and 12th. The **Richmond National Battlefield Park Visitor Center** ⑩ is close to the river near 5th and Tredegar streets.

You could also stretch your legs walking the 12 blocks to the next site, but it's probably best to retrieve the car. Drive west on Broad Street, turn right on 2nd Street, and drive four blocks north to visit the **Maggie L. Walker National Historic Site** ⑪, in Jackson Ward, honoring the achievements of a pioneering black entrepreneur. Next go west on Leigh

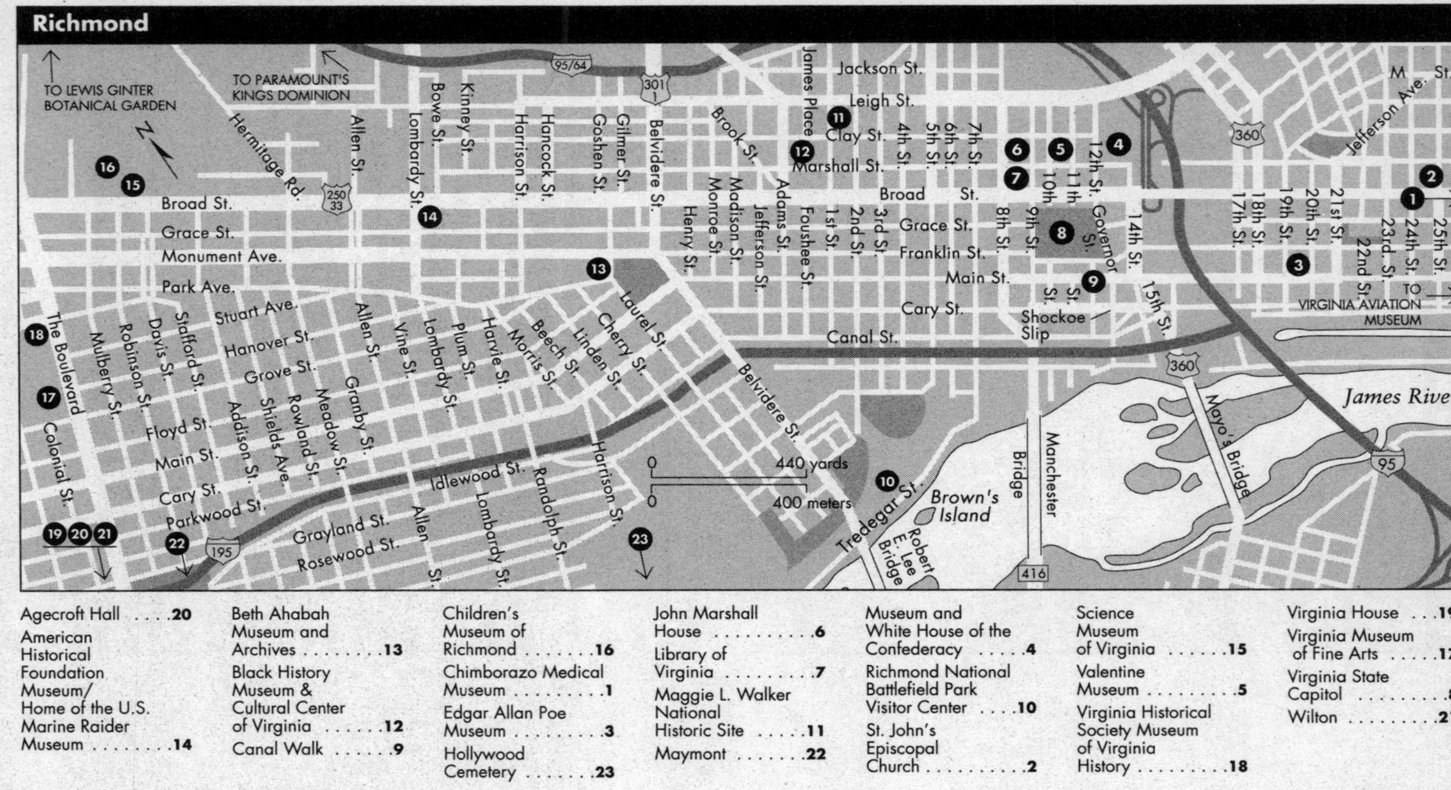
Richmond
TO LEWIS GINTER BOTANICAL GARDEN
TO PARAMOUNT'S KINGS DOMINION
TO VIRGINIA AVIATION MUSEUM
James River
Mayo's Bridge
Manchester Bridge
Brown's Island
Robert E. Lee Bridge
Tredegar St.
Shockoe Slip
Hermitage Rd.
Broad St.
Grace St.
Monument Ave.
Park Ave.
Stuart Ave.
Hanover St.
Grove St.
Floyd St.
Main St.
Cary St.
Parkwood St.
Grayland St.
Rosewood St.
Idlewood St.
The Boulevard
Colonial St.
Mulberry St.
Robinson St.
Davis St.
Stafford St.
Addison St.
Shields Ave.
Rowland St.
Meadow St.
Granby St.
Allen St.
Vine St.
Lombardy St.
Plum St.
Harvie St.
Morris St.
Beech St.
Linden St.
Cherry St.
Laurel St.
Belvidere St.
Harrison St.
Randolph St.
Kinney St.
Bowe St.
Hancock St.
Goshen St.
Gilmer St.
Henry St.
Monroe St.
Madison St.
Jefferson St.
Adams St.
Foushee St.
Brook St.
James Place
Jackson St.
Leigh St.
Clay St.
Marshall St.
1st St.
2nd St.
3rd St.
4th St.
5th St.
6th St.
7th St.
8th St.
9th St.
10th St.
11th St.
12th St.
Governor St.
14th St.
15th St.
17th St.
18th St.
19th St.
20th St.
21st St.
22nd St.
23rd. St.
24th St.
25th St.
Jefferson Ave.
M St.
Franklin St.
Canal St.
440 yards
400 meters
Agecroft Hall 20
American Historical Foundation Museum/ Home of the U.S. Marine Raider Museum 14
Beth Ahabah Museum and Archives 13
Black History Museum & Cultural Center of Virginia 12
Canal Walk 9
Children's Museum of Richmond 16
Chimborazo Medical Museum 1
Edgar Allan Poe Museum 3
Hollywood Cemetery 23
John Marshall House 6
Library of Virginia 7
Maggie L. Walker National Historic Site 11
Maymont 22
Museum and White House of the Confederacy 4
Richmond National Battlefield Park Visitor Center 10
St. John's Episcopal Church 2
Science Museum of Virginia 15
Valentine Museum 5
Virginia Historical Society Museum of Virginia History 18
Virginia House . . .19
Virginia Museum of Fine Arts 17
Virginia State Capitol 8
Wilton 21

Street and turn left on Saint James Place to the **Black History Museum & Cultural Center of Virginia** ⑫, on Clay Street.

TIMING

To visit all these sites would take an entire day. Allow at least an hour for each site or museum—two hours for the Museum and White House of the Confederacy. If you plan to do research at the Library of Virginia, allow a half day there.

Sights to See

12 **Black History Museum & Cultural Center of Virginia.** The goal of this museum in the Jackson Ward is to gather visual, oral, and written records and artifacts that commemorate the lives and accomplishments of blacks in Virginia. On display are 5,000 documents, fine art objects, traditional African artifacts, textiles from various ethnic groups throughout Africa, and artwork by artists Sam Gilllam, John Biggers, and P. H. Polk. ⊠ *00 Clay St., at Foushee St.,* ☎ *804/780–9093,* WEB *www.blackhistorymuseum.org.* 🎟 *$4.* ⏲ *Tues.–Sat. 10–5.*

9 **Canal Walk.** The 1¼-mi Canal Walk meanders through downtown Richmond along the Haxall Canal, the James River, and the Kanawha Canal, and can be enjoyed on foot or in boats. Along the way, look for history exhibits such as the Flood Wall Gallery, bronze medallions, and other exhibits placed on Brown's Island and Canal Walk by the Richmond Historical Riverfront Foundation. Many sights intersect with Canal Walk, including the Richmond National Battlefield Park Civil War Visitor Center and those places at which 5th, 7th, Virginia, 14th, 15th, and 17th streets meet the water.

The James River–Kanawha Canal was proposed by George Washington to bring ships around the falls of the James River. Brown's Island hosts festivals and concerts in warmer months. **Richmond Canal Cruises** (⊠ 139 Virginia St., ☎ 804/649–2800) operates a 35-minute ride on the canal in a 38-seat open boat. Tours, which cost $5, depart from the Turning Basin near 14th and Virginia streets. If you're in a car, try to find the site before parking. Lack of prominent signage makes it challenging to find, and parking lots are a few blocks away.

1 **Chimborazo Medical Museum.** This was once the Civil War's largest and best-equipped hospital. Chimborazo opened in 1861 and treated more than 76,000 Confederate soldiers between 1862 and 1865. It could house more than 3,000 patients in its 100 wards. This site—once more than 40 acres—now houses a National Park Service visitor center and a small medical museum that tells the story of the patients, hospital, and physicians through uniforms, documents and other artifacts. ⊠ *3215 Broad St.,* ☎ *804/226–1981,* WEB *www.nps.gov/rich.* 🎟 *Free.* ⏲ *Daily 9–5.*

3 **Edgar Allan Poe Museum.** Richmond's oldest residence, the Old Stone House in the Church Hill Historic District just east of downtown, now holds a museum honoring the famous writer. Poe grew up in Richmond, and although he never lived in this 1737 structure, his disciples have made it a shrine with some of the writer's possessions on display. The Raven Room has illustrations inspired by his most famous poem. ⊠ *1914 E. Main St.,* ☎ *804/648–5523 or 888/213–2763,* WEB *www.poemuseum.org.* 🎟 *$6.* ⏲ *Tues.–Sat. 10–5, Sun. noon–5 (last tour departs at 4).*

6 **John Marshall House.** John Marshall was chief justice of the U.S. Supreme Court for 34 years—longer than any other. He built his red-brick Federal-style house with neoclassical motifs in 1790. Appointed to the court by President John Adams, Marshall also served as secretary of state and ambassador to France. The house, fully restored and

furnished, has wood paneling and wainscoting, narrow arched passageways, and a mix of period pieces and heirlooms. The house has been a beautifully maintained museum since 1913. ✉ *9th and Marshall Sts.,* ☎ *804/648–7998,* WEB *www.apva.org/apva/marshall.html.* *$5.* ⏲ *Tues.–Sat. 10–5; Sun. noon–5.*

7 **Library of Virginia.** As the official state archive, this library preserves and provides access to more than 83 million manuscript items documenting four centuries of Virginia history. The library also houses and makes available to researchers more than 1½ million books, bound periodicals, microfilm reels, newspapers, and state and federal documents. Its collections include 240,000 photographs, prints, engravings, posters, and paintings. The building has free underground parking. ✉ *800 E. Broad St.,* ☎ *804/692–3500,* WEB *www.lva.lib.va.us.* *Free.* ⏲ *Mon.–Sat. 9–5.*

11 **Maggie L. Walker National Historic Site.** From 1904 to 1934, this restored 25-room brick building was the home of a pioneering African-American businesswoman and educator whose endeavors included banking, insurance, and a newspaper. You can take a 30-minute tour of the house and see a movie about her accomplishments. ✉ *110½ E. Leigh St.,* ☎ *804/771–2017,* WEB *www.nps/gov/malw.* *Free.* ⏲ *Wed.–Sun. 9–5.*

★ 4 **Museum and White House of the Confederacy.** These two buildings provide a look at a crucial period in the city's history. The museum (a good place to start) has elaborate permanent exhibitions on the Civil War era. The "world's largest collection of Confederate memorabilia" includes such artifacts as the sword Robert E. Lee wore to the surrender at Appomattox. Next door, the "White House" has in fact always been painted gray. Made of brick in 1818, the building was stuccoed to give the appearance of large stone blocks. Preservationists have painstakingly re-created the interior as it was during the Civil War, when Jefferson Davis lived in the house. During the 45-minute guided tour, you'll see the entry hall's period 9-ft-tall French rococo mirrors and its floor cloth, painted to resemble ceramic tiles. You can park free in the adjacent hospital parking garage; the museum will validate tickets. ✉ *1201 E. Clay St.,* ☎ *804/649–1861,* WEB *www.moc.org.* *Combination ticket $9.50; museum only, $6; White House only, $7.* ⏲ *Mon.–Sat. 10–5, Sun. noon–5.*

10 **Richmond National Battlefield Park Visitor Center.** Inside what was once the Tredegar Iron Works, this is the best place to get maps and other materials on the Civil War battlefields and attractions in the Richmond area. A self-guided tour and optional tape tour for purchase covers the two major military threats to Richmond—the Peninsula Campaign of 1862 and the Overland Campaign of 1864—as well as the impact on Richmond's home front. Three floors of exhibits in the main building include unique artifacts on loan from other Civil War history institutions. Other original buildings on the site are a carpentry shop, gun foundry, office, and company store.

Built in 1837, the ironworks, along with smaller area iron foundries, made Richmond the center of iron manufacturing in the southern United States. When the Civil War began in 1861, the ironworks geared up to make the artillery, ammunition, and other matériel that sustained the Confederate war machine. Its rolling mills provided the armor plating for warships, including the ironclad CSS *Virginia.* The works—saved from burning in 1865—went on to play an important role in rebuilding the devastated South; it also produced munitions in both world wars. A bookstore and café are adjacent to the visitor center. If you're lucky, you may still find free on-street parking; a pay lot at the visitor center costs $4. ✉ *5th and Tredegar Sts.,* ☎ *804/771–2145.* 🎟 *Free.* ⏲ *Daily 9–5.*

❷ **St. John's Episcopal Church.** For security reasons, the rebellious Second Virginia Convention met in Richmond instead of at Williamsburg; it was in this 1741 church on March 23, 1775, that Patrick Henry delivered the speech in which he declared, "Give me liberty or give me death!" His argument persuaded the Second Virginia Convention to arm a Virginia militia. The speech is reenacted May–September on Sunday at 2 PM. The cemetery includes the graves of Edgar Allan Poe's mother, Elizabeth Arnold Poe, and many famous early Virginians, notably George Wythe, a signer of the Declaration of Independence. The chapel gift shop, in the old Victorian gothic house on the grounds, has Colonial crafts and and other items for sale. Guided tours are led on the half hour; those planning a Saturday visit should call ahead, especially in May and June; weddings often close the church to the public. ✉ *2401 E. Broad St., at 24th St.,* ☎ *804/648–5015.* 🎟 *$3.* ⏲ *Mon.–Sat. 10–4, Sun. 1–4.*

❺ **Valentine Museum.** This museum impressively documents the life and history of Richmond with exhibits that cover topics from architecture to race relations. **Wickham House** (1812), a part of the Valentine, is more rightly a mansion; it was designed by architect Alexander Parris, the creator of Boston's Faneuil Hall. John Wickham was Richmond's wealthiest citizen of the time, and Daniel Webster and Zachary Taylor were frequent guests. The house interiors are stunning, but not everything at the museum is opulent: the slave quarters, also meticulously restored, provide a chilling contrast to the mansion's splendor. ✉ *1015 E. Clay St.,* ☎ *804/649–0711,* WEB *www.valentinemuseum.org.* 🎟 *$5.* ⏲ *Tues.–Sat. 10–5, Sun. noon–5.*

OFF THE BEATEN PATH

VIRGINIA AVIATION MUSEUM – The legendary SR-71 Blackbird spy plane is the newest permanent addition to this hangar-style museum east of downtown. Able to travel faster than three times the speed of sound and at an elevation of more than 85,000 ft (near the edge of the earth's atmosphere), the U.S. Air Force's 32 Blackbirds were used on reconnaissance missions from 1964 to 1990. The museum also has Captain Dick Merrill's 1930s open cockpit mail plane; airworthy replicas of the Wright brothers' 1900, 1901, and 1902 gliders; and a World War I SPAD VII in mint condition. Virginia's Aviation Hall of Fame is also housed at this branch of the Science Museum of Virginia. To get here, take Exit 197 off I–64E and follow signs to the museum. ✉ *Richmond International Airport, 5701 Huntsman Rd.,* ☎ *804/236–3622,* WEB *www.smv.org.* 🎟 *$4.* ⏲ *Mon.–Sat. 9:30–5; Sun. noon–5.*

★ ❽ **Virginia State Capitol.** Thomas Jefferson designed this grand edifice in 1785, modeling it on a Roman temple—the Maison Carrée—in Nîmes, France. The capitol, the seat of the oldest lawmaking body in the United States, is still in use by the state government. It contains a wealth of sculpture: busts of each of the eight presidents that Virginia has given the nation, and a famous life-size—and lifelike—statue of George Washington by Houdon. In the old Hall of the House of Delegates, Robert E. Lee accepted the command of the Confederate forces in Virginia (a bronze statue marks the spot where he stood). Free guided tours of the capitol lasting 20–30 minutes are conducted weekdays 9 to 5. Elsewhere on the grounds, at the Old Bell Tower at 9th Street, you can get travel information for the entire state. ✉ *Capitol Sq.,* ☎ *804/698–1788.* 🎟 *Free.* ⏲ *Apr.–Nov., daily 9–5; Dec.–Mar., Mon.–Sat. 9–5, Sun. 1–5.*

The Fan District

To the west of downtown, Monument Avenue, 140 ft wide and divided by a verdant median, is lined with statues of Civil War heroes and the stately homes of some of the first families of Virginia. A block south, a series of streets fanning out southwesterly from Park Avenue near Virginia Commonwealth University creates the Fan District, a treasury of restored turn-of-the-20th-century town houses that has become a popular neighborhood. Adjacent to it is Carytown, a restored area of shops and eateries along Cary Street.

A Good Tour

Follow Broad Street west, and turn left on Laurel Street to reach the **Beth Ahabah Museum and Archives** ⑬. For the **American Historical Foundation Museum/Home of the U.S. Marine Raider Museum** ⑭, continue west on Broad, turn left on Lombardy Street, and drive one block before turning left into the museum. Plan to spend a couple of hours at the **Science Museum of Virginia** ⑮, about five blocks farther west on Broad Street. Next door is the **Children's Museum of Richmond** ⑯. There's lots of free parking here. After your visit, take the Boulevard south to the **Virginia Museum of Fine Arts** ⑰. In the same block is the **Virginia Historical Society Museum of Virginia History** ⑱. Trendy Cary Street is just four blocks farther south.

TIMING

Even if you select only two or three museums to visit, allow four–five hours for this tour.

Sights to See

⑭ **American Historical Foundation Museum/Home of the U.S. Marine Raider Museum.** Housing the largest collection of military knives and bayonets in the United States, this museum also contains personal artifacts of Confederate general J. E. B. Stuart and Confederate partisan John S. Mosby. Other exhibits chronicle the deeds of the World War II Marine Raiders, a group started by Colonel Evan Carlson to raid Pacific Islands such as Makin. ✉ *1142 W. Grace St.,* ☎ *804/353–1812,* WEB *www.ahfrichmond.com/museum.html.* 🎫 *Free.* ⏲ *Weekdays 9–5.*

⑬ **Beth Ahabah Museum and Archives.** This repository contains articles and documents related to the Richmond and southern Jewish experience, including the records of two congregations. ✉ *1109 W. Franklin St.,* ☎ *804/353–2668,* WEB *www.bethahaba.org.* 🎫 *Free, $3 donation suggested.* ⏲ *Sun.–Thurs. 10–3.*

⑯ **Children's Museum of Richmond.** A welcoming, hands-on place for children and families, the museum is a place to climb, explore, experiment, and play until every surface area is smudged with fingerprints. Bright, colorful, and crowded, the museum's different sections keep an eye out for a child's best interests. How It Works lets children experiment with tools, materials, and their own endless energy. The Feeling Good Neighborhood has a functioning apple orchard as well as a monster-size digestive system. Our Great Outdoors houses the museum's most popular attraction, The Cave, where children explore a 40-ft replica of a Virginia limestone cave and are introduced to earth science, oceanography, and rock collecting. In the Art Studio, the paint gets on someone else's walls for a change. Specific exhibits include Children's Bank, Health and Safety, TV Studio, SuperMarket, Computer Station, Art Studio, StagePlay, and In My Own Backyard (for toddlers). ✉ *2626 W. Broad St.,* ☎ *804/474–2667 or 877/295–2667,* WEB *www.c-mor.org.* 🎫 *$6.* ⏲ *Mon.–Sat. 9:30–5, Sun. noon–5.*

OFF THE BEATEN PATH **LEWIS GINTER BOTANICAL GARDEN** – Among the extensive gardens here are numerous specialty collections of ivy, narcissus, azaleas, rhododendrons, daylilies, and roses. Special areas include the Healing Garden (medicinal plants), the Children's Garden, Asian Valley, Flagler Perennial, English Cottage, and Tea House. The huge visitor center houses meeting facilities, gallery space for exhibitions, a gift shop, and a café open for lunch daily. A 36,000-square-ft education and library complex was completed in the fall of 2002, and a spectacular glass conservatory with a 63–ft-tall dome is slated for completion in 2003. The garden is northwest of downtown. ✉ *1800 Lakeside Ave.,* ☎ *804/262–9887,* WEB *www.lewisginter.org.* 🎫 *$7.* ⏲ *Daily 9–5.*

★ 👆 ⓯ **Science Museum of Virginia.** Aerospace, astronomy, electricity, physical sciences, computers, crystals, telecommunications, and a Foucault pendulum are among the subjects covered in exhibits here, many of which strongly appeal to children. The biggest spectacle is in the Universe Theater, also a planetarium, where an Omnimax theater (like IMAX but with a curved screen) draws the audience into the movie or astronomy show. The museum is in a former train station with a massive dome. ✉ *2500 W. Broad St.,* ☎ *804/367–1080,* WEB *www.smv.org.* 🎫 *Museum $6; museum, Omnimax, and planetarium $12.* ⏲ *Mon.–Wed. 9:30–5, Thurs.–Sun. 11:30–5.*

⓲ **Virginia Historical Society Museum of Virginia History.** With 7 million manuscripts and 125,000 books, the library here is a key stop for researchers and genealogists. The visitor-friendly museum mounts regularly changing exhibits and has permanent exhibitions that include an 800-piece collection of Confederate weapons and equipment and "The Story of Virginia, an American Experience," which covers 16,000 years of history and has galleries on topics such as Becoming Confederates and Becoming Equal Virginians. ✉ *428 N. Boulevard, at Kensington Ave.,* ☎ *804/358–4901,* WEB *www.vahistorical.org.* 🎫 *$4.* ⏲ *Mon.–Sat. 10–5; Sun., galleries only, 1–5. Research library closed Sun.*

★ ⓱ **Virginia Museum of Fine Arts.** The collections here are rich in diversity, from African masks to art nouveau furniture. The museum's most startling pieces are Duane Hanson's super-realistic sculptures; their everyday attire and poses frequently lead visitors to think the figures are living people. Five Fabergé eggs are some of the museum's most treasured works. Among other important works are Roman statuary; paintings by Goya, Renoir, Monet, and van Gogh; and art from the Far East, ancient America, the Orient, Africa, and Egypt. ✉ *Boulevard and Grove Ave.,* ☎ *804/340–1400,* WEB *www.vmfa.state.va.us.* 🎫 *Free; $5 suggested donation.* ⏲ *Tues.–Sun. 11–5.*

Richmond's Estates

Not far from downtown are mansions and country estates, two with buildings transported from England. Presidents and Confederate leaders are buried in Hollywood Cemetery.

A Good Drive

Virginia House, Agecroft Hall, and Wilton are on the west side of Richmond, about 10 minutes from the Museum of Fine Arts. Take Boulevard south to Grove Avenue and turn right. Turn left on Malvern Avenue (which turns into Canterbury, then Sulgrave Road) to visit **Virginia House** ⑲ and **Agecroft Hall** ⑳. To see **Wilton** ㉑, follow Berkshire Street to Route 147 and turn left. Turn left again at Wilton Road; the historic house is at the end of the road. If you want to visit **Maymont** ㉒, drive back out on Wilton Road and turn right on Route 147. After reaching Carytown, turn right on Pump House Road to visit Maymont's petting zoo or continue straight and turn right on Meadow Street to see the mansion. **Hollywood Cemetery** ㉓ will be on the left side of Meadow Street.

TIMING

To visit each mansion, allow anywhere from 30 to 60 minutes for its guided tour. Additionally, Virginia House and Maymont have extensive gardens to wander. Most of these country estates are closed on Monday.

Sights to See

⑳ **Agecroft Hall.** Built in Lancashire, England, in the 15th century during the reign of King Henry VIII, Agecroft Hall was transported here in 1926. It is the finest Tudor manor house in the United States. Set amid gardens planted with specimens typical of 1580–1640, the house contains an extensive assortment of Tudor and early Stuart art and furniture (1485–1660) as well as a few priceless collector's items. ✉ *4305 Sulgrave Rd.,* ☎ *804/353–4241,* WEB *www.agecrofthall.com.* 🎟 *$7.* ⏲ *Tues.–Sat. 10–4, Sun. 12:30–5.*

㉓ **Hollywood Cemetery.** Many noted Virginians are buried here, including presidents John Tyler and James Monroe; Confederate president Jefferson Davis; generals Fitzhugh Lee, J. E. B. Stuart, and George E. Pickett; the statesman John Randolph; and Matthew Fontaine Maury, a naval scientist. ✉ *Cherry and Albemarle Sts.,* ☎ *804/648–8501.* 🎟 *Free.* ⏲ *Mon.–Sat. 7–5; Sun. 8–5.*

㉒ **Maymont.** On this 100-acre Victorian estate is the lavish Maymont House museum, a carriage collection, and elaborate Italian and Japanese gardens. A true family attraction, Maymont's complex includes the new Nature & Visitor Center, native wildlife exhibits, and a children's farm. A café is open for lunch. Tram tours and carriage rides are available. ✉ *2201 Shields Lake Dr.,* ☎ *804/358–7166,* WEB *www.maymont.org.* 🎟 *Free; donation suggested.* ⏲ *Grounds daily 10–7; mansion, nature center, and barn Tues.–Sun. noon–5.*

⑲ **Virginia House.** Built in 1119, this English monastery-turned–country house was saved from a 1925 demolition. Its new owners, Alexander and Virginia Weddell, had it dismantled stone by stone, and seven ships carried the components across the Atlantic and up the James River. After three years of reconstruction, the Weddells had their house (named for Mrs. Weddell, not the state), a re-creation of a European estate with lush gardens. After the couple's death in a train crash, the house was bequeathed to the Virginia Historical Society. The mansion is furnished with treasures acquired worldwide during Weddell's career in the diplomatic service. Mansion tours are given on the hour. Extensive gardens have seasonal flowerings year-round. ✉ *4301 Sulgrave Rd.,* ☎ *804/353–4251.* 🎟 *$5.* ⏲ *Fri.–Sat. 10–4, Sun. 12:30–5; last tour begins 1 hr before closing.*

㉑ **Wilton.** William Randolph III built this elegant Georgian house in 1753 on the only James River plantation in Richmond. Once 14 mi downriver, the home was moved brick by brick to its current site when industry encroached upon its former location. Wilton is the only house in Virginia completely paneled floor to ceiling in every room, and the pastel-painted panels and sunlit alcoves are part of its beauty. The home's 1815 period furnishings include the family's original desk bookcase and an original map of Virginia drawn by Thomas Jefferson's father. The Garden Club of Virginia landscaped the terraced lawns that overlook the James River. ✉ *215 S. Wilton Rd., off Cary St.,* ☎ *804/282–5936,* WEB *www.wiltonhousemuseum.org.* 🎟 *$5.* ⏲ *Mar.–Jan., Tues.–Sat. 10–4:30 (last tour at 3:45); Sun. 1:30–4:30.*

Dining

$$$–$$$$ ✕ **La Petite France.** The walls are emerald green at this formal, traditional French restaurant three blocks off West Broad Street near Staples Mill Road. Reproductions of 18th-century English landscapes and portraits hang on the walls. Panache of lobster (lobster poached in vermouth with truffles and whiskey sauce over pasta) is a popular entrée; other specialties are chateaubriand for two and Dover sole amandine. ✉ *2108 Maywill St.,* ☎ *804/353–8729,* WEB *www.lapetitefrance.net. AE, DC, MC, V. Closed Sun.–Mon.*

$$$–$$$$ ✕ **Lemaire.** The formal rooms of the grandest restaurant in Richmond have an elegant glass conservatory highlighted with ornamental iron and a copper roof. Named for the chef Jefferson employed while president, Lemaire serves a seasonal menu with a French accent as well as a deep Virginia drawl. Local Virginia specialties and produce appear throughout: mainstays include Virginia peanut soup, smoked local trout, roasted boneless rack of Virginia lamb, and Chesapeake crab cakes. Three meals a day are served. ✉ *Jefferson Hotel, 101 W. Franklin St., at Adams St.,* ☎ *804/788–8000,* WEB *www.jefferson-hotel.com. AE, D, DC, MC, V.*

$$$ ✕ **Amici Ristorante.** Game specialties such as pheasant ravioli, stuffed quail, buffalo with Gorgonzola, and ostrich appear regularly on the menu along with osso buco and other northern Italian dishes. In the cozy first floor of this Carytown restaurant, the walls around the booths are adorned with flowered tapestries and oil paintings of Italy. The second floor is more formal, and the white walls trimmed with stenciled grapes and vines. ✉ *3343 W. Cary St.,* ☎ *804/353–4700. AE, MC, V.*

$$–$$$ ★ ✕ **Europa.** At this Mediterranean café and tapas bar, there are plenty of enticing main dishes, but many diners opt for making a meal from the extensive list of tapas priced in the single digits, including Spanish meats and cheeses, lamb meatballs, codfish fritters, and stewed squid. Housed in a former warehouse in Shockoe Bottom just a few blocks from the capitol, the lively restaurant has a quarry-tile floor and original brick walls. Paella fanciers can choose from three versions: "La Valencia" (the traditional meats, fish, and shellfish); "La Marinera" (fish and shellfish); or "La Barcelonesa" (chicken, chorizo, and lamb). ✉ *1409 E. Cary St.,* ☎ *804/643–0911,* WEB *www.europarichmond.com. AE, MC, V. Closed Sun.*

$–$$$ ✕ **The Tobacco Company.** A tobacco warehouse built in the 1860s houses this popular spot. Prime rib (seconds on the house), fresh seafood, and daily specials are the pride of the menu. Perennials include chicken Chesapeake (with crabmeat) and veal marsala. The Atrium has live music nightly. ✉ *1201 E. Cary St.,* ☎ *804/782–9431,* WEB *www.thetobaccocompany.com. AE, D, MC, V.*

$–$$ ✕ **Joe's Inn.** Spaghetti is the specialty—especially the Greek version, with feta and provolone cheese baked on top—and sandwiches (around $5) are distinguished for their generous proportions. Regulars predominate at this local Fan District hangout, but they make newcomers feel right at home. Brunch is served on Sunday. ✉ *205 N. Shields Ave.,* ☎ *804/355–2282. AE, MC, V.*

$–$$ ✕ **Mamma Zu's.** Dine early to avoid a wait at this local favorite, a well-kept secret in the Oregon Hill neighborhood. Jaguars and BMWs stand out when parked alongside this worse-for-wear building. The shabbiness continues indoors with the peeling, painted concrete floor and artsy doodles on orange walls. There's only one menu—myriad hand-chalked items in Italian on a blackboard over the bar—and only one word for the authentic Italian food: outstanding. Service, however, can vary in quality. Dishes change, but you'll always find pasta and seafood.

✉ 501 Pine St., ☎ 804/788–4205. Reservations not accepted. AE. Closed Sun.

Lodging

Of the nearly 150 hotels and motels in the Richmond area, these are among the most noteworthy.

$$$–$$$$ ★ **Jefferson Hotel.** The staircase of 36 steps in the lobby of this famous downtown beaux arts–style hotel resembles the one in the movie *Gone with the Wind.* A National Historic Landmark, the Jefferson (1895) has an opulent grand entrance and indoor swimming pool and terrace; the lobby courtyard is skylit. Yellow, blues, mauves, and dark woods dominate in the guest rooms, which have reproduction 19th-century furnishings. The Lemaire restaurant is highly respected. *✉ 101 W. Franklin St., at Adams St., 23220, ☎ 804/788–8000 or 800/424–8014, FAX 804/225–0334, WEB www.jefferson-hotel.com. 275 rooms, 27 suites. 2 restaurants, room service, indoor pool, health club, bar. AE, D, DC, MC, V.*

$$$ ★ **Commonwealth Park Suites Hotel.** You can rub elbows with the senators and representatives who make this their home when the state legislature is in session. The original brick structure was established in 1846 primarily as a saloon that offered rooms for its drunk clientele. It burned during the Civil War battle for Richmond and was rebuilt around 1896 as a 10-story hotel. Just across the street from the capitol and its magnolia-filled park, the hotel could be somewhere in Europe; still, its reproduction 18th-century mahogany furniture, museum prints, and brass chandeliers confirm that you are in a southern state. All suites are equipped with coffeemakers, hair dryers, irons, and ironing boards. A deluxe Continental breakfast is included weekdays. *✉ 901 Bank St., 23219, ☎ 804/343–7300 or 888/343–7301, FAX 804/343–1025. 59 suites. In-room data ports, minibars, dry cleaning, laundry service, meeting rooms; no-smoking rooms. AE, D, DC, MC, V.*

$$–$$$ ★ **Berkeley Hotel.** Built in 1995 to blend in with the rest of Richmond's buildings, this handsome, European-style hotel combines intimacy with the services of a much larger property—and it's just two blocks from the capitol. Each room has a coffeemaker, iron, ironing board, and hair dryer; passes to the Capitol Club health club are free. *✉ 1200 E. Cary St., 23219, ☎ 804/780–1300, FAX 804/343–1885. 54 rooms, 1 suite. Restaurant, in-room data ports, gym, lobby lounge, dry cleaning, laundry service, concierge, meeting rooms; no-smoking rooms. AE, D, DC, MC, V.*

$–$$$ ★ **Linden Row Inn.** Edgar Allan Poe played in the garden that became the beautiful brick courtyards within this row of 1840s Greek revival town houses. The main building is furnished in antiques and period reproductions; the carriage-house garden quarters are decorated in Old English style and have homemade quilts. Mornings begin with a free newspaper and deluxe Continental breakfast; afternoons end with a wine-and-cheese reception in the beautiful parlor. Also complimentary are transportation to nearby historic attractions and passes to the YMCA's health club. The inn's dining room—open for breakfast, lunch, and dinner—is in the former stables. *✉ 101 N. 1st St., at Franklin St., 23219, ☎ 804/783–7000 or 800/348–7424, FAX 804/648–7504, WEB www.lindenrowinn.com. 60 rooms, 10 suites. Restaurant, in-room data ports, dry cleaning, laundry service; no-smoking rooms. AE, D, DC, MC, V. CP.*

$–$$$ **Omni Richmond.** This luxury hotel in the James Center is next to Shockoe Slip and close to numerous small restaurants and shops. The impressive coral marble lobby has a mural of old Richmond along the river. The rooms are furnished in contemporary style with a honey-and-peach color scheme. You may even want to bring binoculars to enjoy the spectacular view from the upper floors, particularly from rooms facing the James River. Guest privileges at the capitol health club are available for a day fee. ✉ *100 S. 12th St., 23219,* ☎ *804/344–7000,* FAX *804/648–6704,* WEB *www.omnihotels.com. 361 rooms, 12 suites. 2 restaurants, room service, in-room data ports, indoor-outdoor pool, gym, sauna, bar, meeting rooms, parking (fee). AE, D, DC, MC, V.*

$–$$ **Fairfield Inn Richmond West.** This basic Marriott offering with exterior corridors is near I–64 and five full-service restaurants. ✉ *7300 W. Broad St., 23294 (Exit 183C off I–64, 6 mi from downtown),* ☎ *804/672–8621 or 800/228–2800,* FAX *804/755–7155,* WEB *www.fairfieldinn.com. 124 rooms, 1 suite. In-room data ports, pool; no-smoking rooms. AE, D, DC, MC, V. CP.*

$ **Best Western Hanover House.** At this reasonably priced lodging, rooms are done in a pleasant pale blue and have balconies or patios. Some rooms have entrances on the parking lot. The in-room cable TV carries HBO and Disney channels. Two restaurants are within walking distance. Also nearby is the Virginia Center Commons shopping mall; Kings Dominion and Richmond are both about 10 mi away. ✉ *10296 Sliding Hill Rd. (I–95, Exit 86), Ashland 23005,* ☎ *804/550–2805 or 800/528–1234,* FAX *804/550–2104,* WEB *www.bestwestern.com. 93 rooms. Cable TV, pool, gym, laundry facilities, meeting rooms, free parking; no-smoking rooms. AE, D, DC, MC, V. CP.*

$ **Comfort Inn Executive Center.** On the northwest side of Richmond, this three-building redbrick motel is near the University of Richmond and convenient to I–95 and I–64. Its appearance from the street is very attractive, but the motel appears deceptively small; you see only the first of three buildings. The others stretch away from the street in a sort of private cul-de-sac. A deluxe Continental breakfast is included. Thirty rooms have whirlpool bathtubs. ✉ *7201 W. Broad St., 23294,* ☎ *804/672–1108,* FAX *804/755–1625,* WEB *www.comfortinn.com. 123 rooms. Pool, gym, lobby lounge, laundry facilities. AE, D, DC, MC, V. CP.*

Nightlife and the Arts

Bars

Bogart's (✉ 203 N. Lombardy St., ☎ 804/353–9280) is a tiny club with late-night jazz on weekends and a $2 cover charge. **Potter's Pub** (✉ Village Shopping Center, 7007 Three Chopt Rd., ☎ 804/282–9999) encourages audience participation in its folk music fests.

Theater

Barksdale Theatre (✉ 1601 Willow Lawn Dr., ☎ 804/282–2620), the area's oldest not-for-profit theater, began in 1953. Performances ranging from classics to innovative new works are staged Thursday through Saturday evenings and on Sunday afternoon. **Carpenter Center** (✉ 600 E. Grace St., ☎ 804/225–9000, WEB www.carpentercenter.org), a restored 1928 motion picture palace, is now a performing-arts center that puts on opera, traveling shows, symphonic music, and ballet.

Outdoor Activities and Sports

Participant Sports

GOLF

In Richmond you'll see aficionados teeing off most of the year. The area has 24 golf courses open to the public—the **Virginia State Golf Association** (WEB www.vsga.org) has a good handle on them all; its Web site even allows you to book tee times on-line.

RAFTING

Richmond Raft (☎ 804/222–7238 or 800/540–7238, WEB www.richmondraft.com) conducts white-water rafting trips through the city on the James River (Class III and IV rapids), as well as float trips from March through November.

Spectator Sports

The **Richmond Coliseum** (✉ 601 E. Leigh St., ☎ 804/780–4970) hosts ice shows, basketball, wrestling, and tennis tournaments.

AUTO RACING

NASCAR races are held at the **Richmond International Raceway** (✉ Laburnum Ave. exit, off I–64, ☎ 804/345–7223, WEB www.rir.com), usually in June, September, and October.

BASEBALL

The Richmond Braves, a Triple-A farm baseball team for Atlanta, play at the **Diamond** stadium (✉ 3001 N. Boulevard, ☎ 804/359–4444, WEB www.rbraves.com).

Shopping

Sixth Street Marketplace has specialty shops, chain stores, and eating places. **Shockoe Slip** (✉ E. Cary St. between 12th and 15th Sts.), a neighborhood of tobacco warehouses during the 18th and 19th centuries, is now full of boutiques and branches of upscale specialty stores.

The open-air **Farmers' Market** (✉ 17th and Main Sts.), beside the old Main Street Station, is surrounded by art galleries, boutiques, and antiques shops, many in converted warehouses and factories.

PETERSBURG

24 Historic **Petersburg,** 20 mi south of Richmond on I–95, lies along the Appomattox River. During the Civil War, the city was under siege by Union forces from June 1864 to April 1865—the so-called last stand of the Confederacy. A major railroad hub, the city was a crucial link in the supply chain for Lee's army, and its capitulation precipitated the evacuation of Richmond and the surrender at Appomattox.

A number of Petersburg attractions are within the Old Towne area; visitor centers sell various passes that allow for reduced admission to many of them. The centers also have information about Lee's Retreat Trail, a 26-stop driving tour around the area. Free parking is plentiful around town.

To walk **Petersburg National Battlefield** is to be where more than 60,000 Union and Confederate soldiers died during the siege of the city. A pronounced depression in the ground is the eroded remnant of the Crater, the result of a 4-ton gunpowder explosion set off by Union forces in one failed attack. The 1,500-acre park is laced with several miles of earthworks and includes two forts. In the visitor center, maps and models convey background information vital to the self-guided driving tour, during which you park at specified spots on the tour road and proceed on foot to nearby points of interest. ✉ *Rte. 36, 2½ mi east of downtown,* ☎ *804/732–3531.* *$4 car, $2 cyclist or pedestrian.* ⏲ *Park mid-June–Labor Day, daily 8:30–dusk; Labor Day–mid-June, daily 8–5. Visitor center daily 8:30–5:30.*

★ The **Siege Museum** in Old Towne examines the Civil War from a purely local perspective. Exhibits at the museum concentrate on details of ordinary civilian life in embattled Petersburg during the last year of the war. A 15-minute movie narrated by Petersburg-born actor

Joseph Cotten dramatizes the upheaval. ✉ *15 W. Bank St.,* ☎ *804/733–2404.* 🎫 *$3.* ⏲ *Daily 10–5.*

Centre Hill Mansion (1823) is furnished with turn-of-the-20th-century Victorian antiques, including a 9-ft-long grand piano. ✉ *1 Centre Hill Circle,* ☎ *804/733–2401.* 🎫 *$3.* ⏲ *Daily 10–5.*

The Federal-style brick **Farmers Bank** (1817), one of the oldest bank buildings in the nation, was restored by the Association for the Preservation of Virginia Antiquities. ✉ *19 Bollingbrook St.,* ☎ *804/733–2400.* 🎫 *$3.* ⏲ *Apr.–Oct., Fri.–Mon. 10–5.*

Old Blandford Church is today a Confederate shrine. The graves of 30,000 Southern dead are in the memorial area behind the church. The church's 15 spectacular stained-glass windows by Louis Comfort Tiffany are memorials donated by the Confederate states. The Memorial Day tradition is said to have begun in this cemetery in June 1866. ✉ *319 S. Crater Rd. (2 mi south of town),* ☎ *804/733–2396.* 🎫 *$3.* ⏲ *Daily 10–5.*

★ On April 2, 1865, in what is now **Pamplin Historical Park,** Union troops successfully attacked General Robert E. Lee's formerly impenetrable defense line, forcing Lee to abandon Petersburg. Today you are greeted by the 300-ft-long facade of the Battlefield Center, a concrete representation of the Confederate battle lines. Besides the center, which focuses on the April 2 battle, there's a 2-mi battle trail with 2,100 ft of 8-ft-high earthen fortifications, reconstructed soldier huts, and original picket posts. Also on the grounds is Tudor Hall, an 1812 plantation home that served as the 1864 headquarters for Confederate general Samuel McGowan. Costumed interpreters bring the era to life, and reconstructed outbuildings have exhibits and displays. The **National Museum of the Civil War Soldier** on the grounds has interactive displays and nearly 1,000 artifacts. You can select an audio guide that includes the actual letters and diaries of a soldier. The park also has a café and a large store. Allow at least two hours to visit the park and museum. ✉ *6125 Boydton Plank Rd., off U.S. 1, I–85 S. to Exit 63A,* ☎ *804/861–2408 or 877/726–7546,* WEB *www.pamplinpark.org.* 🎫 *$10.* ⏲ *Daily 9–5; call for extended summer hrs.*

Dining and Lodging

$$–$$$ ✕ **Alexander's Fine Food.** White tablecloths flare from beneath glass tops at the tables of this Greek-American restaurant, which also has a bar. A souvlaki platter, leg of lamb, and Athenian-style chicken are specialties. ✉ *101 W. Bank St.,* ☎ *804/733–7134. No credit cards. Closed Sun. No dinner Mon.–Tues.*

$–$$ ✕ **Leonardo's Deli & Cafe.** Rag-painted cherry walls contrast with white wooden booths at this casual deli and café, which serves meals from breakfast through dinner. The tin ceiling and ceiling fans point to the building's age, and the *Mona Lisa* copy on the wall alludes to the café's namesake. ✉ *7 Bollingbrook St.,* ☎ *804/863–4830. AE, MC, V.*

$–$$ 🏨 **Hampton Inn.** Near the front door of this chain hotel, large greenhouse windows frame a bright breakfast room for the extensive Continental breakfast. Each room has a hair dryer, iron, ironing board, and coffeemaker. The inn is between two interstates (Exit 9B off I–295 and Exit 52 off I–95), 4 mi from downtown Petersburg and near the Petersburg National Battlefield. Several restaurants are nearby. A shuttle runs to the Fort Lee army base in the morning and returns in the afternoon. ✉ *5103 Plaza Dr., Hopewell 23860,* ☎ *804/452–1000 or 800/426–7866,* FAX *804/541–8584,* WEB *www.hamptoninn.com.* 72

rooms, 2 suites. In-room data ports, refrigerators, in-room VCRs, pool, gym, sauna, dry cleaning, laundry facilities, meeting rooms; no-smoking rooms. AE, D, DC, MC, V. CP.

$–$$ **The High Street Inn.** This beautiful Queen Anne house with a turret was built in 1895 and is just a few blocks from Petersburg's historic area. The bed-and-breakfast, furnished mainly with antiques, has large bedrooms. The home-cooked breakfast is expansive. If you're allergic, note that two dogs reside here. ✉ *405 High St., 23803,* ☎ *804/733–0505; 888/733–0505 outside VA,* FAX *804/862–0694,* WEB *www.highstreetinn.com. 4 rooms, 2 with bath. No smoking. D, MC, V. BP.*

$ **Best Western Steven Kent.** This pristine two-story motel has a home-style family restaurant, an Olympic-size swimming pool, and and nearly 20 acres of recreational facilities. Local calls and newspapers are free, and rooms have a coffeemaker, microwave, hair dryer, iron, and ironing board. ✉ *12205 S. Crater Rd., 23805,* ☎ *804/733–0600 or 800/284–9393,* WEB *www.bestwestern.com,* FAX *804/862–4549. 133 rooms. Restaurant, in-room data ports, putting green, 2 tennis courts, pool, basketball, horseshoes, bar, lounge, playground, laundry facilities, business services, meeting rooms. AE, D, DC, MC, V. CP.*

FREDERICKSBURG

Halfway between Richmond and Washington near the falls of the Rappahannock River, Fredericksburg is a popular destination for history buffs. The town's 40-block National Historic District contains more than 350 original 18th- and 19th-century buildings, including the house George Washington bought for his mother; the Rising Sun Tavern; and Kenmore, the magnificent 1752 plantation owned by George Washington's sister. The town is a favorite with antiques collectors, who cruise the dealers' shops along Caroline Street on land once used by Native American tribes as fishing and hunting ground.

Although the area was visited by explorer Captain John Smith as early as 1608, the town of Fredericksburg wasn't founded until 1728. Established as a frontier port to serve nearby tobacco farmers and iron miners, Fredericksburg took its name from England's crown prince at the time, Frederick Louis, the eldest son of King George II. The streets still bear names of his family members: George, Caroline, Sophia, Princess Anne, William, and Amelia.

George Washington knew Fredericksburg well, having grown up just across the Rappahannock on Ferry Farm—his residence from age 6 to 20. (The myths about chopping down a cherry tree and throwing a coin across the Rappahannock—later described as the Potomac—refer to this period of his life.) In later years Washington often visited his mother here on Charles Street.

Fredericksburg prospered in the decades after independence, benefiting from its location midway along the route between Washington and Richmond—an important intersection of railroad lines and waterways. When the Civil War broke out, it became the linchpin of the Confederate defense of Richmond and therefore the target of Union assaults. In December 1862, Union forces attacked the town in what was to be the first of four major battles fought in and around Fredericksburg. In the battle of Sunken Road, Confederate defenders sheltered by a stone wall at the base of Marye's Heights mowed down thousands of Union soldiers who charged across the fields.

At Chancellorsville in April 1863, General Robert E. Lee led 60,000 troops to a brilliant victory over a much larger Union force of 134,000, and this resulted in Lee's invasion of Pennsylvania. The following year,

Grant's troops battled Lee's Confederates through the Wilderness, a region of dense thickets and overgrowth south of the Rapidan River, then fought them again at Spotsylvania. Although neither side was victorious, Grant continued heading his troops toward the Confederate capital of Richmond.

By the war's end, fighting in Fredericksburg and at the nearby Chancellorsville, Wilderness, and Spotsylvania Court House battlefields resulted in more than 100,000 dead or wounded. Fredericksburg's cemeteries hold the remains of 17,000 soldiers from both sides. Miraculously, despite heavy bombardment and house-to-house fighting, much of the city remained intact.

Today the city is being overrun for a different reason. The charming, historic town appeals to commuters fleeing the Washington, D.C., area for kinder, less expensive environs. The railroad lines that were so crucial to transporting Civil War supplies now bring workers to and from the nation's capital an hour away, and the sacred Civil War battlegrounds share the area with legions of shopping centers.

Numbers in the text correspond to numbers in the margin and on the Fredericksburg map.

A Good Tour

Begin at the **Fredericksburg Visitor Center** ㉕ to get maps or directions, or to join a tour. Walk northwest on Caroline Street to the **Hugh Mercer Apothecary Shop** ㉖, passing numerous antiques shops and boutiques along the way. Continue another three blocks to the **Rising Sun Tavern** ㉗, built by George Washington's brother. Walk back to Lewis Street, turn right, and walk two blocks to the **Mary Washington House** ㉘. Continue on Lewis Street and turn right on Washington Avenue to the entrance of **Kenmore** ㉙, where George's sister lived. To see the **Mary Washington Grave and Monument** ㉚, turn right on Washington Avenue and walk two blocks. On the southern end of Washington Avenue is the **Confederate Cemetery** ㉛. From the cemetery take William Street back toward the center of town. At Charles Street turn right to reach the **James Monroe Museum and Memorial Library** ㉜. Return to the corner of Charles and William and walk one block to Princess Anne Street to visit the **Fredericksburg Area Museum and Cultural Center** ㉝. To return to the visitor center, walk two more blocks along Princess Anne, turn left on Hanover, and right on Caroline Street. To return to the visitor center, turn left on Hanover and right on Caroline Street. To get to the **Mary Washington College Galleries** ㉞, it's best to drive unless you want to walk almost a mile from where you are now. Drive five blocks northwest on Caroline Street and turn left on Amelia. Follow Amelia and turn left on Washington Avenue. One block later, turn right onto William Street. At College Avenue, turn right and drive ½ mi to the gallery on your right. Parking (on College Avenue and two reserved spots in the staff lot at the corner of College and Thornton Street) may be tight on weekdays when the college is in session. The galleries have a fine collection of Asian art, as well as works by modern masters.

TIMING

A walking tour through the town proper takes three to four hours. A self-guided tour of the Mary Washington College galleries takes about 30 minutes. Spring and fall are the best times to tour Fredericksburg on foot, but because Virginia weather is temperate intermittently in winter, you may find some suitable walking days then. Summers—especially August—can be hot, humid, and not very pleasant for a long walk.

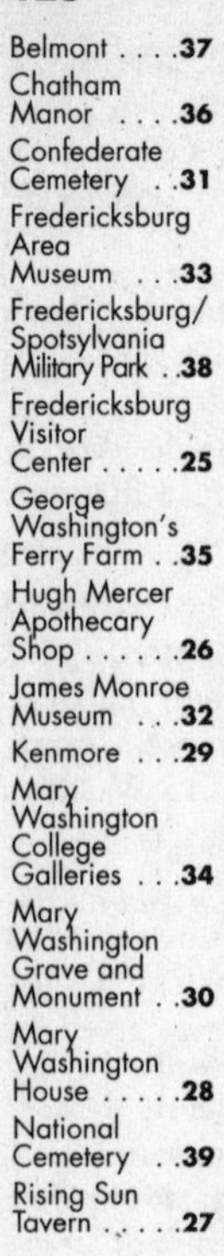

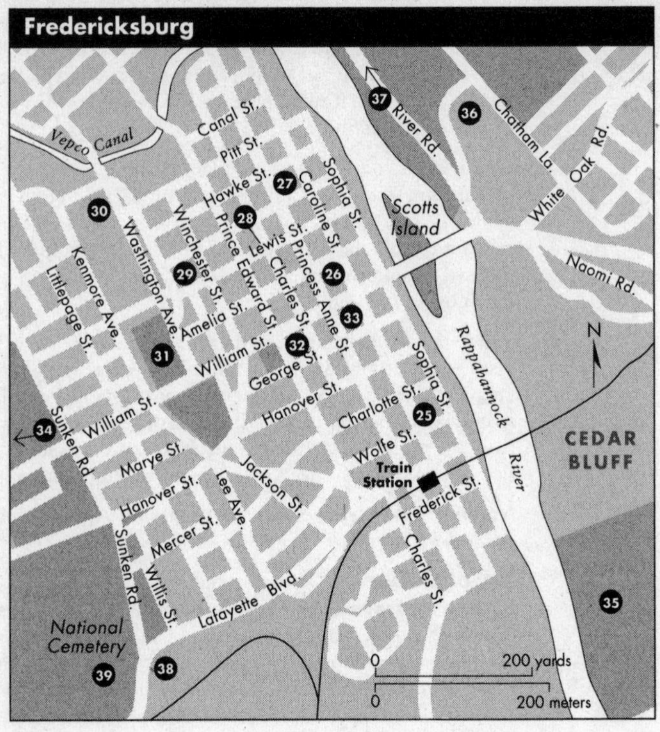

Sights to See

31 **Confederate Cemetery.** This cemetery contains the remains of more than 2,000 soldiers (most of them unknown) as well as the graves of generals Dabney Maury, Seth Barton, Carter Stevenson, Daniel Ruggles, Henry Sibley, and Abner Perrin. ✉ *1100 Washington Ave., near Amelia St., Historic District.* ⏲ *Daily dawn–dusk.*

★ 33 **Fredericksburg Area Museum and Cultural Center.** In an 1816 building once used as a market and town hall, this museum's six permanent exhibits tell the story of the area from prehistoric times through the Revolutionary and Civil wars to the present. Displays include dinosaur footprints from a nearby quarry, Native American artifacts, an 18th-century plantation account book with an inventory of slaves, and Confederate memorabilia. ✉ *907 Princess Anne St., Historic District,* ☎ *540/371–3037,* WEB *www.famcc.org.* 🎫 *$5.* ⏲ *Apr.–Nov., Mon.–Sat. 9–5, Sun. 1–5; Dec.–Mar., Mon.–Sat. 10–4, Sun. 1–4.*

25 **Fredericksburg Visitor Center.** Besides housing the usual booklets, pamphlets, and maps, this visitor center has passes that enable you to park for a whole day in what are usually two-hour zones as well as money-saving passes to city attractions ($24 for entry to nine sights; $16 for four sights). Before heading out on a tour, you may want to see the orientation slide show. The center building itself was constructed in 1824 as a residence and confectionery; during the Civil War it was used as a prison. ✉ *706 Caroline St., Historic District,* ☎ *540/373–1776 or 800/678–4748,* WEB *www.fredericksburgvirginia.net.* ⏲ *Memorial Day–Labor Day, daily 9–7; Labor Day–Memorial Day, daily 9–5.*

NEED A BREAK? Have an old-fashioned malt in **Goolrick's Pharmacy** (✉ 901 Caroline St., Historic District, ☎ 540/373–9878), a 1940s drugstore with a soda fountain. In addition to malts and egg creams (made of seltzer and milk, not egg or cream), Goolrick's serves light meals weekdays 8:30–7 and Saturday 8:30–6.

26 **Hugh Mercer Apothecary Shop.** Offering a close-up view of 18th- and 19th-century medical instruments and procedures, Hugh Mercer Apothecary Shop was established in 1771 by Dr. Mercer, a Scotsman who served as a brigadier general of the Continental Army (he was killed at the Battle of Princeton). Dr. Mercer may have been more careful than other Colonial physicians, but his methods still might make you cringe. A costumed hostess explicitly describes amputations and cataract operations before the discovery of anesthetics. You can also hear about therapeutic bleeding, see the gruesome devices used in dentistry, and watch leeching being demonstrated. ✉ *1020 Caroline St., at Amelia St., Historic District,* ☎ *540/373–3362.* 🎫 *$4.* ⏲ *Apr.–Nov., Mon.–Sat. 9–5; Sun. 11–5; Dec.–Mar., Mon.–Sat. 10–4; Sun. 12–4.*

32 **James Monroe Museum and Memorial Library.** This tiny one-story building—on the site where Monroe, who became the fifth president of the United States, practiced law from 1787 to 1789—contains many of Monroe's possessions, collected and preserved by his family. They include a mahogany dispatch box used during the negotiation of the 1803 Louisiana Purchase (Monroe was minister to France under Thomas Jefferson) and the desk on which Monroe signed the doctrine named for him. ✉ *908 Charles St., Historic District,* ☎ *540/654–2110.* 🎫 *$4.* ⏲ *Mar.–Nov., daily 9–5; Dec.–Feb., daily 10–4.*

★ 29 **Kenmore.** Named Kenmore by a later owner, this house was built in 1775 on a 1,300-acre plantation owned by Colonel Fielding Lewis, a patriot, merchant, and brother-in-law of George Washington. Lewis sacrificed much of his fortune to operate a gun factory that supplied the American forces during the Revolutionary War. As a result, his debts forced his widow to sell the home after his death. Kenmore's plain exterior belies its lavish interior. The plaster ceiling moldings are outstanding and even more ornate than those at Mount Vernon. It's believed that the artisan responsible for the ceilings worked frequently in both homes, though his name is unknown, possibly because he was an indentured servant. Most of the lavish furnishings are in storage until about 2005 while the mansion undergoes a $5 million restoration. Guided 30-minute architectural tours of the home are conducted by docents, and the subterranean Crowninghield museum on the grounds displays some of the furniture, family portraits, and changing exhibits of Fredericksburg life. ✉ *1201 Washington Ave., Historic District,* ☎ *540/373–3381,* WEB *www.kenmore.org.* 🎫 *$6.* ⏲ *Mar.–Nov., Mon.–Sat. 10–5, Sun. noon–5; Jan.–Feb., weekdays by reservation only; Sat. noon–4.*

34 **Mary Washington College Galleries.** On campus are two art galleries. The Ridderhof Martin Gallery hosts exhibitions of art from various cultures and historical periods. The duPont Gallery, in Melchers Hall, displays paintings, drawings, sculpture, photography, ceramics, and textiles by art faculty, students, and contemporary artists. Free gallery-visitor parking is available in the lot at the corner of College Avenue at Thornton Street. ✉ *College Ave., Historic District,* ☎ *540/654–1013.* 🎫 *Free.* ⏲ *During college sessions, Mon., Wed., and Fri. 10–4; weekends 1–4.*

30 **Mary Washington Grave and Monument.** A 40-ft granite obelisk, dedicated by President Grover Cleveland in 1894, marks the final resting place of George's mother at "Meditation Rock," a place on her daughter's property where Mrs. Washington liked to read. It replaced a previous marble monument cornerstone laid by President Andrew Jackson

in 1833, which was damaged by the Civil War bombardment of Fredericksburg. ✉ *Washington Ave. and Pitt St., Historic District.*

㉘ **Mary Washington House.** George purchased a three-room cottage for his mother in 1772 for 225 pounds, renovated it, and more than doubled its size with additions. She spent the last 17 years of her life here, tending the charming garden where her original boxwoods still flourish today, and where many a bride and groom now exchange their vows. The home has been a museum since 1930. Inside, displays include Mrs. Washington's "best dressing glass," a silver-over-tin mirror in a Chippendale frame; her teapot; Washington family dinnerware; and period furniture. The kitchen and its spit are original. Tours begin on the back porch with a history of the house. From there you can see the brick sidewalk leading to Kenmore, the home of Mrs. Washington's only daughter, Betty Washington Lewis. ✉ *1200 Charles St., Historic District,* ☎ *540/373–1569.* 🎫 *$5.* ⏲ *Apr.–Nov., Mon.–Sat. 9–5, Sun. 11–5; Dec.–Mar., Mon.–Sat. 10–4, Sun. noon–4.*

㉗ **Rising Sun Tavern.** In 1760 George Washington's brother Charles built as his home what later became the Rising Sun Tavern, a watering hole for such patriots as the Lee brothers (the only siblings to sign the Declaration of Independence); Patrick Henry, the five-term governor of Virginia who said, "Give me liberty or give me death"; and future presidents Washington and Jefferson. A "wench" in period costume leads a tour without stepping out of character. From her you hear how travelers slept and what they ate and drank at this busy institution. In the taproom you're served spiced tea. ✉ *1304 Caroline St., Historic District,* ☎ *540/371–1494.* 🎫 *$5.* ⏲ *Apr.–Nov., Mon.–Sat. 9–5, Sun. 11–5; Dec.–Mar., Mon.–Sat. 10–4, Sun. noon–4.*

Around Fredericksburg

Surrounding the town of Fredericksburg are historic sites and beautiful vistas where, in 1862, Union forces once stood. Today you see only the lively Rappahannock and beautiful homes on a lovely drive across the river.

A Good Drive

From downtown Fredericksburg, drive east on William Street (Route 3) across the Rappahannock River a mile to **George Washington's Ferry Farm** ㉟, which will be on the right. Return on Route 3 toward Fredericksburg and turn right at the signs to **Chatham Manor** ㊱, just east of the river, where Washington and Jefferson both dined. From Chatham Manor, take River Road (Route 607) 1½ mi along the river, crossing U.S. 1 (Jefferson Davis Highway) to Route 1001 to reach the galleries of **Belmont** ㊲, a spacious Georgian house from the 1790s. Return to Route 1 via Route 1001 and turn right (south) and cross the river. Turn left on Princess Anne Street and drive 1½ mi to the railroad station. This takes you past many old homes, churches, and the main business district. Turn right on Lafayette Boulevard: the **Fredericksburg/Spotsylvania National Military Park** ㊳ and **National Cemetery** ㊴ are ½ mi ahead.

TIMING

Allow five minutes to drive to Ferry Farm from downtown and 10 minutes each to drive to Chatham Manor and Belmont. A tour of Belmont takes about an hour. There's no tour at Chatham Manor, but strolling through the garden and small museum takes about 30 minutes. The battlefields of the Wilderness, Chancellorsville, and Spotsylvania Court House are each within 15 mi of Fredericksburg. It can take one to several hours to tour each one, depending on your level of interest. At the

Fredericksburg battlefield-park visitor center, allow an hour or two—there's a 22-minute video and a small museum, and frequent walking tours are offered.

Sights to See

37 **Belmont.** The last owner of this 1790s Georgian-style house was American artist Gari Melchers, who was chairman of the Smithsonian Commission to establish the National Gallery of Art in Washington; his wife, Corinne, deeded the 27-acre estate and its collections to Virginia. Belmont is now a public museum and a Virginia National Historic Landmark administered by Mary Washington College. You can take a one-hour tour of the spacious house, which is furnished with a rich collection of antiques. Galleries in the stone studio, built by Melchers in 1924, house the largest repository of his work. An orientation movie is shown in the reception area, which was once the carriage house. ✉ *224 Washington St., Falmouth,* ☎ *540/654–1015.* 🎫 *$6.* ⏲ *Mar.–Nov., Mon.–Sat. 10–5, Sun. 1–5; Dec.–Feb., Mon.–Sat. 10–4, Sun. 1–4.*

★ 36 **Chatham Manor.** A fine example of Georgian architecture, Chatham Manor was built between 1768 and 1771 by William Fitzhugh on a site overlooking the Rappahannock River and the town of Fredericksburg. Fitzhugh, a noted plantation owner, frequently hosted such luminaries as George Washington and Thomas Jefferson. During the Civil War, Union forces commandeered the house and converted it into a headquarters and hospital. President Abraham Lincoln conferred with his generals here; Clara Barton (founder of the American Red Cross) and poet Walt Whitman tended the wounded. After the war, the house and gardens were restored by private owners and eventually donated to the National Park Service. The home itself is now a museum housing exhibits spanning several centuries. Concerts are often held here in summer. ✉ *Chatham La., Falmouth,* ☎ *540/371–0802.* 🎫 *$4 (includes Fredericksburg/Spotsylvania National Military Park).* ⏲ *Daily 9–5.*

★ 38 **Fredericksburg/Spotsylvania National Military Park.** The 9,000-acre park actually includes four battlefields and three historic buildings, all accessible for a single admission price. At the Fredericksburg and Chancellorsville visitor centers you can learn about the area's role in the Civil War by watching a 22-minute video at Fredericksburg and a 12-minute slide show at Spotsylvania, and by viewing displays of soldiers' art and battlefield relics. In season, park rangers lead walking tours. The centers offer tape-recorded tour cassettes ($4.95 rental, $7.50 purchase) and maps that show how to reach hiking trails at the Wilderness, Chancellorsville (where General Stonewall Jackson was mistakenly shot by his own troops), and Spotsylvania Court House battlefields (all within 15 mi of Fredericksburg).

Just outside the Fredericksburg battlefield park visitor center is Sunken Road, where from December 11 to 13, 1862, General Robert E. Lee led his troops to a bloody but resounding victory over Union forces attacking across the Rappahannock (there was a total of 18,000 casualties on both sides). Much of the stone wall that protected Lee's sharpshooters is now a re-creation, but 100 yards from the visitor center, part of the original wall overlooks the statue *The Angel of Marye's Heights,* by Felix de Weldon (sculptor of the famous *Marine Corps War Memorial* statue in Arlington). This memorial honors Sergeant Richard Kirkland, a South Carolinian who risked his life to bring water to wounded foes; he later died at the Battle of Chickamauga. ✉ *Fredericksburg battlefield-park visitor center, Lafayette Blvd. and Sunken Rd.,* ☎ *540/373–6122; Chancellorsville Battlefield visitor center, Rte. 3 W,* ☎ *540/786–2880.* 🎫 *$4 (includes all 4 battlefields, Chatham Manor,* *and other historic buildings). ⌚ Visitor centers daily 9–5, driving and walking tours daily dawn–dusk.*

35 **George Washington's Ferry Farm.** But for the outcries of historians and citizens, a Wal-Mart store would have been built on this site of our first president's boyhood home. The land was saved by the Historic Kenmore Foundation, and the discount store found a location farther out on the same road. Ferry Farm, which once consisted of 600 acres, is just across the Rappahannock River from downtown Fredericksburg and was the site of a ferry crossing. Living here from age 6 to 19, Washington received his formal education and taught himself surveying while *not* busy chopping a cherry tree or throwing a dollar across the Rappahannock—legends concocted by Parson Weems. The mainly archaeological site has an exhibit on "George Washington: Boy Before Legend," and ongoing excavations. Colonial games are held daily June through August. Ferry Farm became a major artillery base and river-crossing site for Union forces during the Battle of Fredericksburg. ✉ *Rte. 3 E, 268 Kings Hwy. at Ferry Rd.,* ☎ *540/370–0732,* WEB *www.kenmore.org.* 🎟 *$3.* ⌚ *Mid-Feb.–late May and early Sept.–Dec., 11–4; late May–early Sept., 10–5 daily.*

39 **National Cemetery.** The National Cemetery is the final resting place of 15,000 Union dead, most of whom were never identified. ✉ *Lafayette Blvd. and Sunken Rd.,* ☎ *540/373–6122.* ⌚ *Daily sunrise–sunset.*

Dining

$$–$$$ ✕ **Claiborne's.** On the walls of this swank eatery in the 1910-era Fredericksburg train station are historic train photographs. The restaurant—decorated in a dark green-and-navy color scheme with mahogany-and-brass bars—specializes in low-country Southern cuisine. Accompanying the steaks, chops, and seafood are ample vegetable side dishes served family style. ✉ *200 Lafayette Blvd., Historic District,* ☎ *540/371–7080,* WEB *www.claibornesrestaurant.com. AE, DC, MC, V. No lunch Mon.–Sat., no dinner Sun.*

$$–$$$ ✕ **La Petite Auberge.** Housed in a pre-Revolutionary brick general store, this white-tablecloth restaurant actually has three dining rooms, as well as a small bar. Specialties such as house-cut beef, French onion soup, and seafood are all served with a Continental accent. A prix-fixe ($14) three-course dinner is served from 5:30 to 7 Monday through Thursday. ✉ *311 William St., Historic District,* ☎ *540/371–2727. AE, D, MC, V. Closed Sun.*

$$–$$$ ✕ **Merriman's Restaurant & Bar.** Although housed in a historic brick storefront, Merriman's "fresh natural cuisine" is served in a dining room painted bright yellow. The eclectic menu features Mediterranean dishes such as linguine Mykonos, Greek salad, and Middle Eastern hummus as well as classic Virginia meats and seafood. Desserts are made fresh daily. ✉ *715 Caroline St., Historic District,* ☎ *540/371–7723. AE, D, DC, MC, V.*

$$–$$$ ✕ **Ristorante Renato.** This family-owned restaurant, decorated with lace curtains, red carpeting, and walls covered with paintings, specializes in Italian cuisine, including veal and seafood dishes. ✉ *422 William St., Historic District,* ☎ *540/371–8228. AE, MC, V. No lunch weekends.*

$$–$$$ ✕ **The Riverview.** There's a view of the Rappahannock River and Chatham Manor from both the dining room, which has a cozy fireplace, and the brick patio—a lovely place to eat alfresco in summer. The Riverview describes its offerings as "The Best of Beef, Bay, and Bottle," and its specialties are prime rib and fresh seafood. The restaurant has been a favorite with locals for years. ✉ *1101 Sophia St., Historic District,* ☎ *540/373–6500. AE, D, DC, MC, V.*

$$–$$$ ✕ **The Smythe's Cottage & Tavern.** Taking a step into this cozy little building of several small dining rooms—once a blacksmith's house—is like taking a step back in time. The surroundings are Colonial; the lunch and dinner menus, classic Virginia: seafood pie, quail, stuffed flounder. ✉ *303 Fauquier St., Historic District,* ☎ *540/373–1645. MC, V. Closed Tues.*

Lodging

$$–$$$ **Kenmore Inn.** The front porch seems to beckon you up to the door of this historic home that's a few blocks from the visitor center downtown. Inside, antique furniture abounds. Four guest rooms have working fireplaces. On weekends, you can head to the English pub for live music. The restaurant ($$–$$$), which serves traditional Virginia cuisine, is open Tuesday through Saturday. ✉ *1200 Princess Anne St., Historic District, 22401,* ☎ *540/371–7622,* FAX *540/371–5480,* WEB *www.kenmoreinn.com. 9 rooms. Restaurant, pub; no room TVs. AE, D, DC, MC, V. CP.*

$–$$$ **The Richard Johnston Inn.** This elegant B&B was constructed in the late 1700s and served as the home of Richard Johnston, mayor of Fredericksburg from March 1809 to March 1810. Guest rooms are decorated with period antiques and reproductions. The aroma of freshly baked breads and muffins entices you to breakfast in the large Federal-style dining room set with fine china, silver, and linens. The inn is just across from the visitor center and two blocks from the train station. ✉ *711 Caroline St., Historic District, 22401,* ☎ *540/899–7606,* WEB *www.bbonline.com. 6 rooms, 2 suites. Free parking; no room phones, no TV in some rooms, no smoking. AE, MC, V. BP.*

$ **Fredericksburg Colonial Inn.** This 1920s motel with moss-green siding and forest-green awnings conceals a center staircase popular for weddings. Rooms are furnished with authentic antiques and appointments from the Civil War period, and the lobby has an old-time upright piano. Breakfast includes beverages, cereal, and coffee cake. ✉ *1707 Princess Anne St., Historic District, 22401,* ☎ *540/371–5666. 30 rooms. Refrigerators; no smoking. AE, MC, V. CP.*

THE NORTHERN NECK

Between Fredericksburg and the Chesapeake Bay is the "Northern Neck," an area attractive to nature lovers, anglers, and boaters. This 90-mi-long, million-acre peninsula is bathed on three sides by the Potomac and Rappahannock rivers, and the mighty Chesapeake Bay. Settled more than 300 years ago, the Northern Neck is the birthplace of presidents George Washington, James Monroe, and James Madison as well as General Robert E. Lee and Washington's mother, Mary Ball.

The Northern Neck peninsula is as unspoiled today as when Captain John Smith first visited in 1608. Even at the peninsula's start, the area is forested and tranquil. You'll find plenty of charming B&Bs; fresh-off-the-boat seafood; dozens of marinas; excursion boats to islands in the Chesapeake Bay; historic homes and museums; and places to commune with nature.

If you plan to cook in or camp out, bring your favorite staples from home or stop in either Heathville, Kilmarnock, or Warsaw, where full-service supermarkets can be found. In the summer, just-picked local produce is sold at numerous roadside stands and farmers' markets.

The sites below are listed in geographical order beginning at the intersection of Routes 3 and 301. Though it's unusual that three presidents' birthplaces are in such proximity, that of James Madison and

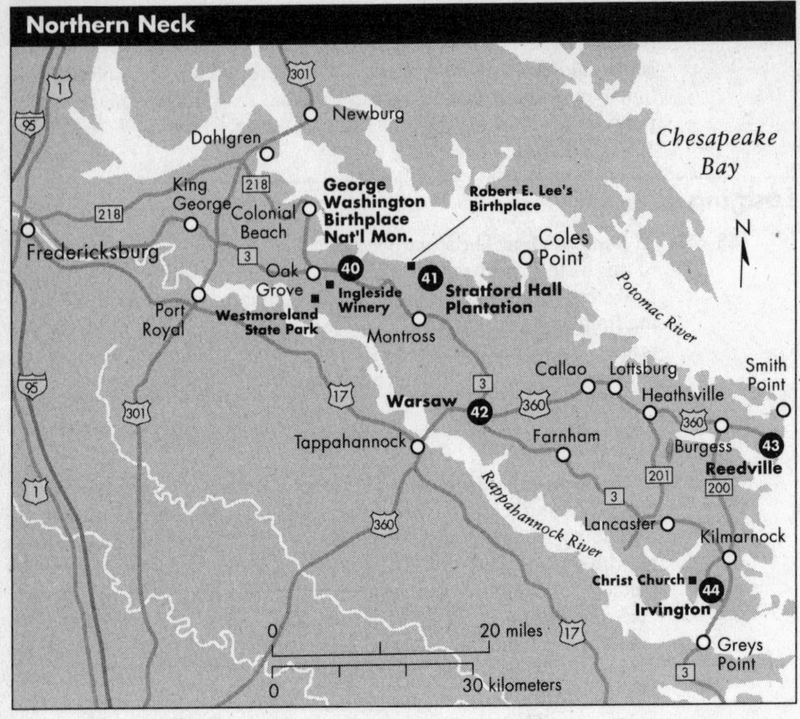

James Monroe are just markers off the highway, whereas Washington's is a national monument. A marker on Highway 301 in Port Conway, King George County, memorializes the onetime plantation where James Madison was born in 1751; an outline of the house and a marker in neighboring Westmoreland County identifies the birthplace of James Monroe, born in 1758, on Highway 205 between Oak Grove and Colonial Beach.

Numbers in the text correspond to numbers in the margin and on the Northern Neck map.

George Washington Birthplace National Monument

40 *32 mi east of Fredericksburg on Rte. 3.*

After you pass the town of Oak Grove on Route 3, all signs point to the national park on the Potomac River. At Pope's Creek, **George Washington Birthplace National Monument** is a 550-acre park mirroring the peaceful rural life our first president preferred. The house in which Mary Ball Washington gave birth to George in 1732 burned in 1779, but native clay was used to make bricks for a representative 18th-century plantation home. Costumed interpreters lead tours through the house, which has items dating from the time of Washington's childhood. The grounds include a kitchen, garden, cemetery with 32 Washington family graves, and the Colonial Living Farm, worked by methods employed in Colonial days. Picnic facilities are available year-round. ✉ *Rte. 3,* ☎ *804/224–1732,* WEB *www.nps.gov/gewa.* 🎟 *$3.* ⏲ *Daily 9–5.*

Lodging

$ **Westmoreland State Park.** This 1,300-acre, full-service park is one of Virginia's most beautiful campgrounds, with hiking trails winding through marshlands, woods, meadows and along the Potomac River.

There are also places to fish, rent boats or kayaks, or simply picnic. The comfortable, climate-controlled cabins have complete kitchens with microwave oven and toaster, dishes, silverware, and cooking utensils (but bring dishwashing supplies). Living rooms have a sofa, dining table, and working fireplace. The basic furnishings include linens for four beds. Westmoreland also has 118 campsites available. ✉ *1650 State Park Rd., Rte. 1, Box 600, Montross 22520-9717,* ☎ *804/493–8821 or 800/933–7275,* FAX *804/493–8329,* WEB *www.dcr.state.va.us/parks/westmore.htm. Grocery, picnic area, kitchens, pool, boating, fishing, hiking, laundry facilities; no phones, no TV. 27 cabins. AE, MC, V. Closed Nov.–Apr.*

Westmoreland State Park campsites. In addition to sites for RVs and tents, Westmoreland also has six camping cabins that provide a shelter but few other amenities. *Flush toilets. 42 partial hook-ups (electric and water). Drinking water, laundry facilities, showers. Fire grates, grills, picnic tables. Electricity. General store. Swimming (river). 42 partial hook-ups, 74 without hook-ups, 129 tent sites, 6 cabins.* ✉ *1650 State Park Rd., Rte. 1, Box 600, Montross 22520-9717,* ☎ *804/493–8821 or 800/933–7275,* FAX *804/493–8329,* WEB *www.dcr.state.va.us/parks/westmore.htm.* *Partial hook-ups $21, no hook-ups and tent sites $16. AE, MC, V.* *Open Mar.–Nov.*

En Route If you'll be camping or staying in a cabin, a good place to pick up groceries is **Westmoreland Berry Farm and Orchard** (✉ Rte. 3, ☎ 800/997–2377), near Oak Grove.

Stratford Hall Plantation

41 *8 mi east of George Washington Birthplace National Monument via Rte. 3.*

Robert E. Lee, who became the commander of the Confederate Army, was born in the Great House of **Stratford Hall Plantation,** one of the country's finest examples of Colonial architecture. Eight chimneys in two squares top the H-shape brick home, built in the 1730s by one of Lee's grandfathers, Colonial governor Thomas Lee. The house contains Robert E. Lee's crib, original family pieces, and period furnishings. The working Colonial plantation covers 1,600 acres and has gardens, a kitchen, smokehouse, laundry, orangery, springhouses, coach house, stables, slave quarters, and a gristmill that operates Saturdays May through October from 1:30 to 3:30. A plantation luncheon and à la carte items ($1.50–$5.75) are served daily from 11:30 to 3 in a large log cabin restaurant. Its outdoor screened deck overlooks the woodlands. ✉ *Rte. 3, Stratford,* ☎ *804/493–8038.* *$7.* *Daily 9–5.*

Lodging

Cole's Point Plantation. This 110-acre wooded campground on the Potomac River has a 575-ft fishing pier, a boat ramp, and a 120-slip full-service marina. The facility has four log cabins that can sleep 4–13 people. *Flush toilets, full hook-ups, partial hook-ups (electric and water). Pool, swimming (river). Restaurant, pool, boating, marina, fishing, bicycles. 74 full hook-ups or tent sites, 35 partial hook-ups or tent sites, 1 tent site, 4 cabins.* ✉ *Rte. 612, north of Rte. 202, Rte. 728, Box 77, Coles Point 22442,* ☎ *804/472–3955,* FAX *804/472–4488,* WEB *www.colespoint.com.* *Cabins $50, full hook-ups $26, partial hook-ups $21, tent sites $19. Reservations essential. AE, MC, V.* *Open May–Oct.*

Warsaw

42 *15 mi southeast of Stratford Hall via Rte. 3.*

The county seat of Richmond County, Warsaw is a pleasant town of 7,000 with recreation facilities that include boat ramps, picnic areas, and sporting fields, and a good selection of grocery stores and small shops. The town, shaded by large oak trees, is near the U.S. 360 bridge over the Rappahannock and is therefore closer to the city of Tappahannock (on the other side) than to its fellow towns on the Northern Neck.

A cruise 20 mi up the river to Ingleside Plantation—a Virginia winery—leaves from Tappahannock. **Rappahannock River Cruises** enlists its ship *Capt. Thomas* to take passengers on the narrated day cruise. A buffet lunch is served at the winery ($9.95), or you can bring your own. To reach the dock, take Highway 17 south from Tappahannock to Hoskins Creek. The cruise departs daily at 10, returning at 4. ✉ *Hoskins Creek,* ☎ *804/453–2628,* WEB *www.tangiercruise.com.* 🎫 *$20.* ⏲ *May–Oct., daily tour at 10.*

Ingleside Plantation Vineyards is one of Virginia's oldest and largest wineries. It produces one of the few sparkling wines from Virginia. There are also white wines (viognier, sauvignon blanc, pinot gris, and chardonnay) and reds (sangiovese, cabernet franc, and sauvignon). The vineyards cover about 50 acres of gently rolling countryside that, with its climate and sandy loam soil, is similar to that in Bordeaux, France. The winery has a tasting bar; a gift shop with grape-related gifts; a large outdoor patio with umbrella tables and a fountain; and a large indoor room for group tastings and buffet lunch. The winery is about 40 minutes east of Fredericksburg and only a few miles from the Washington Birthplace National Monument. ✉ *5872 Leedstown Rd., Oak Grove (from Rte. 3, turn south on Rte. 638 at the winery's signpost),* ☎ *804/224–8687.* 🎫 *$2.* ⏲ *Mon.–Sat. 10–5, Sun. noon–5.*

Camping

$ **Heritage Park Resort.** On Menokin Bay, this campground has panoramic views overlooking the Rappahannock River and scenic wildlife settings. The rustic, wooden, two-bedroom cottages are heated and air-conditioned so they can be rented year-round. Each has a living room with navy plaid chairs and sofa, a dining room, and a fully equipped kitchen. With its banquet facilities for 300, the resort is a good place for picnics, receptions, and family reunions. There are also 78 campsites, some of which have full hook-ups or partial hook-ups. ✉ *2570 Newland Rd. (Rte. 674 2½ mi west of U.S. 360), Warsaw 22572,* ☎ *804/333–4038,* FAX *804/333–4039,* WEB *www.heritagepark.com. 5 cottages. Kitchens, tennis court, pool, boating. AE, D, MC, V.*

Reedville

43 *31 mi from Warsaw via U.S. 360, 46 mi from Stratford Hall via Rtes. 202 and 360.*

This small town at the eastern tip of the Northern Neck was the home of wealthy fishermen and businessmen who made their fortunes from the menhaden fish abundant in the nearby Chesapeake Bay and Potomac waters. Many of their Victorian mansions are now B&Bs.

In the historic district is the educational and activity-oriented **Reedville Fishermen's Museum,** housed in a restored fisherman's home and a larger building. Permanent and rotating exhibits document the area's fishing industry. ✉ *Main St.,* ☎ *804/453–6529.* 🎫 *$2.* ⏲ *May–early Nov., daily 10:30–4:30; early Nov.–late Dec., Fri.–Mon. 10:30–4:30; late Dec.–early Mar., by appt.; early Mar.–Apr., weekends 10:30–4:30.*

Popular cruises to Smith and Tangier islands in the Chesapeake Bay leave from Reedville. The 150-passenger ship *Captain Evans* of **Smith Island and Chesapeake Bay Cruises** sails from the KOA Kampground at Smith Point on Route 802, departing at 10 AM and returning at 3:45 PM daily. The 13½-mi trip takes 1½ hours and passes a 5,000-acre waterfowl and wildlife refuge. Now a part of Maryland, Smith Island—a Methodist colony settled by British Colonists from Cornwall—can also be reached from Crisfield, on Maryland's Eastern Shore. Lunch is available at several restaurants on the island. ✉ *382 Campground Rd., behind the KOA Kampground, Rte. 1, Box 1910,* ☎ *804/453–3430,* WEB *www.eaglesnest.net/smithislandcruise.* 🎫 *$18.50.* ⏲ *May–mid-Oct. Reservations required.*

Tangier is a Virginia island in the Chesapeake Bay named by Captain John Smith. This largely unspoiled fishing village with quaint, narrow streets has a small airport for private planes and can be reached by the ship *Chesapeake Breeze* of **Tangier Island & Chesapeake Cruises** (or from Onacock, Virginia, and Crisfield, Maryland, on the Eastern Shore). The ship departs at 10 AM and returns at 3:45 PM daily, cruising 1½ hours each way. The island has several restaurants serving lunch. From the intersection of Highways 360 and 646, drive 1½ mi; then turn left on Highway 656 (Buzzard's Point Road), which leads to the dock. ✉ *468 Buzzard's Point Rd.,* ☎ *804/453–2628,* WEB *www.tangiercruise.com.* 🎫 *$20.* ⏲ *May–Oct. daily tour at 10. Reservations required.*

Lodging

$$ **The Gables.** A four-story redbrick Victorian mansion from the 1890s, the Gables was built by Captain Albert Fisher, one of the founders of the local fishing industry. The house has been lovingly restored and has period antiques throughout. There are two guest rooms in the main house and four more in the adjacent carriage house. The Gables has its own deepwater dock on Cockrell's Creek with easy access to the Chesapeake Bay. ✉ *Main St., 22539,* ☎ *804/453–5209. 6 rooms. Dock. MC, V. BP.*

$ **Bay Motel.** A basic one-story motel with no landscaping, the Bay does have nice rooms and a friendly innkeeper. It's quite close to the Chesapeake Bay cruise lines. ✉ *Rte. 1, Box 210 (18754 Northumberland Hwy.), 22539,* ☎ *804/453–5171. 20 rooms. Cable TV, pool. DC, MC, V.*

En Route After leaving Reedville on Route 360, turn left on Route 200 and drive 13 mi to Kilmarnock. Turn right on Route 3 and drive to the little town of Lancaster, home of the **Mary Ball Washington Museum and Library.** This four-building complex honors George Washington's mother, who was born in Lancaster County. Lancaster House, built about 1798, contains Washington family memorabilia and historic items related to the county and the Northern Neck. The Steuart-Blakemore Building houses a genealogical library, and the Old Jail is a lending library and archives. ✉ *8346 Mary Ball Rd., Lancaster,* ☎ *804/462–7280,* WEB *www.mbwm.org.* 🎫 *Free.* ⏲ *Dec.–Mar., Tues.–Fri. 9–5; Apr.–Nov., Tues.–Fri. 9–5, Sat. 10–3.*

Irvington

44 *5 mi from Kimarnock.*

For more than 50 years, Irvington has been associated with the golf and sports resort Tides Inn. The lovely town—much older than the resort—also has many B&Bs and marinas.

The **Historic Christ Church** was completed in 1735, when George Washington was three years old. The Georgian-style structure, on the National Register of Historic Places, was built by Robert "King" Carter and contains a rare "triple decker" pulpit made of native walnut. Bricks for the church were fired in a great kiln near the churchyard. A

12-minute video is screened in the museum. ✉ *420 Christ Church Rd. (from Irvington drive 1½ mi north on Rte. 200),* ☎ *804/438–6855,* WEB *www.christchurch1735.org.* *Free.* *Church Apr.–Nov., daily; museum Apr.–Nov., Mon.–Sat. 10–4, Sun. 2–5.*

Dining and Lodging

$ ✕ **White Stone Wine & Cheese.** This shop offers Mediterranean sandwiches, soups, baked goods—and of course, wine and cheese, and tables at which to eat. ✉ *101 William St.,* ☎ *540/371–2233. MC, V. Closes at 5 daily.*

$$$$ ★ **The Tides Inn.** This elegant inn completed an extensive multimillion-dollar renovation in 2002, with the addition of a spa. The inn's 18-hole "Golden Eagle" is one of Virginia's best golf courses. Dinners are served in a plush room overlooking the yacht basin. All rooms have hair dryers and coffeemakers. There's dancing in the Chesapeake Club seven nights a week. Amenities include free use of bicycles, paddleboats, canoes, sailboats, daily yacht excursions, and water taxi service to the marina. ✉ *480 King Carter Dr., 22480,* ☎ *804/438–5000 or 800/843–3746,* FAX *804/438–5222,* WEB *www.tidesinn.com. 106 rooms. 5 restaurants, in-room data ports, 9-hole golf course, 18-hole golf course, 4 tennis courts, 3 pools, spa, gym, boating, bicycles, croquet, horseshoes, shuffleboard, lounge, dance club, shops, baby-sitting, children's programs (4–12), laundry facilities, airport shuttle. AE, D, DC, MC, V.*

$$$ **The Hope and Glory Inn.** This 1890 schoolhouse is now a pale-honey color Victorian B&B. The first-floor classrooms have been opened into an expansive, columned lobby with a painted checkerboard floor. The upstairs bedrooms and small cottages behind the inn are decorated in what might be called California romantic, with pastel painted floors and interesting (nonruffled) window treatments. ✉ *634 King Carter Dr., 22480,* ☎ *804/438–6053 or 800/497–8228,* FAX *804/438–6053,* WEB *www.hopeandglory.com. 7 rooms, 4 cottages. MC, V. BP.*

$–$$ **Windmill Point Resort & Marina.** This "last resort" on the Northern Neck is its eastmost point. The beachfront hotel has 1 mi of white sand beach on the Bay and 150 transient boat slips at its marina. The rooms are basic motel style. Drive east on SR 695 to get here: it's 7 mi from White Stone. ✉ *56 Windjammer La., SR 695, Box 368, White Stone 22578,* ☎ *804/435–1166,* FAX *804/435–0789. 61 rooms. Restaurant, 9-hole golf course, 3 tennis courts, 2 pools, boating, marina, bicycles, meeting rooms. AE, MC, V.*

RICHMOND, FREDERICKSBURG, AND THE NORTHERN NECK A TO Z

To research prices, get advice from other travelers, and book travel arrangements, visit www.fodors.com.

AIRPORTS

Richmond International Airport, 10 mi east of the city, Exit 197 off I–64, has scheduled flights by nine airlines.

➤ AIRPORT INFORMATION: **Richmond International Airport** (✉ Airport Dr., ☎ 804/226–3000).

TRANSFERS

A taxi ride to downtown Richmond from the airport costs $18–$20.

BIKE TRAVEL

Multiuse trails throughout the region offer mountain bikers, cyclists, hikers, and runners a wide variety of urban and rural settings for enjoying their sports. Richmond's Forest Hill Park, Dorey Park in

Henrico County, Poor Farm Park in Hanover County, and Pocahontas State Park in Chesterfield County are some of the most popular sites for bicyclists. For more information about area bicycling, contact the Richmond Area Bicycling Association or Mountain Bike Virginia.

There are no shops that rent bicycles in Richmond.

➤ CONTACTS: **Mountain Bike Virginia** (WEB www.mountainbikevirginia.com). **Richmond Area Bicycling Association** (☎ 804/266–BIKE, WEB www.raba.org).

BUS TRAVEL WITHIN FREDERICKSBURG

FRED is Fredericksburg's excellent regional transit bus.

FARES AND SCHEDULES

A ride on FRED costs only 25 cents. Six lines—red, yellow, blue, orange, green, and purple—serve the region and stop at all historic sites as well as shopping malls and other modern areas of the city from 7:30 AM to 8:30 PM.

➤ BUS INFORMATION: **FRED** (☎ 540/372–1222, WEB www.efredericksburg.com/directory/transit).

CAR RENTAL

Most major car rental companies are represented at Richmond Airport. The smaller Autorent firm has two locations in downtown Richmond and one in Fredericksburg.

➤ CONTACTS: **Autorent** (✉ 8406 W. Broad St., Richmond, ☎ 877/467–3681 or 804/270–4200; ✉ 1051 E. Cary St., #166, Richmond, ☎ 877/467–3681 or 804/643–0444; ✉ 5305 Jefferson Davis Hwy., Fredericksburg, ☎ 877/467–3681 or 540/898–8418).

CAR TRAVEL

Having a car is advisable in Richmond and Fredericksburg. It's essential for touring outlying attractions, including historic homes and battlefields, and the Northern Neck.

Richmond is at the intersection of Interstates 95 and 64, which run north–south and east–west, respectively. U.S. 1 also runs north–south past the city. To drive to **Fredericksburg** from Washington, D.C., take I–95 south to Route 3 (Exit 130-A), turn left, and follow the signs. The drive takes about an hour one way; add 45 minutes during rush hour.

To reach the **Northern Neck** from Fredericksburg either take Route 3 South or U.S. 17 to Route 360, crossing the Rappahannock River at the Tappahannock bridge. Driving north from Williamsburg and Hampton roads, cross the river at Greys Point by driving north on Route 3. Access from Maryland and Washington, D.C., is over the Potomac River toll bridge on Route 301. If you cross here, you'll shortly come upon Virginia's Potomac Gateway Visitors Center in King George.

DISCOUNTS AND DEALS

A Historic Downtown Richmond Block Ticket, which costs $15 and is good for 30 days, allows for admission to any five of nearly 20 museums and cultural attractions in downtown Richmond. The block ticket is available at the attractions themselves.

EMERGENCIES

Fredericksburg's Medic 1 Clinic is open weekdays 8 AM–9 PM, Saturday 9–7, and Sunday 9–3.

➤ CONTACT: **Ambulance, Fire, Police** (☎ 911).

➤ HOSPITALS: **Medical College of Virginia Hospital** (✉ 401 N. 12th St., Richmond, ☎ 804/828–9000). **Medic 1 Clinic** (✉ 3429 Jefferson Davis Hwy., Fredericksburg, ☎ 540/371–1664).

➤ 24-Hour Pharmacies: **CVS Pharmacy** (✉ 2738 W. Broad St., Richmond, ☎ 804/359–2497).

TAXIS

Cabs are metered in Richmond; they charge $3 for the first mile and $1.50 for each additional mile.

➤ Taxi Companies: **Bumbreys Independent Cab Service** (✉ 209 Lafayette Blvd., Fredericksburg, ☎ 540/373–6111). **Colonial Cab** (✉ Richmond, ☎ 804/264–7960). **Groome Transportation** (✉ Richmond Airport, Richmond, ☎ 804/222–7222). **Metro Taxicab Service** (✉ 2405 Westwood Ave., Richmond, ☎ 804/353–5000). **Old Dominion Taxi** (✉ Richmond, ☎ 804/266–0328). **Yellow Cab of Fredericksburg** (✉ 2217 Princess Anne St., Fredericksburg, ☎ 540/368–8120). **Yellow Cab Service Inc.** (✉ 3203 Williamsburg Rd., Richmond, ☎ 804/222–7300).

TOURS

In Richmond, Annabel Lee Riverboat Cruises ply the James River from April to December, with lunch, brunch, dinner, dancing, live riverboat shows, and plantation cruises that run from $23 to $33.

Fredericksburg Carriage Tours depart from the visitor center for leisurely paced, narrated tours of downtown in horse-drawn carriages. Tours last about 45 minutes and cost $10.

Lee's Retreat is a 26-stop self-guided driving tour from Petersburg to Appomattox. For a route map and other information, contact the Petersburg Visitor Center (☞ Visitor Information).

Historic Richmond Tours organizes tours on subjects such as women of Richmond, architecture, the Civil War, the Revolution, homes and gardens, and battlefields, as well as walking tours ($5). It also runs daily two- to four-hour driving tours of the city in air-conditioned vans for $16–$22. Reservations are required.

Richmond Discoveries is a private company that offers excursions in the Richmond area, including trips that highlight Civil War history, horseback tours, and customized rambles for large groups or small families.

You can take a 75-minute narrated tour of Fredericksburg's most important sights on the Trolley. Tours, which are conducted April through November, cost $12.50 and leave from the visitor center daily at 10, noon, 1:30, and 3:30 June through October, and daily at 11 and 1:30 in April, May, and November.

The Living History Company of Fredericksburg conducts walking tours that are tailored to the desires of those taking them. The tour coordinator at the Fredericksburg Visitor Center can arrange a group walking tour of the city as well as of battlefields and other historic sites to which you can drive. Reservations are required. The Fredericksburg Department of Tourism (in the visitor center) publishes a booklet that includes a short history of Fredericksburg and a self-guided tour covering 29 sights.

➤ Boat Tours: ***Annabel Lee* Riverboat Cruises** (✉ 4400 E. Main St., ☎ 804/644–5700 or 800/752–7093).

➤ Carriage and Trolley Tours: **Fredericksburg Carriage Tours** (✉ (1700 Caroline St., ☎ 540/752–5567, WEB www.carriagetours.com). **Trolley** (☎ 540/898–0737).

➤ Guided Tours: **Historic Richmond Tours** (☎ 804/780–0107, WEB www.historicrichmond.com). **Richmond Discoveries** (☎ 804/795–5781).

➤ WALKING TOURS: **The Living History Company of Fredericksburg** (☎ 540/898–0737, WEB www.historyexperiences.com).

TRAIN TRAVEL

Amtrak trains operate between Washington's Union Station, Alexandria, Fredericksburg, Richmond, and a number of commuter stops several times daily. Richmond's train station is north of town. The unmanned Fredericksburg station is two blocks from the historic district.

A one-way ticket costs $14–$18 between Fredericksburg and Washington and $21–$26 between Washington and Richmond. Amtrak service between New York City and Newport News or Florida passes through Richmond daily.

The Virginia Rail Express, which uses the same tracks and station as Amtrak, provides workday commuter service between Fredericksburg and Washington's Union Station with additional stops near hotels in Crystal City, L'Enfant Plaza, and elsewhere. A round-trip ticket from Washington's Union Station to Fredericksburg costs $13.40.

There is no mass transit to the Northern Neck, but you can take the train to Fredericksburg and rent a car.

➤ TRAIN STATIONS: **Fredericksburg station** (✉ Caroline St. and Lafayette Blvd.). **Richmond train station** (✉ 7519 Staples Mill Rd., ☎ 804/553–2903).

➤ TRAIN LINES: **Amtrak** (☎ 800/872–7245). **Virginia Rail Express** (VRE; ☎ 703/658–6200 or 800/743–3873).

VISITOR INFORMATION

Northern Neck Visitor Information is available at the Potomac Gateway Visitor Center and at the Northern Neck Tourism Council. There is no tourist bureau at Reedville, but tourist brochures are available in the Reedville Fishermen's Museum.

Richmond tourist brochures are available at the National Park Service's five Richmond area visitor centers (*see* Richmond National Battlefield Park Civil War Visitor Center *and* Chimborazo Medical Museum).

➤ TOURIST INFORMATION: **Fredericksburg Visitor Center** (✉ 706 Caroline St., 22401, ☎ 540/373–1776 or 800/678–4748, FAX 540/372–6587, WEB www.fredericksburgva.com). **Hanover Visitor Center** (✉ 112 N. Railroad Ave. [I–95, Exit 92B], Ashland, ☎ 804/752–6766 or 800/897–1479, WEB www.town.ashland.va.us). **Metro Richmond Visitors Centers** (✉ 405 N. Third St., 23210, ☎ 804/358–5511, 804/782–2777, or 888/742–4663, FAX 804/780–2577). **Petersburg Visitor Center,** (✉ 425 Cockade Alley, ☎ 804/733–2400 or 800/368–3595, WEB www.petersburg-va.org; information by mail, ✉ 15 Bank St., Petersburg 23803, ☎ 804/733–2402, FAX 804/861–0883). **Potomac Gateway Visitor Center** (✉ 3540 James Madison Parkway, King George 22485, ☎ 540/663–3205, WEB www.northernneck.org). **Reedville** (✉ Box 312, Reedville 22539, ☎ 800/453–6167). **Reedville Fishermen's Museum** (✉ Main St., ☎ 804/453–6529). **Richmond National Battlefield Park Civil War Visitor Center** (✉ 5th and Tredegar Sts., ☎ 804/771–2145; ⏲ Daily 9–5). **Virginia Tourism Corporation** (✉ 901 E. Byrd St., Richmond, ☎ 800/932–5827, WEB www.richmondva.org; ✉ Bell Tower at Capitol Sq., 9th and Franklin Sts., Richmond, ☎ 804/648–3146; information by mail: ✉ 403 N. Third St., 23219).

6 WILLIAMSBURG AND HAMPTON ROADS

The eastern end of Virginia's Tidewater—the historic name for the coastal plain—is rich in history and sights. The Virginia peninsula, which extends southeast into the Chesapeake Bay, defines the port of Hampton Roads on the north and contains the cities of Newport News and Hampton. On the southern side of Hampton Roads are Norfolk, Portsmouth, and the popular ocean resort Virginia Beach.

Updated by Gail Doyle

PERHAPS NO OTHER REGION IN VIRGINIA contains more variety and options than its eastern coastline. Colonial Williamsburg has evoked the days of America's forefathers since the 1920s. Jamestown and Yorktown also help to make the area one of the most historically significant in the United States. When it's time for pure recreation, you can head to theme parks such as Busch Gardens Williamsburg and resort areas, including Virginia Beach.

Where Colonial Williamsburg now stands was once the capital of the Virginia Colony. Its 173-acre village contains re-created and restored structures peopled with costumed interpreters. Everything from momentous political events to blacksmithing is portrayed. Just a short drive along the tree-lined Colonial Parkway is Jamestown, the first permanent English settlement. Completing the "historic triangle" is Yorktown, the site of the battle that ended the war for independence from England. Several 18th- and 19th-century plantations lie west of Williamsburg, along the James River.

At the end of the Virginia peninsula is the enormous Hampton Roads harbor, where the James, Elizabeth, and Nansemond rivers flow together and on into Chesapeake Bay. Hampton Roads has also played a crucial role in the discovery and settlement of the nation, its struggle for independence, and the conflict that nearly dissolved the Union.

This entire area, known as the Tidewater, is technically defined as the area in which all river flow is eastward, toward the Chesapeake Bay. The cities in southeast Virginia are defined by their proximity to the Chesapeake Bay and the rivers that empty into it. Hampton contains the world's largest naval base, and enormous shipbuilding yards are in Norfolk and Newport News. The area is also committed to recreation and tourism: there are many resort hotels, a bustling beachfront, and boardwalk attractions. Virginia Beach, which in the 1950s claimed to have the world's longest public beach, is now working hard to fight oceanfront erosion and rebuild its once showy boardwalk.

Linked to the Hampton Roads area by the unusual Chesapeake Bay Bridge-Tunnel is Virginia's "other coastline," the quiet, largely untrafficked Eastern Shore.

Pleasures and Pastimes

Dining

CATEGORY	COST*
$$$$	over $32
$$$	$22–$32
$$	$12–$22
$	under $12

**per person for a main course at dinner*

Lodging

CATEGORY	COST*
$$$$	over $225
$$$	$150–$225
$$	$100–$150
$	under $100

**All prices are for a standard double room, excluding state tax.*

Exploring Williamsburg and Hampton Roads

To keep the chronology straight, visit Virginia's "historic triangle" in the order of Jamestown, Williamsburg, and then Yorktown. Although Jamestown is somewhat overshadowed by the much-larger Williamsburg, Jamestown Island became the first permanent English settlement (1607) in North America. Subsequently Williamsburg grew into the political and economic center of the Virginia Colony. West of Williamsburg, historic plantations line the James River. Yorktown, site of the final major battle in the American War of Independence, is where the Colonies won their freedom from England. South of Yorktown are Newport News, the shipbuilding capital of Virginia, and Hampton. To see the rest of this waterfront area of Virginia, you can cross the James River at Hampton and visit Norfolk, Portsmouth, and, to the east, the Virginia Beach resort area.

JAMESTOWN, WILLIAMSBURG, AND YORKTOWN

Colonial Williamsburg, a careful restoration of the former Virginia capital, gives you the chance to walk into another century and see how earlier Americans lived. The streets may be unrealistically clean for that era, and you'll find hundreds of others exploring the buildings with you, but the rich detail of the re-creation and the sheer size of the city could hold your attention for days. A ticket or pass (price is based on the number of attractions and the duration of visit) admits the holder to sites in the restored area, but it costs nothing just to walk around and absorb the atmosphere.

The 23-mi Colonial Parkway joins Williamsburg with two other significant historical sites on or near the peninsula bounded by the James and York rivers. Historic Jamestowne was the location of the first permanent English settlement in North America, and it's an excellent place to begin a visit to the area; Yorktown was the site of the final major battle in the American Revolutionary War. The sites themselves are maintained today by the National Park Service. Close by are Jamestown Settlement and the excellent Yorktown Victory Center, both run by the Jamestown-Yorktown Foundation. Like Colonial Williamsburg, these two sights re-create the buildings and activities of the 18th century, using interpreters in period dress.

Numbers in the margin correspond to points of interest on the Williamsburg and Environs map.

Jamestown

❶ *9 mi southwest of Colonial Williamsburg (via Colonial Pkwy.).*

Jamestown takes you to the beginnings of English settlement in this country: its two major sights are places to explore the early relationship between the English and Native Americans.

Historic Jamestowne, separated from the mainland by a narrow isthmus, was the site of the first permanent English settlement in North America (1607) and the capital of Virginia until 1699. The first settlers' bitter struggle for survival here, on the now uninhabited land, makes for a visit that stirs the imagination. Redbrick foundation walls roughly outline the settlement, and artists' conceptions of the original buildings can be seen at several locations. The only standing structure is the ruin of a church tower from the 1640s, now part of the Memorial Church built in 1907; the markers within indicate the original

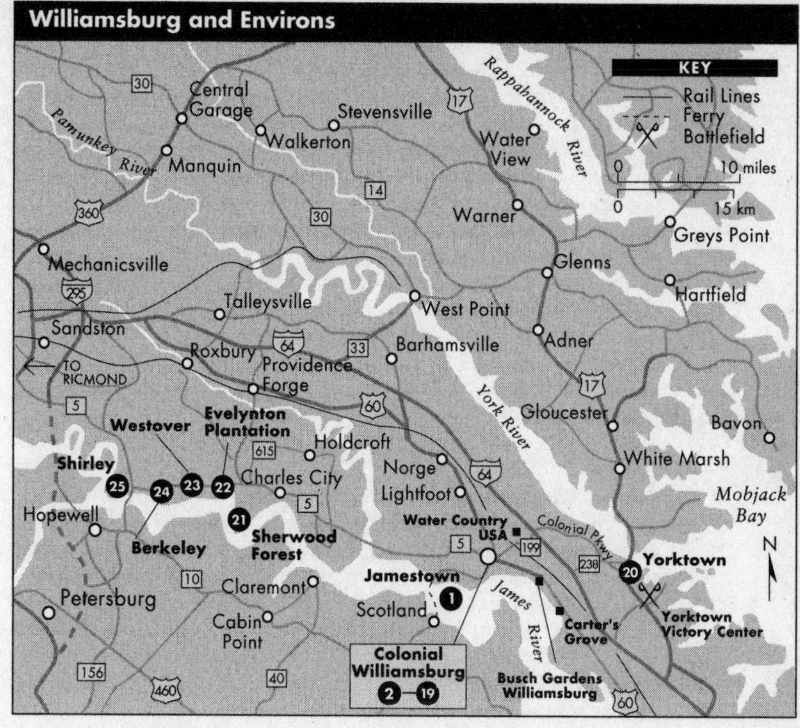

church's foundations. Other monuments around the site also date from the tercentenary celebration in 1907. Statues portray the founder of Jamestown, Captain John Smith, and his advocate, the Native American princess Pocahontas, whose pleas saved Smith from being beheaded.

Along with Yorktown, Historic Jamestowne is part of Colonial National Historical Park, run by the National Park Service. Ranger-guided tours take place daily, and audio stations also narrate the evolving story of Jamestown. Living-history programs are presented daily in summer and on weekends in spring and autumn.

The museum in the visitor center contains one of the most extensive collections of 17th-century artifacts in the United States, and on-site archaeologists continue to dig up evidence of the Colonists' and Native Americans' way of life.

A 5-mi nature drive that rings the island is posted with informative signs and paintings. On leaving Historic Jamestowne, you can stop at the reconstructed Glasshouse to observe a demonstration of glassblowing, an unsuccessful business venture of the early Colonists. The products of today are for sale in a gift shop. ✉ *Off Colonial Pkwy.,* ☎ *757/898–2410.* 🎫 *$6.* ⏲ *Daily 9–5 (gates close at 4:30).*

Adjacent to Historic Jamestowne, but not to be confused with it, a mainland living-history museum called **Jamestown Settlement** holds a version of the early James Fort. Within it, interpreters in costume cook, make armor, and describe their hard life living under thatch roofs and between walls of wattle and daub (stick framework covered with mud plaster). The largest structure in the complex is the church, where attendance was required twice a day. In the Powhatan Indian Village you can enter a "yehakin," or house, and see buckskin-costumed interpreters cultivate a garden and make tools and dugout canoes. This is one museum where everything may be handled—children especially enjoy this. At the pier are full-scale reproductions of the ships in which the settlers arrived: *Godspeed, Discovery,* and *Susan Constant*. The *Godspeed* retraced the original voyage in 1985, and all the vessels are seaworthy. You may climb aboard the *Susan Constant* and find out more from the sailor-interpreters. Indoor exhibits examine the lives of the Powhatans and their English-born neighbors, their interaction, and world conditions that encouraged colonization. There's also a 20-minute docudrama called *Jamestown: The Beginning*. Thursdays and Fridays in April–May and October–November bring lots of school groups, so it's best to arrive after 2 PM on those days. ✉ *Rte. 31, off Colonial Pkwy.,* ☎ *757/253–4838 or 757/229–1607,* WEB *www.historyisfun.org.* *$10.75; combination ticket with Yorktown Victory Center $16.* ⏲ *Daily 9–5.*

Colonial Williamsburg

51 mi southeast of Richmond (via I–64).

★ **Colonial Williamsburg** is a convincing re-creation of the late-18th-century city. This was the capital of Virginia from 1699 to 1780, after Jamestown and preceding Richmond. Williamsburg has long ceased to be politically important, but now that it resembles itself in its era of glory, it's a jewel of the commonwealth. The restoration project, begun in 1926, was inspired by a local pastor, W. A. R. Goodwin, and financed by John D. Rockefeller Jr. The work of the archaeologists and historians of the Colonial Williamsburg Foundation continues to this day, and the restored area of the city is operated by the foundation as a living-history museum. Outside the restored area is a modern city with plenty of dining and lodging options and attractions, including outlet shops and a large water park.

In Colonial Williamsburg, 88 original 18th-century and early 19th-century structures have been meticulously restored, and another 40 have been reconstructed on their original sites. There is one architectural anachronism here: a 19th-century Federal house, privately owned and closed to the public. In all, 225 period rooms have been furnished from the foundation's collection of more than 100,000 pieces of furniture, pottery, china, glass, silver, pewter, textiles, tools, and carpeting.

Period authenticity also governs the landscaping of the 90 acres of gardens and public greens. The restored area covers 173 acres; surrounded by another greenbelt, it's controlled by the foundation, which guards against development that could mar the illusion of the colonial city.

Despite its huge scale, Colonial Williamsburg can seem almost cozy. One million people come here annually, and all year long hundreds of costumed interpreters, wearing bonnets or three-corner hats, rove and ride through the streets (you can even rent outfits for your children). Dozens of skilled craftspeople, also in costume, demonstrate and explain their trades inside their workshops. They include the shoemaker, the cooper (he makes barrels), the gunsmith, the blacksmith, the musical instrument maker, the silversmith, and the wig maker. Their wares are for sale nearby. Four taverns serve food and drink that approximate the fare of more than 220 years ago.

Colonial Williamsburg makes an effort to not just represent the lives of a privileged few, and to not gloss over disturbing aspects of the country's history. Slavery, religious freedom, family life, commerce and trade, land acquisition, and the Revolution are portrayed in four living-history demonstrations. In the 1-½-hour "About Town" walking tour, you can be personally escorted by such famous patriots as Thomas

Jefferson or Martha Washington. In "Talk of the Town" you can get a firsthand account of the events that were important to the community, and the nation, in the spring of 1774. Free black and enslaved men struggle with issues of identity and survival in "Among the Dipping Gourds." At the meetinghouse, you can step into the controversial world of the Reverend James Waddell, a "Licensed Dissenter."

The vignettes that are staged throughout the day take place in the streets and in public buildings. These may include dramatic afternoon court trials or fascinating estate appraisals. Depending on the days you visit, you may see the House of Burgesses dissolve, its members charging out to make revolutionary plans at the Raleigh Tavern. There's even a love story at play as Mr. Drinkard and Miss Grant become involved in a terrible miscommunication before the eyes of camera-clad tourists.

Because of the size of Colonial Williamsburg and the large crowds (especially in the warmer months), the best plan may be to begin a tour early in the day; it's a good idea to spend the night before in the area. The foundation suggests allowing three or four days to do Colonial Williamsburg justice, but that will depend on your own interest in the period—and that interest often increases on arrival. Everyone should allow at least one full day to tour the city. A number of guided walks or tours are available. Museums, exhibits, and stores close at 5 PM, but the town is open 24 hours, and walks and events take place in the evenings, usually ending by 10 PM. Some sites close in winter on a rotating basis.

All vehicular traffic is prohibited to preserve the Colonial illusion. Shuttle buses run continuously to and from the visitor center. Vans for people with disabilities are permitted by prior arrangement, and some structures have wheelchair ramps. Wheelchairs can also be rented (☎ 757/229–1000). Printed versions of the film "Williamsburg: The Story of a Patriot" and special headsets are available for the hearing impaired. Signing interpreters are also offered by calling in advance (☎ 757/220–7612).

Numbers in the margin correspond to points of interest on the Colonial Williamsburg map.

❷ The **Visitor Center** is the logical first stop at Colonial Williamsburg. Here you can park free; buy tickets; see a 35-minute introductory movie, *Williamsburg—the Story of a Patriot*; and pick up the very useful *Visitors Companion*, which has a list of regular events and special programs and a map of the Historic Area. ✉ *102 Information Center Dr., off U.S. 60,* ☎ *757/220–7645 or 800/447–8679,* WEB *www.colonialwilliamsburg.com.* 🎫 *Annual Passes, $39–$59, good for 1 year, admit bearer to every Colonial Williamsburg–run site. General admission, $33 for the first day, can be upgraded to annual pass and include all museums and exhibitions. Various less-expensive tickets allow for more restricted visits. Tickets also sold at the Lumber House in historic area and at the Williamsburg Attraction Center.* ⏲ *Daily 9–5.*

The spine of Colonial Williamsburg's restored area is the broad, 1-mi-long **Duke of Gloucester Street.** On Saturday at noon, from March to October, the Junior Fife and Drum Corps marches the length of the street and performs a stirring drill. Along this artery alone, or just off it, are two dozen attractions. Walking west on Duke of Gloucester Street from the Capitol, you'll find a dozen 18th-century shops—including those of the apothecary, the wig maker, the silversmith, and the milliner.

❸ The **Capitol** is the building that made this town so important. It was here that the pre-Revolutionary House of Burgesses (dominated by the ascendant gentry) challenged the royally appointed council (an almost

Colonial Williamsburg

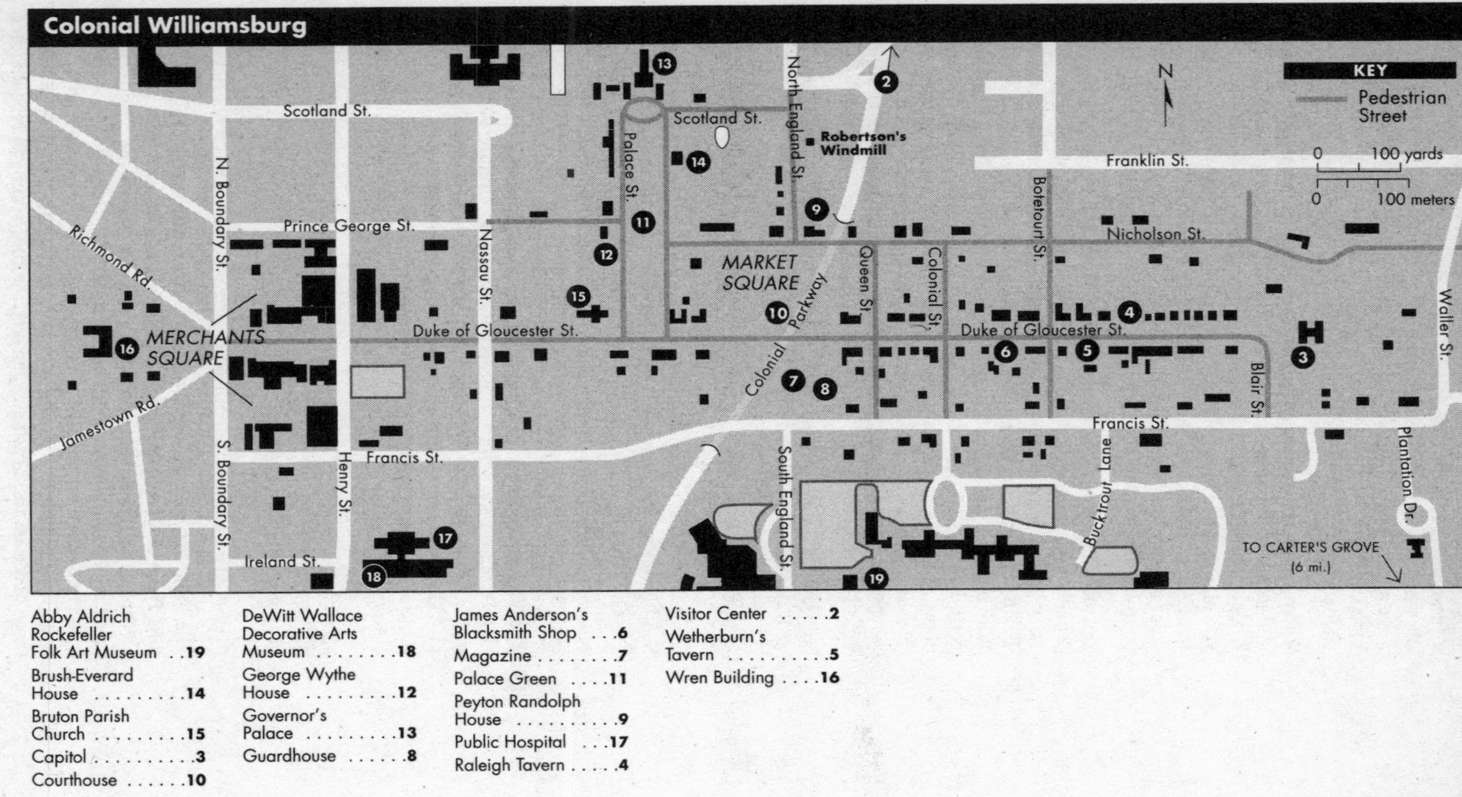

Abby Aldrich Rockefeller Folk Art Museum . . **19**	DeWitt Wallace Decorative Arts Museum **18**	James Anderson's Blacksmith Shop . . . **6**	Visitor Center **2**
Brush-Everard House **14**	George Wythe House **12**	Magazine **7**	Wetherburn's Tavern **5**
Bruton Parish Church **15**	Governor's Palace **13**	Palace Green **11**	Wren Building **16**
Capitol **3**	Guardhouse **8**	Peyton Randolph House **9**	
Courthouse **10**		Public Hospital . . . **17**	
		Raleigh Tavern **4**	

medieval body made up of the bigger landowners). In 1765, the House eventually arrived at the resolutions, known as Henry's Resolves (after Patrick Henry), that amounted to rebellion. An informative tour explains the development, stage by stage, of American democracy from its English parliamentary roots. In the courtroom a guide recites the harsh Georgian sentences that were meted out: for instance, theft of more than 12 shillings was a capital crime. Occasional reenactments, including witch trials, dramatize the evolution of American jurisprudence.

What stands on the site today is a reproduction of the 1705 structure that burned down in 1747. Dark-wood wainscoting, pewter chandeliers, and towering ceilings contribute to a handsome impression. That an official building would have so ornate an interior was characteristic of aristocratic 18th-century Virginia. This was in telling contrast to the plain town meeting halls of Puritan New England, where other citizens were governing themselves at the same time. ✉ *East end of Duke of Gloucester St.*

4 **Raleigh Tavern** was the scene of pre-Revolutionary revels and rallies that were often joined by Washington, Jefferson, Patrick Henry, and other major figures. The spare but elegant blue-and-white Apollo Room is said to have been the first meeting place of Phi Beta Kappa, the scholastic honorary society founded in 1776. The French general Marquis de Lafayette was feted here in 1824. In 1859 the original structure burned, and today's building is a reconstruction based on archaeological evidence and period descriptions and sketches of the building. ✉ *Duke of Gloucester St., west of the Capitol.*

5 **Wetherburn's Tavern,** which offered refreshment, entertainment, and lodging beginning in 1743, may be the most accurately furnished building in Colonial Williamsburg, with contents that conform to a room-by-room inventory taken in 1760. Excavations at this site have yielded more than 200,000 artifacts. The outbuildings include the original dairy and a reconstructed kitchen. Vegetables are still grown in the small garden. ✉ *Duke of Gloucester St., across from Raleigh Tavern.*

6 At **James Anderson's Blacksmith Shop,** smiths forge the nails, tools, and other iron hardware used in construction throughout the town. The shop itself was reconstructed by costumed carpenters using 18th-century tools and techniques—a project featured on public television. ✉ *Between Botetourt and Colonial Sts., on the south side of Duke of Gloucester St.*

7 The original **Magazine** (1715), an octagonal brick warehouse, was used for storing arms and ammunition—at one time, 60,000 pounds of gunpowder and 3,000 muskets. It was used for this purpose by the British, then by the Continental army, and again by the Confederates during the Civil War. Today, 18th-century firearms are on display within the arsenal. ✉ *West of Queen St., on the south side of Duke of Gloucester St.*

8 The **Guardhouse** once served in the defense of the Magazine's lethal inventory; now it contains a replica fire engine (1750) that is seen on the town streets in the warmer months. Special interpretive programs about the military are scheduled here. ✉ *Duke of Gloucester St. near Queen St.*

In **Market Square,** an open green between Queen and Palace streets along Duke of Gloucester, cattle, seafood, dairy products, fruit, and vegetables were all sold—as were slaves. Both the market and slave auctions are sometimes reenacted.

9 The **Peyton Randolph House** was the home of a prominent Colonist and revolutionary who served as attorney general under the British, then as Speaker of the House of Burgesses, and later as president of the first and second Continental Congresses. The oak-paneled bedroom and Randolph family silver are remarkable. ✉ *Nicholson St. at N. England St.*

East of the Peyton Randolph House, on Nicholson Street, is the **military encampment,** where you can get a feeling for military life in the 1700s. During warm weather, "Join the Continental Army," an interactive theater performance, lets you experience military life on the eve of the Revolution. Under the guidance of costumed militiamen, drill and make camp in a 45-minute participatory program. If you want to join the ranks for a little while, you can volunteer at the site.

On the outskirts of the Historic Area, you can follow the pleasant fragrance of wood burning to **Robertson's Windmill,** where rural trades such as basket making, pit sawing (two men on either side of a long saw in a pit), and coopering (barrel making) are demonstrated. When the weather is willing, the windmill powers the fires inside that tradespeople use for their craft. The coopers smolder metal strands that wrap around the barrels, keeping them taut. ✉ *N. England St.*

10 The original **Courthouse** of 1770 was used by municipal and county courts until 1932. Civil and minor criminal matters and cases involving slaves were adjudicated here; other trials were conducted at the Capitol. The stocks once used to punish misdemeanors are outside the building: they can make for a perverse photo opportunity. The courthouse's exterior has been restored to its original appearance. Visitors often participate in scheduled reenactments of court sessions. ✉ *North side of Duke of Gloucester St., west of Queen St.*

11 The handsome **Palace Green** runs north from Duke of Gloucester Street up the center of Palace Street, with the Governor's Palace at the far end and a notable historic house on either side.

12 The **George Wythe House** was the residence of Thomas Jefferson's law professor; Wythe was also a signer of the Declaration of Independence. General Washington used the house as a headquarters just before his victory at Yorktown. The large brick structure, built in the mid-18th century, is conspicuously symmetrical: each side has a chimney, and each floor has two rooms on either side of a center hallway. The garden in back is similarly divided. The outbuildings, including a smokehouse, kitchen, laundry, outhouses, and a chicken coop, are reconstructions. ✉ *West side of Palace Green.*

13 His Majesty's Governor Alexander Spotswood built the original **Governor's Palace** in 1720, and seven British viceroys, the last of them Lord Dunmore in 1775, lived in this appropriately showy mansion. The 800 guns and swords arrayed on the walls and ceilings of several rooms herald the power of the Crown. Some of the furnishings are original, and the rest are matched to an extraordinary inventory of 16,000 items. Lavishly appointed as it is, the palace is furnished to the time just before the Revolution. During the Revolution, it housed the commonwealth's first two governors, Patrick Henry and Thomas Jefferson. The original residence burned down in 1781, and today's reconstruction stands on the original foundation.

A costumed guide greets you at the door for a tour through the building, offering commentary and answering questions. Notable among the furnishings are several pieces made in Williamsburg and actually owned by Lord Dunmore. Social events are described on the walk through the great formal ballroom, where you might even hear the sounds of an 18th-century harp, clavichord, or piano, or see colonists dancing to the hit tunes of the times. The supper room leads to the formal garden and the planted terraces beyond. ✉ *Northern end of Palace Green.*

14 The **Brush-Everard House** was built in 1717 by John Brush, a gunsmith, and later owned by Thomas Everard, who was twice mayor of Williamsburg. The yellow wood-frame house contains remarkable, ornate carving work but is open only for special-focus tours. Temporary exhibits and vignettes on slaves' lives are held here during the summer. ✉ *Scotland St. and Palace Green.*

15 The lovely brick Episcopal **Bruton Parish Church** has served continuously as a house of worship since it was built in 1715. One of its 20th-century pastors, W. A. R. Goodwin, provided the impetus for Williamsburg's restoration. The church tower, topped by a beige wooden steeple, was added in 1769; during the Revolution its bell served as the local "liberty bell," rung to summon people for announcements. The white pews, tall and boxed in, are characteristic of the starkly graceful Colonial ecclesiastical architecture of the region. When sitting in a pew, listening to the history of the church, keep in mind that you could be sitting where Thomas Jefferson, Ben Franklin, or George Washington once listened to sermons. The stone baptismal font is believed to have come from an older Jamestown church. Many local eminences, including one royal governor, are interred in the graveyard. The fully operational church is open to the public; contributions are accepted. ✉ *Duke of Gloucester St. west of Palace St.*

NEED A BREAK? At the west end of Duke of Gloucester Street, for a block on both sides, **Merchants Square** has more than 40 shops and restaurants, some serving fast food. Services also include three banks and a drugstore.

16 The **Wren Building** is part of the College of William and Mary, founded in 1693 and the second-oldest college in the United States after Harvard University. The campus extends to the west; the Wren Building (1695) was based on the work of the celebrated London architect Sir Christopher Wren. Its redbrick outer walls are original, but fire gutted the interiors several times, and the current quarters are largely reconstructions of the 20th century. The faculty common room, with a table covered with green felt and an antique globe, suggests Oxford and Cambridge universities, the models for this New World institution. Jefferson studied and later taught law here to James Monroe and others. Tours, led by undergraduates, include the chapel where Colonial leader Peyton Randolph is buried. ✉ *West end of Duke of Gloucester St.*

17 The **Public Hospital,** a reconstruction of a 1773 insane asylum, provides an informative, shocking look at the treatment of the mentally ill in the 18th and 19th centuries. It also serves as cover for a modern edifice that houses very different exhibitions; entrance to the DeWitt Wallace Decorative Arts Museum is through the hospital lobby. ✉ *Francis St.*

18 The **DeWitt Wallace Decorative Arts Museum** adds another cultural dimension that goes well beyond Colonial history. Grouped by medium are English and American furniture, textiles, prints, metals, and ceramics of the 17th to the early 19th century. If you're yawning at the thought of fancy tableware, stop: you'll be surprised at the exhibits' creative presentations. Prizes among the 8,000 pieces in the collection are a full-length portrait of George Washington by Charles Willson Peale and a royally commissioned case clock surmounted by the detailed figure of a Native American. You can enter the museum through the Public Hospital. ✉ *Francis St.*

19 The **Abby Aldrich Rockefeller Folk Art Museum** showcases American "decorative usefulware"—toys, furniture, weather vanes, coffeepots, and quilts—within typical 19th-century domestic interiors. There are also folk paintings, rustic sculptures, and needlepoint pictures. Since the 1920s, the 2,000-piece collection has grown from the original 400 pieces acquired by the wife of Colonial Williamsburg's first and principal benefactor. ✉ *S. England St.*

The reconstructed **Carter's Grove plantation,** created after extensive archaeological investigation, examines 400 years of history, starting in 1619 with the fortified hamlet called Wolstenholme Towne. Exhibits in the **Winthrop Rockefeller Archaeology Museum** provide further insight. The 18th century is represented by slave dwellings on their original foundations, where costumed interpreters explain the crucial role African-Americans played on plantations. Dramatic plays take place here during the evening. Finally, you may tour the **mansion,** built in 1755 by Carter Burwell, whose grandfather, "King" Carter, made a fortune as one of Virginia's wealthiest landowners and greatest explorers. The mansion was extensively remodeled in 1919, and further additions were made in the 1930s. The interior is notable for the original wood paneling and elaborate carvings. A one-way scenic country road, also used for biking, leads from Carter's Grove through woods, meadows, marshes, and streams back to Williamsburg. ✉ *U.S. 60, 6 mi east of Colonial Williamsburg,* ☎ *757/229–1000.* *$18 (included in any regular Williamsburg pass). Play $10.* ⏲ *Mid-Mar.–Dec., Tues.–Sun. 9–5.*

OFF THE BEATEN PATH

WILLIAMSBURG WINERY – Carrying on a Virginia tradition of wine making that began with early settlers, the winery offers guided tours, a well-stocked wine shop, a unique 17th-century tasting room, and a museum of wine-making artifacts. A casual luncheon is served in the Gabriel Archer Tavern. Be sure to give the cabernets and merlots a try. ✉ *5800 Wessex Hundred, off Lake Powell Rd. and Rte. 199, Williamsburg,* ☎ *757/229–0999.* *$6 (includes tasting of 5–7 wines and a souvenir glass).* ⏲ *Mid-Feb.–mid-Jan., Mon.–Sat. 10:30–5:30, Sun. 11–5:30.*

Dining and Lodging

Dining rooms within walking distance of Colonial Williamsburg's restored area are often crowded, and **reservations** (☎ 800/447–8679) are necessary. Many nationally known chain eateries line both sides of U.S. 60 on the east side of the city. There's enough demand to support a score of pancake houses.

Dining

$$–$$$$ ✕ **Aberdeen Barn.** Saws, pitchforks, oxen yokes, and the like hang on the barn walls, but the wood tables are lacquered, and the napkins are linen. Specialties include slow-roasted prime rib of beef; baby-back Danish pork ribs barbecued with a sauce of peach preserves and Southern Comfort; and shrimp Dijon. An ample but not esoteric wine list is dominated by California vintages (there are Virginia selections, too). ✉ *1601 Richmond Rd.,* ☎ *757/229–6661. AE, D, MC, V. No lunch.*

$$–$$$$ ✕ **Le Yaca.** A mall of small boutiques is the unlikely location for this French-country eatery. The dining room has soft pastel colors, hardwood floors, candlelight, and a central open fireplace. The menu is arranged in the French manner, with four prix-fixe menus and 10 entrées, including whole duck breast with black truffle sauce, leg of lamb with rosemary garlic sauce, and fresh scallops and shrimp with champagne sauce. The restaurant is in the Village Shops at Kingsmill, on U.S. 60 East, near Busch Gardens. ✉ *1915 Pocahontas Trail,* ☎ *757/220–3616. AE, D, DC, MC, V. Closed Sun. and first 2 wks of Jan.*

$$–$$$$ ★ ✕ **Regency Room.** This restaurant in the Williamsburg Inn is known for its elegance, its attentive service, and quality cuisine. Among crystal chandeliers, Asian silk-screen prints, and full silver service, you can sample chateaubriand carved tableside, as well as lobster bisque and rich ice cream desserts. It may almost seem as if you're treated like royalty. A jacket and tie are required at dinner and Sunday brunch. ✉ *Williamsburg Inn, 136 E. Francis St.,* ☎ *757/229–1000. Reservations essential. AE, D, DC, MC, V.*

$$–$$$$ ★ ✕ **The Trellis.** With vaulted ceilings and hardwood floors, the Trellis is an airy and pleasant place for romantic dinners. The imaginative lunch and dinner menus change with the seasons. A dazzling wine list complements such tasty morsels as homemade tomato bisque, wild boar, and soft-shell crabs. The seafood entrées are particularly good, and many patrons wouldn't leave without ordering the rich Death by Chocolate, the restaurant's signature dessert. ✉ *Merchants Sq.,* ☎ *757/229–8610. AE, MC, V.*

$$–$$$ ✕ **Berret's Restaurant and Raw Bar.** One of the most reliable seafood spots around, Berret's is in Merchants Square. Upscale but casual, the restaurant lights crackling fires during colder months and opens up its pleasant outdoor patio when it's warm. Entrées and appetizers employ fresh Chesapeake Bay seafood. It's usually a sure bet to try any of the nightly specials of fresh fish, which often include perfectly prepared tuna. The she-crab soup, a house favorite, is a blend of crabmeat, cream, and crab roe with just a hint of sherry. ✉ *199 Boundary St.,* ☎ *757/253–1847. AE, D, DC, MC, V. Closed Mon. Jan.–early Feb.*

$$ ✕ **The Seafare of Williamsburg.** Here in one of the area's few places for "fine dining," the waiters are tuxedo-clad, the tablecloths crisp linen. The staff dote on patrons with painstaking attentiveness. Food offerings have all the elements of dining on a luxury ocean liner. Rum buns are the prelude to the meal. Highlights include enormous crab cakes and filet mignon filled with crabmeat and rich béarnaise sauce. Order one of the showy flambé desserts, which are prepared tableside. ✉ *1632 Richmond Rd.,* ☎ *757/229–0099. AE, D, DC, MC, V.*

$$ ★ ✕ **The Whaling Company.** Fresh seafood is the drawing card at this large wooden building, which wouldn't look out of place in a New England fishing village. Despite its out-of-town look, the restaurant has an authenticity sometimes hard to find in touristy towns. Locals come in for the fresh scallops, fish, and other tasty morsels from the sea. Steaks are available, but no poultry or other meats are served. The restaurant is off U.S. 60 West just after the Route 199 interchange. ✉ *494 McLaws Circle,* ☎ *757/229–0275. AE, DC, MC, V. No lunch.*

$–$$ ✕ **Sal's Restaurant by Victor.** Locals love this family Italian restaurant and pizzeria. Victor Minichiello and his staff cook in a wood-fired oven and serve up pasta, fish, chicken, and veal dinners as well as subs and pizzas. The restaurant delivers free to nearby hotels. ✉ *1242 Richmond Rd.,* ☎ *757/220–2641. AE, D, MC, V.*

$ ✕ **College Delly.** It's easy to forget that this is a college town, but this cheerful dive keeps up the school spirit. The white-brick eatery with forest-green canvas awnings is fairly dark and scruffy inside. Walls are hung with fraternity and sorority pictures, graduation snapshots, and sports-team photos. Booths and tables are in the William and Mary colors of green and gold. Deli sandwiches, pasta, stromboli, and Greek dishes are all prepared with fresh ingredients and are unfailingly delicious, and there is a wide selection of beers on tap. The Delly delivers orders free to nearby hotels from 6 PM to 1 AM. ✉ *336 Richmond Rd.,* ☎ *757/229–6627. MC, V.*

$ ✕ **Old Chickahominy House.** Reminiscent of old-fashioned Virginia tearooms, this Colonial-style restaurant has delectable goodies served up by sweet, grandmotherly types. For breakfast there's Virginia ham and eggs, made-from-scratch biscuits, country bacon, sausage, and grits. Lunch brings Brunswick stew, Virginia ham biscuits, fruit salad, and homemade pie. ✉ *1211 Jamestown Rd.,* ☎ *757/229–4689. MC, V. No dinner.*

COLONIAL TAVERNS

The four reconstructed "taverns" in Colonial Williamsburg are essentially restaurants with beer and wine available. Colonial-style food is served at lunch, dinner, and Sunday brunch. The dishes are a bit overpriced, but a meal at any tavern is a good way to get into the spirit of the era.

No reservations are taken for lunch, but it's recommended that you make dinner reservations up to two or three weeks in advance. Hours also change according to season, so check by calling the reservations number (☎ 800/447–8679). Smoking is not permitted in any of the taverns.

$$–$$$ ✕ **Chownings Tavern.** A reconstructed 18th-century alehouse, Chownings serves dishes such as Brunswick stew, Welsh rabbit, oyster fritters, and sandwiches—all complemented by especially good bread and drink. Follow the meal with a slice of peanut pie or black-walnut ice cream with gingersnaps. In summer, you may eat outside under the arbor. ✉ *Duke of Gloucester St. AE, D, DC, MC, V.*

$$–$$$ ✕ **Christiana Campbell's Tavern.** George Washington's favorite tavern is across the street from the Capitol. Chesapeake Bay seafood appears in period (crab cakes) and nonperiod (spicy jambalaya) dishes. The Carolina seafood "muddle"—a stew of fresh fish and shellfish—is particularly good, as is the hickory-grilled rib eye. Fig ice cream is the tavern's special flavor. ✉ *Waller St. AE, D, DC, MC, V.*

$$–$$$ ✕ **Kings Arms.** The genteel surroundings and fare here mimic those experienced by George Washington and Thomas Jefferson when they sat down to eat Virginia ham, meat pies, and Sally Lunn bread amid a political discussion. The Arms is now famous for peanut soup; chicken breast with crab stuffing; cavalier's rack of lamb; and a venison, rabbit, and duck game pie. Williamsburg pecan pie is its dessert specialty. Weather permitting, you may eat light meals in a garden behind the tavern. ✉ *Duke of Gloucester St. AE, D, DC, MC, V.*

$$–$$$ ✕ **Shields Tavern.** The only tavern to serve breakfast is named after the bar-owner James Shields. Start with a Shields Sampler, a collection of tantalizing tastes re-created from 18th-century recipes. Some good choices are oyster salad, baked rockfish, and a mixed grill of wild boar sausage and quail. Outdoor seating is available. ✉ *Duke of Gloucester St. AE, D, DC, MC, V.*

Lodging

$$$$ ★ **Williamsburg Inn.** This grand hotel from 1937 is owned and operated by Colonial Williamsburg. Rooms are beautifully and individually furnished with reproductions and antiques in the English Regency style, and genteel service and tradition reign. Rooms come with such perks as complimentary morning coffee and afternoon tea, a free daily newspaper, turndown service, and bathrobes. The Providence Wings, adjacent to the inn, are less formal; rooms are in a contemporary style with Asian accents and overlook the tennis courts, a private pond, and a wooded area. ✉ *136 E. Francis St., Box 1776, 23187-1776,* ☎ *757/229–1000 or 800/447–8679,* FAX *757/220–7096,* WEB *www.colonialwilliamsburg.com. 62 rooms, 14 suites. Restaurant, room service, in-room VCRs, 2 18-hole golf courses, 9-hole golf course, tennis court, 2 pools (1 indoor), gym, spa, croquet, hiking, lawn bowling, lounge, piano, children's programs (ages 5–12), dry cleaning, laundry service, concierge, meeting rooms; no-smoking rooms. AE, D, DC, MC, V.*

$$$ ★ **Kingsmill Resort.** This manicured, 3,000-acre resort on the James River has everything, even a marina and boat ramp. Home to the largest golf resort in Virginia, this is where the Michelob Championship on the PGA tour is held each year. You can play year-round on three championship courses; a fourth course—a par-3, 9-hole gem—is free if you stay here. The numerous brands of beer served at the property's Moody's Tavern are a clue to the acreage's owner: they're all Anheuser-Busch products. Accommodations include beautifully decorated guest rooms and one- to three-bedroom suites with fully equipped kitchens and washers and dryers. The menu at the expensive Bray Dining Room includes inventive dishes that employ seafood, game birds, and steak. A free shuttle bus travels several times daily to and from Williamsburg, Busch Gardens (also owned by Anheuser-Busch), and Water Country USA. ✉ *1010 Kingsmill Rd., Williamsburg 23185,* ☎ *757/253–1703 or 800/832–5665,* FAX *757/253–8246,* WEB *www.kingsmill.com. 235 rooms, 175 suites. 5 restaurants, in-room data ports, 3 18-hole golf courses, 9-hole golf course, putting green, 15 tennis courts, 2 pools (1 indoor), wading pool, health club, sauna, spa, steam room, beach, boating, fishing, billiards, bar, baby-sitting, dry cleaning, laundry service, concierge, business services, meeting rooms. AE, D, DC, MC, V.*

$$$ ★ **Liberty Rose.** Century-old beeches, oaks, and poplars surround this slate-roof, white-clapboard house on a hilltop-acre 1 mi from the restored area of Williamsburg. The inn was constructed in the early 1920s; furnishings include European antiques and plenty of silk and damask. Most remarkable is that every room has windows on three sides. The large room on the first floor has a unique bathroom with a claw-foot tub, a red-marble shower, and antique mirrors. Breakfast is served on a sunporch. ✉ *1022 Jamestown Rd., 23185,* ☎ *757/253–1260 or 800/545–1825,* WEB *www.libertyrose.com. 4 rooms. No smoking. AE, MC, V. BP.*

$$–$$$ ★ **Colonial Houses.** A stay here seems particularly moving at night, when the town's historic area is quiet and you have Williamsburg pretty much to yourself. Five of the 25 homes and two lodging taverns are 18th-century structures; the others have been rebuilt on their original foundations. Lodgings are furnished with antiques, period reproductions, and 20th-century amenities such as hair dryers, irons, ironing boards, and coffeemakers; the staff is costumed. A very hospitable touch is the complimentary fruit basket and bottle of wine delivered to each room. The Colonial Houses share the facilities of the adjacent Williamsburg Inn, and the Williamsburg Lodge. ✉ *136 E. Francis St., Box 1776, 23187-1776,* ☎ *757/229–1000 or 800/447–8679,* FAX *757/565–8444,* WEB *www.colonialwilliamsburg.com. 77 rooms. Room service, dry cleaning; no smoking. AE, D, DC, MC, V.*

$$–$$$ **Williamsburg Lodge.** At this larger establishment there's none of the formality of the Williamsburg Inn across the street, but the furnishings are just as interesting. Reproductions from the adjacent Abby Aldrich Rockefeller Folk Art Museum accent the rooms, which are getting a bit worn. The paneled lobby, where there's a fireplace, is cozy. The expansive health club is shared by those staying at the Williamsburg Inn and Colonial Houses. Every room has a hair dryer, iron, and ironing board; some rooms have coffeemakers. Nightly entertainment includes music or plays (free with special expanded passes) in the lobby lounge. ✉ *310 S. England St., 23187-1776,* ☎ *757/229–1000 or 800/447–8679,* FAX *757/220–7799,* WEB *www.colonialwilliamsburg.com. 264 rooms, 2 suites. 2 restaurants, 2 18-hole golf courses, 9-hole golf course, 2 pools (1 indoor), health club, sauna, bicycles, lobby lounge, dry cleaning, laundry facilities, laundry service, concierge, business services, meeting rooms; no-smoking rooms. AE, D, DC, MC, V.*

$$–$$$ ★ **Williamsburg Sampler Bed & Breakfast Inn.** Charming and hospitable, this redbrick inn near the historic district is modeled after an 18th-century, plantation-style home. Rooms have 18th- and 19th-century antiques, pewter pieces, four-poster beds, and pleasant views of the city. The suites are particularly inviting: each has a separate sitting room, French doors, and a porch overlooking gardens. ✉ *922 Jamestown Rd., 23185,* ☎ *757/253–0398 or 800/722–1169,* FAX *757/253–2669,* WEB *www.williamsburgsampler.com. 4 rooms, 2 suites. Dining room; no smoking. AC, D, DC, MC, V. BP.*

$–$$$ **Howard Johnson's–Historic Area.** Not your typical chain hotel, this family-run franchise inn is a change of pace for the road-weary. Washers and dryers on each floor, spacious guest rooms, and a friendly staff make this a particularly good choice for families. Colonial furnishings, marble fireplaces, and high-back wooden chairs in the lobby lend the hotel some charm. Take time out in the pool or exercise room when you need a break from sightseeing. ✉ *7135 Pocahontas Trail, 23185,* ☎ *800/841–9100,* FAX *757/220–3211,* WEB *www.hojo.com. 96 rooms, 4 suites. Pool, gym, video game room, laundry facilities, concierge, business services. AE, D, DC, MC, V.*

$–$$ **War Hill Inn.** This inn was designed by a Colonial Williamsburg architect to resemble a period structure: the two-story redbrick building at the center has two wood-frame wings. Inside are appropriate antiques and reproductions. The War Hill is inside a 32-acre operating cattle farm, 4 mi from the Colonial Williamsburg information center. Those in search of privacy will want one of the cottages or the first-floor suite (other rooms open onto a common hallway). ✉ *4560 Long Hill Rd., 23188,* ☎ *757/565–0248 or 800/743–0248,* WEB *www.warhillinn.com. 6 rooms, 2 cottages. Cable TV. MC, V.*

$–$$ **Woodlands Hotel and Suites.** An official Colonial Williamsburg property, this motel's various buildings are in a pine grove adjacent to the visitor-center area. Furnishings are contemporary. ✉ *102 Visitor Center Dr., 23185,* ☎ *757/229–1000 or 800/447–8679,* FAX *757/565–8797,* WEB *www.colonialwilliamsburg.com. 204 rooms, 96 suites. Restaurant, pool, horseshoes, Ping-Pong, lobby lounge, playground. AE, D, DC, MC, V. CP.*

$ **Governor Spottswood Motel.** This one-story redbrick motel has been extended gradually, section by section, since the 1950s. Furnishings reflect the influence of Colonial Williamsburg. In classic motel style, each room faces its parking space. There's lawn space and a sunken garden area for the swimming pool. Seven cottages sleep four to seven people, and 14 rooms have kitchens. It's a good value for the location. ✉ *1508 Richmond Rd., 23185,* ☎ *757/229–6444 or 800/368–1244,* FAX *757/253–2410. 78 rooms. Pool, playground. AE, DC, MC, V.*

Outdoor Activities and Sports

AMUSEMENT PARKS

Busch Gardens Williamsburg, a 100-acre amusement and theme park, has more than 35 rides and nine re-creations of European and French Canadian hamlets. In addition to roller coasters, bumper cars, and water ride, the park has also added a small, walk-through nature preserve, the highlight of which is gray wolves. Costumed actors add character to the theme areas, and two covered trains circle the park while cable-car gondolas pass overhead. ✉ *U.S. 60, 3 mi east of Williamsburg,* ☎ *757/253–3350 or 800/343–7946,* WEB *www.buschgardens.com.* *$42.99; parking $7.* ⏲ *Apr.–mid-May, Sat. 10–10, Sun. 10–7; mid-May–mid-June, Sun.–Fri. 10–7, Sat. 10–10; mid-June–July, daily 10–10; Aug., Sun.–Fri. 10–10, Sat. 10–midnight; Sept.–Oct., Fri. 10–6, weekends 10–7.*

At **Water Country USA,** the more than 30 water rides and attractions, live entertainment, shops, and restaurants have a colorful 1950s and '60s surf theme. The Meltdown is a four-person toboggan with 180-degree turns and a 76-ft drop. The Nitro Racer is a super-speed slide down a 382-ft drop into a big splash. The largest attraction is a 4,500-square-ft heated pool. ✉ *Rte. 199, 3 mi off I–64, Exit 242B,* ☎ *757/253–3350 or 800/343–7946,* WEB *www.4adventure.com.* 💵 *$31.99.* ⏲ *May, Fri.–Sun. 10–6; June, daily 10–6; mid-June–July, daily 10–8; Aug., daily 10–7.*

GOLF

Colonial Williamsburg (☎ 757/220–7696 or 800/447–8679) operates three courses—the excellent 18-hole Golden Horseshoe Course; the 18-hole Golden Horseshoe Green; and the 9-hole Spottswood Course. **Kingsmill Resort** (✉ 1010 Kingsmill Rd., ☎ 757/253–3906), near Busch Gardens, has three 18-hole golf courses and a par-3, 9-hole course.

Shopping

Merchants Square, on the west end of Duke of Gloucester Street, has non-Colonial, upscale shops such as Laura Ashley, the Porcelain Collector of Williamsburg, and the J. Fenton Gallery. There's also Quilts Unlimited and the Campus Shop, which carries William and Mary gifts and clothing.

CRAFTS

Nine stores and shops in Colonial Williamsburg imitate those once run in the 1700s. Among the typical wares are silver tea services, jewelry, pottery, pewter and brass items, ironwork, tobacco and herbs, candles, hats, baskets, books, maps and prints, and baked goods. Two **crafts houses** sell approved reproductions of the antiques on display in the houses and museums. ✉ *Craft House, Merchants Sq.,* ☎ *757/220–7747;* ✉ *Craft House Inn, S. England St.,* ☎ *757/220–7749.*

OUTLETS

On the outskirts of Williamsburg, less than 10 minutes west of the Historic Area in the tiny town of Lightfoot, are many **outlet malls.** Stores include Ralph Lauren, J. Crew, and Coach. If you are driving from Richmond to Williamsburg on I–64, go west at Exit 234 to Lightfoot. When you reach U.S. 60 (Richmond Road), the outlets—both freestanding and in shopping centers—are on both sides of the road. Most outlet shops are open Monday–Saturday 10–9, Sunday 10–6. In January and February, some stores close weekdays at 6.

The **Williamsburg Pottery Factory** (✉ U.S. 60 W, Lightfoot, ☎ 757/564–3326), an attraction in itself, has a parking area that is usually crammed with tour buses. Covering 200 acres, the enormous outlet store sells luggage, clothing, furniture, food and wine, china, crystal, and—its original commodity—pottery. Individual stores such as Pfaltzgraff and Banister Shoes are within the compound.

At the **Candle Factory Outlet** (✉ 7521 Richmond Rd., Lightfoot, ☎ 757/564–3354), you can watch candles being made. The **Williamsburg Outlet Mall** (✉ U.S. 60 W, Lightfoot, ☎ 888/746–7333) has more than 60 shops, including the Jockey Store, Linens 'N Things, Farberware, Levi's, and Bass.

The largest of the outlets, **Prime Outlets at Williamsburg** (✉ U.S. 60, Lightfoot, ☎ 757/565–0702) has more than 85 stores. Liz Claiborne, Jones New York, Royal Doulton, L. L. Bean, Waterford-Wedgwood, Mikasa, Eddie Bauer, Tommy Hilfiger, Brooks Bros., Nike, Guess, Nautica, and Cole Haan are all here. It's also the country's only outlet for Lladro, known for its figurines.

Yorktown

 *14 mi northeast of Colonial Williamsburg (via Colonial Pkwy.).*

It was at Yorktown that the combined American and French forces surrounded Lord Cornwallis's British troops in 1781—this was the end to the Revolutionary War. In Yorktown today, as at Jamestown, two major attractions complement each other. Yorktown Battlefield, the historical site, is operated by the National Park Service; and Yorktown Victory Center, an informative entertainment, is operated by the state's Jamestown–Yorktown Foundation.

Yorktown remains a living community, albeit a small one. Route 238 leads into town, where along Main Street are preserved 18th-century buildings on a bluff overlooking the York River. Its quiet character is actually distinctive amid the theme park–like attractions of the area.

Settled in 1691, Yorktown had become a thriving tobacco port and a prosperous community of several hundred houses by the time of the Revolution. Nine buildings from that time still stand, some of them open to visitors. **Moore House,** where the terms of surrender were negotiated, and the elegant **Nelson House,** the residence of a Virginia governor (and a signer of the Declaration of Independence), are open for tours in summer and are part of the Yorktown Victory Center's entrance fee.

The **Swan Tavern,** a reconstruction of a 1722 structure, houses an antiques shop. **Grace Church,** built in 1697 and damaged in the War of 1812 and the Civil War, was rebuilt and has an active Episcopal congregation; its walls are made of native marl (a mixture of clay, sand, and limestone containing fragments of seashells). On Main Street, the **Somerwell House,** built before 1707, and the **Sessions House** (before 1699) are privately owned and closed to the public: they're the oldest houses in town. The latter was used as the Union's local headquarters during General George McClellan's Peninsula Campaign of the Civil War.

Yorktown Battlefield preserves the land where the British surrendered to American and French forces in 1781. The museum in the visitor center has on exhibit part of General George Washington's original field tent. Dioramas, illuminated maps, and a short movie about the battle make the sobering point that Washington's victory was hardly inevitable. A look around from the roof's observation deck can help you visualize the events of the campaign. Guided by an audio tour ($2) rented from the gift shop, you may explore the battlefield by car, stopping at the site of Washington's headquarters, a couple of crucial redoubts (breastworks dug into the ground), and the field where surrender took place. ✉ *Rte. 238 off Colonial Pkwy.,* ☎ *757/898–2410.* 🎟 *$5.* ⏲ *Visitor center daily 9–5 (extended hrs during the summer).*

★ On the western edge of Yorktown Battlefield, the **Yorktown Victory Center** has wonderful exhibits and demonstrations that bring to life the American Revolution. Textual and graphic displays along the Road to Revolution walkway cover the principal events and personalities. The trail enters the main museum, where the story of Yorktown's critical role in the achievement of American independence is told. Life-size tableaux show 10 "witnesses," including an African-American patriot, a loyalist, a Native American leader, two Continental army soldiers, and the wife of a Virginia plantation owner. The exhibit galleries contain more than 500 period artifacts, including many recovered during underwater excavations of "Yorktown's Sunken Fleet" (British ships lost during the siege of 1781). Outdoors, in a Continental army encampment, interpreters costumed as soldiers and female auxiliaries reenact and discuss daily camp life. In another outdoor area, interpreters re-create 18th-century farm life. ✉ *Rte. 238 off Colonial Pkwy.,* ☎ *757/253–4838 or 888/593–4682.* *$8.25; combination ticket for Yorktown Victory Center and Jamestown Settlement, $16.* ⏲ *Daily 9–5.*

Dining and Lodging

$$–$$$$ ✕ **Nick's Seafood Pavilion.** This local landmark has been around since the 1940s. Long lines form for its fish and shellfish. The menu includes seafood shish kebab, a buttery lobster pilaf, Chinese dishes, and baklava for dessert. ✉ *Water St. at foot of bridge,* ☎ *757/887–5269. AE, D, DC, MC, V.*

$–$$ **Marl Inn.** Far from the crowds of the Historic Triangle, this 20th-century stone inn is nevertheless steeped in history: it's on the grounds of the last battle of the Revolution. The white picket-fence house run by owner Eugin Marlin resembles an English manor more than an inn and has antique and 18th-century reproduction furnishings inside. ✉ *220 Church St., 23690,* ☎ *757/898–3859 or 800/799–6207,* WEB *www.marlinnbandb.com. 1 room, 2 suites. Bicycles, some pets allowed. AE, MC, V. BP.*

$ **Duke of York Motel.** All rooms in this classic 1960s motel face the water and are only a few steps from a public beach. The motel also has a swimming pool and a restaurant that serves breakfast and lunch daily. ✉ *508 Water St., 23690,* ☎ *757/898–3232,* FAX *757/898–5922. 57 rooms. Restaurant, pool. AE, D, DC, MC, V.*

Charles City County

35 mi northwest of Colonial Williamsburg (via Rte. 5).

Colonists founded Charles City County in 1616. Today you can get a taste of those early days by following Route 5 on its scenic route, parallel to the James River, past nine plantations—some of which are now bed-and-breakfasts. Block (combination) tickets for admission to Berkeley, Evelynton, Sherwood Forest, and Shirley plantations cost $37 and are sold at each of the sites; MasterCard and Visa are accepted.

21 **Sherwood Forest** (1720), at 300 ft said to be the longest wood-frame house in the United States, was the retirement home of John Tyler (1790–1862), 10th president of the United States. Tyler, who came into office in 1841 when William Henry Harrison died a month after inauguration, was a Whig who dissented from his party's abolitionist line in favor of the proslavery position of the Democrats. He died in 1862, having served briefly in the congress of the Confederate States of America. His house remains in the Tyler family and is furnished with heirloom antiques; it's surrounded by a dozen acres of grounds and the five outbuildings, including a tobacco barn. ✉ *Rte. 5 (14501 John Tyler Memorial Hwy.), Charles City,* ☎ *804/829–5377.* *Grounds $4, house tour $10.50.* ⏲ *House and grounds daily 9–5.*

22 **Evelynton Plantation** originally was part of Westover estate and is believed to have been part of the dowry of William Byrd II's eldest daughter, Evelyn. However, her father refused to allow her to wed her favorite suitor, and she never married. The plantation was purchased in 1846 by the Ruffin family, which had settled on the south shore of the James River in the 1650s. Edmund Ruffin, a celebrated agronomist prior to the Civil War, was a strident secessionist who fired the first shot at Fort Sumter. Evelynton was the scene of fierce skirmishing during the 1862 Peninsula Campaign; the manor house and outbuildings were destroyed during the war.

The present Colonial revival–style house on a hill at the end of a cedar-and-dogwood alley was built two generations later, using 250-year-old brick, under the direction of renowned architect Duncan Lee. The house is furnished with 18th-century English and American antiques and has a handsomely landscaped lawn and gardens. Since it opened to the public in 1986, it has earned a reputation for artistic, abundant flower arrangements in every season. The house, gardens, and grounds are part of a 2,500-acre working plantation still operated by Ruffin descendants. Afternoon tea is held on the terrace during Historic Garden Week and the Christmas season. Flower arranging seminars are held three times a year; call for details. ✉ *Rte. 5 (6701 John Tyler Memorial Hwy.), Charles City,* ☎ *804/829–5075 or 800/473–5075.* 🎟 *$10.50.* ⏲ *Daily 9–5.*

23 **Westover** was built in 1735 by Colonel William Byrd II (1674–1744), an American aristocrat who spent much of his time and money in London. He was in Virginia frequently enough to serve in both the upper and lower houses of the Colonial legislature at Williamsburg and to write one of the first travel books about the region (as well as a notorious "secret diary," a frank and thorough account of plantation life and Colonial politics). Byrd lived here with his beloved library of 4,000 volumes. The house, celebrated for its moldings and carvings, is open only during Garden Week in late April. The grounds are arrayed with tulip poplars at least 100 years old, and gardens of roses and other flowers are well tended. Three wrought-iron gates, imported from England by the colonel, are mounted on posts topped by figures of eagles with spread wings. Byrd's grave is here, inscribed with the eloquent, immodest, lengthy, and apt epitaph he composed for himself. ✉ *Rte. 5, 7000 Westover Rd., Charles City,* ☎ *804/829–2882.* 🎟 *$2.* ⏲ *Grounds daily 9–6, house daily in late Apr. (call for hrs).*

24 Virginians say that the first Thanksgiving was celebrated at **Berkeley** on December 14, 1619, not in Massachusetts in 1621. This plantation was the birthplace of Benjamin Harrison, a signer of the Declaration of Independence, and of William Henry Harrison, who was briefly president in 1841. Throughout the Civil War, the Union general George McClellan used Berkeley as headquarters; during his tenure, his subordinate general Daniel Butterfield composed the melody for taps on the premises. The brick Georgian house, built in 1726, has been carefully restored following a period of disrepair after the Civil War. It is furnished with period antiques. The gardens are in excellent condition, particularly the boxwood hedges. A restaurant has seating indoors and out. ✉ *Rte. 5 (12602 Harrison Landing Rd.), Charles City,* ☎ *804/829–6018.* 🎟 *$10.50.* ⏲ *Daily 9–5.*

★ 25 **Shirley,** the oldest plantation in Virginia, has been occupied by a single family, the Carters, for 10 generations. Their claim to the land goes back to 1660, when it was settled by a relative, Edward Hill. Robert E. Lee's mother was born here, and the Carters seem to be related to every notable Virginia family from the Colonial and antebellum periods. The approach to the elegant 1723 Georgian manor is a dramatic one: the house stands at the end of a drive lined by towering Lombardy poplars. Inside, the hall staircase rises for three stories with no visible support. Family silver is on display, ancestral portraits are hung throughout, and rare books line the shelves. ✉ *501 Shirley Plantation Rd., Charles City,* ☎ *804/829–5121.* 🎟 *$10.50.* ⏲ *Daily 9–5; last tour begins at 4:45.*

Lodging

$$–$$$ 🏨 **Edgewood Plantation.** Three stories high, the Victorian Edgewood sits behind a porch on 5 largely wooded acres, ½ mi west of Berkeley Plantation and less than an hour from Williamsburg. The house includes a graceful three-story staircase and 10 fireplaces (four in bedrooms) and is furnished with antiques and country crafts. Rooms have 18th- and 19th-century canopied king or queen beds and Oriental rugs; period clothing is used as decoration. Breakfast is served in the formal dining room. Two gazebos sit in the English garden. Even if you don't stay here, you may tour this 1849 Victorian wood house (daily, house $8, grounds $2). ✉ *Rte. 5 (4800 John Tyler Memorial Hwy.), Charles City 23030,* ☎ *804/829–2962 or 800/296–3343,* FAX *804/829–2962. 8 rooms. Dining room, pool. AE, MC, V. BP.*

$$ ★ **North Bend Plantation Bed & Breakfast.** This historic inn is a sight to behold. As a working farm, it stands out from other plantation B&Bs. An example of the Academic Greek revival style, its wide, white-frame structure and pitched roof are imposing. Inside, antebellum-era antiques, as well as Civil War maps and artifacts adorn every room. Room amenities include robes and TVs. In the morning, you'll be treated to a Southern breakfast of buttermilk biscuits, Smithfield ham, apple butter, bacon, and grits, along with strong coffee. ✉ *12200 Weyanoke Rd., Box 13A, Charles City 23030,* ☎ *804/829–5176,* FAX *804/829–6828. 4 rooms, 1 suite. Pool, bicycles, croquet, horseshoes. MC, V. BP.*

HAMPTON ROADS AREA

The region known today as the Hampton Roads Area is made up of not only the large natural harbor, into which five rivers flow, but of the peninsula to the north that extends southeast from Williamsburg, and the Tidewater area between the mouth of the harbor and the Atlantic Ocean. On the peninsula are the cities of Newport News and Hampton; to the south and east are Norfolk, Portsmouth, Chesapeake, and Virginia Beach. These cities have been shaped by their proximity to the Chesapeake Bay and the rivers that empty into it, either as ports and shipbuilding centers or, in the case of Virginia Beach, as a hugely popular beach town. Hampton and Norfolk are the "old" cities of this area; recent development and revival efforts have made them worthy of a second look.

During the Civil War, the Union waged its thwarted 1862 Peninsula Campaign here. General George McClellan planned to land his troops on the peninsula in March of 1862 with the help of the navy, and then press westward to the Confederate capital of Richmond. Naval forces on the York and James rivers would protect the advancing army. However, starting with the stronghold that the ironclad CSS *Virginia* (formerly the USS *Merrimack*) held on the James until May, events and Confederates conspired to lengthen and foil the campaign.

Numbers in the margin correspond to points of interest on the Hampton Roads Area map.

Newport News

26 *23 mi southeast of Williamsburg.*

Newport News stretches for almost 35 mi along the James River from near Williamsburg to Hampton Roads. Known mostly for its struggling shipbuilding industry, the city is largely residential and is a suburb for both Williamsburg and the Tidewater area. Newport News has a number of Civil War battle sites and a splendid municipal park. The fabulous Mariners' Museum may be the best museum in the state. Close by, the Virginia Living Museum is a pleasant zoo experience that children will love. The city's small, but busy, airport is convenient to both Williamsburg and the beach, making it an ideal location from which to see both areas.

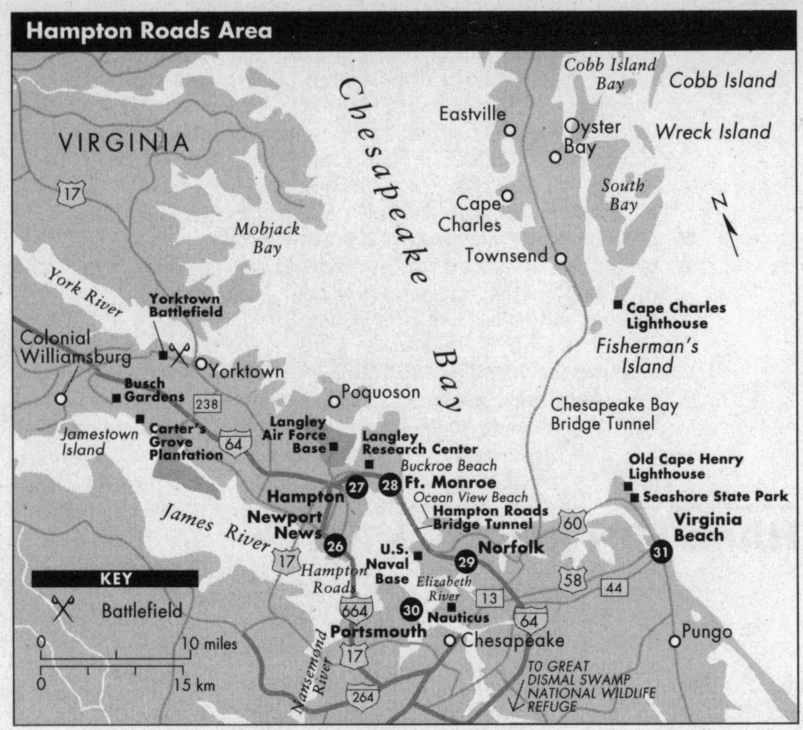

Newport News first appeared in the Virginia Company's records in 1619. It was probably named after Christopher Newport, captain of the *Susan Constant*, largest of the three ships in the company of Captain John Smith that landed at Jamestown in 1607. Newport News Shipbuilding is one of the largest privately owned shipyards in the world, and with approximately 18,000 employees, probably the second-largest employer in Virginia. It is the only shipyard in the country capable of building nuclear aircraft carriers.

A world history of seagoing vessels and the people who sailed them ★ occupies the outstanding **Mariners' Museum,** which is in a 550-acre park. An alliance between the museum and the South Street Seaport Museum in New York City allows the two institutions to share collections, exhibitions, and educational programs. Many of the authentic scale models hand-carved by August Crabtree are so tiny that you must view them through magnifying glasses; they portray shipbuilding accomplishments from those of ancient Egypt to 19th-century Britain. Among the more than 50 full-size craft on display are a Native American bark canoe, a sailing yacht, a speedboat, a gondola, a Coast Guard cutter, and a Chinese sampan. In separate galleries you can often watch the progress of a boat under construction; view ornate and sometimes huge figureheads; examine the watermen's culture of the Chesapeake Bay; and learn about the history of the U.S. Navy.

Such nautical gear as trail boards, rudder heads, and paddle boxes are on display, along with a selection of the intricate whale-tusk carvings called scrimshaw. Photographs and paintings recount naval history and the story of private-sector seafaring. The museum also holds artifacts from the RMS *Titanic* and the ironclad USS *Monitor*, which served in the 1862 Peninsula Campaign and today lies off the coast of North

Carolina. ✉ *100 Museum Dr. (I–64, Exit 258A),* ☎ *757/595–0368 or 800/581–7245,* WEB *www.mariner.org.* 🎫 *$6.* ⏲ *Daily 10–5.*

The **Virginia War Museum** houses more than 60,000 artifacts from all over the world. The collection includes a graffiti-covered section of the Berlin Wall, a Civil War blockade runner's uniform, weapons, uniforms, wartime posters, photographs, and other memorabilia. It traces military history from 1775 to the Gulf War and includes an outdoor exhibition of seven tanks and cannons, and the history of African-Americans and women in the military. Several war memorials are on the grounds of Huntington Park. An annual "Christmas in the Field" Civil War reenactment is performed the second weekend of December. ✉ *9285 Warwick Blvd. (Rte. 60),* ☎ *757/247–8523,* WEB *www.warmuseum.org.* 🎫 *$5.* ⏲ *Mon.–Sat. 9–5, Sun. 1–5.*

The **U.S. Army Transportation Museum,** at Fort Eustis, traces the history of army transportation by land, sea, and air, beginning with the Revolutionary War era. More than 90 vehicles, including experimental craft and numerous locomotives and trains dating to the 1800s, are on display. The museum's Korean War and World War II–era tanks can be toured inside and out. ✉ *Besson Hall, Bldg. 300 (I–64, Exit 250A),* ☎ *757/878–1115.* 🎫 *Free.* ⏲ *Tues.–Sun. 9–4:30.*

At the **Virginia Living Museum,** animals indigenous to the region live in wild or simulated lakefront habitats that allow you to observe their natural behavior. A trail leads to the water's edge, where otters and blue herons can be spotted, then upland past de-scented skunks, lame bald eagles (wounded by hunters), and cute but unpettable bobcats. A 40-ft-tall outdoor aviary re-creates a wetlands habitat. Indoors, the Planetarium (children under three not admitted) offers more celestial sights; call for show times. The tacky Safari minigolf site may be fun for children, but it lessens the splendor of the environment. ✉ *524 J. Clyde Morris Blvd.,* ☎ *757/595–1900.* 🎫 *Museum $9, planetarium $3, combination ticket $11.* ⏲ *Memorial Day–Labor Day, daily 9–6; Labor Day–Memorial Day, Mon.–Sat. 9–5, Sun. noon–5.*

Dining and Lodging

$–$$$ ★ ✕ **Herman's Harbor House.** You may think you've gone off course as you drive through this residential neighborhood, but just keep going. Herman's, at the end of Deep Creek Road, serves the area's best crab cakes, accompanied by ample portions of vegetables. The diverse menu also includes other Tidewater-style seafood dishes as well as steak, veal, and pasta, and desserts made in-house. This is a local favorite, so expect crowds even on weekday nights. ✉ *663 Deep Creek Rd. (I–64, Exit 258A, to Warwick Blvd. to Deep Creek Rd.),* ☎ *757/930–1000. AE, D, MC, V.*

$–$$ ★ ✕🏨 **Omni Newport News Hotel.** The mauve and marble art deco–style atrium lobby of this contemporary hotel looks over the indoor pool below. Rooms, done in soft colors, have cherry furnishings, brass fixtures, and sitting areas with sofas. Mitty's Ristorante and Piano Lounge ($$–$$$) serves regional Italian cuisine and local seafood, with exceptional homemade pasta and veal dishes. Specialties include ziti with broccoli and shrimp Capri (shrimp paired with spinach and fresh Italian herbs). To reach the hotel, take Exit 258A off I–64 and make the first right; turn right at the hotel sign. ✉ *1000 Omni Blvd., 23606,* ☎ *757/873–6664 or 800/873–6664,* FAX *757/873–1732,* WEB *www.omnihotels.com. 183 rooms, 4 suites. Restaurant, in-room data ports, indoor pool, gym, sauna, bar, lobby lounge, nightclub, laundry facilities, business services, meeting rooms; no-smoking rooms. AE, D, DC, MC, V.*

$–$$ 🏨 **Ramada Inn and Conference Center.** Its contemporary exterior a takeoff on the typical column porticos of nearby plantation homes, this hotel's rooms have patterned spreads and wallpaper above the chair rails. The ideal location makes it a good alternative to the high-priced summer rates of Williamsburg hotels. ✉ *950 J. Clyde Morris Blvd., Exit 256B off I–64, 23601,* ☎ *757/599–4460 or 800/841–1112,* FAX *757/599–4336,* WEB *www.ramada.com. 149 rooms. Restaurant, in-room data ports, indoor pool, gym, business services, airport shuttle; no-smoking rooms. AE, D, DC, MC, V.*

Outdoor Activities and Sports

FISHING AND BOATING

Around Newport News you can expect excellent catches of striper, flounder, and the occasional catfish. The **Mariners' Museum** (✉ 100 Museum Dr., ☎ 757/591–7799, WEB www.mariner.org) rents boats for use on Lake Maury (on the museum's grounds). The lake is open for fishing during spring and summer. Encircling the lake is the 5-mi Noland Trail.

The **James River Bridge Fishing Pier** (☎ 757/247–0364) is open year-round; call for hours.

Hampton

27 *5 mi north of Newport News, 16 mi northwest of Norfolk.*

Founded in 1610, Hampton is the oldest continuously existing English-speaking settlement in the United States. It also holds the country's first aviation research facility, NASA Langley Research Center. The center was headquarters for the first manned space program in the United States: Astronauts for the *Mercury* and *Apollo* missions trained here.

Hampton was one of Virginia's major Colonial cities. In 1718, the pirate William Teach (better known as Blackbeard) was killed by Virginia sailors in a battle off North Carolina. As a warning to other pirates, they brought his head back and mounted it on a pole at the entrance to the Hampton River (now Blackbeard Point, a residential area).

The city has been partially destroyed three times: by the British during the Revolution and again during the War of 1812, then by Confederates preempting Union invaders during the Civil War. Since the mid-1990s, Hampton has been undergoing a face-lift. It hosts many summer concerts and family festivals.

★ The **Virginia Air and Space Center** traces the history of flight and space exploration. The nine-story, futuristic, $30 million center is the official repository of the NASA Langley Research Center. Its space artifacts include a 3-billion-year-old moon rock, the *Apollo 12* command capsule, and a lunar lander. The center also holds a dozen full-size aircraft, southeast Virginia's only IMAX theater, and hands-on exhibits that let you see yourself as an astronaut. The **Hampton Roads History Center** (inside the museum and included in its admission charge) depicts the area's colorful history through archaeological and audiovisual exhibitions that include partial reproductions of Colonial buildings. Full-scale reproductions of the gun turret of the USS *Monitor* and a portion of the CSS *Virginia* casemate show how the two ironclads changed the course of naval history at the start of the 1862 Peninsula Campaign in Hampton Roads. ✉ *Downtown Waterfront, 600 Settlers Landing Rd. (I–64, Exit 267),* ☎ *757/727–0800,* WEB *www.vasc.org.* *Space Center $6.50, Space Center and 1 IMAX movie $9.50.* *Memorial Day–Labor Day, Mon.–Wed. 10–5, Thurs.–Sun. 10–7; Labor Day–Memorial Day, daily 10–5.*

In a waterfront park near the Virginia Air and Space Center is the **Hampton Carousel.** Its prancing steeds and bright-color chariots carry riders round and round to the tunes of carnival music. Expert artisans have meticulously restored the 1920 carousel, which was a fixture at the city's former Buckroe Beach Amusement Park for 60 years. ✉ *602 Settlers Landing Rd.,* ☎ *757/727–6381.* 🎫 *$1.* ⏲ *May–Sept., Mon.–Wed. noon–5, Thurs.–Sun. noon–7; call for fall and winter hrs.*

Little of early Hampton has survived the shellings and conflicts of the past, but the brick walls of **St. John's Church** (1728) have. Today a stained-glass window honors Pocahontas, the Native American princess who is said to have saved the life of Captain John Smith in 1608. The communion silver on display, made in London in 1618, is the oldest such service still used in this country. The parish, founded in the same year as the city (1610), also claims to be the oldest in continuous service in America. You may listen to a taped interpretation or take a guided tour (by arrangement) and visit a small museum in the parish house. ✉ *100 W. Queens Way,* ☎ *757/722–2567.* 🎫 *Free.* ⏲ *Weekdays 9–3, Sat. 9–noon.*

Hampton University was founded in 1868 as a freedmen's school, and ever since has had a distinguished history as an institution of higher education for African-Americans. Booker T. Washington was an early graduate. The **Hampton University Museum,** on the riverfront campus, is most notable for its extensive and diverse collection of African art, which includes 2,000 pieces from 87 ethnic groups and cultures. Other valuable holdings include Harlem Renaissance paintings, Native American artwork and crafts, and art from Oceania. ✉ *Museum, Huntington Bldg., off Tyler St. (I–64, Exit 267, to campus),* ☎ *757/727–5308.* 🎫 *Free.* ⏲ *Weekdays 8–5, Sat. noon–4.*

Dining and Lodging

$$$ ✕ **Captain George's.** Although there is an ample à la carte menu, the main pull at this smorgasbord restaurant is the 70-item, all-you-can-eat buffet of fried, steamed, and broiled seafood. Highlights are steamed Alaskan crab legs, steamed shrimp with Old Bay seasoning (a locally made favorite), broiled flounder, steamed mussels, and she-crab soup. Among the 15 desserts are baklava and five fruit cobblers. A mural of the Chesapeake Bay dominates the largest of four dining rooms, which has tables with tops embedded with seashells. ✉ *2710 W. Mercury Blvd.,* ☎ *757/826–1435. AE, MC, V. No lunch Mon.–Sat.*

$$–$$$ ✕ **The Grate Steak.** Farm implements and unfinished pine walls decorate the four dining rooms, which are casual and boisterous. You may choose your own steak and then grill it yourself on a huge barbecue grill. The menu also includes fried shrimp, grilled tuna, and salad bars. Prime rib, served on the bone if you like, is slowly roasted by a professional chef. ✉ *1934 Coliseum Dr.,* ☎ *757/827–1886. AE, D, DC, MC, V. No lunch.*

$$ ✕ **Fisherman's Wharf.** Decorated with ship figureheads and other seagoing paraphernalia, this restaurant is on the second floor of a building on the working waterfront. A seafood-heavy buffet of up to 75 items, including Dungeness or snow crab legs, mussels, cherrystone clams, fish, and prime rib, is set up nightly in a large boat in the dining room. ✉ *14 Ivy Home Rd.,* ☎ *757/480–3113. AE, D, DC, MC, V. Closed Mon. No lunch Mon.–Sat.*

$ ✕ **The Grey Goose Tearoom.** An enticing aroma and a gift shop displaying tea-related items greet patrons of this cozy tearoom decorated with Victorian tea-party prints in gilded frames, antique teapots, and knickknacks. Brunswick stew, creamy Hampton blue-crab soup, and biscuits are permanent fixtures on the "everything homemade" menu, and daily specials are posted on the wall. Desserts are especially good, but avoid the canned fruit salad on iceberg lettuce. The tearoom is open for lunch daily and some weekend nights for "Dinnertainment." ✉ *1101-A W. Queens Way,* ☎ *757/723–7978. AE, D, DC, MC, V. Closed Sun.*

$$–$$$ **Radisson Hotel Hampton.** The nine-story Radisson has the premier location in town, right at a marina and a block away from the Virginia Air and Space Center. Most rooms look over the harbor or the handsome plaza in front of the space center. ✉ *700 Settlers Landing Rd., 23669,* ☎ *757/727–9700 or 800/333–3333,* FAX *757/722–4557,* WEB *www.radisson.com. 172 rooms. Restaurant, café, pool, gym, bar. AE, D, DC, MC, V.*

$$ **Holiday Inn Hampton.** Halfway between Colonial Williamsburg and Virginia Beach, this complex of buildings stands on 13 beautifully landscaped acres. About half the rooms have a pink-and-green color scheme; others have a darker look, with cherrywood dressers and tables. Sofas convert into extra beds in many rooms. Some rooms overlook the indoor pool in the atrium, and others have doors that open, motel-style, directly onto the parking lot. ✉ *1815 W. Mercury Blvd., 23666,* ☎ *757/838–0200 or 800/842–9370,* FAX *757/838–4964,* WEB *www.sixcontinentshotels.com. 320 rooms. Restaurant, 2 pools (1 indoor), gym, sauna, bar. AE, D, DC, MC, V.*

$–$$ **Courtyard by Marriott.** The smell of homemade chocolate cookies greets you at the front desk of this modern hostelry where the chef refills a bottomless basket. It may be a chain hotel, but as the naval items on the walls suggests, it takes in the local influence. Contemporary guest rooms have coffeemakers, hair dryers, irons, and ironing boards. The restaurant serves breakfast only. ✉ *1917 Coliseum Dr., 23666,* ☎ *757/838–3300,* FAX *757/838–6387,* WEB *www.courtyard.com. 146 rooms. Breakfast room, pool, health club, dry cleaning, laundry service. AE, D, DC, MC, V.*

$ ★ **Arrow Inn.** Near Williamsburg and many of the golf and fishing sites, this centrally located, inexpensive hotel is a great place for an extended getaway. Refrigerators and microwaves are available in some rooms. Pets are also welcome for a small fee. ✉ *7 Semple Farm Rd., off I–64 take Exit 261 B,* ☎ *757/865–0300 or 800/833–2520,* WEB *www.arrowinn.com. 59 rooms. Some kitchenettes, refrigerators, laundry facilities; no-smoking rooms. AE, D, DC, MC, V.*

Outdoor Activities and Sports

SPECTATOR SPORTS

Langley Speedway (✉ 3165 N. Armistead Ave., ☎ 757/865–1100) has the NASCAR Weekly Racing Series from April through October. Its nightly races are moderately priced.

Ft. Monroe

28 *Inside Hampton, at the end of Mercury Blvd.*

The channel between Chesapeake Bay and Hampton Roads is the "mouth" of Hampton Roads. On the north side of this passage, Hampton's Ft. Monroe, built in stages between 1819 and 1834, is the largest stone fort in the country and the only one on active duty that is enclosed by a moat. Robert E. Lee and Edgar Allan Poe served here in the antebellum years, and it remained a Union stronghold in Confederate territory throughout the Civil War. After the war, Confederate president Jefferson Davis was imprisoned for a time in one of the fort's casemates (a chamber in the wall); his cell and adjacent casemates now house the Casemate Museum. Exhibits of weapons, uniforms, models, drawings, and extensive Civil War relics retell the fort's history, depict coastal artillery activities, and describe the military lifestyle through the Civil War years. ✉ *Rte. 258 (Mercury Blvd.),* ☎ *757/788–3391.* *Free.* ⏲ *Daily 10:30–4:30.*

Norfolk

29 *16 mi southeast of Hampton.*

Norfolk is reached from the peninsula by the Hampton Roads Bridge-Tunnel (I–64) as well as Route 460. There's plenty to see in this old navy town, but the sites are rather spread out. Like many other old Southern towns, Norfolk has undergone a renaissance, epitomized by the charming shops and cafés in the historic village of Ghent.

The springtime Azalea Festival is one highlight of the lovely 175-acre **Norfolk Botanical Garden** on the eastern edge of the city. Besides growing an abundance of azaleas, rhododendrons, and camellias, the garden has a fragrance garden for the blind, with identification labels in Braille. A delicately landscaped Japanese garden has trees native to that country, including unusual strains of cherry and maple. From mid-March to October, boats and trams carry you along routes to view seasonal plants and flowers, including 4,000 varieties of roses on 3½ acres. Year-round, you can stroll 12 mi of paths. Eleven marble statues of famous artists, carved in the late 19th century by Moses Ezekiel, enhance the natural beauty of the gardens. The lakeside is ideal for picnics. ✉ *6700 Azalea Garden Rd.,* ☎ *757/441–5831,* WEB *www.virginiagarden.org.* 🎫 *Garden $6, boat tours $3.* ⏲ *Mid-Apr.–mid-Oct., daily 9–7, mid-Oct.–mid-Apr., daily 9–5.*

Occupying a 16th-century English Tudor–style house that was reproduced by a textile tycoon at the turn of the 20th century, the **Hermitage Foundation Museum** contains the largest privately owned collection of Asian art in the United States—including ivory and jade carvings, ancient bronzes, and a 1,400-year-old marble Buddha from China. The decorative-art collections include Tiffany glass, Persian rugs, and furniture from the Middle East, India, Europe, and America. You may picnic on the grounds along the Lafayette River. ✉ *7637 N. Shore Rd.,* ☎ *757/423–2052.* 🎫 *$4.* ⏲ *Mon.–Sat. 10–5, Sun. 1–5.*

★ By any standard the **Chrysler Museum of Art** downtown qualifies as one of America's major art museums. The permanent collection includes works by Rubens, Gainsborough, Renoir, Picasso, van Gogh, Andy Warhol, and Pollock—a list that suggests the breadth you'll find here. Classical and pre-Columbian civilizations are also represented. The decorative-arts collection includes exquisite English porcelain and art nouveau furnishings. Every American glassmaker between 1825 and 1950 is represented in the glass collection, which has an extensive number of Tiffany pieces, as well as artifacts from ancient Rome and the Near and Far East. ✉ *245 W. Olney Rd.,* ☎ *757/664–6200,* WEB *www.chrysler.org.* 🎫 *$7.* ⏲ *Wed. 10–9, Thurs.–Sat. 10–5, Sun. 1–5.*

The federal redbrick **Moses Myers House,** built by its namesake in 1792, is exceptional, and not just for its elegance. In the long Adam-style dining room, a wood writing desk holds a collection of fine china—and a set of silver kiddush cups (Moses Myers was Norfolk's first permanent Jewish resident). A transplanted New Yorker, Myers made his fortune in Norfolk in shipping, then served as a diplomat and a customhouse officer. His grandson married James Madison's grandniece, his great-grandson served as mayor, and the family kept the house for five generations. The furnishings, 70% of them original, include family portraits by Gilbert Stuart and Thomas Sully. ✉ *331 Bank St.,* ☎ *757/333–1085.* 🎫 *$5, includes admission to Willoughby-Baylor House; $10, combination ticket with Chrysler Museum.* ⏲ *Wed.–Sat. 10–4, Sun. 1–4.*

The **Douglas MacArthur Memorial** is the burial place of the controversial war hero. An "army brat" with no hometown, General MacArthur

(1880–1964) designated this navy town as the site for a monument to himself because it was his mother's birthplace—and perhaps because no one as well known as he had a monument nearby (MacArthur's ego was formidable). In the rotunda of the old City Hall, converted according to MacArthur's design, is the mausoleum; 11 adjoining galleries house mementos of MacArthur's career, such as his signature corncob pipe and the Japanese instruments of surrender that concluded World War II. Next door the general's staff car is on display, and a 24-minute biography is screened. ✉ *Bank St. and City Hall Ave.,* ☎ *757/441–2965.* 🎫 *By donation.* ⏲ *Mon.–Sat. 10–5, Sun. 11–5.*

St. Paul's Church, constructed in 1739, was the only building in town to survive the bombardment and conflagration of New Year's Day 1776; a cannonball fired by the British fleet remains embedded in the southeastern wall. An earlier church had been built on this site in 1641, and the churchyard contains graves dating from the 17th century. ✉ *St. Paul's Blvd. and City Hall Ave.,* ☎ *757/627–4353.* 🎫 *By donation.* ⏲ *Tues.–Fri. 10–4.*

Built in 1794, the **Willoughby-Baylor House** is a redbrick town house that combines Federal and Georgian styles. The authentic period antiques are not original to the house, but they follow an inventory made in 1800 on the death of Captain William Willoughby, who built the house. The herb-and-flower garden is also in keeping with the era. ✉ *601 E. Freemason St.,* ☎ *757/622–1211.* 🎫 *$5, includes admission to the Moses Myers House; $10, combination ticket with the Chrysler Museum.* ⏲ *Wed.–Sat. 10–4, Sun. 1–4.*

The **Waterside Festival Hall** is a mixture of stores and entertainment. Waterside has become the nightlife hot spot of the area, with 11 restaurants and bars, including Jillian's and Bar Norfolk. Musical performances and temporary art exhibitions take place in the public spaces, and there are restaurants and plenty of places to snack as you shop. The **Hampton Roads Transit kiosk** (☎ 757/623–3222) is a source of visitor information and the launching point for various tours of the city. ✉ *Waterfront, 333 Waterside Dr.,* WEB *www.watersidemarketplace.com.*

The **Norfolk Naval Base,** on the northern edge of the city, is an impressive sight, holding as it does more than 100 ships of the Atlantic Fleet. Among them is the USS *Theodore Roosevelt,* a nuclear-powered aircraft carrier with a crew of 6,300, one of the largest warships in the world. The submarine piers and the heliport are also memorable sights. Tour buses operate year-round, departing from the naval-base tour office. ✉ *9079 Hampton Blvd.,* ☎ *757/444–7955; visitors office 757/444–1577,* WEB *www.navstanorva.navy.mil/tour.* 🎫 *Tour $5.* ⏲ *Tours daily 9–3 on the half hour.*

A popular attraction on Norfolk's much-redeveloped waterfront is **Nauticus,** the National Maritime Center. With more than 70 high-tech exhibits on three "decks," the site displays concepts as ancient as shipbuilding right next to interactive displays that encompass the modern naval world. The battleship USS *Wisconsin* has found a home here. Its enormous gun turrets and conning tower are impressive up-close. Weather satellites, underwater archaeology, and the Loch Ness Monster all come together here in a stimulating and informative environment. There are additional fees for the AEGIS Theater and Virtual Adventures. ✉ *1 Waterside Dr.,* ☎ *757/664–1000,* WEB *www.nauticus.org.* 🎫 *$9.50.* ⏲ *Memorial Day–Labor Day, daily 10–6; Labor Day–Memorial Day, Tues.–Sat. 10–5, Sun. noon–5.*

Virginia Zoological Park, the largest in the state, has more than 100 species living on 55 acres—including rhinos and ostriches as well as such domesticated animals as sheep. With the assistance of docents, children may handle some animals. Elephant demonstrations are scheduled regularly during summer months. ✉ *3500 Granby St.,* ☎ *757/441–2706.* *$3.50.* ⏲ *Daily 10–5.*

Dining and Lodging

$$–$$$ ★ ✕ **La Galleria.** This restaurant has earned a reputation as one of the best in Norfolk. The interior, not done in the usual homey Southern style, may appear cold, but it is impressive. Decorations include Corinthian columns and large urns imported from Italy. A pianist entertains with soft music. Among the menu choices are *vongole al casino* (baked clams sprinkled with herbs, garlic, and bread crumbs) as an appetizer, and many excellent pastas and main courses, such as salmon sautéed in herbs, garlic, and white wine. A predinner visit can be made to the d'Art Center across the street, a working community for the visual arts. ✉ *120 College Pl.,* ☎ *757/623–3939. AE, DC, MC, V.*

$$–$$$ ★ ✕ **The Ship's Cabin.** The Cabin is best known for its seafood but has good steaks as well. For an appetizer try the Oysters Bingo—Eastern Shore salt oysters lightly rolled in batter, sautéed in butter, and served hot in the shell with bits of scallions and parsley in white wine. The New York strip steak makes a fine entrée. Bread served with the meal is baked fresh daily on site; the blueberry bread is almost a dessert in itself. Window-side booths in one room overlook the Chesapeake Bay and the narrow ship channel over the Chesapeake Bay Bridge-Tunnel; the other dining rooms, lit by fireplaces and candles, are cozy. ✉ *4110 E. Ocean View Ave.,* ☎ *757/362–4659. AE, D, DC, MC, V. No lunch Mon.–Sat.; Sun. brunch 11–3.*

$–$$ ✕ **Basil's.** Fresh seafood dishes are this eatery's specialty, but the freshly made pastas stand out as well. Try the ravioli à la basil for a starter and the tuna *romanga* to get a real taste for the kitchen's strengths. Marble columns and fine wood furnishings make the place perfect for a quiet evening. ✉ *Clarion James Madison Hotel, 345 Granby St.,* ☎ *757/622–6682. AE, D, DC, MC, V.*

$–$$ ★ ✕ **Freemason Abbey Restaurant and Tavern.** This former church building has 40-ft-high cathedral ceilings and large windows that look onto the historic business district. There's intimate dining at the reconstructed-steel mezzanine; downstairs you can get lighter fare. Regular appetizers include artichoke dip and ham-wrapped scallops. There's a lobster special on Wednesday, and on Thursday prime rib heads the menu. The wild game nights are quite an occasion: wild boar, alligator, and any other type of meat you can think of is served. Call ahead to find out when the special meals take place. ✉ *209 W. Freemason St.,* ☎ *757/622–3966. AE, D, DC, MC, V.*

$–$$ ★ ✕ **The Wild Monkey.** From its scrumptious "$10 Meatloaf" to the smoked salmon with blue cheese, this Ghent restaurant wows to the last bite. Its ever-changing wine list is bountiful, and there's even a board with recommended wine and food pairings. For a starter, try the pork and ginger dumplings; end with the pecan pie. If you go for Sunday brunch, the Cuban is a fine sandwich, and the frittata is a unique take on a traditional Mexican dish. Make sure to get here early; the tiny Monkey doesn't take reservations. ✉ *Colley Ave.,* ☎ *757/627–6462. Reservations not accepted. AE, MC, V. No dinner Sun.*

$ ★ ✕ **Doumar's.** After he introduced the world to its first ice cream cone at the 1904 World's Fair in St. Louis, Abe Doumar founded this drive-in institution in 1934. It's still operated by his family. Waitresses carry to your car the specialties of the house: barbecue, limeade, and ice cream in waffle cones made according to an original recipe. ✉ *20th St. and Monticello Ave.,* ☎ *757/627–4163. No credit cards. Closed Sun.*

$$–$$$$ **Norfolk Waterside Marriott.** This 1991 addition to the redeveloped downtown area is connected to the Waterside Festival Hall shopping area by a ramp and is close to Town Point Park, site of many festivals. The handsome lobby, with wood paneling, a central staircase, silk tapestries, and Federal-style furniture, sets a high standard that continues throughout the hotel. Rooms are somewhat small, but each has most everything the business traveler could ask for—including two telephones and voice mail. ✉ *235 E. Main St., 23510,* ☎ *757/627–4200 or 800/228–9290,* FAX *757/628–6452,* WEB *www.marriott.com. 396 rooms, 8 suites. 2 restaurants, in-room data ports, indoor pool, lobby lounge. AE, D, DC, MC, V.*

$$–$$$ **Holiday Inn Select Airport.** Surprisingly plush for a Holiday Inn property, this new airport location welcomes business travelers with an elegant lobby bar and fireplace. Rooms are outfitted with all the technological conveniences of an office, including two phone lines with data port, voice mail, and high-speed Internet access. ✉ *Lake Wright Executive Center, 1570 N. Military Hwy., 23502,* ☎ *757/213–2231,* FAX *757/213–2232,* WEB *www.sixcontinentshotels.com. 147 rooms. Restaurant, in-room data ports, microwaves, refrigerators, indoor pool, gym, hot tub, lobby lounge, Internet, business services, meeting rooms, airport shuttle. AE, D, DC, MC, V.*

$$–$$$ **Sheraton Norfolk Waterside Hotel.** Modern is the word for the way this hotel is furnished, from the bright, spacious lobby to the ample rooms and large suites. A ground-floor bar with dramatic 30-ft windows overlooks the Elizabeth—many rooms also have a beautiful view over the water. This property is convenient to the Waterside Festival Hall shopping area. ✉ *777 Waterside Dr., 23510,* ☎ *757/622–6664,* FAX *757/625–8271,* WEB *www.sheraton.com. 426 rooms, 20 suites. Restaurant, pool, lounge. AE, D, DC, MC, V.*

$–$$ ★ **Clarion James Madison Hotel.** In the early 1900s, this hotel was the skyscraper of Norfolk—coming in at eight stories. The renovated boutique hotel still maintains a domineering presence downtown. You can sip a microbrew on a leather seat in the lobby's lounge, where exquisite Tiffany chandeliers, mahogany wood pillars, and Oriental rugs recall the Jazz Age. Rooms, however, have ordinary traditional hotel furnishings, except for the original claw-foot sinks in the bathrooms. ✉ *345 Granby St., 23510,* ☎ *757/622–6682 or 888/402–6682,* FAX *757/683–5949,* WEB *www.jamesmadisonhotel.com. 127 rooms, 54 suites. Restaurant, in-room data ports, cable TV with video games, lobby lounge, dry cleaning, laundry facilities, concierge, meeting rooms, free parking. AE, D, MC, V.*

Nightlife and the Arts

Town Point Park (✉ Waterfront), between Nauticus and Waterside Festival Hall, is the site of many free outdoor festivals and concerts, including Harborfest in spring. You'll find fun, food, and music most Fridays from May through October.

DINNER CRUISE

The ***Spirit of Norfolk*** (✉ 333 Waterside Dr., Norfolk, ☎ 757/625–1748, WEB www.spiritcruises.com) operates the area's only dinner-dance cruises with live music and entertainment. Lunch and brunch cruises are also available.

MUSIC

The **Virginia Opera Company** (✉ 160 E. Virginia Beach Blvd., ☎ 757/623–1223, WEB www.vaopera.org) is often joined by major guest artists during its season (October through March). The elegant Harrison Opera House has superb acoustics and intimate seating.

Outdoor Activities and Sports

BASEBALL

Gleaming over the Norfolk harbor area is Harbor Park, home to the **Norfolk Tides** (✉ Waterside Dr., ☎ 757/622–2222, WEB www.norfolktides.com). The Tides are the International League, Triple-A team for the New York Mets. Harbor Park seats 13,000 fans and has a full-service restaurant and bar. For added fun, travel to the ball game via the Elizabeth River Ferry. Ferries leave every 30 minutes on game days from the North Landing Pier in Olde Towne Portsmouth.

FISHING

Charters and pier fishing are offered in season at **Harrison Boat House** (✉ 414 W. Ocean View Ave., ☎ 757/588–9968). **Willoughby Bay Marina** (✉ 1651 Bayville St., ☎ 757/588–2663) has fishing charters.

Shopping

An eclectic mix of chic shops, including antiques stores and eateries, are in **Ghent,** a turn-of-the-20th-century neighborhood that runs from the Elizabeth River to York Street, to West Olney Road and Llewellyn Avenue. Colley Avenue and 21st Street is the hub.

You can watch painters, sculptors, glassworkers, quilters, and other artists at work in their studios at the **d'Art Center** (✉ 125 College Pl., ☎ 757/625–4211); the creations are for sale in two galleries on the premises.

MacArthur Center Mall (✉ 300 Monticello Ave., ☎ 757/627–6000, WEB www.shopmacarthurmall.com) is the center of Norfolk's downtown and hosts more than 100 upscale stores, plus anchors Nordstrom and Dillard's. Restaurants inside such as Johnny Rocket's and Castaldi's are good value for the food and price.

In Ghent, the upscale clothing and shoe boutiques at **The Palace Shops** (✉ 21st St. and Llewellyn Ave., ☎ 757/622–9999) will please shoppers looking for some finery. Antiques hunters will probably want to check out the **Ghent Market and Antique Center** (✉ 1400 Granby St., ☎ 757/625–2897) with a full city block of goods. Fine kitchen equipment and accessories can be found at the lovely **Bouillabaisse** (✉ 1611 Colley Ave., #A, ☎ 757/627–7774).

Rowena's Jam and Jelly Factory (✉ 758 W. 22nd St., ☎ 757/627–8699) tempts your sweet tooth with factory tours Monday through Wednesday; make arrangements in advance. For sale in the shop are homemade jams, cooking sauces, fruit curds, and cookies.

Portsmouth

30 *6 mi southwest of Norfolk (via I–264).*

Portsmouth, across the Elizabeth River from Norfolk, has a well-maintained historic area called Olde Towne, which has handsome buildings from the 18th and 19th centuries. A five-minute pedestrian ferry makes traveling between Portsmouth and Norfolk easy.

The **Portsmouth Naval Shipyard Museum,** on the waterfront, has exhibits on naval history that include models of 18th-century warships. You can board the retired Coast Guard lightship (a floating lighthouse), whose quarters below deck have been furnished authentically. The museum is close to the pedestrian ferry landing. ✉ *2 High St.,* ☎ *757/393–8591.* *$1.* *Tues.–Sat. 10–5, Sun. 1–5.*

The **Portsmouth Children's Museum** has rooms where children can learn engineering and scientific principles by playing with bubbles and blocks. ✉ *221 High St.,* ☎ *757/393–8393.* *$5 (includes Portsmouth Naval Shipyard Museum).* ⏲ *Mon.–Sat. 9–5, Sun. 11–5.*

Lodging

$$ **Holiday Inn Olde Towne.** With the Portsmouth waterfront just out the door, and Olde Towne's attractions so nearby, this hotel is very well situated. The undistinguished appearance of the building hides pleasant things inside: public and guest rooms vary in size, but all have a modern look, and some private guest rooms share water views from a balcony. The restaurant overlooks the Elizabeth River and Norfolk's downtown skyline on the opposite shore. ✉ *8 Crawford Pkwy., 23704,* ☎ *757/393–2573 or 800/465–4329,* FAX *757/399–1248,* WEB *www.sixcontinentshotels.com. 210 rooms, 5 suites. Restaurant, in-room data ports, pool, gym, lobby lounge, laundry facilities, laundry service, meeting rooms. AE, D, DC, MC, V.*

Nightlife and the Arts

Inside the restored 1945 **Commodore Theatre** (✉ 421 High St., ☎ 757/393–6962), crystal chandeliers and wall murals provide a handsome setting for light dinner fare and first-run movies. There are tables on the main floor, and the balcony has traditional theater seating.

OFF THE BEATEN PATH

GREAT DISMAL SWAMP NATIONAL WILDLIFE REFUGE – The forbidding name was assigned to the area by William Byrd on one of his early 18th-century surveying expeditions. George Washington once hoped to drain it. Today the swamp is a 106,000-acre refuge that harbors bobcats, black bears, and more than 150 varieties of birds. A remarkably shallow lake—3,000 acres, 6 ft deep—is surrounded by skinny cypress trees that lend the scene a primeval quality. One hundred miles of hiking and biking trails, including a wheelchair-accessible boardwalk, make this a spectacular contrast to nearby downtown Portsmouth and Norfolk. ✉ *Follow signs from Rte. 32, Suffolk 23434,* ☎ *757/986–3705.* ⏲ *Apr.–Sept., daily 6:30–8; Oct.–Mar., daily 6:30–5.*

Virginia Beach

31 *18 mi east of Norfolk (via I–64 to Rte. 44).*

The heart of Virginia Beach—a stretch of the Atlantic shore from Cape Henry south to Rudee Inlet—has been a popular summertime destination for years. With 6 mi of crowded public beach, high-rises, amusements, and a busy 40-block boardwalk, Virginia's most populated city is now a place for peaceful communion with nature. The Boardwalk and Atlantic Avenue have teak benches, an oceanfront park, and a 3-mi bike trail. As for getting into the water, there's plenty of access to sailing, surfing, and scuba equipment rentals. The farther north you go, the more beach you'll find in proportion to bars, T-shirt parlors, and video arcades. Most activities and events in town are oriented toward families.

Along the oceanfront, the **Old Coast Guard Station,** set in a 1903 Seatack Lifesaving Station, contains photographic exhibits, examples of lifesaving equipment, and a gallery that depicts German U-boat activity off the coast during World War II. ✉ *24th St. and Atlantic Ave.,* ☎ *757/422–1587.* *$3.* ⏲ *Mon.–Sat. 10–5, Sun. noon–5.*

Inland from the shore is the late-17th-century **Adam Thoroughgood House,** named for the prosperous plantation owner who held a land grant of 5,350 acres and died in 1640. This little (45-by-22-ft) brick house, probably constructed by a Thoroughgood grandson, recalls the English cottage architecture of the period, with a protruding chimney and a steeply pitched roof. The four-room early plantation home has a 17th-century garden with characteristic hedges. ✉ *1636 Parish Rd.,* ☎ *757/460–7588.* 🎟 *$2.* ⏲ *Tues.–Sat. 10–5, Sun. noon–5.*

★ The sea is the subject at the popular **Virginia Marine Science Museum,** a massive facility with more than 200 exhibits. This is no place for passive museum goers; many exhibits require participation. You can use computers to predict the weather and solve the pollution crisis, watch the birds in the salt marsh through telescopes on a deck, handle horseshoe crabs, take a simulated journey to the bottom of the sea in a submarine, and study fish up close in tanks that re-create various underwater environments. The museum is almost 2 mi inland from Rudee Inlet at the southern end of Virginia Beach. ✉ *717 General Booth Blvd.,* ☎ *757/425–3474.* 🎟 *$9.95.* ⏲ *Daily 9–5 (until 7 Mon.–Sat., mid-June–Labor Day).*

Sandwiched between high-rise hotels is the **Atlantic Wildfowl Heritage Museum,** which holds fine waterfowl art and artifacts, including decoys (thousands of waterfowl migrate through eastern Virginia on their way north and south). The building, a small renovated cottage built in 1895 by Virginia Beach's first mayor and postmaster, Bernard Holland, is the oldest building of its kind on the oceanfront. Purchased in 1909 by a Norfolk banker and cotton broker, it is known as the de Witt Cottage on the National Register of Historic Places. ✉ *1113 Atlantic Ave.,* ☎ *757/437–8432.* 🎟 *Free.* ⏲ *Memorial Day–Sept., Mon.–Sat. 10–5, Sun. noon–5; Oct.–Memorial Day, Tues.–Sat. 10–5, Sun. noon–5.*

At the northeastern tip of Virginia Beach, on the cape where the mouth of the bay meets the ocean, the historic **Old Cape Henry Lighthouse** is near the site where the English landed on their way to Jamestown in 1607. This lighthouse, however, didn't light anyone's way until 1792. You can still climb to the top of the old lighthouse in summer; a new, working lighthouse is closed to visitors. ✉ *U.S. 60,* ☎ *757/422–9421.* 🎟 *$3.* ⏲ *Mid-Mar.–Oct., daily 10–5; Nov. and Jan.–mid-Mar., daily 10–4.*

Botanists will have a field day at **First Landing State Park,** which is inland from the Cape Henry lighthouses and the army installation at Ft. Story. Spanish moss grows no farther north than here, and blue spruce appears no farther south. The park is also a haven for red and gray foxes, raccoons, opossums, water snakes, and other denizens of swamp and dune. Boardwalks built just above the water level let you get close to flora and fauna while keeping your feet dry, and there are campgrounds, picnic areas, and guided tours. ✉ *2500 Shore Dr. (U.S. 60),* ☎ *757/412–2300.* 🎟 *Apr.–Oct., weekdays $3 per car, weekends $4; Nov.–Mar., $2.* ⏲ *Apr.–Oct., park daily 8 AM–dusk, visitor center weekdays 8–4, weekends 9–4; Nov.–Mar., park Sun.–Fri. 8 AM–dusk, visitor center weekdays 8–4, Sun. 9–4.*

Dining and Lodging

$$–$$$ ✕ **The Lighthouse.** Many oilcloth-covered tables in these six nautically themed dining rooms overlook the ocean or the inlet. The floors are red clay tile; the walls have dark-wood paneling. But the main attraction here is the seafood. If you can't decide whether you want Maine lobster, chicken, shrimp, or crab cakes, you can try the mixed grill, where you can mix and match any two items. ✉ *1st St. and Atlantic Ave.,* ☎ *757/428–7974. AE, D, DC, MC, V.*

$–$$$ ✕ **Croaker's.** A great local favorite, Croaker's isn't a restaurant that many people passing through the area know about. Far from the crowds, it's at the north end of Shore Drive. Along with melt-in-your-mouth crab cakes, Croaker's serves up a mean Oysters William (oysters with white wine, butter, and shallots). Another surprise is the excellent steaks, which are cut to order. ✉ *3629 Shore Dr.,* ☎ *757/363–2490. AE, D, DC, MC, V. No lunch.*

$$ ★ ✕ **Coastal Grill.** Though it's in a mall, this place has a warm, even elegant look, with a big, open bar and artful lighting. But food is the reason to come: chef-owner Jerry Bryan prepares American classics with an innovative, irresistible twist. Spinach salad is paired with sautéed chicken liver and balsamic vinaigrette; New York strip steak comes with sautéed onions and horseradish cream; and the fresh seafood dishes—including seasonal oysters on the half shell—are sublime. The moderately priced wine list comes with suggestions for wine-and-food pairings. Come early and expect a wait. ✉ *1427 Great Neck Rd.,* ☎ *804/496–3348. Reservations not accepted. AE, D, DC, MC, V. No lunch.*

$$ ★ ✕ **Havanna's.** This upbeat bistro serves up Cuban-inspired cuisine in fun, tropical surroundings. The cedar furnishings and low-hanging lights over the long tables make this local favorite look sophisticated. With dishes such as grilled flank steak mojo (marinated with peppers and spices), saffron-infused bouillabaisse, and *picadillo* (spicy ground beef), this tony place leaves you craving a cigar and a cocktail. If you like both, you're in luck: there's a fine line of cigars as well as an assortment of margaritas. ✉ *1423 N. Great Neck Rd.,* ☎ *757/496–3333. AE, D, MC, V.*

$–$$ ✕ **Rockafeller's.** The Down East architecture of this local favorite with double-deck porches hints at the seafood that's available. The restaurant has a bar, a raw bar, and alfresco dining in good weather (in cool weather, the large window wall still gives you a water view). Seafood, pasta, chicken, and beef share the menu with salads and sandwiches. This eatery (and several others) are tucked away on Rudee Inlet. To get here, go south on Pacific Avenue and turn right on Winston-Salem immediately before the Rudee Inlet bridge. The street ends at Mediterranean Avenue. ✉ *308 Mediterranean Ave.,* ☎ *757/422–5654. AE, D, DC, MC, V.*

$$–$$$$ ★ **Ramada Plaza Resort Oceanfront.** With its 17-story tower, this Ramada is the tallest hotel in the city. Rooms that do not face the ocean directly have either a partial view or overlook the swimming pool, where there's a summer swim-up bar. The modern lobby is dressed in mauve and emerald and has a skylit atrium. Each guest room has a coffeemaker, iron, ironing board, and hair dryer. Beds have quilted spreads and striped draperies. Gus' Mariner Restaurant, a fancy spot with prices to match, serves excellent seafood. ✉ *57th St. and Oceanfront, 23451,* ☎ *757/428–7025 or 800/365–3032,* FAX *757/428–2921,* WEB *www.ramada.com. 247 rooms. 2 restaurants, microwaves, refrigerators, in-room safes, indoor-outdoor pool, gym, sauna, bar, dry cleaning, laundry service, convention center, meeting rooms; no-smoking rooms. AE, D, DC, MC, V.*

$$–$$$ **Cavalier Hotels.** In the quieter north end of town, this 18-acre resort complex combines the original Cavalier Hotel of 1927, a seven-story redbrick building on a hill, with an oceanfront high-rise built across the street in 1973. The clientele is about evenly divided between conventioneers and families. F. Scott and Zelda Fitzgerald stayed regularly in the older section (it has since been lavishly refurbished). If you stay on the hilltop, you can see the water—and get to it easily by shuttle van or a short walk. The newer building overlooks 600 ft of private beach. There is a fee for tennis, but the other athletic facilities are free. ✉ *Atlantic Ave. and 42nd St., 23451,* ☎ *757/425–8555 or 888/746–2327,* FAX *757/425–0629,* WEB *www.cavalierhotel.com. 400 rooms. 5 restaurants, in-room data ports, putting green, 4 tennis courts, 2 pools (1 indoor), wading pool, gym, beach, croquet, volleyball, baby-sitting, playground; no-smoking rooms. AE, D, DC, MC, V.*

$ ★ **Clarion Hotel Town Center Virginia Beach.** This sparkling white, modern hotel is well situated for business and pleasure, midway between Norfolk and the beach and 15 mi from Norfolk International Airport.

The skylit lobby overlooks a glassed-in indoor pool. Rooms have a sitting area with sofa and desk; there are floral spreads and moss-color carpeting, with prints of flowers on the wall. Every room has a hair dryer, iron, ironing board, and coffeemaker. Coffee in the lobby is complimentary. ✉ *4453 Bonney Rd., 23462,* ☎ *757/473–1700 or 800/847–5202,* FAX *757/552–0477,* WEB *www.clarionhotels.com. 149 rooms. Restaurant, in-room data ports, refrigerators, pool, gym, hot tub, lobby lounge, dry cleaning, laundry service, meeting rooms; no-smoking rooms. AE, D, DC, MC, V.*

$ **Extended Stay America.** Designed for business travelers and their long-term stays, this affordable lodging is clean, with weekly rates from $349 to $399. Decorated with white walls with burgundy patterned spreads and cherrywood furniture, the large rooms have a kitchen with a microwave, coffeemaker, and cooking utensils. The hotel is midway between Norfolk and Virginia Beach. ✉ *4548 Bonney Rd., 23462,* ☎ *757/473–9200 or 800/398–7829,* WEB *www.extstay.com. 120 rooms. In-room data ports, kitchenettes, laundry facilities; no-smoking rooms. AE, D, DC, MC, V.*

Nightlife

There's free nightly entertainment from April through Labor Day weekend at the 24th Street stage or 24th Street Park on the Boardwalk. **Harpoon Larry's** (✉ 24th and Pacific Sts., ☎ 757/422–6000) is a local watering hole with true character, not a tourist trap. Don't be surprised to see a great white shark staring back at you as you eat a juicy piece of that shark's cousin (mahimahi) stuffed with fresh Chesapeake Bay crabmeat, or enjoy raw oysters and a cold Corona. Some come just for the pool table.

Outdoor Activities and Sports

BOATING AND CANOEING

For canoe rentals, try **Munden Point Park** (☎ 757/426–5296).

GOLF

There are four public golf courses in Virginia Beach, each with their own moderately priced fees. Except for Kempsville Greens, all ask that you reserve a tee time one week in advance. **Cypress Point Country Club** (✉ 5340 Club Head Rd., ☎ 757/490–8822) has greens fees of $29 for weekdays and $39 for weekends. Caddies are available. **Hell's Point** (✉ PU–2700 Atwoodtown Rd., ☎ 757/721–3400) has power carts, which are included in the greens fees ($52 weekdays and $62 weekends). **Honey Bee Golf Club** (✉ PU–5016 S. Independence Blvd., ☎ 757/471–2768) has a greens fee of weekdays $20–$32, weekends $25–$39. Inquire about caddies, if you want one. **Kempsville Greens Municipal Golf Course** (✉ 4840 Princess Anne Rd., ☎ 757/474–8441) is the least expensive course (weekdays $19, weekends $21). There are no caddies; power carts cost $12 per person. There's open play on weekdays, and weekend times are taken beginning at 8 AM on Friday.

WATER SPORTS

Chick's Beach Sailing Center (☎ 757/460–2238) offers Hobie Cat and Windsurfer rentals and lessons. You can use **Wild River Outfitters** (☎ 757/431–8566) for guided kayak tours, dolphin tours, and more. **Lynnhaven Dive Center** (☎ 757/481–7949) leads dives and gives lessons.

WILLIAMSBURG AND HAMPTON ROADS A TO Z

To research prices, get advice from other travelers, and book travel arrangements, visit www.fodors.com.

AIRPORTS

The three major airports in the region are served by many national and international carriers. Ticket prices are often much less expensive flying out and into Norfolk and Newport News than nearby Richmond. All three airports are relatively small and are easy to navigate in and around.

Newport News/Williamsburg International Airport is served primarily by US Airways. Norfolk International Airport, between Norfolk and Virginia Beach, is served by major carriers as well as several smaller ones. Limousine service is available. Richmond International Airport, 10 mi east of Richmond, off I–64 at Exit 197, is about 45 mi from Williamsburg.

➤ AIRPORT INFORMATION: **Newport News/Williamsburg International Airport** (✉ 12525 Jefferson Ave., at I–64, Newport News, ☎ 757/877–0221). **Norfolk International Airport** (✉ Norview Ave., ☎ 757/857–3351). **Richmond International Airport** (✉ Airport Dr., ☎ 804/226–3000, daily 8:30–5).

BIKE TRAVEL

Biking around Colonial Williamsburg is a wonderful way to explore its 173 acres. Rental bikes are available for those staying at the Williamsburg Inn, Lodge, or Colonial Inns. Bikesmith, in Williamsburg, rents bikes to all. Bike rentals are also available from Bikebeat, about 3 mi from the restored area. The pamphlet "Biking through America's Historic Triangle" maps a 20-mi route along the bike path of the scenic Colonial Parkway, which goes past Williamsburg, Yorktown, and Jamestown. The guide is available at area bike shops.

In Virginia Beach, there are numerous locations along the boardwalk where you can rent bikes. The covered multiperson bikes are especially fun for families.

➤ BIKE RENTALS: **Bikebeat** (✉ 4640-9B Monticello Ave., Williamsburg, ☎ 757/229–0096). **Bikesmith** (✉ 515 York St., Williamsburg, ☎ 757/229–9858). **Jamestown Bicycle Rental Co.** (✉ Jamestown, ☎ 757/291–2266). **Ocean Rentals Beach Service** (✉ (Virginia Beach, ☎ 757/481–5191). **Seashore Bike Shop** (✉ Virginia Beach, ☎ 757/491–9312). **Williamsburg Lodge** (✉ 310 S. England St., ☎ 757/229–1000, WEB www.colonialwilliamsburg.com).

BOAT AND FERRY TRAVEL

The Elizabeth River Ferry conveys pedestrians from Waterside Festival Hall, in Norfolk, to Portsmouth's Olde Towne. Taking the five-minute ferry trip is more fun than driving through the tunnel; it departs Norfolk 15 minutes before and after every hour.

➤ BOAT AND FERRY LINES: **Elizabeth River Ferry** (☎ 757/222–6100; 75¢; ⏲ daily 7:15 AM–11:45 PM).

BUS TRAVEL

Greyhound Lines typically has half a dozen or so departures daily from Hampton, Norfolk, Virginia Beach, Suffolk, and Williamsburg.

➤ BUS DEPOTS: **Williamsburg Transportation Center** (✉ 468 N. Boundary St., Williamsburg, ☎ 757/229–1460 or 800/231–2222). **Charles Carr/Hampton Depot** (✉ 2 W. Pembrook Ave., Hampton, ☎ 757/722–9861). **Greyhound Norfolk Depot** (✉ 701 Monticello Ave., Norfolk, ☎ 757/625–7500). **Myles of Travel** (✉ 1017 Laskin Rd., Virginia Beach, ☎ 757/422–2998). **Newbreed Travel Center** (✉ 1562 Holland Rd., Suffolk, ☎ 757/934–8068).

➤ BUS LINES: **Greyhound Lines** (☎ 800/231–2222).

CAR RENTALS

Car rental agencies are numerous throughout the region, especially near the three area airports. You should be able to rent a car easily and have a good deal of choice in the make, even during peak summer tourism months.

CAR TRAVEL

Williamsburg is west of I–64, 51 mi southeast of Richmond; the Colonial Parkway joins Williamsburg with Jamestown to the southwest and Yorktown to the east.

The I–664 road creates a circular beltway through the Hampton Roads area. I–664 connects Newport News and Norfolk, via Suffolk. I–64 runs northwest through Norfolk to intersect with I–664 in Hampton and I–95 at Richmond. U.S. 58 and what was once I–44 is now just an extension of I–264 (part of I–64).

PARKING

Parking near the Colonial Williamsburg historic area can be difficult during summer months and special events. It is best, if you are touring the historic area, to park at the visitor center and ride the shuttle to the park. The parking lot behind the Merchants Square shopping area is a good bet if you are planning a short visit or to dine around the area.

In Virginia Beach, there is no shortage of public parking lots and spaces. The cost for a day of parking is approximately $7.50 and includes free trolley passes for up to four people to travel up and down Atlantic Avenue Municipal lots/decks are at 4th Street (metered only), 9th Street and Pacific Avenue, 19th Street and Pacific Avenue, 25th Street and Pacific Avenue, 31st Street and Atlantic Avenue, and Croatan and Sandbridge beaches. Metered spaces have a three-hour limit.

TRAFFIC

The area is well served with expressways and interstate highways, but you'll have to share these routes with a lot of local drivers. Because the ragged coastline is constantly interrupted by water, driving from one town to another usually means going through a tunnel or over a bridge, either one of which may create a traffic bottleneck. The entrance to the tunnel between Hampton and Norfolk can get very congested, especially on weekends, so listen to your car radio for updated traffic reports.

Williamsburg, despite a wealth of tourist attractions, is still a small town of sorts. You can travel from Colonial Williamsburg to Busch Gardens in 10–20 minutes, depending on traffic conditions. All attractions are well signed and it is difficult to get lost.

The Tidewater area, however, is another story. With a long list of tunnels and bridges connecting a myriad of waterways, it is easy to find yourself headed in the wrong direction. Highways have adequate signs, but sometimes it may be too late to merge before entering a tunnel/bridge. Traffic is highly congested during rush hour and during peak summer months, when the beach traffic can grind everything to a halt.

In congested periods, use the less-traveled I–664. The 17½-mi Chesapeake Bay Bridge-Tunnel is the only connection between the southern part of Virginia and the Eastern Shore; U.S. 13 is the main route up the spine of the Eastern Shore peninsula into Maryland.

DISABILITIES AND ACCESSIBILITY

In Colonial Williamsburg, vans for people with disabilities are allowed by prior arrangement. Some structures in the park have wheelchair ramps. For more information on special services for people with disabilities, call Colonial Williamsburg at 757/229–1000 Ext. 2473.

In Virginia Beach, there are access ramps for the disabled on every beach from 1st to 58th streets. There are handicap-accessible wooden walkways that extend from the boardwalk to the water at 8th, 17th, 24th and 30th streets. There is also designated on-street parking for people with disabilities at the Rudee Loop, between 2nd and 38th streets. Designated handicap parking is also available at all off-street municipal parking lots.

➤ LOCAL RESOURCES: **Al's Wheelchair Transportation** (✉ Virginia Beach, ☎ 757/474–1968). **Association of Retarded Citizens of The Virginia Peninsula** (✉ Williamsburg, ☎ 757/826–6461). **Peninsula Center for Independent Living** (✉ Williamsburg, ☎ 757/827–0275 or 757/564–1880). **TLC Transportation** (✉ Virginia Beach, ☎ 757/449–4852).

DISCOUNTS AND DEALS

At Colonial Williamsburg, there are a number of all-inclusive tickets that cost just a bit more than a $33 one-day pass. The Freedom Pass ($39) allows you to visit for one full year and includes admission to special events as well. The Liberty Pass ($69) is also valid for a year and includes all the benefits of The Freedom Pass plus admission to all special events, access to a VIP visitors' lounge, and special discounts. Discount coupons for Busch Gardens and Water Country USA can be found at several area restaurants and retailers.

By ordering a visitor packet from the Virginia Beach Convention and Visitors Bureau, travelers receive a coupon booklet with discounts at restaurants, shops, and rental facilities.

➤ CONTACT: **Colonial Williamsburg** (✉ Williamsburg, ☎ 800/441–2613, WEB www.colonialwilliamsburg.com).

EMERGENCIES

➤ CONTACT: **Ambulance, Fire, Police** (☎ 911).

➤ DOCTORS AND DENTISTS: **Physicians Referral Services of Williamsburg** (✉ Williamsburg, ☎ 757/229–4636). **Virginia Beach Medical Referral Service** (✉ Virginia Beach, ☎ 757/640–1958).

➤ HOSPITALS: **Riverside Regional Medical Center** (✉ 500 J. Clyde Morris Blvd., ☎ 757/594–2000; 757/594–2050 emergency room). **Sentara Bayside Hospital** (✉ 800 Independence Blvd., Virginia Beach, ☎ 757/363–6137). **Sentara Norfolk General Hospital** (✉ 600 Gresham Dr., ☎ 757/668–3551). **Williamsburg Community Hospital** (✉ 301 Monticello Ave., Williamsburg, ☎ 757/259–6000; 757/259–6005 emergency room).

➤ 24-HOUR PHARMACIES: **Rite Aid** (✉ 525 W. 21st St., Norfolk, ☎ 757/625–6073; ✉ 801 Frederick Blvd., Portsmouth, ☎ 757/397–5981; ✉ 5795 Princess Ann Rd., Virginia Beach, ☎ 757/490–0307).

LODGING

With more than 200 hotel properties in Williamsburg, there are many hotel rates and amenities to choose from. For a complete list of hotels, contact the Williamsburg Area Convention and Visitors Bureau.

APARTMENT AND HOUSE RENTALS

Apartment and house rentals are not common in the Williamsburg area, but quite the thing to do at Virginia Beach. There's a great range in size, cost, and relative amount of luxury, so research possible rentals thoroughly.

➤ LOCAL AGENTS: **Long and Foster Real Estate** (✉ 317 30th St., Virginia Beach, ☎ 757/428–4600 or 800/941–3333). **Siebert Realty** (✉ 601 Sandbridge Rd., Virginia Beach, 23456, ☎ 757/426–6200 or 877/422–2200, WEB www.siebert-realty.com).

BED-AND-BREAKFASTS

There are many bed-and-breakfasts in the Williamsburg area, especially near the James River Plantations off Route 10. Most are housed in historic properties with charming antiques. Most rates include a full country breakfast.

Reservations at inns can be made through the Virginia Division of Tourism Reservation Service. Virginia Beach Reservations can make a reservation in your choice of about 75 hotels. Williamsburg Vacation Reservations, representing more than 70 hostelries, provides free lodging reservation services.

➤ RESERVATION SERVICES: **Virginia Beach Reservations** (☎ 800/822–3224). **Virginia Division of Tourism Reservation Service** (☎ 800/934–9184). **Williamsburg Vacation Reservations** (☎ 800/446–9244).

MEDIA

The main local newspaper in Williamsburg and Newport News is the *Newport News Daily Press*. The *Virginia Gazette* is published in Williamsburg. The *Virginian-Pilot* is the main paper for the entire Tidewater region.

TAXIS

You don't see their cars often, but there are a few taxi companies in Williamsburg. Norfolk and Virginia Beach have quite a few more because of airport traffic and the military bases. Unless you're at Newport News/Williamsburg International Airport or Norfolk International Airport, you will need to phone for a cab. Rates are metered and tipping is expected.

➤ TAXI COMPANIES: **Beach Taxi** (✉ Virginia Beach, ☎ 757/486–6585). **Beach Yellow Cab** (✉ Virginia Beach, ☎ 757/460–0606). **Black and White Cabs** (✉ Norfolk, ☎ 757/855–4444). **Groome Transportation** (✉ Williamsburg, ☎ 757/877–9477). **Yellow Cab** (✉ Norfolk, ☎ 757/622–3232). **Yellow Cab** (✉ Williamsburg, ☎ 757/722–1111).

TOURS

Most Williamsburg tours depart from the Greenhow Lumber House, where you can purchase tickets and make reservations.

American Rover Sailing Tours, which offers boat tours aboard a striking 135-ft topsail schooner, cruises around Hampton Roads's nautical historical landmarks and the Norfolk naval base. The *Carrie B,* a scaled-down reproduction of a Mississippi riverboat, cruises Hampton Roads for 2½ hours to give you a look at the naval shipyard and the site of the encounter of the USS *Monitor* and the CSS *Virginia* during the Civil War. A luxury yacht's Discovery Cruise explores Virginia Beach's Broad Bay.

Carriage and wagon rides are available daily, weather permitting. General ticket holders may purchase tickets on the day of the ride at the Lumber House.

The Hampton Circle Tour is a self-guided driving route that passes all of Hampton's attractions. Maps are available from the Visitors Bureau. The Virginia Beach Tour driving trip goes past both beach and historic points. Maps are available at the visitor center, but signs also mark the route.

Lanthorn Tours take you on an evening walking tour of trade shops where jewelry and other products are made in 18th-century style. The separate ticket required for this program may be purchased at the visitor center or from the Greenhow Lumber House.

The Norfolk Trolley has a guided tour of the historic downtown area that allows you to get on and off as you please. Tickets are available at the Hampton Roads Transit kiosk at Waterside Festival Hall. Portsmouth's Olde Towne Trolley Tour gives you the inside story of major historical events. It departs from various points in downtown on Sunday and Wednesday at 10:45.

Hour-long guided walking tours of the historic area depart from the Greenhow Lumber House daily from 9 to 5. Reservations should be made on the day of the tour at the Lumber House and can be made only by those with tickets to Colonial Williamsburg. "The Original Ghosts of Williamsburg" Candlelight Tour is based on the book of the same name by L. B. Taylor Jr. The tour is offered every evening at 8 (there's also an 8:45 tour June–August). The 1¼-hour, lantern-lit guided tour through historic Williamsburg costs $8.50. Interpreters well versed in Williamsburg and Colonial history are available to lead groups on tours of the Historic Area.

➤ BOAT TOURS: **American Rover Sailing Tours** (☎ 757/627–7245). ***Carrie B*** (☎ 757/393–4735). **Discovery Cruise** (☎ 757/422–2900).

➤ DRIVING TOURS: **Hampton Circle Tour** (☎ 757/727–1102). **The Virginia Beach Tour** (☎ 757/473–4888 or 800/822–3224).

➤ TROLLEY TOURS: **Norfolk Trolley** (✉ 333 Waterside Dr., ☎ 757/640–6300). **Olde Towne Trolley Tour** (✉ 6 Crawford Pkwy., ☎ 757/393–5111. (✉ 6 Crawford Pkwy., ☎ 757/393–5111).

➤ WALKING TOURS: **Greenhow Lumber House** (✉ Duke of Gloucester St., ☎ 757/220–7645 or 800/447–8679). **Interpreters** (☎ 800/228–8878).**"The Original Ghosts of Williamsburg" Candlelight Tour** (☎ 757/253–1058).

TRAIN TRAVEL

Amtrak trains stop in Williamsburg on their way from Boston; New York; Philadelphia; Washington, D.C.; and Richmond to Newport News, with one train daily in each direction. At Newport News, a shuttle bus connects to Norfolk. Trains stop at Williamsburg on their way from New York, Washington, and Richmond to Newport News.

➤ TRAIN STATIONS: **Newport News Amtrak Station** (✉ NPN; 9304 Warwick Blvd., ☎ 757/245–3589). **Williamsburg Transportation Center** (WBG; ✉ 468 N. Boundary St., ☎ 757/229–8750).

Train Lines**Amtrak** (☎ 800/872–7245).

VISITOR INFORMATION

Visitor Information Centers throughout the area generally operate daily 9–5. Call ahead to get visitor packets from Colonial Williamsburg and Virginia Beach: they both include a wealth of information and great maps. The Virginia Beach packet also includes a useful coupon booklet.

➤ TOURIST INFORMATION: **Colonial National Historical Park** (✉ Box 210, Yorktown 23690, ☎ 757/898–3400, WEB www.apva.org). **Colonial Williamsburg Dining and Lodging Reservations** (☎ 800/447–8679). **Colonial Williamsburg Visitor Center** (✉ Box 1776, Williamsburg 23187-1776, ☎ 800/246–2099, WEB www.history.org). **Hampton Convention and Visitors Bureau** (✉ 710 Settlers Landing Rd., Hampton 23669, ☎ 757/727–1102 or 800/800–2202, WEB www.hampton.va.us/tourism). **Newport News Tourism and Conference Bureau** (✉ 2400 Washington Ave., Newport News 23607, ☎ 757/928–6843 or 888/493–7386, WEB www.newport-news.org). **Newport News Visitor Information Center** (✉ 13560 Jefferson Ave. [1–64, Exit 250B], ☎ 757/886–7777 or 888/493–7386). **Norfolk Convention and Visitors Bureau** (✉ End of 4th View St., 23503, ☎ 757/441–1852 or 800/368–3097, WEB www.norfolkcvb.com). **Portsmouth Convention and Visitors**

Bureau (✉ 505 Crawford St., Suite 2, Portsmouth 23704, ☎ 757/393–5327 or 800/767–8782, WEB www.ci.portsmouth.va.us). **Virginia Beach Visitor Information Center** (✉ 2100 Parks Ave., Virginia Beach 23451, ☎ 757/437–4888, WEB www.vbfun.com). **Williamsburg Area Convention and Visitors Bureau** (✉ 201 Penniman Rd., Box 3585, Williamsburg 23187-3585, ☎ 757/253–0192 or 800/368–6511). **Williamsburg Attraction Center** (✉ 5715-62A U.S. 60, Prime Outlets, Williamsburg 23187, ☎ 757/253–1058).

7 BALTIMORE

Harborplace and the Inner Harbor, Oriole Park at Camden Yards, the Maryland Science Center, the National Aquarium in Baltimore, the American Visionary Art Museum—these and other attractions have transformed Baltimore. Equally lively are the historic neighborhoods, including Federal Hill, named to commemorate Maryland's 1788 ratification of the U.S. Constitution, and Fells Point, the center of Baltimore's thriving shipbuilding industry in the 18th and 19th centuries.

Updated by Michelle Gienow

BALTIMORE IS A CITY OF NEIGHBORHOODS. From the cobblestone streets of historic Fells Point and Federal Hill, up the wide avenues of wealthy Mount Vernon, and across the countless modest blue-collar enclaves, the city wears many different faces. On the east and west sides, seamless blocks of the city's trademark redbrick row houses, each fronted by white marble steps, radiate outward from the modern towers of downtown Baltimore. Uptown, marble mansions, grand churches, and philanthropic institutions proudly bearing their founders' names mark the city's progress: fortunes earned on the harbor flowed north to create these monuments to wealth and power.

It's true that the city has faced some difficult times. After World War II, a steady flow of residents to the newly developed suburbs slowly drained the city of vitality as well as population; the loss of manufacturing jobs also hurt this blue-collar town, and many neighborhoods declined. However, 1980's christening of Harborplace symbolized and was instrumental to the revival of Baltimore's Inner Harbor and the rejuvenation of surrounding neighborhoods. Hotels, office buildings, and attractions such as the Maryland Science Center, the stellar National Aquarium, and Oriole Park at Camden Yards were built around Inner Harbor; just north of the harbor, the high-rise towers at Charles Center modernized the city's office space stock and became Baltimore's most prestigious business address. Restaurants and shops proliferated in the once-downtrodden downtown area and then beyond, and the city's historic structures and neighborhoods received unprecedented numbers of visitors.

Twenty years later, momentum continues to build through the city's Digital Harbor initiative, which attempts to lure existing technology firms to Baltimore while also supporting those that are newly founded. Neighborhoods hosting the Digital Harbor "incubators," such as Canton and Locust Point, are becoming increasingly trendy and prestigious—as well as expensive—addresses for the young entrepreneurs drawn back to city life.

At the same time, Baltimore's image has received a boost from the arrival of a professional football franchise expansion team: the Baltimore Ravens, whose name draws on the city's association with Edgar Allan Poe. The Ravens began their 1996 season at Memorial Stadium, the former home of the Colts and the Orioles. The team played there until their new football stadium was completed in 1998; in 2001 they won Super Bowl XXXV.

In a sense, the city has come full circle since its early, prosperous days. Baltimore was established by the Colonial government in 1729, at the end of the broad Patapsco River that empties into the Chesapeake Bay. Named for George Calvert, the first Lord Baltimore and the founder of Maryland, the town grew as a port and shipbuilding center and enjoyed booming business during the War of Independence.

A quantum leap came at the turn of the 19th century: from 6,700 in 1776, the population reached 45,000 by 1810. Because it was the home port for U.S. Navy vessels and for the swift Baltimore clipper ships that often preyed on British shipping, the city was a natural target for the enemy during the War of 1812. After capturing and torching Washington, D.C., the British fleet sailed up the Patapsco River and bombarded Baltimore's Fort McHenry, but in vain. The 30- by 42-ft, 15-star, 15-stripe flag was still flying "by the dawn's early light," a spectacle that inspired "The Star-Spangled Banner."

After the War of 1812, Baltimore prospered as a slave market, and during the Civil War the population's sympathies were divided between North and South, provoking riots. Frederick Douglass escaped his childhood enslavement in the shipyards of Fells Point to become a famed orator and abolitionist. The first bloodshed of the Civil War occurred in Baltimore when the Sixth Massachusetts Regiment was stoned by an angry group of Baltimoreans. (This is a town whose regional identity has always been, and remains, ambiguous.) Soon after, President Lincoln, mistrusting the loyalty of certain city officials, had them summarily detained—an act that was no doubt strategically effective but was probably unconstitutional.

After the war, Baltimore became a manufacturing center of iron, steel, chemical fertilizer, and textiles. It also became the oyster capital of the world, packing more of those tasty mollusks in 1880 than anywhere else. After a 1904 fire destroyed 1,500 structures, Baltimore rebuilt valiantly and rode the economic roller coaster over two world wars and the Great Depression. The city's manufacturing base became a liability in the 1950s and '60s as U.S. competitiveness in that area faltered. But the massive revitalization efforts of the '80s has helped the city get back on its feet.

Today, Baltimore's Inner Harbor serves as the pulse of not only a vibrant, growing metropolis but of the city's environs as well. The downtown renaissance at Charles Center and Inner Harbor spurred a growth in tourism. Historic neighborhoods such as Federal Hill, Fells Point, Canton, and wealthy Roland Park (developed by Frederick Law Olmsted, designer of New York City's Central Park) are now the home of businesspeople and families who only a few years ago might have lived in the suburbs.

EXPLORING BALTIMORE

The city of Baltimore fans out northward from the Inner Harbor, with attractions such as the National Aquarium and Oriole Park at Camden Yards at the center, and residential neighborhoods and historic sites out near the edges. Downtown streets are laid out in a grid, although it is by no means regular. From Pratt Street, which runs east along Inner Harbor, the major northbound artery is Charles Street; many attractions, dining, and lodging options are either directly on or just steps away from Charles. Cross streets' addresses are marked "East" or "West" according to which side of Charles Street they are on; similarly, Baltimore Street marks the dividing line between north and south.

It's easy to explore downtown, the Inner Harbor, and individual neighborhoods such as Mount Vernon or Charles Village by foot, but for traveling between most of these areas a car is by far the most efficient means of transportation. Water taxis ply the harbor and are an enjoyable means of travel between waterfront attractions such as Fort McHenry and Fells Point, and efficient light-rail runs north–south along Howard Street.

Mount Vernon

Baltimore's cultural center, Mount Vernon has remained the city's most fashionable address since the neighborhood's beginnings in the early 1800s. Many of Baltimore's museums, galleries, and theaters were founded here, along with the city's most notable 19th-century historic and architectural landmarks. The neighborhood was at the heart of this bustling port town's transformation into a prosperous, prominent metropolis. Wealthy and artfully designed, Mount Vernon was named for the nation's first significant monument to George Washington, erected at the neighborhood's center in Mount Vernon Place.

North of the Inner Harbor, Charles Street provides the ideal route for a leisurely stroll. Of special interest is the nearly mile-long stretch of Charles Street between Saratoga and Biddle streets: it is a veritable restaurant row. Here, dozens of eateries of all sorts are interspersed with intriguing boutiques and art galleries.

Fans of director John Waters will recognize some Mount Vernon sites featured in his movies, including the Washington Monument.

Numbers in the text correspond to numbers in the margin and on the Baltimore map.

A Good Tour

This tour is best accomplished with a car, though you may want to park along Charles Street somewhere between Mulberry and Madison streets and walk to the first seven attractions. Begin at the intersection of Charles and Baltimore streets at Charles Center and head north, walking uphill. At Saratoga Street, you'll pass one of the many historic churches in Baltimore, St. Paul's Episcopal Church, begun in 1854. The **Basilica of the Assumption** ①, the nation's oldest Catholic cathedral, is one block west of Charles Street on Mulberry Street. West of the basilica is the **Enoch Pratt Free Library** ②, the nation's first free public library. Returning to Charles Street, notice the First Unitarian Church, at Franklin Street, one block up: designed by Maximilian Godefroy in 1819, the church that year was the site for the sermon that definitively established Unitarianism as a denomination (the sermon was given by the church's founder, Dr. William Ellery Channing). About two blocks north is the **Walters Art Museum** ③, an impressive museum with more than 30,000 paintings, sculpture, and other artworks. The gallery marks the southern end of **Mount Vernon Square,** where a series of lovely parks is dominated by the **Washington Monument** ④. The Peabody Conservatory of Music and the **Peabody Library** ⑤ are on the southeast side of Mount Vernon Square. Head west on Mount Vernon Place, which turns into Monument Street, to visit the **Maryland Historical Society** ⑥ for an intriguing look at the past.

Return to your car and drive north on Charles Street 1½ mi to the **Baltimore Museum of Art** ⑦, where an excellent art collection is housed in a John Russell Pope–designed building. The art museum is contiguous to the Homewood campus of Johns Hopkins University, where the exquisite **Homewood House Museum** ⑧, the historic house of John Carroll Jr., is open to the public.

From Johns Hopkins University, turn left on Charles Street and drive several blocks north to Stratford. Turn right on Stratford and drive to where it intersects with Greenway to reach **Sherwood Gardens** ⑨, an urban garden oasis where tulips and azaleas abound each spring. Backtrack one block to St. Paul Street, which then curves northwest to meet Charles Street; two blocks north of that intersection, at Charles Street and Cold Spring Lane, stands the grand **Evergreen House** ⑩, where a guided tour will give you a sense of the lives of the rich and famous at the turn of the 20th century.

TIMING

The many sights of historic Mount Vernon merit at least an entire morning. Save the afternoon for the Baltimore Museum of Art and the Homewood campus of Johns Hopkins University.

American Visionary Art Museum 15
Babe Ruth Birthplace and Museum 28
Baltimore City Hall 23
Baltimore Civil War Museum - President Street Station 20
Baltimore Maritime Museum 18
Baltimore Museum of Art 7
Baltimore Public Works Museum 19
Basilica of the Assumption 1
B&O Railroad Museum 30
B. Olive Cole Pharmacy Museum 27
Davidge Hall 25
Dr. Samuel D. Harris National Museum of Dentistry 26
Enoch Pratt Free Library 2
Evergreen House . . .10
Federal Hill Park 14
Harborplace and The Gallery 11
Homewood House Museum 8
Maryland Historical Society 6
Maryland Science Center 13
Mount Clare Museum House 29
National Aquarium in Baltimore 17
Peabody Library 5
Port Discovery–The Baltimore Children's Museum 21
Sherwood Gardens 9
Star-Spangled Banner House 22
USS *Constellation* . . .12
Walters Art Museum 3
Washington Monument 4
Westminster Cemetery and Catacombs 24
World Trade Center 16

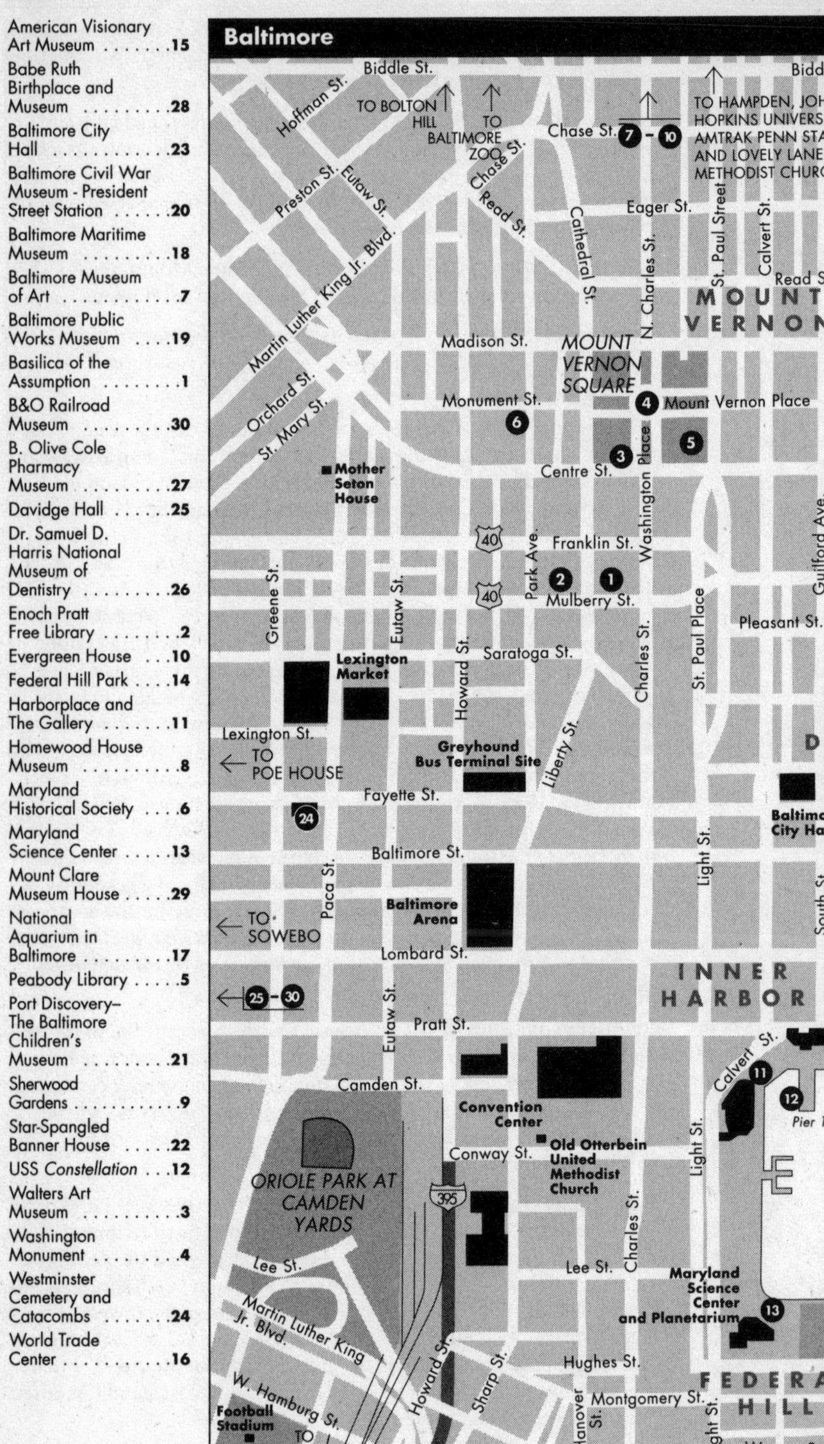

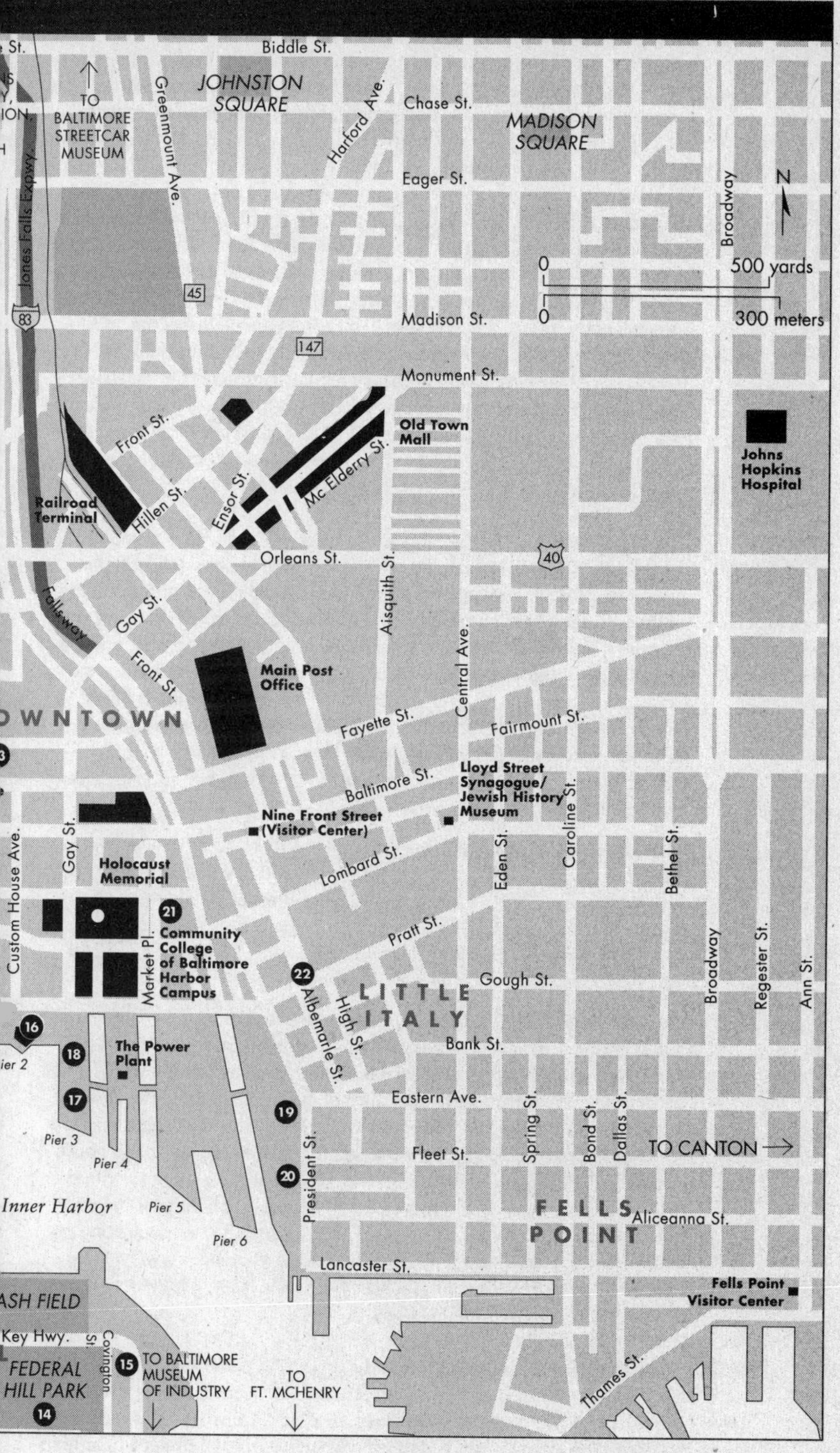

Biddle St.
JOHNSTON SQUARE
TO BALTIMORE STREETCAR MUSEUM
Greenmount Ave.
Harford Ave.
Chase St.
MADISON SQUARE
Eager St.
Broadway
N
0
500 yards
0
300 meters
Jones Falls Expwy.
83
45
Madison St.
147
Monument St.
Old Town Mall
Front St.
Mc Elderry St.
Ensor St.
Hillen St.
Railroad Terminal
Johns Hopkins Hospital
Orleans St.
40
Aisquith St.
Fallsway
Gay St.
Front St.
Main Post Office
Central Ave.
DOWNTOWN
Fayette St.
Fairmount St.
Baltimore St.
Lloyd Street Synagogue/ Jewish History Museum
Nine Front Street (Visitor Center)
Caroline St.
Custom House Ave.
Gay St.
Holocaust Memorial
Lombard St.
Eden St.
Bethel St.
21
Community College of Baltimore Harbor Campus
Market Pl.
Pratt St.
22
Albemarle St.
High St.
LITTLE ITALY
Gough St.
Broadway
Regester St.
Ann St.
16
Pier 2
18
The Power Plant
Bank St.
17
Eastern Ave.
19
Pier 3
Pier 4
President St.
Fleet St.
Spring St.
Bond St.
Dallas St.
TO CANTON
20
Inner Harbor
Pier 5
FELLS POINT
Aliceanna St.
Pier 6
Lancaster St.
Fells Point Visitor Center
ASH FIELD
Key Hwy.
Covington St.
FEDERAL HILL PARK
14
15
TO BALTIMORE MUSEUM OF INDUSTRY
TO FT. MCHENRY
Thames St.

Sights to See

7 **Baltimore Museum of Art.** Works by Matisse, Picasso, Cézanne, Gauguin, van Gogh, and Monet are among the 100,000 paintings, sculptures, and decorative arts on exhibit at this impressive museum, near Johns Hopkins University. Particular strengths include an encyclopedic collection of postimpressionist paintings donated to the museum by the Cone sisters, Baltimore natives who were pioneer collectors of early 20th-century art. The Cone Wing, greatly expanded in 2001, has four sequential galleries that include works that have never been publicly shown before. The museum also owns the world's second-largest collection of Andy Warhol works, and many pieces of 18th- and 19th-century American painting and decorative arts. The museum's neoclassical main building was designed by John Russell Pope, the architect of the National Gallery in Washington; the modern aluminum and concrete wing houses the contemporary art collection. From Gertrude's, the museum restaurant, you can look out at 20th-century sculpture displayed in two landscaped gardens. ✉ *10 Art Museum Dr., Charles Village,* ☎ *410/396–7100.* *$7; free first Thurs. of month.* *Wed.–Fri. 11–5, weekends 11–6, first Thurs. of month 11–8.*

OFF THE BEATEN PATH

AMERICAN DIME MUSEUM – Named for traveling collections of man-made and natural curiosities popular in the 19th century (called "dime museums" after the typical cost of admission) Baltimore's most eccentric museum is dedicated to the art of the carnival sideshow, displaying a collection of colorful artifacts such as sideshow banners, props, and believe-it-or-not displays that include a "genuine" unicorn. Exhibitions explain the attractions and even let you in on the secrets of the business. Sword swallowers, contortionists, and other sideshow professionals occasionally perform. ✉ *1808 Maryland Ave., Midtown,* ☎ *410/230–0263,* WEB *www.dimemuseum.com.* *$5.* *Wed.–Fri. noon–3, weekends noon–5.*

BALTIMORE STREETCAR MUSEUM – This often-overlooked museum lets you travel back to an era when streetcars dominated city thoroughfares. A film traces the vehicle's evolution, and there are beautifully restored streetcars to explore. Best of all, you can actually take unlimited rides on a working streetcar. ✉ *1901 Falls Rd., Midtown,* ☎ *410/547–0264.* *$6.* *Sun. noon–5; June–Oct., Sat. noon–5.*

THE BALTIMORE ZOO – The 150 acres of the Baltimore Zoo—the third-oldest zoo in the country—make a natural stomping ground for little ones, who enjoy the spectacle of elephants, lions, giraffes, hippos, and penguins, among the 2,000 animals that make this their home. Don't miss the warthog exhibit, said to be the nation's only dedicated environment for the bumpy beasts. Favorite sights include a chimpanzee house and leopard lair, river otters in an outdoor pond, a petting zoo with a re-created barnyard, and a Maryland Wilderness exhibit with animals native to the state. A ride on "Zoo-Choo" provides further diversion. ✉ *Druid Hill Lake Dr., Druid Hill,* ☎ *410/366–5466,* WEB *www.baltimorezoo.org.* *$10.* *Nov.–Apr., daily 10–4; May–Oct., weekdays 10–4, Sat. 10–8, Sun. 10–5.*

1 **Basilica of the Assumption.** Completed in 1821, the Catholic Basilica of the Assumption is the oldest cathedral in the United States. Designed by Benjamin Latrobe, architect of the U.S. Capitol, it stands as a paragon of neoclassicism, with a grand portico fronted by six Corinthian columns suggesting an ancient Greek temple. Two towers are surmounted by cupolas. Twenty-four original skylights in the dome, covered over after World War II, are being restored; completion is slated for 2006, the bicentennial of the laying of the church's cornerstone.

Bells ring the Angelus daily at 6 AM, noon, and 6 PM. ✉ *Mulberry St. at Cathedral St., Mount Vernon,* ☎ *410/727–3564.* ⏲ *Weekdays 7:30–5, weekends 7:30–6:30.*

❷ **Enoch Pratt Free Library.** Donated to the city of Baltimore in 1882 by its namesake, a wealthy merchant, the Enoch Pratt Free Library was the country's first free-circulation public library and remains one of its largest. The Pratt was remarkable for allowing any citizen to borrow books at a time when only the wealthy could afford to buy them. When the collection outgrew its original fortresslike rococo structure in 1933, Pratt's democratic ideals were incorporated into the new building's grand yet accessible design. Innovations such as a sidewalk-level entrance and department store–style exhibit windows set the standard for public libraries across the country. The building is still a treat to explore. A huge skylight illuminates the grand Central Hall's marble floors, gilded fixtures, mural panels depicting the history of printing and publishing, and oil portraits of the Lords Baltimore. An especially charming touch is the fishpond in the Children's Department. ✉ *400 Cathedral St., Midtown,* ☎ *410/396–5500,* WEB *www.pratt.lib.md.us.* ⏲ *Mon.–Wed. 10–8, Thurs.–Sat. 10–5, Sun. 1–5.*

❿ **Evergreen House.** Built in the 1850s, this 48-room Italianate mansion was the home of the 19th-century diplomat and collector John Work Garrett, whose father was president of the Baltimore and Ohio Railroad (the Garrett family continued to live here until the 1950s). Garrett bequeathed the house, its contents (an exquisite collection of books, paintings, and porcelain), and 26 acres of grounds to Johns Hopkins University. He required that the estate remain open to "lovers of music, art, and beautiful things." A tour of the mansion provides a fascinating look at the luxury that surrounded a rich American family at the turn of the 20th century. ✉ *4545 N. Charles St., Roland Park,* ☎ *410/516–0341.* 🎟 *$6.* ⏲ *Weekdays 10–4, weekends 1–4.*

❽ **Homewood House Museum.** This elegant Federal-period mansion was once the home of Charles Carroll Jr., son of Charles Carroll of Carrollton, a signer of the Declaration of Independence. Deeded to Johns Hopkins University in 1902 along with 60 acres, the house served as faculty club and offices before being fully restored to its 1800 grandeur (it's one of the finest examples of the neoclassical architecture of the period). Also on campus is the Lacrosse Hall of Fame, the only national museum dedicated to the sport. ✉ *3400 N. Charles St., at 34th St., Charles Village,* ☎ *410/516–5589,* FAX *410/516–7859.* 🎟 *$6.* ⏲ *Tues.–Sat. 11–4, Sun. noon–4.*

Lovely Lane Methodist Church. Built in 1882, Lovely Lane Methodist Church is honored with the title "The Mother Church of American Methodism." Stanford White designed the Romanesque sanctuary after the basilicas of Ravenna, Italy; the stained-glass windows are excellent examples of Italian mosaic art. The buildings to the north that resemble the church are the original campus of the Women's College of Baltimore, now Goucher College. Dr. Goucher, the college's founder, was a pastor at Lovely Lane. ✉ *2200 St. Paul St., Charles Village,* ☎ *410/889–1512.* ⏲ *Weekdays 9–4. Tours of church and Methodist Historical Society by appointment.*

❻ **Maryland Historical Society.** More than 200,000 objects, including period furnishings, textiles, costumes, and toys, serve to celebrate Maryland's history and heritage at this museum. The Radcliffe Maritime Collection tells the history of Maryland's Chesapeake Bay and the Port of Baltimore. Featured are portraits by the Peale family and Joshua Johnson, America's first African-American portrait artist. Two major attractions are the original manuscript of "The Star-Spangled Banner" and the world's largest collection of 19th-century American silver. ✉ *201 W. Monument St., Midtown,* ☎ *410/685–3750,* WEB *www.mdhs.org.* 🎟 *$4.* ⏲ *Wed.–Fri. 10–5, Sat. 9–5, Sun. 11–5.*

Mother Seton House. This modest brick house was the Baltimore home of Elizabeth Ann Seton, the first saint to be born in America, who later moved to Emmitsburg and established the nation's first parochial school. ✉ *600 N. Paca St., Downtown,* ☎ *410/523–3443.* 🎟 *Free.* ⏲ *Weekends 1–4 and by appointment.*

★ **Mount Vernon Square.** One of the most beautifully designed public spaces in the world, Mount Vernon Square acquired its ground and name when John Eager Howard donated the highest point in Baltimore as a site for a memorial to George Washington. With the monument as its center, the square is composed of four parks, each a block in length, that are arranged around Mount Vernon Place (which goes east–west) and Washington Place (north–south). The sculptures in the parks deserve a close look; of special note is a bronze lion by Barye in the middle of West Mount Vernon Place. Northeast of the monument is Mount Vernon Methodist Church, built in the mid-1850s on the site of Francis Scott Key's home and place of death. Take a moment to admire the brownstones along the north side of East Mount Vernon Place. They're excellent examples of the luxurious mansions built by 19th-century residents of Baltimore's most prestigious address.

5 **Peabody Library.** Adjacent to the Peabody Conservatory of Music, the Peabody Library is a fine example of neo-Renaissance architecture. Its stunning reading room reflects the scholarly interests of the 19th century, with more than a quarter of a million books lining the shelves. Most impressive, though, are the cast-iron balconies towering above the black-and-white marble floor. A skylight, 61 ft above, brightens the library, which some have called "the most beautiful room in Baltimore." ✉ *17 E. Mount Vernon Pl., Mount Vernon,* ☎ *410/659–8179.* 🎟 *Free.* ⏲ *Weekdays 9–3.*

9 **Sherwood Gardens.** A popular spring destination for Baltimore families, this 6-acre park contains more than 80,000 tulips that bloom in late April. Azaleas peak in late April and the first half of May. The gardens are usually at their best around Mother's Day. ✉ *Stratford Rd. and Greenway, east of St. Paul St., Guilford,* ☎ *410/323–7982.* 🎟 *Free.* ⏲ *Daily dawn–dusk.*

★ 3 **Walters Art Museum.** The Walters's prodigious collection of more than 30,000 artworks provides an organized overview of human history over 5,500 years, from the 3rd millennium BC to the early 20th century. The original museum (1904) houses the museum's major collections of Renaissance and baroque paintings as well as a sculpture court. In two other buildings are Egyptian, Greek and Roman, Byzantine, and Ethiopian art collections, among the best in the nation, along with many 19th-century paintings. There are also medieval armor and artifacts, jewelry, and decorative works; Egyptology exhibits; and a wonderful gift shop. ✉ *600 N. Charles St., Mount Vernon,* ☎ *410/547–9000,* WEB *www.thewalters.org.* 🎟 *$8; free Sat. 11–1.* ⏲ *Tues.–Sun. 10–5.*

4 **Washington Monument.** Completed on July 4, 1829, Baltimore's Washington Monument was the first monument dedicated to the nation's first president. The 160-ft white marble tower is capped with an 18-ft statue depicting Washington in 1783 as he resigned his position as the commander in chief of the Continental Army at the Annapolis statehouse. A total of 228 steps spiral up to the top of the monument, where incomparable views of the city are available from four portals. The tower

was designed and built by Robert Mills, the first architect born and educated in the United States; 19 years after completing Baltimore's Washington Monument, Mills designed and erected the national Washington Monument in the District of Columbia. ✉ *Mount Vernon Pl., Mount Vernon,* ☎ *410/396–0929.* 💵 *$1.* ⏲ *Wed.–Fri. 10–5, weekends noon–5.*

Woman's Industrial Exchange. This Baltimore institution was organized in 1882 as a way for destitute women, many of them Civil War widows, to support themselves in a ladylike fashion through sewing and other domestic handiworks. To this day patrons can still purchase handmade quilts, exquisitely embroidered baby clothes, endearing sock monkeys, and many other fine crafts, but most come to lunch in the tearoom where old-fashioned menus that your grandmother would recognize—and adore—are served by solicitous uniformed waitresses in a setting that has altered very little since its founding. Breakfast is served, but the emphasis is on genteel ladies' luncheon fare such as tomato aspic, chicken salad, and light-as-air yeast rolls. The sublime homemade baked goods and desserts are a special treat. It's closed on weekends. ✉ *333 N. Charles St., Mount Vernon,* ☎ *410/685–4388.* ⏲ *Weekdays 7:30–2:30 (bakery and gift shop open until 3:30).*

Inner Harbor

The Inner Harbor is Baltimore's first-choice destination for residents and tourists alike. The city's largest concentration of restaurants, hotels, shopping, and major cultural attractions is arrayed around the sparkling waters of the same deepwater port that drew the area's first settlers more than 300 years ago. Now one of the city's liveliest districts, it's also a working port where merchant ships unload cargo or undergo dry-dock repairs while, nearby, luxurious pleasure boats tie up for a visit along the promenade. Landlubbers can enjoy Baltimore's maritime scene as well; sailboat tours, water taxis, and boat rentals let you tour the city by sea.

South of the Inner Harbor, and best accessed by car or water taxi, **Fort McHenry**—now preserved as a national monument—was bombarded by the British during the War of 1812. During a long night's siege by cannon and artillery the fort never fell, and the sight of the just-designed American flag flying above the fort's walls inspired Francis Scott Key to pen a poem that became the national anthem.

A Good Walk

You can spend an entire day simply strolling along the brick promenades that outline Baltimore's waterfront; if you're feeling ambitious, however, you can cover the Inner Harbor itself in the morning and then spend the afternoon visiting various attractions nearby. Begin at the northwest corner of the Inner Harbor at **Harborplace and The Gallery** ⑪, where two glass-enclosed market pavilions invite you to graze at the food stalls and boutiques. Tour the **USS *Constellation*** ⑫, a restored 1854 wooden naval warship docked at the heart of Harborplace. Walk down to the southwest corner of Inner Harbor, to the **Maryland Science Center** ⑬, where an IMAX movie theater and hundreds of hands-on exhibits engage both children and adults. From there it's just a short walk to the best view in Baltimore at **Federal Hill Park** ⑭ and the adjacent **American Visionary Art Museum** ⑮, Baltimore's most unusual major attraction.

Return to Harborplace and walk east along the northern edge of Inner Harbor to Pier 2: here, at the **World Trade Center** ⑯, you can enjoy the panoramic vista from 27 floors up. At Piers 3 and 4 is the **National**

Aquarium in Baltimore ⑰, with its thousands of colorful fish, sharks, dolphins, jellyfish, reptiles, and amphibians. Docked just to the west on Pier 3 is the **Baltimore Maritime Museum** ⑱, whose three vessels include the USS *Torsk,* the submarine credited with sinking the last two Japanese warships during World War II. On Pier 4 is a dining and entertainment complex, the **Power Plant.** It's an option if you want to break for lunch, although Harborplace offers a wider selection of eateries. If time allows, there are two small museums at the east end of the Inner Harbor. Just past Pier 6 the **Baltimore Public Works Museum** ⑲ offers a peek at the city's underground workings, from steam pipes to sewers. A block farther east, at President and Fleet streets, the **Baltimore Civil War Museum-President Street Station** ⑳ considers Baltimore's divided sympathies during the War Between the States.

Cross Pratt Street to **Port Discovery—The Baltimore Children's Museum** ㉑, which the young and young-at-heart climb, crawl, slide, and swing their way through. If you're ready for more, head east on Pratt Street to Albemarle Street and the **Star-Spangled Banner House** ㉒. The American flag that flew at Fort McHenry when Francis Scott Key wrote "The Star-Spangled Banner" was sewn here. Four blocks north, at Baltimore Street, **Nine Front Street** is a visitor information center housed inside a circa-1790 town house. **Baltimore City Hall** ㉓ is one block north and four blocks west on Lombard Street.

TIMING

Allow a whole day for Inner Harbor attractions, by far Baltimore's busiest area. Arrive early at the National Aquarium to ensure admission, which is by timed intervals; by noon, the wait is often two or three hours.

Sights to See

★ ⓯ **American Visionary Art Museum.** The nation's official museum and education center for self-taught or "outsider" art has won great acclaim by both museum experts and those who don't even consider themselves art aficionados. Seven galleries exhibit the unusual creations—paintings, sculptures, relief works, and pieces that defy easy classification—of untrained "visionary" artists working outside the mainstream art world. In addition to the visual stimulation of amazingly intricate or refreshingly inventive works, reading the short bios of artists will give you insight to their often moving spiritual and expressive motivations. The museum's unusual, playful philosophy extends outside its walls, with large exhibits installed in a former whiskey warehouse and a 55-ft whirligig twirling in the museum's plaza. The Joy America Cafe has a view of the Baltimore Harbor and an exuberant menu to match its playful name. ✉ *800 Key Hwy., Federal Hill,* ☎ *410/244–1900,* WEB *www.avam.org.* 🎫 *$8.* ⏲ *Tues.–Sun. 10–6.*

㉓ **Baltimore City Hall.** Built in 1875, Baltimore City Hall consists of mansard roofs and a gilt dome over a 110-ft rotunda, all supported by ironwork. In addition to its own grand architecture, City Hall has tours of the chambers and exhibits on Baltimore's history. Directly across the street is City Hall Plaza, on what was originally the site of the Holliday Street Theatre. The theater was owned and operated by the Ford brothers; they also operated Ford's Theatre in Washington, D.C., where President Lincoln was assassinated. "The Star-Spangled Banner" was first publicly sung here. Now chess enthusiasts gather here for impromptu outdoor matches. ✉ *100 N. Holliday St., Downtown,* ☎ *410/396–3100.* 🎫 *Free.* ⏲ *Weekdays 8–4:30.*

⑳ **Baltimore Civil War Museum-President Street Station.** President Street Station offers a glimpse of the violence and divided loyalties that the war caused in Maryland, a state caught in the middle. Originally the Baltimore terminus of the Philadelphia, Wilmington, and Baltimore Railroad, the relocated station, built in 1849, contains exhibits that depict the events that led to mob violence. It began when troops from the Sixth Massachusetts Regiment bound for Washington, D.C., walked from this station to the Camden Station (near Oriole Park). In what would be the first bloodshed of the Civil War, four soldiers and 12 civilians were killed; 36 soldiers and a number of civilians were wounded. The riot lasted for several hours and inspired the secessionist poem "Maryland, My Maryland," today the state song. Guided tours of the route of the Sixth Massachusetts are offered at 1 PM on weekends. ✉ *601 President St., Inner Harbor East,* ☎ *410/385–5188.* 🎫 *$3; guided tour $5.* ⏲ *Tues.–Sun. 10–5. Guided tour $5.*

18 **Baltimore Maritime Museum.** Consisting of three docked vessels and a restored lighthouse, this museum gives a good sense of Baltimore's maritime heritage as well as American naval power. On the west side of the pier, the submarine USS *Torsk,* the "Galloping Ghost of the Japanese Coast," is credited with sinking the last two Japanese warships in World War II. The lightship *Chesapeake,* built as a floating lighthouse in 1930 and now out of commission, remains fully operational. The *Taney* is a Coast Guard cutter that saw action at Pearl Harbor. Built in 1856, the Seven Foot Knoll Lighthouse marked the entrance to the Baltimore Harbor from the Chesapeake Bay for 133 years before its move to the museum. ✉ *Pier 3, Inner Harbor,* ☎ *410/396–3453,* WEB *www.baltomaritimemuseum.org.* 🎫 *$6.* ⏲ *Mar.–Dec., Sun.–Thurs. 10–5:30, Fri.–Sat. 10–6:30; Jan.–Feb., Fri.–Sun. 10:30–5.*

OFF THE BEATEN PATH

BALTIMORE MUSEUM OF INDUSTRY – Housed in an 1865 oyster cannery, the fascinating Baltimore Museum of Industry covers the city's industrial and labor history and is worth the ½-mi walk south of the Inner Harbor along Key Highway. Here, you can watch and help operate the functional re-creations of a machine shop circa 1900, a print shop, a cannery, and a garment workroom. A restored steam-driven tugboat that plied the waterfront for the first half of this century is docked outside. ✉ *1415 Key Hwy., Federal Hill,* ☎ *410/727–4808,* WEB *www.charm.net/~bmi.* 🎫 *$6.* ⏲ *Mon.–Sat. 10–5, Sun. noon–5.*

19 **Baltimore Public Works Museum.** Just a short walk east of the Inner Harbor, this museum is an unusual collection of artifacts displayed in an unusual location: the 80-plus-year-old Eastern Avenue Sewage Pumping Station. Here you can examine several generations of water pipe, including wood piping nearly 200 years old. Other exhibits tell the history of such city services as trash removal. Outdoors, a life-size model reveals what lies underneath Baltimore streets. ✉ *751 Eastern Ave., Inner Harbor,* ☎ *410/396–5565.* 🎫 *$2.50.* ⏲ *Tues.–Sun. 10–4.*

14 **Federal Hill Park.** On the south side of Inner Harbor, Federal Hill Park was named in 1788 to commemorate Maryland's ratification of the U.S. Constitution. Later it was the site of Civil War fortifications, built by less-than-welcome Union troops under the command of Major General Benjamin "Spoonie" Butler. Until the early 1900s, a signal tower atop Federal Hill displayed the "house" flags of local shipping companies, notifying them of the arrival of their vessels. Some of the oldest homes in Baltimore surround the park, and its summit provides an excellent view of the Inner Harbor and the downtown skyline. The best vantage point for photographing Baltimore, it is also a favorite spot for watching holiday fireworks. ✉ *Battery Ave. and Key Hwy., Federal Hill.*

★ **Fort McHenry.** This star-shape brick fort is forever associated with Francis Scott Key and "The Star-Spangled Banner," which Key penned while watching the British bombardment of Baltimore during the War of 1812. Key had been detained onboard a truce ship, where he had been negotiating the release of one Dr. William Beanes, when the bombardment began; Key knew too much about the attack plan to be released. Through the next day and night, as the battle raged, Key strained to be sure, through the smoke and haze, that the flag still flew above Fort McHenry—indicating that Baltimore's defenders held firm. "By the dawn's early light" of September 14, 1814, he saw the 30-ft by 42-ft "Star-Spangled Banner" still aloft and was inspired to pen the words to a poem (set to the tune of an old English drinking song). The flag that flew above Fort McHenry that day had 15 stars and 15 stripes, and was hand-sewn for the fort. A visit to the fort includes a 16-minute history film, guided tour, and frequent living history displays (including battle reenactments) on weekends. To see how the formidable fortifications might have appeared to the bombarding British, catch a water taxi from the Inner Harbor to the fort instead of driving. ✉ *E. Fort Ave., Locust Point (from Light St., take Key Hwy. for 1½ mi and follow signs),* ☎ *410/962–4290,* WEB *www.nps.gov/fomc.* *$5.* ⏲ *Memorial Day–Labor Day, daily 8–8; Labor Day–Memorial Day, daily 8–5.*

11 **Harborplace and The Gallery.** This 1980 development began the Baltimore renaissance, a legendary urban renewal success story. Two airy, glass-enclosed marketplaces offer a plethora of shops and eateries: the Light Street Pavilion has two stories of food courts and restaurants and the Pratt Street Pavilion is dedicated mainly to retail stores. More than a dozen restaurants, including the Capitol City Brewing Company, Phillips, and City Lights, offer waterfront dining, and such local specialty shops as Celebrate Baltimore and Maryland Bay Company carry unusual and interesting souvenirs. Jugglers, bands, and other street performers entertain the crowd at an outdoor amphitheater between the two pavilions, and paddleboats are available for rent south of the Pratt Street building. A skywalk from the Pratt Street Pavilion leads to **The Gallery**, an upscale four-story shopping mall with 70 more shops, including April Cornell, J. Crew, Coach, and Godiva Chocolatiers. ✉ *100 Pratt St., Inner Harbor,* ☎ *410/332–4191,* WEB *www.harborplace.com.* ⏲ *Mon.–Sat. 10–9, Sun. 10–6. (Harborplace and The Gallery have extended summer hrs; some restaurants open earlier for breakfast, and most close very late.)*

Lloyd Street Synagogue. Built in 1845, this was the first synagogue in Maryland and the third in the United States. Now restored and part of the Jewish Museum of Maryland, the artworks, photographs, and documents exhibited cover the Jewish experience in Baltimore. ✉ *15 Lloyd St., Inner Harbor East (follow Pratt St. east from Inner Harbor, turn left on Central Ave., left again onto Lombard St., and then right onto Lloyd St.)* ☎ *410/732–6400,* WEB *www.jhsm.org.* *$4.* ⏲ *Tues.–Thurs. and Sun. noon–4 and by appointment.*

13 **Maryland Science Center.** Originally known as the Maryland Academy of Sciences, this 200-year-old institution is one of the oldest scientific institutions in the United States. Now housed in a contemporary building, the three floors of exhibits on the Chesapeake Bay, applied science, dinosaurs, and outer space are an invitation to engage, experiment, and explore. The center has a planetarium, a simulated archaeological dinosaur dig, and an IMAX movie theater with a screen five stories high. ✉ *601 Light St., Inner Harbor,* ☎ *410/685–5225,* WEB *www.mdsci.org.* *$8; IMAX tickets $9.* ⏲ *Weekdays 10–5, Sat. 10–6, Sun. noon–6.*

★ 17 **National Aquarium in Baltimore.** The most-visited attraction in Maryland has more than 10,000 fish, sharks, dolphins, and amphibians dwelling in 2 million gallons of water. They're joined by the reptiles, birds, plants, and mammals inhabiting the center's rain-forest environment, a glass pyramid 64 ft high. This ecosystem harbors two-toed sloths in calabash trees, parrots in the palms, iguanas on the ground, and red-bellied piranhas in a pool (a sign next to it reads DO NOT PUT HANDS IN POOL). In the Marine Mammal Pavilion, seven Atlantic bottlenose dolphins give several entertaining presentations a day that highlight their agility and intelligence. The aquarium's famed shark tank and Atlantic coral reef exhibits are spectacular; you can wind through an enormous glass enclosure on a spiral ramp while hammerheads and brightly hued tropical fish glide by. Hands-on exhibits include such docile sea creatures as horseshoe crabs and starfish, and the outdoor seal pool is always popular. ✉ *Pier 3, Inner Harbor,* ☎ *410/576–3800,* WEB *www.aqua.org.* 🎟 *$17.50.* ⏲ *Mar.–June and Sept.–Oct., Sat.–Thurs. 9–5, Fri. 9–8; July–Aug., Mon.–Thurs. 9–6, Fri.–Sun. 9–8; Nov.–Feb., Sat.–Thurs. 10–5, Fri. 10–8; visitors may tour for up to 2 hrs after closing. Timed tickets may be required on weekends and holidays; purchase these early in the day.*

Nine Front Street. This cute two-story brick town house, built in 1790, was once the home of Mayor Thorowgood Smith. The Women's Civic League restored it and maintains it as a visitor information center. ✉ *9 Front St., Inner Harbor East,* ☎ *410/837–5424.* ⏲ *Tues.–Fri. 9–3.*

Old Otterbein United Methodist Church. In the shadow of the Baltimore Convention Center and near Harborplace, the oldest ecclesiastical building in Baltimore was built in 1785. ✉ *112 W. Conway St., Downtown,* ☎ *410/685–4703.* ⏲ *Sun. after 11 AM services; Apr.–Oct., Sat. 11–3.*

★ 21 **Port Discovery—The Baltimore Children's Museum.** Designed to offer a different experience for every visitor, this interactive museum is like no other—and adults are encouraged to play every bit as much as the children. A favorite attraction is the three-story KidWorks, a futuristic jungle gym on which the adventurous can climb, crawl, slide, and swing their way through stairs, slides, ropes, zip-lines, and tunnels, and even traverse a narrow footbridge three stories up; there is a miniversion of KidWorks especially for toddlers. In Miss Perception's Mystery House, youngsters help solve a mystery surrounding the disappearance of the Baffeld family by sifting through clues; some are written or visual, and others are gleaned by touching and listening. At the R&D Dreamlab you can make wind-driven machines and other imaginative objects to take home, and Adventure Expeditions takes you to ancient Egyptian ruins where hieroglyphics must be deciphered to find a hidden pharaoh's tomb. ✉ *35 Market Pl., Inner Harbor,* ☎ *410/727–8120,* WEB *www.portdiscovery.com.* 🎟 *$11.* ⏲ *Memorial Day–Labor Day, daily 10–6; Labor Day–Memorial Day, Tues.–Sat. 10–5, Sun. noon–5.*

The Power Plant. What was once the city's power plant is now a bustling day- and nighttime retail and dining complex that includes a Hard Rock Cafe, a Barnes & Noble, and an ESPN Zone, 35,000 square ft devoted to sports, entertainment, and dining. Designed by Disney and ESPN, the two-level facility is supposed to feel like a stadium. Diners can participate in virtual-reality sports activities or watch their favorite teams on TV. ESPN occasionally broadcasts live from the Zone, especially during and after Baltimore Orioles baseball games or other local sporting events. ✉ *Pier 5, 601 E. Pratt St., Inner Harbor,* ☎ *no phone.*

22 **Star-Spangled Banner House.** Built in 1793, this Federal-style home was where Mary Pickersgill hand-sewed the 15-star, 15-stripe flag that survived the British bombardment of Fort McHenry in 1814 and inspired Francis Scott Key to write "The Star-Spangled Banner." The house contains Federal furniture and American art of the period, including pieces from the Pickersgill family. Outdoors, a map of the United States has been made of stones from the various states. A museum connected to the house tells the history of the War of 1812. ✉ *844 E. Pratt St., Inner Harbor East,* ☎ *410/837–1793,* WEB *www.flaghouse.org.* 🎫 *$5.* ⏲ *Tues.–Sat. 10–4.*

12 **USS *Constellation*.** Launched in 1854, the USS *Constellation* was the last—and largest—all-sail ship built by the U.S. Navy. Before the Civil War, as part of the African Squadron, she saw service on antislavery patrol; during the war, she protected Union-sympathizing U.S. merchant ships from Confederate raiders. The warship eventually became a training ship for the navy before serving as the relief flagship for the Atlantic Fleet during World War II, finally arriving in Baltimore in 1955 for restoration to her original condition. You can tour the USS *Constellation* for a glimpse of life as a 19th-century navy sailor, and children can muster to become Civil War–era "powder monkeys." Recruits receive "basic training," try on replica period uniforms, participate in a gun drill, and learn a sea chantey or two before being discharged and paid off in Civil War money at the end of their "cruise." ✉ *Pratt and Light Sts., Inner Harbor,* ☎ *410/539–6238,* WEB *www.constellation.org.* 🎫 *$6.50.* ⏲ *May–mid-Oct., daily 10–6; mid-Oct.–Apr., daily 10–4.*

★ 16 **World Trade Center.** With 32 stories, this is the world's tallest pentagonal building. The 27th-floor observation deck ("Top of the World") allows an unobstructed view of Baltimore and beyond from 423 ft. Multimedia presentations focus on local economic growth and on Baltimore's sister cities in other nations. ✉ *401 E. Pratt St., Inner Harbor,* ☎ *410/837–8439,* WEB *www.bop.org/topworld.* 🎫 *$4.* ⏲ *Memorial Day–Labor Day, daily 9–9; Apr.–May and Sept.–Oct., Wed.–Sun. 10–7.*

Fells Point

One of the city's earliest settlement sites, Fells Point is a Colonial-era neighborhood once populated by shipbuilders and sailors and now rich in history, immigrant enclaves, and offbeat characters. Weekend nights find Fells Point's cobblestone streets flooded with fun-seekers headed to its many bars, clubs, and restaurants. Beyond the honky-tonks and dining, however, there lies a National Register Historic District neighborhood of 18th-century brick homes, appreciated by its diverse residents as a very livable community where individuality is welcome.

The neighborhood was founded in 1726 when Englishman William Fell purchased the peninsula, seeing its potential for shipbuilding and shipping. Beginning in 1763, his son Edward and his wife, Ann Bond Fell, divided and sold the land; docks, shipyards, warehouses, stores, homes, churches, and schools sprang up, and the area quickly grew into a bustling seaport. Fells Point was famed for its shipyards (the notoriously speedy clipper ships built here so irritated the British during the War of 1812 that they tried to capture Baltimore, a move resulting in Fort McHenry's bombardment). During the 1830s Frederick Douglass, former slave turned orator and Baltimore's most famous civil rights activist, was employed at a shipyard at the end of Thames Street.

Today people come to Fells Point simply to enjoy themselves rather than to visit historic sites. There are no museums to speak of; the major activity is strolling the waterfront promenade, choosing one restaurant from the many, and browsing shop windows. Cultural attractions include two theaters, art galleries, and a large number of live music venues. There are dozens of unique small stores selling everything from handmade clothing to brassware, souvenirs to skateboards. The neighborhood is also a major center for antiques merchants.

A fun way to reach Fells is via an Inner Harbor water taxi. Alternatively, the neighborhood is a five-minute cab ride from downtown. Main thoroughfares are Thames (pronounced with a long "a") Street, running east–west, and Broadway, running north–south. Most bars, restaurants, and shops are on these arteries.

A Good Walk

For a historic walking tour map, stop by the **Fell's Point Visitor Center** on South Ann Street. Next door is the small **Robert Long House Museum,** the city's oldest home. From there, turn right on cobblestone Thames Street, flanked on the north by blocks of small shops and restaurants and on the south by sailboats and working tugs docked along the harbor. The neighborhood's hub of action is at the intersection of Thames and Broadway. To the south, Broadway becomes a pier from which water taxis depart, and to the north it encloses a pedestrian promenade that holds the **Broadway Market.** Shops and taverns line Broadway as well.

Sights to See

Broadway Market. For a drink or light snack, visit the twin pavilions, which have provided neighborhood residents with fresh produce, fish, meat, and flowers for more than 100 years. You can buy a pastry or a sandwich, eat oysters at a raw bar, or pick up a can of Maryland's signature seafood spice mix, Old Bay Seasoning, by the fishmonger's stall. ✉ *Broadway, between Fleet and Lancaster Sts., Fells Point.*

Fell's Point Visitor Center. This visitor center is also the home of the Society for the Preservation of Federal Hill and Fell's Point, which is why the center uses the apostrophe in "Fell's" (it's not commonly used). There's a gift shop here and a historic walking tour brochure for the taking. Neighborhood tours depart from here on Friday evening and Saturday morning and focus on topics such as maritime history or slavery and Frederick Douglass's tenure in Fells Point. ✉ *808 S. Ann St., Fells Point,* ☎ *410/675–6750,* WEB *www.preservationsociety.com.* ⏲ *Daily noon–4.*

Robert Long House Museum. The city's oldest existing residence, this small brick house was built in 1765 as both home and business office for Robert Long, a merchant and quartermaster for the Continental Navy who operated a wharf on the waterfront. Furnished with Revolutionary War–era pieces, the parlor, bedroom, and office seem as if Long himself just stepped away. A fragrant herb garden flourishes in warm months. ✉ *812 S. Ann St., Fells Point,* ☎ *410/675–6750.* 🎫 *$3.*

OFF THE BEATEN PATH

GREAT BLACKS IN WAX MUSEUM – Overseeing the entrance to this successful, homespun museum is North African general Hannibal, astride his life-size elephant. Behind him, more than 100 wax figures and dioramas are on display. Though not as convincing as the likenesses at a Madame Tussaud's, they do a good job of recounting the triumphs and trials of Africans and African-Americans. The wax figures are accompanied by text and audio. The slave ship exhibit depicts the atrocities endured on the Middle Passage from Africa to the Caribbean and North America. Baltimoreans honored include Frederick Douglass, who as a youth lived and worked in Fells Point, singer Billie Holiday, and jazz composer Eubie

Blake. Civil rights leaders and Harriet Tubman's role in the Underground Railroad network are also on display. To get here from Fells Point, take Broadway north and turn left at North Avenue. ✉ *1601 E. North Ave., East Baltimore,* ☎ *410/563–3404,* WEB *www.greatblacksinwax.org.* *$6.* ⏲ *Mid-Jan.–mid-Oct., Tues.–Sat. 9–6, Sun. noon–6; mid-Oct.–mid-Jan., Tues.–Sat. 9-5, Sun. noon–5. Closed Mon. except during Feb., July, Aug., Martin Luther King Jr. Day, and most federal holidays (holiday hrs 10–4).*

West Baltimore

Despite their proximity to the Inner Harbor, the neighborhoods farther west are often overlooked by those making their first trip to Baltimore. Yet some of the city's most colorful residents have lived in these working-class areas, where museums commemorate them today. Babe Ruth was born in a house that still stands as a museum to one of baseball's greatest; it's just a few blocks from Oriole Park at Camden Yards.

A Good Drive

Because the sights are far apart in this area and the streets are less safe than those in downtown Baltimore, West Baltimore is best visited by car. Start this tour at Fayette and Greene streets, where the **Westminster Cemetery and Catacombs** ㉔ hold the remains of Edgar Allan Poe—perhaps Baltimore's most renowned literary figure. Just up Paca Street you can buy a fine lunch at the Lexington Market. Less than a mile away—follow Greene Street north, turn left on Saratoga Street, and follow it just a few blocks to Amity Street—you'll find the **Poe House,** where Edgar Allan Poe wrote his first horror story. Because of the possibility of street crime in this area, take safety precautions: don't go alone, and don't go at night.

Next, venture farther into the outskirts of town, toward the University of Maryland Hospital complex. Those of a medical bent will appreciate **Davidge Hall** ㉕, the oldest building in the United States used continuously for teaching medicine, and the adjacent **Dr. Samuel D. Harris National Museum of Dentistry** ㉖. A block away is the **B. Olive Cole Pharmacy Museum** ㉗.

Just south of Pratt Street, on Emory Street, is the **Babe Ruth Birthplace and Baseball Center** ㉘, only three blocks from Oriole Park. After a tour of **Oriole Park at Camden Yards,** one of baseball's most revered ballparks, drive west on Pratt Street to Martin Luther King Boulevard, turn left and go two blocks, then turn right onto Washington Boulevard. At the eighth traffic light, turn into Carroll Park on the right. At the top of the hill you'll find the **Mount Clare Museum House** ㉙, which once belonged to Charles Carroll, a member of the Continental Congress. Return downtown by driving east along Pratt Street to the **B&O Railroad Museum** ㉚, the birthplace of railroading in America.

TIMING

Several hours should suffice to cover all the sights on this tour. Reserve an extra hour around lunchtime to stroll among the food stands at Lexington Market. Sights are dispersed on the drive, and the neighborhoods are less safe than downtown Baltimore.

Sights to See

㉘ **Babe Ruth Birthplace and Museum.** This modest brick row house, just three blocks from Oriole Park at Camden Yards, was the birthplace of "the Bambino." Although Ruth was born here in 1895, his family never lived in the home; they lived in a nearby apartment, above a tavern run by Ruth's father. The row house and the adjoining buildings make up a museum devoted to Ruth's life and to the local Orioles baseball club. Film clips, rare photos of Ruth, Yankees payroll checks, a scorebook from Ruth's first professional game, and many other artifacts can be found here, along with Orioles memorabilia that includes bats and other items associated with Cal Ripken Jr. ⊠ *216 Emory St., Downtown,* ☎ *410/727–1539,* WEB *www.baberuthmuseum.com.* *$6.* ⏲ *Apr.–Oct., daily 10–5; Nov.–Mar., daily 10–4; until 7 before Orioles home games.*

★ 30 **B&O Railroad Museum.** The famous Baltimore and Ohio Railroad was founded on the site that now houses this museum, which contains more than 120 full-size locomotives and a great collection of railroad memorabilia, from dining car china and artwork to lanterns and signals. The 1884 roundhouse (240 ft in diameter and 120 ft high) adjoins one of the nation's first railroad stations. From this station, the legendary race between the *Tom Thumb* (a working replica of the steam locomotive is inside) and a gray horse took place: the horse won when *Tom Thumb* lost a fan belt. Samuel Morse's first transmission of Morse code, WHAT HATH GOD WROUGHT?, in 1844, passed through wires here, en route from Washington to the B&O Pratt Street Station. Train rides are available on weekends. ⊠ *901 W. Pratt St., West Baltimore,* ☎ *410/752–2490,* WEB *www.borail.org.* *$8.* ⏲ *Daily 10–5.*

27 **B. Olive Cole Pharmacy Museum.** This endearing museum contains a replica of an early 19th-century pharmacy and paintings that relate to the history of pharmacies. ⊠ *650 W. Lombard St., Downtown,* ☎ *410/727–0746.* *Free.* ⏲ *Weekdays by appointment.*

25 **Davidge Hall.** Built in 1812 for $35,000, this green-dome structure has been used for teaching medicine for nearly two centuries. Part of the downtown campus of the University of Maryland at Baltimore, Davidge Hall is a relic of the days when dissection was illegal; the acoustically perfect anatomy theater was lighted by skylights instead of windows so that passersby would not witness students working on cadavers. ⊠ *522 W. Lombard St., Downtown,* ☎ *410/706–7454.* *Free.* ⏲ *Weekdays 8:30–4:30.*

26 **Dr. Samuel D. Harris National Museum of Dentistry.** Appropriately, this unusual museum, which has a set of George Washington's dentures, is on the Baltimore campus of the University of Maryland, the world's first dental school. Housed in a Roman Renaissance revival–style building, the museum has exhibits on the anatomy and physiology of human and animal teeth and the history of dentistry; you can also play a tune on the "Tooth Jukebox." One popular exhibit displays the dental instruments used in treating Queen Victoria in the mid-19th century. ⊠ *31 S. Greene St., Downtown,* ☎ *410/706–0600.* *$4.50.* ⏲ *Wed.–Sat. 10–4, Sun. 1–4.*

29 **Mount Clare Museum House.** One of the oldest residences in Baltimore, this elegant mansion was begun in 1754. It was the home of Charles Carroll, author of the Maryland Declaration of Independence, member of the Continental Congress, and one of Maryland's major landowners. The state's first historic museum house has been carefully restored to its Georgian elegance; more than 80 percent of the 18th-century furniture and artifacts, including rare pieces of Chippendale and Hepplewhite silver, crystal, and Chinese export porcelain, were owned and used by the Carroll family. Washington, Lafayette, and John Adams were guests here. The greenhouses are famous in their own right: they provided rare trees and plants for Mount Vernon. ⊠ *1500 Washington Blvd., Southwest Baltimore,* ☎ *410/837–3262.* *$6.* ⏲ *Tues.–Fri. 11–4, weekends 1–4.*

★ **Oriole Park at Camden Yards.** Since its opening in 1992, this nostalgically designed baseball stadium has inspired other cities to emulate its neotraditional architecture and state-of-the-art amenities. Home of the Baltimore Orioles, Camden Yards bustles on game days but is accessible in the off-season as well. The Eutaw Street promenade, between the warehouse and the field, is open daily and has a view of the stadium; look for the brass baseballs embedded in the sidewalk that mark where home runs have cleared the fence, or visit the Orioles Hall of Fame display and the monuments to retired Orioles. Daily tours take fans to every nook and cranny of the ballpark, from the immense JumboTron scoreboard to the dugout to the state-of-the-art beer delivery system. You may even spot former Oriole Boog Powell at his concession stand, Boog's BBQ. ✉ *333 W. Camden St., Downtown,* ☎ *410/685–9800 general information; 410/547–6234 tour times; 410/481–7328 tickets to Orioles home games,* WEB *www.theorioles.com.* 🎫 *Eutaw St. promenade free; tour $5.* ⏲ *Eutaw St. promenade daily 10–3, otherwise during games and tours.*

Poe House. Though the "Master of the Macabre" lived in this tiny row house only three years, he wrote "MS Found in a Bottle" and his first horror story, "Berenice," in the tiny garret chamber that's now furnished in an early 19th-century style. Besides visiting this room, you can view changing exhibits and a video presentation about Poe's short, tempestuous life. Because of the possibility of crime, it's best to visit this neighborhood during daylight hours as part of a group. ✉ *203 N. Amity St., West Baltimore,* ☎ *410/396–7932,* WEB *www.eapoe.org/balt/poehse.htm.* 🎫 *$3.* ⏲ *Wed.–Sat. noon–3:45.*

24 **Westminster Cemetery and Catacombs.** The city's oldest cemetery is the final resting place of Edgar Allan Poe and other famous Marylanders, including 15 generals from the American Revolution and the War of 1812. Dating from 1786, the cemetery was originally known as the Old Western Burying Grounds. In the early 1850s a city ordinance demanded that burial grounds be part of a church, so a building was constructed above the cemetery, creating catacombs beneath it. In the 1930s the schoolchildren of Baltimore collected pennies to raise the necessary funds for Poe's monument. In one of Baltimore's quirkier traditions, each year on Poe's birthday a mysterious stranger leaves three roses and a bottle of cognac on the writer's grave. ✉ *W. Fayette and Greene Sts., Downtown,* ☎ *410/706–2072.* ⏲ *Daily 8–dusk.*

NEED A BREAK?

Founded in 1782, **Lexington Market** (✉ Lexington St. between Paca and Eutaw Sts., Downtown, ☎ 410/685–6169, WEB www.lexingtonmarket.com) is just north of Westminster Cemetery. With more than 150 vendors, there's plenty of everything for anyone's taste. The modern structure holds a busy scene, but be careful in the surrounding neighborhood.

DINING

It's easy to eat well in Baltimore, where the dining scene offers the cosmopolitan dining advantages commonly found in major cities: kitchens that operate until 10 PM or later, especially on weekends; a large number of restaurants within a compact central area; and cuisines, from traditional to ethnic to the newest of nouveau.

North of Saratoga Street in Mount Vernon, Charles Street is chockablock with restaurants. If you're interested in local flavor, visit Little Italy at the eastern end of the Inner Harbor, where Italian restaurants near the intersection of Pratt and High streets cover every possible price range and regional variation (although most tread the classic Southern Italian, spaghetti-with–garlic-bread road). A very short drive, cab ride, or water taxi cruise to the east of Little Italy, Fells Point has a concentration of interesting local restaurants as well, many with outdoor or waterfront dining.

CATEGORY	COST*
$$$$	over $32
$$$	$22–$32
$$	$12–$22
$	under $12

**per person for a main course at dinner*

Mount Vernon

$$–$$$$ ★ ✕ **The Prime Rib.** Bustling and crowded, this luxuriously dark dining room is just north of Mount Vernon Square and only five minutes from the Inner Harbor. Tables are set close together under a low ceiling, keeping things intimate for bankers and lawyers, as well as couples on expensive dates. A piano and bass combo provides quiet jazz music every night. Consistently ranked among the city's best restaurants, the Prime Rib has a traditional menu headed by a sterling prime rib and an even better filet mignon; the jumbo lump crab cakes are also great. The wine list is surprisingly short and predominantly Californian. ✉ *1101 N. Calvert St., Mount Vernon,* ☎ *410/539–1804,* WEB *www.theprimerib.com. Reservations essential. Jacket required. AE, D, DC, MC, V.*

$$–$$$ ✕ **The Brewer's Art.** This tastefully redone mansion houses a pair of elegant dining rooms, but look closely—the Brewer's Art is serious about its mission, and there's a copper-tank brew house in the back. The restaurant cultivates a young, urbane air, with an ambitious menu, a clever wine list, and the Belgian-style beers it brews: try the potent Resurrection ale. The menu of seasonal dishes uses high-quality, locally available ingredients to create European-style country fare that is both hearty and sophisticated. The classic steak frites are a best bet, as are the fresh homemade ravioli made with seasonal ingredients such as pumpkin in autumn and tomatoes and artichokes in the summer. ✉ *1106 N. Charles St., Mount Vernon,* ☎ *410/547–6925,* WEB *www.belgianbeer.com. AE, D, DC, MC, V. Closed Mon.*

$$–$$$ ✕ **Spike & Charlie's Restaurant and Wine Bar.** In 1991, the Gjerde brothers opened their first eatery here, and it wasn't just the great location that brought them success. Across from the Meyerhoff Symphony Hall and near the Lyric Theater, the innovative kitchen whips the mashed potatoes to order, makes the condiments from scratch, and still gets patrons to performances on time. Dishes range from roasted butternut squash soup with ancho chile and pears to duck breast in a golden raisin and horseradish sauce. No time for dinner? Stop in for one of more than 200 well-chosen wines and delicious desserts (Spike began his career as a pastry chef). ✉ *1225 Cathedral St., Mount Vernon,* ☎ *410/752–8144,* WEB *www.spikeandcharlies.com. AE, D, MC, V. Closed Mon.*

$$–$$$ ✕ **Tio Pepe.** Candles illuminate the whitewashed walls of these cellar dining rooms, which are usually hopping (the Shawl Room is quietest). The menu covers all regions of Spain. The staple is *paella à la Valenciana* (chicken, sausage, shrimp, clams, and mussels with saffron rice); a less-well-known Basque preparation is red snapper with clams, mussels, asparagus, and boiled egg. For appetizers, try the mushrooms from the caves of Segovia. The short but diverse wine list has many Spanish vintages, and there is a more expensive reserve list. Make dinner reservations well in advance; walk-in weekday lunch seating is usually

Dining
- Acropolis 41
- Akbar 14
- Babalu Grill 21
- The Bicycle 29
- The Black Olive 44
- Blue Agave 30
- The Blue Moon Dining House 43
- Bo Brooks 49
- The Brass Elephant 9
- The Brewer's Art 10
- Charleston 37
- Chiapparelli's 38
- Hamilton's 45
- Hamptons 28
- Joy America Cafe 33
- Kawasaki 18
- La Tavola 39
- Loco Hombre 7
- Louisiana 42
- McCafferty's 1
- McCormick & Schmick's 34
- O'Bryckis Crab House 40
- Polo Grill 6
- The Prime Rib 4
- Red Maple 9
- Rusty Scupper 32
- Ruth's Chris Steak House 21
- SOIGNE 31
- Spike & Charlie's 11
- Tio Pepe 17

Lodging
- The Admiral Fell Inn 45
- Biltmore Suites Hotel 13
- Celie's Waterfront Bed & Breakfast 46
- Courtyard by Marriott Hunt Valley 3
- Courtyard by Marriott Baltimore Inner Harbor 36
- Days Inn Inner Harbor 25
- Doubletree Inn at the Colonnade 5
- Hampton Inn Hunt Valley 2
- Harbor Court 28
- Hyatt Regency 27
- Inn at 2920 47
- Inn at Henderson's Wharf 48
- Inner Harbor Marriott . .24
- Marriott Baltimore Waterfront 35
- Mount Vernon Hotel . . .16
- Mr. Mole Bed & Breakfast 12
- Peabody Court 15
- Quality Inn at the Carlyle 8
- Radisson Plaza Lord Baltimore 23
- Renaissance Harborplace Hotel . . .26
- Tremont Hotel 19
- Tremont Plaza Hotel .20
- Wyndham Inner Harbor 22

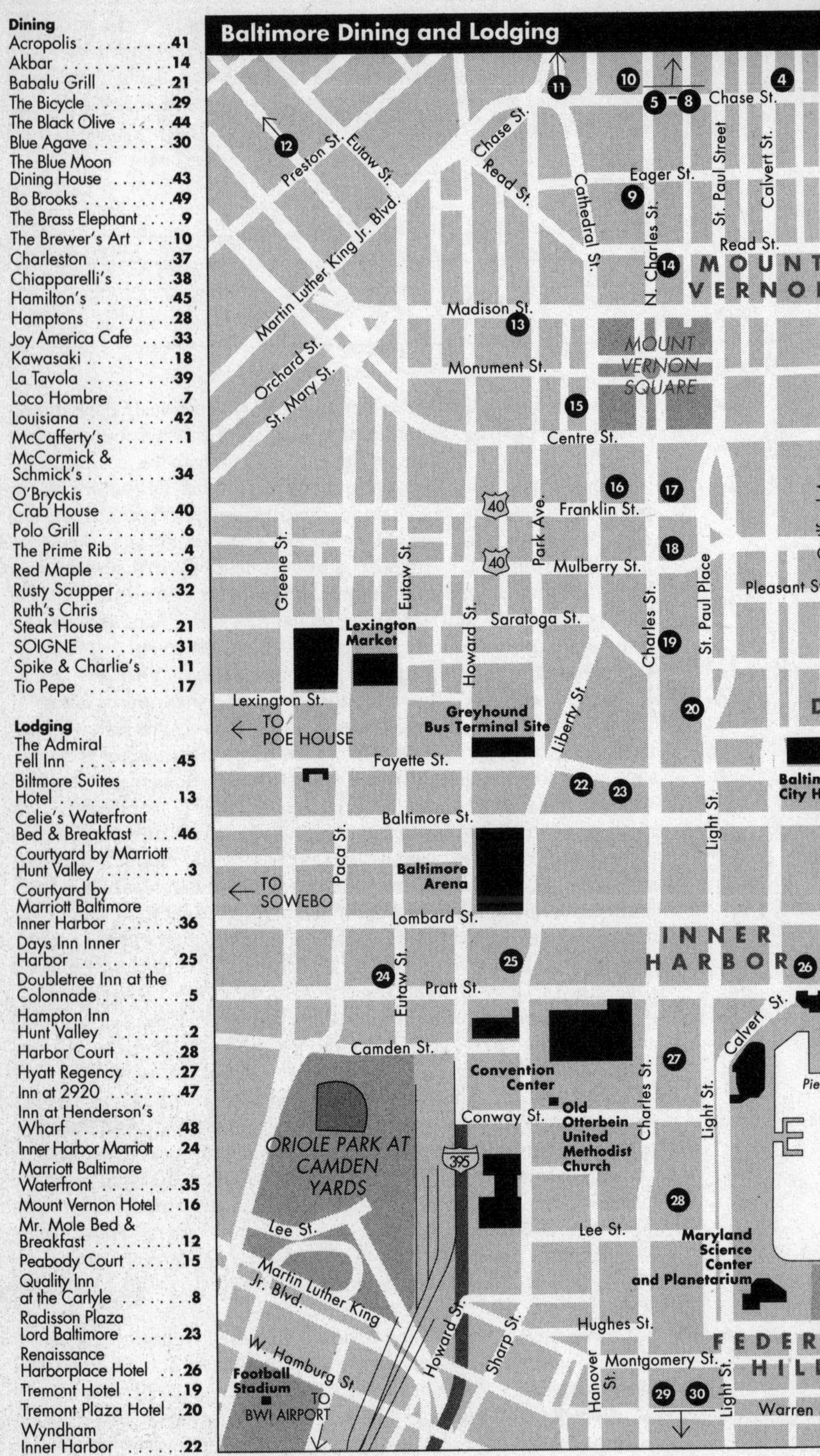

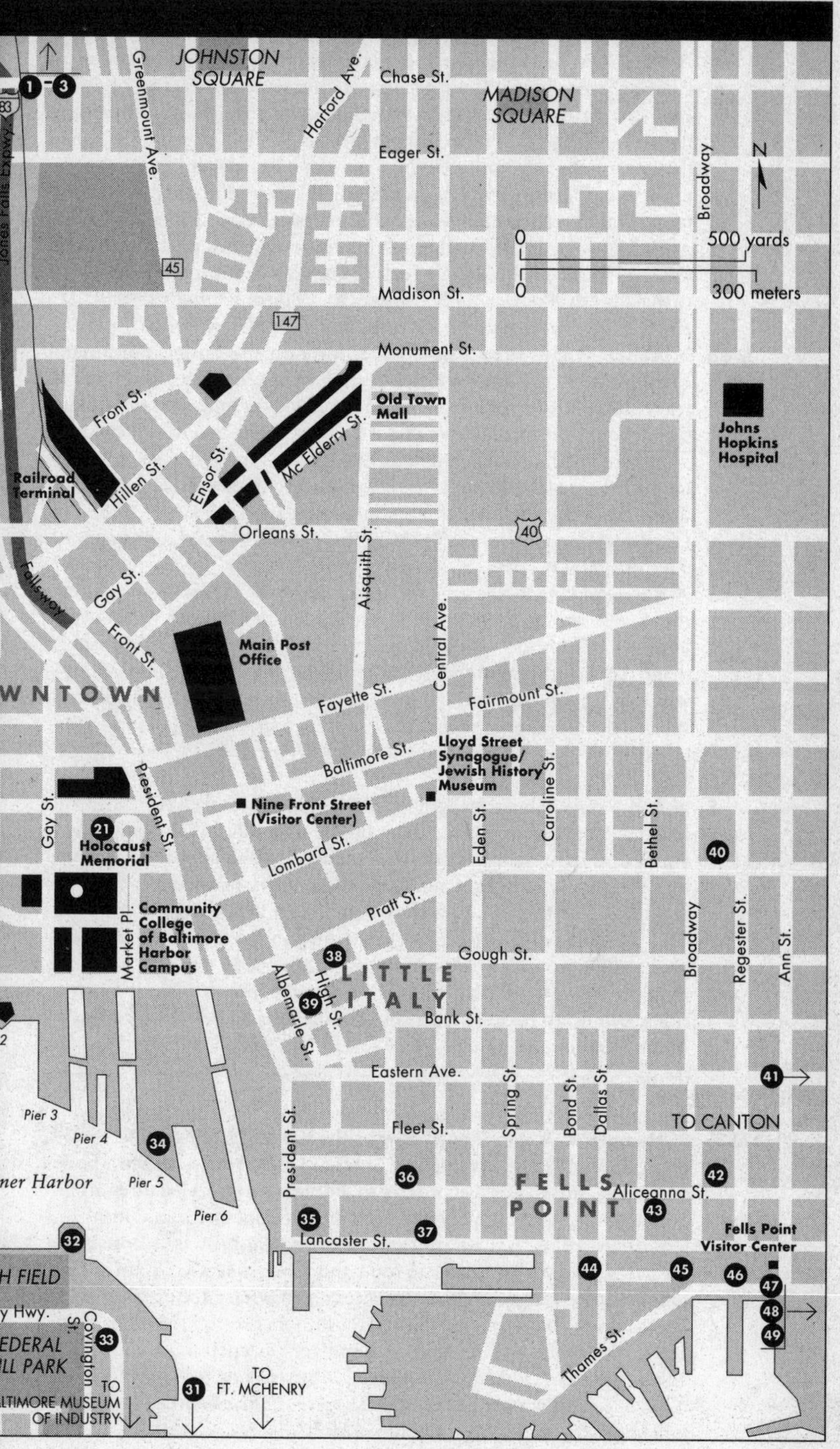
JOHNSTON SQUARE
MADISON SQUARE
Chase St.
Harford Ave.
Greenmount Ave.
Eager St.
Broadway
N
0
500 yards
0
300 meters
Jones Falls Expwy.
83
45
Madison St.
147
Monument St.
Front St.
Old Town Mall
Johns Hopkins Hospital
Mc Elderry St.
Ensor St.
Hillen St.
Railroad Terminal
Orleans St.
40
Aisquith St.
Fallsway
Gay St.
Front St.
Central Ave.
Main Post Office
WNTOWN
Fayette St.
Fairmount St.
Baltimore St.
Lloyd Street Synagogue/ Jewish History Museum
Caroline St.
President St.
Nine Front Street (Visitor Center)
Gay St.
Holocaust Memorial
Lombard St.
Eden St.
Bethel St.
Community College of Baltimore Harbor Campus
Market Pl.
Pratt St.
Gough St.
Broadway
Regester St.
Ann St.
LITTLE ITALY
Albemarle St.
High St.
Bank St.
Eastern Ave.
Pier 3
Pier 4
Pier 5
Pier 6
ner Harbor
President St.
Fleet St.
Spring St.
Bond St.
Dallas St.
TO CANTON
FELLS POINT
Aliceanna St.
Lancaster St.
Fells Point Visitor Center
H FIELD
y Hwy.
EDERAL LL PARK
Covington St.
TO ALTIMORE MUSEUM OF INDUSTRY
TO FT. MCHENRY
Thames St.
1
3
2
21
31
32
33
34
35
36
37
38
39
40
41
42
43
44
45
46
47
48
49

available. ✉ *10 E. Franklin St., Mount Vernon,* ☎ *410/539–4675. Reservations essential. Jacket and tie. AE, D, DC, MC, V.*

$$ ★ ✕ **The Brass Elephant.** The rooms of this grand antebellum house on Charles Street are filled with classical music and the chatter of diners (the Teak Room is the quietest, the Oak Room the noisiest). An atrium meant to suggest a Venetian café has moss painted on pink walls, and the rest of the interior, including the elephant sconces, is just as remarkable. The northern Italian menu includes traditional piccatas and marinaras as well as updated versions of Italian classics, such as homemade cannelloni filled with duck confit, woodland mushrooms, and ricotta. Upstairs, the softly lit Tusk Lounge is a comfortable, classy spot to meet for drinks. ✉ *924 N. Charles St., Mount Vernon,* ☎ *410/547–8480,* WEB *www.brasselephant.com. AE, DC, MC, V.*

$–$$ ✕ **Akbar.** A few steps below street level on the business-and-retail Charles Street corridor, this small restaurant is usually crowded and always filled with pungent aromas and the sounds of Indian music. Among the vegetarian dishes, *alu gobi masala,* a potato-and-cauliflower creation, is prepared with onions, tomatoes, and spices. Tandoori chicken is marinated in yogurt, herbs, and strong spices, then barbecued in a charcoal-fired clay oven. Try Akbar for an interesting Sunday brunch. ✉ *823 N. Charles St., Mount Vernon,* ☎ *410/539–0944,* WEB *www.akbar-restaurant.com. AE, D, DC, MC, V.*

$–$$ ✕ **Kawasaki.** Amid the art galleries and shops of North Charles Street, this lively dining room is good for a convivial dinner or weekday lunch. Cases on the wall hold the personal chopsticks of Kawasaki's many regulars. Menu standouts are sparkling fresh sushi and sashimi—without a doubt the best in town. Try one of the creative sushi rolls, such as the Number 5, with scallops, orange slices, and Japanese mayonnaise. ✉ *413 N. Charles St., Mount Vernon,* ☎ *410/659–7600. AE, DC, MC, V. Closed Sun.*

$ ✕ **Red Maple.** Theatrical, stylish Red Maple doesn't have a sign out front: a small red maple tree icon on the front door is the only way it announces its presence. Inside, the striking, minimalist space is warmed by a fireplace, candlelight, and sumptuous suede banquettes. The food is equally arresting: Asian-inspired tapas, artfully conceived and beautifully presented. Consider the tiny whole ginger-garlic baby vegetables, spilling from a faux "grocery sack" fashioned from a crisp wonton wrapper. The 16 different small plates are inexpensive, but it's easy to run up your tab because each is so compelling. ✉ *930 N. Charles St., Mount Vernon,* ☎ *410/547–0149. AE, DC, MC, V. No lunch.*

Inner Harbor

$$$$ ★ ✕ **Hamptons.** A panoramic view of the Inner Harbor competes with the restaurant's elegant interior: Sheraton-style tables, set with bowls of flowers, are spaced generously in a dining room styled after an English country house. Lauded by both the national media and local gastronomes alike, Baltimore's foremost restaurant is a consistent award-winner for its exquisite food and flawless service. Expect carefully composed seasonal cuisine at once contemporary and classic: roasted pheasant with butternut squash and mushroom risotto in Madeira demiglacé, for instance. The Sunday champagne brunch is a major draw. ✉ *Harbor Court Hotel, 550 Light St., Inner Harbor,* ☎ *410/347–9744,* WEB *www.harborcourt.com/restrnt. Reservations essential. Jacket and tie required. AE, D, MC, V. Closed Mon.*

$$–$$$$ ✕ **Babalu Grill.** High-spirited Babalu Grill is one of the most entertaining restaurants in town. From the prominent portrait of Desi Arnaz to the conga drum bar stools to the live salsa music on weekends, this place is about fun. The house cocktail, the *mojito,* is a rum, sugarcane, and mint drink sure to help you catch the Babalu spirit. Many of the classic Cuban dishes on the menu come from owner Steve DeCastro's family recipes, such as savory *ropa vieja* (a stew of shredded beef) and seafood paella, brimming with shrimp, shellfish, and chorizo. The bar serves an impressive array of obscure rums and tequilas, and the wine list focuses on South American and Spanish vintages. ✉ *32 Market Pl., Inner Harbor,* ☎ *410/234–9898,* WEB *www.serioussteaks.com/Babalu. AE, D, DC, MC, V.*

$$–$$$$ ✕ **Rusty Scupper.** A perennial tourist favorite, the Rusty Scupper undoubtedly has the best view along the waterfront; sunset here is magical, with the sun sinking slowly into the harbor as lights twinkle on in the city's skyscrapers. The interior is decorated with light wood and windows from floor to ceiling; the house specialty is seafood, particularly the jumbo lump crab cake, but the menu also offers beef, chicken, and pasta. Reservations are essential on Friday and Saturday. ✉ *402 Key Hwy., Inner Harbor,* ☎ *410/727–3678. AE, D, DC, MC, V.*

$$–$$$$ ✕ **Ruth's Chris Steak House.** One of Baltimore's best steak houses, Ruth's Chris is just a couple of blocks north of the Inner Harbor. The two-story dining room, decorated in dark florals with matching carpet and cushioned chairs and booths, is dominated by an intricate wood staircase that came from a local railroad museum. The menu is primarily custom-aged steaks cut by hand, broiled, and served sizzling on heated plates, with some seafood. Potatoes, salads, and vegetables are served à la carte. There is a free shuttle to and from area hotels. Reservations are essential for Friday and Saturday. ✉ *600 Water St., Inner Harbor,* ☎ *410/783–0033,* WEB *www.serioussteaks.com. Jacket and tie. AE, D, DC, MC, V. No lunch.*

$$–$$$ ✕ **McCormick & Schmick's.** McCormick & Schmick's is a chain restaurant, but a very good one. Their expansive Baltimore location at the end of Pier 5, on the east side of the busy waterfront, offers a terrific harbor view; ask to be seated on the waterfront patio. More than two dozen varieties of fish and seafood, available on a daily basis, are flown in from all over the world. The large menu changes daily, depending on what's best and freshest. Choose from the more than half-dozen choices of oysters available on the half shell, or go for the signature cedar-planked wild Oregon king salmon. ✉ *711 Eastern Ave., Inner Harbor,* ☎ *410/234–1300,* WEB *www.mccormickandschmicks.com. AE, D, MC, V.*

Federal Hill

$$–$$$ ✕ **The Bicycle.** A hip part of the city's restaurant scene, bright, energetic, and often noisy Bicycle offers intelligent, creative cuisine. Caribbean, Asian, and Southwestern flavors influence the brief but engaging menu, which is supplemented by specials that make use of the freshest seafood and local seasonal produce available each day. The wine list reflects the restaurant's fun, accessible attitude toward dining: there are 18 different bottles of wine available for $18 as well as a longer roster of well-chosen, variably priced vintages. Tables are close in this small bistro, but proximity enhances its vivaciousness. ✉ *1444 Light St., Federal Hill,* ☎ *410/234–1900,* WEB *www.bicyclebistro.com. Reservations essential. AE, D, MC, V. Closed Sun.–Mon. No lunch.*

$$–$$$ ★ ✕ **Joy America Cafe.** Baltimore's most creative kitchen overlooks the harbor from the offbeat American Visionary Art Museum, and the appropriately unconventional menu does the place justice. The food is inspired by the New World: South and Central America, Cuba, and the Caribbean all influence the kitchen. Exuberant flavors abound, such as the chile-spiced shrimp ceviche with lime and coconut milk. Sunday brunch fare includes interesting twists such as crab omelets and *huevos rancheros* (country-style fried eggs) with sweet potatoes. ✉ *American Visionary Art Museum, 800 Key Hwy., Federal Hill,* ☎ *410/244–6500. AE, DC, MC, V. Closed Mon.*

$$ ✕ **Soigné.** Polished yet relaxed, like a bit of New York's SoHo in South Baltimore, Soigné presents an Asian- and French-influenced fusion menu in attractively spare, comfortable surroundings. The creative menu attempts (and succeeds beautifully with) such ambitious dishes as seared foie gras with scallops, the combined richness of which is leavened with carmelized mango in a saki-spiked demi-glacé. The lemongrass sorbet, with pineapple-mint salsa and rose peppercorns, is one of the most fascinating (and delicious) desserts in town. ✉ *554 E. Fort Ave., Federal Hill,* ☎ *410/659–9898. Reservations essential. AE, D, MC, V. Closed Sun. No lunch.*

$–$$ ✕ **Blue Agave.** To create his authentic regional Mexican and American Southwestern dishes, chef and owner Michael Marx flies in chiles from New Mexico and spices and chocolate from Oaxaca. Every sauce and salsa is made daily to create pure, concentrated flavors—the traditional mole sauces in which the restaurant specializes are delicious. Dishes such as grilled quail served with both green and spicy yellow moles, or the more familiar chicken enchiladas with mole poblano, demonstrate the kitchen's command of this rich, complex concoction. More than 80 different kinds of tequila are available, and you won't find a finer margarita anywhere; try the deep purple version made from prickly-pear juice. ✉ *1032 Light St., Federal Hill,* ☎ *410/576–3938,* WEB *www.blueagaverestaurant.com. AE, D, MC, V. Closed Tues.–Wed. No lunch.*

Little Italy

$$–$$$ ✕ **Chiapparelli's.** At this neighborhood favorite, families come to celebrate milestones—baptisms, communions, graduations, and such. Pictures of the Baltimore landscape adorn the redbrick walls, and some white-clothed tables overlook one of Little Italy's main streets. The reasonably priced pasta selections rely on standards, but there's also more upscale fare such as chicken Giuseppe, breaded chicken breast with spinach, crabmeat, and provolone in a lemon wine sauce. There's an extensive selection of Italian red and white wines to accompany your meal. ✉ *237 S. High St., Little Italy,* ☎ *410/837–0309,* WEB *www.chiapparellis.com. AE, D, DC, MC, V.*

$$ ✕ **La Tavola.** Specializing in homemade, inventive pasta dishes, La Tavola is a cut above other Little Italy spaghetti houses. Owner Piero Conti pays careful attention to every facet of his restaurant, and it shows in the attractive surroundings, attentive service, and terrific food. Don't miss the *mafalde alla fiorentina,* wide pasta with spinach, ricotta, pine nuts, and raisins in a nutmeg-scented cream sauce. Veal cannelloni in béchamel tomato sauce is another standout on the consistently creative and excellent menu. If you're still hungry after one of La Tavola's generous plates of pasta, the fresh fish is a good bet, as is the roasted veal chop. ✉ *248 Albemarle St., Little Italy,* ☎ *410/685–1859,* WEB *www.la-tavola.com. AE, D, DC, MC, V.*

Fells Point

$$$–$$$$ ★ ✕ **The Black Olive.** One of the best Greek restaurants in the country, the Black Olive specializes in impeccably fresh seafood. Let the waiter give you a guided tour of the catch of the day, which reclines on a sparkling bed of ice in the kitchen case. Enjoy your selection simply grilled, lightly dressed, and filleted for you table-side, accompanied by a glass from the wine list's intelligent selection of oft-neglected Greek vintages. For an appetizer be sure to try the *kakavia,* a spicy Greek bouillabaisse served with irresistible bread warm from the brick oven. ✉

814 S. Bond St., at Shakespeare St., Fells Point, ☎ *410/276–7141,* WEB *www.theblackolive.com. Reservations essential. AE, D, MC, V. Closed Mon. No lunch.*

$$$ ★ ✕ **Charleston.** The kitchen here may have a South Carolina low-country accent, but it's also fluent in the fundamentals of French cooking. Inside the glowingly lit dining room, such classics as she-crab soup, crisp cornmeal-crusted oysters, and spoon bread mesh beautifully with more elegant fare, such as squab roasted with apples. Best bets are Southern-inspired dishes such as shrimp sautéed with andouille and Cajun ham served over creamy grits. The wine list offers more than 250 vintages, and the superb waitstaff provides attentive yet unobtrusive service. ✉ *1000 Lancaster St., Fells Point,* ☎ *410/332–7373,* WEB *www.charlestonrestaurant.com. Reservations essential. AE, D, MC, V. Closed Sun. No lunch.*

$$–$$$ ✕ **Hamilton's.** In the basement of an inn that's more than 200 years old, Hamilton's low-ceilinged dining room is as warm and inviting as the food is accomplished. The seasonally influenced "New American" board of fare changes frequently, but the focus is on local produce and regional Chesapeake seafood. Flavor is as important as presentation here, and the kitchen never loses its focus on quality. At the Sunday champagne brunch are stunning views from the inn's rooftop terrace and live chamber music. Complimentary valet parking is provided for Hamilton's patrons. ✉ *Admiral Fell Inn, 888 S. Broadway, Fells Point,* ☎ *410/522–2195. AE, DC, MC, V.*

$$–$$$ ✕ **Louisiana.** Fells Point's most elegant dining room has the feel of a spacious, opulent antebellum parlor. The menu mixes Creole and French with a touch of New American, and is accompanied by an expansive, thoughtful wine list. The lobster bisque, with a dollop of aged sherry added at the table by one of Louisiana's impeccable waiters, is sublime, and crawfish étouffée is a worthy follow-up course. ✉ *1708 Aliceanna St., Fells Point,* ☎ *410/327–2610. AE, DC, MC, V. No lunch.*

$$–$$$ ✕ **O'Brycki's Crab House.** For 50 years this has been Baltimore's crab house of choice; once you taste the steamed crabs you'll understand why. Beyond that, the seafood menu is standard and the food fair. Talk-show host Oprah Winfrey, once a Baltimore television personality, still orders crab cakes from here by mail. ✉ *1727 E. Pratt St., Fells Point,* ☎ *410/732–6399,* WEB *www.obryckis.com. AE, D, DC, MC, V. Closed mid-Dec.–early Mar.*

$–$$ ✕ **Acropolis.** East of Fells Point, Greektown (15 minutes by cab from Inner Harbor hotels) has ethnic restaurants that cost less than those in Little Italy. In this festive, informal restaurant, you'll find murals and music of Greece, and a clientele composed largely of families. Portions are generous, with rockfish and red snapper leading the fresh seafood menu. Try shrimp oregano—jumbo shrimp sautéed in white wine and served with a tomato-feta sauce over rice pilaf; or lamb Giouvetsi—baby lamb braised in olive oil and baked with orzo. ✉ *4718 Eastern Ave., Greektown,* ☎ *410/675–3384. AE, D, DC, MC, V.*

$ ✕ **Blue Moon Dining House.** A cozy café charmingly decorated in a celestial motif appropriate to its name, the Blue Moon is a favorite local spot for breakfast, served until 3 PM every day of the week. Start with one of the wonderful, enormous homemade cinnamon rolls, but save room for excellent brunch-quality fare such as crab Benedict and sky-high French toast topped with fruit compote. On Fridays and Saturdays the Moon reopens at 11 PM and stays open all night, attracting revelers from Fells Point's many clubs and bars. On weekend mornings there's often a line to get a table in this tiny café, but it's well worth the wait. ✉ *1621 Aliceanna St.,* ☎ *410/522–3940. No reservations accepted. AE, D, MC, V.*

Canton

$–$$$ ✕ **Bo Brooks.** Picking steamed crabs on Bo Brooks's waterfront deck with a pitcher of cold beer at hand as sailboats and tugs ply the harbor is a quintessential Baltimore pleasure. Brooks serves its famous crustaceans year-round, along with a menu of Chesapeake seafood classics. Locals know to stick to the Maryland crab soup, jumbo lump crab cakes, and fried oysters. ✉ *2701 Boston St., Canton,* ☎ *410/558–0202,* WEB *www.bobrooks.com. AE, D, MC, V.*

Baltimore North

$$–$$$$ ★ ✕ **Polo Grill.** Near the Johns Hopkins University campus, this is Baltimore's most prestigious see-and-be-seen dining room. Despite the highrollers at the next table and the masculine hunt club interior, it's still a warm and comfortable place for dinner. Hosts Lenny and Gail Kaplan—and the talented kitchen staff—live up to their formidable reputation with popular dishes such as the house specialty: fried lobster tail. There is an extensive wine list, with many vintages available by the glass, and the service is top-notch. ✉ *Doubletree Inn at the Colonnade, 4 W. University Pkwy., Charles Village,* ☎ *410/235–8200,* WEB *www.polo-grill.com. AE, D, DC, MC, V.*

$$–$$$ ✕ **McCafferty's.** Named for former Baltimore Colts coach Don McCafferty, this is a haven for fans of both pigskin and beef. The house specialty is aged prime beef, which receives unanimous raves. The menu also includes seafood and poultry. What really draws attention are the items on the restaurant walls: football helmets, signed baseballs, caricatures, and jerseys are all on display. From some tables, you can watch ESPN and Orioles games running concurrently on the bar's two TVs. ✉ *1501 Sulgrave Ave., Mount Washington,* ☎ *410/664–2200. AE, D, DC, MC, V. No lunch weekends.*

$–$$ ✕ **Loco Hombre.** This popular restaurant is packed for Sunday brunch, when the menu features such favorites as white-corn cakes with maple syrup, red banana–stuffed French toast, and burritos and enchiladas stuffed with eggs, breakfast meats, refried beans, and cheeses. Lunch and dinner bring spicy, imaginative versions of Southwestern classics, such as sautéed rock shrimp enchiladas or snapper with green chiles and goat cheese. Loco Hombre is often overlooked by visitors because of its distance from the Inner Harbor, but it's worth a visit. ✉ *413 W. Cold Spring La., Roland Park,* ☎ *410/889–2233,* WEB *www.locohombre.com. AE, D, DC, MC, V.*

LODGING

All hotels listed are within a short drive or a half hour's walk of the Inner Harbor. Fells Point is less than a mile from downtown Baltimore and the Inner Harbor—a commute that is especially enjoyable by water taxi. Lodging reservations must be made well in advance for Preakness weekend, the third weekend in May. Hunt Valley, an attractive rural suburb 30 minutes' drive north of Baltimore on Interstate 83, offers convenient budget options.

CATEGORY	COST*
$$$$	over $225
$$$	$150–$225
$$	$100–$150
$	under $100

**All prices are for a standard double room, excluding state (5% in Maryland) and Baltimore City tax (7.5%) for a total of 12.5% room tax.*

Mount Vernon

$$$$ **Peabody Court.** Built as a luxury apartment house in 1924, this 13-story hotel (renovated in 2002) faces the Washington Monument. The hotel retains its original distinguished lobby and other period touches such as marble bathrooms. Business travelers will be at home here, since rooms have desks and two-line speakerphones with data ports; a lobby business center has a fax machine, copier, and computer station. Rooms with park views are the best choice. A courtesy shuttle will ferry you to destinations within a 2-mi radius. The hotel bistro, George's on Mount Vernon Square, offers American and Italian cuisine. ✉ *612 Cathedral St., Mount Vernon, 21201,* ☎ *410/727–7101,* FAX *410/789–3312,* WEB *www.clarionhotel.com. 104 rooms. In-room data ports, gym, library, parking (fee). AE, D, DC, MC, V. CP.*

$$$ ★ **Tremont Hotel.** Built in the 1960s as an apartment house, the 13-story Tremont is now a European-style all-suites hotel that's elegant but still comfortable. The lobby and hotel restaurant, 8 East, are intimate and private—qualities attracting guests who might be easily recognized. The suites come in two sizes: both have a toaster oven and a coffeemaker (complete with freshly ground beans). The Tremont is strategically located near Mount Vernon's cultural attractions and restaurants, and the concierge will also help you arrange local transportation, which in most cases is free of charge. ✉ *8 E. Pleasant St., Downtown, 21202,* ☎ *410/576–1200 or 800/873–6668,* FAX *410/244–1154,* WEB *www.tremontsuitehotels.com. 60 suites. Restaurant, microwaves, kitchens, gym, bar, concierge, parking (fee). AE, D, DC, MC, V.*

$$$ ★ **Tremont Plaza Hotel.** This 37-story building, once an apartment building, is in the densest part of the business district. Its plain facade and minuscule brass-and-marble lobby belie the tasteful earth-tone guest rooms, which are a favorite of musicians and actors performing at local theaters. The suites come in six sizes. The best views, of the city and the small park in the center of St. Paul Place, are from rooms with numbers ending in 06. The restaurant, Tugs, has a nautical theme and a menu rich in seafood. ✉ *222 St. Paul Pl., Downtown, 21202,* ☎ *410/727–2222 or 800/873–6668,* FAX *410/685–4215,* WEB *www.tremontsuitehotels.com. 253 suites. Restaurant, kitchens, pool, gym, sauna, bar, parking (fee). AE, D, DC, MC, V.*

$$–$$$ **Mr. Mole Bed & Breakfast.** This elegant town house in an exclusive neighborhood just west of Mount Vernon gets its name from a character in the classic children's book *The Wind in the Willows.* Each of the six guest rooms is whimsically decorated, and comes with fresh flowers and a direct-dial phone with voice mail. Typically, the Dutch-style breakfast consists of fresh fruits, Amish cheeses and meats, homemade breads, and coffee cake. Mr. Mole is within walking distance of the Lyric Opera House, Myerhoff Symphony Hall, and Howard Street's Antique Row. ✉ *1601 Bolton St., Bolton Hill, 21217,* ☎ *410/728–1179,* FAX *410/728–3379,* WEB *www.mrmolebb.com. 6 rooms. Dining room, free parking; no kids under 10, no smoking. AE, D, DC, MC, V. CP.*

$–$$$ **Mount Vernon Hotel.** One of the city's unique lodgings, Mount Vernon Hotel is owned and operated by Baltimore International College, a school for culinary arts and hospitality training; the professional hotel staff is supplemented with student interns learning the hotel and restaurant business hands-on. The nine-story hotel, originally the city's YMCA, offers sunny, warm-hued rooms with traditional cherry furnishings. Ask for one of the extraordinary loft rooms, with split sleeping and living levels illuminated by one enormous window. The hotel is in the heart of the Mount Vernon cultural district, with the Inner Harbor eight blocks away. ✉ *24 W. Franklin St., Mount Vernon,*

21201, ☎ 410/727–2000 or 800/245–5256, FAX 410/576–9300, WEB www.bichotels.com/mtvernon. 134 rooms. Restaurant, gym, business services. AE, MC, V.

$$ **Biltmore Suites Hotel.** On a tree-lined side street, this small, tasteful hotel offers some of the quietest lodgings in Baltimore. Since 1880 the building has housed travelers in opulent Victorian decor. All rooms have coffeemakers. Nearby attractions include Meyerhoff Symphony Hall, the Lyric Opera House, the Walters Art Museum, and many restaurants. A nearby light-rail stop provides easy transportation to downtown and the Inner Harbor. ✉ *206 W. Madison St., Mount Vernon, 21201,* ☎ *410/728–6550,* FAX *410/728–5829,* WEB *www.biltmoresuites.com. 13 rooms, 12 suites. Some kitchenettes, refrigerators, meeting rooms, some pets allowed (fee). AE, D, DC, MC, V. CP.*

Inner Harbor

$$$$ ★ **Harbor Court.** The entrance to the most prestigious hotel in Baltimore is set back from the street by a brick courtyard that provides an immediate sense of tranquillity. A grand spiral staircase dominates the lobby, which is decorated in English country opulence. All guest rooms include such deluxe touches as twice-daily maid service, plush bathrobes, and televisions in the bathrooms; upscale suite amenities also include 6-ft marble tubs with separate shower, canopied four-poster beds, and CD players. Waterside rooms offer a commanding view of the harbor, but courtyard rooms are quietest. ✉ *550 Light St., Inner Harbor, 21202,* ☎ *410/234–0550 or 800/824–0076,* FAX *410/659–5925,* WEB *www.harborcourt.com. 195 rooms, 8 suites. 2 restaurants, tennis court, indoor pool, health club, sauna, racquetball, bar, library, concierge, parking (fee). AE, D, DC, MC, V.*

$$$$ **Hyatt Regency.** This stretch of Light Street is practically a highway, but the unenclosed skyways allow ready pedestrian access to both Inner Harbor attractions and the convention center. Rooms have rich gold and black-purple prints, cherrywood furniture, and marble in the bathrooms; most rooms have views of the harbor or the city. The lobby has glass elevators and the chain's trademark atrium. The 12th floor is the club level, with complimentary breakfast, evening hors d'oeuvres, and a private concierge available. Atop the hotel, Pisces restaurant and lounge provides stunning city views, especially at night. ✉ *300 Light St., Inner Harbor, 21202,* ☎ *410/528–1234 or 800/233–1234,* FAX *410/685–3362,* WEB *baltimore.hyatt.com. 486 rooms, 25 suites. 2 restaurants, 3 tennis courts, pool, gym, sauna, 2 bars, parking (fee). AE, D, DC, MC, V.*

$$$$ **Marriott Baltimore Waterfront.** The city's tallest hotel and the only one directly on the inner harbor itself, this upscale 32-story Marriott has an elegant, neoclassical interior that uses multihued marbles, rich jewel-tone walls, and interesting photographs of Baltimore architectural landmarks. Although it is at the eastern end of the Inner Harbor, all downtown attractions are within walking distance; there is also a water taxi stop right by the front door. Most rooms offer spectacular, unobstructed views of the city and harbor; ask for one that faces west toward downtown for a splendid panorama of the waterfront and skyscrapers. ✉ *700 Aliceanna St., Inner Harbor East, 21202,* ☎ *410/385–3000,* FAX *410/895–1900,* WEB *www.marriotthotels.com/BWIWF. 750 rooms. Restaurant, coffee shop, indoor pool, health club, lounge, business services, parking (fee). AE, D, DC, MC, V.*

$$$$ **Radisson Plaza Lord Baltimore.** Baltimore's historic landmark hotel, the Radisson extends its Jazz Age elegance to the guest rooms, which have been restored to their original style. Built in 1928, this 23-story hotel is distinguished by an elegantly gilded art deco lobby. Rooms on

the south side have the best view, and from the top three floors you can see the harbor. The hotel is quiet and comfortable, and the location is central, just three blocks from the Baltimore Convention Center or Harborplace. ✉ *20 W. Baltimore St., Downtown, 21202,* ☎ *410/539–8400,* FAX *410/625–1060,* WEB *www.radisson.com/lordbaltimore. 224 rooms, 20 suites. 2 restaurants, gym, sauna, bar, parking (fee). AE, D, DC, MC, V.*

$$$$ **Renaissance Harborplace Hotel.** The most conveniently located of the Inner Harbor hotels—across the street from the shopping pavilions, where the harbor-based Baltimore renaissance began—the Renaissance Harborplace meets the needs of tourists, business travelers, and conventioneers alike. The guest rooms are light and cheerful with amenities that include coffeemakers, terry-cloth robes, hair dryers, and ironing boards. Most rooms have a view of the harbor or an indoor courtyard. The staff here is attentive and cordial. The hotel adjoins The Gallery, a four-story shopping mall. ✉ *202 E. Pratt St., Inner Harbor, 21202,* ☎ *410/547–1200 or 800/468–3571,* FAX *410/539–5780,* WEB *www.renaissancehotels.com/BWISH. 622 rooms, 60 suites. Restaurant, indoor pool, gym, sauna, bar, parking (fee). AE, D, DC, MC, V.*

$$$–$$$$ **Courtyard by Marriott Baltimore Inner Harbor.** One block from the Inner Harbor waterfront and adjacent to Little Italy, this lodging is the farthest east of the Inner Harbor hotels. Built in 2000 with sunny rooms decorated in soothing neutral tones, the Courtyard Inner Harbor is a comfortable and attractive alternative to more central hotels with similar amenities and higher rates. Most downtown attractions are still within walking distance, though the stadiums and convention center are more comfortably reached by car or cab. Many dining and nightlife options are nearby. ✉ *1000 Aliceanna St., Inner Harbor East, 21202,* ☎ *443/923–4000,* FAX *443/923–9970,* WEB *www.courtyard.com/BWIDT. 205 rooms. Restaurant, in-room data ports, pool, gym, business services, parking (fee). AE, D, DC, MC, V.*

$$$–$$$$ **Inner Harbor Marriott.** This centrally located 10-story hotel is a block away from Oriole Park at Camden Yards, Harborplace, and the convention center. The public areas are nondescript but surprisingly tranquil, as are the pastel-hue rooms decorated in teal, mauve, and gray. The best views are from those rooms that face the Inner Harbor and the ballpark. Those staying on the 10th floor enjoy concierge-level privileges. ✉ *Pratt and Eutaw Sts., Inner Harbor, 21201,* ☎ *410/962–0202 or 800/228–9290,* FAX *410/625–7832,* WEB *www.marriotthotels.com/BWIIH. 524 rooms, 34 suites. Restaurant, in-room data ports, indoor pool, gym, sauna, bar, parking (fee). AE, D, DC, MC, V.*

$$$–$$$$ **Wyndham Inner Harbor.** One of Baltimore's largest, this hotel (four blocks from the harbor) divides its rooms between two towers and also houses the largest ballroom in the city, which makes it especially popular with conventioneers. Rooms, decorated in light colors, have a contemporary flair and marble-floor bathrooms. Amenities include in-room voice mail, modem jacks, hair dryers, and ironing boards. The hotel restaurant is Don Shula's Steak House, where the menu is presented on an official NFL football autographed by Shula, a former coach for the Baltimore Colts. ✉ *101 W. Fayette St., Downtown, 21201,* ☎ *410/752–1100,* FAX *410/752–0832,* WEB *www.wyndham.com/BaltimoreInnerHarbor. 707 rooms, 21 suites. 2 restaurants, in-room data ports, pool, gym, bar, parking (fee). AE, D, DC, MC, V.*

$$–$$$ **Days Inn Inner Harbor.** Less than three blocks from the Inner Harbor, this nine-story redbrick building provides reliable and relatively economical accommodations in the center of town. The utilitarian, pastel-hue guest rooms are sparsely furnished, but each has a small desk and phone with voice mail and data port. Rooms on the west side have

views of the stadium. ✉ *100 Hopkins Pl., 21201,* ☎ *410/576–1000,* FAX *410/576–9437,* WEB *www.daysinnerharbor.com. 250 rooms, 8 suites. Restaurant, refrigerators, pool, bar. AE, D, DC, MC, V.*

Fells Point

$$$–$$$$ **The Admiral Fell Inn.** This elegant inn is an upright anchor at the center of action in funky Fells Point. No place is more convenient to this port city's nightlife, and none better evokes its past. By cleverly joining together buildings constructed between the late 1770s and the 1920s, the owners created a structure that resembles a small, European-style hotel. The rooms, which vary in shape, all have four-poster canopy beds. Three suites and eight rooms have whirlpool baths. Some hallways have a few stairs, and some rooms face a quiet, interior courtyard: if steps or street noise are a hindrance to your comfort, let the reservation agent know. ✉ *888 S. Broadway, Fells Point, 21231,* ☎ *410/522–7377 or 800/292–4667,* FAX *410/522–0707,* WEB *www.admiralfell.com. 80 rooms. 2 restaurants, in-room data ports, bar, meeting rooms, free parking. AE, DC, MC, V. CP.*

$$$–$$$$ **Inn at Henderson's Wharf.** Built in the mid-1800s as a B&O Railroad tobacco warehouse, this richly decorated, warmly inviting B&B–style inn has harbor or garden views from all of its rooms. The inn is at the water's edge, on the very peninsula that gave Fells Point its name. Adjacent to the inn is a marina with slips to 150 ft; all possible amenities are available to visiting yachtsmen. Baltimore's best nightlife is also nearby. ✉ *1000 Fell St., Fells Point, 21231,* ☎ *410/522–7777 or 800/522–2088,* FAX *410/522–7087,* WEB *www.hendersonswharf.com. 38 rooms. Gym, concierge, meeting rooms, free parking; no smoking. AE, DC, MC, V. CP.*

$$–$$$$ **Celie's Waterfront Bed & Breakfast.** Proprietor Celie Ives oversees every detail of this small inn, which is right on the waterfront. The sunny guest rooms, all with private bath, are tastefully decorated with antiques and fresh flowers, and no two are alike. Upscale amenities include down comforters, terry bathrobes, fireplaces, and whirlpool baths. The B&B surrounds a flower-filled private courtyard, and a rooftop deck provides a wonderful view of Baltimore's skyline and harbor. The hearty Continental breakfast, which includes home-baked bread, is served in your room, in the garden, on the roof, or by a crackling fire in the dining room. ✉ *1714 Thames St., Fells Point, 21231,* ☎ *410/522–2323 or 800/432–0184,* FAX *410/522–2324,* WEB *www.celieswaterfront.com. 7 rooms. Dining room, free parking. AE, D, MC, V. CP.*

Canton

$$$ **Inn at 2920.** In the heart of one of the city's trendiest neighborhoods, this stylish B&B is dedicated to tranquil, luxurious living. Low-allergen surroundings (natural fiber carpeting, low-chemical cleaning products, purified air) and high thread-count sheets are standard amenities, and each room has a Jacuzzi bathtub, satellite television with VCR, and CD player. Business travelers receive complimentary cell phones and wireless Internet access during their stay. Full-course breakfasts generally include fresh fruit salad, omelets, and waffles or pancakes. ✉ *2920 Elliott St., 21224,* ☎ *410/342–4450,* FAX *410/342–6436,* WEB *www.theinnat2920.com. 4 rooms. Cable TV with movies, hot tub, free parking; no smoking. AE, MC, V. BP.*

North Baltimore

$$–$$$$ **Doubletree Inn at the Colonnade.** Directly across the street from Johns Hopkins and within walking distance of the Baltimore Museum of Art, this hotel is also just 10 minutes north of downtown. Rooms are

welcoming, with rich, warm furnishings, and there are extras such as a glass-dome swimming pool, whirlpools, and free transportation to center-city destinations. The hotel restaurant, the Polo Grill, is one of the best in town. ✉ *4 W. University Pkwy., Charles Village, 21218,* ☎ *410/235–5400,* FAX *410/235–5572,* WEB *www.doubletree.com. 106 rooms, 19 suites. Restaurant, in-room data ports, indoor pool, gym, hot tub, lobby lounge, business services, meeting rooms, parking (fee). AE, D, DC, MC, V.*

$$ **Courtyard by Marriott Hunt Valley.** About 30 minutes from downtown, in an affluent suburb that is a growing corporate center, this motel is comfortable and affordable. The simple guest rooms are as standardized as Courtyard's signature white-stucco exterior; coffeemakers, ironing boards, and hair dryers are added conveniences. The neighbors are office buildings, which means that all rooms enjoy quiet nights but uninteresting views. The nearby York and Shawan road corridors offer diverse dining options, and there's public transportation to downtown via the light-rail Hunt Valley stop. ✉ *221 International Circle, Hunt Valley, 21030,* ☎ *410/584–7070,* FAX *410/584–8151,* WEB *www.marriotthotels.com/BWIHU. 146 rooms, 12 suites. Restaurant, in-room data ports, indoor pool, gym, hot tub, bar, free parking. AE, D, DC, MC, V.*

$–$$ **Hampton Inn Hunt Valley.** Guest rooms at this suburban hotel are brightly decorated with basic furnishings. The property is within walking distance to a light-rail station for transportation to downtown Baltimore; the city is an easy 25-minute drive directly down I–83. Although there is no restaurant in the hotel, a free breakfast bar is available every morning, and many restaurants are nearby. ✉ *11200 York Rd., Hunt Valley, 21031,* ☎ *410/527–1500,* FAX *410/771–0819,* WEB *www.hamptoninn.com. 120 rooms. In-room data ports, refrigerators, free parking. AE, D, DC, MC, V. CP.*

$–$$ **Quality Inn at the Carlyle.** Surrounded by parks and tree-lined streets, this basic, comfortable lodging is adjacent to the Johns Hopkins University Homewood campus. The secure high-rise building combines hotel, apartments, and retail businesses. Nearby attractions include the Baltimore Zoo and Baltimore Museum of Art; downtown and the Inner Harbor are 10 minutes away. ✉ *500 W. University Pkwy., Charles Village, 21210,* ☎ *410/889–4500,* FAX *410/467–3073,* WEB *www.qualityinn.com. 38 rooms, 42 suites. Restaurant, pool, gym, hair salon, sauna, parking (fee). AE, D, DC, MC, V.*

NIGHTLIFE AND THE ARTS

The most comprehensive and complete calendar for Baltimore events appears in the *City Paper* (www.citypaper.com), a free weekly distributed in shops and yellow street-corner machines; it's published every Wednesday. Other event listings appear in the "Maryland Live" Thursday supplement to the *Baltimore Sun* and the monthly *Baltimore* magazine.

Fells Point, just east of the Inner Harbor, is the center of Baltimore's nightlife; the waterfront neighborhood's scores of bars, restaurants, and clubs attract a rowdy, largely collegiate, crowd. Those seeking quieter surroundings tend to head for the upscale comforts of downtown or Mount Vernon clubs and watering holes.

Bars and Lounges

The Brewer's Art (✉ 1106 N. Charles St., Mount Vernon, ☎ 410/547–6925, WEB www.belgianbeer.com) is one of the hippest spots in Baltimore. Upstairs there's an elegant bar and lounge with armchairs, marble pillars, and chandeliers, plus a gracious dining room with terrific food. Dark and cavelike, the basement bar specializes in Belgian-style beers. Six blocks north of The Brewer's Art, at the funkier (and slightly seedier) **Club Charles** (✉ 1724 N. Charles St., Mount Vernon, ☎ 410/727–8815), Maryland Institute College of Art students hang out in stylized art deco surroundings and wait for local underground cinema director John Waters to appear here (it's his favorite watering hole). The **Hippopotamus** (✉ 1 W. Eager St., Mount Vernon, ☎ 410/547–0069, WEB www.clubhippo.com) is Baltimore's longest-reigning, and by far most popular, gay bar. A comfortable saloon-style front bar offers drinks, pool tables, and a relative lack of noise, and the cavernous dance club pulses with a high-energy crowd. The city's hottest nightspot is **Redwood Trust** (✉ 202 E. Redwood St., Downtown, ☎ 410/659–9500, WEB www.trustbaltimore.com). What was once a bank building has been renovated into a dazzling dance club with three floors, numerous bars, and a VIP mezzanine level. Gilded columns, velvet sofas, and theatrical lighting create a glamorous space enhanced by a state-of-the-art sound system and 38-ft floating circular dance floor.

Since the 1970s the funky, friendly **Cat's Eye Pub** (✉ 1730 Thames St., Fells Point, ☎ 410/276–9866, WEB www.catseyepub.com) has been Fells Point's main destination for live music. Every night brings a different band playing anything from blues to zydeco to jazz to Irish folk on the tiny stage. There are more than 40 different beers on tap. The **Horse You Came In On** (✉ 1626 Thames St., Fells Point, ☎ 410/327–8111) is a neighborhood tradition. A dim, quiet neighborhood tavern during the week, "The Horse" explodes into packed, raucous life on the weekends as young professionals meet and greet, listen to live music, and drink vast numbers of pints. Happy hour runs until 9 PM during the week.

8x10 (✉ 8 E. Cross St., Federal Hill, ☎ 410/625–2000, WEB www.the8by10.com) emphasizes the blues, but rock, alternative rock, and occasional jazz can also be heard here. Monday is open mike night, bringing local talent and $1 drafts. At **Bayou Blues Cafe** (✉ 1636 Thames St., Fells Point, ☎ 410/342–3220) live blues bands play Thursday through Sunday nights, and a Cajun food menu accompanies the music.

At **DSX** (✉ 200 W. Pratt St., Downtown, ☎ 410/659–5844), sports fans banter about trivia, dispute scores, and commiserate over scandals. This is a favorite postgame hangout for Orioles and Ravens fans. The **ESPN Zone** (✉ 601 E. Pratt St., Inner Harbor, ☎ 410/685–3776, WEB espn.go.com/espninc/zone/baltimore.html) brings every conceivable sport to its scores of television screens, but the true attraction is the arcade, where fans can indulge in virtual versions of rock climbing, bass fishing, and motorcycle racing as well as team sports such as baseball and football.

Comedy Clubs

The Comedy Factory (✉ 36 Light St., Downtown, ☎ 410/752–4189) is one of the best local spots. Part of the national comedy outlet chain, **The Baltimore Improv** (✉ 6 Market Pl., Inner Harbor, ☎ 410/727–8500, WEB www.symfonee.com/Improv/Baltimore) brings up-and-coming national acts to its stage.

Music

Meyerhoff Symphony Hall (✉ 1212 Cathedral St., Mount Vernon, ☎ 410/783–8000, WEB www.baltimoresymphony.org) is the city's principal concert hall. It's the home of the Baltimore Symphony Orchestra, led by maestro Yuri Temirkanov. The outdoor **Pier Six Concert Pavilion** (✉ Pier 6 at Pratt St., Inner Harbor, ☎ 410/752–8632, WEB www.bop.org/calendar/events/pier6.html) offers both pavilion and lawn seating for concerts showcasing top national musicians and groups. Concerts are held from June to September.

Theater

Center Stage (✉ 700 N. Calvert St., Mount Vernon, ☎ 410/332–0033), the state theater of Maryland, performs works by Shakespeare and Samuel Beckett as well as contemporary playwrights. The intimate **Fells Point Corner Theater** (✉ 251 S. Ann St., Fells Point, ☎ 410/276–7837), an 85-seat venue dedicated to acting and directing workshops, stages eight off-Broadway productions a year, along with readings and poetry slams. **Lyric Opera House** (✉ 140 W. Mt. Royal Ave., Mount Vernon, ☎ 410/685–5086) hosts plays and musicals in addition to opera productions.

OUTDOOR ACTIVITIES AND SPORTS

Participant Sports

Bicycling

Baltimore lacks any kind of defined network of bicycling paths; those wanting to explore the region on two wheels will need to ride on the city streets (a frequently hazardous experience) or head out of town to dedicated cycling trails.

Baltimore and Annapolis Trail (✉ Rte. 50 in Arnold to Dorsey Rd., BWI Airport, ☎ 410/222–6244) includes 13 mi of paved trails, open space, bridges, and woodlands. Shops along the trail have bikes to rent. You can pick up the trail near BWI airport, just outside the city; call for directions. The 21-mi **Northern Central Railroad Hike and Bike Trail** (☎ 410/592–2897, WEB www.dnr.state.md.us/publiclands/central/gunpowder.html) extends along the old Northern Central Railroad to the Maryland-Pennsylvania line, beginning at Ashland Road, just east of York Road in Hunt Valley, and heading north 20 mi to the Pennsylvania border. Parking is available at seven points along the way. It was on this line that President Lincoln rode to deliver the Gettysburg Address and on which—after his assassination—his body was carried to Gettysburg and on to Illinois, his home state. For more information and a map, contact Gunpowder Falls State Park.

Fishing

The **Fishin' Shop** (✉ 9026C Pulaski Hwy., East Baltimore, ☎ 410/391–0101) is a bait-and-tackle shop that can advise on local fishing holes. **Tochterman's** (✉ 1925 Eastern Ave., Fells Point, ☎ 410/327–6942), a large tackle shop, also provides personal guides for fly-fishing and other fishing on the Chesapeake Bay and its tributaries.

Water Sports

Directly north of the city, **Loch Raven Reservoir** (✉ 12101 Dulaney Valley Rd., Loch Raven, ☎ 410/887–7692) is more than just Baltimore's reserve drinking water. This lovely lake is open for fishing, canoeing, and the use of boats with electric motors, with rentals available daily 7 AM–6 PM from April to December. **Springriver Corp.** (✉ 6434 Baltimore National Pike, Ellicott City, ☎ 410/788–3377) rents rafts, canoes, and sea and white-water kayaks for day use on bay tributaries and lakes in the region. The enthusiastic staff will recommend destinations and help draw up plans for your outing.

Spectator Sports

Baseball

The **Baltimore Orioles** (✉ Oriole Park at Camden Yards 333 W. Camden St., Downtown, ☎ 410/685–9800 general information; 410/481–7328 for tickets, WEB www.theorioles.com), sometime contenders in the American League East division, play in their beautiful ballpark from early April until early October. Think twice about settling on a hot dog and Budweiser for your meal: the stadium also sells lump-meat crab cakes, former Orioles first baseman Boog Powell's barbecued pork loin and beef, and local microbrews.

Football

Professional football returned to Baltimore in 1996, when Cleveland Browns owner Art Modell moved his team here. Rechristened the **Baltimore Ravens** (✉ 1101 Russell St., Downtown, ☎ 410/261–7283, WEB www.ravenszone.net) the team plays in a state-of-the-art stadium from August to January.

Horse Racing

On the third Saturday in May the prestigious Preakness Stakes, part of racing's Triple Crown, is run at Baltimore's **Pimlico Race Course** (✉ Hayward and Winner Aves., West Baltimore, ☎ 410/542–9400, WEB www.marylandracing.com). The course has additional Thoroughbred racing from April through June. Race days are Wednesday through Sunday, and full card simulcasting is open Tuesday through Sunday year-round.

SHOPPING

Shopping Districts and Malls

The Pratt Street and Light Street pavilions of **Harborplace and The Gallery** (☎ 410/332–4191) contain almost 200 specialty shops that sell everything from business attire to children's toys. The eateries include national restaurant chains, one-of-a-kind pushcart vendors, and fancy sit-down restaurants.

Heading up **Charles Street** from downtown north through the upper reaches of Mount Vernon, you'll come across many unique and interesting boutiques, shops, and arts and crafts galleries.

The up-and-coming neighborhood of **Hampden** (the "p" is silent), northwest of Johns Hopkins University, holds funky, engaging shops selling everything from housewares to housedresses along its main drag, 36th Street. A small nexus of antiques shops, art galleries, and cafés are turning this area into one of the city's most interesting retail corridors. (Hampden will appeal to John Waters fans, because it was the setting for his 1998 film *Pecker.*)

Owings Mills Town Center (✉ Owings Mills exit from I–795, Owings Mills, 20 min northwest of the Inner Harbor, ☎ 410/363–1234, WEB www.owingsmillsmall.com) has Macy's and Hecht's department stores; specialty clothing stores; and shoe, toy, and bookstores as well as a multiplex cinema with stadium seating. Both fast-food and formal restaurants are among the numerous eating options. The mall is at the northern terminus of the region's subway/metro system. **Towson Town Center** (✉ Dulaney Valley Rd. and Fairmount Ave., ½ mi south of I–695 at Exit 27A, Towson, ☎ 410/494–8800, WEB www.towsontowncenter.com) is one of the mid-Atlantic's largest malls, with nearly 200 specialty shops spread over a million square feet. Hecht's and Nordstrom are the center's anchor department stores. **Village of Cross Keys** (✉ 5100 Falls Rd., North Baltimore, ☎ 410/323–1000), about 6 mi from downtown off I–83, is an eclectic collection of 30 boutiques and stores: women's, men's, and children's clothing shops, a flower shop, bookstore, and restaurants are all here. The attractive, open-air court is the site for occasional outdoor spring and summer concerts and promotional events.

Department Stores

At **Hecht's,** merchandise includes men's, women's, and children's clothing along with housewares, furniture, and the best gift departments in town. There are five locations around Baltimore, including ones in Owings Mills Town Center and Towson Town Center.

You can shop for top-name designer goods accompanied by courteous, service-oriented sales staff and live music from a grand piano in **Nordstrom** (✉ Towson Town Center, 825 Dulaney Valley Rd., Towson, ☎ 410/494–9111).

Food Markets

All year long, indoor food markets, all of which are at least 100 years old, accommodate vendors of fresh flowers, fish, meat, and produce. Lexington Market is the largest and most famous, and Broadway and Cross Street markets are close behind in terms of fresh, local, taste-tempting foods. City markets are open Monday–Saturday 8:30–6.

Broadway Market (✉ Broadway and Fleet St., Fells Point) has many stalls with fresh fruit, prepared foods, a raw bar, and baked goods that can be eaten at counters or taken outside for picnics along the waterfront. **Cross Street Market** (✉ Light and Cross Sts., Federal Hill) has a terrific sushi bar along with produce, sandwich, and bakery stands. Cross Street is open late on Fridays and Saturdays when the market hosts one of the city's most popular happy hour scenes, attracting crowds of youngish professionals. The city's oldest and largest public market, **Lexington Market** (✉ Lexington St. between Paca and Eutaw Sts., Downtown, ☎ 410/685–6169, WEB www.lexingtonmarket.com) has more than 150 vendors selling fresh meat, produce, seafood, baked goods, delicatessen items, poultry, and food products from around the world. Don't miss the world-famous crab cakes at Faidley's Seafood; other local specialties with market stalls are Rheb's chocolates, Polock Johnny's Polish sausages, and the decadent chocolate-iced vanilla wafer cookies at Berger's Bakery.

Specialty Stores

Antiques

Most of Baltimore's antiques shops can be found on historic Antique Row, which runs along the 700 and 800 blocks of North Howard Street and has 40 shops representing more than 70 dealers. Shops include cluttered kitsch boutiques as well as elegant, high-end galleries of furniture and fine art. Fells Point shops, which mostly carry antique accessories and knickknacks, are concentrated on Eastern, Fleet, and Aliceanna streets. The second and fourth Sunday of the month, a flea market takes place on Broadway, across from Fells Point's waterfront.

In Federal Hill, **Gaines McHale Antiques and Home** (✉ 836 Leadenhall St., Federal Hill, ☎ 410/625–1900, WEB www.gainesmchale.com) brings new meaning to the word "recycling." Owners Jean and Mike McHale build new pieces with old wood, turning antique armoires, for example, into entertainment centers, wet bars, computer desks, and other furniture that fulfills contemporary needs. There is also a large selection of unaltered, high-quality country and traditional antiques from England and France.

Books

Atomic Books (✉ 1100 W. 36th St., Hampden, ☎ 410/662–4444, WEB www.atomicbooks.com) sells "literary finds for mutated minds"—in other words, head to this fun, colorful shop for obscure titles and small-press publications, including independent comics and 'zines, along with videos. There is also a formidable selection of pop-culture toys such as lunch boxes, cookie jars, and stickers. Those who like Atomic Books really, really like it. **Barnes & Noble** (✉ 601 E. Pratt St., Inner Harbor, ☎ 410/385–1709), in the Power Plant complex at the Inner Harbor, is the city's largest general-interest bookseller.

Baltimore has some very good locally owned specialty bookstores. **Mystery Loves Company** (✉ 1730 Fleet St., Fells Point, ☎ 410/276–6708, WEB www.mysterylovescompany.com) specializes in books and gifts for whodunit fans; the shop stocks an excellent selection of works by Baltimore native son (and inventor of the genre) Edgar Allan Poe. **The Children's Bookstore** (✉ 737 Deepdene Rd., ☎ 410/532–2000) is a cozy, well-stocked resource for current and classic children's literature that will delight readers of all ages.

The **Kelmscott Bookshop** (✉ 32 W. 25th St., Charles Village, ☎ 410/235–6810, WEB www.kelmscottbookshop.com) is known for its enormous, well-preserved stock of old and rare volumes in every major category, especially art, architecture, American and English literature, and travel. The books are clearly organized in 12 rooms on two floors of two converted town houses. The shop also provides a diligent search service for out-of-print titles.

Gifts

A can of Old Bay seasoning, the spice mix locals use for steaming crabs and shrimp, makes a practical and tasty souvenir. If you don't get a chance to buy a can from a local grocery store, there are several **Celebrate Maryland** shops in Baltimore-Washington International Airport (one on each pier) that sell Old Bay and other Maryland products. **Celebrate Baltimore** (✉ 301 S. Light St., ☎ 410/752–3838) carries unique, high-quality city-related souvenirs and local specialty products. For unique, truly local mementos of Baltimore, **Hometown Girl** (✉ 1001 W. 36th St., Hampden, ☎ 410/662–4438, WEB www.celebratebaltimore.com) is the place to go. Take home with you the city's quirkier local traditions with a screen painting how-to video, a kit for cleaning rowhouse marble steps, and crab-shaped twinkle lights. The shop also stocks local history books and Baltimore guidebooks.

The **Tomlinson Craft Collection** (✉ The Rotunda, 711 W. 40th St., Hampden, ☎ 410/338–1572) in Roland Park is a gallery of local artisan handiworks with a wonderful selection of functional and decorative gifts. There is an especially good collection of jewelry, from elegant to funky; blown glass from nationally recognized artists; and ceramics, textiles, and metalwork. The **Store Ltd.** (✉ Village of Cross Keys, North Baltimore, ☎ 410/323–2350) is actually a retail museum of top-quality (and pricey) collections, including handcrafted jewelry designs by local artist Betty Cook, perpetual calendars, stationery, and women's sportswear. You'll also find kitchen gadgets, coffee-table books, hats, whimsical lawn items, and lifelike stuffed animals.

Jewelry

Amaryllis (✉ 200 E. Pratt St., ☎ 410/576–7622) specializes in incredibly feminine handcrafted jewelry from more than 400 artists; the store also has a marvelous selection of antique and vintage jewelry, plus luxurious women's accessories. **Beadazzled** (✉ 501 N. Charles St., Mount Vernon, ☎ 410/837–2323, WEB www.beadazzled.net) carries contemporary and vintage jewelry. Designers come from all over the world for the incredibly wide selection of beads; select from the striking necklaces, bracelets, and earrings on hand, or let the talented staff help you design your own creation. **Marley Gallery of Contemporary**

Jewelry, Inc. (✉ Festival at Woodholme Gallery, 1809 Reisterstown Rd., Pikesville, ☎ 410/486–6686) sells fine designer jewelry from leading contemporary artists, and original designs by Marley Simon. All work is done in-house.

Men's Clothing

Jos. A. Bank's Clothiers (✉ 100 E. Pratt St., Inner Harbor, ☎ 410/547–1700) is a century-old Baltimore source for men's tailored clothing and casual wear.

Women's Clothing

Several shops within the Village of Cross Keys shopping court carry women's clothing on par in both style and price with that of New York's 5th Avenue boutiques. Try **Jones and Jones** (☎ 410/532–9645) for stylish business and casual wear. **Ruth Shaw** (☎ 410/532–7886) carries cruise wear, evening attire, and casual clothing.

The **White House, Inc.** (✉ Pavilion at Harborplace, 201 E. Pratt St., Inner Harbor, ☎ 410/659–0283; ✉ Owings Mills Town Center, Owings Mills, ☎ 410/363–0036) boutiques carry white (and some cream and light silver) clothing, lingerie, and accessories for women, as well as pearl and crystal jewelry and other gift items. The adjacent Black Market companion stores work the same theme.

Hampden's eclectic, arty attitude comes through in the charming boutique **Oh! Said Rose** (✉ 840 W. 36th St., Hampden, ☎ 410/235–5170). The small shop is crowded with flowing feminine clothing, unusual imported perfumes, irresistible trinkets, and one-of-kind items such as beaded wire hair accessories.

SIDE TRIPS FROM BALTIMORE

Not far from Baltimore, Maryland's landscape is dotted with well-preserved 18th- and 19th-century towns. In Harford County, Havre de Grace, at the top of the bay, and nearby Aberdeen, with its legacy of military history, make for an ideal day trip.

Havre de Grace

40 mi northeast of Baltimore (via I–95).

On the site of one of Maryland's oldest settlements is the neatly laid-out town Havre de Grace, reputedly named by the Marquis de Lafayette. Because this "harbor of mercy" on the Chesapeake Bay at the mouth of the Susquehanna River was shelled and torched by the British in the War of 1812, few structures predate that period.

Havre de Grace is about a 40-minute drive from downtown Baltimore. From downtown, take I–395 to I–95; pick up I–95 north to New York and follow it to Harford County and Havre de Grace. Route 155 off Exit 89 leads to downtown Havre de Grace.

One of the few 18th-century structures in Havre de Grace—and the town's most historically significant building—is the **Rodgers House** (✉ 226 N. Washington St.), a two-story redbrick Georgian town house topped by a dormered attic. This was the home of Admiral John Rodgers, who fired the first shot in the War of 1812; like most of the other historic houses of Havre de Grace, it is closed to the public but still worth a drive past.

The **Havre de Grace Decoy Museum,** housed in a converted power plant, has 1,200 facsimiles of ducks, geese, and swans made from wood, iron, cork, papier-mâché, and plastic. Three classes—decorative, decorative floater, and working decoys—are represented. A permanent exhibit of six human figures portrays 20th-century carvers, including the prolific R. Madison Mitchell, and a recorded narration covers the lore of the craft. On weekends, decoy carvers demonstrate their art in the museum basement. A festival during the first full weekend in May includes carving contests and demonstrations by retrievers. ✉ *Giles and Market Sts.,* ☎ *410/939–3739,* WEB *www.decoymuseum.com.* 🎫 *$4.* ⏲ *Daily 11–4.*

The **Susquehanna Museum,** at the southern terminal of the defunct Susquehanna and Tidewater Canal, tells the history of the canal and the people who lived and worked there. From 1839 until 1890 the canal ran 45 mi north to Wrightsville, Pennsylvania. It was a thoroughfare for mule-drawn barges loaded with iron ore, coal, and crops. The museum, in a lock tender's cottage built in 1840, is partially furnished with modest midcentury antiques that recall its period of service. Outdoors, a pivot bridge across the lock has been restored and the original wooden gates have been dragged up onto land. There are demonstrations of a reconstructed lock, with vessels passing up this small segment of the canal. A 10-minute video explains the operation of the canal. ✉ *Erie and Conesto Sts.,* ☎ *410/939–5780.* 🎫 *$2.* ⏲ *May–Oct., weekends 1–5; candlelight tour 2nd Sun. in Dec.*

The conical **Concord Point Lighthouse** is the oldest continuously operated lighthouse on the Chesapeake Bay. Built in 1827, it was restored in 1980. You can climb up 30 ft for views of the bay, the river, and the town. ✉ *Concord and Lafayette Sts. at the Susquehanna River, Havre de Grace,* ☎ *410/939–9040.* 🎫 *Free.* ⏲ *Apr.–Oct., weekends 1–5.*

The **Steppingstone Museum** is a 10-acre complex of seven restored turn-of-the-20th-century farm buildings plus a replica of a canning house. Among the 12,000-plus artifacts in the collection are a horse-drawn tractor and an early gas-powered version, manual seeders and planters, and horse-drawn plows. A blacksmith, a weaver, a wood-carver, a cooper, a dairymaid, and a decoy artisan regularly demonstrate their trades in the workshops. ✉ *Susquehanna State Park, 461 Quaker Bottom Rd.,* ☎ *410/939–2299.* 🎫 *$2.* ⏲ *May–Oct., weekends 1–5.*

★ The **Ladew Topiary Gardens** hold America's finest display of topiary—the life's work of Harvey Smith Ladew. The trees and shrubs are sculpted into geometric forms and lifelike renditions of animals such as a fox and hounds, swans, and even a seahorse. The 15 different formal gardens cover 22 acres. Besides the amazing topiary displays are rose, berry, and herb gardens, and a tranquil Japanese garden with pagoda, lily ponds, and lush flowers. In summer, there are special events such as concerts and polo matches. The 18th-century manor house is filled with English antiques, paintings, photographs, and fox-hunting memorabilia. The standout room is the Oval Library, one of the most beautiful rooms in America. A summer concert series brings live music to Ladew on alternating Sunday evenings, with the gardens providing ideal picnic grounds (a café on the grounds serves lunch and light snacks). The gardens are 14 mi north of the Baltimore beltway. ✉ *3535 Jarrettsville Pike, Monkton,* ☎ *410/557–9466,* WEB *www.ladewgardens.com.* 🎫 *House and gardens $12, gardens only $8.* ⏲ *Mid-Apr.–Oct., weekdays 10–4, weekends 10:30–5.*

Dining and Lodging

$$–$$$$ ✕ **Josef's Country Inn.** This tidy restaurant would not be out of place in the Bavarian countryside. The menu is heavily German, but also serves such old-school Continental fare as pâté maison, veal Oscar, and beef tournedos. There is a pleasant garden patio for outdoor dining. ✉ *2410 Pleasantville Rd., Fallston,* ☎ *410/877–7800. AE, D, DC, MC, V.*

$$–$$$ ★ ✕ **Crazy Swede.** A nautical theme prevails in this restaurant in a former hotel on a tree-lined avenue. Windows and mirrors on all sides keep the dining room well lighted regardless of whether the sailboat lanterns at the tables are burning. On the menu, beef, seafood, and pasta dishes are all well represented. Veal Havre de Grace, served with shrimp and lump crabmeat in a Chablis cream sauce, is a specialty. ✉ *400 N. Union Ave., Havre de Grace,* ☎ *410/939–5440,* WEB *www.crazyswederestaurant.com. AE, MC, V.*

$$–$$$ ✕ **MacGregor's.** Behind the redbrick facade of a bank built in 1928, MacGregor's occupies two dining rooms on two levels, with glass walls on three sides looking onto the Chesapeake Bay. The interior is adorned with carved duck decoys, mounted guns, and antique prints of the town; there's also outdoor dining on a deck with a gazebo. Seafood is the specialty, and the kitchen claims to have the best crab cakes on the bay. ✉ *331 St. John's St.,* ☎ *410/939–3003,* WEB *www.macgregorsrestaurant.com. AE, D, DC, MC, V.*

$–$$$ **Vandiver Inn.** This three-story wood house, built in 1886 and listed on the National Register of Historic Places, is 1½ blocks from the bay. Green with a dark green trim on the outside, the inn has a Victorian look, with antique beds and other period pieces. The O'Neil and the Rodgers suites have their own porches. Another porch extends the width of the house front, and the gazebo in the backyard is as old as the house itself. The Murphy and Kent guest suites, adjacent to the original inn, have Jacuzzi tubs. ✉ *301 S. Union Ave., Havre de Grace, 21078,* ☎ *410/939–5200 or 800/245–1655,* WEB *www.vandiverinn.com. 9 rooms, 4 suites. Breakfast room. AE, D, MC, V. BP.*

$–$$ ★ **Spencer-Silver Mansion.** This house was built in 1886 from gray granite quarried at nearby Port Deposit—the same kind of granite used to build the Brooklyn Bridge. Characteristic Victorian details include stained-glass windows, a wraparound porch, and a turret. One guest room is a round turret room; another has a queen-size brass bed and a view of the garden. The carriage house is a lovely two-story stone cottage with loft bedroom, a Jacuzzi, and a fireplace; it sleeps up to four but is ideal for couples seeking a romantic hideaway. All rooms are furnished with period antiques supplemented by select reproductions. ✉ *200 S. Union Ave., 21078,* ☎ *410/939–1097,* WEB *www.spencersilvermansion.com. 4 rooms, 1 suite. No smoking. AE, MC, V. BP.*

Aberdeen

30 mi northeast of Baltimore.

A site for artillery testing since 1917, Aberdeen celebrates its heritage every year on Armed Forces Day (the third Saturday in May) with tank parades and firing demonstrations. The town is also the birthplace of "Iron Man" Cal Ripken Jr., who made baseball history in 1995 by breaking Lou Gehrig's record for most consecutive games played.

Aberdeen loves its native son so much that they gave part of City Hall to honor the legendary Baltimore Oriole shortstop. The small but heartwarming **Ripken Museum** holds memorabilia from Cal's career with the team, both major- and minor-league, as well as items pertaining to brother Billy, who played for the O's, and father Cal Sr., who coached and managed the team. A gift shop sells autographed baseballs and other Ripken mementos. ✉ *8 Ripken Plaza,* ☎ *410/273–2525.* *$3.* ⏲ *Memorial Day–Labor Day, daily 11–3; Labor Day–Apr., Fri. and Mon. 11–3, Sat. 11–4, Sun. noon–3:30; May–Memorial Day, Thurs.–Fri. and Mon. 11–3, Sat. 11–4, Sun. noon–3:30.*

Opened in June 2002, **Cal Ripken Stadium** (✉ 937 Gilbert Rd., ☎ 410/297–9292, WEB www.ripkenbaseball.com) brings Single-A baseball to town with the IronBirds, an Orioles minor-league affiliate team. Owned by Cal Ripken, the team plays short-season ball every June to September in Ripken Stadium, a 5,500-seat venue complete with skyboxes. The stadium and minor-league team are just the first phase of Ripken's planned 50-acre sports complex, which will include a youth baseball academy. A miniature replica of Camden Yards, complete with a warehouse in right field, is already under construction, and five more youth-scale versions of classic stadiums (including Fenway Park and Wrigley Field) will follow.

BALTIMORE A TO Z

To research prices, get advice from other travelers, and book travel arrangements, visit www.fodors.com.

ADDRESSES

Laid out in a more-or-less regular grid pattern, Baltimore is fairly easy to navigate. The navigational center of town is the intersection of Charles and Baltimore streets; all east–west demarcations use Charles Street as the starting (zero) block, and north–south distinctions originate at Baltimore Street. The major downtown north–south thoroughfares are Charles and Saint Paul (north of Baltimore Street) and Light Street (south of Baltimore). Downtown, east–west traffic depends heavily on Pratt and Lombard streets. The downtown area is bounded by Martin Luther King Boulevard on the west and by the Jones Falls Expressway (President Street) on the east.

North Baltimore begins at University Parkway; north of North Avenue, in central Baltimore, streets are numbered beginning with 20th Street. South Baltimore's upper boundary is Key Highway, and West Baltimore begins at Martin Luther King Boulevard.

The Inner Harbor is that area of downtown Baltimore directly on the waterfront; its boundaries are Pratt Street to the north, Key Highway to the south, Light street to the west and President Street to the east. Inner Harbor East refers to waterfront areas east of President Street but west of Fells Point; this area encompasses Little Italy. Fells Point, the city's entertainment district, lies directly east from downtown and the Inner Harbor, along the waterfront.

Mount Vernon is directly north up Charles Street from the downtown and Inner Harbor areas; the neighborhood's south boundary lies at Saratoga Street, its north at Mount Royal Avenue, and east and west are demarcated by the Jones Falls Expressway and Cathedral Street, respectively.

Charles Village, home of Johns Hopkins University, is north of Mount Vernon; its southern boundary is 25th Street, and University Parkway marks its northern extreme.

AIRPORTS

Most travel within the Virginia-Maryland region is done by car or train. For arrival by air, Baltimore's major airport is Baltimore-Washington International Airport (BWI), just south of town. BWI is easily reached by car, taxi, or light-rail; for most agencies, rental cars are returned to lots off the airport premises.

➤ AIRPORT INFORMATION: **Baltimore-Washington International Airport** (BWI; ✉ 10 mi south of Baltimore off Rte. 295/Baltimore-Washington Pkwy., ☎ 410/859–7111 for information and paging).

TRANSFERS

By Bus: **BWI Super Shuttle** provides van service between the airport and downtown hotels, every half hour, 4 AM–midnight. Travel time is about 30 minutes; the fare is $20 for the first person, $5 per additional passenger. Hotel vans, which operate independently of the hotels, take 30 minutes on average. Some hotels may provide complimentary limousine service.

By Limousine: **Carey Limousines** provides both limousine and van service, which cost $40–$55 per hour; make reservations 24 hours in advance.

By Taxi: **Airport Taxis** stand by to meet arriving flights. The ride into town on I–295 takes 20 minutes; a trip between the airport and downtown costs about $20. Airport Taxi service is available only *from* BWI; for transportation to the airport, consult a local cab company such as **Jimmy's Cab Co.** or **Arrow Taxicab.**

By Train: Quick, convenient light-rail train service connects the airport with downtown Baltimore, Penn Station (which connects with Amtrak), and other destinations every 17 minutes. The fare is $1.35 one way, $2.70 round-trip, or $3 for a one-day multiride pass. For information and schedules, contact the **Maryland Transit Administration.**

Amtrak service between the BWI Airport rail station and Penn Station is available daily at irregular intervals, so call ahead. The ride takes 10–15 minutes and costs $5. **Maryland Area Rail Commuter** trains travel between the BWI Airport and Penn Station in about 20 minutes, weekdays 7 AM–10 PM, at a fare of $3.25.

➤ CONTACTS: **Airport Taxis** (☎ 410/859–1100). **Arrow Taxicab** (☎ 410/358–9696). **Amtrak** (☎ 800/872–7245). **BWI Airport rail station** (☎ 410/672–6167). **BWI Super Shuttle** (☎ 410/859–0800). **Carey Limousines** (☎ 410/880–0999 or 800/336–4646). **Jimmy's Cab Co.** (☎ 410/296–7200). **Maryland Area Rail Commuter** (MARC; ☎ 800/325–7245). **Maryland Transit Administration** (MTA; ☎ 410/539–5000, WEB www.mtamaryland.com). **Penn Station** (✉ Charles St. and Mt. Royal Ave., Mount Vernon, ☎ 410/291–4269).

BIKE TRAVEL

Navigating Baltimore by bicycle is an uneasy proposition. The vast majority of residents rely on four-, rather than two-wheeled, vehicles, and local drivers are infamous for their lack of willingness to share the road with bicycles. There are practically no bike-oriented amenities such as bicycle lanes or even bike racks. However, with caution and awareness on the part of the rider, the compact center core of the city, where most of the attractions, restaurants, and hotels are, can be navigated and even enjoyed on two wheels.

➤ BIKE RENTALS: **Light Street Cycles** (✉ 1015 Light St., Federal Hill, ☎ 410/685–2234).

BUS TRAVEL

Travel to Baltimore by bus is easy and convenient. Passengers can arrive at the downtown bus terminal or at the Baltimore Travel Plaza on I–95; the plaza has long-term parking and local bus service to downtown and other destinations. Greyhound Lines has scheduled daily service to and from major cities in the United States and Canada. Peter Pan Bus Lines offers slightly cheaper travel to many destinations in the Northeast, including Washington, D.C., New York, and Boston.

➤ BUS DEPOTS: **Baltimore Travel Plaza** (✉ 5625 O'Donnell St., at I–95, East Baltimore, ☎ 800/231–2222). **Greyhound Lines Downtown Bus Terminal** (✉ 210 W. Fayette St., Downtown, ☎ 800/231–2222).

➤ BUS LINES: **Greyhound Lines** (☎ 800/231–2222, WEB www.greyhound.com). **Maryland Transit Administration** (MTA; ☎ 410/539–5000, WEB www.mtamaryland.com). **Peter Pan Bus Lines** (☎ 800/237–8747).

BUS TRAVEL WITHIN BALTIMORE

Buses provide an easy, inexpensive way to see much of Baltimore. The Maryland Transit Administration has more than 70 bus routes. There is also MTA bus service between Baltimore and Annapolis.

FARES AND SCHEDULES

Route and schedule information is available by contacting the Maryland Transit Administration. Bus and transit schedules are also available inside the Charles Center metro station (Charles and Baltimore streets downtown), but sometimes these run out and are not immediately replaced. Fare is $1.35. All-day passes are $3 and can be used with light-rail or metro travel. Some routes have service 24 hours daily.

➤ INFORMATION: **Maryland Transit Administration** (MTA; ☎ 410/539–5000, WEB www.mtamaryland.com).

CAR RENTALS

Baltimore is served by all major car rental agencies; of these, Enterprise and Thrifty have the most numerous and convenient locations around town.

➤ AGENCIES: **Enterprise** (☎ 800/736–8222, WEB www.enterprise.com). **Thrifty** (☎ 410/859–4900, WEB www.thrifty.com).

CAR TRAVEL

From the northeast and south, I–95 cuts across the city's east side and the harbor; Route 295, the Baltimore–Washington Parkway, follows a similar route farther to the east and is the best route downtown from the airport. From the north, I–83, also called the Jones Falls Expressway, winds through Baltimore and ends at the Inner Harbor. I–395 serves as the primary access to downtown from I–95. From the west, I–70 merges with the Baltimore Beltway, I–695. Drivers headed downtown should use I–395.

PARKING

Parking in downtown Baltimore tends to be difficult; on weekdays, many garages fill up early with suburban commuters. When the Orioles or Ravens play a home game, parking around the Inner Harbor can be nearly impossible to find. Best bets for parking are hotel garages, which seem to almost always have spaces available. Attended parking lots are located around the downtown periphery and cost less than garages.

Though widespread, metered parking spaces are not the best option. Most meters charge 25¢ per 20-minute period and have a two-hour limit; around the Inner Harbor vicinity meters are in effect 24 hours a day.

TRAFFIC

Weekday rush hour traffic can be quite heavy, particularly around the I–95 tunnels and on the Jones Falls Expressway. However, tie-ups generally don't last longer than an hour. When the Orioles or Ravens play a home game, the stadium area becomes extremely congested, and it's better to avoid driving in that vicinity as well as on I–295 (the most convenient entrance/exit area for the stadiums) altogether.

CHILDREN IN BALTIMORE

BABY-SITTING

Baltimore lacks a baby-sitter referral service. Most hotels provide child-care referral services for guests; check with the concierge desk. Rates range from $8 to $20 per hour.

DISABILITIES AND ACCESSIBILITY

Major attractions and points of interest in Baltimore, from the 18th-century fortifications at Ft. McHenry to Ravens Stadium, are accessible to those with disabilities; many have especially helpful resources. The National Aquarium, for example, offers Assistive Listening Devices, ASL interpreters, audio and Braille tours, express entry for visitors with special needs, and reserved seating for the dolphin show. Local organizations such as LINC (Learning Independence Through Computers) are the best source for getting information on accessibility at area hotels, restaurants, and attractions; LINC's Web site carries a comprehensive list of local support organizations and accessible facilities in the Baltimore area.

Baltimore's Center Stage, Mechanic Theater, and Lyric Opera House all provide accessible performances, which include audio description, Braille, and large-print programs for events. The group Maryland Arts Access works to make arts, recreation, and cultural activities throughout the state available to all, regardless of disability.

➤ LOCAL RESOURCES: **LINC** (✉ 1001 Eastern Ave., East Baltimore, ☎ 410/659–5462, WEB www.linc.org/TextOnly/mdres_text.html). **Maryland Arts Access** (✉ 1 N. Charles St., Downtown, ☎ 410/347–1650, WEB www.mdtap.org/md_arts.html).

DISCOUNTS AND DEALS

It is already one of the most affordable cities on the eastern seaboard, but nevertheless there are ways to save money when visiting Baltimore. The Baltimore Area Convention and Visitors Association offers special hotel packages that combine discounted rooms with tickets to local attractions or events: packages change frequently, so contact them for details.

Numerous Web sites offer discounted hotel rooms in Baltimore, but fewer sites do the same thing for dining. If you're willing to dine at off-peak hours to save up to 30% off your dinner bill, visit the Dinner Broker Web site, where you can see what restaurants participate and make free on-line reservations.

➤ CONTACT: **Baltimore Area Convention and Visitors Association** (✉ 451 Light St., ☎ 877/225–8466 [877/BALTIMORE], WEB www.baltimore.org/pages/group_packages.htm#downtown). **Dinner Broker** (✉ ☎ 888/432–8288 [888/IEATAT8], WEB www.dinnerbroker.com).

EMERGENCIES

Baltimoreans are typically helpful, vocal, and concerned in emergency situations and do not hesitate to get involved. To report non-life-threatening situations that are nonetheless of concern, the Baltimore City Police Department operates an alternative phone line, **311,** that connects directly to a police operator.

Police, fire, or ambulance response is almost always immediate.

Mercy Medical Center has set up a "Dial a Downtown Doctor" hot line for physician referrals and appointments. The service is available around the clock, seven days a week. Also downtown, the University of Maryland Medical Center operates a similar service from 7 AM to 7 PM daily, and can provide access to dentists as well as medical doctors.

➤ CONTACT: **Ambulance, fire, police** (☎ 911).

➤ DOCTORS AND DENTISTS: **Dial a Downtown Doctor** (✉ ☎ 800/636–3729, WEB www.mdmercy.com). **University of Maryland Find a Doctor** (✉ ☎ 800/492–5538, WEB www.umm.edu/findadoctor).

➤ HOSPITALS: **Johns Hopkins Hospital** (✉ 600 N. Wolfe St., East Baltimore, ☎ 410/955–2280). **Mercy Medical Center** (✉ 301 St. Paul Pl.,

Downtown, ☏ 410/332–9000). **University of Maryland University Hospital** (✉ 22 S. Greene St., West Baltimore, ☏ 410/328–8667).
➤ 24-HOUR PHARMACIES: **Rite Aid** (✉ 250 W. Chase St., Mount Vernon, ☏ 410/752–4473; ✉ Rotunda shopping center, 711 W. 40th St., Charles Village, ☏ 410/467–3343).

LODGING

Central Maryland, including Baltimore, does not have an endless number of B&Bs, but there are still enough to suit most travelers' tastes. Maryland Lodging is a free state-sponsored referral service, affiliated with the Maryland Hotel and Lodging Association, which provides information and reservations for hotels, B&Bs, and other accommodations in the region. The service is available daily 9–9.

BED-AND-BREAKFASTS

➤ RESERVATION SERVICES: **Maryland Lodging** (☏ 800/634–7386, WEB www.mdlodging.org).

MAIL AND SHIPPING

Baltimore's main post office is convenient to downtown and open 24 hours. Federal Express and other major shippers have offices downtown, and operators such as Kinko's and Mail Boxes Etc. offer packing and shipping services.

Free public Internet access is available at the Enoch Pratt Free Library. For those who would like to sip a latte while surfing on-line, Funk's Democratic Coffee Spot in Fells Point is open until 11 PM weeknights and Sunday, midnight Friday and Saturday.
➤ CONTACTS: **Main Post Office** (✉ 900 E. Fayette St., Inner Harbor East, ☏ 410/347–4425). **FedEx** (✉ 36 S. Charles St., ☏ 800/463–3339). **Kinko's** (✉ 300 N. Charles St., Downtown, ☏ 410/223–2000). **Mail Boxes Etc.** (✉ 211 E. Lombard St., Downtown, ☏ 410/659–9360).
➤ INTERNET CAFÉS: **Enoch Pratt Free Library** (✉ 400 Cathedral St., Midtown, ☏ 410/396–5500). **Funk's Democratic Coffee Spot** (✉ 1818 Eastern Ave., Fells Point, ☏ 410/276–3865).

OUTDOORS AND SPORTS

Given its location on the Chesapeake, the largest watershed in the continental United States, Baltimore enjoys water sports above all others. Sailing is the most popular way to float, and kayaking, sculling, and canoeing are also pursued. The Downtown Sailing Center is a nonprofit, volunteer-run sailing organization with about 550 members. The center offers inexpensive adult and junior sailing lessons, recreational sailing, racing, and cruising.

Publicly accessible kayaking is available through the Canton Kayak Club, a nonprofit organization founded in 1999 that encourages residents to paddle Baltimore's myriad waterways.
➤ SAILING: **Downtown Sailing Center** (✉ 1425 Key Hwy., Federal Hill, ☏ 410/727–2884, WEB www.downtownsailing.org).
➤ KAYAKING: **Canton Kayak Club** (✉ 2809 Boston St., Canton, ☏ 410/534–3451, WEB www.cantonkayakclub.com).

SIGHTSEEING TOURS

Tours of Baltimore, on foot or four wheels, run from traditional surveys of historic buildings and sites to quirkier explorations such as the Fells Point Ghost Tour.

BUS TOURS

The Baltimore Shuttle offers an upbeat 90-minute narrated bus tour of Baltimore's various neighborhoods and attractions seven days a week

aboard comfortable 25-passenger minibuses. Tours depart from the visitor center at Harborplace, next to the Phillips restaurant, but hotel pickups can be arranged; ask the concierge for a brochure. Group tours are available and can be customized for specific interests.
➤ CONTACTS: **The Baltimore Shuttle** (☎ 410/732–5098, WEB www.baltimoretransportation.com/narratedtours.htm).

WALKING TOURS

For a general overview of Baltimore, energetic, irrepressible Zippy Larson is by far the city's most engaging tour guide. She offers many different walking tours with historic, cultural, and architectural themes. Zippy's witty, well-researched tours start at $55 per person (which includes a restaurant meal) and take you outside the tourist bubble. Group tours can also be arranged through Baltimore Rent-A-Tour, which customizes an itinerary concentrating, for example, on architecture, history, sports, or shopping.

Many tours cater to more specific interests as well. One favorite is the Fells Point Ghost Tour, which interweaves narrative about the maritime neighborhood's colorful past with tales of its spectral inhabitants. Tours, which are suitable for children, run every Friday evening from March to November and cost $12 per adult; reservations are recommended. Other Fells Point walking tours are offered through the Fells Point Visitors Center and focus on such topics as maritime history, slavery, and immigration.

For building buffs, the Baltimore Architectural Foundation sponsors monthly walking tours of the historic and architecturally significant neighborhoods of Federal Hill and Mount Vernon; reservations are required. A particularly fascinating experience is local historian Wayne Schaumburg's guided tour to Greenmount Cemetery. Baltimore's largest and most prestigious burial ground is the final resting place of John Wilkes Booth, Johns Hopkins, and other native sons and daughters. Tours take place in May and October.
➤ CONTACTS: **Baltimore Architectural Foundation** (☎ 410/539–7772, WEB www.baltimorearchitecture.org). **Baltimore Rent-A-Tour** (☎ 410/653–2998, WEB www.baltimorerent-a-tour.com). **Fells Point Ghost Tours** (☎ 410/522–7400, WEB www.fellspointghost.com). **Fells Point Visitors Center Tours** (☎ 410/675–6750, WEB www.preservationsociety.com). **Greenmount Cemetery Tours** (☎ 410/256–2180, WEB home.earthlink.net/INSERT TILDEwschaumburg). **Zippy Larson's Shoe Leather Safaris** (☎ 410/817–4141, WEB www.bcpl.net/INSERT TILDEzipbooks).

WATER TOURS

There are numerous ways to explore the harbor and the nearby Chesapeake Bay by water. Most cruise and tour boats depart from docks in the Inner Harbor. The tall ship *Clipper City* offers excursions around the harbor aboard a 158-ft replica of an 1850s topsail schooner. Harbor Cruises, Ltd. presents lunch, dinner, and evening cruises around the harbor aboard the *Bay Lady* and *Lady Baltimore*. Based along the historic Fells Point waterfront, Schooner Nighthawk Cruises offers cruises and moonlight buffet sailings aboard a restored U.S. merchant marine passenger vessel built in 1880.
➤ CONTACTS: **Clipper City** (✉ Inner Harbor, ☎ 410/539–6277, WEB www.sailingship.com). **Harbor Cruises, Ltd.** (☎ 410/727–3113 or 800/695–2628, WEB www.harborcruises.com). **Schooner Nighthawk Cruises** (✉ Thames St., Fells Point, ☎ 410/276–7447, WEB www.a1nighthawkcruises.com).

SUBWAY TRAVEL

The Baltimore metro serves those coming into the city from the suburban northwest. Stops include Charles Center and Lexington Market, both within walking distance of the Inner Harbor. The single line runs from Owings Mills to Johns Hopkins Hospital, east of downtown.

FARES AND SCHEDULES

Fare is $1.35. Trains run weekdays 5 AM–midnight, Saturday and Sunday 6 AM–midnight.

➤ INFORMATION: **Maryland Transit Administration** (MTA; ☎ 410/539–5000, WEB www.mtamaryland.com).

TAXIS

Taxis in Baltimore are not usually flagged or hailed in the street. Instead, call to have a cab pick you up, ask your hotel concierge or doorman to summon a taxi, or go to the cab stand at Pratt and Light streets in the center of the Inner Harbor zone. Local companies include Arrow Taxicab and Jimmy's Cab Co.

➤ TAXI COMPANIES: **Arrow Taxicab** (☎ 410/358–9696). **Jimmy's Cab Co.** (☎ 410/296–7200).

TRAIN TRAVEL

All Amtrak trains on the northeast corridor between Boston and Washington stop at Baltimore's Penn Station.

Light-rail is an easy, comfortable way to reach downtown from the northern and southern suburbs. Stops near downtown include Oriole Park at Camden Yards, Howard Street, and Centre Street near Mount Vernon. The city's cultural center can be reached by the Cathedral Street stop. Light-rail has been extended to Hunt Valley, BWI Airport, and Glen Burnie. The fare is $1.35.

➤ TRAIN STATIONS: **Penn Station** (✉ Charles St. and Mt. Royal Ave., Mount Vernon, ☎ 410/291–4269).

➤ TRAIN LINES: **Amtrak** (800/872–7245). **Maryland Transit Administration** (MTA; ☎ 410/539–5000, WEB www.mtamaryland.com).

TRANSPORTATION AROUND BALTIMORE

The majority of Baltimore's attractions are within walking distance or a short cab ride from the Inner Harbor. Beyond that area a car is useful. The clean, speedy metro (subway) and light-rail lines are somewhat limited, and riding public buses can involve a number of transfers. Parking rates downtown are about $18 a day. Inner Harbor sites and other downtown attractions are best reached on foot or by water taxi.

VISITOR INFORMATION

Contact the Baltimore Area Convention and Visitors Association for information on the city. A live operator will answer your questions weekdays 8:30–5:30; otherwise an automated system is in place. The drop-in visitor center is open Monday through Saturday 9–5, and Sunday 10–5. Metered parking is nearby.

The Baltimore Office of Promotion's Web site has the most detailed information on city events such as New Year's Eve, the Waterfront Festival, the Book Festival, and the Thanksgiving Parade (the Saturday before Thanksgiving).

Fell's Point Visitor Center has information particular to the neighborhood, including a handout that covers many buildings' histories and architecture.

For more information on Havre de Grace and Aberdeen, contact the Discover Harford County Tourism Council.

➤ TOURIST INFORMATION: **Baltimore Area Convention and Visitors Association** (✉ 100 Light St., Baltimore 21202, ☎ 888/225–8466, WEB www.baltconvstr.com). **Baltimore Office of Promotion** (WEB www.bop.org). **Baltimore Visitor Center** (✉ 451 Light St. [west shore of Inner Harbor, next to Phillips Harborplace], Inner Harbor, ☎ 877/225–8466). **Discover Harford County Tourism Council** (✉ 121 N. Union Ave., Suite B, Havre de Grace 21078, ☎ 410/939–3336 or 800/597–2649, WEB www.harfordmd.com). **Fell's Point Visitor Center** (✉ 808 S. Ann St., Baltimore 21231, ☎ 410/675–6750).

WATER TAXIS

Uniquely Baltimorean, Ed Kane's Water Taxis are a fun and convenient way to get around the Inner Harbor. They make stops at 16 points along the waterfront, including Fells Point, the National Aquarium, museums, restaurants, and Fort McHenry. The Seaport Taxi makes the same stops using larger pontoon boats. All-day tickets for both services are $5.

Both the water taxis and harbor shuttle are a respite from the busy city streets and give you a great view of the city's skyline and harbor. Look for stops, marked with signs, all along the waterfront; depending on season, boats arrive every 10–15 minutes or you can call to be picked up at a particular location.

➤ CONTACTS: **Ed Kane's Water Taxis** (☎ 410/563–3901, WEB www.thewatertaxi.com). **Seaport Taxi** (☎ 410/675–2900, WEB www.natlhistoricseaport.org/taxi.html).

8 FREDERICK AND WESTERN MARYLAND

Mountains, forests, and unspoiled rivers cover westernmost Maryland, where fertile valleys were first farmed in the 1700s. The 250-year-old town of Frederick has a 50-block historic district and was the site of repeated clashes in the Civil War. Also in the vicinity are Antietam National Battlefield, where Union and Confederate troops fought on the bloodiest single day of the war, and Cumberland, where you can still see remnants of the historic Chesapeake and Ohio Canal.

By Greg Tasker

THE MARYLAND MOUNTAINSIDE—it's the state's best-kept secret. Stretching from the rolling farmland of the Piedmont region to the remote mountaintops of Garrett County and the heights of the Appalachians, the region is full of historic towns, Civil War battlefields, and miles of hardwood forests where white-tail deer, wild turkey, and even black bear roam among vast stretches of oaks, hickories, and maples. The nation's first pioneers crossed these worn, majestic mountains as they made their way westward on the National Pike, the nation's first federally funded highway. Today, campers, hikers, hunters, and those seeking an escape from Baltimore, Washington, and the suburbs head to these hills.

In the early 1700s, Germans and other immigrants came to farm the fertile valleys of Frederick and Washington counties, where large dairy farms still dot the pastoral landscape. The Irish and Scots arrived in the first half of the 19th century to help build railroads, the National Pike, and the Chesapeake and Ohio (C&O) Canal. This nearly 185-mi-long waterway paralleled the meandering Potomac River from Washington's Georgetown to Cumberland, Maryland. Remnants of it remain, and today the canal's towpath is a popular hiking and biking trail.

Because of its proximity to Baltimore and Washington, Frederick, the region's largest city, became a staging area for many important events in American history. Ben Franklin helped plan aspects of the French and Indian War from Braddock Heights, a mountain on Frederick's western edge. Meriwether Lewis stopped by before meeting up with William Clark on their trek westward. During the Civil War, Confederate and Union troops clashed on the streets of Frederick, on their way to the battles of South Mountain and Antietam.

The region's other big towns, Hagerstown and Cumberland, were transportation hubs in earlier centuries. Though the railroad plays a less important role in both cities today, its past is used to lure visitors. Hagerstown is known for its Roundhouse Museum, which has an extensive collection of railroad memorabilia, history books, and a miniature railroad layout. Cumberland is in the midst of a multimillion-dollar project to turn the western terminus of the Chesapeake and Ohio Canal into a heritage and recreational area. A new visitor center has already opened at the C&O Canal National Historical Park. The city's Victorian-era train station has been restored and is the starting point of a popular excursion up the mountains. Eventually, a stretch of the canal will be restored for tours on replicas of the original canal boats.

The region's mountains, forests, and world-famous rivers are an equally important draw. Kayakers and white-water rafters rave about the rapids on the Savage River and the north-flowing Youghiogheny River, and hikers, bicyclists, and campers flock to state parks throughout the region. Deep Creek Lake, the state's largest, is frequented by boaters and anglers.

Disagreement lingers on just where western Maryland begins. For Baltimoreans, more familiar with the Eastern Shore and Ocean City, anything west of their beltway is western Maryland. Washingtonians, on the other hand, tend to lump Frederick and points west together as a distinct region. For the people who live in the hills of Allegany and Garrett counties, western Maryland begins just west of a man-made cut in a mountain called Sideling Hill. This unusual geological formation has become an attraction among motorists tooling along Interstate 68. Passing rock formations several million years old, the highway opens to sweeping views of mountain ridges, shaded blue in the fading sunset. These are the Alleghenies, Maryland's mountainside.

Pleasures and Pastimes

Dining

CATEGORY	COST*
$$$$	over $32
$$$	$22–$32
$$	$12–$22
$	under $12

**per person for a main course at dinner*

Lodging

CATEGORY	COST*
$$$$	over $225
$$$	$150–$225
$$	$100–$150
$	under $100

**All prices are for a standard double room, excluding state tax.*

Exploring Frederick and Western Maryland

Frederick, Maryland's second-largest city, is surrounded by rolling farmlands and rugged mountains where outdoor activities beckon. In Washington County, northwest of Frederick, Hagerstown is the county seat and a great base for excursions to the C&O Canal, various state parks, and the Appalachian Trail. Farther west, the rugged mountains of Allegany County are traversed by the Old National Highway: today the site of a scenic railroad excursion, this is the very route that westward pioneers traveled in covered wagons. Maryland's westernmost county, Garrett County, was once the vacation destination of railroad barons and Washington's high society; today it's a big destination for boaters, fishermen, and outdoors enthusiasts.

FREDERICK

Frederick has one of the best-preserved historic districts in Maryland, perhaps second only to Annapolis. Within the 50-block district, tree-shaded streets are lined with buildings from the 18th and 19th centuries, and brick walks connect lovely courtyards. Eclectic shops, museums, antiques stores, and fine restaurants attract crowds of weekend visitors.

Numbers in the text correspond to numbers in the margin and on the Frederick map.

A Good Walk

Frederick's Historic District is easily accessible by foot, though not all the worthwhile sites are within walking distance. Begin a leisurely tour at the **Frederick Visitor's Center** ①, which is located downtown amid restaurants, boutiques, and shops. A few must-see historic sites and museums are nearby. South of the visitor center on Patrick Street, scene of a skirmish between Union and Confederate troops before the Battle of Antietam in 1862, is the **National Museum of Civil War Medicine** ②. A few blocks west of the museum is the **Barbara Fritchie House and Museum** ③, where the bold, patriotic Fritchie waved a Union flag outside her window as Confederate troops marched through town. A few blocks south of the Fritchie home on Bentz Street is the

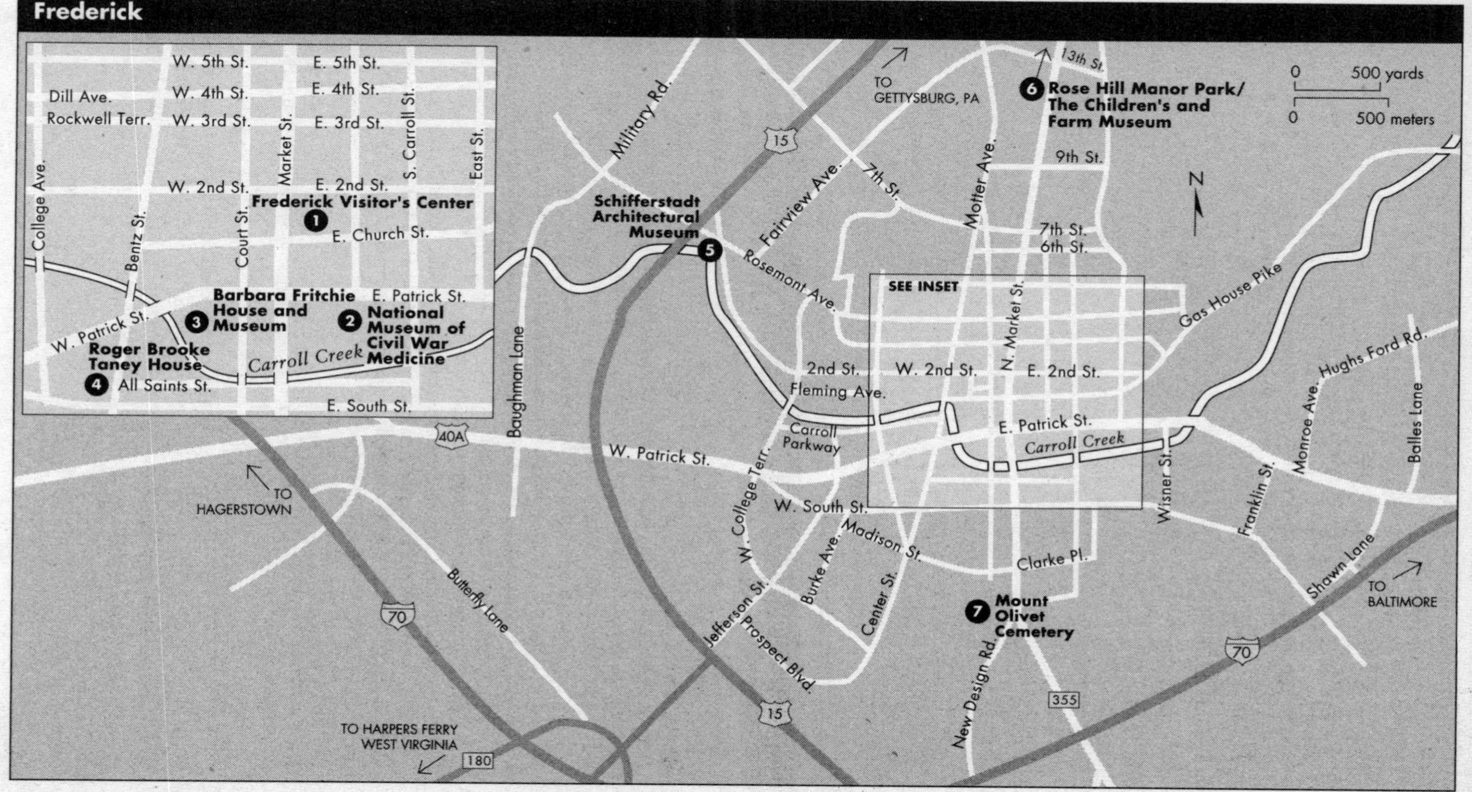
Frederick
W. 5th St.
E. 5th St.
Dill Ave.
W. 4th St.
E. 4th St.
Rockwell Terr.
W. 3rd St.
E. 3rd St.
Market St.
S. Carroll St.
East St.
College Ave.
W. 2nd St.
E. 2nd St.
Frederick Visitor's Center
1
E. Church St.
Court St.
Bentz St.
Barbara Fritchie House and Museum
3
E. Patrick St.
2 National Museum of Civil War Medicine
W. Patrick St.
Roger Brooke Taney House
Carroll Creek
4 All Saints St.
E. South St.
Military Rd.
Baughman Lane
Schifferstadt Architectural Museum
5
15
TO GETTYSBURG, PA
Fairview Ave.
7th St.
Motter Ave.
6 Rose Hill Manor Park/ The Children's and Farm Museum
13th St.
9th St.
7th St.
6th St.
0 500 yards
0 500 meters
N
Rosemont Ave.
SEE INSET
N. Market St.
Gas House Pike
2nd St.
W. 2nd St.
E. 2nd St.
Fleming Ave.
Hughs Ford Rd.
Monroe Ave.
Balles Lane
Carroll Parkway
E. Patrick St.
Carroll Creek
40A
W. Patrick St.
TO HAGERSTOWN
W. College Terr.
W. South St.
Madison St.
Wisner St.
Franklin St.
Clarke Pl.
Burke Ave.
Center St.
Jefferson St.
7 Mount Olivet Cemetery
Shawn Lane
TO BALTIMORE
70
Butterfly Lane
Prospect Blvd.
New Design Rd.
70
15
355
TO HARPERS FERRY WEST VIRGINIA
180

Roger Brooke Taney House ④, a museum dedicated to Supreme Court Justice Taney and his brother-in-law, Francis Scott Key.

TIMING

It will take three to four hours to cover these sights.

Sights to See

★ ❸ **Barbara Fritchie House and Museum.** This is one of Frederick's most popular attractions. After you visit this modest brick cottage, a reproduction of the original, it's easy to imagine Dame Fritchie sticking her white-capped head out of a second-floor window and waving a Union flag at Confederate troops. Poet John Greenleaf Whittier made her famous; his poem "Barbara Fritchie" appeared in the *Atlantic Monthly* a year after Confederate troops passed through Frederick. His stirring account of Fritchie defiantly waving the flag at the invading Confederates stirred patriotism and made the 95-year-old woman a heroine. Her unusual life, at least as told by Whittier, has fascinated history enthusiasts around the world. Even British prime minister Winston Churchill visited the house; on his way to Camp David with President Franklin Roosevelt, he stood outside and recited Whittier's poem: "Shoot if you must, this old gray head, but spare your country's flag. . . ." A tea set Fritchie used to serve George Washington is on display. ✉ *154 W. Patrick St.,* ☎ *301/698–0630.* 🎟 *$2.* ⏲ *Apr.–Sept., Mon. and Thurs.–Sat. 10–4; Oct.–Nov., Sat. 10–4, Sun. 1–4.*

❶ **Frederick Visitor's Center.** At the center you can pick up brochures of historic sites and maps for a self-guided tour or join a guided 90-minute walking tour with costumed guides. Tours begin at 1:30 PM and are offered on holidays and weekends April through December. ✉ *19 E. Church St.,* ☎ *301/228–2888 or 800/999–3613,* WEB *www.visitfrederick.org.* 🎟 *Tour $5.50.* ⏲ *Daily 9–5.*

❷ **National Museum of Civil War Medicine.** With historic photographs, artifacts, and documents, the complicated story of medicine, including the evolution of practices in use today, is told by following the journey of Peleg Bradford, a young Union private from Maine. The war, in which two-thirds of the 620,000 fatalities resulted from disease, led to advances in the transportation of the wounded, hospital care, surgery, and prostheses. More than 3,000 medical artifacts are on display—including the only known surviving Civil War surgeon's tent, as well as a Civil War ambulance. The building housing the museum was used to embalm the dead after the Battle of Antietam. ✉ *48 E. Patrick St.,* ☎ *301/695–1864,* WEB *www.civilwarmed.org.* 🎟 *$6.50.* ⏲ *Mon.–Sat. 10–5, Sun. 11–5.*

❹ **Roger Brooke Taney House.** A two-story Federal-style house contains a museum dedicated to Taney (1777–1864) and his brother-in-law Francis Scott Key, author of the "Star-Spangled Banner." History remembers Supreme Court Justice Taney as the author of the 1857 Dred Scott Decision, which stated that blacks had no constitutional rights. Taney and Key practiced law together in Frederick; their office still stands across from City Hall. Personal belongings of both men are on display at the Taney House. Behind the home is the former slave quarters, one of the few such surviving structures in the region. The house is open by appointment; the first weekend in April; and the second Saturday of December, during the Museums by Candlelight tour. ✉ *121 S. Bentz St.,* ☎ *301/228–2888.* 🎟 *Donation requested.* ⏲ *By appointment.*

A Good Drive

Begin at the **Schifferstadt Architectural Museum** ⑤ on the city's west side, near Baker Park. Drive back toward downtown along Rosemont Avenue. Turn right onto Rockwell Terrace and then left on Market Street and head north to the **Rose Hill Manor Park/The Children's and Farm Museum** ⑥, the home of Maryland's first governor. Finally, retrace the drive south via Court Street. Turn left on South Street and then right on Market Street through the heart of the Historic District to **Mount Olivet Cemetery** ⑦, where two of the city's most famous citizens, Francis Scott Key and Barbara Fritchie, are buried.

TIMING

It will take about three hours to cover these sights.

Sights to See

❻ **Rose Hill Manor Park/The Children's and Farm Museum.** Although this lovely Georgian manor is intended as a place for elementary-school children to study local and regional history, it's more than just this. Maryland's first governor, Thomas Johnson, lived here from 1798 to 1819. Guided tours of the gracious home focus on the early 19th century, covering the manor's owners and their lifestyles. During the tour, children can card wool, weave on a table loom, play with reproductions of old toys, and dress in period costumes. Also open are several outbuildings, including a log cabin, ice house, smokehouse, blacksmith shop, and large shed housing a carriage collection. You can also wander through herb, vegetable, and rose gardens. *1611 N. Market St., ☎ 301/694–1648, WEB www.co.frederick.md.us/govt/parks/rosehill.html. $4. Apr.–Oct., Mon.–Sat. 10–4, Sun. 1–4; Nov., Sat. 10–4, Sun. 1–4.*

❼ **Mount Olivet Cemetery.** Some of Frederick's most famous sons and daughters rest here, including Francis Scott Key and Barbara Fritchie. The cemetery also shelters the graves of more than 800 Confederate and Union soldiers killed during the battles of Antietam and Monocacy. ✉ *515 S. Market St., ☎ 301/662–1164. Daily.*

❺ **Schifferstadt Architectural Museum.** Believed to be the oldest house in Frederick, this unusual stone structure was built in 1756 by German immigrants. Spared from the wrecking ball two decades ago by preservation-minded citizens, the house is considered one of the finest examples of German architecture in Colonial America. Because the rooms are barren, it's easy to observe structural details such as the sandstone walls, which are 2½-ft thick. ✉ *1110 Rosemont Ave., ☎ 301/663–3885. $3. Apr.–mid-Dec., Tues.–Sat. 10–4, Sun. 1–4.*

Dining and Lodging

$$–$$$$ ✕ **The Red Horse.** A local institution and landmark—note the red horse on the roof—the Red Horse is primarily a steak house. The dining room is rustic with a stone fireplace, rafters, and large wagon-wheel chandelier. The service is first-rate; you can watch your steak being grilled from behind a window. A lower-level cigar parlor serves cognac, ports, sherries, and bourbons. ✉ *996–998 W. Patrick St., ☎ 301/663–3030. AE, MC, V.*

$–$$$ ✕ **Cafe Kyoko.** Located above a downtown Frederick bakery, Cafe Kyoko overlooks busy Patrick Street. The dining room is sparsely decorated but inviting with wooden booths along the window front, exposed rafters, and ceiling fans. The menu is a mix of Japanese, Thai, and other Asian cuisine. Sushi and Thai-curry dishes are popular choices. The less adventurous will find chicken teriyaki, steak, and seafood entrées. The wine and beer selection is limited. ✉ *10 E. Patrick St., ☎ 301/695–9656. AE, MC, V.*

$–$$$ ✕ **Isabella's.** The 2002 opening of this Spanish eatery added some flair to downtown Frederick's predominantly American restaurant scene. Most people head here for the tapas—little appetizers that originated in the Andalusia region of Spain. Isabella's tapas may include lamb, beef, chicken, and seafood with various spices, herbs, and wonderful sauces. Try the littleneck clams steamed in beer, garlic, cilantro, pepper, and tomato or the grilled lamb chops, served with a black currant sauce. Three or four tapas makes a meal. ✉ *44 N. Market St.,* ☎ *301/698–8922. AE, D, DC, MC, V. Closed Mon.*

$–$$ ✕ **Firestone's.** In a 1920s-era building that in earlier incarnations was a bank, a sporting goods store, and an Irish pub, Firestone's is a casual, slightly upscale place for good American fare. At first glimpse, it seems more like a local pub, with a wooden bar dominating the main floor. Look more closely, and you'll see the white linens covering the tables. Steak and seafood are plentiful on the menu, which also offers a few surprises, including marinated and roasted Portobello mushrooms stacked with onions, peppers, eggplant, and zucchini. Desserts are homemade. ✉ *105 N. Market St.,* ☎ *301/663–0330. AE, D, MC, V. Closed Mon.*

$$$–$$$$ ★ ✕ **Antrim 1844.** Once part of a 2,500-acre plantation, this pre–Civil War mansion, less than 10 mi from Gettysburg, is an elegant retreat. The owners have re-created the genteel spirit of a 19th-century estate. The nine mansion guest rooms are furnished with period antiques, working fireplaces, canopy feather beds, and marble baths or whirlpools. Other guest rooms are in a restored 19th-century carriage house, and buildings that were once an ice house and a plantation office. Don't miss the prix-fixe, six-course dinner ($62), an evening-long event. The menu includes seafood, beef, and poultry, all served with exquisite sauces. ✉ *30 Trevnanion Rd., Taneytown 21787,* ☎ *410/756–6812 or 800/858–1844,* FAX *410/756–2744,* WEB *www.antrim1844.com. 22 rooms. Restaurant, putting green, tennis court, pool, croquet, lawn bowling, bar; no room TVS, no kids under 12; no smoking. AE, MC, V. BP.*

$$$–$$$$ ★ ✕ **Stone Manor.** Part of a 114-acre working farm, this inn is inside an 18th-century stone home (with later additions). The majestic Stone Manor, with 10 working fireplaces, has six suites individually decorated with floral-print armchairs and sofas, antique reproductions, and canopy or carved poster beds. Breakfast is served in one of the three lovely dining rooms or in the suites—but the five-course dinner ($69) is the main event. Herbs from the chef's garden figure in all the dishes, from wild game and fowl to seafood and beef. Lunch is available by advance reservation. ✉ *5820 Carroll Boyer Rd., Middletown 21769,* ☎ *301/473–5454,* FAX *301/371–5622,* WEB *www.stonemanor.com. 6 suites. Restaurant, in-room VCRs, business services, meeting rooms; no room phones, no smoking. AE, D, DC, MC, V. BP.*

$$–$$$ ✕ **Turning Point Inn.** A prominent doctor once lived in this Edwardian-era home, which is now a bed-and-breakfast inn. Flowering trees, lilacs, and rhododendrons line the long driveway, setting the stage for a relaxing weekend getaway. The main house's four rooms are painted in rose, gray, and white and are furnished with antique reproductions. The bowls of fruit in each room are a nice touch. Two other rooms are in a cottage and dairy house. The inn's excellent restaurant ($$–$$$) has an enclosed garden patio that overlooks well-manicured wildflower and rose gardens. The menu includes Chesapeake Bay seafood, roast duckling, and beef; almost everything is prepared with local produce and herbs. ✉ *8406 Urbana Pike, Urbana 21704,* ☎ *301/831–8232,* FAX *301/831–8092,* WEB *www.theturningpointinn.com. 4 rooms, 2 cottages. Restaurant, bar. AE, D, DC, MC, V. Restaurant closed Mon. BP.*

Nightlife and the Arts

The **Frederick Coffee Co. and Café** (✉ 100 East St., ☎ 301/698–0039) is in a renovated garage whose bays are now windows overlooking the

Everedy Square & Shab Row complex. Folk and jazz musicians perform Saturday night.

The **Weinberg Center for the Arts** (✉ 20 W. Patrick St., ☎ 301/228–2828) was a movie house in the 1920s. Now the theater offers plays, musicals, and concerts throughout the year.

Outdoor Activities and Sports

Hiking

The famed **Appalachian Trail** traverses the spine of South Mountain just west of Frederick, from the Potomac River to the Pennsylvania line. Several well-known viewpoints can be found along Maryland's 40-mi stretch, including Annapolis Rocks and Weverton Cliffs. The best access points that have parking available are Gathland State Park, Washington Monument State Park, and Greenbrier State Park. For more information, contact the **Appalachian Trail Conference** (✉ 799 Washington St., Harpers Ferry, WV 25425, ☎ 304/535–6331, WEB www.atconf.org).

Shopping

In downtown Frederick, **Everedy Square & Shab Row** was once a complex of buildings that manufactured kitchen utensils and wares; now it's a center for retail shops, restaurants, and boutiques. At the family-owned **Candy Kitchen** (✉ 52 N. Market St., ☎ 301/698–0442) you can get hand-dipped chocolates.

The area's best outdoor store, **The Trail House** (✉ 17 S. Market St., ☎ 301/694–8448) sells and rents quality hiking, backpacking, camping, and cross-country skiing equipment. The store also stocks a nice selection of maps and books. The **Museum Shop** (✉ 20 N. Market St., ☎ 301/695–0424) sells museum-quality ceramics, sculpture, handcrafted jewelry, Whistler etchings, and Japanese woodcuts.

Away from downtown, **Wonder Book & Video** (✉ 1306 W. Patrick St., ☎ 301/694–5955) stocks more than 600,000 new and used books, videos, and compact discs.

SIDE TRIPS FROM FREDERICK

Not only is Frederick within easy driving distance of Baltimore and Washington, D.C., but it's also surrounded by other areas of interest, including historic towns, scenic parks, and national battlefields.

Numbers in the margin correspond to points of interest on the Side Trips from Frederick map.

Monocacy National Battlefield

8 *2 mi south of Frederick (via Rte. 355).*

Monocacy National Battlefield was the site of a little-known, hugely mismatched confrontation between 12,000–13,000 Confederates and 5,800 Union troops on July 9, 1864; many historians believe the Union victory thwarted a Confederate invasion of Washington, D.C. Although the Union troops were outnumbered, they delayed the Rebels by burning a bridge along the Monocacy. This tactic, along with some intensive fighting in the river, delayed the Confederates' approach to Washington, allowing the federal government time to bolster its forts. The farmland surrounding the battlefield remains largely unchanged. An electronic map in the visitor center explains the battle. ✉ *4801 Ur-*

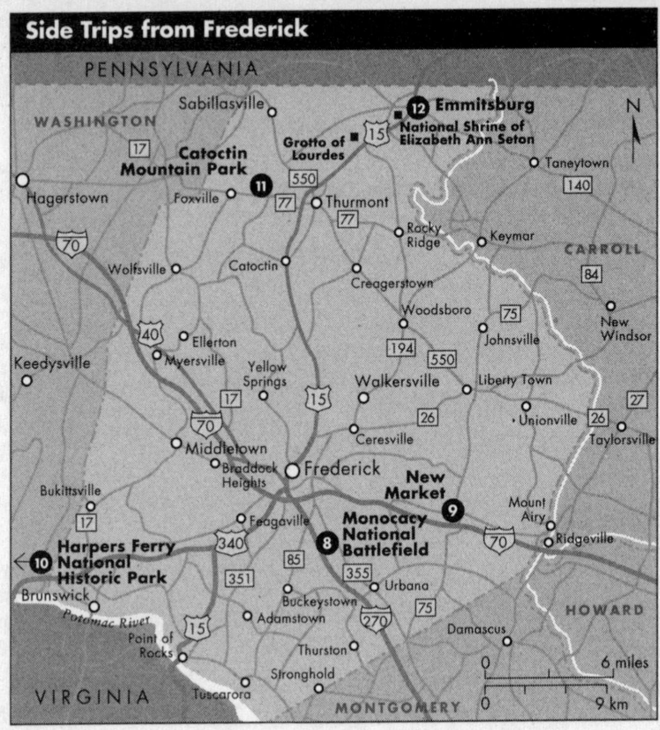

bana Pike, ☎ *301/662–3515,* WEB *www.nps.gov/mono/home.htm.* Free. ⏲ *Daily 8–4:30 (until 5:30 Memorial Day–Labor Day).*

New Market

❾ *8 mi east of Frederick (via Rte. 70).*

The self-proclaimed antiques capital of Maryland, New Market is a 200-year-old village surrounded by farmland. Though some things have remained the same for the past two centuries, a new addition to town is the throngs of tourists walking Main Street in search of furnishings and knickknacks.

Dining

$$–$$$ ✕ **Mealey's.** Once a store and hotel on the National Pike, Mealey's today is a busy restaurant in the heart of New Market, appropriately decorated with antiques. A large stone fireplace dominates the spacious main dining room, which is often filled to capacity on weekend evenings and Sunday afternoon; smaller dining rooms offer more privacy. Beef and Chesapeake Bay seafood are the specialties. Desserts are worth saving room for—especially the bread pudding, served with a bourbon vanilla sauce. ✉ *8 Main St.,* ☎ *301/865–5488. AE, D, DC, MC, V.*

Harpers Ferry National Historical Park

❿ *24 mi southwest of Frederick (via Rte. 340).*

Less than a mile from both Maryland's and Virginia's state lines is Harpers Ferry National Historic Park in West Virginia. Thomas Jefferson described the area that makes up the park best: "On your right comes up the Shenandoah, having ranged along the foot of the mountains a hundred miles to seek a vent. On your left approaches the Potomac, in quest of a passage also. In the moment of their junction they rush together against the mountain, rend it asunder, and pass off to the sea. . . . This scene is worth a voyage across the Atlantic." The spot where these rivers converge so dramatically is also where, on October 16, 1859, the radical abolitionist John Brown led his 21-man assault on the Harpers Ferry arsenal. Today, much of Harpers Ferry has been restored as it was during the time of John Brown's raid, and historic markers and exhibits tell the story of that infamous event and the town's tumultuous involvement in the Civil War.

The township of **Harpers Ferry** grew around a U.S. armory built in 1740, and many buildings have been preserved. Lining the cobblestone streets are shops and museums, where park employees in period costume demonstrate Early American skills and interpret the evolution of American firearms. Each second Saturday in October the park service stages Election Day 1860, when the presidential candidates on the slate in the region (Stephen Douglas, John Bell, and John Breckinridge—Abraham Lincoln was not on this ballot) again debate the hot topic of their day: states' rights versus a strong federal union. ✉ *Parking lot 1 mi past Shenandoah bridge on Rte. 340, Harpers Ferry, WV,* ☎ *304/535–6298,* WEB *www.nps.gov/hafe.* 🎫 *$5 per vehicle, $3 per person arriving by other means.* 🕓 *Daily 8–5.*

Above the park on High Street is the small, memorable **John Brown Wax Museum,** which depicts the abolitionist's raid on the town and the highlights of his life. ✉ *High St.,* ☎ *304/535–6342.* 🎫 *$4.50.* 🕓 *Daily 9–4:30; closed mid-Dec.–mid-Mar.*

Catoctin Mountain Park

⓫ *15 mi north of Frederick (via Rte. 15).*

Hidden within this park is Camp David, the presidential retreat that was the site of the famous peace accords between Egypt and Israel. You won't find the camp, which has been used by presidents since Franklin D. Roosevelt, and even if you come close, you'll run into security officers. What you will find are 6,000 acres of rocky outcrops and thick forests traversed by 20 mi of moderate to strenuous hiking trails, the most popular of which have scenic overlooks. A small visitor center has exhibits on the area's wildlife. Across Route 77 is **Cunningham Falls State Park,** the site of a cascading 78-ft waterfall and a man-made lake. Both parks have camping facilities. ✉ *Rte. 77, west of Rte. 15, Thurmont,* ☎ *301/663–9330,* WEB *www.nps.gov/cato.* 🎫 *Free.* 🕓 *Visitor center weekdays 10–4:30, weekends 8:30–5. Park daily dawn–dusk.*

Catoctin Wildlife Preserve & Zoo, 6 mi from the park, holds more than 350 animals on 30 acres. The zoo is easily navigable by children, and the tall trees and winding paths make for comfortable walking. Exotic animals here include tigers, macaws, monkeys, and boas. A petting zoo allows children to mingle with goats and other small animals. Throughout the summer there are interactive shows, when children can touch snakes, talk to tigers, and learn about grizzlies. ✉ *13019 Catoctin Furnace Rd., Thurmont,* ☎ *301/271–3180,* WEB *www.cwpzoo.com.* 🎫 *$11.95.* 🕓 *Mar., daily 10–4; Apr. and Oct., daily 10–5; early to late May and early to late Sept., daily 9–5; Memorial Day–Labor Day, daily 9–6.*

Dining

$–$$ ✕ **Cozy Restaurant.** A local institution, the Cozy Restaurant became internationally famous during the 1979 Camp David Accords, when hordes of reporters stayed at the adjacent inn to cover the Israeli-Egyptian peace talks. Photographs, newspaper clippings, and memorabilia from that era are on display in the restaurant's entrance halls. The 750-seat restaurant is best known these days for its all-you-can-eat buffets, which often include seafood, steaks, and fried chicken. ✉ *103 Frederick Rd., Thurmont,* ☎ *301/271–7373,* WEB *www.cozyvillage.com. AE, MC, V.*

En Route Two of Frederick County's three covered bridges span creeks near Thurmont. The **Loy's Station Covered Bridge,** originally built in 1848 and recently reconstructed after a fire, is east of Thurmont off Route 77. **Roddy Road Covered Bridge,** built in 1856, is north of Thurmont, just off Route 15. Picnic areas are near both bridges.

Emmitsburg

12 *24 mi north of Frederick (via Rte. 15).*

By the foothills of the Catoctin Mountains, Emmitsburg, founded in 1757, was the site of the first parochial school in the United States and the final home of the first American saint. Its Main Street remains a showcase of fine examples of Federal, Georgian, and Victorian architecture; many of the buildings are still in use as homes and businesses.

The **National Shrine Grotto of Lourdes** reproduces the famous grotto in France where a peasant girl saw visions of the Virgin Mary. The grotto, tucked into a mountain overlooking Mount Saint Mary's College, draws more than 1 million visitors a year, and a sunrise Easter service attracts a crowd. Beautifully landscaped paths lead to the grotto and a small chapel. ✉ *U.S. Rte. 15,* ☎ *301/447–5318,* WEB *www.msmary.edu/grotto.* ⏲ *Daily dawn–dusk.*

The **National Shrine of St. Elizabeth Ann Seton** contains the home of the first American-born saint, who came to the Maryland mountains to establish the Sisters of Charity and the nation's first parochial school. Born to wealth in New York City, Elizabeth Ann Seton (1774–1821) was widowed with five children before her experiences in Italy led her to convert to Catholicism. A short film and exhibits tell her story, and a classroom contains authentic furnishings. She is buried in a small graveyard on the well-maintained and shaded grounds. She was canonized in Rome in 1975; Pope John Paul II designated the chapel of her shrine a minor basilica in 1991. ✉ *333 S. Seton Ave.,* ☎ *301/447–6606,* WEB *www.setonshrine.org.* ⏲ *May–Oct., daily 10–4:30; Nov.–mid-Jan. and Feb.–Apr., Tues.–Sun. 10–4:30.*

WESTERN MARYLAND

The South Mountains that divide Frederick and Washington counties once sheltered Confederates, who formed a defensive line against advancing Union soldiers just before the Battle of Antietam. Only a few monuments and road signs mark this lesser-known battle site today. Hikers and cyclists come to travel the South Mountains' Appalachian Trail and marvel at panoramic views of the Potomac River and the valley that surrounds Hagerstown to the west.

Numbers in the margin correspond to points of interest on the Western Maryland map.

Hagerstown

13 *25 mi west of Frederick (via I–70), 75 mi west of Baltimore (via I–70).*

Once a prosperous railroad hub and manufacturing center, Hagerstown is striving to redefine itself, spending millions refurbishing downtown buildings for offices and retail stores. Chic restaurants have opened along the Public Square, and plans call for the creation of an arts and entertainment district around the venerable Maryland Theatre. The re-

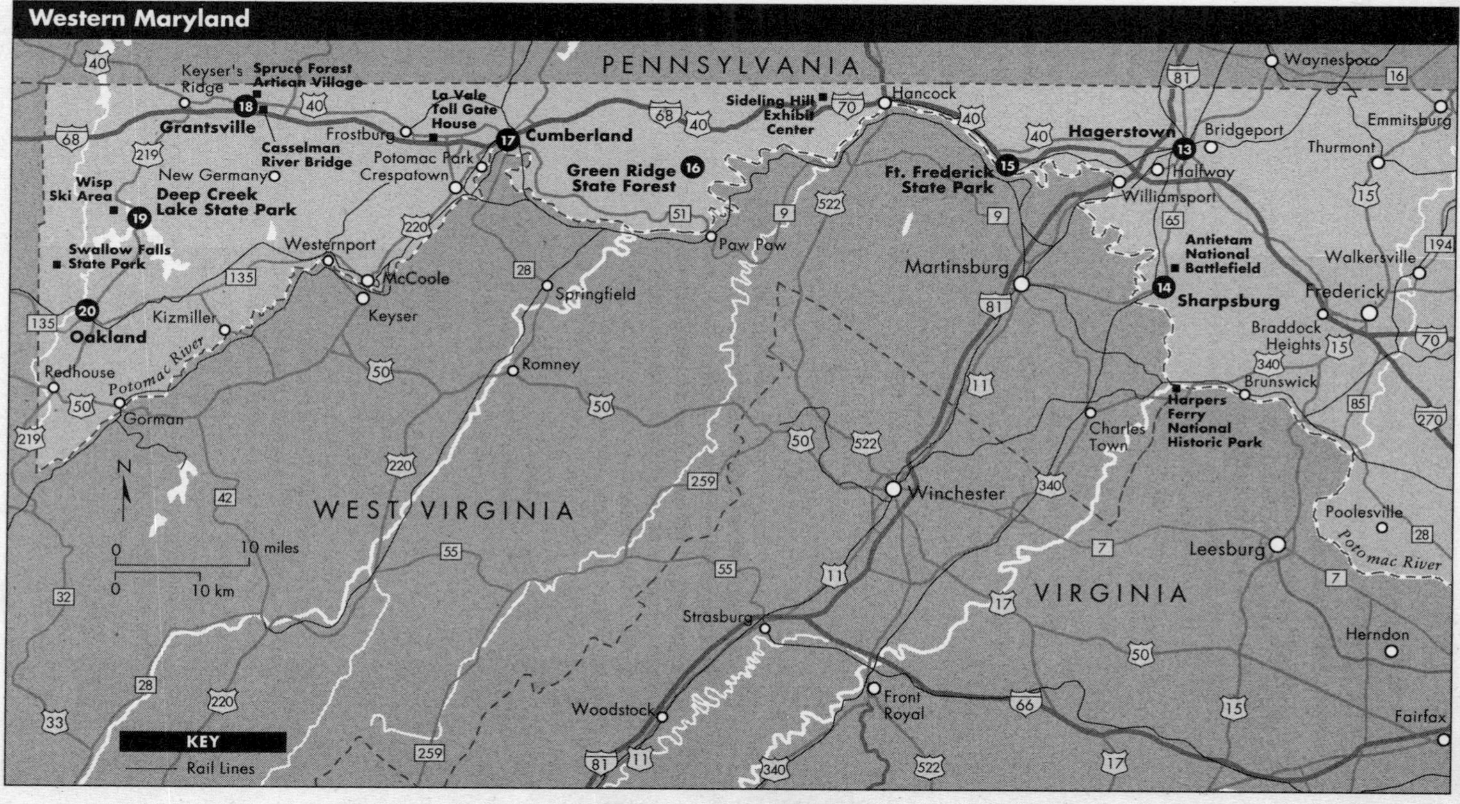
Western Maryland
PENNSYLVANIA
WEST VIRGINIA
VIRGINIA
Keyser's Ridge
Spruce Forest Artisan Village
Grantsville
Casselman River Bridge
La Vale Toll Gate House
Frostburg
Cumberland
Potomac Park
Crespatown
New Germany
Wisp Ski Area
Deep Creek Lake State Park
Swallow Falls State Park
Westernport
McCoole
Keyser
Kizmiller
Oakland
Redhouse
Potomac River
Gorman
Green Ridge State Forest
Sideling Hill Exhibit Center
Hancock
Paw Paw
Springfield
Romney
Ft. Frederick State Park
Hagerstown
Bridgeport
Halfway
Williamsport
Martinsburg
Antietam National Battlefield
Sharpsburg
Waynesboro
Emmitsburg
Thurmont
Walkersville
Frederick
Braddock Heights
Brunswick
Harpers Ferry National Historic Park
Charles Town
Winchester
Poolesville
Potomac River
Leesburg
Herndon
Fairfax
Strasburg
Front Royal
Woodstock
N
0
10 miles
0
10 km
KEY
Rail Lines

gion lost its bid to create a national Civil War museum, but did gain the headquarters of the nation's largest Civil War battlefield preservation group, the Association for the Preservation of Civil War Battlefields. The group has spent thousands of dollars to help preserve land at the nearby Antietam National Battlefield in Sharpsburg.

Hagerstown may have lesser ties to the Civil War than Frederick, but the city's past is being tapped as a tourism magnet—and there's some justification. The Battle of Antietam and the lesser-known Battle of South Mountain were both fought just outside Hagerstown, and Confederates occasionally came through town, most noticeably in 1864, when they threatened to burn the city. The Rebels relented after city officials paid a $20,000 ransom.

The **Washington County Museum of Fine Arts** has an impressive collection of American paintings, drawings, prints, and sculpture from the 18th century to the present that includes the work of Benjamin West, James McNeill Whistler, and Norman Rockwell. The museum's holdings also include two portraits by Joshua Johnson, believed to be the first African-American portrait artist. The building is inside Hagerstown's beautiful **City Park,** a 27-acre wooded and landscaped haven with two small, man-made lakes—they're filled with ducks, geese, and swans during the spring and fall. ✉ *91 Key St.,* ☎ *301/739–5727,* WEB *www.washcomuseum.org.* 🎫 *Free.* ⏲ *Tues.–Sat. 10–5, Sun. 1–5.*

The **Hager House and Museum** is the original home of the town's founder, Jonathan Hager, who built the home in 1739 over two springs to give his family a protected water supply and an indoor springhouse (used to refrigerate food). Built of uncut fieldstones, the house has 22-inch-thick walls and 18th-century furnishings. Colonial-style flower and herb gardens surround it. A small museum next to the house contains an extensive collection of 18th- and 19th-century coins, forks, and combs made of bone, pottery, buttons, and ironwork. The items were excavated during the house's 1953 restoration. ✉ *110 Key St.,* ☎ *301/739–8393.* 🎫 *$4.* ⏲ *Apr.–Dec., Tues.–Sat. 10–4, Sun. 2–5.*

Hagerstown Roundhouse Museum. Although the city's 89-year-old roundhouse was demolished in 1999, photographs, artifacts, and memorabilia from Hagerstown's railroading heyday can be found in this two-story museum, inside a former office of the Western Maryland Railway. Lights, lanterns, bells, and whistles are among the artifacts, and model railroad layouts add to the fun. ✉ *300 S. Burhans Blvd.,* ☎ *301/739–4665,* WEB *www.roundhouse.org.* 🎫 *$3.* ⏲ *Fri.–Sun. 1–5.*

Dining and Lodging

$–$$ ✕ **Roccoco.** In downtown Hagerstown, this restaurant bills itself as "a grand brasserie." The selections here go beyond the usual, including country garlic soup, crispy duck spring rolls, garlic chicken, and avocado pizza. Entrée standouts include a smoked chicken-mascarpone–pine nut ravioli with a truffle cream sauce and veal scallopini with mushrooms and Madeira wine sauce. Pastries and desserts are made on the premises. ✉ *20 W. Washington St.,* ☎ *301/790–3331. AE, D, MC, V. Closed Sun.*

$$ **Wingrove Manor Bed & Breakfast.** The large, inviting front porch on this Victorian house on the north side of town has a brick stairway leading up to it, adding to the general grandeur. The four guest rooms are stately and dignified, but they do include televisions and VCRs (there's a large video library) for unwinding. Two rooms have Jacuzzis. Breakfast is served in the main dining room. ✉ *635 Oak Hill Ave., Hagerstown 21740,* ☎ *301/797–7769,* FAX *301/797–8659,* WEB *www.wingrovemanor.com. 4 rooms. In-room VCRs. AE, DC, MC, V. BP.*

$ **Four Points Sheraton Hotel.** Blue and mauve color schemes and touches of wood in these rooms keep things looking warm for guests, many of whom stay here for business. Some business suites have Murphy beds and conference tables. ✉ *1910 Dual Hwy., Hagerstown 21740,* ☎ *301/790–3010,* FAX *301/733–4559,* WEB *www.sheraton.com. 108 rooms. Restaurant, room service, in-room data ports, pool, gym, sports bar, business services, meeting rooms. AE, D, DC, MC, V.*

Shopping

Prime Outlets (✉ 495 Prime Outlets Blvd., ☎ 888/883–6288) can occupy your day with more than 100 designer and specialty outlet stores with men's, women's, and children's clothing, housewares, electronics, gifts, shoes, and accessories.

Sharpsburg

14 *10 mi south of Hagerstown (via Rte. 65), 20 mi west of Frederick (via Alt. Rte. 40 to Rte. 34).*

Among the cornfields and woods that surround Sharpsburg is the ★ **Antietam National Battlefield,** where Union and Confederate troops clashed on September 17, 1862. It was the single bloodiest day of the war: more than 23,000 men were killed or wounded. Landmarks on the largely undisturbed battlefield include the Burnside Bridge, Dunkard Church, and Bloody Lane. The Union's victory at Sharpsburg gave President Abraham Lincoln the momentum to announce on September 22 that unless the Confederacy stopped fighting and rejoined the Union, an "Emancipation Proclamation" would be issued on January 1 that would free all slaves in Confederate states. At the visitor center are Civil War artifacts, a short film about Lincoln's visit, an hour-long documentary about the battle (shown at noon daily), and rental cassettes for narrated driving tours. An overlook provides a panoramic view of the battlefield and the countryside. ✉ *Rte. 65, Sharpsburg Pike,* ☎ *301/432–5124,* WEB *www.nps.gov/anti.* *$3.* *Battlefield daily dawn–dusk; visitor center Labor Day–Memorial Day, daily 8:30–5; Memorial Day–Labor Day, daily 8:30–6.*

Dining and Lodging

$$–$$$ ✕ **Old South Mountain Inn.** Built in 1732, the South Mountain Inn was a trading post in its early days. Now a restaurant, the 18th-century stone structure is atop South Mountain along the National Pike (now Route 40). In addition to an indoor dining room, there's also an enclosed garden patio with white wicker furniture and plants as well as a garden patio. Highlights on the Continental menu include chicken saltimbocca, a boneless breast sautéed in butter and topped with fontina cheese and prosciutto, and Brace of Quail, quail stuffed with the inn's own sausage and braised in a wild mushroom and red wine sauce. ✉ *6132 Old National Pike, Boonsboro 21713,* ☎ *301/432–6155,* FAX *301/432–2211. AE, DC, MC, V. Closed Mon.*

$$–$$$ **Inn at Antietam.** Built in 1908, this Victorian home sits on 8 acres. The site was once the campgrounds of Gen. George Pickett during the Battle of Antietam. Next door is the Antietam National Cemetery. Common areas include a solarium, parlor, and wraparound porch. The Gen. Burnside Smokehouse Suite has a sleeping loft and a brick fireplace. Breakfast, with a menu that changes daily, often includes favorites such as blueberry pancakes, eggs Benedict, and Belgian waffles. ✉ *220 E. Main St., Sharpsburg 21782,* ☎ *877/835–6011,* FAX *301/432–5981,* WEB *www.innatantietam.com. 5 suites. Library; no TV in some rooms, no kids under 6, no smoking. AE, MC, V. Closed Jan.*

$ **Piper House Bed & Breakfast.** This 1840 farmhouse on the Antietam battlefield is furnished simply, as it would have been during the war. An extensive collection of Civil War books and memorabilia is in the library, and breakfast is served in a country kitchen. Not only did this house survive the bloody daylong battle, but it also served as the headquarters of Confederate Gen. James Longstreet and as a hospital for wounded Union and Rebel soldiers. ✉ *Antietam National Battlefield, Rte. 65, Sharpsburg 21782,* ☎ *301/797–1862. 3 rooms. Library; no room phones, no room TVs, no smoking. MC, V.*

Ft. Frederick State Park

⓯ *17 mi west of Hagerstown (via I–70), 40 mi west of Frederick (via I–70).*

Along the Potomac River stands one of the few surviving stone forts from the French and Indian War. Built in 1756, the barracks were reconstructed in the 1930s by the Civilian Conservation Corps, to whom a small museum here is dedicated. A visitor center displays artifacts from the French and Indian War and the Colonial era. ✉ *11100 Ft. Frederick Rd., Big Pool,* ☎ *301/842–2155.* *$3.* ⏲ *Apr.–Oct., daily 8 AM–dusk; Nov.–Mar., weekdays 8 AM–dusk, weekends 10 AM–dusk.*

En Route Interstate 68 cuts through Sideling Hill—the mountain that separates Washington and Allegany counties—thus exposing nearly 850 vertical ft of sedimentary rock formed 350 million years ago. At the top of the mountain is the **Sideling Hill Exhibit Center,** which seeks to explain one of the best rock exposures in the eastern United States. The four-story visitor center also has interpretive exhibits of animals native to western Maryland. Forty-minute tours that cover the center and the mountain's geology are offered at 11, 1, and 3 daily. Picnic areas overlook the stunning valleys. ✉ *I–68, 5 mi west of Hancock,* ☎ *301/678–5442.* *Free.* ⏲ *Daily 9–5.*

Green Ridge State Forest

⓰ *23 mi west of Ft. Frederick State Park (via I–70 to I–68), 62 mi west of Frederick (via I–70 to I–68).*

Maryland's second-largest forest—nearly 40,000 acres—stretches across most of eastern Allegany County. Its vast stands of oak, maple, hickory, and pine attract those from Baltimore, who come here to hunt, bike, and camp in the fall and spring. Beneath the forest growth, decaying tombstones and crumbling stone foundations are remnants of the lives of the immigrants who worked on the C&O Canal and the railroad. Within the forest is a Potomac River overlook, where Union soldiers once stood on the lookout for Confederate saboteurs. A *Baltimore Sun* columnist called one of the park's overlooks, just off the interstate, "the best deck in Maryland" because of its phenomenal view of heavily wooded mountains. ✉ *28700 Headquarters Dr. NE, Flintstone,* ☎ *301/478–3124.* *Free.* ⏲ *Park office daily 8–4.*

Cumberland

⓱ *17 mi west of Green Ridge State Park via I–68; 89 mi west of Frederick (via I–70 to I–68), 142 mi west of Baltimore (via I–70 to I–68).*

Cradled in the Allegheny Mountains, Cumberland was once America's gateway to the west. Pioneers, and later, trains and motorists, took advantage of a 1-mi-long natural pass in the mountains—the Narrows—to make their way west. The National Pike, the first federally funded highway, appropriated by Congress in 1806; the Chesapeake and Ohio Canal; and the Baltimore and Ohio Railroad all converged here in the mid-19th century. When the B&O Railroad beat the canal to Cumberland, it doomed the waterway as the future transportation route.

Today, Cumberland is revisiting its transportation heritage to help its economy and attract tourists. A two-lane highway and an excursion train now cross through the 900-ft-deep Narrows, whose exposed red shale and sandstone cliffs above make for a scenic ride. In addition, millions of dollars are being spent to restore a stretch of the canal and offer mule-drawn barge rides to visitors. The city's historic train station has been restored, and by 2007, the entire complex, known as Canal Place, will be completed and include recreational areas, pedestrian bridges, and other attractions.

In the mid- to late 19th century, Cumberland's leading politicians, doctors, lawyers, and businessmen lived in the **Washington Street Historic District,** which stretches along Washington Street from Wills Creek to Allegany Street and from Greene Street to Fayette Street. The six-block district, on the National Register of Historic Places, still reflects the architecture of the period, with prominent Federal, Greek revival, Italianate, Queen Anne, and Georgian revival homes. Of particular interest is the **Emmanuel Episcopal Church and Parish Hall** (✉ 16 Washington St.). It was built in 1849–50 on the site of the former Ft. Cumberland, a frontier outpost during the French and Indian War. The Gothic revival church was built of native sandstone and contains three large Tiffany windows.

The only surviving structure from Ft. Cumberland, **George Washington's Headquarters** (✉ Washington and Greene Sts., ☎ 301/777–5132; 🎫 free; ⏲ by appointment) was used by the future president and military hero when he was an aide to General Braddock. The one-room cabin, built in 1754–55, stands at Prospect Square in Riverside Park, downhill from where Ft. Cumberland once stood.

The Second Empire–style **Gordon-Roberts House** was built in 1867 by Josiah Gordon, president of the C&O Canal, on fashionable Washington Street. Today it's the home of the Allegany County Historical Society, and a repository for hundreds of items of local and national significance, including furniture, clothing, hats, accessories, and toys. ✉ *218 Washington St.,* ☎ *301/777–8678,* WEB *www.historyhouse.allconet.org.* 🎫 *$3.* ⏲ *June–Oct., Tues.–Sat. 10–5, Sun. 1–5.*

The **Western Maryland Scenic Railroad** allows riders to relive the glory days of trains in Cumberland. A 1916 Baldwin locomotive, once used in Michigan's Upper Peninsula, carries you uphill through the Narrows and up scenic mountains on a 32-mi round-trip to Frostburg. A 90-minute layover in Frostburg allows time for lunch at one of the many restaurants on the city's main street, just up the hill. A diesel engine typically runs on weekdays, with the more popular steam engine saved for weekends. Also in Frostburg, the **Thrasher Carriage Collection Museum** (✉ 19 Depot St., ☎ 301/689–3380, WEB www.thrashercarriagemuseum.com; 🎫 $2; ⏲ May–Sept., Tues.–Sun. 11–3; Oct., daily 11–3; Nov.–Dec., weekends 11–3) contains almost every style of horse-drawn vehicle, including carriages, milk wagons, sleighs, and funeral wagons. These vehicles from another era were collected by James R. Thrasher, a local blacksmith's son who became a successful businessman. Museum admission is included in the train fare. ✉ *13 Canal St.,* ☎ *301/759–4400 or 800/872–4650,* WEB *www.wmsr.com.* 🎫 *$19.* ⏲ *Departures at 11:30 AM: May–Sept., Wed.–Sun; Oct., daily; Nov.–mid-Dec., weekends.*

The **Cumberland Visitors Center—C&O Canal National Historical Park** explains Cumberland's role as the western terminus of the C&O Canal. Interactive exhibits relate to boatbuilding at the Cumberland boatyards and the regional coal industry, which used the canal to transport coal to D.C. You can walk through a re-created Paw Paw Tunnel, one of the landmarks along the nearly 185-mi canal. ✉ *Western Maryland Railway Station, 13 Canal St.,* ☎ *301/722–8226,* WEB *www.canalplace.org.* 🎫 *Free.* ⏲ *Daily 9–5.*

Dining and Lodging

$$–$$$ ✕ **J. B.'s Steak Cellar.** A blazing fireplace, dark paneling, and cushioned chairs keep this basement-level restaurant cozy in winter, when skiers returning home from the Wisp Ski Area in neighboring Garrett County stop by. Cuts of beef and fresh seafood are displayed in a glass case in one of the two small dining rooms, and steaks are grilled in front of diners. The menu, predominantly beef, chicken, and seafood, also includes pasta dishes such as seafood Alfredo and Portobello mushroom linguine. Prime rib remains a favorite. ✉ *12801 Ali Ghan Rd. NE, Cumberland (Exit 46, I–68, 1 mi east of Cumberland),* ☎ *301/722–6155. AE, D, DC, MC, V.*

$–$$$ ✕ **Au Petit Paris.** Murals of Paris street scenes welcome diners to this restaurant, whose three intimate dining rooms are decorated with pictures of the City of Light. Duckling, lamb, veal, and seafood are the specialties here. Signature dishes include ostrich medallions served in a wine sauce with mushroom caps, and baked shrimp stuffed with crab. The chateaubriand steak serves two and must be ordered 24 hours in advance. Desserts include bananas Foster and cherries jubilee. ✉ *86 E. Main St., Frostburg,* ☎ *301/689–8946. Reservations essential. AE, D, DC, MC, V. Closed Sun.–Mon.*

$–$$ ✕ **City Lights.** This casual restaurant, inside a two-story, century-old building, has wooden booths and tables covered in white linens. Seafood, hand-cut steaks, and pasta dishes are the dinner staples here. The lasagna Florentine, an eye-popping 32-layer spinach lasagna, attracts attention most evenings. Homemade New York–style cheesecakes are among the desserts. ✉ *59 Baltimore St.,* ☎ *301/722–9800. AE, D, DC, MC, V. Closed Sun.*

$$–$$$ 🏨 **Rocky Gap Lodge and Golf Resort.** With Evitts Mountain and Lake Habeeb as a backdrop, this resort is in one of the state's most idyllic locales. The lobby, dining room, and lounge overlook a 243-acre man-made lake. In keeping with the nature outside, greens and browns are used throughout the six-story hotel. Rooms, larger than most, are appointed with Shaker-style furniture; most have views of a breathtaking ridge of mountains. Suites include a gas fireplace and sitting area. You can try your swing on the 18-hole golf course, hike the park's trails, or boat, fish, and swim. ✉ *Rocky Gap State Park, 16701 Lakeview Rd., Box 1199, Flintstone 21530,* ☎ *301/784–8400 or 800/724–0828,* FAX *301/784–8408,* WEB *www.rockygapresort.com. 203 rooms, 15 suites. 2 restaurants, 18-hole golf course, 3 tennis courts, indoor-outdoor pool, lake, gym, beach, boating, fishing, hiking, bar, business services, meeting rooms. AE, D, DC, MC, V.*

$–$$ 🏨 **Holiday Inn-Downtown.** Cumberland's only downtown hotel is within walking distance of the downtown mall, historic sites, and the C&O Canal. The hotel caters to many business travelers and offers the usual Holiday Inn amenities: in-room coffeemaker, hair dryer, iron, and ironing board. Rooms on the west side of the six-story hotel come with a panoramic view of the mountains. Passing night trains can sometimes be a disturbance to those sleeping on the opposite side. ✉ *100 S. George St., 21502,* ☎ *301/724–4001,* FAX *301/724–4001,* WEB *www.cumberlandmdholidayinn.com. 130 rooms. Restaurant, room service, pool, gym, bar, business services, meeting rooms, airport shuttle, some pets allowed. AE, MC, V.*

$-$$ **Inn at Walnut Bottom.** Within two 19th-century row houses connected by a modern addition, this charming country inn is within walking distance of Cumberland's historic district. Antiques and reproductions of 19th-century country furniture are standard in each of the guest rooms. Lemonade, apple cider, and homemade sweets are served every afternoon in an upstairs sitting room that's filled with games, puzzles, books, and magazines. You can rent bicycles for a ride along the flat towpath of the C&O Canal or opt for the inn's Afspaending treatment, a kind of massage therapy. ✉ *120 E. Greene St., 21502,* ☎ *301/777–0003 or 800/286–9718,* FAX *301/777–8288,* WEB *www.iwbinfo.com. 12 rooms. Bicycles; no smoking. AE, D, MC, V. BP.*

Outdoor Activities and Sports

Adventure Guides & Travel (✉ 113 E. Main St., Frostburg, ☎ 301/689–0345) provides instruction and rental equipment in rock and ice climbing, caving, rappelling, kayaking, canoeing, scuba, snorkeling, and trout and bass fishing.

Allegany Expeditions Inc. (✉ 10310 Columbus Ave. NE, Cumberland, ☎ 301/722–5170, WEB www.alleganyexpeditions.com) offers guided backpacking, caving, canoeing, fishing, and kayaking tours. The company also rents out camping equipment.

Grantsville

18 *21 mi west of Cumberland (via I–68).*

Two miles south of the Mason-Dixon Line, Grantsville is a village amid some of the most productive farmland in the region. It is also in the heart of the county's Amish and Mennonite communities. To the west and south is Maryland's largest forest, the 53,000-acre Savage River State Forest. Mostly undeveloped, it's used by hikers, campers, anglers, and, in the winter, cross-country skiers. Also nearby is New Germany State Park, which has hiking trails, campsites, and cabins.

By the time you see the **Casselman River Bridge** (✉ Rte. 40), you're almost in Grantsville. This single-span stone arch bridge ½ mi east of town was built in 1813; at the time it was the largest of its kind. Though the bridge is no longer in use, it serves as the backdrop for a small state park and picnic area.

The history and craftsmanship of Upper Appalachia are exhibited at the rustic **Spruce Forest Artisan Village and Penn Alps,** a museum village where spinners, weavers, potters, stained-glass workers, wood sculptors, and bird carvers demonstrate their skills. The Winterberg House, a log stagecoach stop, is the last remaining log tavern along the Old National Pike. It is now used as a crafts store and restaurant. ✉ *Rte. 40,* ☎ *301/895–3332,* WEB *www.spruceforest.org.* *Free.* *Mon.–Sat. 10–5.*

In the northern end of Savage River State Forest, the much smaller **New Germany State Park** (400 acres) contains stands of hemlocks and pines planted in the late 1950s. In winter, this popular hiking spot's 8 mi of trails are groomed for cross-country skiing. A 13-acre manmade lake is available for swimming, fishing, and boating. The park also has picnic shelters, 39 campsites, and 11 rental cabins, fully equipped for year-round use. ✉ *349 Headquarters La., 25 mi southwest of Cumberland via I–68 and Lower New Germany Rd. (Exit 24),* ☎ *301/895–5453,* WEB *www.dnr.state.md.us.* *$2, Memorial Day–Labor Day only.* *Daily dawn–dusk.*

Lodging

$$$ **Savage River Lodge.** Hidden in Maryland's largest state forest, this rustic retreat on a plot of 45 acres has 18 cozy, upscale cabins; each

comfortably sleeps four. The handsome three-story lodge, with an inviting stone fireplace, is a short walk from the cabins. The cabins contain oversize furniture, queen-size beds in a loft, and gas log fireplaces and ceiling fans. Muffins and orange juice are delivered to your room every morning. ✉ *1600 Mount Aetna Rd., Grantsville 21536, 5.2 mi off I–68, Exit 29,* ☎ *301/689–3200,* FAX *301/689–2746,* WEB *www.savageriverlodge.com. 18 cabins. Restaurant, fishing, mountain bikes, hiking, cross-country skiing, bar, library, business services, meeting rooms, some pets allowed (fee); no room TVs. AE, D, MC, V.*

Shopping

Yoder Country Market (✉ Rte. 669, ☎ 301/895–5148), open Monday through Saturday, began as a butcher shop on a Mennonite family farm in 1947. Today, the market sells homemade breads, cookies, pies, and pastries baked on the premises. There's also a nice selection of bulk groceries, local food products, meats, and homemade jams and jellies. A Mennonite kitchen serves a limited menu.

Deep Creek Lake State Park

19 *21 mi southwest of Grantsville via I–68 and Rte. 219.*

Garrett County's greatest asset, the 3,900-acre Deep Creek Lake was created in the 1920s as a water source for a hydroelectric plant on the Youghiogheny (pronounced "Yok-a-gainy") River—a favorite among kayakers and white-water rafters. Though much of Deep Creek Lake's 65-mi shoreline is inaccessible to the public, it's visible from Route 219 and from numerous restaurants and motels, many of which have private docks.

For best public access, visit **Deep Creek Lake State Park** (✉ 898 State Park Road, ☎ 301/387–4111, WEB www.dnr.state.md.us). The 1,818-acre park hugs the eastern shore of the lake and has a public boat launch, small beach, and picnic and camping sites. At the park's Discovery Center are hands-on educational activities for children, a freshwater aquarium, native animals on display, and a small gift shop. The center also is a staging area for organized outdoor activities, including lake boat tours.

Near Deep Creek Lake is Maryland's only alpine ski resort, the **Wisp Ski & Golf Resort,** atop 3,080-ft Marsh Mountain. Called "the Wisp" by locals, the mountain has a humble history: its eastern face was once a cow pasture. Today it's one of the area's most popular destinations.

Dining and Lodging

$–$$$ ✕ **Deep Creek Brewing Co.** Just off Route 219 above Deep Creek Lake, this brew pub pours a fine selection of eight or so handcrafted beers—golden and pale ales and stouts, named after local landmarks—and above-average pub fare. Wild stew—venison, elk, and ostrich in a beer base—stands out from more usual appetizers and soups. The menu includes fish-and-chips and many hearty sandwiches; steak, chicken, fresh seafood, and pasta round out the entrée choices. No alcohol is served on Sunday. ✉ *75 Visitors Center Dr., McHenry,* ☎ *301/387–2182. AE, D, MC, V.*

$–$$ ✕ **Bumble Q's.** The Texas flavor of the barbecue here may seem out of place in Appalachia, but owner and Garrett County native Vivian Padgett spent some time cooking on a Texas ranch. Taste her pulled pork sandwich or BBQ ribs and you'll know why the unassuming joint is a local favorite. Her chili contains three types of beans and chopped roast beef. Desserts are homemade. ✉ *145 Bumblebee Rd., just off Rte. 219,* ☎ *301/387–7667. No credit cards. No dinner Sun.–Tues.*

$$–$$$ **Carmel Cove Inn.** Come to this former monastery retreat for tranquillity and first-rate amenities. The inn is on a ridge above a Deep Creek Lake cove, and those staying here have free use of canoes, rafts, fishing equipment, mountain bikes, and cross-country skis and snowshoes. The chapel has been converted into an English-style great room, where you can play billiards or board games, watch movies, listen to music, or browse through magazines. A communal refrigerator is stocked with wine and beer. Breakfast can be taken in the small, bright dining room; guest rooms; or on the deck, weather permitting. Some rooms have private decks and fireplaces. ✉ *290 Marsh Hill Rd., Oakland 21550,* ☎ *301/387–0067,* FAX *301/387–4127,* WEB *www.carmelcoveinn.com. 10 rooms. Tennis court, lake, outdoor hot tub, dock, boating, fishing, bicycles, cross-country skiing; no room TVs, no smoking. D, MC, V. BP.*

$$–$$$ **Savage River Inn.** Way off the beaten path within the Savage River State Forest, this inn began as a farmhouse in 1934. Additions since have created a modern, four-story structure. The great room has a large stone fireplace and splendid views of mountain scenery. Outside, enjoy a landscaped garden, pool, and hot tub. Rooms are decorated with country furnishings, and two have sitting areas and fireplaces. ✉ *Rte. 495 S to Dry Run Rd., Box 147, McHenry 21541,* ☎ *301/245–4440,* WEB *www.savageriverinn.com. 4 rooms. Pool, hot tub, bicycles, hiking. MC, V. BP.*

Outdoor Activities and Sports

BICYCLING

High Mountain Sports (✉ 21327 Garrett Hwy., McHenry, ☎ 301/387–4199, WEB www.highmountainsports.com) rents mountain bikes, snow and water skis, kayaks, and snowboards and sells outdoor gear and equipment. Kayak, mountain bike, and other outdoor tours are available as well.

BOATING

At the docks at Deep Creek Lake State Park, **Nature Lake Tours** (✉ 898 State Park Rd., ☎ 301/746–8782) offers sunrise, nature, dinner, and family-oriented tours of the lake daily from April through October.

Oakland

20 *11 mi southwest of Deep Creek Lake State Park (via Rte. 219).*

Though it's the Garrett County seat, the town of Oakland keeps a low profile. Tucked away in Maryland's extreme southwestern corner, the town sits atop a mountain plateau, 2,650 ft above sea level. Oakland prospered during the last half of the 19th century, when the famous Baltimore and Ohio Railroad reached town, bringing summer vacationers. Trains no longer bring tourists, but Oakland survives as the government and commercial center of the county.

At **Swallow Falls State Park,** paths wind along the Youghiogheny River, past shaded rocky gorges and rippling rapids, to a 63-ft waterfall. The park is also known for its stand of 300-year-old hemlocks and for its excellent camping, hiking, and fishing facilities. ✉ *222 Herrington La., off Rte. 219, Oakland,* ☎ *301/334–9180,* WEB *www.dnr.state.md.us.* *Memorial Day–Labor Day, $2; Labor Day–Memorial Day, $1.* ⏲ *Daily dawn–dusk.*

Dining

$$–$$$ ✕ **Deer Park Inn.** French-born chef and owner Pascal Fontaine uses locally grown produce in many of his dishes at this French country restaurant. His favorite dish is confit of duck, which he marinates in its own juices after curing it overnight. Beef, seafood, chicken, and lamb round

out the entrée choices. Dessert highlights include crêpes and a strawberry and rhubarb tart with crème fraîche. The restored Victorian mansion lies between Deep Creek Lake and Oakland. During the area's off-season months, the restaurant may be closed Monday–Wednesday, so call ahead. ✉ *65 Hotel Rd., Deer Park,* ☎ *301/334–2308. AE, D, MC, V. Closed Sun. No lunch.*

$$–$$$ ✕ **Cornish Manor.** Built in 1868, this ornate Victorian house was once the home of a Washington, D.C., judge. Today, the 7-acre grounds and expansive home have been turned into one of the area's best-known dining destinations. Many entrées have whimsical French-American names such as "Are you game? *Cailles à la Crème et Champignons de Paris,*" quail in a cream and mushroom sauce. The less adventurous will find steak selections, pasta, and seafood. The bakery on the premises sells bread, rolls, muffins, croissants, fruit tarts, and imported cheese. ✉ *Memorial Dr.,* ☎ *301/334–6499. AE, D, MC, V. Closed Sun. and Mon.*

FREDERICK AND WESTERN MARYLAND A TO Z

To research prices, get advice from other travelers, and book travel arrangements, visit www.fodors.com.

AIR TRAVEL

Frederick, Hagerstown, and Cumberland are all served by regional airports. Hagerstown has commuter flights to the Baltimore-Washington International Airport (BWI) and Pittsburgh International Airport.

BUS TRAVEL

Greyhound Lines provides daily transportation to Frederick, Hagerstown, Cumberland, and Keysers Ridge in Garrett County, from Baltimore; Washington, D.C.; and Pittsburgh, Pennsylvania.

Greyhound Lines has daily runs to Hagerstown, Cumberland, Frostburg, and Keysers Ridge. Frederick, Hagerstown, and Cumberland all operate municipal bus lines. Fares vary.

Frederick Transit provides bus service within Frederick and to outlying towns, including Thurmont, Emmitsburg, Jefferson, and Walkersville. Shuttle buses transport commuters to the Washington Metro at Shady Grove and Maryland's commuter train at Point of Rocks. The shuttle fare is $1.

➤ Bus Depots: **Frederick Train Station** (✉ 100 S. East St., Frederick, ☎ 301/663–3311).

➤ Bus Lines: **Frederick Transit** (☎ 301/694–2065). **Greyhound Lines** (☎ 800/231–2222, WEB www.greyhound.com).

CAR RENTALS

➤ Agencies: **Avis Rent-A-Car** (✉ Washington County Regional Airport, 18434 Showalter Rd., Hagerstown, ☎ 800/831–2847). **Hertz** (✉ 322 S. Center St., Cumberland, ☎ 301/777–1525).

CAR TRAVEL

The best way to see western Maryland is by car. Interstate 70 links Frederick to Hagerstown and intersects with Route 15 and I–270, the main highway to Washington, D.C. West of Hagerstown, I–68—the main road through western Maryland—passes through some of the most scenic stretches of the state. Follow Route 219 off I–68 to reach Deep Creek Lake and the more remote areas of Garrett County.

EMERGENCIES

➤ EMERGENCY SERVICES: **Ambulance, fire, police** (☎ 911).
➤ HOSPITALS: **Frederick Memorial Hospital** (✉ 400 W. 7th St., Frederick, ☎ 301/698–3300). **Garrett County Memorial Hospital** (✉ 251 N. 4th St., Oakland, ☎ 301/533–4000). **Memorial Hospital** (✉ Memorial Ave., Cumberland, ☎ 301/777–4000). **Sacred Heart Hospital** (✉ 900 Seton Dr., Cumberland, ☎ 301/759–4200).

TOURS

Heritage Koaches provides horse-drawn trolley, carriage, and stagecoach tours of Cumberland. Mountain Getaway Tours offers guided bus tours of the mountains and historic sites in Allegany and Garrett counties and West Virginia and Pennsylvania. Westmar Tours conducts group bus tours of the Allegheny Mountain region and the Shenandoah Valley, led by guides in Colonial and 19th-century garb.

In Frederick, costumed guides lead walking tours ($5.50) that focus on the town's 250 years of history. Tours start at the visitor center, which also has brochures that outline a self-guided tour.
➤ BUS TOURS: **Heritage Koaches** (✉ 13 Canal St., Cumberland, ☎ 301/777–0293). **Mountain Getaway Tours** (☎ 800/459–0510). **Westmar Tours** (✉ 13 Canal St., Cumberland 21501, ☎ 301/777–0293).

TRAIN TRAVEL

The Maryland Area Rail Commuter line runs from Frederick southwest to Point of Rocks on the Potomac River and then onto Washington, D. C. Amtrak service is available from Washington, D.C., to Cumberland.
➤ TRAIN LINES: **Maryland Area Rail Commuter** (MARC, ☎ 800/325–7245). **Amtrak** (☎ 800/872–7245) service is available from Washington, D.C., to Cumberland.
➤ TRAIN STATIONS: **Cumberland Station** (✉ E. Harrison St. and Queen City Dr., Cumberland). **Frederick Train Station** (✉ 100 S. East St., Frederick, ☎ 301/663–3311). **Point of Rocks Station** (✉ Clay St.).

VISITOR INFORMATION

➤ TOURIST INFORMATION: **Allegany County Convention & Visitors Bureau** (✉ 13 Canal St., Cumberland 21502, ☎ 301/777–5138, WEB www.mdmountainside.com). **Garrett County Chamber of Commerce** (✉ 15 Visitors Center Dr., McHenry 21541, ☎ 301/387–4386, WEB www.garrettchamber.com). The **Tourism Council of Frederick County** (visitor center; ✉ 19 E. Church St., Frederick 21701, ☎ 301/228–2888, WEB www.visitfrederick.org). **Hagerstown/Washington County Convention & Visitor's Bureau** (✉ 16 Public Sq., Hagerstown 21740, ☎ 301/791–3246).

9 ANNAPOLIS AND SOUTHERN MARYLAND

Its more than 50 pre-Revolution buildings lend Annapolis an appropriate dignity. But the capital also has an unstoppable liveliness: City Dock draws pleasure seekers for outdoor dining and concerts, and its sailboat and powerboat shows receive national coverage. South of Annapolis lie the more rural lands of Calvert, Charles, and St. Mary's counties. In southern Maryland, ancient trees shade a cypress swamp sanctuary, and clay cliffs, some 100 ft tall, tower over Calvert Cliffs State Park.

Updated by Greg Tasker

THE PAST IS NEVER FAR AWAY from the present among the coves, rivers, and creeks of the Chesapeake Bay's lesser known *western* shore. Colonial Maryland asserts itself in the lively port of Annapolis. Today, "Crabtown," as the state capital is sometimes called, has one of the highest concentrations of 18th-century buildings in the nation, including more than 50 that predate the Revolutionary War.

The region south of Annapolis and D.C. is a peninsula cleft by the Patuxent River, a 110-mi-long tributary to the Bay. The counties of Anne Arundel, Calvert, Charles, and St. Mary's, which make up the area, have all been supported since their founding in the 1600s through tobacco fields and fishing fleets. More recently, the northern parts of the counties have emerged as prime residential satellites for the Annapolis-Baltimore-Washington, D.C., metro triangle—but despite the subdivisions and concomitant shopping centers, southern Maryland retains much of its rural character. Save for the fair-weather getaway enclave, Solomons Island, and the archaeological site-in-progress, Historic St. Mary's City, the region remains largely undiscovered. All the better for travelers who do come to enjoy stunning water vistas, miles of scenic roads, dozens of historic sites, and a plethora of inns and bed-and-breakfasts on the water, in tiny towns, or nestled in the fields and woodlands of its unspoiled countryside.

Pleasures and Pastimes

Dining

In the beginning, there was crab: crab cakes, crab soup, whole crabs to crack. This Chesapeake Bay specialty is still found in abundance, but Annapolis has broadened its horizons to include eateries—many in the Historic District—that offer many sorts of cuisines. Ask for a restaurant guide at the visitor center.

Dinner reservations in Annapolis are recommended throughout the summer and at times of Naval Academy events.

CATEGORY	COST*
$$$$	over $32
$$$	$22–$32
$$	$12–$22
$	under $12

**per person for a main course at dinner*

Lodging

There are many places to stay near the heart of the city, as well as area B&Bs and chain motels a few miles outside town (some of which offer free transportation to the downtown historic area).

Hotel reservations are necessary, even a year in advance, during the sailboat and powerboat shows in the spring and fall and Naval Academy commencement in May.

CATEGORY	COST*
$$$$	over $225
$$$	$150–$225
$$	$100–$150
$	under $100

**All prices are for a standard double room, excluding state tax.*

Exploring Annapolis and Southern Maryland

Annapolis and southern Maryland encompass the western shore of the Chesapeake Bay, an area within easy driving distance of Baltimore and Washington, D.C. Annapolis, on a peninsula bounded by the Severn and South rivers and the Chesapeake Bay, is a mid-Atlantic sailing capital and the gateway to southern Maryland. Calvert County, just south of Annapolis, promises compelling Bayside scenery that includes the imposing Calvert Cliffs and several miles of bay beaches. Beyond the Patuxent River, across the 1⅓-mi Thomas Johnson Bridge, lies St. Mary's County, a peninsula that protrudes farther into the Chesapeake, with the Patuxent and the Potomac rivers on either side of it.

ANNAPOLIS

In 1649 a group of Puritan settlers moved from Virginia to a spot at the mouth of the Severn River, where they established a community called Providence. Lord Baltimore—who held the royal charter to settle Maryland—named the area around this town Anne Arundel County, after his wife; in 1684 Anne Arundel Town was established across from Providence on the Severn's south side. Ten years later, Anne Arundel Town became the capital of Maryland and was renamed Annapolis—for Princess Anne, who later became queen. It received its city charter in 1708 and became a major port, particularly for the export of tobacco. In 1774 patriots here matched their Boston counterparts (who had thrown their famous tea party the previous year) by burning the *Peggy Stewart,* a ship loaded with taxed tea. Annapolis later served as the nation's first peacetime capital (1783–84).

The city's considerable Colonial and early republican heritage is largely intact and, because it's all within walking distance, highly accessible. Maryland is the only state in which the homes of all its signers of the Declaration of Independence still exist—they're all in Annapolis. You can tour three of the four—the homes of Charles Carroll, Samuel Chase, and William Paca.

Although it has long since been overtaken by Baltimore as the major Maryland port, Annapolis is still a popular pleasure-boating destination. On warm sunny days, the waters off City Dock become center stage for an amateur show of powerboaters maneuvering through the heavy traffic. Annapolis's enduring nautical reputation derives largely from the presence of the United States Naval Academy, whose strikingly uniformed midshipmen throng the city streets in crisp white uniforms during the summer and navy blue in winter.

Numbers in the text correspond to numbers in the margin and on the Annapolis map.

A Good Tour

You can see Annapolis in a single well-planned day. To get maps, schedules, and information about guided tours all year-round, it's best to begin your walking tour at the **Annapolis & Anne Arundel County Conference & Visitors Bureau** ①. Exit the visitor center, then turn left at West Street and walk to **St. Anne's Church** ②, straight ahead a half block. The edifice incorporates walls from a former church that burned in 1858; a congregation has worshiped here continuously since 1692. Off Church Circle, take Franklin Street one block to the **Banneker-Douglass Museum** ③, which portrays African-American life in Maryland, and return to the circle after a visit. Continue around the circle to the Maryland Inn and walk to the end of Main Street—passing many boutiques and small restaurants—and the **Historic Annapolis**

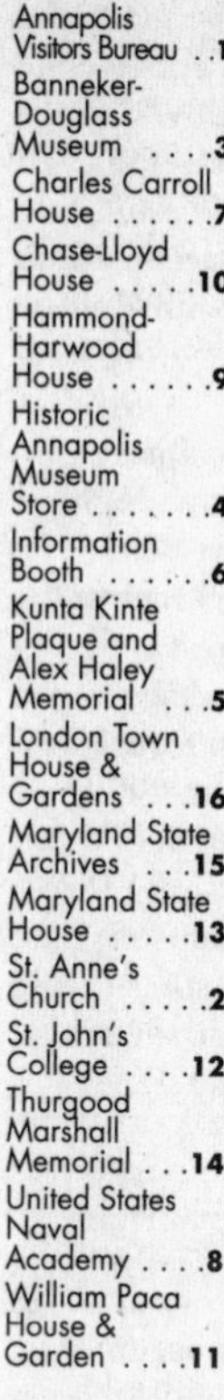

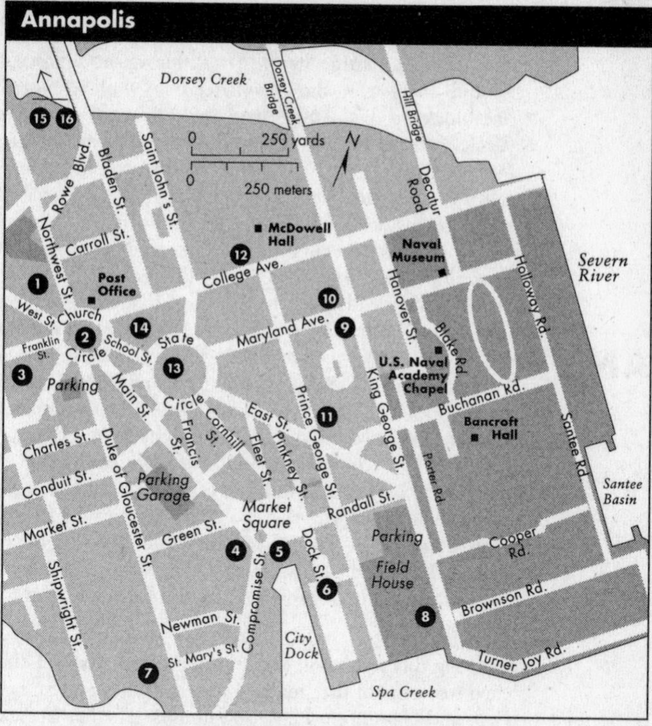

Foundation Museum Store ④, where you can rent audiotapes for self-guided walking tours. Farther down, past the Market House, which has many places to stop for a snack, look down to see the **Kunta Kinte Plaque and Alex Haley Memorial** ⑤, which commemorates the 1767 arrival of the slave portrayed in Alex Haley's *Roots.* On the other side of City Dock in front of the harbormaster's office, there's an **information booth** ⑥ where you can get maps and information from April to October.

To see the **Charles Carroll House** ⑦, return to Market Square and walk down Compromise Street. Turn right at St. Mary's Street, which dead-ends at Duke of Gloucester Street (the house is across this street, behind St. Mary's Church). Retrace your steps and turn right at Market Square onto Randall Street. Walk two blocks to the Naval Academy wall and turn right, entering the gate to the **United States Naval Academy** ⑧ and its Armel-Leftwich Visitor Center. Here you can join a tour or continue solo through the academy grounds where future U.S. Navy and Marine Corps officers are trained. Walk toward the Naval Academy Chapel dome and turn right on Buchanan Road and again at the Tecumseh statue, figurehead of the USS *Delaware,* to visit the academy's dormitory, Bancroft Hall. Return to Tecumseh and take the curvy walkway to the left to the chapel. From the chapel entrance the Naval Academy Museum is a half block to the left in Preble Hall.

From the museum, leave through Gate 3 to your right and walk to the **Hammond-Harwood House** ⑨ and the **Chase-Lloyd House** ⑩, both designed by Colonial America's foremost architect, William Buckland. The two homes are across the street from each other in the second block of Maryland Avenue. Continue on Maryland Avenue a block to Prince George Street; turn left and walk a block to the **William Paca House and Garden** ⑪, home of a signer of the Declaration of Independence.

Retrace your route and continue a block past Maryland Avenue to the campus of **St. John's College** ⑫, directly ahead at the College Avenue end of Prince George Street. After touring the campus, follow College Avenue away from the Naval Academy wall to North Street and go one block up to the **Maryland State House** ⑬ in the middle of State Circle. After touring the capitol, stop and visit the **Thurgood Marshall Memorial** ⑭ in State House Square, close to Bladen Street and College Avenue. Then turn back toward State Circle and turn right, exiting State Circle via School Street. Notice the beautiful wrought-iron fencing that surrounds Government House, a Georgian mansion with sculpture gardens that's the home of Maryland's governor. Walk down School Street, which leads back to Church Circle and West Street where the tour began. From here you can drive to the **Maryland State Archives** ⑮, where you can search for family history or do historical research. It's on the right as you leave downtown on Rowe Boulevard, heading toward Route 50. Farther west on U.S. Route 50 is **London Town House and Gardens** ⑯. At Maryland's largest archaeological excavation, digging goes on in search of the abandoned town of London. The public can participate on scheduled dig days, and docents lead tours of a three-story brick home built there in 1760. To get here from Route 50, take Exit 22 onto Highway 665 and turn right onto Highway 2 south; cross the South River Bridge and turn left at Mayo Road; in less than a mile, turn left onto Londontown Road and follow it 1 mi to the site.

TIMING

Walking this route will take about an hour. Budget another half hour each for tours of the smaller historic homes and an hour each for the Paca and Hammond-Harwood houses. The Naval Academy deserves about two hours, plus another half hour if you visit the museum. The capitol takes a quarter hour to see. The drive to the Maryland Archives takes about five minutes; it's another 15 minutes to London Town. Plan on 1½ hours for taking the tour and wandering the grounds. Note that traffic and parking in downtown Annapolis can be difficult, especially on weekends and during good weather.

Sights to See

❶ **Annapolis & Anne Arundel County Conference & Visitors Bureau.** Start your visit at Annapolis's main visitor center. Here you can pick up maps and brochures or begin a guided tour. ✉ *26 West St., Historic District,* ☎ *410/280–0445,* WEB *www.visit-annapolis.org.* ⏲ *Daily 9–5.*

❸ **Banneker-Douglass Museum.** This museum, in a former church, has changing exhibits, lectures, films, and literature about the African-American experience in Maryland. It's named for Benjamin Banneker, a Maryland astronomer, surveyor, and mathematician who lived during the 18th and 19th centuries, and Frederick Douglass, the 19th-century abolitionist, politician, and writer. ✉ *84 Franklin St., Historic District,* ☎ *410/216–6180,* WEB *www.marylandhistoricaltrust.net/bdm.htm.* 🎟 *Free.* ⏲ *Tues.–Fri. 10–3, Sat. noon–4.*

❼ **Charles Carroll House.** This birthplace and city home of the only Catholic to sign the Declaration of Independence has 18th-century terraced gardens that overlook Spa Creek. One of the wealthiest men in Colonial America, Carroll was educated abroad, studying law in France and England. He served in the Maryland legislature and later became one of the state's first two U.S. senators. After leaving public office, he became a businessman and entrepreneur. The restored 1720 house's wine cellar was added in the 19th century. ✉ *107 Duke of Gloucester St., Historic District,* ☎ *410/269–1737 or 888/269–1737,* WEB *www.carrollhouse.com.* 🎟 *$5.* ⏲ *Labor Day–July 3, Fri. and Sun. noon–4, Sat. 10–2; July 4–Labor Day, daily 10–4; other times by appointment.*

⑩ **Chase-Lloyd House.** William Buckland, a prominent Colonial architect, built the Chase-Lloyd House. In 1774 the tobacco planter and revolutionary Edward Lloyd IV completed work begun five years earlier by Samuel Chase, a signer of the Declaration of Independence and future Supreme Court justice. The first floor is open to the public and contains more of Buckland's handiwork, including a parlor mantelpiece with tobacco leaves carved into the marble. (Buckland was famous for his interior woodwork; you can see more of it in the Hammond-Harwood House, across the street, and in George Mason's Gunston Hall in Mason Neck, Virginia.) The house, furnished in a mixture of 18th-, 19th-, and 20th-century pieces, has a staircase that parts dramatically around an arched triple window. For more than 100 years the house has served as a home for elderly women, who live upstairs. ✉ *22 Maryland Ave., Historic District,* ☎ *410/263–2723.* 🎫 *$2.* ⏲ *Mar.–Dec., Mon.–Sat. 2–4.*

★ ⑨ **Hammond-Harwood House.** Ninety percent of this 1774 home is original. One of the States' finest examples of Colonial five-part Georgian architecture (a single block with two connecting rooms and wings on each side), the Hammond-Harwood House is the only verifiable full-scale example of William Buckland's work. It was also his final project, as he died the year the house was completed. Exquisite moldings, cornices, and other carvings appear throughout (note especially the garlands of roses above the front doorway). The house was meant to be a manorial wedding present from Matthias Hammond, a planter and revolutionary, to his fiancée, who jilted him before the house was finished. Hammond died a bachelor in 1784. The Harwoods took over the house toward the turn of the 19th century. Today it's furnished with 18th-century and early 19th-century furniture and paintings, including portraits by Charles Willson Peale. The garden is tended with regard to period authenticity. ✉ *19 Maryland Ave., Historic District,* ☎ *410/269–1714,* WEB *www.hammondharwoodhouse.org.* 🎫 *$6; $10 combination ticket with William Paca House.* ⏲ *May–Oct., daily noon–5; Nov.–Dec. and Mar.–Apr., daily noon–4; Jan.–Feb., weekends noon–4; (last tours leave at 3).*

④ **Historic Annapolis Foundation Museum Store.** The Historic Annapolis Foundation operates its museum store in a warehouse that held supplies for the Continental Army during the Revolutionary War. Here you can shop, check out a diorama of the city's 18th-century waterfront, and rent taped narrations for the 90-minute walking tours. ✉ *77 Main St., Historic District,* ☎ *410/268–5576,* WEB *www.hafmuseumstore.com.* 🎫 *Free.* ⏲ *Sun.–Thurs. 10–6, Fri.–Sat. 10–9. Variable extended hrs in summer.*

⑥ **Information Booth.** From April to October the information booth on City Dock, adjacent to the harbormaster's office, is open and stocked with maps and brochures. ✉ *Dock St. parking lot, Historic District,* ☎ *410/280–0445.*

NEED A BREAK? The reconstructed **Market House Pavilion** (✉ City Dock, Historic District), a collection of about 20 market stalls in the center of Market Square, sells baked goods, fast food, and seafood (prepared or to cook at home). There's no seating; set up your picnic anywhere on the dock.

⑤ **Kunta Kinte Plaque and Alex Haley Memorial.** The three-sided obelisk and plaque beyond Market Square at the head of City Dock commemorates the 1767 arrival of the African slave immortalized in Alex Haley's *Roots*. A 14-ft-wide granite "compass rose" with a bronze globe centered on Annapolis allows you to face the country of your family's origins. The memorial to Alex Haley includes bronze statues of Haley reading to three children of different ethnic backgrounds. WEB *www.kintehaley.org.*

16 **London Town House and Gardens.** Maryland's largest archaeological site, this National Historic Landmark is on the South River, 8 mi from Annapolis. The three-story waterfront brick house, built by William Brown in 1760, has 8 acres of woodland gardens. The 17th-century tobacco port of London, made up of 40 dwellings, shops, and taverns, disappeared in the 18th century, when its buildings were abandoned and left to decay. The excavation of the town is still going on. From April to September, you can join the dig one Saturday each month (call for schedule). Docents conduct 30- to 45-minute house tours; allow more time to wander the grounds. From March 15 to December, house tours leave on the hour (the last is at 3). ✉ *839 Londontown Rd., Edgewater,* ☎ *410/222–1919,* WEB *www.historiclondontown.com.* *$6.* *Hourly house tours mid-Mar.–Dec., Tues.–Sat. 10–4, Sun. noon–4 (last tour leaves at 3); Jan.–mid-Mar. by appointment.*

15 **Maryland State Archives.** Genealogists use the public search room for family history and historical research. Collections include original land, court, government, business, and church records; newspapers; photographs; and maps. In the lobby are changing exhibits and a gift shop. ✉ *350 Rowe Blvd., West Side,* ☎ *410/260–6400 or 800/235–4045,* WEB *www.mdarchives.state.md.us.* *Free.* *Wed.–Fri. 8–4:30, Sat. 8:30–noon and 1–4:30 (closed first Sat. of each month).*

★ 13 **Maryland State House.** Completed in 1780, the State House is the oldest state capitol in continuous legislative use; it's also the only one in which the U.S. Congress has sat (1783–84). It was here that General George Washington resigned as commander in chief of the Continental Army and where the Treaty of Paris was ratified, ending the Revolutionary War. Both events took place in the Old Senate Chamber, which is filled with intricate woodwork (featuring the ubiquitous tobacco motif) attributed to Colonial architect William Buckland. Also decorating this room is Charles Willson Peale's painting *Washington at the Battle of Yorktown,* a masterpiece by the Revolutionary War period's finest portrait artist. The Maryland Senate and House now hold their sessions in two other chambers in the building. Also on the grounds is the oldest public building in Maryland, the tiny redbrick **Treasury,** built in 1735. Nearby on Lawyers Mall is the impressive Thurgood Marshall Memorial. ✉ *State Circle, Historic District,* ☎ *410/974–3400.* *Free.* *Weekdays 8:30–5; weekends 10–4, ½-hr tour daily at 11 and 3.*

NEED A BREAK? Deli sandwiches, subs, milk shakes, and other ice cream concoctions are the bill of fare at **Chick and Ruth's Delly** (✉ 165 Main St., ☎ 410/269–6737), a longtime counter-and-table institution with friendly waitstaff and sandwiches named for state politicos.

2 **St. Anne's Church.** St. Anne's Episcopal parish was founded in 1692; King William III donated the Communion silver. The first St. Anne's Church, built in 1704, was torn down in 1775. The second, built in 1792, burned down in 1858. Parts of the walls survived and were incorporated into the present structure, built the next year. The churchyard contains the grave of the last Colonial governor, Sir Robert Eden. ✉ *Church Circle, Historic District,* ☎ *410/267–9333.* *Free.* *Daily 8–5:30.*

12 **St. John's College.** Here is the alma mater of Francis Scott Key, lyricist of "The Star-Spangled Banner." However, since 1937, the college

has been best known as the birthplace of the Great Books curriculum, which includes reading the works of great authors from Homer to Faulkner and beyond. All students at the college follow the same curriculum for four years, and classes are conducted as discussions rather than lectures. Climb the gradual slope of the long, brick-paved path to the impressive golden cupola of **McDowell Hall,** the third-oldest academic building in the country, just as St. John's is the third-oldest college in the country (after Harvard and William and Mary, respectively). Founded as King William's School in 1696, it was chartered under its current name in 1784. St. John's grounds once held the last living Liberty Tree (the trees under which the Sons of Liberty convened to hear patriot-orators plan the Revolution against England). Wounded in a 1999 hurricane, the 400-year-old tulip poplar was removed; its progeny stands to the left of McDowell Hall. The **Elizabeth Myers Mitchell Art Gallery** (☎ 410/626–2556), on the east side of Mellon Hall, presents exhibits and special programs that relate to the fine arts. Down King George Street toward the water is the **Carroll-Barrister House,** now the college admissions office. The house was built in 1722 at Main and Conduit streets and was moved onto campus in 1957. Charles Carroll (not the signer of the Declaration but his cousin), who helped draft Maryland's Declaration of Rights, was born here. ✉ *60 College Ave., at St. John's St., Historic District,* ☎ *410/263–2371,* WEB *www.sjca.edu.*

⓮ **Thurgood Marshall Memorial.** Born in Baltimore, Maryland, Thurgood Marshall (1908–93) was the first African-American Supreme Court Justice and was one of the 20th century's foremost leaders in the struggle for equal rights under the law. Marshall won the decision in Brown v. Board of Education of Topeka in which the Supreme Court in 1954 overturned the doctrine of "separate but equal." He was appointed as United States solicitor general in 1965 and to the Supreme Court in 1967 by President Lyndon B. Johnson. The 8-ft statue depicts Marshall as a young lawyer. ✉ *State House Sq., bordered by Bladen St., School St., and College Ave., Historic District.*

★ ❽ **United States Naval Academy.** Probably the most interesting and important site in Annapolis, the Naval Academy runs along the Severn River and abuts downtown Annapolis. Midshipmen enter from every part of the United States and many foreign countries to undergo rigorous study in subjects that range from literature to navigation to nuclear engineering. The academy, established in 1845 on the site of a U.S. Army fort, occupies 329 scenic waterfront acres. The centerpiece of the campus is the bright copper-clad dome of the interdenominational **U.S. Naval Academy Chapel.** Beneath it lies the crypt of the Revolutionary War naval officer John Paul Jones, who, in a historic naval battle with a British ship, uttered the inspirational words, "I have not yet begun to fight!"

Near the chapel in Preble Hall is the **U.S. Naval Academy Museum & Gallery of Ships** (✉ 118 Maryland Ave., Historic District, ☎ 410/293–2108), which tells the story of the U.S. Navy through displays of model ships and memorabilia from naval heroes and fighting vessels. The U.S. Naval Institute and Bookstore (WEB www.usni.org) is also in this building. This 85,000-member professional association, which has advanced scientific and literary knowledge of the sea services since 1873, houses more than 450,000 historic images. Admission for the museum, institute, and bookstore is free; hours are Monday through Saturday from 9 to 5 and Sunday from 11 to 5.

On the grounds midshipmen go to classes, conduct military drills, and practice for or compete in intercollegiate and intramural sports. **Bancroft Hall** is one of the largest dormitories in the world (it houses the entire 4,000-member Brigade of Midshipmen). You may view a midshipman's room just inside the hall. Always subject to inspection, rooms here are quite a bit neater than typical dorm rooms. The **Statue of Tecumseh,** in front of Bancroft Hall, is a bronze replica of the USS *Delaware*'s wooden figurehead, "Tamanend." It's decorated by midshipmen for athletics events, and for good luck during exams, students pitch pennies into his quiver of arrows. If you're there at noon in fair weather you can see midshipmen form up outside Bancroft Hall and parade to lunch to the beat of the Drum and Bugle Corps. The USNA Armel-Leftwich Visitor Center has exhibits of midshipmen life and the *Freedom 7* space capsule. ✉ *52 King George St., Historic District,* ☎ *410/263–6933,* WEB *www.navyonline.com.* 🎫 *Grounds tour $6.* ⏲ *Visitor Center: Mar.–Dec., daily 9–5; Jan.–Feb., daily 9–4. Guided walking tours Mar.–Dec., Mon.–Sat. 10–2 on the hr, Sun. 12:30–2:30 on the half hr; Jan.–Feb., weekdays hourly 10–3, Sat. 9:30–2:30 on the half hr, Sun. 12–3 every half hr. Call ahead to confirm.*

★ ⓫ **William Paca House and Garden.** Paca (pronounced "PAY-cuh") was a signer of the Declaration of Independence and a Maryland governor from 1782 to 1785. His house was built in 1765, and its original garden was finished in 1772. Inside, the main floor (furnished with 18th-century antiques) retains its original Prussian-blue and soft-gray color scheme. The second floor contains a mixture of 18th- and 19th-century pieces. The adjacent 2-acre gentlemen's pleasure garden provides a longer perspective on the back of the house, plus worthwhile sights of its own: parterres (upper terraces), a Chinese Chippendale bridge, a pond, a wilderness area, and formal arrangements. An inn, Carvel Hall, once stood on the gardens. After the inn was demolished in 1965, it took eight years to rebuild the gardens, which are planted in 18th-century perennials. ✉ *186 Prince George St., Historic District,* ☎ *410/263–5553,* WEB *www.annapolis.org.* 🎫 *House and garden $8; combination ticket with Hammond-Harwood House $10.* ⏲ *House and garden mid-Mar.–Dec., Mon.–Sat. 10–5, Sun. noon–5; Jan.–mid-Mar., Fri.–Sat. 10–4, Sun. noon–4.*

Dining

$$–$$$$ ✕ **Ristorante Piccola Roma.** Amid the sophisticated black-and-white interior of the cozy "Little Rome" Restaurant, you can feast on authentic Italian food. Silva Recine prepares the recipes—specialties are antipasti, salads, pasta, veal, and fish—and supervises the fine dining staff. ✉ *200 Main St., Historic District,* ☎ *410/268–7898. AE, D, DC, MC, V.*

$–$$$$ ✕ **Middleton Tavern Oyster Bar and Restaurant.** Horatio Middleton began operating this "inn for seafaring men" in 1750; Washington, Jefferson, and Franklin were among its patrons. Today, two fireplaces, wood floors, paneled walls, and a nautical theme give it a cozy charm. Seafood tops the menu; the Maryland crab soup and broiled Chesapeake Bay rockfish are standouts. Try the tavern's own Middleton Pale Ale, perhaps during a weekend blues session in the upstairs piano bar. Brunch is served on weekends, and you can dine outdoors in good weather. ✉ *2 Market Space, City Dock at Randall St., Historic District,* ☎ *410/263–3323. AE, D, MC, V.*

$$$ ✕ **Breeze.** The blues, sand tones, teak, and beach glass employed all create a contemporary flair at this relaxed restaurant. Chef Shane Henderson taps into the rich bounty of the Chesapeake region—from both water and land. His menu includes rockfish with fried green tomatoes and a leek and lobster salad. A favorite is Crab 3 Ways: crab cake, crab dip, and crabmeat in a champagne-butter sauce. ✉ *Loews Annapolis Hotel, 126 West St.,* ☎ *410/295–3232. AE, D, DC, MC, V.*

$$–$$$ ✕ **aqua terra.** This funky restaurant gives history-minded Annapolis an alternative to the Colonial flavor found at most other downtown eateries. Inside are bare floors, blond-wood furniture, an open kitchen, and a handsome granite counter under a row of blue teardrop-shape lamps. The menu changes with each season, but each employs seafood, beef, and pasta as regular features. A summer menu included Cajun New York strip: a handsome cut of beef topped with pink curls of shrimp, butter, and chopped garlic. The summer's linguine was tossed with lumps of crab, fresh tomatoes, and shallots. ✉ *164 Main St.*, ☎ *410/263–1985. AE, MC, V.*

$$–$$$ ✕ **Café Normandie.** Ladder-back chairs, wooden beams, skylights, and a four-sided fireplace make this French restaurant homey. Out of the open kitchen—with its blue-and-white ceramic tiles—comes an astonishingly good French onion soup, made daily from scratch. Puffy omelets, crepes, and seafood dishes are other specialties. The restaurant's brunch (Friday through Sunday) offers American and French dishes, including poached eggs in ratatouille, eggs Benedict, seafood omelets, pancakes, waffles, and croissants and muffins made from scratch. ✉ *185 Main St., Historic District,* ☎ *410/263–3382. AE, D, DC, MC, V.*

$$–$$$ ✕ **Carrol's Creek.** You can walk, catch a water taxi from City Dock, or drive over the Spa Creek drawbridge to this local favorite in Eastport. Whether you dine indoors or out, the view of historic Annapolis and its harbor is spectacular. All-you-can-eat Sunday brunch is of special note, as are the seafood specialties. A menu standout is macadamia-encrusted mahimahi, which is served over sweet mashed potatoes with a mango compote. ✉ *410 Severn Ave., Eastport,* ☎ *410/263–8102,* WEB *www.carrolscreek.com. AE, D, DC, MC, V.*

$–$$$ ✕ **Rams Head Tavern.** A traditional English-style pub also houses the Fordham Brewing Company, which you can tour. The Rams Head serves better-than-usual tavern fare, including spicy shrimp salad, crab cakes, beer-battered shrimp, as well as more than 170 beers—26 on tap—from around the world. Brunch is served on Sunday. The nightclub-like Rams Head Tavern On Stage brings in nationally known folk, rock, jazz, country, and bluegrass artists. Dinner-show combo specials are offered; the menu has light fare. ✉ *33 West St., Historic District,* ☎ *410/268–4545,* WEB *www.ramsheadtavern.com. AE, D, MC, V.*

$–$$ ✕ **McGarvey's Saloon and Oyster Bar.** An Annapolis institution since 1975, this dockside eatery and watering hole is full of good cheer, great drink, and grand food. A heritage of seasonal shell- and finfish dishes, the finest burgers and steaks, as well as unstinting appetizers, make the McGarvey's menu one of the most popular in the area. The full menu is available daily until 11 PM. ✉ *8 Market Space,* ☎ *410/263–5700. AE, DC, MC, V.*

Lodging

$$$$ **The Annapolis Inn.** An extraordinarily elegant B&B, this circa 1770 house has an intimate and richly colored dining room and parlors, all decorated in a style in keeping with the era of the original home. The master suite has a formal sitting room and two of the inn's five working fireplaces. Each suite has a king-size bed with imported luxury linens. Among the fixtures in the bathrooms are hand showers, bidets, and neck rolls for the two whirlpool baths. The towel holders and marble floors are heated. The third-floor suite's sundeck offers a close-up view of the domes of the Naval Academy Chapel and the state capitol as well as a glimpse of the harbor. There's generally a two-night minimum on weekends. ✉ *144 Prince George St., 21401,* ☎ *410/295–5200,* FAX *410/295–5201,* WEB *www.annapolisinn.com.*

3 suites. Dining room, in-room data ports, free parking; no kids, no smoking. AE, MC, V. BP.

$$$$ **Annapolis Marriott Waterfront.** You can practically fish from your room at the city's only waterfront hotel. Rooms, done in a modern style with mauve quilted bedspreads, have either balconies over the water or large windows with views of the harbor or the historic district. The outdoor bar by the harbor's edge is popular in nice weather. ✉ *80 Compromise St., Historic District, 21401,* ☎ *410/268–7555 or 800/336–0072,* FAX *410/269–5864,* WEB *www.annapolismarriott.com. 150 rooms. Restaurant, in-room data ports, gym, boating, 2 bars, laundry service, concierge, business services, meeting rooms, parking (fee); no-smoking rooms. AE, D, DC, MC, V.*

$$$$ **O'Callaghan Hotel.** When this Irish-owned and -operated hotel opened in 2002, it was the city's first new downtown hotel in more than two decades. The lush carpets, in deep blues, golds, and other colors, and floor-length drapes were custom-made in Ireland (most of the attentive staff is from the Emerald Isle as well). Meeting rooms are named after counties in Ireland, and maps and pictures of the Old Country adorn the elegant guest rooms. The first-floor restaurant and bar overlooks West Street and carries a limited but fine selection of entrées. ✉ *174 West St., 21401,* ☎ *410/263–7700,* FAX *410/990–1400,* WEB *www.ocallaghanhotels-us.com. 120 rooms, 2 suites. Restaurant, cable TVs with movies and video games, health club, bar, concierge, laundry services, business services, meeting rooms, parking (fee). AE, MC, V.*

$$$–$$$$ **Historic Inns of Annapolis.** A stay in one of these three 18th-century inns will add still more historic charm to your Annapolis visit. Registration for all three is at the 51-room **Governor Calvert House,** built in 1727 for the Maryland chief executive, who was also cousin to the fifth Lord Baltimore. At 23 State Circle, the 25-room **Robert Johnson House** was built for the Annapolis barber in 1772 by his grandson. The **Maryland Inn,** with 34 guest rooms and 10 suites, has some rooms that date back to the Revolutionary era. It's at 16 Church Circle (the entrance is on Main Street). The Treaty of Paris Restaurant, the King of France Tavern, and the Drummer's Lot Pub serve all three inns. Guest rooms are individually decorated with antiques and reproductions; all have coffeemakers and hair dryers, and some have kitchenettes, sitting suites, or whirlpools. ✉ *58 State Circle, 21401,* ☎ *410/263–2641 or 800/847–8882,* FAX *410/268–3613,* WEB *www.annapolisinns.com. 110 rooms, 10 suites. Restaurant, in-room data ports, some kitchenettes, health club, bar, pub, laundry service, concierge, business services, meeting rooms, parking (fee); no-smoking rooms. AE, D, DC, MC, V.*

$$–$$$$ **William Page Inn.** Built in 1908, this dark-brown, cedar-shingle, wood-frame structure was the local Democratic party clubhouse for 50 years. Today its wraparound porch is furnished with Adirondack chairs. The slope-ceiling third-floor suite with dormer windows includes an Italian-marble bathroom with whirlpool. Breakfast is served in the common room. There's a two-night minimum for weekend stays. ✉ *8 Martin St., 21401,* ☎ *410/626–1506 or 800/364–4160,* WEB *www.williampageinn.com. 4 rooms, 2 with shared bath, 1 suite. Free parking; no-smoking rooms. MC, V. BP.*

$$–$$$ **Loews Annapolis Hotel.** Although its redbrick exterior blends with the city's 18th-century architecture, the interior is airy, spacious, and modern. The lobby's color scheme employs celadon and light brown; the parquet floor has a herringbone pattern. Guest rooms—done in beige fabrics in various textures and shades—have coffeemakers and terry robes. A free hotel shuttle bus takes you anywhere you want to go in Annapolis, and a complimentary breakfast is served in the Corinthian restaurant for those staying at the "concierge" level. ✉ *126 West St.,*

West Side, 21401, ☎ 410/263–7777 or 800/235–6397, FAX 410/263–0084, WEB www.loewsannapolis.com. 210 rooms, 7 suites. 2 restaurants, room service, in-room data ports, minibars, gym, hair salon, bar, dry cleaning, laundry service, concierge, concierge floor, business services, meeting rooms, airport shuttle, parking (fee); no-smoking floors. AE, D, DC, MC, V.

$–$$$ **Gibson's Lodgings.** Three detached houses from three decades—1780, 1890, and 1980—are operated together as a single inn. One of the houses' hallways is strikingly lined with mirrors. Guest rooms are furnished with pre-1900 antiques. One first-floor room, which has a private bath and porch, is designed for disabled access. Free parking in the courtyards is a big advantage in the heart of this small Colonial-era city (the houses are opposite the U.S. Naval Academy). Continental breakfast is served in the formal dining room of the 18th-century Patterson House. ✉ *110–114 Prince George St., 21401, ☎ 410/268–5555 or 877/330–0057, FAX 410/268–2775, WEB www.avmcyber.com/gibson. 21 rooms, 4 with shared bath. Meeting rooms, free parking. AE, MC, V. CP.*

$–$$$ **Sheraton–Barcelo Hotel.** Traffic and parking in downtown Annapolis can be difficult. Adjacent to the Annapolis Mall and Westfield Shoppingtown, in the midst of numerous chain restaurants, is this large hostelry with a free hourly shuttle bus to and from downtown. The Sheraton's lobby is outfitted with marble floors, fresh flowers and ferns, and two sitting areas among marble columns. The café is adjacent to the lobby. Rooms are furnished with blond woods, geometric carpeting, and burgundy-print bedspreads. ✉ *173 Jennifer Rd., West Side, 21401, ☎ 410/266–3131 or 888/627–8980, FAX 410/266–6247, WEB www.starwood.com/sheraton. 196 rooms. Café, room service, in-room data ports, indoor pool, gym, lobby lounge, business services, meeting rooms, free parking; no-smoking rooms. AE, D, DC, MC, V.*

$–$$ **Best Western Annapolis.** This two-story motel is a good value. Set away from traffic intersections but just 3 mi from the U.S. Naval Academy, it's a well-maintained hostelry. Guest rooms, entered from the parking lot, are decorated in forest green with quilted floral bedspreads. There's an outdoor covered deck for enjoying the complimentary Continental breakfast or your own picnic. From U.S. 50, take Exit 22 and follow the signs to Riva Road north. The motel is in a business park on your left. ✉ *2520 Riva Rd., Parole, 21401, ☎ 410/224–2800 or 800/638–5179, FAX 410/266–5539, WEB www.bestwestern.com. 142 rooms. In-room data ports, pool, gym, laundry service, meeting rooms, free parking. AE, D, DC, MC, V. CP.*

Nightlife and the Arts

Bars and Clubs

The lounge at **Harry Browne's** (✉ 66 State Circle, ☎ 410/263–4332) gives people something to do on Monday night: listen to live Irish music. The mid-18th-century **King of France Tavern** (✉ 16 Church Circle, ☎ 410/263–2641) is adjacent to the Treaty of Paris Restaurant in the landmark Maryland Inn. In addition to live jazz on Friday and Saturday and blues on Sunday, local artists sponsored by radio station WRNR (for "Rock 'N' Roll") perform on Monday. The tavern was home to late jazz guitar great Charlie Byrd, and General George Washington is said to have lost a horse in a poker game here.

Middleton Tavern (✉ City Dock, ☎ 410/263–3323) presents local and regional acoustic musicians nightly at its Oyster Bar lounge. The Oyster Shooter—raw oysters served in a shot glass with vodka and cocktail sauce and washed down with beer—supposedly originated here. The upstairs piano bar is open on Friday and Saturday nights.

The **Rams Head Tavern on the Stage** (✉ 33 West St., Historic District, ☏ 410/268–4545, WEB www.ramsheadtavern.com) hosts nationally known folk, rock, jazz, country, and bluegrass groups. Past performers include Lyle Lovett, Ralph Stanley, and Linda Thompson. Dinner combinations are available; the area is nonsmoking.

Music and Theater

Annapolis Summer Garden Theater (✉ 143 Compromise St., at Main St., ☏ 410/268–9212, WEB www.summergarden.com) stages a mix of musicals and plays outdoors (May–September), including occasional works by local playwrights. The **Colonial Players** (✉ 108 East St., ☏ 410/268–7373, WEB www.cplayers.com/pol.html) active since the 1940s, is the city's principal theater troupe.

Entertainment at the **Naval Academy** (☏ 410/293–2439 for schedules; 800/874–6289 for tickets) includes the Distinguished Artists Series, The Masqueraders (the Academy's theatrical club), chamber music recitals, and Glee Club concerts. **Naval Academy Band** (☏ 410/293–0263) concerts, many held outside during fair weather, are free.

Outdoor Activities and Sports

Sandy Point State Park (✉ 1100 E. College Pkwy. [Rte. 50], 12 mi east of Annapolis, ☏ 410/974–2149, WEB www.dnr.state.md.us) has beaches for fishing and swimming, 22 launching ramps for boats, rock jetties extending into the bay, and a fishing pier. Admission is $3 on weekdays and $4 on weekends from April to October; from November to March admission is $1 per vehicle.

Participant Sports

BICYCLING

The **Baltimore and Annapolis (B&A) Trail** (✉ Earleigh Heights Rd., Severna Park, ☏ 410/222–6244, WEB www.aacpl.lib.md.us/rp) runs through 13 mi of farmland and forests as well as urban and suburban neighborhoods, from Annapolis to Glen Burnie. It follows the old Baltimore and Annapolis Railroad and is linked directly to the 12½-mi trail encircling Baltimore-Washington International Airport. The trail is open sunrise to sunset to hikers, bikers, runners, and rollerbladers. Access to the southern end of the trail is via Boulters Way off Route 450 near the Scenic Overlook and World War II Memorial. Parking there is free.

Pedal Pushers Bike Shop (✉ 546 Baltimore and Annapolis Blvd. [Rte. 648], Severna Park, ☏ 410/544–2323) rents bikes for the B&A Trail.

FISHING

Anglers (✉ 1456 Whitehall Rd., ☏ 410/757–3442) sells equipment for archery and hunting as well as for fresh- and saltwater fishing. Anglers is also a full-service Orvis fly-fishing dealer.

SAILING

Annapolis Sailing School (✉ 601 6th St., ☏ 800/638–9192 or 410/267–7205, WEB www.annapolissailing.com) bills itself as America's oldest and largest sailing school. The inexperienced can take a two-hour basic lesson. In addition, live-aboard, cruising, and advanced-sailing programs are available, as are boat rentals.

Run by women and primarily for women who want to go on multiday sails, **Womanship** (✉ 137 Conduit St., ☏ 410/267–6661 or 800/342–9295, WEB www.womanship.com) also has programs for girls (ages 12–17), for mother/daughter partners, for couples, and for family groups, and can custom-design classes for special needs or desires. Men are welcome to take classes as half of a couple or as part of a group.

Spectator Sports

The teams of the **United States Naval Academy Athletic Association (NAAA)** (☎ 800/874–6289 ticket office, WEB www.navysports.com) compete in about 20 varsity sports, most notably football. The team plays home games in the fall at the Navy–Marine Corps Stadium on Rowe Boulevard in Annapolis.

JOUSTING

The **Amateur Jousting Club of Maryland** (✉ Box 315, Crownsville 21032, ☎ 410/266–7304, WEB blackbox.psyberia.com/~AJC) can provide details on about 48 jousting tournaments and events that take place from April through November. The longest-running tournament of the state sport is held the last Saturday in August at Christ Episcopal Church in Port Republic.

Shopping

Along Maryland Avenue as well as on Main Street in downtown Annapolis you'll find antiques and fine art, fashions, arts and crafts, home furnishing, and gifts and souvenirs as well as nautical clothing and other necessities for seasoned salts and would-be sailors alike.

A destination in itself, the **Arundel Mills** (✉ 7000 Arundel Mills Circle, Hanover, ☎ 410/540–5100) shopping mall holds more than 200 well-known retailers and eateries, including Ann Taylor Loft, Kenneth Cole, Bass Pro Shops, Saks Fifth Avenue Outlet, and T. J. Maxx. In 2002, the first-of-its-kind Crayola Works Creativity Studio and Store opened.

Antiques

Dealers in fine antiques abound along Annapolis's "other main street," Maryland Avenue. Other shops are in nearby West Annapolis. **Annapolis Antique Gallery** (✉ 2009 West St., ☎ 410/266–0635) is a consortium of 35–40 dealers with an inventory that includes Victorian and art deco pieces. **Ron Snyder Antiques** (✉ 2011 West St., ☎ 410/266–5452) specializes in 18th- and 19th-century American furniture displayed in seven tastefully decorated rooms.

CALVERT COUNTY

The long, narrow peninsula between the Patuxent River and the Chesapeake Bay is Calvert County, an area that has not been completely overrun by tourism. Two principal routes—Route 2 from Annapolis and Route 4 from Washington, D.C.—merge near Sunderland and continue on together to the county's southern tip. Exploring the Bayside and riverside communities to either side of the highway, as well as the inland sites and attractions, will immerse you quickly in the tangible history and heritage of agriculture and fishing.

North Beach

17 *31 mi south of Annapolis (via Rte. 2, Rte. 260, and Rte. 261).*

North Beach was founded in 1900 as a resort for family summer vacations. Amusement centers, bingo halls, theaters, and bathhouses defined the town until the Great Depression. Then, in 1933, a hurricane ravaged the beach and destroyed the pier and boardwalk as well as many buildings. Post-WWII programs sponsored by the Veterans Administration facilitated an unprecedented building boom, turning North Beach into a year-round community.

Southern Maryland

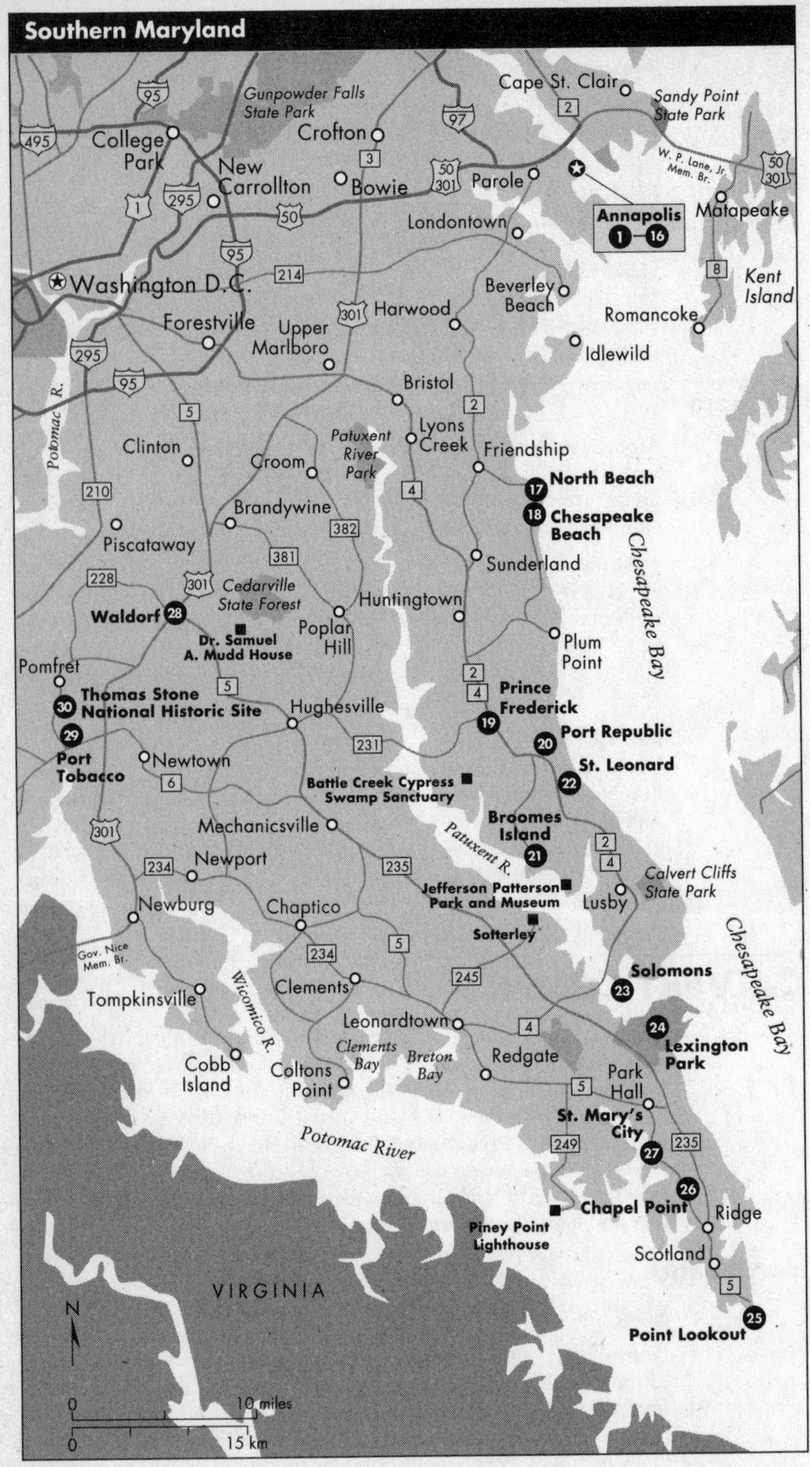

Dining and Lodging

$–$$ ✕ **Neptune's.** One of two restaurants in tiny North Beach, modest Neptune's claims to prepare "the world's best mussels," which do make the trip worth it to many. There are also seafood pastas, burgers, and curs of Angus beef. The small restaurant and bar with its wooden tables and brick floor is friendly and informal. ✉ *8800 Chesapeake Ave., at 1st St.,* ☎ *410/257–7899. AE, D, MC, V.*

Chesapeake Beach

18 *1 mi south of North Beach (via Rte. 261), 32 mi south of Annapolis (via Rte. 2, Rte. 260, and Rte. 261).*

This charming little town beside the Bay was founded at the close of the 19th century as a resort to rival those along the French Riviera. It was served by steamboats from Baltimore and by a railroad from Washington, D.C., built by Colorado tycoons. Steamboat service diminished over time and the railroad failed in 1935, but the town survived as private automobiles became more readily available. It boomed again in 1948 with the legalization of slot machines, although they lasted only 20 years.

The **Chesapeake Bay Railway Museum,** housed in the railroad's 1898 trackside terminus, provides memorable glimpses of the onetime resort's turn-of-the-20th-century glory days. Among its exhibits are a glass-enclosed model of the town of Chesapeake Beach, a gleaming, black Ford Model T that once carried guests from the station to their hotels, a hand-carved horse from the magnificent carousel, and a slot machine as well as photos of early vacationers. One of the railroad's passenger cars rests nearby. ✉ *4155 Mears Ave. (Rte. 261),* ☎ *410/257–3892.* 🎟 *Free.* ⏲ *May–Sept., daily 1–4; Apr. and Oct., weekends 1–4 and by appointment.*

Dining

$$–$$$ ✕ **Rod 'n' Reel.** This family-owned restaurant opened optimistically in 1936, the year after the demise of the railroad from Washington, and since then it has remained synonymous with superb seafood. The indoor bar is welcoming, as is the large outdoor one, which overlooks a beach rife with wildfowl. Broad views of the Bay can be had from any table in the expansive dining room. The extensive menu includes succulent southern Maryland specialties such as rockfish stuffed with crab imperial, fried oysters, and the region's ubiquitous crab cakes as well as entrées adopted from other maritime communities: Alaskan crab legs, Cajun-seasoned roasted shrimp, and Maine lobster. ✉ *Rte. 261 and Mears Ave.,* ☎ *410/257–2735,* WEB *www.rodnreelinc.com. AE, D, MC, V.*

En Route The brick **All Saints Episcopal Church,** built in the 1770s, replaced a log building that served as the sanctuary of a parish founded in 1692. The hilltop site seems farther than it really is from a busy junction nearby. A simple, classic look is evident inside and out. The church sits amid mature trees and wrought iron–fenced family grave sites dating to the 1700s. Indoors, the clay-tile floor, classic white box pews, and plain windows set off the subtle blue-and-rose stained-glass window over the altar. ✉ *Junction of Rtes. 2 and 4,* ☎ *410/257–6306,* WEB *www.allsaintssunderland.ang-md.org.* ⏲ *Daily 10–5. Services Sun. 8 AM and 10:30 AM.*

Prince Frederick

19 *10 mi south of Sunderland; 38 mi south of Annapolis (via Rte. 2 and Rte. 2/4).*

Prince Frederick, the Calvert County seat, has been consumed by fire—and rebuilt—three times. Today, the white-column brick courthouse on Main Street is one of the town's older buildings, dating to 1916.

Dining and Lodging

$$–$$$ ✕ **Old Field Inn.** In this converted wood-frame home from the late 1800s, three dining rooms are filled with historic family portraits and linen-covered candlelit tables. Oriental carpets enhance the hardwood floors in two of the rooms. Veal Wellington is a chef's specialty. Another is filet mignon stuffed with herbed cream cheese and a merlot sauce. The seafood sampler—an appetizer for two—includes clams casino, shrimp, and escargot. ✉ *485 Main St.,* ☎ *410/535–1054,* WEB *www.oldfieldinn.com. AE, D, MC, V. No lunch.*

$$ **Serenity Acres B&B.** Set on 5 acres of wood, Serenity Acres is about 6 mi north of Prince Frederick. Its understated rooms, all with queen-size beds, are genuinely homey. The year-round, screened-in hot tub, sunk into a wooden deck, and the in-ground pool are refreshing after a long day of touring. ✉ *4270 Hardesty Rd., Huntingtown 20639,* ☎ *800/485–4251 or 410/535–3744,* FAX *410/535–3835,* WEB *www.bbonline.com/md/serenity. 4 rooms. In-room VCRs, pool, exercise equipment, hot tub; no-smoking rooms. MC, V. BP.*

Battle Creek Cypress Swamp Sanctuary

6 mi southwest of Prince Frederick.

With the northernmost naturally occurring stand of bald cypress trees in the United States, the 100-acre Battle Creek Cypress Swamp Sanctuary provides close-up looks at the forest primeval. A ¼-mi elevated boardwalk at the bottom of a steep but sturdy column of steps gives you a good vantage point to see the swamp, thick with 100-ft trees that are more than a thousand years old. Guides at the nature center can alert you to the seasonal permutations of the vegetation and the doings of squirrels, owls, and other wildlife. Indoor exhibits focus on the area's natural and cultural history. ✉ *Sixes Rd. (Rte. 506),* ☎ *410/535–5327,* WEB *www.calvertparks.org.* *Free.* *Tues.–Sat. 10–4:30, Sun. 1–4:30.*

Port Republic

20 *5 mi east of Battle Creek Cypress Swamp Sanctuary.*

Christ Episcopal Church traces its origins to 1672, when a log-cabin church stood at the site. Its 1772 brick replacement, coated with plaster, is notable for its biblical garden, planted with species mentioned in the scriptures. Port Republic School No. 7 is on the church's property. Since immediately after the Civil War the grounds have been a venue for jousting (Maryland's state sport) on the last Saturday in August. ✉ *3090 Broomes Island Rd. (Rte. 264),* ☎ *410/586–0565.* *Free.* *Daily dawn–dusk.*

Port Republic School No. 7, a classic one-room schoolhouse built in the 1880s, looks for all the world as if today's lesson could begin any minute. Here, you'll find a restored classroom with archetypal desks, inkwells, and a school bell. Until 1932 a single teacher taught children in seven grades here. ✉ *3100 Broomes Island Rd. (Rte. 264),* ☎ *410/586–0482.* *Free.* *Memorial Day–Labor Day, Sun. 2–4 and by appointment.*

Broomes Island

21 *7 mi south of Port Republic (via Rte. 264).*

An area without specific boundaries, Broomes is not even an island per se, except during a very high tide or in a strong storm. Made up of little more than a few houses and stores, a post office, a church, and an oyster-packing plant, this little area at the mouth of Island Creek is partly a portrait in the decline of a water-dependent community.

Dining

$-$$ ✕ **Stoney's Seafood House.** Popular with sailors, this restaurant overlooks Island Creek, which flows into the Patuxent River. There's ample seating—and a tiki bar—outside. Stoney's is worth a visit for its hefty crab cakes alone, made with plenty of back fin meat and little filler. Oyster sandwiches and Stoney's Steamer—handpicked selections of fresh seafood—make other good seafood choices. Homemade desserts such as the strawberry shortcake and the Snickers pie are not for the faint of heart. ✉ *Oyster House Rd.,* ☎ *410/586–1888. AE, D, MC, V. Closed Nov.–early Mar.*

St. Leonard

㉒ *2 mi south of Port Republic, 43 mi south of Annapolis (via Rte. 2/4).*

Behind 2½ mi of scenic Patuxent riverfront stretch 544 acres of woods and farmland. The 70-odd archaeological sites have yielded evidence of 9,000 years of human habitation—from prehistory on through to Colonial times. At the **Jefferson Patterson Park and Museum,** you can follow an archaeology trail to inspect artifacts of the successive hunter-gatherer, early agricultural, and plantation societies that once roamed and settled this land. Displays include primitive knives and axes, fragments of Native American pottery, and Colonial glassware. Stroll along the nature trails to take a look at wildlife, antique agricultural equipment, and fields of crops. ✉ *10115 Mackall Rd. (Rte. 265),* ☎ *410/586–8500,* WEB *www.jefpat.org.* 🎫 *Free.* ⏲ *Mid-Apr.–mid-Oct., Wed.–Sun. 10–5.*

On the forested heights of Calvert Cliffs overlooking the Chesapeake Bay, **Flag Ponds Nature Park** was a busy fishery until the 1950s. Today, it beckons with one of Calvert County's few public bay beaches, a fishing pier, 3 mi of gently graded hiking trails, observation decks at two ponds, a boardwalk through wetlands, and indoor wildlife exhibits. Soaring cliffs, flat marshland, and wildflowers (including the Blue Flag Iris, for which the park is named) provide stunning contrasts, and the shoreline trail here is not seashells but abundant fossils dating to the Miocene age, 10–20 million years ago, when southern Maryland was covered by an ocean. ✉ *Rte. 2/4, Lusby,* ☎ *410/586–1477,* WEB *www.calvertparks.org.* 🎫 *$6 per vehicle April–Oct.; $3 per vehicle Nov.–Mar.* ⏲ *Memorial Day–Labor Day, weekdays 9–6, weekends 9–8; Labor Day–Memorial Day, weekends 9–6.*

Nightlife and the Arts

For a taste of the tropics *and* the Far East along St. Leonard's Creek, wet your lips with an umbrella-topped cocktail at **Vera's White Sands** (✉ Rte. 4, Lusby, ☎ 410/586–1182), a celebration of owner Vera Freeman's world travels and exotic tastes. For years, clad in her trademark long gowns and feather boas, she's taken her place at the piano and entertained diners and bar patrons. Open May through October, Vera's maintains a swimming pool that is, as Vera says, "for all the fun times" and a deepwater (15-ft) marina with 84 slips. Lusby is 6 mi southeast of St. Leonard.

Solomons

㉓ *13 mi southeast of St. Leonard, 59 mi south of Annapolis (via Rte. 2/4).*

On the tip of the peninsula, Solomons is where the Patuxent empties into the Chesapeake. The town has become a popular getaway for sailors, boaters, and affluent professionals. But it's still a laid-back waterfront town—at least, compared with, say, Annapolis or St. Michaels.

Several excellent boatyards and marinas cater to powerboaters and sailors, with nautical services from the simplest to the most sophisticated. There are several antiques, book, gift, and specialty shops and galleries side by side, parallel to the boardwalk. Wherever you go, you'll be surrounded by stunning views at nearly every turn.

★ The **Calvert Marine Museum** is concerned with the history of both the river and the Bay. The bright, spacious exhibition hall contains models and life-size examples of historically significant types of working and pleasure boats. A grouping of 15 tanks holds various examples of marine life; the river otters here are often at play. The jaws of a white shark open above an exhibit on fossils, and children can sift through sharks' teeth and other specimens and examine them under microscopes. Outside, small craft of different periods are on display in a waterside shed, and on many summer afternoons you can take a cruise aboard a converted 1899 bugeye sailboat, *William B. Tennison*. There's also a restored hexagonal lighthouse from 1883 that's perched like an insect on six slender legs. The **J. C. Lore & Sons Oyster House** (June–Aug., daily 1–4:30, May and Sept., weekends 1–4:30), operated by the museum, was a processing plant built in 1934 and converted to a museum of the local seafood industries. This National Historic Landmark displays the tools used by oystermen, crabbers, and fishermen. ✉ *Rte. 2 at Solomons Island Rd.,* ☎ *410/326–2042 or 410/326–8217 weekends,* WEB *www.calvertmarinemuseum.com.* *$5.* *Daily 10–5.*

A world-class sculpture and botanical venue, **Annmarie Garden on St. John** is a 30-acre property on the St. John Creek. The sculptural art is by artists both local and from around the world. One of the more intriguing installations is a series of 13 "Talking Benches." Each tells an ecological story by depicting a plant that grows in southern Maryland, including dogwood, loblolly pines, papaw trees, and tobacco. Smooth, user-friendly pathways curve through the grounds. Little here is off-limits, and picnickers are welcome to settle in virtually anywhere. Be sure to visit the mosaic-filled rest rooms. ✉ *Dowell Rd.,* ☎ *410/326–4640,* WEB *www.annmariegarden.org.* *Free.* *Daily 10–4.*

Dining and Lodging

$$–$$$$ ✕ **Lighthouse Inn.** The bar is a reproduction of an oyster boat, and fishing nets and pictures of old Solomons set the mood. Gas lanterns illuminate the polished wood tables and the exposed ceiling beams. Diners on the first floor have a view of Solomons Harbor on Back Creek; on the second floor, patrons look onto the creek toward the Patuxent River. The catch of the day is frequently sautéed, and the chef's crab cakes' recipe is closely guarded. On weekends in the warmer months you can order lighter fare on the partially covered "quarterdeck." ✉ *14636 Solomons Island Rd.,* ☎ *410/326–2444,* WEB *www.lighthouse-inn.com. AE, D, DC, MC, V. No lunch.*

$$–$$$ ✕ **DiGiovanni's Dock of the Bay.** Rare is the place you can enjoy elegant waterside dining and professional service at budget prices. The Venetian chef creates succulent Italian dishes using fresh herbs and spices. The *cacciucco* (seafood soup) alone is worth a special trip, as is the linguini Neri with scallops. A folk singer entertains on Wednesday and Friday evenings. ✉ *14556 Solomons Island Rd.,* ☎ *410/394–6400. AE, MC, V. No lunch weekdays. Closed 1st 2 wks in Jan.*

$–$$$ ★ **Back Creek Inn.** Built as a waterman's home in 1880, this wood-frame house sits on well-tended grounds that lead to the edge of Back Creek. There's an outdoor deck next to a beautiful perennial garden, and you can soak in the open-air hot tub. Three rooms look out on the Patuxent River or Back Creek, and one opens onto the garden. Breakfast is served in the dining room or by the lily pond. ✉ *Calvert and*

Alexander Sts., 20688, ☎ 410/326–2022, FAX 410/326–2946, WEB www.bbonline.com/md/backcreek. 4 rooms, 2 suites, 1 cottage. Dining room, cable TV, outdoor hot tub, bicycles; no-smoking rooms, no kids under 12. MC, V. Closed mid-Dec.–early Jan. BP.

$$ **Holiday Inn Select Conference Center and Marina.** In this five-story waterfront hotel, every guest room has a water view (if you count the swimming pool); rooms look onto the cove, the open creek, or the courtyard. Whirlpools are available in some suites. Designed to accommodate convention and meeting business, the hotel is often heavily booked, so try to reserve early. ✉ *155 Holiday Dr., Box 1099, 20688, ☎ 410/326–6311 or 800/356–2009, FAX 410/326–1069, WEB solomonsmd.hiselect.com. 276 rooms, 50 suites. Restaurant, room service, in-room data ports, some kitchenettes, 2 tennis courts, pool, gym, sauna, volleyball, 2 bars, shop, laundry facilities, business services, meeting rooms; no-smoking rooms. AE, D, DC, MC, V.*

ST. MARY'S COUNTY

"Just at the mouth of the river, we observed the natives in arms. That night, fires blazed through the whole country and since they had never seen such a large ship, messengers were sent in all directions, who reported that a 'canoe' like an island had come with as many as there were trees in the woods."—Father Andrew White, recounting the arrival of the *Ark* and the *Dove* in 1634.

Father White arrived in the New World in 1634 as a member of Lord Baltimore's contingent of 140 colonists. The two "canoes" the Native Americans spotted were the tiny sailing vessels that had just crossed the Atlantic to reach the southernmost tip of Maryland's western shore, where the Potomac River meets the Chesapeake Bay. The peninsula between the Potomac and the Patuxent rivers is today St. Mary's County, easily one of the state's most beautiful regions, and gradually attracting development because of its easy access to Washington, D.C., to the north.

Like so much of Maryland south of Annapolis and Washington, many scenic drives throughout St. Mary's County bring together charming inland and waterside towns and historic sites. Hearty food and homey accommodations are readily found.

Lexington Park

24 *9 mi southeast of Solomons, 68 mi south of Annapolis (via Rte. 2/4 to Rte. 235).*

The **Patuxent Naval Air Museum** houses items from the research, development, test, and evaluation of naval aircraft. Seventeen vintage aircraft are displayed outside. Inside, you may climb into a cockpit trainer and view some of the more improbable creations that never passed muster, such as the Goodyear "Inflatoplane" and a portable helicopter. ✉ *Patuxent River Naval Air Station, Rte. 235 (Three Notch Rd.), ☎ 301/863–7418, WEB www.paxmuseum.com. Free. Tues.–Sun. 10–5.*

OFF THE BEATEN PATH

SOTTERLEY – The distinguished house on the grounds of this 18th-century plantation is the earliest known (1717) post-in-ground structure in the United States: in place of a foundation, cedar timbers driven straight into the ground support it. The house is a sampler of architectural styles and interior design from the last two centuries. On the grounds of this National Historic Landmark are other buildings from the 18th through early 20th centuries, including a Colonial customs warehouse, a smokehouse, a "necessary" (an outhouse), and a restored slave cabin. ✉ *Rte.*

245 near Hollywood, 12 mi north of Lexington Park via Rte. 235 and Rte. 245, ☎ 301/373–2280, WEB www.sotterley.com. $7. ⏲ May–Oct., Tues.–Sat. 10–4, Sun. noon–4.

Lodging

$–$$ ★ **Potomac View Farm Bed & Breakfast.** Construction of this white wood-frame "telescope" house (built in progressively smaller sections) began in 1830. It's a farmhouse, not a manor, and is furnished with handsome, simple oak furniture and decorative quilts. The rooms have some elegant touches, such as 10-ft ceilings with crown moldings. One of the restored outbuildings, originally the gardener's cottage, is now a room with its own bath. A one-bedroom kitchenette apartment attached to the main house also has its own bath. The waterside inn sits on 120 acres of farmland planted with corn and soybeans. The proprietors also operate the marina, where charters can be arranged. ✉ *44477 Tall Timbers Rd., Tall Timbers 20690, ☎ 301/994–2311. 5 rooms without bath, 1 suite, 1 cottage. Restaurant, pool, beach, boating, marina, bar, laundry service. AE, D, MC, V. BP.*

Point Lookout

㉕ *20 mi south of Lexington Park, 88 mi south of Annapolis (via Rte. 2/4 and Rte. 235 to Rte. 5).*

When Father Andrew White came to Point Lookout and saw the Potomac at its side, he mused that the Thames was a mere rivulet in comparison. Instead of being overwhelmed by the wilderness of the New World, he observed that "fine groves of trees appear . . . growing in intervals as if planted by the hand of man."

On the approach to **Point Lookout State Park,** two memorial obelisks remind travelers of the dark history of this starkly alluring point of land. Beginning in 1863, a Union prison stood at the farthest tip of the peninsula, just across the Potomac from Confederate Virginia. During those last two years of the conflict, nearly 4,000 of the 50,000 Confederate soldiers here died because of poor conditions. All that remains of the prison are some earthen fortifications, partially rebuilt and known as Fort Lincoln, with markers noting the sites of hospitals and other buildings. A small museum supplies some of the details. The 500-acre state park has boating facilities, nature trails, and a beach for swimming. The RV campground, with hook-ups, is open year-round; tent camping facilities close from early November through late March. ✉ *Rte. 5, ☎ 301/872–5688, WEB www.dnr.state.md.us. Weekends and holidays May–Sept. $3. ⏲ Year-round, daily dawn–dusk.*

Dining and Lodging

$–$$$ ★ ✕ **Spinnakers Restaurant at Point Lookout Marina.** This restaurant has brought the best of southern Maryland to the shores of Smith Creek. Specialties include grilled rockfish, Kansas City steaks, and excellent crab cakes. Subdued lighting, fresh flowers, and linen-covered tables make for an elegant, casual space. The enthusiastic staff makes dining here a comfortable experience. Sunday brunch is a local tradition. ✉ *Point Lookout Marina, 32 Millers Wharf Rd., Ridge, ☎ 301/872–4340, WEB www.spinnakersrestaurant.com. AE, D, DC, MC, V. Closed Jan.–mid-Feb.*

$ **St. Michael's Manor & Vineyard.** Joe and Nancy Dick have run their B&B on Long Neck Creek since the early 1980s—and they've harvested grapes from their 3 acres of vines nearly as long as that. Rooms overlook the water and are decorated with antiques and family heirlooms, the beds covered with hand-sewn quilts. There is a working fireplace at each end of the public space on the ground floor in the Georgian-style main building. Nancy's eggs Benedict are always popular, and her airy Austrian puff pancakes over fresh apples or peaches are delicious. ✉ *50200 St. Michael's Manor Way, Scotland 20687,* ☎ *301/872–4025,* WEB *www.stmichaels-manor.com. 4 rooms. Pool, bicycles, some pets allowed; no smoking. No credit cards. Closed Jan.–Feb. BP.*

Outdoor Activities and Sports

Scheibel's (✉ Wynne Rd., Ridge, ☎ 301/872–5185) will arrange fishing charters.

Chapel Point

26 *9 mi northwest of Point Lookout (via Rte. 5), 77 mi south of Annapolis.*

St. Ignatius Church, built in 1758, is all that survives of the pre-Revolutionary plantation of St. Inigoes. A church dating from the 1630s had stood where this church, named for the founder of the Jesuits, stands now; the graveyard is one of the oldest in the United States. Several veterans of the Revolution are buried here, alongside Jesuit priests who served here. To see inside the church, ask for the key at the sentry box of the naval installation next door. ✉ *Villa Rd., off Rte. 5,* ☎ *301/872–5590.* *Donation requested.* *By appointment.*

St. Mary's City

27 *4 mi northwest of Chapel Point (via Rte. 5), 73 mi south of Annapolis (via Rte. 2/4 to Rte. 235 to Rte. 5 North).*

After their sighting of what is today Point Lookout, an intrepid group of 140 English settlers sailed the *Ark* and the *Dove* up the Potomac, where they landed on an island that became St. Clement's. Their exploration, however, soon found them on a course into a tributary of the Potomac, the St. Mary's River. About halfway up, on an east bank, they founded St. Mary's City, the fourth permanent settlement in British North America and eventually the first (and short-lived) capital of Maryland.

Long before a Constitution or a Bill of Rights, the first law of religious tolerance in the New World was enacted in St. Mary's City, guaranteeing the freedom to practice whatever religion one chose. Here, too, almost three centuries before American women achieved suffrage, Mistress Margaret Brent challenged the status quo and requested the right to vote (she didn't get it). The settlement served as Maryland's capital city until 1695, when the legislature moved to Annapolis and the county seat moved to Leonardtown. St. Mary's City virtually vanished, its existence acknowledged only in historical novels and textbooks.

In 1934, a first step in the rebirth of St. Mary's was taken. In commemoration of the 300th anniversary of Maryland, the Colony's imposing State House, originally built in 1676, was reconstructed. In the early 1970s, a vast archaeological-reconstruction program began in earnest, a project that has revealed nearly 200 individual sites. The entire 800-plus acres have become a living-history museum and archaeological park called **Historic St. Mary's City.** ★

The historic complex includes several notable reconstructions and reproductions of buildings. The **State House of 1676,** like its larger and grander counterpart in Williamsburg, has an upper and a lower chamber for the corresponding houses of Parliament. This 1934 reproduction is based on court documents from the period; the original was dismantled in 1829 (many of the bricks were used for Trinity Church nearby). The small square-rigged ship, ***Maryland Dove,*** docked behind the State House, is an accurate replica of one of the two vessels that conveyed the original settlers from England. The nearby **Farthing's Ordinary** is a reconstructed inn.

Godiah Spray Tobacco Plantation depicts life on a 17th-century tobacco farm in the Maryland wilderness. Interpreters portray the Spray family—the real family lived about 20 mi away—and its indentured servants, enlisting passive onlookers in such household chores as cooking and gardening or in working the tobacco field. The buildings, including the main dwelling house and outbuildings, were built with period tools and techniques.

Throughout Historic St. Mary's City, you're encouraged to explore other sites and exhibits-in-progress such as the town center, the location of the first Catholic church in the English Colonies, a "victualing" and lodging house (a Colonial-era B&B), and the woodland Native American hamlet. Historic interpreters in costume—and in character—add realism to the experience. ✉ *Rte. 5,* ☎ *240/895–4990 or 800/762–1634,* WEB *www.stmaryscity.org.* 🎫 *$7.50.* 🕑 *Call for exhibit hours.*

OFF THE BEATEN PATH

PINEY POINT LIGHTHOUSE – The first permanent lighthouse constructed on the Potomac River is now the center of a small, 6-acre park. A museum includes lighthouse history and artifacts from Maryland's first historic shipwreck dive preserve—the remains of the U-1105 Black Panther German submarine. After the U.S. Navy tested the U-boat's capabilities, it sank it here. ✉ *Lighthouse Road, Piney Point,* ☎ *301/769–2222,* WEB *www.co.saint-marys.md.us/recreate/museums.* 🎫 *Donation requested.* 🕑 *May–Oct., Fri.–Mon. noon–5.*

Dining and Lodging

$$–$$$ ✕🏨 **Brome-Howard Inn.** Set on 30 acres of farmland, this 19th-century farmhouse provides a trip through time to life on a tobacco plantation. Rooms are decorated with original family furnishings. Relax on one of the big outdoor porches or patios and watch the lazy St. Mary's River nearby. In the evening, there are two candlelit dining rooms—the foyer or the formal parlor. Five miles of hiking trails lead to St. Mary's City, and the inn has bikes for the use of guests. The restaurant ($$$–$$$$) specializes in seafood and occasionally serves such exotic items as bison, ostrich, or shark. ✉ *18281 Rosecroft Rd., 20686,* ☎ *301/866–0656,* FAX *301/866–9660,* WEB *www.bromehowardinn.com. 3 rooms, 1 suite. Restaurant, bicycles, hiking, library. AE, MC, V. BP.*

CHARLES COUNTY

To the north of St. Mary's County and about 35 mi southwest of Annapolis, relatively rural Charles County is flanked on its west by the Potomac River's big bend as it flows south from Washington, D.C. This is tobacco country, dotted with depot towns, riverfront ports-of-call, wildlife preservation centers, and unsung historical sites. Less-traveled county and state roads crisscross the pristine countryside.

Waldorf

28 *40 mi south of Annapolis on Rte. 301.*

The **American Indian Cultural Center and Piscataway Indian Museum** strives to be a source for information on the art and culture of the Piscataway Native Americans; the museum emphasizes the life of Maryland's indigenous people prior to the 17th century. Artifacts, tools, and weapons are on display, and there is a full-scale reproduction of a traditional longhouse. ✉ *16816 Country La.,* ☎ *301/372–1932.* 🎫 *$3.* 🕑 *By appointment.*

The **Dr. Samuel A. Mudd House** is where John Wilkes Booth ended up at 4 AM on Good Friday, 1865, his leg broken after having leaped from the presidential box at Ford's Theater. Most likely, the 32-year-old Dr. Mudd had no idea his patient was wanted for the assassination of Abraham Lincoln. Nonetheless, Mudd was convicted of aiding a fugitive and sentenced to life in prison. (President Andrew Jackson pardoned him in 1869.) Today the two-story house set on 10 rolling acres in Charles County looks as if the doctor is still in. The dark purple couch where Mudd examined Booth remains in the downstairs parlor, 18th-century family pieces fill the rooms, and the doctor's crude instruments are displayed. There is a 30-minute guided tour of the house, an exhibit building, and Mudd's original tombstone. ✉ *14940 Hoffman Rd.,* ☎ *301/645–6870,* WEB *www.somd.lib.md.us/MUSEUMS/Mudd.htm.* 🎫 *$3.* ⏲ *Apr.–late Nov., Wed. and weekends 11–4.*

Port Tobacco

29 *11 mi southwest via Rte. 301 and Rte. 6 from Waldorf.*

One of the oldest communities in the East, Port Tobacco first existed as the Native American settlement of "Potopaco." (The similarity between this Native American name—meaning "the jutting of water inland"—and the name for the plant that was to become a cornerstone of the region's economy—is purely coincidental.) Potopaco was colonized by the English in 1634, and later in the century emerged as the major seaport of Port Tobacco. The Historic District includes the reconstructed early 19th-century courthouse; Catslide House, one of the area's four surviving 18th-century homes; and a restored one-room schoolhouse, dating to 1876 and used as such until 1953.

★ 30 **Thomas Stone National Historic Site,** built in the 1770s, was the Charles County home of Thomas Stone, one of four Maryland signers of the Declaration of Independence. It has been painstakingly rebuilt after a devastating fire left it a shell in the late 1970s. The restoration re-created the distinctive five-part Georgian house inside and out. The two-story main plantation house is linked to the two wings and adjoining hallways in an arc rather than a straight line. All the rooms have exquisite details, such as built-in cabinets, elaborate moldings, a table set in fine china, gilded mirrors, and a piano. The house overlooks terraced fields and the family grave site. ✉ *6655 Rose Hill Rd., between Rtes. 6 and 225, 4 mi west of La Plata,* ☎ *301/392–1776,* WEB *www.nps.gov/thst.* 🎫 *Free.* ⏲ *Mid-June–Aug. daily 9–5; Sept.–mid-June, Wed.–Sun. 9–5.*

ANNAPOLIS AND SOUTHERN MARYLAND A TO Z

To research prices, get advice from other travelers, and book travel arrangements, visit www.fodors.com.

AIRPORTS

Baltimore-Washington International Airport is convenient to Annapolis and attractions in southern Maryland.

➤ AIRPORT INFORMATION: **Baltimore-Washington International Airport** (BWI; ✉ Exit 2 off Baltimore-Washington Pkwy., ☎ 410/859–7100, WEB www.bwiairport.com).

TRANSFERS

The most convenient way to get to Annapolis is by car or taxi. From BWI, follow airport exit signs and then take I–97 south to Route 50 east. Take Exit 24 onto Rowe Boulevard and follow signs to the Annapolis visitor center.

You can also reach Annapolis by bus or shuttle. The Sky Blue Bus Route runs from the International Terminal Bus Stop to Annapolis. You can transfer from the Spa Road stop to other routes, several of which stop near the visitor center.

BWI Ground Transportation has information on Super Shuttle and Airport Vans.

➤ CONTACTS: **BWI Ground Transportation** (☎ 800/435–9294). **Sky Blue Bus Route (Dept. of Public Transportation)** (☎ 410/263–7964).

BIKE TRAVEL

Take a Step, an Annapolis brochure that has biking maps and more information, is available by visiting the visitor center or contacting the Department of Public Transportation.

➤ INFORMATION: **Department of Public Transportation** (☎ 410/263–7964). **Washington Area Bicyclist Association** (WEB www.waba.org).

BOAT AND FERRY TRAVEL

To get around the Annapolis waterfront, call the Jiffy Water Taxi.

➤ BOAT AND FERRY LINES: **Jiffy Water Taxi** (☎ 410/263–0033, WEB www.watermarkcruises.com/taxi.shtml).

BUS TRAVEL

Maryland's Mass Transit Administration offers regularly scheduled bus service from Baltimore to Annapolis (about one hour and 20 minutes one-way from downtown Annapolis).

Bus service between Washington, D.C., and Annapolis is geared toward commuters rather than vacationers. Weekday mornings and afternoons, buses arrive at and depart from the Navy–Marine Corps Stadium parking lot, from College Avenue by the state buildings, and also from St. John's College. On weekends Greyhound makes one trip daily, arriving at and departing from the stadium.

➤ BUS LINES: **Dillons Bus Service** (☎ 800/827–3490 or 410/647–2321, WEB www.dillonbus.com). **Greyhound** (☎ 800/231–2222, WEB www.greyhound.com). **Mass Transit Administration** (MTA; ☎ 410/539–5000, WEB www.mtamaryland.com).

FARES AND SCHEDULES

The Annapolis Department of Public Transportation has a shuttle bus service (75¢) in the downtown area between 6:30 AM and 8 PM.

➤ INFORMATION: **Department of Public Transportation** (☎ 410/263–7964).

CAR TRAVEL

Annapolis is normally 35–45 minutes by car from Washington, D.C., on U.S. 50 (Rowe Boulevard exit). During rush hour (weekdays 3:30–6:30 PM), however, it takes about twice as long.

From Baltimore, following Routes 3 and 97 to U.S. 50, travel time is about the same. To tour southern Maryland, follow Route 2 south from Annapolis, and Route 4, which continues through Calvert County.

PARKING

Parking spots on Annapolis's historic downtown streets are scarce, but you can pay $4 ($8 for recreational vehicles) to park at the Navy–Marine Corps Stadium (to the right of Rowe Boulevard as you enter town from Route 50), and ride a shuttle bus downtown for 75¢. Parking is also available at garages on Main Street and Gott's Court (adjacent to the visitor center); on weekdays parking is free for the first hour and $1 an hour thereafter; on weekends it costs $4 a day.

EMERGENCIES

➤ CONTACTS: **Ambulance, Fire, Police** (☎ 911).

➤ HOSPITALS: **Anne Arundel Medical Center** (✉ 2001 Medical Pkwy. [off Jennifer Rd.], Annapolis, ☎ 443/481–1000). **Calvert Memorial Hospital** (✉ 100 Hospital Rd., Prince Frederick, ☎ 410/535–8344). **St. Mary's Hospital** (✉ 25500 Point Lookout Rd. [Rte. 5], Leonardtown, ☎ 301/475–8981).

LODGING

BED-AND-BREAKFASTS

Two reservation services operate in Annapolis. Annapolis Accommodations can book you into bed-and-breakfasts, hotels, and vacation homes. Annapolis Bed & Breakfast Association books lodging in the old section of town, which has many restaurants and shops as well as the Maryland State House and the City Dock. The U.S. Naval Academy and St. John's College serve as the northern and western boundaries of the territory.

➤ RESERVATION SERVICES: **Annapolis Accommodations** (✉ 41 Maryland Ave., 21401, ☎ 410/263–3262, WEB www.stayannapolis.com). **Annapolis Bed & Breakfast Association** (☎ 410/295–5200, WEB www.annapolisbandb.com).

MAIL AND SHIPPING

➤ POST OFFICE: **Annapolis Main Office** (✉ 1 Church Cir., 21401, ☎ 410/263–9291 or 877/877–7833 TTY).

TAXIS

Downtown Annapolis is accessible by foot, but to reach the malls and outlying attractions, a car or taxi is necessary. The Annapolis Cab Company provides taxi service in and around Annapolis.

➤ TAXI COMPANIES: **Annapolis Cab Company** (☎ 410/268–0022).

TOURS

Besides private charters, the 74-ft, three-masted *LIBERTÉ, The Schooner* offers Sunday brunch sails between May and June. Captain Chris lives on the schooner and is the captain for all sails. The *Schooner Woodwind* and the *Schooner Woodwind II* are twin 74-ft boats that have two to four sails a day (except Monday) between April and October, and some overnight trips.

When the weather's good, Watermark Cruises runs boat tours that last from 40 minutes to 7½ hours and go as far as St. Michaels on the Eastern Shore, where there's a maritime museum, yachts, dining, and boutiques. Prices range from $6 to $35.

Discover Annapolis Tours leads one-hour narrated minibus tours ($12) that introduce you to the history and architecture of Annapolis. Tours leave from the visitor center daily April through November and most weekends December through March.

Guided walking tours are a great way to see Annapolis's Historic District. The Historic Annapolis Museum Store rents two self-guided (with audiotapes and maps) walking tours: "Historic Annapolis Walk with Walter Cronkite" and "Historic Annapolis African-American Heritage Audio Walking Tour." The cost for each is $5.

Several tours leave from the visitor center at 26 West Street. On Annapolis Walkabout tours ($8), experts on historic buildings take you around the Historic District and the U.S. Naval Academy. Tours are held weekends from April to October.

Guides from Three Centuries Tours wear Colonial-style dress and take you to the state house, St. John's College, and the Naval Academy. The cost is $9. Tours depart daily April through October at 10:30 from the visitor center and at 1:30 from the information booth, City Dock.

Legacy Promotions offers historic walking tours of streets not often visited by most tourists. Their walks incorporate information about the town's African-American heritage.

➤ BOAT TOURS: ***LIBERTÉ***, The Schooner, (✉ Chart House Restaurant dock, Eastport, ☎ 410/263–8234, WEB www.theLiberte.com). ***Schooner Woodwind*** and ***Schooner Woodwind II*** (✉ Annapolis Marriott Hotel dock, Annapolis, ☎ 410/263–7837, WEB www.schooner-woodwind.com). **Watermark Cruises** (✉ Box 3350, 21403; City Dock, Historic District, ☎ 410/268–7600 or 410/268–7601, WEB www.watermarkcruises.com).

➤ BUS TOURS: **Discover Annapolis Tours** (✉ 31 Decatur Ave., Historic District, ☎ 410/626–6000, WEB www.discover-annapolis.com).

➤ WALKING TOURS: **Annapolis Walkabout** (✉ 223 S. Cherry Grove Ave., Historic District, ☎ 410/263–8253; ⏲ Apr.–Oct., weekends 11:30). **Historic Annapolis Foundation Walking Tours** (✉ 77 Main St., Historic District, ☎ 410/268–5576, WEB www.annapolis.org). **Legacy Promotions** (✉ 835 Spa Rd., ☎ 410/280–9745). **Three Centuries Tours** (✉ 48 Maryland Ave., Historic District, ☎ 410/263–5401, FAX 410/263–1901, WEB www.annapolis-tours.com).

VISITOR INFORMATION

Crain Memorial Welcome Center is a good place to pick up information if you're traveling north from Virginia.

➤ TOURIST INFORMATION: **Annapolis–Anne Arundel County Conference and Visitors Bureau** (✉ 26 West St., Annapolis 21401, ☎ 410/280–0445, WEB www.visit-annapolis.org). **Calvert County Dept. of Economic Development & Tourism** (✉ County Courthouse, Prince Frederick 20678, ☎ 410/535–4583 or 800/331–9771). **Charles County Office of Tourism** (✉ 8190 Port Tobacco Rd., Port Tobacco 20677, ☎ 800/766–3386). **Crain Memorial Welcome Center** (✉ U.S. Rte. 301/12480 Crain Hwy., near Newburg, 1 mi north of Governor Nice bridge over the Potomac River, ☎ 301/259–2500). **St. Mary's County Tourism** (✉ 23115 Leonard Hall Dr., Leonardtown 20650, ☎ 301/475–4411).

10 THE EASTERN SHORE

Cross the Chesapeake Bay from Annapolis, or from Norfolk and Virginia Beach, Virginia, or exit Interstate 95 as it emerges out of northern Delaware, and the pace feels slower and more relaxed. Eastern Shore towns are born on and sustained by the water; historic churches and mansions tucked amid fertile, flat fields; waterside cafés and shops; appealing B&Bs and luxury inns. But in the Atlantic coast resort of Ocean City, Maryland, the pace picks up again.

Updated by
Pete Nelson

SAILING THE CHESAPEAKE BAY nearly four centuries ago in search of new territory for his English king, Captain John Smith wrote that "heaven and earth never agreed better to frame a place for man's habitation." Today the counties of Maryland and Virginia on the eastern side of the Bay retain an enchanting culture and landscape of calm despite their proximity to Baltimore and Washington, D.C.

The Eastern Shore's first permanent English settlement—indeed, the first in Maryland and one of the earliest along the Atlantic—took root on Kent Island, now Queen Anne's County, in 1631. The region's long heritage is not only recorded in architecture and on paper and canvas, but continues to reveal itself through recent archaeological research, such as that being done at East New Market. Many Eastern Shore families have been here for many generations; current residents are therefore often an important link to the region's history.

A well-rounded visit to the Shore might consist of exploring hospitable communities and historic sites, strolling through wildlife parks and refuges, pausing at a few of the myriad shops, dining at third-generation-owned waterfront restaurants, and overnighting at inns and bed-and-breakfasts. One of the region's most popular summertime destinations is Ocean City, which clings to a narrow barrier island off the southeastern edge of Maryland's Eastern Shore. Its ocean-side culture differs dramatically from that of the Chesapeake, lacking as it does the early American aura that pervades the rest of the peninsula.

To understand the Eastern Shore, look to the Bay. The Chesapeake is 195 mi long and the nation's largest estuary (a semi-enclosed body of water with free connection to the open sea). Freshwater tributaries large and small flow south and west into the Bay, ensuring the agricultural wealth of the peninsula as well as the bounty of the Bay ("Chesapeake" is an Algonquian word meaning "great shellfish"). At day's end look west across Chesapeake Bay and you can see the sun set over water—a rare sight for any East Coast resident.

Pleasures and Pastimes

Dining

CATEGORY	COST*
$$$$	over $32
$$$	$22–$32
$$	$12–$22
$	under $12

**per person for a main course at dinner*

Lodging

CATEGORY	COST*
$$$$	over $225
$$$	$150–$225
$$	$100–$150
$	under $100

**All prices are for a standard double room, excluding state tax.*

Exploring the Eastern Shore

The Eastern Shore takes up most of the Delmarva (for Delaware-Maryland-Virginia) Peninsula, which reaches down from Pennsylvania and stretches some 200 mi to its tip just above Norfolk and Virginia Beach, Virginia. Only two bridges connect the Eastern Shore to the western and southern mainland. To the north, the William Preston Lane Jr. Bridge, or "the Bay Bridge," crosses just above Annapolis, its dual spans stretching 4½ mi across. To the south, the impressive, 17½-mi Chesapeake Bay Bridge-Tunnel connects Norfolk, Virginia Beach, and other Tidewater-area towns with the peninsula.

Whether you choose road, air, or water, it's easy to get around on the Eastern Shore. The rural roads make for pleasant driving and easy cycling, the airports allow for regional air service, and the dozens of marinas have many years' experience with almost every vessel type.

For glimpses into the past, stop by towns with roots deep in early American history, including Chestertown, Easton, Oxford, and St. Michaels. The life of the waterman—as Bay fishermen are traditionally known—still reigns in Crisfield, on Smith Island, and on Tilghman Island. A visit to Virginia's Eastern Shore, the slim peninsula running from the Maryland line to the Chesapeake Bay Bridge-Tunnel, calls for getting off U.S. 13 to take in the 300-year-old port town of Onancock, secluded Tangier Island, popular Chincoteague Island, and the Chincoteague National Wildlife Refuge.

QUEEN ANNE'S COUNTY

The eastern landfall of the Bay Bridge, which carries U.S. 50/301, is Kent Island, near the hamlets of Stevensville and Chester. This island gateway is 5 mi wide where U.S. 50/301 crosses it, and 14 mi long. William Claiborne established Maryland's first permanent settlement here in 1631 as part of Virginia. Today, the small towns in this one-time trading post all have their share of churches and homes that recall the region's past.

Numbers in the margin correspond to points of interest on the Maryland's Eastern Shore map.

Stevensville

1 *10 mi east of Annapolis (via U.S. 50/301).*

Tiny Stevensville, just north of the Bay Bridge's eastern landfall, is emerging as an enclave of artisans and craftspeople. Its galleries and studios sell original pottery, stained glass, and painted furniture as well as antiques and fine art. Its historic center has been on the National Register since 1986.

The **Old Stevensville Post Office,** now owned by the Kent Island Heritage Society, is a small building from the late 1800s. On a narrow lot, the structure stands with its side facing the street. ✉ *Love Point Rd.,* ☎ *410/643–5969.* 🎫 *Free.* ⏲ *Sat. 10–4, or by appointment, June through Sept.*

Dining and Lodging

$$–$$$ ✕ **Tavern on the Bay.** The menu at the Tavern ranges from succulent steaks to well-made crab cakes, but don't overlook the daily "fresh-line" fish specials. ✉ *Chesapeake Bay Beach Club, 500 Marina Club Rd., off Rte. 18 near Rte. 50/301,* ☎ *410/604–1933,* WEB *www.chesapeakebaybeachclub.com. AE, MC, V.*

$–$$$ ✕ **Hemingway's.** A broad veranda and an upper-level section indoors both have great views west across the Bay, at its narrowest here, and of Annapolis beyond. The sunsets can rival those off Key West, home of the restaurant's namesake. This long-popular restaurant serves tapas, soups, and salads; entrées include Atlantic salmon and coconut sesame shrimp. In summer a very informal bar and grill opens on the

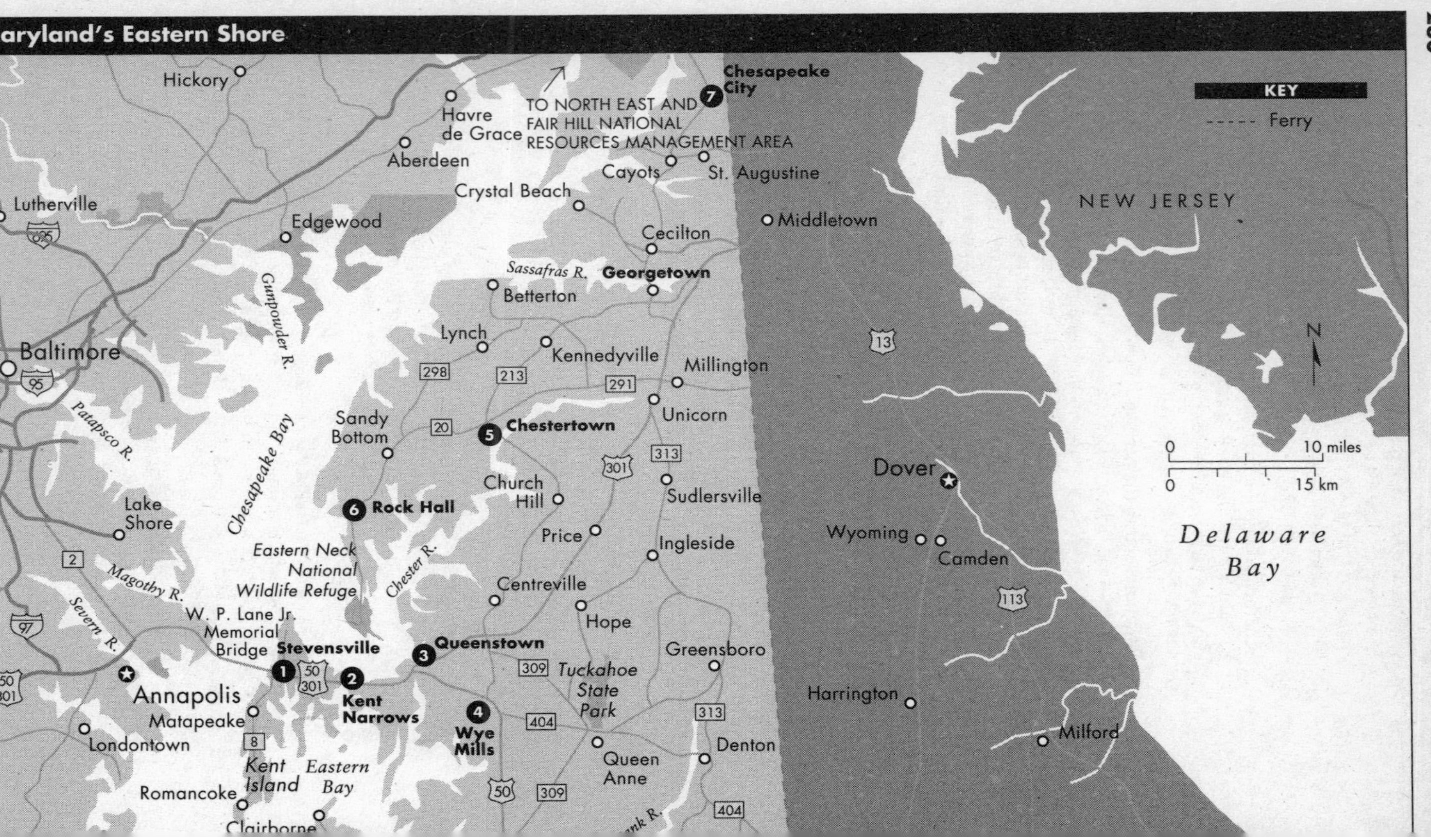

Maryland's Eastern Shore
KEY
Ferry
Hickory
Chesapeake City
TO NORTH EAST AND FAIR HILL NATIONAL RESOURCES MANAGEMENT AREA
Havre de Grace
Aberdeen
Cayots
St. Augustine
Crystal Beach
Middletown
NEW JERSEY
Lutherville
83
695
Edgewood
Cecilton
Sassafras R.
Georgetown
Betterton
Gunpowder R.
Lynch
Kennedyville
Baltimore
95
298
213
291
Millington
13
N
Unicorn
Patapsco R.
Sandy Bottom
20
Chestertown
Chesapeake Bay
313
301
0 10 miles
0 15 km
Church Hill
Sudlersville
Dover
Lake Shore
Rock Hall
Price
Ingleside
Wyoming
Camden
Delaware Bay
Eastern Neck National Wildlife Refuge
2
Chester R.
Magothy R.
Centreville
113
Severn R.
W. P. Lane Jr. Memorial Bridge
Hope
97
Stevensville
Queenstown
Greensboro
50 301
309
Tuckahoe State Park
Annapolis
Kent Narrows
Harrington
Matapeake
Wye Mills
404
313
Londontown
8
Milford
Denton
Kent Island
Eastern Bay
Queen Anne
Romancoke
50
309
404

Chesapeake Beach
Tilghman Island
Neavitt
Bellevue
Oxford
Preston
Federalsburg
Bridgeville
Georgetown
Milton
Seaford
Millsboro
Laurel
Choptank R.
Spocott Windmill
Cambridge
East New Market
Prince Frederick
Chesapeake Bay
St. Leonard
Church Creek
Vienna
Taylors Island
Bucktown
Hebron
Delmar
Bishop
Patuxent R.
Cove Point
Quantico
Salisbury
Willards
Assawoman Bay
Ocean City
Berlin
Honga
Blackwater National Wildlife Refuge
Fishing Bay Wildlife Management Area
Lakesville
Fishing Bay
Nanticoke R.
Wicomico R.
Powellville
Lexington Park
Honga R.
Eden
Longridge
Newark
Park Hall
Hooper Str.
Princess Anne
Pocomoke State Forest
Furnace Town
Assateague Island National Seashore
Snow Hill
Spence
Potomac River
Chesapeake Bay
Wenona
Manokin R.
Westover
Chincoteague Bay
Tangier Sound
Point Lookout
Pocomoke City
Stockton
See Virginia's Eastern Shore 23—25
Smith Island
Crisfield
VIRGINIA

lower level, with tables on the lawn adjacent to its private dock. Live music on weekends enhances its simple soup and sandwich menu. ✉ *Pier One Rd., off Rte. 18, ☎ 410/643–2722. AE, D, MC, V.*

$$–$$$$ ★ ✕🏨 **Kent Manor Inn & Restaurant.** A summer hotel through most of the 20th century, this imposing antebellum manor house is on 226 acres of farmland along Thompson Creek, near the Chesapeake Bay. Many guestrooms have cozy window seats, others Italian marble fireplaces. All rooms on the upper floors open onto semiprivate verandas. The restaurant ($$–$$$) serves meals in two elegant Victorian dining rooms or in an enclosed porch. Roasted rack of lamb, topped with a pomegranate glaze and served with shiitake mushroom compote, and the shrimp, brushed with horseradish sauce and wrapped in bacon, are but two of its finest entrées. ✉ *500 Kent Manor Dr., 21666, ☎ 410/643–5757 or 800/820–4511.* WEB *www.kentmanor.com. 20 rooms, 4 suites. Restaurant, cable TV, dock, croquet, volleyball, bar, meeting rooms; no smoking. AE, D, MC, V. Restaurant closed Mon.–Tues. (except for guest breakfast). BP.*

Nightlife

The **Chesapeake Bay Beach Club** (✉ 500 Marina Club Rd., off Rte. 18, near Rte. 50/301, ☎ 410/604–1933, WEB www.chesapeakebaybeachclub.com) is a happening place open year-round, but summer brings the liveliest times here. It includes two pubs, the Sunset Bar, and a shrimp shack. Live music on weekends spans the generations, and when the weather cooperates, the buff and the not-so gather for sports in, nearby, and on the water, including beach volleyball. The beach is free and open to the public.

Outdoor Activities and Sports

You can stroll or roll along the **Cross Island Trail** between Kent Narrows on the western edge of Kent Island—5½ mi wide here—and Bay beachfront on its eastern side. Here the smoothly paved or hard-packed trail joins the **Terrapin Nature Area,** 279 flat, lush acres that hug the Chesapeake Bay. The area, made up of five identifiable habitats, including wetlands, woodlands, and wildflower meadows, as well as tidal ponds and sandy beaches, has ample parking at both of its ends.

Shopping

Ye Olde Church House (✉ 426 Love Point Rd., ☎ 410/643–6227) in old Stevensville is just that, but now it's a shop filled with crafts and hand-spun yarn, hand-dipped candles, old-fashioned soap and candy, and the occasional antique. With sheep grazing in the pasture next door, it's hard to miss and worth seeking out.

Kent Narrows

❷ *5 mi east of Stevensville, 15 mi east of Annapolis (via U.S. 50/301).*

Kent Narrows is a slim, but vital, channel between Kent Island and the mainland of Maryland's Eastern Shore, near the town of Grasonville. A number of eclectic bars and restaurants have congregated at this intersection of road- and waterway traffic.

Exploration Hall (✉ 425 Piney Narrows Rd., Chester 21619, ☎ 410/604–2100 or 888/400–7787, WEB www.qac.org), the county's visitor center, has an interactive exhibit on Chesapeake Bay ecology and history.

Dining

$$$–$$$$ ✕ **The Narrows.** Overlooking the namesake waterway separating Kent Island from the Eastern Shore, this restaurant has views that included the home port of one of the region's largest commercial fishing fleets. The atrium of the contemporary dining room, with a skylight and large

windows, is airy. Specialties include a Caesar salad with fried oysters and grilled peppered tuna, sérved over sautéed spinach. ✉ *3023 Kent Narrows Way S, Grasonville,* ☎ *410/827–8113. AE, D, DC, MC, V.*

$$–$$$$ ★ ✕ **Harris Crab House.** On the mainland side of Kent Narrows, this family-friendly institution provides ample docking space for diners arriving by boat. Some of the seafood comes directly from local watermen. Cream-of-crab soup and back-fin crab cakes are among the best around—the cakes are spicy enough to promote plenty of beer drinking. A nautical theme prevails in the large dining room; oyster cans and other relics from an adjacent abandoned oyster house are all on display. You can get expansive water views from a table on the deck. ✉ *433 Kent Narrows Hwy., Grasonville,* ☎ *410/827–9500,* WEB *www.harriscrabhouse.com. MC, V.*

Outdoor Activities and Sports

BOATING

Queen Anne's County has 18 public landings for boats of all sizes. Of these, nine have trailer launching ramps, but the others are "unimproved" and can be used only for canoes, kayaks, and other small boats that can be carried to the water. A seasonal or daily permit is required to launch a boat from public landing ramps and for parking at these sites. For locations where permits may be purchased, contact **Parks and Recreation** (☎ 410/758–0835).

C & C Charters (✉ Mears Point Marina, 506 Kent Narrows Way N, ☎ 410/827–7888 or 800/733–7245, FAX 410/827–5341, WEB www.cccharters.com) has an extensive fleet of power- and sailboats over 30 ft. It's one of the northern Bay's most experienced and hospitable boat firms. Join Captain Michael Hayden as part of the crew of ***Nellie L. Byrde*** (☎ 410/886–2906) part of the Bay's historic skipjack fleet.

Queenstown

❸ *11 mi east of Stevensville, 21 mi east of Annapolis (via U.S. 50/301).*

The cove of Queenstown's harbor is protected by a bend of the mouth of the Chester River. Established in 1707 as "Queen Anne's Town," it became an important enough port to be attacked by the British during the War of 1812. A pleasantly sleepy little community, it's worth a short visit.

Lodging

$$$ **Lands End Manor on the Bay.** Set on 17 secluded acres on Eastern and Prospect bays, a 10-minute drive east of Queenstown, this stunningly decorated former hunting lodge has see-forever views from its three spacious rooms, which all have king-size beds. The cozy common areas include a great room, gun room, and solarium. When evening arrives, homemade cookies and sherry are set out. Deep-draft docking is available for guests. ✉ *232 Prospect Bay Dr., Grasonville 21638,* ☎ *410/827–6284. 3 rooms. Refrigerators, pool, dock, boating, bicycles; no smoking. MC, V. BP.*

Wye Mills

❹ *5 mi south of Queenstown, 14 mi southeast of Stevensville.*

The **gristmill** for which this village is named was built—and rebuilt—in the late 1600s. It supplied flour to George Washington's troops during the War of Independence. The first and third Saturdays of each month, from mid-April to early November, you can still buy fresh cornmeal as well as whole-wheat and buckwheat flour. ✉ *Rte. 662,*

☎ *410/827–6909 or 410/685–2886.* 🎫 *Free.* ⏲ *Mid-Apr.–early Nov., Mon.–Thurs. 10–1, Fri.–Sun. 10–4.*

Lodging

$$$$ 🏨 **Manor House.** This imposing 1930s English Tudor–style structure is perched on the end of an idyllic peninsula in the Wye River. The English club touches include overstuffed seating and Oriental rugs. A broad, fully furnished verandah stretches the width of the house. Guest room furnishings are conservatively contemporary with nautical accents. Vistas, most over the water, are stunning from any window. A full breakfast is served on weekends. ✉ *511 Pintail Point La. (near Rte. 50),* ☎ *410/827–7029,* FAX *410/827–7052,* WEB *www.pintailpoint.com. 2 rooms, 1 suite, 1 cottage. Cable TV, pool, outdoor hot tub, bicycles, billiards, library, kennel; no room phones, no smoking. D, MC, V. CP.*

$–$$$$ 🏨 **Irishtown B&B.** Operated by the Pintail Point resort, this renovated but still rustic early 1900s farmhouse can sleep 6 to 10 people. Rates are $500 per night for up to 6, then $50 per person up to a maximum of 10. ✉ *511 Pintail Point La. (near Rte. 50),* ☎ *410/827–7029,* FAX *410/827–7052,* WEB *www.pintailpoint.com. 1 house. Bicycles, kennel; no room phones, no room TVs, no smoking. D, MC, V. CP.*

Outdoor Activities and Sports

The **Pintail Point** complex (✉ 511 Pintail Point La., near Rte. 50, ☎ 410/827–7029, WEB www.pintailpoint.com) on the Wye River defies easy definition. It's a semiprivate resort with two hostelries open year-round (Irishtown B&B and Manor House). There's shooting and fly-fishing instruction, sporting clay shooting and lessons, upland game and waterfowl hunting, freshwater pond fishing, and a four-boat charter boat fleet for Chesapeake Bay fishing as well as for catered meals and receptions. Biking and hiking trails as well as canoeing creeks abound. An 18-hole golf course, Hunters Oak, is adjacent.

Shopping

Browse among acres of objects, from genuine antiques to everyday "other ★ people's treasures," then bid against amateurs and pros alike at **Dixon's Furniture** (✉ 2017 Dudley Corner Rd. [intersection of Rtes. 290 and 544], Crumpton, ☎ 410/928–3006), an institution of wide renown. It's much more than just furniture. Some of the food and beverage concessions here are run by members of the local Amish community. The auction takes place every Wednesday from dawn to dusk.

KENT COUNTY

The communities on the upper reaches of Maryland's Eastern Shore are steeped in history and determined to preserve it. Those in Kent County, whose idyllic location between the Chester and Sassafras Rivers is enhanced by a long, ragged Chesapeake Bay shoreline, are among the most fiercely protective. Hidden hamlets untouched by time savor their quiet anonymity; others struggle to balance acceptance of their recent renown with a heritage of 300 years.

Chestertown

❺ *47 mi northeast of Annapolis (via U.S. 50/301 to Rte. 213), 24 mi north of Wye Mills (via U.S. 50 to Rte. 213).*

Chestertown was a major international port in Colonial days: a tall, brick customhouse continues to dominate the High Street waterfront. Still the home of families whose local roots go back many generations, the town has its share of newer residents, many of them retirees. Today, venerable inns and good restaurants, fine art galleries and antiques shops line the brick pavements of High Street, Chestertown's broad, tree-lined main street. To walk along its narrow streets, some of them cobbled, is to commune quietly with some of the country's oldest history. At the northern edge of Chestertown is **Washington College,** one of the nation's oldest liberal-arts institutions. George Washington helped found the college in 1782 through a gift of 50 guineas.

Geddes-Piper House, home of the Historical Society of Kent County, is a splendid Federal-style home containing 18th-century furniture and an impressive teapot collection, a historical library, and shop. It is a good place to begin a visit to Chestertown. ✉ *Church Alley,* ☎ *410/778–3499,* WEB *www.hskcmd.com.* *$3.* ⏲ *Tues.–Sun. 9–4.*

The *Sultana,* a reproduction of a 1768 Colonial schooner by the same name, was launched in 2001. With a length of only 97 ft, the original *Sultana* was the smallest schooner ever registered on the Royal Navy Lists. The mission of this "Schoolship of the Chesapeake" is to provide unique, hands-on educational experiences in Colonial history and environmental science. Several two-hour public sails are available each month from April through November (adults, $25; children, $15). Day-long and multiday public sails are also scheduled regularly. The *Sultana* can be seen close-up when she is anchored in the Chester River, at the end of Cannon Street. ✉ *105 S. Cross St.,* ☎ *410/778–5954,* WEB *www.schoonersultana.com.*

Dining and Lodging

$$–$$$ ✕ **Blue Heron Café.** This relaxed, contemporary dining room has high, sloped ceilings and skylights. Among the café's most sought-after entrées is baked rockfish, but don't overlook the oyster fritters, a signature dish. The service here is genuine and attentive. ✉ *236 Cannon St.,* ☎ *410/778–0188. AE, MC, V. Closed Sun.*

$$–$$$ ✕ **Kennedyville Inn.** In a little town 8 mi north of Chestertown, the Kennedyville is known for its pit barbecue and microbrewed beers as well as daily seafood specials and light fare. The polished service and personal attention are as fine as the food, and the wine and spirits selection has been carefully chosen. It's not open long hours: seating is Wednesday and Thursday 5–8, Friday and Saturday 5–9, and Sunday 1–6. ✉ *Rte. 213, east side, Kennedyville,* ☎ *410/348–2400. D, MC, V. Closed Mon.–Tues. No lunch Mon.–Sat.*

$ ✕ **Play It Again, Sam.** This is one of those card shop/bookshop/coffee shop/snack shop/general store enterprises that can provide some insight into a community's character. Washington College students and others mingle happily at sidewalk tables when weather permits and in the "reading room" when it doesn't. ✉ *108 S. Cross St.,* ☎ *410/778–2688. No credit cards.*

$–$$$ ✕🏨 **Imperial Hotel and Restaurant.** This three-story brick structure at the intersection of Chestertown's two main downtown streets was built in 1903. Guest rooms and suites are decorated with original artwork, authentic period furnishings, and custom-designed and handcrafted pieces, some of which hide TVs and telephones. The hotel's two dining rooms ($$$) are bright and airy, both serving regional dishes such as rack of lamb with toasted pecans and peanuts as well as Asian-Mediterranean cuisine. Don't overlook the creations of the restaurant's own pastry chef. ✉ *208 High St., 21620,* ☎ *410/778–5000,* FAX *410/778–9662,* WEB *www.imperialchestertown.com. 11 rooms, 2 suites. Restaurant, cable TV, meeting room; no smoking. AE, D, MC, V. Restaurant closed Mon.–Tues. No lunch, except Sun.*

$$–$$$ ★ 🏨 **White Swan Tavern.** Step back in time at this inn, restored to its appearance circa 1790. Built as a home in 1733, it was a tavern, then a general store; it may be the town's oldest building. Brick fireplaces and deep window seats, an old writing desk, and pewter candleholders are all in keeping with its Colonial past. The original kitchen, shaded by a giant elm, is the inn's most requested guest room. Its rough ceiling beams, brick floor, and large fireplace attest to its antiquity. Afternoon tea is served in the dining room, on the rear stone patio, or in guest rooms. ✉ *231 High St., 21620,* ☏ *410/778–2300,* FAX *410/778–4543,* WEB *www.chestertown.com/whiteswan. 4 rooms, 2 suites. Meeting room; no room phones, no room TVs, no smoking. MC, V. CP.*

$$ ★ **Hill's Inn.** Before they began the restoration of this Victorian inn, the proprietors already had the set of 1870s stained-glass windows that are now installed here. On the ground floor are painted faux fireplaces and hand-painted plaster ceilings; "Jenny Doors" (tall, wide windows that open upward to create doorways) lead to a gracious veranda. All rooms are furnished with period antiques and have queen- or king-size beds. An English tea, complete with clotted cream and scones made from scratch, is part of the experience, as is a glass of sherry in the evening beside the fireplace. Therapeutic massages are available on request. ✉ *114 Washington Ave., 21620,* ☏ *410/778–1926,* FAX *410/778–3606. 4 rooms. No room phones, no room TVs, no kids under 12, no smoking. MC, V. BP.*

Nightlife and the Arts

Younger and older "C'town" residents alike head to **Andy's** (✉ 337½ High St., ☏ 410/778–6779) when they're looking for an unpretentious nightspot. Its simple menu ($) includes burgers, pizza, and "blue plate specials." Bluegrass, country, folk, jazz, rock, and pop bands play on Friday and Saturday. Andy's is closed on Sunday and serves no lunch.

Shopping

Robert Ortiz Studio (✉ 207 S. Cross St., ☏ 410/810–1400, WEB www.ortizstudios.com) is a place to find uncommonly handsome handcrafted furniture.

Rock Hall

❻ *13 mi southwest of Chestertown (via Rte. 291 to Rte. 20).*

No longer just a side trip, Rock Hall, its hardy maritime character intact, has emerged as a viable destination in its own right, to be reached either by road or by boat. It reveres its heritage, despite the pleasure boats anchored in its waters and moored at its docks that far outnumber actual working fishing boats.

The **Waterman's Museum** profiles the hard life on the Bay in absorbing detail, celebrating a Chesapeake way of life that in many ways is dying out. On display are exhibits on oystering and crabbing that include historical photos and local carvings, as well as preserved examples of his all-important boats and a reproduction of a waterborne shanty. ✉ *20880 Rock Hall Ave.,* ☏ *410/778–6697. Free. May–Sept., daily 8–5; Oct.–Apr., weekdays 8–5, Sat. 9–5, Sun. 10–4.*

At the tip of the Eastern Neck peninsula, at the mouth of the Chester River, is the superb **Eastern Neck National Wildlife Refuge.** This 2,285-acre park, 8 mi south of Rock Hall, is a prime place to spot migratory waterfowl, wild turkey, Delmarva fox squirrels, and southern bald eagles, undeterred by the experimental power-generating solar panels and wind turbines installed nearby. Nearly 6 mi of roads and trails and an observation tower provide excellent vantage points. ✉ *1730 Eastern Neck Rd.,* ☏ *410/639–7056,* WEB *easternneck.fws.gov. Daily dawn–dusk.*

Dining and Lodging

$–$$$ ✕ **Waterman's Crabhouse.** This casual dockside restaurant looking out toward the Chesapeake Bay Bridge has lots of local color. The menu includes ribs, steaks, and fried oysters, but its crab dishes are legendary: so are its homemade cheesecake and key lime pie. Warm summer weekends mean live entertainment and seating on the 40-ft deck. There's a deep-draft dock for diners arriving by boat. ✉ *21055 Sharp St.,* ☎ *410/639–2261. AE, D, MC, V. Closed Jan.–Feb.*

$$ ✕🏨 **The Inn at Osprey Point.** On 30 lush acres along Swan Creek, this stately Colonial-style building has brick fireplaces and exposed beams. It's worth staying here for the views alone. Rooms have four-poster, canopied beds; the spacious two-room Escapade suite has French doors and a marble bath with a whirlpool hot tub. At the inn's restaurant ($$–$$$; closed Tues.–Wed.), fine regional fare is served. The cream-of-crab soup with sherry is a favorite among regulars, as are entrées such as Maryland jumbo lump crab cakes and pan-seared duck breast. ✉ *20786 Rock Hall Ave., 21661,* ☎ *410/639–2194,* WEB *www.ospreypoint.com. 6 rooms, 1 suite. Restaurant, picnic area, cable TV, pool, marina, meeting rooms; no room phones, no kids, no smoking. D, MC, V. CP.*

Outdoor Activities and Sports

Canoeing and kayaking on quiet creeks and rivers throughout the Eastern Shore's ragged western shorelines are popular pastimes here. Two firms in Kent County provide rentals, tours, and lessons for the area: they're also good sources for waterside camping advice. One is **KayakCanoe LLC,** 4 mi north of Rock Hall, (✉ Swan Creek Rd., ☎ 410/639–9000, WEB www.kayakcanoe.com). The other is **Chester River Kayak Adventures,** (✉ 5758 Main St., Rock Hall, ☎ 410/639–2001, WEB www.crkayakadventures.com). These entrepreneurs also operate two B&Bs. Canoes and kayaks are also available to guests of some B&Bs and in some nature parks.

CECIL COUNTY

Cecil County includes the northern extremities of Chesapeake Bay. Its western boundary with Harford County, the Susquehanna River, is the Bay's principal northern tributary. Its southern boundary with Kent County is another tributary, the Sassafras River. The all-important Chesapeake and Delaware (C&D) Canal is cut between Cecil's third major river, the Elk, and the Delaware River, a major shipping route that connects Chesapeake Bay with Delaware Bay and the Atlantic Ocean. Some 12,000 acres of public parks and forests in addition to a wildlife management area help preserve connections with nature and the outdoors.

Chesapeake City

❼ *31 mi north of Chestertown (via Rte. 213).*

A town split dramatically in two by the C&D Canal, Chesapeake City homes and businesses face each other across the busy waterway. Those sitting at the restaurants and taverns next to the canal often marvel at the giant oceangoing vessels that slide by—seemingly within arm's reach. Chesapeake City's own well-protected harbor cove welcomes visiting pleasure craft virtually year-round.

Dining and Lodging

$$–$$$ ★ ✕ **The Bayard House.** One of the few restaurants in Chesapeake City, the Bayard House's cuisine and service would stand out almost anywhere. Patrons in the know travel to this canal-shop eatery for dishes such as grilled breast of duck; tournedos Baltimore, twin fillets of beef

topped with crab and lobster; and the de rigueur Maryland crab cakes. The Maryland crab soup is even more widely renowned. ✉ *11 Bohemia Ave.,* ☎ *410/885–5040. AE, D, MC, V.*

$$–$$$ **Ship Watch Inn.** Three levels of broad decks mean that every room has a place from which to relax and watch international watercraft sail in and out of the C&D Canal just yards away. (A canal-side hot tub offers an even closer view.) Built as a residence in 1920, the elegant, eclectic furnishings of this waterfront B&B blend well with the modern amenities. The decades-old black-and-white photos hanging in the public areas reveal much about the roles the owner-innkeepers' families played in the history of Chesapeake City. ✉ *401 First St., 21915,* ☎ *410/885–5300,* WEB *www.shipwatchinn.com. 8 rooms. Cable TV, meeting rooms; no smoking. AE, MC, V. BP.*

Outdoor Activities and Sports

Chesapeake Horse Country Tours (✉ Uniglobe Hill Travel, 200 Bohemia Ave., Chesapeake City 21915, ☎ 410/885–2795, WEB www.uniglobehill.com) allow you to roll through Cecil's stunning acres of emerald grassland. The tours head to horse farms that have produced such notable racing legends as Northern Dancer and Kelso.

North East

12 mi northwest of Chesapeake City (via Rte. 213 and Rte. 40).

Uncommon neighborliness along a main street of antiques and collectibles shops and homey eateries gives Cecil's riverside county seat its welcoming charm.

You could spend a weekend in the **5&10 Antique Market.** Originally the Hotel Cecil, it became Cramer's 5&10, an old fashioned variety store with hard-to-find items, penny candy jars, and a pair of proprietors who themselves became historic treasures. The building's enterprising current owner created an antiques mart but fully restored the building's exterior and retained its well-worn wood flooring, candy jars, and display counters. ✉ *115 S. Main St.,* ☎ *410/287–1250.*

The **Day Basket Factory** has been crafting oak baskets by hand since 1876. Brothers Edward and Samuel Day set up shop in North East partly because the forests along the Susquehanna River were full of white oak, the best kind of wood for baskets. Today skilled craftspeople and weavers use techniques passed down through the generations; you can often watch them as they work. ✉ *714 S. Main St.,* ☎ *410/287–6100,* WEB *www.daybasketfactory.com.* ⏲ *Apr.–Dec., Tues.–Thurs. 10–5, Fri.–Sat. 10–6, Sun. 1–5.*

The two spacious buildings of the **Upper Bay Museum** at the head of the North East River preserves the rich heritage of both the commercial and recreational hunter. This unusual museum houses an extensive collection of boating, fishing, and hunting artifacts native to the Upper Chesapeake Bay: sleek sculling oars, rare working decoys, and the outlawed "punt" gun and "gunning" rigs. ✉ *Walnut St. at Rte. 272,* ☎ *410/287–2675.* ⏲ *May 15–Oct. 31, Wed.–Sun. noon–4.*

About 6 mi south of the town of North East, **Elk Neck State Park** juts into the headwaters of the Chesapeake Bay to its west, with the Elk River flowing along its eastern flank. You can drive almost the length of the peninsula and then walk about a mile through pleasant woodlands to the cliffs on its tip. There you'll find the sparkling-white Turkey Point Lighthouse. No longer in use, it's maintained by volunteers. The 270-plus-degree view from Turkey Point is stunning. Camp sites are available here, as are some charming 1950s-era wooden cabins that are admirably well maintained. Elk Neck is a prime location for picnicking as well as for fishing and swimming off of sandy beaches. ✉ *Route 272 south of North East,* ☎ *410/287–5333 or 888/432–2267,* WEB *www.dnr.state.md.us/publiclands/central/elkneck.html.*

Dining and Lodging

$–$$ ✕ **Woody's Crab House.** You can get the crabs here, of course, and have them served any number of imaginative ways. But slurp one of the thick homemade soups, or down the famous Carolina shrimp burger, and you'll understand why this funky little eatery is so popular. The kids' menu is a thoughtful extra. But go easy on the real food: Woody's ice cream parlor, next door, includes seasonal favorite flavors such as apple, pumpkin, and Fourth of July (a celebration of red, white, and blue ice creams). ✉ *29 S. Main St.,* ☎ *410/287–3541. Reservations not accepted. D, MC, V.*

$$–$$$ ★ **Elk Forge B&B Inn and Retreat.** An easy hour's drive from either Baltimore or Philadelphia, Elk Forge is an appealing destination unto itself. On 5 acres of woods and gardens, the inn is along the Big Elk Creek. Each of the 12 guest rooms is uniquely decorated and well appointed. A daily afternoon tea includes the innkeepers' own herbal blends; services at the Spa in the Garden include Swedish massage and aromatherapy facials. ✉ *807 Elk Mills Rd. (Rte. 316), Elk Mills 21920,* ☎ *410/392–9007 or 877/355–3674,* WEB *www.elkforge.com. 12 rooms. In-room data ports, cable TV, in-room VCRs, outdoor hot tub, massage, spa, badminton, croquet, meeting rooms; no smoking. AE, MC, V. BP.*

TALBOT COUNTY

Water defines the landscape of Talbot County, which has some of the region's most vibrant little towns, including Easton, Oxford, and St. Michaels. The Chesapeake Bay forms its western border, and the meandering Choptank River slices through the Delmarva Peninsula to form its southern and eastern borders. Waterfront hamlets that started as fishing villages now include comfortable inns and downtown B&Bs. Fine waterside restaurants and folksy main street taverns are also part of this comfortably refined region.

Easton

★ 8 *79 mi south of North East and 36 mi south of Chestertown (via Rte. 213 and U.S. 50), 36 mi southeast of Annapolis (via U.S. 50/301 to U.S. 50).*

Well-preserved buildings dating from Colonial through Victorian times still grace the downtown of this affluent, genteel town. Fine art galleries, high-quality antiques shops, and gift boutiques sit side by side along North Harrison Street and others make up the small midtown mall called Talbottown.

Rebellious citizens gathered at the **Talbot County Courthouse** to protest the Stamp Act in 1765 and to adopt the Talbot Resolves, a forerunner of the Declaration of Independence. Today, the courthouse, built in 1712 and expanded in 1794, along with two wings added in the late 1950s, is still in use. The two-tier cupola is topped by a weather vane. ✉ *11 N. Washington St.,* ☎ *410/770–8001.* ⏲ *Weekdays 8–5.*

★ In its 1820s-era renovated schoolhouse, the **Academy Art Museum** houses a permanent collection of fine art by such American artists as James McNeil Whistler, Grant Wood, Lichtenstein, and Rauschenberg, as well as Chagall and Dürer. Special exhibitions often cover Eastern Shore artists, and the juried art show the museum holds in early October is one of the finest in the region. ✉ *106 South St.,* ☎ *410/822–2787 or 410/822–0455,* FAX *410/822–5997,* WEB *www.art-academy.org.* 🎫 *$2.* ⏲ *Mon.–Sat. 10–4, Wed. 10–9.*

A three-story Federal brick house, restored by a Quaker cabinetmaker in 1810, houses the **Historical Society of Talbot County,** which maintains a small museum of local history and manages Tharpe Antiques. The society also operates Three Centuries Tours, a one-hour overview of authentically furnished homes of the 17th through 19th centuries. ✉ *25 S. Washington St.,* ☎ *410/822–0773.* 🎫 *$5.* ⏲ *Tues.–Fri. 11–3, Sat. 10–4. Guided house tours Tues.–Sat. 11:30 and 1:30.*

Dining and Lodging

$$–$$$ ★ ✕ **Mason's.** A family-run landmark for more than 30 years, Mason's uses fresh ingredients from its own garden when making its dishes. Pink snapper, ahi tuna, and Pacific striped marlin from Hawaii are appreciated by seafood lovers, and the restaurant's tenderloin is second to none. Next door is a coffee bar and a food store that sells hard-to-find cheeses and meats, wonderful hand-crafted chocolates, and all manner of esoteric edibles. ✉ *42 E. Dover St.,* ☎ *410/822–3204. AE, D, MC, V. Closed Sun.*

$$–$$$ ✕ **Out of the Fire.** A spare, modern interior sets this neighborhood bistro apart from its Colonial neighbors. Of note is the owner's insistence that all equipment and furnishings—including a trompe l'oeil mural, faux-finish walls, and pottery—be obtained locally. One of the more interesting entrées is Caribbean spiced pork with ginger mango chutney. Breads are baked in a stone-hearth oven; desserts are produced on site. Enjoy one of more than 100 labels at the wine bar or in the overstuffed seating off to one side of the open kitchen. ✉ *22 Goldsborough St.,* ☎ *410/770–4777. AE, D, MC, V. Closed Sun.*

$$–$$$ ★ ✕🏨 **Inn at Easton.** This B&B operates one of the finest restaurants ($$$) in the country. Delightfully imaginative creations include green Thai bouillabaisse, but the signature dish is roasted lamb sirloin with a Dijon herb crust. With a colorful interior that's full of antiques and gracious touches, this circa 1790 Federal mansion is a bit like a boutique hotel. Original paintings by the Russian impressionist Nikolai Timkov are hung in the common areas. Upstairs, the seven rooms and suites skillfully combine old-time charm with modern amenities. ✉ *25 S. Harrison St.,* ☎ *410/822–4910 or 888/800–8091,* FAX *410/820–6961,* WEB *www.theinnateaston.com. 3 rooms, 4 suites. Restaurant; no room TVs, no kids under 9, no smoking. AE, D, MC, V. No lunch. BP.*

$$–$$$ 🏨 **The Tidewater Inn & Conference Center.** This stately four-story brick hotel was built in 1949. Beyond its first-story archways, a Colonial theme pervades its spacious common areas, where there are hurricane lamps, huge fireplaces, and paintings of old Easton. Mahogany reproduction furniture fills the charming rooms, done in greens and golds. In the hotel's full-service dining room, a "hunting breakfast" is available early every morning in season. ✉ *101 E. Dover St., 21601,* ☎ *410/822–1300 or 800/237–8775,* WEB *www.tidewaterinn.com. 114 rooms, 7 suites. Restaurant, cable TV, pool, bar, business services, meeting rooms, kennel; no-smoking floors. AE, D, MC, V.*

St. Michaels

9 *9 mi west of Easton (via Rte. 33), 49 mi southeast of Annapolis.*

St. Michaels, once a shipbuilding center, is today one of the region's major leisure-time destinations. Its ever-growing popularity has brought more and more shops, cafés, waterfront restaurants, and inns. In warmer months, tourists and boaters crowd its narrow streets and snug harbor.

In a 17th-century half-timber cabin, the **St. Mary's Square Museum** preserves local artifacts. The most prominent item in the collection was a shipyard bell that still rings at the start of the workday, at lunch, and at quitting time. The museum also occupies the adjoining Teetotum Building, a yellow clapboard house of the Civil War era named for a children's toy it was thought to resemble. ✉ *St. Mary's Sq.,* ☎ *410/745–9561.* *Donation suggested.* ⏲ *May–Oct., weekends 10–4.*

★ The **Chesapeake Bay Maritime Museum,** one of the region's finest, chronicles the Bay's rich history of boatbuilding, commercial fishing, navigating, and hunting in compelling detail. Exhibits among nine buildings on the 18-acre waterfront site include two of the Bay's unique skipjacks among its more than 80 historic regional boats. There's also the restored 1879 Hooper Strait Lighthouse, a working boatyard, and a "waterman's wharf" with shanties and tools of oystering and crabbing. In the Bay Building, you can see a dugout canoe hewn by Native Americans and a crabbing skiff. The Waterfowl Building contains carved decoys and stuffed birds, including wood ducks, mallards, and swans. ✉ *Mill St. at Navy Point,* ☎ *410/745–2916,* WEB *www.cbmm.org.* *$7.50.* ⏲ *June–Sept., daily 9–6; Oct.–Nov. and Mar.–May, daily 9–5; Dec.–Feb., daily 9–4.*

Dining and Lodging

$$$ ★ ✕ **208 Talbot.** Unobtrusively situated on St. Michaels' busy main street, 208 Talbot has several intimate dining rooms with exposed brick walls and brick floors. Seafood specialties include such starters as baked oysters with prosciutto, pistachio nuts, and champagne, and baked salmon in a tomato, mushroom, and tarragon sauce. Entrées, all served with tossed salad, include roasted halibut with lobster and mashed potatoes. On Saturdays, there's a prix-fixe menu ($50). ✉ *208 N. Talbot St.,* ☎ *410/745–3838,* WEB *www.208talbot.com. D, MC, V. Closed Mon.–Tues.*

$$–$$$ ✕ **Town Dock Restaurant.** Every seat in this vast restaurant overlooks the water, and every window frames its own scene; the deck is also open. Fresh seafood dishes such as local red snapper and rockfish and Atlantic salmon are favorites. For a finale, sample some strawberries hand-dipped in chocolate. ✉ *125 Mulberry St.,* ☎ *410/745–5577,* WEB *www.town-dock.com. AE, D, DC, MC, V. Closed Tues.–Wed. Nov.–Mar.*

$–$$ ✕ **Crab Claw Restaurant.** Owned and operated by the same family since 1965, this St. Michaels landmark started as a clam- and oyster-shucking house for watermen long before that. Diners at both indoor and outdoor tables have panoramic views over the harbor to the river beyond, but eat dockside if you can. As the name suggests, this is *the* down-home place for fresh steamed and seasoned blue crabs. But the extensive menu also includes sandwiches and other light fare as well as other seafood and meat dishes. Children's platters are available, too. ✉ *End of Mill St., at the Harbor,* ☎ *410/745–2900 or 410/745–9366. No credit cards. Closed late Dec.–early Mar.*

$$$$ ★ ✕ **Inn at Perry Cabin.** Set on 25 acres beside the Miles River, this luxury inn employs a nautical theme throughout to elegant effect. Each guest room has unique charm and elegant appointments; standard amenities include heated towel racks, fresh flowers in all rooms, and afternoon tea. Above all, staying here means finding impeccable service under world-class management. Dining at the inn's restaurant with its flawless cuisine and stellar wine selection is an event. The signature crab spring roll with pink grapefruit, avocado, and toasted almonds, and the lamb shank glazed with honey and tarragon are both exquisite. ✉ *308 Watkins La., 21663,* ☎ *410/745–2200 or 800/722–2949,* FAX *410/745–3348,* WEB *www.perrycabin.com. 54 rooms, 27 suites. Restaurant, in-room data ports, pool, pond, exercise equipment,*

Close-Up

THE VENERABLE SKIPJACKS OF THE CHESAPEAKE BAY

SETTLEMENT ALONG THE FERTILE SHORES of the Chesapeake Bay was an obvious choice for 17th-century English immigrants, who soon farmed the cash crop of tobacco and plucked plentiful blue crabs and plump oysters from its bottom. Among the reminders of the Bay's fishing culture, which endures, are its dwindling fleet of native skipjacks: broad, flat-bottom wooden sailing vessels for dredging oysters. Economical to build, skipjacks had the shallowest draft—the distance from the waterline to the lowest point of the keel—of any boat in the Chesapeake Bay. This made them essential for cruising above the grassy shoals favored by oysters.

At first, oyster harvesters would stand in small boats and use simple, long-handle tongs, like a pair of scissored rakes, to grasp clumps of oysters from the bottom and bring them aboard. It was tiresome, difficult work. But in the early 1800s, sturdy Yankee schooners, having left the depleted waters of New England, entered the Chesapeake Bay with dredges, ungainly iron contraptions that dragged up oysters along the bottom. With their first large harvest, Chesapeake's fishing industry changed forever.

Dredging was banned initially as exploitive and intrusive, first by Virginia and later by Maryland, but after the Civil War drained the region's economy, Maryland changed its mind and legalized the practice, allowing it under certain conditions for boats powered only by sails. By 1875, more than 690 dredging licenses were issued to owners of pungies, schooners, and sloops. Soon, more sophisticated dredgers emerged, such as "bugeyes" and "brogans." All were loosely called *bateaux*, French for "boats."

The oyster bounty was not to last. After peaking in 1884 with 15 million bushels, less than a third of that amount was caught in 1891. Despite the growing use of steam and gasoline power on land and water, "only under sail" laws prevailed in the Bay. As the 19th century drew to a close, boatbuilders were forced to experiment with boat designs that were cheap to build and yet had sails that would provide enough power for dredging and transporting the harvests. In 1901, one of these new bateaux appeared in Baltimore's harbor. She caught the eye of a *Baltimore Sun* newspaper reporter, who wrote that their "quickness to go about may have earned for them the name of skipjack . . .applied by fishermen on the New England coast to the bonita, a fly[ing] member of the fish family." The name stuck.

Oysters—and the Chesapeake's renowned blue crab—are still harvested by a dwindling number of watermen, their fleets concentrated in locales such as Crisfield and Kent Narrows, and Smith Island.

Only a dozen sail-powered skipjacks are still working. Taking a ride on one of them (generally from early April through October, when they're not dredging) is an exhilarating way to fully experience the culture and history of the Chesapeake. The region's second-largest working skipjack, the *Nellie L. Byrde,* is docked in front of Explorer Hall beside Kent Narrows. The *Nathan of Dorchester* is berthed in Cambridge. The *Herman M. Krentz,* built in 1955, and the 80-ft *Rebecca T. Ruark,* originally built in 1886, both sail from Tilghman Island or nearby St. Michaels.

massage, sauna, steam room, dock, bar, library, concierge, meeting rooms, helipad; no smoking. AE, DC, MC, V.

$$–$$$$ ★ **Five Gables Inn & Spa.** Three circa 1860 homes are now an elegant comfortable getaway. Some rooms have a private porch or balcony; all are elegantly decorated with working gas fireplaces, antique furnishings, fine linens and towels, and down comforters. Refreshments are served daily at 3. ✉ *209 N. Talbot St., 21663,* ☎ *410/745–0100 or 877/466–0100,* FAX *410/745–2903* WEB *www.fivegables.com. 11 rooms, 3 suites. Dining room, cable TV, some in-room VCRs, pool, sauna, spa, steam room, bicycles, shops, some pets allowed (fee); no phones in some rooms, no smoking. AE, MC, V. CB.*

$$–$$$$ ★ **Wades Point Inn on the Bay.** Five miles northwest of St. Michaels, three brick Colonial and wood-frame Victorian buildings form an exceptional retreat. The stately Main House was built in 1819. In 1890, facilities were added for summertime guests, and Wades Point Farm emerged as a bona fide inn. Combining the serenity of the country and the splendor of the Chesapeake Bay, this uncommon complex is at the heart of 120 acres of fields and woodland. Two sun-bright corner rooms in one wing are closest to the water, but each carefully decorated period room has a private porch or balcony. Cows and goats grazing along a 1-mi trail through the property welcome hikers, joggers, and bird-watchers. ✉ *Wades Point Rd. (Rte. 33, Box 7), 21663,* ☎ *410/745–2500,* WEB *www.wadespoint.com. 23 rooms. Some kitchenettes, pond, dock, hiking, meeting rooms; no a/c in some rooms, no room phones, no room TVs, no kids under 1, no smoking. MC, V. CP.*

$$–$$$ **Victoriana Inn.** Adirondack chairs line a sloping expanse of lawn leading to the formal gardens of what was once a Civil War army officer's home. Set on the town's harbor and across a footbridge from the Maritime Museum, this inn is a relaxing haven. All rooms include queen-size beds; two have fireplaces and three overlook the water. The suite has a private water-view deck and a fireplace as well as a TV. There's a nightly happy hour that includes wine, beer, and light hors d'oeuvres. ✉ *205 Cherry St., 21663,* ☎ *410/745–3368,* WEB *www.victorianainn.com. 6 rooms, 1 suite. Bicycles; no room phones, no TV in some rooms, no kids under 12; no smoking. MC, V. BP.*

Outdoor Activities and Sports

Town Dock Marina (✉ 305 Mulberry St., ☎ 410/745–2400 or 800/678–8980) rents bicycles as well as surrey-top electric boats and small powerboats. ***The Patriot*** (✉ docked near Crab Claw Restaurant and Chesapeake Bay Maritime Museum, St. Michaels, ☎ 410/745–3100, WEB patriotcruises.com), a 65-ft steel-hull yacht, departs four times daily, from April through October, for one-hour cruises on the Miles River. The tour covers the ecology and history of the area as it passes along the tranquil riverfront landscape.

Shopping

Talbot Street, the main street in St. Michaels, is lined with restaurants, galleries, and all manner of shops, including a hardware store that doubles as a retro gift shop. Stroll between Mill Street, the lane to the Chesapeake Bay Maritime Museum, and Willow Street, or head just beyond to Canton Alley.

Tilghman Island

⑩ *13 mi southwest of St. Michaels (via Rte. 33).*

A few small upscale residential communities notwithstanding, a visit to Tilghman Island provides intriguing insight into the Eastern Shore's remarkable character. Leave your car and explore by bike or kayak. A handful of B&Bs and small inns provide excellent accommodations here. A small fleet of working fishing boats, including a few of the region's remaining skipjacks, call Dogwood Harbor "home port."

Dining and Lodging

$$–$$$$ **Lazyjack Inn on Dogwood Harbor.** One of the island's original 1855 homes has been transformed into this charming B&B, which is beside Dogwood Harbor. Tastefully decorated rooms are equipped with down comforters and candles in the windows. Guests are welcomed with fresh flowers and a tray of sherry on the bureau. Both suites include a fireplace and an oversize hot tub. You can reserve a sail on the innkeepers' restored 1935 45-ft boat, the *Lady Patty.* ✉ *5907 Tilghman Island Rd., 21671,* ☎ *410/886–2215 or 800/690–5080,* WEB *www.lazyjackinn.com. 2 rooms, 2 suites. Boating; no room phones, no room TVs, no kids under 12, no smoking. AE, MC, V. BP.*

$$–$$$ **Chesapeake Wood Duck Inn.** Designed in 1890 as a boardinghouse, this inn, beside venerable Dogwood Harbor, also served some time as a bordello as well as a respectable waterman's family residence. Impeccably restored, the nonstuffy inn is enhanced with original artworks. A first-floor fireplace, screened porch, and sunporch make the inn suitable for all seasons. In the elegant dining room, your hosts—one of whom is an experienced professional chef—present wonderful breakfasts that may include crèpes, maple-braised sausage and apples, and eggs whipped with white truffles and served with an Asiago cheese sauce. A prix-fixe dinner with wine is available for 4 to 12 guests by prior arrangement. ✉ *Box 202, Gibsontown Rd., 21671,* ☎ *410/886–2070 or 800/956–2070,* FAX *410/677–7256,* WEB *www.woodduckinn.com. 6 rooms, 1 suite. Dining room; no room TVs, no children under 14, no smoking. MC, V. BP.*

$$–$$$$ ✕ **Tilghman Island Inn.** Warm, welcoming conviviality and casual elegance define this compact, modern resort overlooking the Chesapeake Bay (there are also views of a neighboring waterfowl marsh). Five deluxe waterside rooms have hot tubs, fireplaces, and spacious decks. Dishes served at the Gallery Restaurant ($$–$$$) include the unusual black-eyed pea cake and Oysters Choptank. The 5-acre complex includes a 20-slip transient marina and a small fleet of tandem and single kayaks available for rent. ✉ *Coopertown Rd., Box B, 21671,* ☎ *410/886–2141 or 800/866–2141,* WEB *www.tilghmanislandinn.com. 15 rooms, 5 suites. Restaurant, in-room data ports, cable TV, tennis court, pool, dock, marina, croquet, 2 bars, meeting rooms, some pets allowed; no smoking. AE, D, DC, MC, V. CP.*

Outdoor Activities and Sports

Tilghman Island's tiny Dogwood Harbor is the home port of two of the region's revered skipjacks. They are available for tours between early April and late October. The ***Herman M. Krentz*** (✉ Dogwood Harbor, Tilghman Island, ☎ 410/745–6080, WEB www.oystercatcher.com) is U.S. Coast Guard–certified for 32 passengers. A 2-hour tour costs $30.

The ***Rebecca T. Ruark*** (✉ Dogwood Harbor, Tilghman Island, ☎ 410/886–2176 or 410/829–3976, www.skipjack.org) is U.S. Coast Guard–certified for 49 passengers. (✉ Dogwood Harbor, Tilghman Island, ☎ 410/886–2176 or 410/829–3976, WEB www.skipjack.org; 2-hr hands-on learning cruise $30).

En Route The **Oxford-Bellevue Ferry,** begun in 1683, may be the oldest privately owned ferry in continuous operation in the United States. It crosses the Tred Avon River between Bellevue, 7 mi south of St. Michaels via Routes 33 and 329, and Oxford. ✉ *N. Morris St. at the Strand, Oxford,* ☎ *410/745–9023,* WEB *www.oxfordmd.com/obf.* *Ferry: $5 car and driver one way, $1 pedestrian, $2 bicycle, $3 motorcycle.* *Mar.–Memorial Day and Labor Day–Nov., weekdays 7 AM–sunset,* *weekends 9 AM–sunset; Memorial Day to Labor Day, weekdays 7 AM–9 PM, weekends 9–9.*

Oxford

11 *7 mi southeast of St. Michaels (via Rte. 33 and Rte. 333).*

Tracing its roots to 1683, Oxford remains secluded and untrammeled. Robert Morris, a merchant from Liverpool, lived here with his son, Robert Morris Jr., a signer of the Declaration of Independence. The younger Morris helped finance the Revolution but ended up in debtor's prison after losing at land speculation.

The **Oxford Museum** displays models and pictures of sailboats. Some boats were built in Oxford, site of one of the first Chesapeake regattas (1860). Check out the full-scale racing boat by the door. Other artifacts include the lamp from a lighthouse on nearby Benoni Point, a sail-maker's bench, and an oyster-shucking stall. Docents elaborate on the exhibits, which set the context for a walking tour of nearby blocks. ✉ *Morris and Market Sts.,* ☎ *410/226–5122.* *Free.* ⏲ *Apr.–Oct., Fri.–Sun. 2–5.*

Dining and Lodging

$$–$$$$ ✕ **Robert Morris Inn.** In the early 1700s, this building on the banks of the Tred Avon River was crafted as a home by ships' carpenters using ship nails, hand-hewn beams, and pegged paneling. In 1738, it was bought by an English trading company as a house for its Oxford representative, Robert Morris. Four guest rooms have handmade wall paneling and fireplaces built of English bricks used as boat ballast. Other buildings in the complex include a newer manor house on a private beach. Circa 18th-century murals of river scenes adorn the walls of the main room in the inn's restaurant ($$–$$$), known for its meticulous preparation of the Chesapeake Bay's bounty. ✉ *314 N. Morris St., 21654,* ☎ *410/226–5111,* FAX *410/226–5744,* WEB *www.robertmorrisinn.com. 35 rooms. Restaurant, taproom, Internet, meeting rooms; no room phones, no TV in some rooms, no smoking. AE, MC, V.*

$$$$ ★ **Combsberry.** This 1730 brick home, together with a carriage house and cottage and a formal garden, is set amid magnolias and willows on the banks of Island Creek. Inside are five arched fireplaces, floral chintz fabrics, and polished wood floors. All the rooms and suites of this luxurious B&B have water views and are furnished with English manor–style antiques, including four-poster and canopy beds. Some also have hot tubs and working fireplaces; the two-bedroom Carriage House has a kitchen. ✉ *4837 Evergreen Rd., 21654,* ☎ *410/226–5353,* WEB *www.combsberry.com. 2 rooms, 2 suites, 1-bedroom cottage, 2-bedroom carriage house. Dining room, library, some pets allowed; no room phones, no room TVs, no kids under 12. AE, MC, V. BP.*

DORCHESTER COUNTY

One of the larger, yet sparsely populated counties on Maryland's Eastern Shore, Dorchester retains the aura of early America in its few towns and tiny fishing villages. The expansive Choptank River, its northern boundary, and the rambling 22,000-acre Blackwater National Wildlife Refuge are idyllic locales for biking and boating, hiking and camping, and hunting and fishing (including, of course, crabbing).

Cambridge

12 *15 mi southeast of Oxford (via U.S. 50), 55 mi southeast of Annapolis (via U.S. 50/301 to U.S. 50).*

In this county seat, Annie Oakley used to aim at waterfowl from the ledge of her waterfront home. Graceful Georgian, Queen Anne, and Colonial revival buildings abound: with an art gallery here and a museum there, a night or two in Cambridge can be very refreshing.

The three-story, 18th-century Georgian **Meredith House** is headquarters of the Dorchester County Historical Society. Chippendale, Hepplewhite, and Sheraton period antiques fill the first floor. The Children's Room holds an impressive doll collection, cradles, miniature china, and baby carriages. Portraits and effects of six former Maryland governors from Dorchester County adorn the Governor's Room. There's also a restored smokehouse, blacksmith's shop, and medicinal herb garden. ✉ *902 La Grange Ave.,* ☎ *410/228–7953.* *Free.* *By appointment only.*

The **James B. Richardson Maritime Museum** in downtown Cambridge celebrates and chronicles Chesapeake boatbuilding with impressive, scaled-down versions of boats peculiar to the Chesapeake Bay, such as bugeyes, pungies, skipjacks, and log canoes—and the tools used to build them. Photos, a film, and a model boatbuilding workroom complement the models. ✉ *401 High St.,* ☎ *410/221–1871.* *Free.* *Wed. and weekends 1–4 and by appointment.*

Dining and Lodging

$–$$$ ✕ **Snappers Waterfront Cafe.** Join regulars at this casual waterside restaurant and bar on the edge of town. Choose from an extensive menu of dishes with a Southwestern flavor, healthy portions of steak, and such entrées as baked stuffed shrimp. ✉ *112 Commerce St.,* ☎ *410/228–0112. AE, D, MC, V.*

$$$$ **Hyatt Regency Chesapeake Bay Golf Resort, Spa and Marina.** Beside the Choptank River to the east of downtown Cambridge, this complex is the Eastern Shore's first full-service, year-round resort. Built on nearly 350 acres, the resort includes an 18-acre nature preserve, an 18,000-square-ft spa, and a golf course designed by Keith Foster. The six-story resort makes optimal use of natural light and its spectacular views of the water. All rooms and suites have a private balcony; those on the upper level have raised ceilings. The resort's restaurants include the self-service Bay Country Market and the Blue Point Provision Company for seafood. Two sandstone fireplaces and a 30-ft high wall of windows welcome you to Michener's Library. ✉ *100 Heron Blvd., 21613,* ☎ *410/901–1234,* FAX *410/901–6301,* WEB *chesapeakebay.hyatt.com. 384 rooms, 16 suites. 5 restaurants, snack bar, room service, in-room data ports, in-room safes, refrigerators, cable TV, 18-hole golf course, 4 tennis courts, indoor-outdoor pool, health club, spa, beach, marina, bar, lounge, shops, Internet, concierge, business services, convention center, meeting rooms. AE, D, V, MC.*

$–$$$ **Loblolly Landings and Lodge.** Set amid mature loblolly pines on 170 acres, this burgeoning B&B is a great retreat 1½ mi from Blackwater National Wildlife Refuge. The rooms are spacious and bright; the suite has a hot tub and fireplace. The 900-square-ft great room, which has a stone wall and fireplace, overlooks a stocked fishing pond favored by great blue heron, egrets, and osprey. Cable TV is available in a large common room. Bicycles, canoes, and kayaks may be rented at the Lodge. The complex includes a comfortably air-conditioned and heated bunkhouse that sleeps 10. ✉ *2142 Liners Rd., Church Creek 21622,* ☎ *410/397–3033 or 800/862–7452,* FAX *410/397–3377,* WEB *www.loblollylandingsbandb.com. 3 rooms without bath, 1 suite. Boating, fishing, bicycles, archery, airstrip, some pets allowed; no room phones, no room TVs, no kids under 5, no smoking. D, MC, V. BP.*

$$ **Glasgow Inn.** A long driveway crossing a broad landscaped lawn leads to this stately white plantation house that evokes its genteel 18th-century beginnings. All rooms are filled with period prints and furniture, including four-poster beds. Front rooms look out over the lawn to the Choptank River. ✉ *1500 Hambrooks Blvd., 21613,* ☎ *410/228–0575,* WEB *www.glasgowinncambridge.com. 10 rooms, 5 with bath. Dining room, croquet, meeting rooms; no room phones, no TV in some rooms, no smoking. No credit cards. BP.*

Blackwater National Wildlife Refuge

13 *8 mi south of Cambridge (via Rte. 16 to Rte. 335), 63 mi southeast of Annapolis.*

The largest nesting bald eagle population north of Florida makes Blackwater its home. You'll often see the birds perching on the lifeless tree trunks that poke from the wetlands here, part of nearly 27,000 acres of woods, open water, marsh, and farmland. In fall and spring, some 35,000 Canada and snow geese pass through in their familiar *V* formations to and from their winter home, joining more than 15,000 ducks. The rest of the year, residents include endangered species such as peregrine falcons and silver-haired Delmarva fox squirrels. Great blue heron stand like sentinels while ospreys dive for meals, birds sing, and tundra swans preen endlessly. By car or bike, you can follow a 5-mi road through several habitats or follow a network of trails on foot. Exhibits and films in the visitor center provide background and insight. ✉ *Rte. 335 at Key Wallace Dr.,* ☎ *410/228–2677,* WEB *www.friendsofblackwater.org.* *$3 car, $1 pedestrian or cyclist.* ⏲ *Wildlife drive daily, dawn–dusk. Visitor center weekdays 8–4, weekends 9–5.*

Outdoor Activities and Sports

The ***Nathan of Dorchester*** (✉ Long Wharf, ☎ 410/228–7141), a recently built replica of a skipjack, cruises the Choptank River from Long Wharf at the foot of High Street in Cambridge. In summer the 28-passenger *Nathan* sets sail on most Saturday evenings and Sunday afternoons.

All of the land of the **Fishing Bay Wildlife Management Area,** bordering Blackwater National Wildlife Refuge, is along Fishing Bay at the southern end of Dorchester County. Here you can take a pair of "water trails" through some scenic rivers and streams—it's reminiscent of Florida's Everglades. A short canoeing or kayaking trek down one of these water trails—recommended only for paddlers with some experience—is an exceptional way to experience a salt marsh and the wildlife that lives in one. Contact the Dorchester County Department of Tourism for more information, as well as a waterproof map.

East New Market

14 *15 mi southeast of Oxford (via U.S. 50), 8 mi east of Cambridge (via U.S. 50 to Rte. 16).*

Believed to have been first settled on a Choptank Native American trail in the 1660s, this extraordinary town contains some 75 buildings of historic significance—churches, schools, businesses, and residences—representing three centuries. In this living museum of architecture, every exhibit is in its original location. An illustrated walking-tour map is available from the Dorchester County Tourism office.

THE LOWER EASTERN SHORE

The three counties of Maryland's lower Eastern Shore—Wicomico, Worcester, and Somerset—contain the contrasting cultures of the Chesapeake Bay and the Atlantic coast but still share a common history.

The small towns throughout the region sometimes seem a century away from the oceanfront's summertime bustle. Main Street shops, early America inns, and unsung restaurants are a far cry from the boutiques and galleries, the high-rise hotels and condos, and eateries of nearby Ocean City, which clings to a narrow, sandy strip.

Salisbury

15 *32 mi southeast of Cambridge (via U.S. 50), 87 mi southeast of Annapolis (via U.S. 50/301 to U.S. 50).*

Barges still ply the slow-moving Wicomico River between the Bay and Salisbury, the Eastern Shore's second-largest port after Baltimore. The tree-shaded waterfront is a popular draw for hiking, biking, boating, fishing, and shopping. Antiques shops and galleries, along with some exemplary Victorian architecture, fill the six blocks that make up downtown.

★ Operated in partnership with Salisbury University, the **Ward Museum of Wildfowl Art** presents realistic marshland and wildfowl displays. Two brothers from Crisfield, Lem and Steve Ward, helped transform decoy making from just a utilitarian pu it to an art form; their re-created studio is a must-see exhibit. Besides the premier collection of wildfowl art, the 30,000-square-ft museum has some 2,000 other artifacts as well as a gift shop and library. ✉ *3416 Schumaker Pond, at Beaglin Park Dr.,* ☎ *410/742–4988,* WEB *www.wardmuseum.org.* 🎫 *$7.* ⏲ *Mon.–Sat. 10–5, Sun. noon–5.*

Dining and Lodging

$–$$$ ✕ **The Red Roost.** Inside a former chicken barn, inverted bushel baskets now serve as light fixtures at this down-home crab house, where hammering mallets rival the beat of piano and banjo sing-alongs. The Red Roost gets rave reviews for its seafood specialties and ribs, as well as its meaty steamed crabs. ✉ *Rte. 352 and Rte. 362, Whitehaven,* ☎ *410/546–5443 or 800/953–5443. AE, MC, V.* ⏲ *Dinner only. Closed Mon. and Tues., Labor Day–Memorial Day and Nov.–Mar.*

Furnace Town

16 *15 mi southeast of Salisbury (via Rte. 12), 96 mi southeast of Annapolis.*

Furnace Town is a re-creation of a 19th-century industrial village that grew alongside the huge outdoor Nassawango Iron Furnace. It has a blacksmith shop, a shed used for broom making, a smokehouse, print shop, church, and company store. You can also get a close-up look at nature via the boardwalk and trails that pass through a cypress swamp. Bring mosquito repellent in summer. ✉ *Old Furnace Rd., Rte. 12,* ☎ *410/632–2032.* 🎫 *$3.* ⏲ *Apr.–Oct., daily 11–5.*

Snow Hill

17 *19 mi southeast of Salisbury (via Rte. 12), 106 mi southeast of Annapolis.*

The streets of Snow Hill, the Worcester County seat, are lined with huge sycamores and stately homes the reflect its days as a shipping center in the 18th and 19th centuries.

The redbrick **All Hallows Episcopal Church,** (✉ 109 W. Market, ☎ 410/632–2327) completed in 1756, occupies the site of an earlier sanctuary. Inside is a Bible that belonged to Queen Anne. The church is one of the Snow Hill historic structures that appear in a walking-tour brochure available at the Julia A. Purnell Museum or, on weekdays, at Town Hall, at the corner of Green and Bank.

Outdoor Activities and Sports

CANOEING

Pocomoke River Canoe Company (✉ 312 N. Washington St., Snow Hill, ☎ 410/632–3971, FAX 410/632–2866, WEB www.inntours.com) rents canoes, gives lessons, and leads tours along the Pocomoke River, a habitat for bald eagles, blue herons, and egrets.

Berlin

18 *15 mi northeast of Snow Hill (via Rte. 113), 22 mi east of Salisbury (via U.S. 50); 7 mi west of Ocean City (via U.S. 50).*

Berlin is just a short drive from Ocean City but is far less strident and loud in temperament. Magnolias, sycamores, and ginkgo trees line streets filled with predominantly Federal- and Victorian-style buildings (47 are on the National Register of Historic Places). Berlin—its name derived not from the German city but from Burleigh Inn, a Colonial way station—was the principal location for two recent films: *Runaway Bride* (1998) and *Tuck Everlasting* (2002).

Dining and Lodging

$$–$$$$ ★ ✕🏨 **Atlantic Hotel.** This fully restored 1895 inn blends the taste of grand living with modern conveniences. Guest rooms are spacious and have four-poster beds on hardwood floors. Beneath chandeliers, the hotel's formal dining room ($$–$$$) serves scrumptious entrées that may include a pistachio duck dish or rockfish topped with oysters, ham, and crabmeat. In the tavern, a very talented waiter periodically joins the pianist and sings. The second-floor parlor, done in bold red and green hues with ornate furnishings, is a perfect place to relax. ✉ *2 N. Main St., 21811,* ☎ *410/641–3589 or 800/814–7672,* FAX *410/641–4928,* WEB *www.atlantichotel.com. 17 rooms. Restaurant, café, cable TV, library, meeting rooms; no smoking. AE, MC, V.*

Ocean City

19 *7 mi east of Berlin and 29 mi east of Salisbury (via U.S. 50).*

Stretching some 10 mi along a narrow barrier island just off Maryland's Atlantic coast, Worcester County's Ocean City draws millions annually to its broad beaches and the innumerable activities and amenities that cling to them, as well as to the quiet bayside.

On the older, southern end of the island, where the 3-mi Boardwalk begins, you'll find a restored 19th-century carousel as well as traditional stomach-churning amusement park rides and a fishing pier. The north–south roads, as well as the Boardwalk itself, are crowded with shops selling the prerequisites of resort destinations everywhere, from artwork to T-shirts to snack food to beer. Beyond the northern end of the Boardwalk (27th Street), high-rise condos prevail, and the beaches are less congested.

Lodging options include modern high-rises, sleepy motels, two B&Bs, and older hotels with oceanfront porches filled with wooden chaises longues and rocking chairs. Cuisine here includes Thrasher's renowned "Boardwalk" fries, available from dozens of outlets throughout Ocean City, to fine restaurant fare accompanied with world-class wine lists. Fresh seafood abounds.

A year-round destination, Ocean City is particularly appealing in the fall and early winter, then again in late winter and early spring, when the weather is mild. Most hotels and better restaurants remain open year-round, although the latter may operate on fewer days and/or shorter schedules. Furthermore, many festivals and other special events are scheduled for the off-season.

★ On the southernmost tip of the island, the **Ocean City Life Saving Station Museum** traces the resort to its days as a tiny fishing village in the late 1800s. Housed in an 1891 building that once held the U.S. Lifesaving Service and the Coast Guard, the museum's exhibits include models of the grand old hotels, artifacts from shipwrecks, boat models, and even itchy wool swimsuits and an old mechanical laughing lady from the Boardwalk. Press the button, and you'll be laughing with her. ✉ *Boardwalk at the Inlet,* ☎ *410/289–4991,* WEB *www.ocmuseum.org.* 🎫 *$2.* ⏲ *June–Sept., daily 11–10; May and Oct., daily 10–4; Nov.–Apr., weekends 10–4.*

Trimper's Amusement Park, at the south end of the Boardwalk, has a "boomerang" roller coaster; a double Ferris wheel; and the Hirschell Spellman Carousel, from 1902. The park has been owned by the Trimper family since it opened in 1890. ✉ *Boardwalk and S. 1st St.,* ☎ *410/289–8617.* 🎫 *Pay per ride or attraction.* ⏲ *Memorial Day–Labor Day, weekdays 1 PM–midnight; weekends noon–midnight. Labor Day–Memorial Day indoor portion only, weekends noon–midnight.*

Dining

$$–$$$ ★ ✕ **Fager's Island.** This bayside restaurant gives you white-linen treatment and views of soothing wetlands and stunning sunsets through its large windows. White stucco walls and white columns contrast with red tile floors and brass chandeliers. Entrées include prime rib, fresh mahimahi, and salmon. There's an outside deck for more informal dining and a raw bar with lighter fare. On a whimsical note: in the summer, Tchaikovsky's *1812* Overture is played every evening, with the tumultuous finale timed to coincide with the setting of the sun. ✉ *60th St. at the Bay,* ☎ *410/524–5500,* WEB *www.fagers.com. Reservations essential. AE, D, DC, MC, V.*

$$–$$$ ✕ **Harrison's Harbor Watch Restaurant and Raw Bar.** Overlooking the Ocean City Inlet at the island's southernmost tip, this sprawling, two-story seafood restaurant includes only freshly prepared sauces, soups, breads, and dressings on its menu, with fish and meat cut and prepared daily. A raw bar is also available. Comfortable booths have tile tabletops and clear ocean views. There's seashell-pattern carpeting, ocean scenes on the walls, and huge fish-market signs and lobster artwork hanging from a sloped wood-beam ceiling. ✉ *Boardwalk at the Inlet,* ☎ *410/289–5121. AE, D, MC, V.*

$$–$$$ ✕ **The Hobbit.** Dedicated to Bilbo Baggins and other literary creations of J. R. R. Tolkien, this bayside dining room has murals depicting scenes from the classic novel, and wood table lamps are carved in the shapes of individual Hobbits. The deck is popular with summer diners. Veal with pistachios is sautéed in a sauce of Madeira, veal stock, prosciutto, mushrooms, shallots, and heavy cream. Hobbit Catch is the fish of the day (typically salmon, swordfish, or tuna). Light fare is served in the adjoining bar as well as in the café. A gift shop sells Hobbit-related T-shirts and gifts. ✉ *101 81st St.,* ☎ *410/524–8100,* WEB *www.hobbitgifts.com. AE, D, MC, V.*

$$–$$$ ✕ **Phillips Crab House & Seafood Buffet.** Feast on crab cakes, crab imperial, or stuffed and fried shrimp at the original 1956 home of a restaurant that has since become a chain. The dark-paneled dining room has decorative stone floors, hanging Tiffany-style lamps, stained-glass

windows, and funky wall art. Its wildly popular buffet is served in an upstairs dining room. ✉ *21st St. and Philadelphia Ave.,* ☎ *410/289–6821 or 800/549–2722,* WEB *www.phillipsoc.com. AE, D, MC, V.*

Lodging

During the high-season months of summer, Ocean City has about 10,000 hotel rooms to choose from. A narrow island means that no lodging is far from either the ocean or the bay. Rates vary dramatically through the year, with the lowest typically between mid-November and mid-March, and the highest during the months of July and August. A room with an ocean view will almost always come with a premium rate.

$$$$ ★ **The Edge.** Opened in 2002, the Edge's accommodations here exude quality and style. In this boutique hotel, each of the rooms is uniquely furnished to evoke such locales as Bali or the Caribbean, the French Riviera or southern Italy, and even the *Orient Express.* From queen- and king-size feather beds to gas-fed fireplaces, no amenity is amiss. Windows that take up the entire west-facing room walls allow for panoramic views at sunset. ✉ *56th St. at the Bay, 21842,* ☎ *410/524–5400 or 888/371–5400,* FAX *410/524–3928,* WEB *www.fagers.com. 10 rooms, 2 suites. In-room hot tubs, minibars, refrigerators. AE, D, DC, MC, V.*

$$$–$$$$ ★ **Lighthouse Club Hotel.** This elegant all-suite hotel is a Chesapeake Bay "screwpile" lighthouse look-alike of uncommonly quiet luxury, just blocks from the busy Coastal Highway. Its airy, contemporary suites have high ceilings and views of sand dunes that slope to the Assawoman Bay. Rooms have white-cushioned rattan furniture and marble bathrooms with two-person hot tubs and the convenience of coffeemakers and plush terry robes. Sliding glass doors lead to private decks with steamer chairs. ✉ *56th St. at the Bay, 21842,* ☎ *410/524–5400 or 888/371–5400,* WEB *www.fagers.com. 23 suites. Minibars, refrigerators, hot tubs. AE, D, DC, MC, V.*

$$–$$$$ **Dunes Manor Hotel.** The Victorian theme of the lobby, with immense crystal chandeliers and a carved ceiling, sets the tone for this hotel, built in 1987 to replicate a 19th-century seashore resort. Step beyond the lobby and settle into a green rocking chair overlooking the ocean. All rooms are oceanfront and have two double beds, pickled-pine furniture, and private balconies; suites include a full kitchen. Tea and homemade cookies are served each afternoon. The hotel is a block beyond the north end of the Boardwalk. ✉ *28th St. at the Boardwalk, 21842,* ☎ *410/289–1100 or 800/523–2888,* FAX *410/289–4905,* WEB *www.dunesmanor.com. 160 rooms, 10 suites. Restaurant, microwaves, refrigerators, indoor-outdoor pool, gym, hot tub, bar, free parking. AE, D, DC, MC, V.*

$$ **Atlantic Hotel.** Family owned and operated, the three-story, H-shape frame hotel—Ocean City's oldest—is a replacement of the original Victorian hotel that burned in 1922. Rooms are plainly furnished and decorated just as they were originally, but now with modern comforts, such as air-conditioning. This is oceanside vacationing as it was in a calmer era. ✉ *Boardwalk and Wicomico St., 21843,* ☎ *800/328–5268 or 410/289–9111,* FAX *410/289–2221,* WEB *www.atlantichotelocmd.com. 90 rooms. Cable TV. MC, V. Closed Oct.–Apr.*

$–$$ **The Lankford Hotel & Apartments.** Opened in 1924, the Lankford is still owned by the family of the original owners. Many combinations of rooms in the hotel and the adjacent lodge are available for small groups of friends and families. Bicycle storage and Ocean City Golf Course privileges are included in the rate. Lazing in a rickety rocking chair on the front porch off the small (unair-conditioned) lobby, cooled by overhead fans, is a true throwback to quieter times. (All guest rooms are air-conditioned.) ✉ *8th St. at the Boardwalk, 21842,* ☎ *410/289–4041 or 800/282–9709,* FAX *410/289–4809,* WEB *www.ocean-city.com.*

23 rooms, 28 suites and apartments. Laundry facilities, free parking. No credit cards. Closed Columbus Day weekend through Apr.

Nightlife and the Arts

In summer, Ocean City provides enough entertainment for everyone, ranging from refined to rowdy. Most of Ocean City's many bars and clubs are closed in midwinter, but a popular few remain open a few days a week.

CONCERTS

Northside Park Recreation Center (✉ 125th St. at the Bay, ☎ 410/250–0125) is frequently the site of free outdoor concerts. The family-style free summer concert series, **Sundaes in the Park,** is held at 6 PM every Sunday from late June through late August.

BARS

Open since 1976, the large sports saloon known as the **Greene Turtle** (✉ Coastal Hwy. at 116th St., ☎ 410/723–2120) has been hugely popular.

The **Ocean Club** (✉ Oceanfront at 49th St., ☎ 410/524–7500) is a dancing, dining, imbibing, and people-watching complex made up of Lenny's Front Porch, a Tiki bar, and the rooftop Crow's Nest. Families and those over 30 are unlikely to feel out of place here.

The waterside **Seacrets Bar and Grill** (✉ 49th St. at the Bay, ☎ 410/524–4900) presents live entertainment nightly and draws a crowd ranging from those in their early 20s to baby boomers.

DANCE CLUBS

One of the most versatile complexes (✉ Coastal Hwy. at 17th St., ☎ 410/289–6331) for older teens and those in their twenties includes the **Big Kahuna,** a DJ-driven "party place"; the **Paddock,** also DJ-driven and with a bit more volume and flash; and **Rush,** more subdued and upscale.

During lunchtime, the huge **Bonfire Restaurant & Nightclub** (✉ 71st St. and Ocean Hwy., ☎ 410/524–7171) serves an all-you-can-eat buffet and at dinnertime, an à la carte menu. Families fill the tables at lunch, but in the evening Bonfire caters more to thirties-and-over diners enjoying the live Top 40 music played by local groups five days a week. It's closed Monday–Thursday, mid-October–mid-March.

Outdoor Activities and Sports

Primarily a summertime holiday resort destination, myriad outdoor activities await you in Ocean City and its environs—once you feel like getting up off your beach towel. The Atlantic Ocean and Assawoman Bay are the biggest playgrounds, but besides fishing of many kinds, power boating and sailing, you can also bike and play tennis, volleyball, and (especially) golf.

BICYCLING

A portion of the Coastal Highway has been designated for bus and bicycle traffic. Bicycle riding is allowed on the Ocean City Boardwalk from 5 AM to 10 AM in summer and 5 AM to 4 PM the rest of the year. The bike route from Ocean City to Assateague Island (U.S. 50 to Rte. 611) is a 9-mi trek, and Assateague itself is crisscrossed by a number of clearly marked, paved trails.

Bike rentals are available throughout Ocean City, "every three blocks" according to some. One of the most venerable bike rental, sales, and service enterprises is the highly respected **Mike's Bikes** (✉ N. Division St. and Baltimore Ave., ☎ 410/289–5404; ✉ N. 1st St. at the Boardwalk, ☎ 410/289–4637). Rates range from $4 for the first hour,

$2 for every hour thereafter for regular adult bikes up to $20 an hour for a six-passenger-and-two-toddler "surrey."

BOATING

Assawoman Bay, between the Ocean City barrier island and the mainland, is where you can go deep-sea fishing, sailing, jet skiing, and paragliding. **Sailing, Etc.** (✉ 5305 Coastal Hwy., ☎ 410/723–1144) rents sailboats, catamarans, kayaks, and Windsurfers and teaches sailing and windsurfing.

FISHING

No fishing licenses are required in Ocean City. Public fishing piers on the Assawoman Bay and Isle of Wight Bay are at (south to north) 3rd, 9th, 40th, and 125th streets and at the inlet in Ocean City. Other fishing and crabbing areas include the U.S. 50 bridge, Oceanic Pier, Ocean City Pier at Wicomico Street and the Boardwalk, and Shantytown Village.

GOLF

Now rivaling premier golfing destinations around the United States, Ocean City is within easy driving distance of no fewer than 17 golf courses. For a complete listing of courses and details, contact the Worcester County Tourism office.

VOLLEYBALL

The **Eastern Volleyball Association** (☎ 410/250–2577) coordinates a series of professional and pro/am tournaments at several locations on the beach throughout the summer.

Shopping

Ocean City's 3-mi-long boardwalk is lined with retail outlets for food, gifts, and souvenirs, as well as several specialty stores. Side streets are rife with still more. Shopping malls, including innumerable factory outlets, are along the Coastal Highway, which runs the length of the island.

The Kite Loft (✉ 5th St. at the Boardwalk, ☎ 410/289–6852; ✉ 45th St. Village, ☎ 410/524–0800; ✉ Coastal Hwy. at 131st St., ☎ 410/250–4970) has a dazzling line of kites as well as banners, flags, and wind socks, hammocks and sky chairs, whirligigs and wind chimes.

The Lankford Shops (✉ 8th St. at the Boardwalk, ☎ 410/289–8232), operated by the Lankford Hotel, sell bikinis, handicrafts, hobby supplies—such as miniature furniture for dollhouses—and ocean-side souvenirs.

Shantytown Village (✉ Rte. 50 at Shantytown Rd., West Ocean City) is a replica "storybook" village of some 20 shops for holiday gifts and souvenirs, candy, collectibles, flowers, and wine.

Assateague Island National Seashore

20 *18 mi south of Ocean City.*

The Assateague Island National Seashore occupies the northern two-thirds of the 37-mi-long barrier island: a small portion of the seashore is operated as Assateague State Park. ("Assateague" means "brown or yellow river" or "river beyond.") The southern third of the island is the Chincoteague National Wildlife Refuge, in Virginia. Although most famous for the small, shaggy, sturdy wild horses (adamantly called "ponies" by the public) that roam freely along the beaches and roads, the National Seashore is also worth getting to know for its wildland, wildlife, and opportunities for outdoor recreation. In summer its mild surf is where you'll find shorebirds tracing the lapping waves back down the beach. Behind the dunes, the island's forests and bayside marshes invite exploration.

Swimming, biking, hiking, surf fishing, picnicking, and camping are all available on the island. The visitor center at the entrance to the park has aquariums and hands-on exhibits about the seashore's birds and ocean creatures as well as the famous ponies. ✉ *7206 National Seashore La. (Rte. 611),* ☎ *410/641–1441,* WEB *www.assateagueisland.com.* *7-day pass $5 per vehicle; $2 per person for bicycles and pedestrians.* ⏲ *Visitor center daily 9–5, park daily 24 hrs.*

Crisfield

21 *33 mi southwest of Salisbury (via U.S. 13 to Rte. 413).*

In William W. Warner's study of the Chesapeake Bay, *Beautiful Swimmers,* Crisfield was described as a "town built upon oyster shells, millions of tons of it. A town created by and for the blue crab, Cradle of the Chesapeake seafood industries, where everything was tried first." The number of seafood processing plants here—where workers still pick crabs and shuck oysters as they have for more than a century, by hand—has dwindled to just three from more than 150, but you can still marvel at the craft and listen to workers singing hymns as they work.

Lodging

$ **Bea's B&B.** Sunshine streaming through the stained-glass windows in this 1909 home personifies Bea's cheerful hospitality. There's a screened porch for summer and fireplaces that are soothing in summer. A steam room adds a touch of modernity. ✉ *10 S. Somerset Ave., 21817,* ☎ *410/968–0423,* WEB *www.beasbandb.com. 2 rooms. Cable TV; no room phones, no kids under 10, no smoking. No credit cards. BP.*

Outdoor Activities and Sports

Eco-Tours on the *Learn-It* (✉ Crisfield City Dock, 1021 W. Main St., ☎ 410/968–9870) depart daily at 10 and 1:30 from the Captain's Galley restaurant. Learn about the wildfowl and water creatures of the Chesapeake Bay, find out why bay grasses are important, explore the effects of shoreline erosion, and visit an experienced waterman—as Bay fishermen are known—at work, all while aboard the comfortable 40-ft bay workboat, which has been certified by the U.S. Coast Guard.

Shopping

The Ice Cream Gallery (✉ 5 Goodsell Alley, ☎ 410/968–0809) is a sweets emporium that doubles as a crafts outlet for local artisans. From here there's a spectacular view out over the Bay. **Tropical Chesapeake** (✉ 712 Broadway, ☎ 410/968–3622) prepares oven-baked deli sandwiches and sells gifts and clothing.

Smith Island

22 *10 mi west of Crisfield by boat.*

For more than three centuries, Smith Islanders have made their living coaxing creatures from the Chesapeake Bay. Today, the tiny island's three villages, made up of simple homes, churches, and a few stores, remain reachable only by boat and fiercely independent. Listen for the distinct accents of the residents here, which echo that of their 17th-century English ancestors. A midday visit by passenger ferry allows ample time for a stroll around the island and a leisurely meal overlooking watermen's shanties and workboats. Stop by **Ruke's,** a venerable general store that serves excellent fresh seafood.

Air-conditioned **Smith Island Cruises** leave Crisfield's Somers Cove Marina for the 60-minute trip to Smith Island at 12:30 PM daily from Memorial Day to mid-October. ✉ *Somers Cove Marina, Crisfield,* ☎ *410/425–2771,* WEB *www.smithislandcruises.com.* 🎫 *$20.*

Another way to get to Smith Island is via the mail boat, ***Island Belle*** (☎ 410/968–1118) for $20 round-trip.

Two freight boats, ***Captain Jason I*** and ***Captain Jason II*** (☎ 410/425–4471), also take passengers to Smith Island for $20 round-trip. All three boats depart daily at 12:30 PM and return to Crisfield at 5:15 PM, year-round, weather permitting. You can ride back to Smith Island later in the evening; both captains live on the island.

The **Smith Island Center** traces the island's history through such exhibits as an equipped workboat, photos, a time line, and a 20-minute video narrated by islanders. ✉ *Just off town dock, Ewell,* ☎ *410/425–3351.* 🎫 *$2.* ⏲ *Apr.–Oct., daily noon–4 and by appointment.*

The first privately owned facility of its kind on the island, tiny **Smith Island Marina** hugs the water's edge adjacent to the Ewell Tide Inn and B&B. ☎ *410/425–2141 or 888/699–2141.*

Lodging

An overnight on Smith Island gives new meaning to the term "getaway." Your neighbors include more egrets, heron, osprey, and pelicans than people.

$$ **Inn of Silent Music.** Set in a town that's separated by water from the other two villages on Smith Island, this remote English cottage–style inn takes its soothing name from a phrase in a poem by St. John of the Cross, a Carmelite monk. Tylerton has no restaurants, but the innkeepers will cook a fresh seafood dinner for guests at an extra charge. ✉ *Tylerton 21866,* ☎ *410/425–3541,* WEB *www.innofsilentmusic.com. 3 rooms. Dining room, dock, bicycles; no room phones, no room TVs, no kids under 6, no smoking. No credit cards. Closed mid-Nov.–early Mar. BP.*

$–$$ **Ewell Tide Inn and B&B.** On the northern tip of Smith Island, down-home hospitality is heartily extended by a licensed ferry- and charter-boat captain and his wife. Dinner is available, but must be ordered in advance. Open year-round, the inn welcomes children, as well as pets, on weekdays. This couple also operates Ewell's Driftwood General Store as well as the adjacent marina, a separate operation. ✉ *Ewell 21824,* ☎ *410/425–2141 or 888/699–2141,* WEB *www.smithisland.net. 4 rooms without bath. Dining room, in-room data ports, cable TV, dock, bicycles, pub, meeting rooms, some pets allowed; no room phones, no smoking. AE, MC, V. BP.*

VIRGINIA'S EASTERN SHORE

A narrow 70-mi-long peninsula between the Chesapeake Bay and the Atlantic Ocean, Virginia's Eastern Shore has one main artery bisecting its full length. U.S. 13's occasional gentle curves interrupt an otherwise straight, flat route through unremarkable landscape. To either side, however, tiny hamlets are scattered among farms and protected wildlife habitats, and along the shore watermen still struggle for their living.

At its southernmost tip, the extraordinary Chesapeake Bay Bridge-Tunnel sweeps 17½ miles across the Chesapeake Bay to connect with the Virginia Tidewater towns of Hampton Roads, Norfolk, and Virginia Beach.

Numbers in the margin correspond to points of interest on the Virginia's Eastern Shore map.

Virginia's Eastern Shore

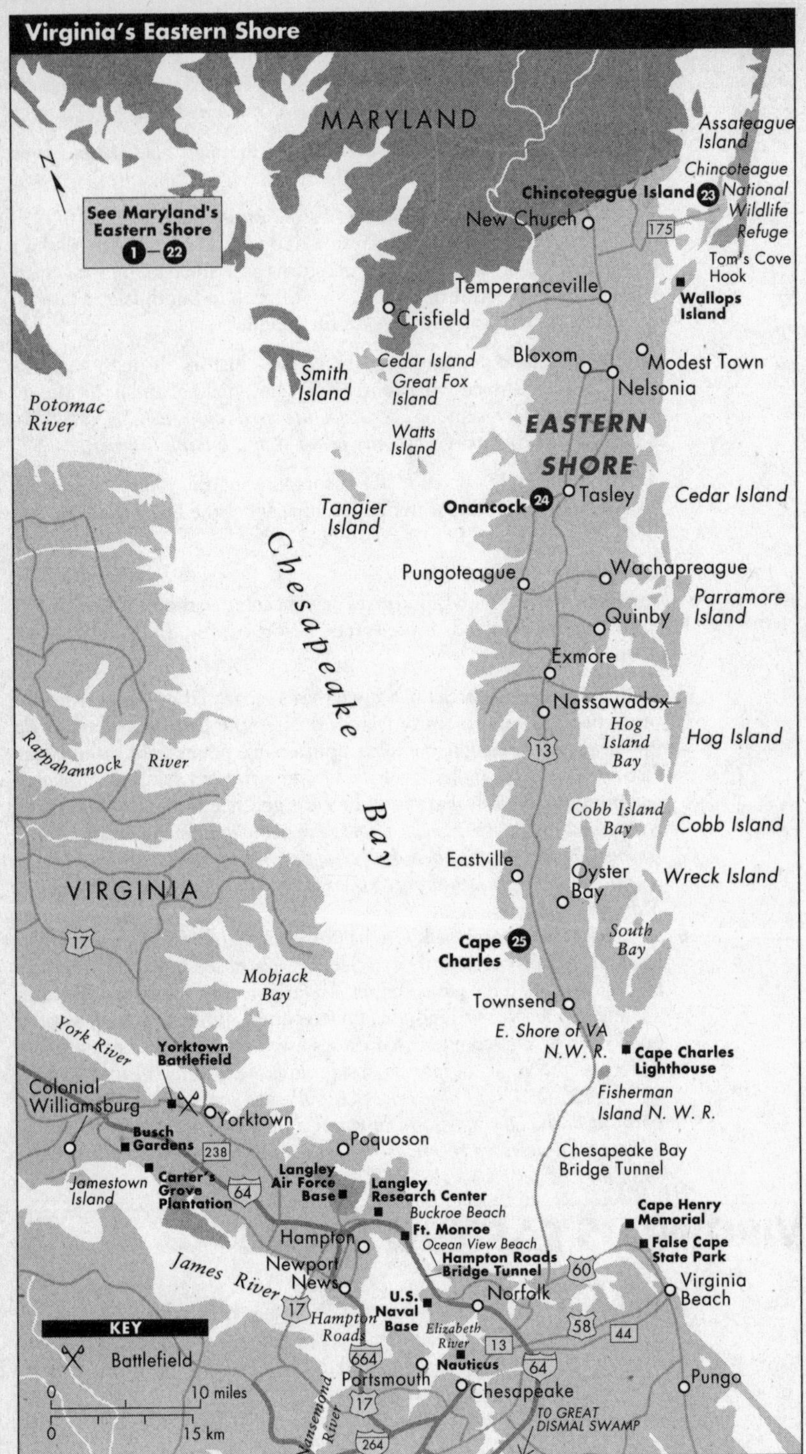

Chincoteague Island

23 *27 mi southeast of Snow Hill, MD (via U.S. 13 to Rte. 175), 43 mi southeast of Salisbury, MD (via U.S. 13 to Rte. 175).*

Just south of the Maryland-Virginia line, the Virginia Eastern Shore's only island resort town (Chincoteague, meaning "large stream or inlet," is pronounced "**shin**-coh-teeg") exudes a pleasant aura of seclusion, despite the renown it has gained since the publication of the 1947 children's book *Misty of Chincoteague,* the story of one of the wild ponies that are auctioned off every summer. Chincoteague Island's inns, restaurants, and shops are eminently reachable by walking; relatively uncrowded beaches stretch out nearby.

Islanders and visitors alike savor one of the shore's specialties during October's **Chincoteague Oyster Festival,** which can sell out months in advance. The Chincoteague Chamber of Commerce (✉ 6733 Maddox Blvd., ☎ 757/787–2460, WEB www.chincoteaguechamber.com) sells tickets.

The **Oyster and Maritime Museum** chronicles the local oyster trade with displays of mostly homemade tools; elaborate, hand-carved decoys; marine specimens; a diorama; and audio recordings based on museum records. *✉ 7125 Maddox Blvd., ☎ 757/336–6117. $3. ⏲ June–Sept., daily 10–5; Mar.–May, Sat. 10–5, Sun. noon–4.*

Most of Virginia's **Chincoteague National Wildlife Refuge** occupies the southern third of Assateague Island, directly off of Chincoteague Island. (The northern two-thirds, part of Maryland, is taken up by the Assateague Island National Seashore.) Created in 1943 as a resting and breeding area for the imperiled greater snow goose as well as other birds, this refuge's location makes it a prime "flyover" habitat. It also protects native and migratory nonavian wildlife, including the small Sika deer that inhabit its interior pine forests. A 3.2-mi self-guided wildlife loop is a great introduction to the refuge. Bike or walk it; it is open to vehicles only between 3 PM and dusk. The Chincoteague ponies (*see* "The Ponies of Assateague") occupy a section of the refuge isolated from the public, but they may still be viewed readily from a number of spots. *✉ Visitor Center and entrance: Maddox Blvd. at Beach Rd., ☎ 757/336–6122, WEB www.assateagueisland.com. $5 per car (valid for 7 days). ⏲ May–Sept., daily 5 AM–10 PM; Oct. and Apr., daily 6 AM–8 PM; Nov.–Mar., daily 6–6.*

Dining and Lodging

$–$$ ✕ **Etta's Channel Side Restaurant.** On the eastern side of the island, along the Assateague Channel, this meticulously maintained family-friendly restaurant has a vista as soothing as its food. Its dishes include pastas and popular meat dishes as well as typical fish and shellfish creations. Its signature dish is flounder stuffed with crab imperial. *✉ 7452 East Side Dr., ☎ 757/336–5644. D, MC, V. Closed Jan.–Feb. No lunch Mon.–Thurs.*

$–$$ ★ ✕ **Shucking House Cafe.** This relaxed eatery is just the place to unwind after a day on the water. Featuring oyster, crab, and fish sandwiches along with fish-and-chips, this café is a pleasant change from fancy restaurants or fast-food franchises. Be sure to try the rich New England or Manhattan clam chowders, both prepared with local mollusks. *✉ Landmark Pl., ☎ 757/336–5145. MC, V.*

$–$$$ **Island Motor Inn Resort.** There are views of the ocean and bay from the private balcony off every room in this three-story motel beside the Intercoastal Waterway. Stroll the inn's private 600-ft boardwalk or relax in the quiet garden area beside the koi pond. One of the two gyms is set aside for weights, with a personal trainer on call. In addition to the pools, there's a hot tub on the third floor. For when you must be inside, every room has a 27-inch cable TV. ✉ *4391 N. Main St., 23336,* ☎ *757/336–3141,* FAX *757/336–1483,* WEB *www.islandmotorinn.com. 60 rooms. Café, room service, in-room data ports, refrigerators, cable TV, 2 pools (1 indoor), 2 gyms, hot tub, laundry facilities, meeting rooms. AE, D, DC, MC, V.*

$$–$$$ ★ **Channel Bass Inn.** This three-story, beige clapboard house just off Chincoteague Bay was built in the 1870s, then expanded and converted to an inn 50 years later. Its luxurious rooms all have comfortable sitting areas. In addition to its full breakfast, the inn serves afternoon tea daily in the public tearoom. Delicacies such as *apfel kuchen* (German apple cake), firm scones, and an extraordinary multilayer trifle, all homemade, are served on Wedgewood china. ✉ *6228 Church St., 23336,* ☎ *757/336–6148 or 800/249–0818,* WEB *www.channelbass-inn.com. 8 rooms, 1 suite. Shop, some pets allowed; no room phones, no room TVs, no kids under 6, no smoking. AE, D, MC, V. BP.*

$–$$$ **The Inn at Poplar Corner and the Watson House.** These two stately structures across the street from each other both look Victorian. But whereas the Watson House is from the 1890s, the Inn at Poplar Corner was built a century later. Both contain impressive Victorian furniture. All four of the Poplar Corner rooms have hot tubs and private showers. Rates include breakfast, served at the Poplar Corner's antique dining table or on the inviting side porch. For visits to the National Wildlife Refuge, you can borrow beach chairs and binoculars. ✉ *4240 Main St. (Box 905), 23336,* ☎ *757/336–1564 or 800/336–6787,* FAX *757/336–5776,* WEB *www.watsonhouse.com. 10 rooms. Bicycles; no room phones, no room TVs, no kids under 10, no smoking. MC, V. Closed Dec.–Mar. BP.*

$–$$$ **Miss Molly's.** Operated by the same innkeepers as the Channel Bass Inn, this unassuming 1886 Victorian inn claims fame as the temporary home of author Marguerite Henry, who wrote *Misty of Chincoteague*. Here, in 1946, she spent two of her six weeks in Chincoteague preparing the background for her renowned children's novel. Miss Molly, the daughter of the home's builder, spent most of her life here. Genuine high tea is served every afternoon at the Channel Bass. ✉ *4141 Main St., 23336,* ☎ *757/336–6686 or 800/221–5620,* FAX *757/336–0600,* WEB *www.missmollys-inn.com. 7 rooms. No room phones, no room TVs, no kids under 6, no smoking. AE, D, MC, V. Closed Jan.–Feb.*

Outdoor Activities and Sports

Nearby beaches open to the public, managed by the National Park Service, are at the eastern end of Beach Road (☎ 757/336–6577).

You can rent boats for fishing or for a spin around the bay from **Captain Bob's** (✉ 2477 S. Main St., ☎ 757/336–6654) or **R&R Boats** (✉ 4183 Main St., ☎ 757/336–5465).

Shopping

Chincoteague Country Corner (✉ 4044 Main St., ☎ 757/336–5771) carries gifts, crafts, and model boats, both assembled and in kits.

Listen for the sounds of fine jazz and inhale the aroma of good coffee that wafts from the windows of the **mainStreet shop & coffeehouse** (✉ 4288 Main St., ☎ 757/336–6782, WEB www.mainstreet-shop.com). This corner venue is a lively mix of color and art and people. The enclosed front porch of this little house has tiny tables for java and munchies. Inside are clothes, shoes, graphics, mirrors, lighting, and more.

The wildlife sculpture by renowned artisan Donald White and the jewelry by Joan's Jems are reason enough to visit **White's Copperworks** (✉ 6373 Maddox Blvd., ☎ 757/336–1588, WEB www.whitescopperworks.

com). Also available are hand-carved wood flowers, wind chimes, matted photos, prints, and puzzles.

OFF THE BEATEN PATH **WALLOPS ISLAND –** NASA's Wallops Flight Facility Visitors Center fires the imagination with full-scale rockets, films on space and aeronautics, and displays on NASA projects. Although this was the site of early rocket launchings and NASA occasionally sends up satellites here, the facility now focuses primarily on atmospheric research. ✉ *Rte. 175, 20 mi southwest of Chincoteague,* ☎ *757/824–2298 or 757/824–1344,* WEB *www.wff.nasa.gov.* 🎫 *Free.* ⏲ *July–Aug., daily 10–4; Sept.–June, Thurs.–Mon. 10–4.*

Onancock

24 *30 mi southwest of Chincoteague (via Rte. 175 to U.S. 13).*

Four miles from the Chesapeake Bay at the mouth of Onancock Creek, Onancock, which means "foggy place," was once the home of a handful of Algonquin families. It was established as a port in 1690 and later emerged as an important ferry link with the burgeoning waterside cities of Maryland and Virginia. Today, this quiet community of 1,600, the second-largest town on Virginia's Eastern Shore, is worth a short visit for a flavor of its past as a transfer point between water and land.

Dining and Lodging

$$ ✕ **Hopkins & Bros. General Store & Eastern Shore Steamboat Co. Restaurant.** Beside the wharf, inside a general store (circa 1842) on the National Register of Historic Places, you can imagine yourself waiting for a steamer to Baltimore. At the charming eatery adjacent to the store, there's fresh baked grouper with locally picked crabmeat stuffing as well as prime meats that are hand cut to order. ✉ *2 Market St.,* ☎ *757/787–3100,* WEB *www.onancock.net. MC, V. Closed Sun. No lunch.*

$–$$ ✕ **Backfins.** This family-run restaurant has prime rib and crab cakes and everything in between, but don't overlook the Barrier Island Soup Collection, a popular choice. ✉ *47 Market St.,* ☎ *757/787–2906,* WEB *www.backfins.com. MC, V.*

$ ★ 🏨 **The Spinning Wheel Bed and Breakfast.** Spinning wheels from the innkeepers' collection complement other local antiques in this restored 1890s Victorian house. Every room has a queen-size bed—and its own wheel. A huge sheepdog, Nelly, waits to welcome you. A stay here is like a visit to Grandmother's house. ✉ *31 North St., 23417,* ☎ *757/787–7311 or 888/787–0337,* FAX *757/787–8555,* WEB *www.1890spinningwheel.com. 5 rooms. Bicycles; no room phones, no kids under 10, no smoking. D, MC, V. Closed mid-Oct.–mid-Apr. BP.*

$–$$ 🏨 **76 Market Street.** Near the ferry to Tangier Island, this circa-1840s Victorian house is pleasantly simple with three warmly welcoming rooms—Blue, Rose, and Yellow—all with queen-size beds and private baths. There's cable TV with a VCR in the common room. Guests regularly rave about the innkeeper's breakfasts. ✉ *76 Market St., 23417,* ☎ *757/787–7600 or 888/751–7600,* FAX *757/787–2744,* WEB *www.76marketst.com. 3 rooms. Croquet, volleyball; no room phones, no TV, no kids under 6, no smoking. MC, V. BP.*

Tangier Island

Crab traps stacked 10 ft high, watermen's shanties on the water, and a landscape virtually devoid of excessive commercialization await those who come to this Virginia fishing community in the Chesapeake Bay. You can't bring a car, but you can join a guided tour near the boat dock, rent a golf cart to roam the few narrow roads, or simply soak in the timelessness on foot. Stop by the Waterfront Sandwich Shop or head to the Islander Seafood Restaurant. As on Maryland's Smith Island, you'll hear the distinct accents that reveal the English origins of the residents' 17th-century ancestors. Note that Tangier Island is "dry"; you may bring your own alcohol for personal use, but you must use discretion.

Narrated trips from Onancock to the island are available on **Tangier-Onancock Cruises** (☎ 757/891–2240) at 10 AM daily Memorial Day–October 15. The return trip leaves Tangier at 2 PM, allowing ample time to explore.

Lodging

$ **Shirley's Bay View Inn.** You may stay in one of two guest rooms in one of the oldest houses on the island and have breakfast on 100-year-old china, hosted by members of the home's original family, or you may stay in one of the adjacent cottages. Either way, an overnight on Tangier Island is an uncommon experience. A visit to Shirley's should include a visit to her ice cream parlor, where music from the 1950s plays. ✉ *16408 West Ridge Rd., 23440,* ☎ *757/891–2396,* WEB *www.tangierisland.net. 2 rooms and 7 cottages. Cable TV, refrigerators, beach; no room phones; no smoking. No credit cards.*

Cape Charles

25 *31 mi south of Onancock (via U.S. 13).*

Cape Charles, established in the early 1880s as a railroad-ferry junction, quieted down considerably after its heyday, but in the past few years its very isolation has begun to attract people from farther and farther away. The town holds one of the largest concentrations of late-Victorian and turn-of-the-20th-century buildings in the region. Clean, uncrowded public beaches beckon, as do a marina, renowned golf course, and the Eastern Shore of Virginia National Wildlife Refuge.

Lodging

$$–$$$ **Wilson-Lee House.** A taste of Cape Charles's gilded age lives on in this turn-of-the-20th-century home, built for a businessman. The six rooms are whimsically decorated with a mélange of periods and styles, with a claw-foot tub in one bathroom, a hot tub in another. Breakfast here is an epicurean event. In good weather, it's served on the screened wraparound porch. Guests may play tennis at a nearby court at no charge; golfing packages for play at the Bay Creek Golf Club are also available. ✉ *403 Tazewell Ave., 23310,* ☎ *757/331–1954,* WEB *www.wilsonleehouse.com. 6 rooms. Golf privileges, boating, fishing, bicycles; no room phones, no room TVs, no kids under 12, no smoking. MC, V.*

$$ **Pickett's Harbor.** Clinging to the southernmost tip of the peninsula, this land parcel is part of a 17th-century grant to the owner's family. The current clapboard B&B was built in 1976 according to a Colonial-era design, with floors, doors, and cupboards from several 200-year-old James River farms reinstalled here. All guest rooms overlook small sand dunes and the Chesapeake; the backyard is actually 27 acres of private beach. Runners and bikers are likely to find the area's long country lanes and untrafficked paved roads a delight. ✉ *Rte. 600, Box 96, Cape Charles 23443,* ☎ *757/331–2212,* WEB *www.pickettsharbor.com. 6 rooms, 4 with bath. Beach, bicycles, some pets allowed; no room phones, no room TVs, no smoking. No credit cards. BP.*

Outdoor Activities and Sports

In 2002, before it had been open even a year, remote **Bay Creek Golf Club** (✉ 1 Clubhouse Way, ☎ 757/331–9000, WEB www.baycreekgolfclub.

com) was lauded by *Golf Magazine* as one of the top 10 new public courses in the United States. The "front 9" of the 18-hole Arnold Palmer course play right along the edge of the Chesapeake Bay. It's a view rivaled by few other courses. Fees (including a cart) are $55 on weekdays and $65 on weekends.

Eastern Shore of Virginia and Fisherman Island National Wildlife Refuges

13 mi south of Cape Charles.

At the southernmost tip of the Delmarva Peninsula, these unique refuges—including nearby Skimore Island and with Fisherman Island National Wildlife Refuge—were established in 1984. Their maritime forest, myrtle and bayberry thickets, grasslands, and croplands, as well as ponds are used by such species as bald eagles and peregrine falcons. Each fall, between late August and early November, migrating birds "stage," or gather in large groups, on refuge lands until favorable winds and weather conditions allow for easy crossing of the Chesapeake Bay. ✉ *Southern extremity of Rte. 13,* ☎ *757/331–2760,* WEB *easternshore.fws.gov.* 🎫 *Free.*

THE EASTERN SHORE A TO Z

To research prices, get advice from other travelers, and book travel arrangements, visit www.fodors.com.

AIRPORTS

The Salisbury–Ocean City–Wicomico Regional Airport is the only airport on Maryland's or Virginia's Eastern Shore with scheduled air traffic.

➤ AIRPORT INFORMATION: **Salisbury–Ocean City–Wicomico Regional Airport** (SBY; ✉ 5485 Airport Terminal Rd., Unit A, Salisbury, MD, ☎ 410/548–4827).

BIKE TRAVEL

Flat and friendly, the Eastern Shore is a great region to go biking. Call Maryland's Department of Transportation for a state bicycle map and for more information.

Bicycles are available for rent at Stevensville's Happy Trails Bike Repair, which is open from 10 to 6 Monday through Saturday. Happy Trails will pick up and drop off bikes for boaters in local marinas and guests at local hotels and B&Bs. On Sunday at 9 AM, Happy Trails also hosts escorted group rides of 15 to 30 miles, when the weather allows.

Chestertown's Bike Work Bicycle Shop rents bikes for adults and children; helmets are included in the rate. A group, open to those just visiting, rides up to 60 miles every Sunday at 8 AM, weather permitting. The shop is open Tuesday through Friday 9–5, Saturday 9–3, and Sunday and Monday by appointment.

➤ CONTACTS: **Bike Work Bicycle Shop** (✉ 208 S. Cross St., Chestertown, ☎ 410/778–6940, WEB www.bikeworkbicycleshop.com). **Happy Trails Bike Repair** ((✉ 111 Cockey La., ☎ 410/643–0670). **Maryland Dept. of Transportation** (☎ 800/252–8776). **Oxford Mews** (✉ 105 Morris St., Oxford, ☎ 410/820–8222).

BUS TRAVEL

Carolina Trailways makes several round-trip runs daily between Baltimore or Washington and Easton, Cambridge, Salisbury, and Ocean City.

Greyhound Lines leaves regularly from Norfolk and Virginia Beach for destinations on the Eastern Shore.

When you're in Ocean City, you can avoid the aggravation of driving in slow-moving traffic by taking **The Bus,** which travels 10-mi-long Coastal Highway 24 hours a day, in its own lane, with service about every 10 minutes. Bus-stop signs are posted every other block, and there are shelters at most locations. A $2 ticket is good for 24 hours.

A park and ride facility on the mainland—on Route 50 just west of Ocean City—has free parking for some 700 vehicles. It's on The Bus's route.

➤ BUS DEPOTS: **Cambridge** (✉ 501 Maryland Ave., ☎ 410/228–4626). **Easton** (✉ FastStop Convenience Store, U.S. 50, 2 mi north of town, opposite airport, ☎ 410/822–3333). **Ocean City** (✉ 2nd St. and Coastal Hwy. at the U.S. 50 bridge, ☎ 410/289–9307). **Salisbury** (✉ 350 Cypress St., ☎ 410/749–4121).

➤ BUS LINES: **The Bus** (☎ 410/723–1607). **Carolina Trailways** (☎ 800/231–2222). **Greyhound Lines** (☎ 800/231–2222).

CAR RENTALS

Avis and Hertz have car rental facilities at the Salisbury–Ocean City–Wicomico Regional Airport.

CAR TRAVEL

A car is indispensable for touring the region. To reach the Eastern Shore from Baltimore or Washington, D.C., travel east on U.S. 50/301 and cross the 4½-mi Chesapeake Bay bridge (toll collected eastbound only, $2.50) northeast of Annapolis.

The extraordinary 17½-mi Chesapeake Bay Bridge-Tunnel, officially the Lucias J. Kellam Jr. Bridge-Tunnel, is the only connection between Virginia's Eastern Shore and Norfolk, Virginia Beach, and other Tidewater-area towns. There's a toll of $10 in either direction.

The bridge and tunnel complex comprises 12 mi of trestled roadway, two mile-long tunnels, two bridges, almost 2 mi of causeway, and four man-made islands, on one of which there is a restaurant and on another a fishing pier. U.S. 13 is the main route up the spine of the peninsula into Maryland.

TRAFFIC

In summer, Friday afternoon eastbound (beach-bound) traffic can be very heavy; conversely, Sunday and sometimes Saturday afternoon westbound traffic (from the beaches toward Baltimore and Washington, D.C.) can be equally congested.

➤ CONTACTS: **Chesapeake Bay Bridge-Tunnel** (☎ 757/331–2960, WEB www.cbbt.com).

DISABILITIES AND ACCESSIBILITY

The B&Bs and small inns that represent the majority of the accommodations throughout Maryland's and Virginia's Eastern Shore may not always be handicapped accessible.

Furthermore, because some of the region's towns are 200–300 years old, sidewalks are often brick, stone stairs are well worn, and roads are sometimes still cobbled.

EMERGENCIES

➤ CONTACT: **Ambulance, Fire, Police** (☎ 911).

➤ HOSPITALS: **Atlantic General Hospital** (✉ 9733 Healthway Dr., Berlin, MD, ☎ 410/641–1100). **Dorchester General Hospital** (✉ 300 Byrn St., Cambridge, MD, ☎ 410/228–5511). **Easton Memorial**

Hospital (✉ 219 S. Washington St., Easton, MD, ☎ 410/822–1000). **Kent & Queen Anne's Hospital** (✉ 100 Brown St., Chestertown, MD, ☎ 410/778–3300). **Northampton-Accomack Memorial Hospital** (✉ 9507 Hospital Ave., Nassawadox, VA, ☎ 757/442–8777). **Peninsula General Hospital** (✉ 100 E. Carroll St., Salisbury, MD, ☎ 410/543–7101).

MEDIA

The *Baltimore Sun* and the *Washington Post* both cover events throughout Maryland's Eastern Shore.

TOURS

Besides any number of tours by boat from several of the waterside towns on Maryland's and Virginia's Eastern Shore, there are day-trip tours into the region from Annapolis and Baltimore. Larger towns, including Annapolis as well as St. Michaels, are home port for diesel- or gasoline-powered tour boats and yachts of various sizes. As part of its Day on the Bay Cruise series, the Annapolis-based Watermark Cruises operates between there and Rock Hall on the last Friday of every month, May through September, a thoroughly enjoyable way to visit one town while staying in the other. It costs $49.50 per adult. Chesapeake Bay Lighthouse Tours offer a rare chance to see the Bay's lighthouses up close. Passengers on the all-day Great Circle Route visit 12 lighthouses, and those on the Passage, a half-day tour, visit five. There is also a "two light" sunset cruise. Bring your camera. A full day costs $120 for an adult, a half day $60, and two hours costs $35. Board the *Cambridge Lady* to explore the Choptank River and its tributaries. In addition to Cambridge, some departures are available from Denton and Oxford. The *Lady* sails from May through October; tours are $20.

Rock Hall Trolleys, with 35 stops, is the way to explore this burgeoning Bayside community (adults, $2; children, $1)—and to travel between here and Chestertown ($4 per person, round-trip). It runs Friday–Sunday.

Historic Chestertown and Kent County Tours schedules guided, narrated walking tours from 1½ to 2 hours that focus on history and architecture, particularly that of the 18th century. Tours are by appointment only. Guided tours of Crisfield are run by the J. Millard Tawes Historical Museum. From May through October, the tours include a visit to a crab processing plant.

➤ BOAT TOURS: ***Cambridge Lady*** (☎ 410/221–0776, WEB www.cambridgelady.com). **Chesapeake Bay Lighthouse Tours** (☎ 410/886–2215 or 800/690–5080, WEB www.chesapeakelights.com). **Watermark Cruises** (☎ 410/268–7601 Ext. 111, WEB www.watermarkcruises.com).

➤ TROLLEY TOURS: **Rock Hall Trolleys** (☎ 410/639–7996 or 866/748–7658, WEB www.rockhalltrolleys.com).

➤ WALKING TOURS: **Historic Chestertown and Kent County Tours** (☎ 410/778–2829). **J. Millard Tawes Historical Museum** (✉ Somers Cove Marina, ☎ 410/968–2501; 🎫 $2.50; ⏲ May–Oct., daily 9–4:30; Nov.–Apr., weekdays 9–4:30).

VISITOR INFORMATION

➤ TOURIST INFORMATION IN MARYLAND: **Bay Country Welcome Center** (✉ 1000 Welcome Center Dr., Centreville, ☎ 410/758–6803). **Cecil County Tourism** (✉ 129 E. Main St., Rm. 324, Elkton 21921, ☎ 410/996–6290 or 800/232–4595, FAX 410/996–5305, WEB www.seececil.org). **Chesapeake House Welcome Center** (✉ Chesapeake House Service Area, I–95 [between exits 93 and 100, near Perryville], ☎ 410/287–2313). **Chincoteague Chamber of Commerce** (✉ 6733 Maddox Blvd., Chincoteague, ☎ 757/336–6161, FAX 757/336–1242,

WEB www.chincoteaguechamber.com). **Dorchester County Department of Tourism** (✉ 2 Rose Hill Pl., Cambridge 21613, ☎ 410/228–1000 or 800/522–8687, FAX 410/228–6848, WEB www.tourdorchester.org). **Eastern Shore of Virginia Chamber of Commerce** (✉ 19056 Industrial Parkway [off Rte. 13], Melfa 23410, ☎ 757/787–2460, FAX 757/787–8687, WEB www.esvachamber.org). **Kent County Office of Tourism** (✉ 100 N. Cross St., Suite 3, Chestertown 21620, ☎ 410/778–0416, FAX 410/778–2746, WEB www.kentcounty.com). **Ocean City Dept. of Tourism and Visitor Information Center** (✉ 4001 Coastal Hwy., at 41st St., Ocean City 21842, ☎ 410/289–8181 or 800/626–2326, FAX 410/289–0058, WEB www.ococean.com). **Queen Anne's County Dept. of Tourism and Visitors Center** (✉ 425 Piney Narrows Rd., Chester 21619, ☎ 410/604–2100 or 888/400–7787, FAX 410/604–2101, WEB www.qac.org). **Salisbury Chamber of Commerce** (✉ 300 E. Main St., ☎ 410/749–0144). **Somerset County Tourism Office and Visitors Center** (✉ 11440 Ocean Hwy., Princess Anne 21853, ☎ 410/651–2968 or 800/521–9189, FAX 410/651–3917, WEB www.visitsomerset.com). **Talbot County Office of Tourism and Visitors Center** (✉ 11 N. Washington St., Easton 21601, ☎ 410/770–8000 or 888/229–7829, FAX 410/770–8057, WEB www.talbotcounty.md). **U.S. 13 Welcome Center** (✉ 144 Ocean Hwy. [Rte. 13; 15 mi south of Snow Hill], Pocomoke City, ☎ 410/957–2484). **Wicomico County Convention & Visitors Bureau and Visitors Center** (✉ 8480 Ocean Hwy., Delmar 21875, ☎ 410/548–4914 or 800/332–8687, FAX 410/341–4996, WEB www.wicomicotourism.org). **Worcester County Tourism Office** (✉ 105 Pearl St., Snow Hill 21863, ☎ 410/632–3617 or 800/852–0335, FAX 410/632–3158, WEB www.visitworcester.org).

➤ TOURIST INFORMATION IN VIRGINIA: **Chincoteague Chamber of Commerce** (✉ 6733 Maddox Blvd., Box 258, Chincoteague 23336, ☎ 757/336–6161, WEB www.chincoteaguechamber.com). **Eastern Shore of Virginia Tourism** (✉ Rte. 13, Box 460, Melfa 23410, ☎ 757/787–2460, WEB www.esvachamber.org).

INDEX

Icons and Symbols

★ Our special recommendations
✕ Restaurant
🏨 Lodging establishment
✕🏨 Lodging establishment whose restaurant warrants a special trip
🦆 Good for kids (rubber duck)
☞ Sends you to another section of the guide for more information
✉ Address
☎ Telephone number
⏲ Opening and closing times
🎟 Admission prices

Numbers in white and black circles ③ ❸ that appear on the maps, in the margins, and within the tours correspond to one another.

A

B

D

E

N

U

V

W